Birth of Modern Facts

Birth of Modern Facts

How the Information Revolution Transformed Academic Research, Governments, and Businesses

James W. Cortada

ROWMAN & LITTLEFIELD
Lanham • Boulder • New York • London

Rowman & Littlefield
Bloomsbury Publishing Inc, 1359 Broadway, New York, NY 10018, USA
Bloomsbury Publishing Plc, 50 Bedford Square, London, WC1B 3DP, UK
Bloomsbury Publishing Ireland, 29 Earlsfort Terrace, Dublin 2, D02 AY28, Ireland
www.bloomsbury.com

Published by Rowman & Littlefield
An imprint of The Rowman & Littlefield Publishing Group, Inc.
4501 Forbes Boulevard, Suite 200, Lanham, Maryland 20706
www.rowman.com
86–90 Paul Street, London EC2A 4NE
Copyright © 2023 by The Rowman & Littlefield Publishing Group, Inc.

All rights reserved. No part of this publication may be: i) reproduced or transmitted in any form, electronic or mechanical, including photocopying, recording or by means of any information storage or retrieval system without prior permission in writing from the publishers; or ii) used or reproduced in any way for the training, development or operation of artificial intelligence (AI) technologies, including generative AI technologies. The rights holders expressly reserve this publication from the text and data mining exception as per Article 4(3) of the Digital Single Market Directive (EU) 2019/790.

British Library Cataloguing in Publication Information available

Library of Congress Cataloging-in-Publication Data

ISBN: 978-1-5381-7390-9 (cloth)
ISBN: 978-1-5381-7391-6 (electronic)

Contents

Preface		vii
1	Defining Information in Modern Times	1
2	Second Industrial Revolution Encounters Information	27
3	How Librarians Organized Information	57
4	Early Encounters by Computer Builders	89
5	Mathematicians and Statisticians Create New Tools	129
6	Scientists and Medical Experts Shape Information	153
7	New Business and Government Information Ecosystems	183
8	What Information Economists Created	213
9	Contributions of Political Scientists and Historians to Modern Information	249
10	How Information Evolved	277
Endnotes		309
For Further Reading		395
Index		427
About the Author		445

Preface

A fact acquires its true and full value only through the idea which is developed from it.

Justus von Liebig (1803–1873)

Information is ubiquitous—it's everywhere, available instantly in vast quantities on almost any subject, both trivial and significant. It is specialized, also broad, accurate and inaccurate, accessible by smartphone, personal computer (PC), books, and paper ephemera. We are hesitant to make decisions without consulting information, and yes, it keeps changing as more and different data, facts, and insights emerge. But, there are two problems: one of immediate practical concern, the other more an issue for historians. Of immediate concern is that humanity has accumulated so much information of a specialized nature that it is becoming increasingly difficult to master enough of it across multiple specialties in order to further optimize its use. So broad patterns of how things work in science or medicine, for example, which would be of great value, are difficult to uncover. Have we become so specialized and narrowly focused that we see the trees but not the forests? Does your doctor not know enough about diabetes *and* the effects of nutrition to treat what is now the most widely diffused human disease? Increasingly, students of information are becoming nervous and worried that we are fixated on trees alone, and not also on forests, hence all the discussions about the need for artificial intelligence (AI) and chaos theories, for instance. The second problem, more for historians, is that it has only been in the past two centuries that we have bulked up on information—hard data, facts—while in the earlier centuries there was simply far less. One of the features of human activities since the early 1800s has been the increased supply of facts intruding into human behavior. That is a relatively new development in human history that is insufficiently recognized, let alone understood.

It should be obvious that the two issues—the historian's and of people in general—are related, and that they need to be understood, as they are not going away. Appreciating how information increased and became more balkanized—specialized—has much to teach us as we continue the rapid and massive collection of evermore information and the development of computing tools to take charge from humans its collection, analysis, and use in the years to come. If humans are to effectively use information in the decades to come, we need to understand how it was created and is evolving. This book is intended to help in that process.

The question of what is information had long been the private preserve of philosophers, priests, and paragons of academic truth until tinkerers, engineers, and computer scientists invented computers, software, and databases. That last set of events occurred over nearly a century, and now with AI experiencing its first real renaissance, the debate about the meaning of information is renewing. There is growing evidence of this trend: best-selling books about AI, journals devoted to the history of information, IEEE Computer Society and Association for Computing Machinery (ACM) journals debating how to create, manage, and analyze information, companies like IBM and Google selling services to manage "Big Data," medical doctors declaring proudly that they are practicing "evidence-based" medicine, and large social media companies fined by governments for selling information about you and I without our permission. Powerful economic and political forces now hide behind many news articles; government policies; authoritarian leaders; and the evolving nature, fragmentation, and transformation of the Internet. For centuries information was seen as transmitted by language and text among humans—an anthropomorphic exclusive—but there is growing scientific evidence that trees and animals communicate with each other.[1]

Growing interest in information as a subject onto itself transcends all parts of society around the world. This conversation is far more expansive than prior more insulated discussions among technologists, academics, and policy makers. Unfolding the results of "fake facts" in American, Asian, and European politics exceeded the lies and propaganda of earlier decades. As the percentage of the world's population graduating from high schools, colleges, and universities continues to increase, people are becoming more aware of the role of information—facts and data—in their lives. It is an awareness that exceeds, but also parallels, the expanded use of handheld information technologies. Their awareness suggests people in many walks of life the need to understand the nature and role of information to a greater extent than in prior times. There is a role for experts on information to play in helping better understand this topic. No longer can one rely just on social media and public policy experts; we need technologists, computer scientists, historians, political scientists, and others to help launch a new form of literacy—information literacy. The world has done this before, first with reading literacy, later mathematical literacy, and most recently computational literacy (i.e., PCs, tablets, and smartphones).

It used to be so easy. Everyone knew what a fact was: George Washington was the first American president; today is Wednesday; the French Revolution began in 1789; and this book was published. Every walk of life had similar absolutes, such as the farmer knew for a fact that the seasons changed, computer scientists that 8 bits made a byte, that numbers could be clustered together into what eventually became known as databases, business management that profits were the financial differences between what it cost to make and sell a product for which it sold. All had a definitive reality to them as certain as the existence of a piece of metal or a wooden board. This was so even though they were ideas—some scholars call them fictions of the mind, therefore solely in our heads, but with the caveat that if one believed them to be real, truthful, that individuals would make decisions and take action based on these then they were not fiction. Actions lead to physical consequences. So facts are part of such realities.

Children engage with the issue, too. For example, as a child raised in the Catholic Church, I was taught—and believed it to be so—that God was kind, that Jesus loved children, that if we confess our sins, these would be forgiven by our kind, just God. A few years later, we learned that this process was not so simple. Our Catholic God is a three-part entity, a trinity, made up of the Father, Son, and Holy Spirit. In pre-Vatican II Catholicism, one accepted that definition, perhaps, for example, in the United States, because the *Baltimore Catechism* had been used to teach this truth to millions of children and many thousands of priests. Similar changes in the presentation of religious facts occurred at synagogues and mosques around the world. All three religions "of the book" were in agreement that, *in fact*, there was a Heaven and a God. Parents did not lie, and they said, "Yes, God is a trinity and there is a Heaven for good children." Facts were certain, straightforward, not complicated. University training and life's experiences then made things complicated.

Only a tiny number of people were concerned or expert on the changing nature of information, largely academics and computer scientists who were proposing new views about information and "feedback loops" and statistics in the 1940s–1960s, such as mathematician Norbert Wiener at MIT, engineer Claude E. Shannon at Bell Labs, and statisticians W. Edwards Deming at the U.S. Department of Agriculture and Walter Shewhart also at Bell Labs. Each became famous and influential in computer science, business, and even in the entire nation. Japan awards the Deming Prize annually for outstanding business management practices, which depend on the effective use of information (data) for decision-making.

Increasingly, today one encounters arguments such as, "Well, it's not so simple," with psychologists arguing that ideas, beliefs, and facts are fictions that only humans are able to conjure up. Some AI experts embrace such notions as they study how the human mind works versus a computer's intelligence. Many scientists and engineers seem in a hurry to resolve the issue, because computers are supposed to be as smart as people by 2050, and the singularity is poised to manifest itself even earlier. If cyborgs and sensors eventually take over most work and even the management of the human race, will people have just erased a category of facts known to billions of folks for thousands of years called religion? Will science facilitate that, and will computer scientists be complicit in such an act?

The general subject of what is information, defining its features, and how these are used is complex and evolving. Scholars and practitioners cannot even settle on the use of one word. Just in the past several paragraphs I used three words for what should be the same idea: information, facts, and data, and even stretched a bit to dabble in beliefs. Across many academic disciplines debate is underway about the nature of information, not simply just concerning its discovery. It includes a shift from uncovering facts to understanding their nature, and it has been computer scientists and to a lesser extent earlier, librarians, who may have started this new round of discussion. The priests of two thousand years ago might finally have had their monopoly on the topic ruptured (at least in the West), after a half-millennium siege through the Counter Reformation and the Enlightenment with its adoption of the scientific method. So far, the humans have been in charge of the process. One sign of this rupture is that physicists and biologists now accept that information exists as part of every object—rocks, planets, atoms, genes—and some even go so far as to argue that all existing material things are extensions of information and as ubiquitous as energy. So the general topic of information has become a heady subject.

I have written this book about information—facts, data—in the belief that understanding how elements of information evolved is useful for those who work in subjects that deal with their very construct and application, such as computer scientists and those exploring social media, and, most recently, history. Because the topic is massive, I chose to write about how information evolved since the mid-nineteenth century. I approach the discussion by situating it into the period of the Second Industrial Revolution. I wrote a history book aimed at those audiences that prefer historical perspective. One of my findings is that scholars in varying disciplines pay attention to the research conducted by colleagues in other disciplines. So, media experts read history; historians pay attention to economics; anthropologists and archaeologists are eager users of computing; and so forth. While each has their body of theories, frameworks, and methodologies, this book tacks closely to history in the belief that telling the story of how information evolved through the activities of key disciplines has much to teach all about how their own bodies of facts and data have been evolving. Historians provide context to inform current activities as does this book.

I purposefully do not engage in the various debates that occur within the intellectual circles of various disciplines. I do not claim to know enough across all these represented to do that. I offer a point of view on how information evolved in their historical space with the understanding that each chapter could be a book of its own, because each topic is that big. Second, I include within one book the developments of information in multiple disciplines, so an expert in one can learn how their corner of the world compares with developments in others, and how one affected each other, because one of my findings is that no discipline's information evolved in isolation from activities elsewhere. I hope that people reading the chapter representing their discipline would conclude I had done merely a rudimentary job, unknowingly including errors in judgment or facts, so that they would proceed to fix problems with their more expanded research on the history of information in their field. I think of this book as a stimulant, because historians of information are today still working out what issues, theories, and frameworks are best suited for understanding the role of information.

Members of a particular discipline might question the decisions I made about where to conduct conversations, such as about topology. Does it belong in the chapter on mathematics or on statistics, or at all? That we could even have such a conversation helps expose how the subject of information's history is not yet stable. That is where historians of, say, these two disciplines—mathematics and statistics—can advance our understanding of the history of information. Similar border issues could be presented as evidence that perhaps more traditional topic boundaries may be in flux; they certainly are in what and how data and information are being used and by whom. Historical research will help us understand how information continues to evolve.

Writing this book has been an intellectual journey not so different than that of many readers. Like others, as a child I grew up in a world without computers; now they hide in almost everything electrical in my home and office. Yet, a week does not go by without one or more books coming into my house, and so it has been for half a century. I was trained in the humanities—European and American political history to be precise—but spent nearly four decades working at IBM, explaining to its customers why and how to use information technologies. To do that, I had to remain current in the evolution of the technology—my latest learning efforts now involve hybrid clouds, quantum computing, and AI (again). As both historian and business writer, I focused the bulk of my attention on the history of information technology (IT), information, and its uses. I journeyed from pre-Vatican II religious instruction to wondering if cyborg movies portended the future. I wondered how such worldviews influenced computer scientists, IT users, and my grandchildren, while trying to help my neighborhood association define what a community membership database should look like. But the central conclusion is that it was always about information, not a particular form of computing.

I carry out the objectives for this book through a combination of revisiting in chronological order earlier thinking about information, focusing on how it evolved as people sought to use it for practical practices. Think of this exercise as a journey documenting society's experience through its disciplines (e.g., scientists, economists, political scientists, librarians) largely applying the methods of an historian. A central question I pose, is information ephemera, tool, or a general-purpose technology? How do these change? For the millions of people still transforming the nature of information, this book is an offering in the form of information prized by scholars and old people for centuries—context.

Because information, hence any discussion of it, is fluid, dynamic, flexible, general-purpose, and most specific, the rest of this book reads more like a combination essay and monograph. I do that because I want to think broadly, to offer a frame of reference. I lay on an historian's view, less to ask that one think chronologically about a series of sequential events, than to stimulate the consideration of variables that evolve as new circumstances warrant, all generated by different academic and professional disciplines. I want historians working in their various specialties to take into consideration the role of information to a greater extent than normally done. This will not be an historiographical discussion about historical evidence per se, rather about information's influence (role) on human affairs.

If you read this book to its end, I hope you will ponder the intended and unintended consequences of your own work with information; reaffirm; and gain a greater confidence in your efforts to understand what it is, how it evolves, and how it fits into the societies in which you plant your results. The first lesson any historian will counsel is that nobody lives in isolation, that everything one does has consequences, and that in one way or another all people are held accountable for their actions. Information is the chariot upon which we ride to our actions and legacies. It has always been so. I will not provide absolute definitions of information, because they keep changing, but will suggest what to keep in mind.

This book should feel like a normal monograph about the history of information since the 1840s. Who participated in the definition then used information varied over time with each constituency approaching the topic in unique ways, often simultaneously, but often, too, apart from each other. As the importance and visibility of information increased during the second half of the twentieth century, more constituencies became engaged in the discussion and use of facts. So, we trace their thinking, arguing that they paid a great deal of attention to the subject and that in time collectively raised the visibility of information as the important topic that it has become today. We have reached a point in the evolution of this discussion about the nature of information where various disciplines are converging. We can see that happen, for example, in universities where computer science departments and library schools are merging, where neuroscientists and experts on the human brain work with software engineers at Google, Amazon, Facebook, and IBM, where journalists and their editors debate what constitutes a lie (fake facts) in discussions with politicos, information science experts, and their internal computing staffs. Today, information is widely seen as in plain sight, important, tangible, fungible, and central in the lives of children, citizens, professionals, and academics. This book helps to describe some of the trends that brought information from between library stacks and academic conferences out into the wider world of contemporary society.

In 2016, I published a broad survey of what kinds of information existed in the United States during the same period as the book you are reading. Entitled *All the Facts*, it described what information existed in the work, public, and private lives of many corners of American society. It demonstrated that the amount of information and the extent of its use were vast, indeed so much that one could no longer ignore its use in any attempt to understand American society. The technological, scientific, and economic changes since the 1870s increased the intensity with which its use expanded. This second book, *Birth of Modern Facts*, builds on the earlier one by examining how those forces—technological, scientific, and economic—affected the kinds of information that became available. This second book demonstrates that one of the reasons Americans and the world at large used so much information in so many new ways is because they were able to organize facts and add to and change them into useful forms. So, we move from demonstrating that there was a great deal of it to a deeper description of its evolving features. As with the earlier book, I discuss the consequences of the transformations when they affected the further evolution of facts. We continue to progress down a path to a deeper understanding of the role of information in modern society, recognizing that these two volumes represent the start of a journey, hardly the complete account. Like *All the Facts*, this book, *Birth of Modern Facts*, raises many questions yet to be answered, suggesting more for scholars exploring the role of facts.

But to clear away some of the intellectual underbrush that may impede the central focus of this book—how and what information emerged and what it looked like—let us dispense with why and purpose questions. I take it as a central motivation that people developed information that they believed would be useful and practical for whatever activities in which they were engaged.

In other words, information is a tool. However, there are large quantities of publications that would argue that it is an insufficient explanation, and they would be right in the particular, but not in the general. In general, people need information to do their jobs, to have their fun, to support their personal lives. However, say in politics and even some business management cases, information is used to impose authority (power) over groups, such as minorities or women. Fake or actual information can be used to sow discord and confusion, as Americans experienced with recent political activities and their responses to Covid-19 vaccination information, which became purposefully politicized. Information has long been used in hostile ways against ethnic and racial groups and harmful to their interests, as happened with eugenics studies of African Americans in the early to mid-twentieth century. Increasingly, too, debates about "White man" colonialism and imperialism are seeping into all manner of academic discussions; information studies are just beginning to get dragged into that vortex. I want to set aside most of those discussions so that we can concentrate on the object itself—information—in the belief that with a better understanding of its nature and evolution, one can be better informed when they engage in these other, and quite interesting, discussions.

HOW THIS BOOK IS ORGANIZED

Because definitions of data, facts, information, and knowledge/wisdom are not set and vary by disciplines, the introduction discusses their meanings. It offers an explanation, too, of why they varied. I argue that these have a profound effect on how computer scientists, scholars in the humanities and social sciences, media, and business management, and public officials engage with the topic. The introduction provides a typology for information useful to multiple disciplines that builds on earlier research I did on the history of information. I address the meaning of the book's title to argue that information comes in many forms and how it transformed in modern times.

Chapter 1 can be seen as a pre-history of our modern concern about information. It demonstrates that the emergence of the Second Industrial Revolution of the nineteenth and early twentieth centuries was a direct result of the expanded use of organized bodies of information in science, engineering, business, economics and public administration, reinforced by extended levels of literacy and education. The next five chapters explore in further detail how major communities of information users dealt with the topic. These chapters demonstrate that various disciplines simultaneously defined and shaped information, some of their work transcending disciplines, others not so much. Chapter 2 focuses on the work of librarians who initiated much of the twentieth-century discussion about the nature of information before computer scientists came to dominate the debate after World War II, but who now are re-engaging in the discourse through their library schools (often now called iSchools). Chapter 3 does the same for computer scientists and engineers, and in chapters 4 and 5, the work of mathematicians, statisticians, and scientists. Businesses and governments became massive users of all manner of data, facts, information, and so forth, also shaping the nature of modern information, so their roles are described in chapter 6. Chapter 7 introduces some of the most recent participants in the conversation—economists—and in chapter 8, the work of political scientists and historians are described.

We then pivot away from groups influencing the nature of information to several themes focusing on how facts/data were appropriated. The agency of use is why one needs information. Chapter 9 looks at how information and computing when combined changed the nature of work. Chapter 10 pulls together our findings and discusses the implications of the history of information's evolution. It is a precursor to future research on current developments in the evolution of information. A bibliographic essay rounds out the book for those interested in exploring further the issues discussed in this book.

I benefitted from many years of help. Nancy Mulhern at the University of Wisconsin library exposed me to massive amounts of U.S. government studies and sources. Wayne A. Wiegand, one of America's great historians of libraries did too, largely through his publications and thinking. Thomas Misa, recently retired historian of technology at the University of Minnesota, made many specific suggestions for the improvement of this manuscript, line by line in many instances. William Aspray, of the University of Colorado, now emeritus, taught me an enormous amount about the nature of information and is about its form today. Many thanks go out to my editor, Jon Sisk, and to his team, for making it possible to publish this book.

The ideas expressed in this book are not necessarily those of Rowman & Littlefield or colleagues who have educated me over the past half-century. Weaknesses found here are of my own making, a testament that it is challenging to get all the facts right. But, let us continue the discussion. I can be reached at jcortada@umn.edu.

James W. Cortada

Chapter 1

Defining Information in Modern Times

Information is the resolution of uncertainty.

Claude E. Shannon (1916–2001)

But Ikujiro Nonaka (b. 1935) is also right when identifying why information is of value: "Whether an order is formed or not depends on whether or not information is created," and "the essence of creating order is in the creation of information." Hundreds of millions of people paused in their daily routines over the evening and next day of November 9–10, 1987, to view the remarkable TV images of young East Germans tearing down the Berlin Wall, the most iconic symbol of the Cold War that had suffused the lives of Europeans and to only a slightly lesser extent North Americans since the early 1960s. While they cheered and danced, many older people around the world waited for East German police to start shooting people, but that never happened. After the shock of what had just transpired sunk in, it seemed political leaders in Europe, North America, Asia, and South America were thinking and saying the same thing: it seemed the Cold War was ending. Over the next couple of years it did. Well-informed, educated adults anywhere recognized that an era had indeed ended. It had been a long one—called the Cold War—that had lasted since the 1940s. It fundamentally shaped what people thought about computers, warfare, all manner of technologies, space travel, education, and information. This contentious era so profoundly influenced the East–West struggle for ideological, military, and economic dominance of the world that it overwhelmed other names bandied about as alternative labels: Nuclear Age (1950s), Computer Age (1960s–1970s), and the Information Age (1980s–2010s). We give names to our pets, children, and our times all for the same reasons: to differentiate one from another and as shorthand descriptors. Yet, so many pundits and citizens of the world would agree that perhaps today they live in the Information Age. Historians dislike that practice—well, at least for "our times." They had seen other eras that were obvious to the masses, but ultimately proved not to be helpful: November 11, 1919, was seen as the end of an era (i.e., Victorian Age) with the declaration of a cessation in military operations in World War I Europe, 1815 (Napoleonic Era) when nearly two decades of Napoleonic empire building ended conclusively with his final military defeat. But there had been other eras less obvious that became more potent to historians: Renaissance (1400s–1500s), Early Modern Europe (1500s–1700s), Enlightenment (1700s), and the Second Industrial Revolution (1840s/1870s–1939/1945). Even with such obvious-in-hindsight labels, they continued to debate their relevance, while the public moved on to other names.

In each era a shaping influence on its identity was the role of information, regardless of who was doing the naming or who was arguing the case for one label over another. That role applies to residents and pundits of our time, many of whom speak of our era as the Information or Internet Age, or some variant, even gracing it with American president Donald J. Trump's name.[1] Each generation's identity of an era served as a lens through which they viewed events and took actions. Science philosopher Thomas Kuhn (1922–1996) spoke of scientists working through the prism of a paradigm, a worldview that was real and relevant to them until new evidence—data, facts, information—demonstrated that it was not so, and then they embraced a new view of the world. The discovery of germs by the early 1800s is an example; the understanding of what DNA is and how it works is another. There was always a constant flow of these changes since at least the Renaissance, but they shared one thing in common: information. How people viewed the nature of information, the extent of its collection, organization and use, and observable effects on one's activities spoke volumes about the history of the human race. Conversely, how one viewed their time—their era—shaped how they perceived, studied, and used it.

In no period did it seem that this was more so than in the late nineteenth and all of the twentieth centuries. In fact, more people were concerned about the nature of information in the past 150 years than probably in any other. The case is obvious: There were more people living than before who could pay attention to the issue; there were more literate educated individuals too; there were more information handling tools and ephemera to work with from paper to computers; there were more jobs and activities that required the use of organized bodies of facts; and there were more facts visible and obvious to all.[2] One factoid: over 130 million different books have been published in the past 500 years. If we multiplied that number by how many copies of each were printed (nearly impossible to do) we would be talking about billions of volumes, and that is before we waded into discussions about how much information existed in digital forms, which would make the number of books seem trivial.

For at least four decades it has been nearly impossible for an author of a book about books, media, the Internet, or computers to resist the temptation to explain how much information there was in the world. We have all done it, and it is fun to try to best an earlier author with bigger numbers or more clever explanations. A couple of examples suffice. To begin with respected historian, senior government official, and successful business start-up executive Tom Wheeler: "Every day the two jet engines on a Boeing 787 Dreamliner generate one terabyte of data—approximately 1 trillion bytes of data," while "tens of billions of microchips are being deployed in the internet of things."[3] Eric Schmidt, former chair of Alphabet Inc. (Google's parent company) quietly, but with his usual authoritative gravitas, opined that "from the dawn of civilization until 2003 human-kind generated about five exabytes of data," or nearly 5 million trillion bytes of information, more fashionably called *data*. Schmidt could not hold back, adding that all that data was equivalent to "all the words ever spoken by humans to date."[4] How he arrived at that conclusion eludes me, but never mind, he made his point: there is a lot of information out there. To put an even finer point on his hype, Schmidt said that in 2010 people were creating an equal amount of data in two days.[5] Wheeler could not resist calling our attention to a comment from the International Data Corporation (IDC) that in 2017—a mere seven years since Schmidt pontificated, humans were creating, "44 exabytes of new data on a daily basis. That's equivalent of 3 million Libraries of Congress being created daily!"[6] And my addition: there is more data on the Internet being sent from one device to another than there are humans doing the same thing over the Web, and that is with over 4 billion people trying.

There seems to be no end in sight to our profoundly obvious awareness that humans swim in an ocean of information and are subject to its practices. Recently we learned, for example, that trees communicate with each other; people long suspected birds and bees did too, but now using "scientific evidence" scientists confirmed that belief.[7] We now know that the over 500 species of organisms in our intestines communicate and coordinate with each other—Claude Shannon and Norbert Wiener would undoubtedly find this fact both fascinating and confirmatory of their own thinking about information.[8]

But all this information carries with it long simmering philosophical concerns, most of which we will not engage with in this book, but that should be acknowledged as existing. For example, and central in philosophy and discussions of what constitutes scientific facts, is the widely accepted notion that a scientific fact exists—that is to say, is true—only when we also know why it exists. This idea has circulated in the world of philosophy and knowledge since Aristotle's time. The German philosopher George Wilhelm

Friedrich Hegel (1770–1831) argued that "pure concepts" were grounded in reality, that is to say, experience, hence factual. French philosopher/sociologist Jacques Ellul (1912–1994) argued that qualitative information ultimately evolves into quantitative facts.[9] A student of Ellul's ideas pointed out that the Frenchman's conclusion was that "the reduction of everything to quantity is partly a cause, and partly an effect, of the modern omnipresence of computing machines and cybernated factories," an issue already evident to him when originally declared in 1954 just when computers were beginning to be used.[10] We encounter the issue of numbers—quantification—all through this book from the eighteenth century to the present. But the point to make is that notions of what constituted truthful facts has long been a contested issue that will not be resolved in this book because information has also been recognized as being useful, productive, disruptive, dangerous, wonderful, and essential. Just as frustrating and confusing is that there is insufficient consensus on what constitutes a working definition of information.[11]

It is all these things as it is to one's well-being that information has the irritating characteristic of there existing so much of it that people have felt compelled to organize it so as to get to what they needed. Typologies, definitions, and other mechanisms for organizing it have been major human interests for centuries. Those activities involved categorizing information, such as in today's modern academic disciplines (e.g., history, computer science, economics), each with a definition of the kind of facts and supporting theories of how they operate, and characterizations of their features (i.e., numeric, textual), and earlier by librarians creating cataloging systems to know where rationally to house books on shelves.

For the Western world the event that symbolized the start of the Enlightenment was the publication of the *Encyclopédie, ou dictionnaire raisonné des sciences, des arts et des métiers* between 1751 and 1772 in twenty-eight volumes and later in multiple editions and translations. It was the eighteenth century's Wikipedia. Besides including contributions from many luminaries in France, crucially its editors recognized that there was now so much information that it had to be an anthology of contributed articles by experts in multiple fields. That conclusion signaled to Europe and its colonies that information had reached some new tipping point. In the words from a prospectus written for the publication, "It is to contain the general principles that form the basis of each science and each art, liberal or mechanical, and the most essential facts that make up the body and substance of each," a recognition that, like the individuals discussed in our twenty-first-century book, a grand topic had become too big for one, or few, people to embrace sufficiently, let alone effectively. Then, as now, these earlier students of information recognized that all these subjects were part of "a chain that binds them together" and that "it would be ignorant and presumptuous to believe that everything is known concerning any subject, whatsoever."[12]

Few historians of information and knowledge dare to start years of serious study of information without genuflecting before this grand project and we do the same here. These eighteenth-century illuminati recognized that the world was filling with what they called a "sea of objects." Ironically, today computer scientists use the same word—*objects*—in a way their earlier counterparts would have understood, as reference to a specific instance of a class, where it represents a combination of variables, actions (functions), or a value stored in memory (computer today, human memory in the 1700s) and relevant for our book, as data structures.[13] When a historian in 2011 spoke about modern online access to the tidal wave of information, he compared the Internet to the *Encyclopédie*.[14] There seemed to be too much information. How to organize it was a problem then as now. Nearly the first one hundred pages of the eighteenth-century encyclopedia even did what we do in this Introduction—discuss the nature of information, its definition, and how best to organize it—as prelude and defense of the organization of the older monumental work.

Since creation and organization of human societies with their languages and written text, people complained of having too much information; the eighteenth-century French did too. Humans long dealt with this problem by organizing information into groups of facts that they could access and use, and that melded with the way their minds functioned. All societies always did this. With so many literate people in the twentieth century, more was being done than before to manage and catalog information. One could opine that it had become nearly impossible to keep up with what everyone else was doing with such efforts, also because there were so many people busily creating information. That latter comment goes far to explain why, for example, a computer scientist at an American university can be forgiven if she is not aware of what librarians were thinking about data sets in the 1920s, or U.S. government statisticians about Big Data (they did not call it so) in the 1930s and 1950s. Yet over time the activities of one community seeped into those of other intellectual disciplines. Some of these overlaps (or shared concerns) surfaced in different epochs but also imbricated in the same periods, as one sees today, for instance, with historians, media experts, and computer scientists all pronouncing on the nature and use of information.

So, what are they talking about? Information? Data? Facts? Knowledge? We think we know what these terms mean—and to a reasonable extent that is the case—but probe further, and one can see there are nuances in definitions that influence the activities of billions of people. In fact, the subject has so expanded that perhaps for the first time in the history of information, we have to qualify the scope of the discussion, by saying that we will only explore how human beings dealt with information. How trees, plants, frogs, whales, and germs handle such issues is beyond your author's knowledge, although other researchers are already exploring those other users of information.[15] In short, we restrict ourselves to the anthropomorphic.

This introductory chapter sets the table for the rest of the book. It begins by exploring the definitions of information and how these relate to other terms used analogously by humans, such as knowledge and wisdom. Key attributes and types of information are next presented to, again, constrain yet sharpen our scope for the anthropomorphic. Brief comments on long-term trends about information help to inform how it is evolving today across disciplines. I focus attention on the methodologies used in this book as these should prove useful to other scholars. The introduction concludes with guidance to inform our journey through the book.

DEFINITIONS OF INFORMATION AND HOW THESE RELATE TO KNOWLEDGE AND WISDOM

As a child in the 1950s and as a college student in the 1960s, I had, of course, been exposed to facts. In the earlier years I went to American, British, and Catholic schools in the United States, Europe, and the Middle East. I attended Randolph-Macon College, a Methodist institution in the United States where I majored (American term, *read* British term) in American and European history and Spanish literature. I lived in a world of information—called "facts" in those days—and we simply accepted their existence without contemplating their nature. They were objects to be memorized and, in history, remembered in chronological order. Of course, our teachers expected us to understand why events (themselves considered facts or information) had unfolded, such as why the American Civil War of the 1860s took place, or why World War I. In mathematics we memorized multiplication tables, while in science the names of major bones in the human body, along with explanations about why specific phenomenon occurred, such as mathematical theorems. These received orthodoxies were accepted as definitive and not subject to possible alternative explanations until one was exposed to variations in college or more normally, in graduate school. Catholic priests teaching us in middle school in Cairo, Egypt, expected us to memorize passages from Shakespeare while in another school in Rome lay teachers hammered into our little heads names of emperors and popes. We did those things without any contemplation that these facts possessed any intrinsic features or alternative identities. Facts were easy in those days, because they were absolutes. Adolph Hitler ruled Germany in the 1930s; Winston Churchill was the British prime minister during World War II;

2 × 2 = 4; water freezes at 32 degrees Fahrenheit; my mother's name was Shirley, mine Jim.

But that easiness, which so effortlessly was how one viewed the bulk of their education and understanding of what they knew, masked a churn underway in academic, scientific, and engineering circles where the realization had been emerging that information per se was more than a recitation of historical dates or scientific data, more than about what the philosophers and priests ruminated. Too many books, magazines, and newspapers, too many schools and universities, and too many scientific discoveries began to make it increasingly evident to both experts and the masses that the world was flooding with more facts—information—by the early 1900s on both sides of the Atlantic and increasingly, too, in Japan, China, and eastward in Europe past Berlin and even Moscow.[16] The Second Industrial Revolution could not happen without new and different facts, too, in engineering, science, accounting, mathematics, business operations, and managerial practices.

Nor could one ignore how to meld all those bodies of emerging facts into practical functions and organizations, what today we call *applications* or by academics *appropriations*. One historian and sociologist, James R. Beniger (1946–2010), caught the essence of it all by stating what in hindsight was obvious: that all these facts were needed to enhance *control* over human business activities, that "the coevolution of energy utilization, processing speed, and control, the gains from control technologies that accrue through increasing reliability and predictability, and the increasing control required of control technologies themselves—account for the Control Revolution that has continued unabated from the 1880s to the present."[17] In the more than three decades since Beniger made this observation, no scholar has questioned his conclusion. And so it was across all new academic fields and sectors of human activities from politics to warfare.[18] Each community saw its identity shaped by what facts it embraced and used to control its own activities and destinies, to understand the larger world and its own ecosystem, to succeed and profit: lawyers the law; engineers how to build bridges, buildings, and machines; business managers how to run enterprises transcending entire continents and shepherding thousands of employees; doctors with medicine; or the military applying the new military killing machines of its day.[19]

People, professions, industries, entire economies, and societies began developing variegated definitions of information. In turn, those definitions helped people to shape what research they did, what facts they prized, what work they performed, and what they valued professionally and personally. The consequences of such bifurcations in what constituted information proved spectacular: invention of nuclear war; development and use of computers; secularization of the Christian world; exploration of space; conquest of diseases like smallpox, plague, and influenza that had periodically killed up to a third of human populations, while increasing the length of healthy lives of people by 25 percent in the past century.[20]

Today the possibilities of more transformations that are both good and bad, positive or negative, advantageous or not for people and Earth ripple through the psyche of entire societies, all based on human use of information. We can call upon computer scientist Ken Steiglitz to explain in his usual clear language what is happening: "Earth has become thoroughly soaked in information-bearing signals" and "algorithms—for hiding and stealing information, for solving problems of biology and physics, and for mimicking thought itself—[these] are becoming our most powerful tools (and weapons)."[21] People recognize that all manner of information is the bases for all their activities so that is why understanding what they mean by information is the central issue discussed in this book. It is also why this volume can essentially only be a brief history of information's definition, coupled with how these evolved. It is not a short book so one might ask why use the word *brief*? It is because information is highly varied and appears in all aspects of life, taking us back to the earlier reference that biologists think trees share data and not just nutrients and that many living creatures chatter all the time, not just birds and squirrels.

Studying information has drawn considerable attention in recent years. Certainly, one can add this book to such a list. Each writer explores the nature of the word, the ideas underlying it, its variants by discipline, and its implications. Most, if not all, readers know what the word means, but probably as much through their work experience and its attendant intellectual and professional paradigms as through the collective understanding of society. So, upon closer examination what constitutes information and its cousins—facts, data, knowledge, and wisdom—actually becomes less clear. Words take on different meanings by discipline. When a scientist characterizes data as uncertain, meaning that a fact is not 100 percent absolute or variable, the proverbial "man on the street" would take it that a fact when said to be *uncertain* means possibly untrue, not really accurate. Yet the poor scientist was simply being very precise in defining the limits of a particular fact, not questioning its truthfulness. We need some clarity that transcends disciplines and what humankind has been experiencing for over the past century. We provide brief definitions so that as the reader proceeds through this book's account of information, all can work with a shared view of the topic, mitigating some fuzziness with this strategy. Let us agree on some fundamental meanings.

Let us acknowledge what has long been recognized: that information is often used interchangeably with cousin words, such as data, facts, and knowledge. Let us also agree that information means facts or data, such as James is my first name, that today's temperature is always a number, and that a number is also a fact.[22] Let us also agree that each fact is a stand-alone entity that does not need context or any other descriptive ornament to make it a reality. James is a name; that it is my name is less important than that it exists on its own. The same applies to a number.

At the other extreme is the requirement that a fact be set within a complex context that can carry on with other facts, mixed with experiences, pattern recognition, categorization within disciplines and topics, and be situated within a specific period in history or society. For that we have the word "knowledge."[23] That word captures the act of taking multiple facts (both similar and not) and placing them within some context relevant to someone's thinking. Causation and conclusions may also be part of context. A publisher's publishing record with books and magazines are collections of facts (i.e., titles, number of sales or subscriptions over specific periods of time) situated within the history of what that press did as an organization and how these publications either supported or inhibited its ability to function, in other words context approaches the concept of knowledge. Answering the question "Why?" is often part of what enters the world of knowledge regardless of the discipline or categories of facts. For a long time it was the preserve of philosophers.[24] The wise and insightful historian and Librarian of Congress Daniel J. Boorstin (1914–2004) in 1980 made a distinction between knowledge and information that helps us understand the significance of our discussion:

> While knowledge is orderly and cumulative, information is random and miscellaneous. We are flooded with messages from the instant-everywhere in excruciating profusion. In our ironic twentieth century version of Gresham's law, information tends to drive knowledge out of circulation. The oldest, the established, the cumulative, is displaced by the most recent, the most problematic. The latest information on anything and everything is collected, diffused, received, stored, and retrieved before anyone can discover whether the facts have meaning.[25]

This is an interesting observation for those concerned about the role of "fake facts" forty years later.

So far definitions of knowledge, however, have been subjects of more debate than notions regarding facts or information. Debates centered on the role of truth—usually has to be there—and the extent that it must be believed by the individual possessing knowledge and those to whom he or she is communicating about it. We will not deal with the nature of truth per se as that could consume hundreds of pages, as it has been a central topic of discussion regarding information, knowledge, and wisdom since at least when humans recorded their thoughts.[26] Like facts, truth and knowledge come in various forms, such as "situated knowledge," "partial knowledge," "scientific knowledge," or "religious knowledge," among others. For our purposes, let us agree that knowledge is both an aggregation of facts relevant to each other and that it reflects a collection of information providing insights on how these are understood or used in a job, discipline, or society. The entire discussion of this book can be seen as an example.

But, what then do we need to say about wisdom? As a general observation, wisdom takes the next step beyond knowledge to answer the question "So what?" It provides meaning and the significance of a body of knowledge. Example: So what that Moore's Law tells us a great deal about how computer technologies evolved since the 1950s? It also speaks to the issue of doing something with knowledge. Moore's Law teaches us to expect a certain pattern to reoccur in the capacity of computer chips to store more data and to operate faster at predictably declining costs, rates, and time—rules of thumb based on experience, observable facts, and numerous "Aha" moments in the lives of computer scientists, chip manufacturers, venture capitalists, and consumers.[27] As the authoritative *Oxford English Dictionary* (*OED*) explains wisdom, it is the "capacity of judging rightly in matters relating to life and conduct; soundness of judgment in the choice of means and ends; sometimes, less strictly, sound sense, especially in practical affairs." The *OED* calls it the opposite of "folly."[28]

Each discipline strives for wisdom. The exponential expansion of data in the past two centuries reinforced methods to measure and apply (operationalize) it. Proponents of Big Data argue that this behavior continues with facts collected electronically.[29] Librarians think of wisdom as the top of any hierarchy of information, as one librarian put it, wisdom is "more an aspirational goal than a concept with a straightforward definition. Here you can use knowledge to see overall patterns and make 'wisest' use of those patterns."[30]

Sandwiched between information and wisdom are facts and data along a continuum that varies by topic, attributes of the data, and how these are analyzed. Are facts and data merely synonyms duplicating words we already have in the very large vocabulary constituting the English language, or do they reflect nuance? One thinks of facts as truthful (realistic) descriptors of a reality, of a circumstance, for instance, that the temperature right now is 48 degrees Fahrenheit. Facts are powerful because they can motivate action, such as to put on a jacket before stepping outdoors.[31] Facts are more narrowly envisioned than information, because often with information one attaches a bit of context, even at the risk of not being necessarily as absolute in its truth: my wife thinks I am wonderful. That probably is true on occasion, but certainly not factual all the time. Such varying ambiguity can generate fuzzy thinking about my behavior open to diverse interpretations: an employee of mine might think I am terrible and have specific facts to prove it, while one of my grandsons may think the opposite and, too, have verifiable evidence to support his claim, such as I frequently buy them candy and take them to movies they want to see that their parents do not have time to view. Facts have the propensity to cause action.

Then, finally, there is data, another term used frequently in this book, particularly when we discuss computing and arrive more closely to the present. Data is often viewed as even narrower than facts. It is more absolute, such as a number or an electrical impulse shared between sensors and software. A fact, say my name is James, carries with it much anthropological and cultural baggage. It can be a variant of Jimmy or Jim or cross languages such as Jaime in Spanish. It has a liturgical heritage since one of the Christian disciples was named James. It is a Western name, and has been attached to good and bad, famous and infamous people in history. Data, on the other hand, is seen as less humanistic or in social forms and more precisely in engineering and scientific terms, most notably a number. Data is seen as individual units of information, much like we think of a *bit* as a unit within a *byte* of digital information.[32] Data is normally viewed as a number describing a discrete reality, such as the temperature at 3:45 PM Greenwich Mean Time in London. When combined with many other data, one has the ability to understand a changing circumstance (i.e., how the weather changed that afternoon in London). The quantity of data even has its own vocabulary.

"Datum" is the word used to describe one piece of data, such as the temperature right now, while "data" is the plural version of the word.[33] We rarely use datum in conversation and so is normally the purview of a book's copyeditor, but not to the rest of we mortals, because people rarely speak of one datum, rather about many datums or, in our parlance, data.[34] Finally, there is metadata, which one student of digital information conveniently defined as "data about data," such as descriptions of other information, documents, and other records. This scholar, Michael Buckland, points out that metadata is more than a description of other data, because if one inverts the relationship between that word and data, the description (datum) "becomes central rather than peripheral," hence a powerful tool for "search and discovery" when using computers to do the seeking.[35]

People are not normally inclined to quote the frightfully complicated yet profoundly important 1948 paper by Claude E. Shannon (1916–2001) for a clear definition of a word, but in this case it is useful to do so. He is considered one of the most important voices in the development of computers. While introducing his theory of communication, thinking in terms of how information could be communicated electronically and moved about, Shannon thought in terms of how best to transmit a *message*, meaning something that had *meaning* (his word). He spoke of "units of messages," something that was *discrete*, such as a number that could be measured; hence recognized as stand-alone ideas that could be converted into electrical impulses on a telephone or telegraph line. But, as more the norm in the 1930s and 1940s, he used the terms *information* and *data* interchangeably, unless he was talking about the mathematics of measuring signals, a discussion taken up in chapter 3. Because his theory was so fully developed with his publication, he had a profound effect on the first generation of engineers who became what we now call computer scientists.[36]

None of these words from information to messages is static in meaning and use. One can study the epistemology of each; most scholars turn to the *OED* to learn about Greek and Roman origins of such terms and for the major European languages to their respective royal society serving as the authority on the meaning and use of a word. These are useful sources for the history of a term and how it has been used since tracking languages at the word level began largely in Europe in the sixteenth century.[37] Moving closer to our time, the word information was not used in the nineteenth century, but became a fashion of the next one. Nor did Europeans, Asians, or Americans use "data" or "facts" so much in the 1800s. They thought and spoke more in terms of "education," "practical knowledge," or "skills." As engineering and scientific knowledge and practices disseminated across disciplines and professions with the emergence of the Second Industrial Revolution, the need for more narrowly and precisely defined terms became necessary, hence the arrival of those newer words. These were often used in the substantially enhanced disciplines of physics, mathematics, accounting, and statistics.[38]

Information served as the most inclusive, if least defined, term to serve as a catchall for all manner of facts, even those not as absolute in their truthfulness. For example, a billionaire might think that the average American or European citizen is reasonably well-off: they were experiencing low unemployment, had strong social and medical safety nets, and people were living longer—all true facts. Therefore, a billionaire's information confirmed that life was good on both sides of the Atlantic Ocean. But present the same facts to someone earning $20,000 in Chicago or €17,000 in Paris, and you get a different story: complaints about the government taking away retirement benefits, attempting to raise tuition at universities, or altering labor laws to make it easier to lay off employees—all true facts, too. Therefore, the French citizen confirms that life on both sides of the Atlantic Ocean could be far better. So, information is in the eye of the beholder, while facts less so, such as the amount of someone's income.

The word "information" is the most widely used term today to express all the various notions defined earlier. In the early twentieth century people spoke about knowledge, today we hear that term less frequently; it is all about information and perhaps increasingly, data. The word *facts* ebbs and flows in popularity, although in the 2010s was adorned with a negative connotation for representing lies, known as *fake facts*.[39] Data is, in the vernacular of popular culture, "hot." Americans, for example, spent billions of dollars on these in both electronic forms (bits and bytes) and paper.[40]

Even the humble word *data* has a pedigree that complicates our study of how information changed over time. In the eighteenth century data evolved from something that could not be discovered to being exactly what one wanted to observe and uncover through scientific experimentation. No longer could one assume a piece of data existed—a given—rather something that now had to be proven. As one scholar observed, now "data became tethered to conceptions of discoverable fact and demonstrable knowledge," reflecting a shift from "assumption to conclusion."[41] That was the major information event in Europe in the 1700s. However, that same scholar, Colin Koopman, argued that data reversed its role: "Data were once again put to work as no longer in need of any epistemic backing. Data were becoming that which can be assumed or given. Thus could data remain perfectly functional despite their being recognized, already by 1911, as 'a wilderness,' or what we today call an 'information overload.'"[42] We encounter this issue in most chapters of this book. The news for data is better, as it has been promoted in recent years from simply collections of signals, numbers, and segregated facts.

There is growing interest in declaring data a cultural artifact. Put together a collection of these regarding you, the reader, and surely we have a cultural collection and so embodiment of truth, for it comes before information. "If we're not careful, in other words, our zeal for more and more data can become a faith in their neutrality and autonomy, their objectivity," warn two experts, because data has its own identity, its own social baggage, its history.[43] Each discipline treats it differently, as the next near-dozen chapters demonstrate. So, data must be viewed as the cultural artifact that it becomes as is the admonition that one should make about information, knowledge, and wisdom.

ATTRIBUTES OF INFORMATION

It helps to contemplate briefly the attributes and types of information that predominated since the end of World War II. It has become so common to describe information as either on paper or electronic that one can embrace subconsciously that perspective as the virtually accepted way to categorize information (facts and data too). Only on occasion are we mildly disabused of this view when we have to pause to acknowledge that information is available simultaneously in print and electronic formats, such as a major newspaper, for example, the *New York Times* or *Le Figaro*. We have coexisted with both formats long enough that they almost seem components of one continuum. Yet, each format has its costs and benefits, its strengths and weaknesses, its attributes. Even a cursory review of the evolution of information in the twentieth century quickly leads to the conclusion that in 1945 the vast majority resided on paper, while radio-delivered facts were ephemeral, gone unless remembered once transmitted or written down. The same applied to telephone conversations, less so with telegraph messages since the input and output of each message was a piece of paper. Television shared the same ephemeral quality as radio, with the addition of much tacit information that could only be communicated by images. The one exception to these generalities was if a radio or TV program was recorded on magnetic tape or later on video or digital formats. With the arrival of computer mainframes in the 1950s, smaller systems in the 1960s, personal computers in the 1970s and 1980s, the Internet in the 1990s, and smartphones in the 2000s, the balance of power between paper and electronic formats changed swiftly. Digitized information rapidly surpassed paper in volume in less than six decades. Yet, the quantity of paper-housed and digitally stored information each continued to increase simultaneously around the world at rates that far exceeded those of any prior time in human history. Here is not the place to explain why, although bits and pieces of that story unfold in subsequent chapters because circumstances evident in earlier times continued to influence events after World War II.[44]

A debate is underway pondering how long paper documentation will last, most notably among librarians, many of whom think the paper book is dead and have started to clean out their libraries, replacing materials with e-books, databases, terminals, and coffee salons. In fairness to them, declining amounts of physical space and shrinking budgets can also be blamed for reinforcing their behavior.[45] But librarians are not alone in the grand conversation. None of the participants has a good track record of predicting accurately future trends. Librarians in the 1930s began tossing out newspapers, thinking that microfilm, then microfiche, would take over; they were wrong, and so we have too few bound sets of old newspapers and too much microfilm copies; the microfilm copies they produced were fuzzy and incomplete.[46] Book publishers were terrified that e-books would overtake paper books, and for a few years it looked that way; readers demonstrated through their purchases, however, that they prefer their paper books, even though they buy e-books too.[47] Computer scientists once envisioned AI taking over many human cognitive functions; they are still waiting expectantly for that to happen.[48] Factory workers worried about being displaced by robots for nearly a century, many convinced this would happen; they were wrong, and today worldwide there are both high-tech and human labor forces.[49] Their managers expected too much from computers, misunderstood what impact they would have, and today work in flatter organizations, while reports coming out of Amazon warehouses mimic the working conditions Charlie Chaplin mocked in his 1936 movie, *Modern Times*.[50]

So, viewing information simply as paper-based or digitally based is not terribly helpful for understanding the role of facts in modern times, nor for comprehending how work and play changed as a result. At best, that old paradigm is useful only to start exploring the greater topic, for which both historians and economists have already spent several decades. All of this investigation of the greater topic—information—has to occur because as MIT's Seth Lloyd described simply, "It is no secret that the world is glutted with information" with the volume "growing exponentially."[51]

One important feature of information manifested in their physical and digital formats is that people appropriated concurrently both in all societies and professions across all industries and human activities. In other words, people used both books *and* computers, read magazines *and* watched television, perused 3" × 5" library catalog files *and* online WorldCat citations, consulted reference books *and* googled Wikipedia. British historian David Edgerton published a book in 2011 entitled *The Shock of the Old: Technology and Global History since 1900*, which, in hindsight, did not seem so profound at the time.[52] He demonstrated that new technologies had not pushed older ones to the trash heap of history. Hammers and nails of old were not fully replaced by hydraulic nail guns; older wood burning stoves were not fully replaced by electric stoves; fountain pens by ball-point versions; push lawn mowers by gas versions, later by electric, and even after by battery-driven models. Rather, "to become widely used, a (new) thing does not have to be massively better than what preceded it; it need only be *marginally* better than alternatives."[53] He celebrated the humble and simple paper clip as a useful technology, even though there were alternatives, such as Sellotape, tags, three-ring binders, and folders.[54] People appropriated the new and the old when either made more practical sense to use. He found evidence of this behavior across all manner of technologies.

His insight applies, too, to paper and digital forms of information. One can purchase a paper birthday greeting card or send a digital version, or simply post a Happy Birthday message on someone's Facebook time line. People still write condolence messages by hand on stationery; doing so on a widow's Facebook page remains borderline inappropriate. Corporations issue paper and digital versions of their annual reports; book publishers offer paper and digital copies of their products but also will sell individual chapters as e-products. Probably most readers of this paragraph have consumed information in both ways and within each format in myriad other forms: in the world of paper handwritten notes, 3" × 5" cards, 8" × 11" formatted manuals, 6" × 9" formatted books, also magazines, flyers, newsletters, catalogs and other advertisements, paper tickets, and so forth.

Nobody, it seems, is exempt from the practice. At the dawn of the new century, in several computer laboratories where high priests of our digital age had been plying their trade for decades, two investigators reported that these experts used a combination of digital and paper files to do their work, even publishing photographs showing incredibly cluttered, sloppy piles of notes, papers, Post-it Notes framing personal computers (PCs), and diskettes scattered about.[55] They were not presenting evidence of chaos, rather interview results that demonstrated that these technologists occupying these crowded spaces found their variously formatted collections of information useful in the way they were preserved and that they knew what they had and where these were located, in other words, in what pile. So, we should break away—but not completely abandon—the descriptions of information as fundamentally paper or digital if we are to uncover other insights about the role of information in modern times. Other attributes may potentially prove of greater utility as we explore how people endowed information with characteristics and roles in the twentieth century.

Already one can observe that information in the twentieth and early twenty-first centuries became more diverse, while people (increasingly, too, software and sensors) used it in more ways. That this behavior became increasingly obvious to the wider public is one reason why so many people believe we live in an Information Age.

There are numerous other attributes to acknowledge; many so familiar that they require minimal explanation. Table 1.1 lists many of these to reinforce that observation. Table 1.2 reminds us of some of the most obvious ways humans interact with information. We encounter observations inherent in these tables in subsequent chapters. They reinforce findings from the *Shock of the Old* and the *Myth of the Paperless Office*, while demonstrating that over time information evolved in format, type, and use, sometimes in collaboration with those who lived in the older paper-based world. These include such examples as accountants in the 1950s with those using computers in the 1960s, book authors of the 1970s who wrote blogs in the 2010s, librarians who loved their paper ephemera and book stacks but increasingly imagined libraries without them.[56]

The first table is long on purpose: to demonstrate that information can be varied, portable, comes in many forms, and can be used in innumerable ways. To a twenty-first-century reader that may seem an obvious statement. However, to residents of the Western world of, say, the early nineteenth century, it would have been a revelation, because their definition of information was narrower, as were their sources. There were fewer books, and less specialized publications, while they drew a great deal of what they learned from the Bible, agricultural newspapers, and through conversations with peers and neighbors.[57] In many parts of Europe, rates of illiteracy remained so high that the bulk of printed information remained unavailable to most people, accessible only to some who worked in government, were professors or priests.[58]

Table 1.1. Attributes of Information

Components	Examples and Explanations
Expresses a reality	Trees have leaves; watches tell time
Text and descriptive	Green house, small dog
Numeric	Temperature, results of a mathematical calculation
Expresses a concept	Theory, hypotheses, thesis
Portable	Does not have to be just in one place, can appear in multiple formats (e.g., in a book and on TV)
Communicable	Can be shared, distributed across space and time
Configurable	Can be grouped with other information in many combinations, such as by discipline, chronology, type, format, forms
Sortable	Can be organized in myriad ways, such as books are by topic in a library, data in a database, disease data by types, standards
Flexible forms	Cooking recipes, laws, narratives
Stored variously	In one's mind, in printed paper form, electronically
Translatable	Can appear in any human and computer programming language and be represented by electronic impulses, such as by sensors
Artifact	Can be stored as an object, such as a book or DVD, data file in a computer, forms
Permanent and ephemeral	Can be stored on a document for centuries or be a name forgotten after an introduction, or erased off a data file after use (i.e., password)
Uses vary	To support a point of view, inform a profession or entertainment, reinforce a belief in politics or religion, sell a product, typically for work, hobbies, sports, religious purpose, and play
Truthful or false	Based on observation and scientific practices (i.e., chemistry, physics, statistics) or purposefully misleading or not true (e.g., misrepresenting a point of view of a political candidate or stating that smoking is not harmful to health)
Accuracy important	To be effective, users must be confident in the reality of a fact and dismissive of false or inaccurate information
Actionable/deployable	A green light at a crossroads allows a driver to pass through an intersection, a medical test result to medication or operation
Accessible by many	Teachers, officials, children, and adults, in multiple languages, from their smartphones or computers
Affordability	Can be free (e.g., a conversation), variously priced, or expensive, but widely affordable
Value-laden	Data considered in context can carry other meanings and values, such as if from New York City a person might be assumed to be a political liberal or critical of the American South; facts can be biased

Table 1.2. Common Human Interactions with Information

Interactions	Examples
To govern society	Laws, manners, game rules in sports, political manifestos
To operate organizations	Accounting, human resource policies, business practices, enforced laws and processes
To inform beliefs	Theology, political party positions, culture, experiences
To support research	Census and economic data, history for historians, science, engineering
To support entertainment	Facts about movies, book reviews, advertisements
To protect	Medical research and cures, environmental facts regarding safety of water and air, military strength of a nation's enemy
To think and act	Human brains used consciously available facts to make decisions (e.g., temperature dictates what to wear) and subconsciously (tacit knowledge, instinct, hunch, based on prior but not consciously articulated facts)

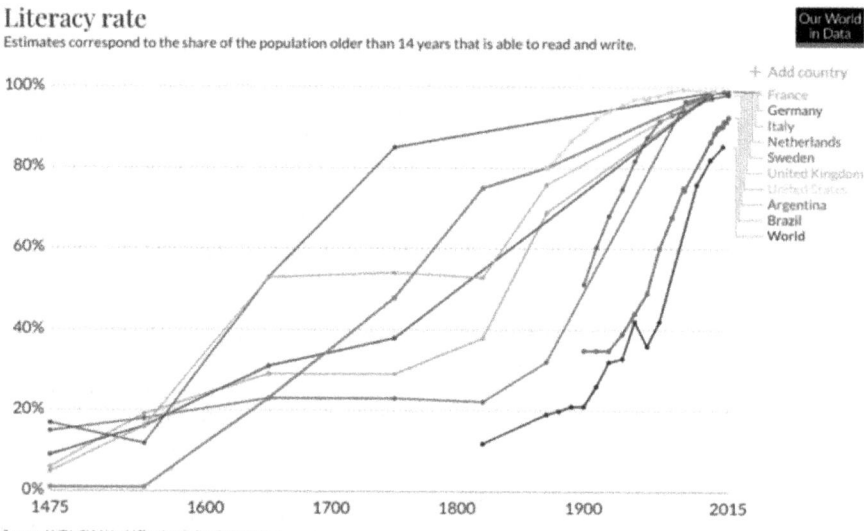

Figure 1.1. Global Literacy Rates, 1474–2015. *Source*: Max Roser and Esteban Ortiz-Ospina (2019). "Literacy." Published online at OurWorldInData.org. Retrieved from: https://ourworldindata.org/literacy (accessed March 7, 2020).

Since literacy was such a compelling force in the creation and use of information of all types, we need to keep that fact in mind as we discuss the evolution of facts in modern times. To put a fine point on the matter, figure 1.1 documents how fast and extensively literacy became ubiquitous. As argued earlier, so much changed during the twentieth century.

Defining Information in Modern Times

A second observation one can make about the contents of table 1.1 is, in the parlance of technologists, information has many of the attributes of a general-purpose technology and indeed, one might eventually be able to argue that it was its massive flexibility that informed the mindset of computer scientists and digital publishers during the second half of the twentieth century and the first decade of the twenty-first century, respectively. As a reminder for those not familiar with the notion of a general-purpose technology, the phrase has essentially two meanings. First, that it can fundamentally transform a society or economy, as did steam engines and later electricity, automobiles, computers, and the Internet. These are recognizable technologies that could be applied broadly in diverse ways and that have, in the language of the economist, spillover effects, which is to say, they cause much change in a society or economic sector.[59] Spillover effects are important because without that potential, one might not have invented the wheel or printing, for instance. Scholars in the twentieth century increasingly viewed general-purpose technologies as taking three forms: products or objects, organizations, and processes.[60] Examples of the first include the automobile, airplanes, and computers, and from the prior century, railroads, telegraph, and telephone. Examples of organizations include mass production factories and later lean manufacturing organizations with workers in the latter playing a greater role in the activities and decisions of the firm than managers.[61] Examples of process changes include the production of genetically modified foods in biotechnology, gene therapy, telecommuting, and now emerging autonomous cars and use of industrial robots applying expert systems software and early forms of AI. All three forms emerged from around the world; the case of lean manufacturing came from Japan; the earliest automobiles from Germany.

A second definition, more narrowly construed, is the same idea applied within a class of technologies, such as in computer science. Here, for example, the computer chip (microprocessor), which is the processing heart and storage medium of a computer, is said to be a general-purpose technology because it can be put into and be used by large mainframe computers (also called *servers* today), personal computers (PCs), tablets, smartphones, and sensors in machinery, trucks, airplanes, traffic lights, and "intelligent" doorbells.[62] Artificial intelligence (AI) is widely considered the next variant of a general-purpose technology, because it can be used in potentially so many ways, most yet unrealized, and that can be seen as hardware, software, and digitized data.[63] The key criterion is flexibility.

As table 1.1 demonstrates, information meets that requirement. That insight has not been lost on the protagonists who appear in the pages of this book. Furthermore, almost every instance of the development and use of general-purpose technologies in the twentieth century relied more extensively than in all prior centuries on bodies of information emanating out of such broad newly recognized disciplines as engineering, physics, mathematics, statistics, biology, medicine, astronomy, electronics, and material sciences, to mention the most obvious. This trend toward the use of ever-larger, more diverse bodies of information had been building for centuries, increasing dramatically in Europe during the eighteenth century and in the United States in the nineteenth century.[64]

The bridge between the two tables, however, is the ability of information to be communicated among people, machines, groups, entire industries, and economies, and, just as important, over time beyond the lifetime of the creator of a fact. That latter point is very much a unique contribution of the human species, beginning more with writing than oral traditions, because the written word could be more precisely preserved than a repeat of memorized or rephrased transmission of information. To be sure, information is transformed through writing and printing too—one has only to look at the history of the Bible as it went through many iterations and translations over the course of nearly two millenniums—but writing was crucial to the process. That was followed by a stream of other developments, such as the invention of paper, the book, moveable print, pamphlets, newspapers, magazines, and most recently such digital mediums as magnetic tape, disk drives, diskettes, compact disks (CDs), digital video disks (DVDs), online databases, and, of course, the Internet. It was the act of physically moving data from one person to another, from one place to another, from one time to another that proved crucial. The ability to combine electricity with telegraphy and telephony and wireless communications, later with computers, then most dramatically with PCs (by the late 1980s) assisted in increasing the availability of inexpensive and massive quantities of information. That expanded body of information made it possible for people to do what is listed in table 1.2. The list is short, powerful, and suggestive; one could imagine it being longer, but the point is made. The ability to package and move information about offered added evidence of its general-purpose attribute, making facts often the tool of choice for conducting human activity.

One additional issue needs to be addressed: Is information an object, a thing, or something else? During the two centuries discussed in this book, the public at large and those working in any job category or discipline overwhelmingly viewed information as a "tool" (their most widely used descriptor of information) that could be applied to improve their work and to make possible many activities, both public and private. They viewed information as if it were an object, a "thing," which they could touch because information came in such physical forms as books and newspapers. Those of us who have studied the nature of information would understand that physical notion but also realize that information is really not a thing, is it? Today, in the hard sciences, there is growing belief that the most prevalent "thing" in the universe may be information and/or energy. So we may be coming back to the notion of information as an object, as a tool. Across a handful of books that I have written, I have taken the position that to understand the role of information in the past two centuries, it is useful to think of information as a tool. A tool is an object one uses to do something. We do this all the time without noticing: it is a number representing a price, bits in software, facts moving from point "a" to point "b" in telecommunications, and so forth.

But all do not embrace the argument of information as an object, and so one should at least understand, too, the alternative. Margaret J. Wheatley has presented one worth exploring, too. We view information so much as an object that she complains that this paradigm prevents one from considering alternative views. She argues that "in the universe that new science is exploring, information is a very different 'thing.'" Rather, "in the new theories of evolution and order, information is a dynamic, changing element, taking center stage. Without information, life cannot give birth to anything new; information is absolutely essential for the emergence of a new order."[65] In the evolution of life, matter comes and goes quickly, such as the cells in our bodies replacing themselves in days, weeks, and months, while the information that makes all that happen survives from one generation of cells to another, what we see happening with DNA, a memory (information) that has constructed a protective housing for it called a cell. But in the end, she perhaps unknowingly gives a feature of physicality: "Information is unique as a resource because it can generate itself. It's the solar energy of organization—inexhaustible, with new progeny possible with every interpretation."[66] While her comment is a peek at what the hard sciences are exploring vis-à-vis information, in the end Wheatley is like the rest of us, anthropomorphic, because she comes back to the more widely held view that it is a thing, even if it cannot be touched and has attributes unseen to the human eye. What the scientists are now discovering is that information may be a much more complex, misunderstood massive entity of reality than we understood to be the case over the previous two centuries.

THE ROLE OF TAXONOMIES

Individuals, entire professions, and disciplines that transformed information engaged in discussions about how to organize facts. Taxonomies are the way information is organized; it is also thought of as both the practice, and in some disciplines the "science" of classifying information. Often the organization of information is referred to as a *schema* or *taxonomic schema*, a way of structuring information. Organizing one's private library of books by subject or in alphabetical order by author are schemas. For our purposes taxonomies are about organizing ideas and facts. Publishers of encyclopedias do this, often with entries presented in alphabetical order. Wikipedia does too and within such categories has rules about how information is presented.[67] We immediately encounter schemas—taxonomies—in chapter 3 as librarians sorted out how best to organize knowledge, from a more practical perspective books and journals. In telecommunications and databases one can have trees and hierarchies that form taxonomies; in mathematics tree structures are especially important. Computer scientists find taxonomies essential to their work, too.[68]

Once established within a discipline, they become the "way things are organized," making them almost an extension of a field's language and code. That is why it often is important for debates to take place as new bodies of information surface or circumstances call for different organization of facts.[69] In this book, we encounter examples of both instances, because information transformed so much. The previous discussion about the differences between data, information, and knowledge was about a taxonomy embraced by most students of information's features. Anytime one sees a list of attributes of information, they are engaged in a discussion about taxonomies. They can be quite diverse. For example, a distinguished information scientist, David G. Luenberger, in the introduction to his book about information makes clear that the entire universe of information can be boiled down to "five essentials": Entropy (the foundation of information), Economics (strategies for value), Encryption (security through mathematics), Extraction (information from data), and Emission (the mastery of frequency).[70] He then imposes on those five essentials "themes of analysis." These concepts involve "average performance," "optimality," "complexity," and "structure."[71]

In this book I am agnostic on the matter of taxonomies, because as an historian it is essential to document as many of these as space permits.[72] Others who want to implement taxonomies in a particular discipline cannot be so sympathetic to the diversity of schema. They must fight intellectual battles, put their careers and successful uses of information on the line, and in some instances, involve with life and death in some fields (e.g., medicine, warfare).

A ROADMAP TO *BIRTH OF MODERN FACTS*

Information is, thus, a far more complex nuanced topic than one might otherwise think possible. A second notion—offered up more forcefully in subsequent chapters—is that there are so many people creating and using information that they largely and unintentionally constructed silos of understanding of information's definition and attributes, although they periodically shared their variations across disciplines, formats, and time. Dueling taxonomies fueled debates, shaped definitions, and stimulated disagreements. The realization that we live in an era when information was so overtly an obvious component of jobs, play, and worldviews grew out of these various activities. Imagine these actions and facts like bricks of a building, and computer scientists and librarians as the bricklayers building today's society, then add the thought of computers, software, books, Internet, and other instrumentalities as comprising the digital plumbing of our age. Information infrastructures have been around for a long time, but far more obvious by today than ever before.[73]

This book describes the evolution of information through the work of various creators and users of facts. For the most part, we discuss groups of protagonists, such as computer scientists, business people, and librarians but also stars within their worlds, such as individual librarians (Melvil Dewey [1851–1931] comes to mind) and others who eventually came to be known as computer scientists, such as Alan M. Turing (1912–1954) and Claude E. Shannon. The order of presentation of these disciplines and their stars is roughly chronological, but they overlap much like the imbrication of shingles overlapping on a roof. So, for example, librarians thought about typologies and hierarchies of information before there were computers, but continued to do so after Turing and Shannon and their colleagues were busy at work. Because historians were the latest to engage on the topic, they are discussed last. We then pivot to a discussion of how computing and digital data played a larger role in human affairs involving all manner of people, professions, industries, and societies. But first, we turn to a time when people were comfortable with steam engines and were becoming so with newly harnessed electricity for telegraphy, when libraries were small, when blackboards in classrooms were the revolutionary screens of their age, and even before the invention of automobiles, computers, and the Internet.

ON THE QUESTION OF METHODOLOGY

Books on broad topics have long posed various problems for their authors, ranging from how to go about the task all the way to how to find a publisher willing to invest in a complicated project. I have discussed these issues elsewhere.[74] Here, I want to focus on the approach taken, because it speaks to how histories of new topics could be studied. The history of information is relatively new, just as feminist history was in the 1990s, reinterpretations of slavery in the 1980s, and statistically rich economic history in the 1970s. When faced with a relatively new topic, a central question is "Where do we begin to tell the story?" Right behind that question is "What do we need to learn?" "What sources do we have upon which to reconstruct the past?"

Indeed, "What is the topic?" All of those questions have to be addressed before scholars can have differing points of view about how to go about the task, what sources to emphasize, or what "schools" of thought should influence interpretation of events. With the history of information I feel like the nineteenth-century librarians who correctly concluded that the first step in getting control over massively growing bodies of information was to categorize facts, organizing them into groups related to each other.

That first step is also what emerging disciplines did by defining what information they worked with, flagging gaps that needed to be filled, then going about creating information shaped to meet their requirements. Over time both the librarians and the disciplines kept reshaping their categories, the first taking the Dewey system, for example, and subdividing it into more categories, while disciplines created sub-disciplines and then from each of those yet narrower disciplines. In both instances, attempts were periodically made to bring these disparate bodies of information back together. In science in the late 1900s it was the Grand Challenge movement, today it is the General Systems Theory, while particle physicists have long been looking for a Grand Unified Theory. For nearly a half-century, cross-disciplinary research and teaching animated those who dared to cross academic boundaries in search of more encompassing truths. Episodically, these groups scored some victories, then retreated back to their narrower, if partially redefined, information ecologies.

As I argued in this book and elsewhere, we are early in the maturation of this subfield of history called information. We are still in the cataloging and characterization phase.[75] It is that realization that affected how this book was organized. I was influenced by an earlier project, where I posited that almost all residents in the United States used enormous amounts of information in all aspects of their lives to such an extent that no future history of the country could ever be written without taking that reality into account. The result was *All the Facts: A History of Information in the United States Since 1870* (2016). I divided the American scene into three very large buckets: information used in the private sector (e.g., jobs and companies), in the public sector (e.g., jobs, agencies, and individual's relations with these), and in private life (e.g., religion, home maintenance, raising children, hobbies). Within each of these three categories I identified professions, types of organizations, then examples of the use of information within them. In every instance that I looked at within this organization of the story, I found vast quantities of information in use in a routine manner as "business as usual," as "this is how we do this." This proved so much the case that one could look at the book as a massive bibliographic study.

There was pitifully little room to engage in the great issues that historians are drawn to. In it you will find little discussion about how men used information to gain political, economic, and sexual power. Only brief acknowledgments can be found about how African Americans were oppressed in part by denying them information; the same for indigenous people and immigrants. There were exceptions, such as my discussion about the information ecosystems children had that extended beyond what existed in schools. I ignored the quality of information, such as false facts and their effects on people and on the affairs of the nation. I knew those all had to be addressed, but later, not then, because at a minimum like the librarians of the 1800s, we needed to know what was in the library to work with and to organize the material so that others could come in and use these.[76] Since then, I have become involved in initiatives to go to the next step that having *All the Facts* made possible, mentioned before. The first book gave future researchers a context, a frame of reference in which to situate their narrower deep-dive histories, such as how women used information or, more recently, the role of fake facts.[77]

Reviews of this first book essentially said its structure worked. But of course, most reviewers wanted to get to the fun part of the topic, such as the effects of the use of information and about the merits of specific types of information, and so forth. An author can tell they are on the right track when reviewers make comments such as "This is an interesting study that opens a broad new field of studies that should (will) be pursued by future historians." So, the next large research initiative had to be about understanding more specifically the features of information, because while writing *All the Facts* it became clear that facts themselves changed over time even if much remained the same. Information evolved to more mathematical forms, was shaped by the needs of new professions and disciplines, and became more voluminous. Few scholars had addressed those developments outside their individual disciplines; one could see that in the endnotes for this volume. More interesting, this behavior was evident everywhere I looked and echoed something I had observed in the early 2000s when I studied how entire industries reshaped their work with the assistance of information technologies. Many industries were appropriating technologies at the same time with little cognizance that others were doing the same. They were doing the same because of underlying motivations and similar technologies influencing one industry after another.[78] I observed the same behavior among the shapers of information in the same historical period I explored in *All the Facts*. I concluded that I had to essentially devote the book you are reading to the same task as before: to provide a high-level overview of broad changes and patterns of behavior with respect to information.

So, I looked at the information groups of users had, added to, and changed over time. I put scientists together, librarians in their own group, business community into another, and so forth, until I had satisfied myself that I had explored enough communities to where I could identify broad patterns of behavior and equally important, write descriptions of changed information. Of course, as in the earlier study, everything was introductory and too brief, but a start for other historians. In each instance, I examined the role of a discipline and its profession, then generalized about how information changed in each of their spheres. Next I looked at specific roles of what in the late twentieth century were fashionably called "thought leaders"—they existed in each discipline—followed by drilling down through their key "journals of record," where new forms of information unfolded before our eyes. It made sense to pick one publication in each discipline since we knew that multiple journals within a field tended to reinforce each other's new trends and to engage in dialogue and debate as this process unfolded. In the history of information, we see this behavior play out again with the publication of *Information & Culture* and *Library & Information History*. I would not be surprised if more journals appeared on the subject slicing the conversation into ever-narrower topics. It happens frequently. In American and West European history, for example, I challenge the reader to find any state or province that does not have a history journal devoted to it; the vast majority were established through local historical societies in the nineteenth and twentieth centuries.[79]

In addition to organizing clusters of information and users, providing more detailed discussions of the role of specific individuals, and examining the output of key journals, you will notice that this book is festooned with endnotes. Done on purpose, these serve as starting points for those wishing to look more thoroughly at, say, how information changed in chemistry or economics. That also explains why we needed an extensive bibliographic essay, again a strategy I employed in half a dozen earlier research projects that reviewers commented were useful for those going forward.

Following this book, I will be exploring contemporary trends in how information is evolving, in the belief that their features are being shaped as much by prior experiences as they are by current innovations in information technology. We tend to hear about the latter, such as about the role of massive computing power and AI, but historians know those two technological influences are never the whole story. Prior experiences, extant professional protocols, and beliefs would surely be as influential, if not more so, than computers or current fashions. It had always been so in all disciplines, so why would it be different for the history of how people shaped information, particularly in times when economic, social, and political changes were as profound as any one could find in earlier centuries?

As historians want to do, my primary objective was to provide both a description—a story—of what happened but also to embed context helpful to other researchers exploring interesting and fashionable topics that simply could not be done within the confines of one book. Information is not simply an abstract cognitive fiction but real as any physical object. I have long viewed information as tools. This book was about introducing the reader to how some of these were made, changed, and for what purposes.

Chapter 2

Second Industrial Revolution Encounters Information

I do not think there is any thrill that can go through the human heart like that felt by the inventor, as he sees some creation of the brain unfolding to success.
What one man calls God, another calls the laws of physics.

Nikola Tesla (1856–1943)

Between the 1920s and the late 1980s American university students were taught that the United States had lived through the Gilded Age, British students the Victorian Age, and the French La Belle Époque between roughly the 1860s and the start of World War I in 1914. This was an era when many Western nations (Japan to an extent too) transformed from agricultural to modern industrial economies, when large information-dependent organizations were first created. American humorist Mark Twain (1835–1910) coined the phrase the "Gilded Age" in 1873. The nickname refers to the act of putting a thin layer of gold on a base metal, which is misleading for suggesting greater wealth than was there, and, the desire of the rich and the ambitious, aspirations that the creation of new information supported. Corruption, wealth inequality, violent labor unrest and racial problems were the bane of the age in the United States, which in time led grudgingly to the emergence of many reforms buttressed by new information. As the developer of alternating electrical current, Nicola Tesla, demonstrated, his was also an era of invention. Students learned that the economies of most Western European countries transformed, including Italy and Russia, but that Americans led the charge.[1] In reality, the Americans took decisive lead only during World War II, although they picked up enormous momentum during World War I.

We did not hear about information beyond medical and scientific research, but a great deal about societal transformations. In 1973, while I was completing a PhD in history, historian Daniel Boorstin described the Gilded Age "as an Age of Revolution—of countless, little-noticed revolutions, which occurred not in the halls of legislatures or on battlefields or on the barricades but in homes and farms and factories and schools and stores, across the landscape and in the air—so little noticed because they came so swiftly, because [they] touched Americans everywhere and every day."[2] In 2016, economic historian Robert J. Gordon called it "the special century," arguing that the transformation was economic, because it freed a "household from an unremitting daily grind of painful manual labor, household drudgery, darkness, isolation, and early death."[3] Both got it right, as far as it goes, and historians of the European experience did too in similar fashion.[4] Too many Europeans, historians, and economists today, however, still think along the lines of the old historians of the 1930s–1970s by focusing on politics, social reforms, and creation of large corporations, but, too, more recently on women, slavery, labor, minorities, ethnic cleansing (including what happened to American Indians as the "West was conquered"), literature, and increasingly science at the expense of understanding how information played an important role in such themes.[5] Most recently, historians around the world have been exploring the expansion of colonial rule in Africa, Asia, and North America as extensions of the economic and political strength of industrializing societies. While their discoveries are documenting extraordinary brutal administration and economic exploitation, worldwide societies and economies were undergoing radical changes in less than a century.

Underpinning all this worldwide transformation was the increased availability and use of information.[6] Nikola Tesla, creator of much new information about electricity, was emblematic of the age when understanding scientific and engineering principles expanded rapidly, helping to change how people viewed facts. People were displacing God's ways with scientific laws. Recently developed information made possible novel ways to grow economies, develop entirely new industries (notably railroad transportation, large manufacturing, electricity and chemicals), and improve the quality of life with the scientific findings saluted by Boorstin and Gordon.[7] Economic prosperity funded what admittedly was often an expensive creation of new information. My research on the history of information and years of observing research and development at IBM and at other large organizations confirmed it was both.

It began with the English harnessing the power of steam to energize new modes of manufacturing and transportation in the first half of the eighteenth century, with uneven development in the Second Industrial Revolution that began between the 1840s and 1870s in various countries.[8] While historians have just about dismissed the old concept of the First Industrial Revolution, they have yet to do so with respect to the Second Industrial Revolution. Behavior tagged to the second one continues to unfold, suggesting that perhaps the forces at work in the past two centuries means that we are still living in the era of the Second Industrial Revolution. We may come to rename it the Second Industrial Evolution as the evidence presented in this book might suggest it would be appropriate. That some economists, like Gordon, might suggest a slowdown in innovation characterizing the Second Industrial Revolution may be unfolding, one has only to see how new medical cures based on knowledge of DNA or deployment of both carbon-based materials and alternative forms of energy are underway to pause and wonder if we are still participating in some still evolution in humankind's way of life. In short, the role of information in whatever this era one wants to label is pervasive and powerful. It cannot be ignored—that is the key finding of our research.

Many historians agree that information, and its dissemination (communication), was one of the glues and impetus for this particularly fertile era in history.[9] The old notion of the "Gilded Age" populated with "robber barons" is retreating, but not fully gone, because it was the desire for success, prosperity, and unfettered business practices in a new economy that helped to shape the emergence of new forms of information. Philosopher Andy Clark, when looking at the role of AI, aptly came up with a useful way to describe what had been going on for over a century before the arrival of AI that we can appropriate when thinking about how to navigate through decades of information's history. He recommended that we think of the subject as a "coadaptive dance of mind, culture, and technology."[10]

All eras come to an end, or at least go through phases. The period from the 1840s to 1914 was one that saw relatively fewer wars than that had occurred before. In 1914, European nations began their collective near-suicide that so profoundly changed their economies, societies, and politics. The experienced British foreign secretary Sir Edward Grey (1862–1933) musing despondently just as the war began that August, turned to a friend and said so presciently, "The lamps are going out all over Europe," and "we shall not see them lit again in our lifetime."[11] Four years later, every European government in the war had collapsed, except for Great Britain's; entire empires evaporated, such as Turkey's in the Middle East and the Balkans'; Europe wallowed in debt; entire societies stumbled out of the war embittered and exhausted. Twenty million people had died. An entire generation of potential future leaders did too in the trenches; subsequent statesmen were unable to prevent the renewal of the world war that led to millions of additional deaths between 1939 and 1945.

Only the United States came out of World War I with a strong economy. It now held much of Allied Europe's debt; it had suffered the fewest war casualties; its economy was intact and wealthy; and it had the capability of using the world's store of newest scientific and technical knowledge.[12] It also possessed the necessary academic and institutional infrastructures to develop and leverage new findings.[13] That is why the majority of this chapter and the rest of this book are largely about the American experience with information. While the rest of the world contributed to the shaping and use of information, bluntly put, it essentially played catch-up with the Americans, applying much of what came out of the United States during its "American Century." It remains a jarring label today. Societies are currently in the process of challenging American hegemony, or themselves are being confronted by North Americans on the battlefield of contemporary information assisted by its supportive technologies. But across the twentieth century the United States had the most information-driven momentum.

This chapter describes how the Second Industrial Revolution emerged and evolved, especially how in the establishment of large businesses, government and university organizations were able to create, organize, and deploy new bodies of information. These institutions recognized that information was an asset. I explain how information made possible the creation of large enterprises. I then argue that government agencies served as some of the most important creators of new information. We then move to the organization of new facts and scientific disciplines, a contribution made by a rapidly expanding number of universities. The private and public sectors developed new tools and machines to use data, setting the table for twentieth-century innovations in telecommunications, data processing, and computers. Much of these economic, social, technological, and institutional developments were American-born, but not completely so. To account for that limitation, this chapter concludes briefly with developments in other countries, most specifically the appropriation of new ways of creating and using information in Europe. The work of all the constituencies described in subsequent chapters was made possible by the activities and assets available during the Second Industrial Revolution. That is why the subject of this chapter is so essential to our understanding of the modern history of information.

But first, I clarify the chronology and language. Historians refer to the First Industrial Revolution as that period in England, then in France, and the rest of Western Europe (later the United States too), as entering this era in the early 1700s. The start of the Second Industrial Revolution is often dated roughly to the 1840s–1880s, depending on what country they are discussing, when a second round of economic, technological, and social changes began built on the momentum of the first revolution. As suggested earlier, we may still be going through that second phase; however, there is increasing support for the idea that sometime after the availability of computers and more advanced telecommunications after World War II, a new period began pushing humankind into the Third Industrial Revolution, say in the 1970s–1980s. No matter if that is the case or not, for convenience I use the label of the Second Industrial Revolution since across the entire period from the mid-1800s to the present people acquired vast quantities of new and changing information. In this book, we pick up the story in the mid-1800s and essentially run it to the end of the 1900s. Future historians will undoubtedly fine-tune this chronology, as they are wont to do, but here we focus on the broader themes and patterns of behavior that can inform their thinking in the twenty-first century. The evolution of information will inform that chronology since many topics have a long history, for example, from the study and use of coal—carbon—in the 1700s to the development of artificial diamonds in the mid-twentieth century to the current construction of airplanes, laptops, and vehicles out of carbon-based materials.[14]

HOW INFORMATION LED TO LARGE ENTERPRISES

Historian Alfred D. Chandler Jr. (1918–2007), who taught several generations of business historians how "a new form of capitalism appeared in the United States and Europe," reflected on the creation of large industrial enterprises run by professional managers. Railroads in the nineteenth century were emblematic.[15] They represented the connection between information and enterprises. The first freight and passenger rail line started operating in 1827, and by 1910 the majority of the American network had been built. Already by 1850, some 9,000 miles of rail had been laid, federal government grants for land and rights of way worked out, and by the 1930s it all peaked with 254,037 miles of track.[16] By 1906 seven firms controlled two-thirds of the railroad industry. The industry had to manage over one million pieces of rolling stock and over a million employees.[17] To create and operate such immense enterprises called for a great deal of varied information.

First, iron tracks did not work well. Development of mass production of steel with the Bessemer process resulted in growing knowledge about how to remove phosphorous from iron and making steel a more durable, stronger, and less expensive alternative; steel rails lasted ten times longer than iron ones. Second, improvements in the engineering of locomotives made them more powerful and efficient. Third, invention of the telegraph and its concurrent deployment along railroad lines provided the communications network needed to coordinate the activities of so many trains. Fourth, new accounting methods and practices tracked rolling stock, sales of passenger tickets, fees, and payments, giving management the tools they needed to scale. Fifth, to collect such information economically these companies needed data processing equipment, such as desktop calculators, adding machines, then telephones, and tabulators—all products of new information in science and technology, of tinkerers, and eventually of such companies as Western Union, AT&T, Burroughs, and the small firms that became progenitors of IBM.[18]

The results of the merging and use of new scientific and engineering information proved nothing less than spectacular. Let Chandler explain the circumstances: "With the completion of the modern transportation and communications networks—the railroad, telegraph, steamship, and cable—and of the organizational and technological innovations essential to operate them as integrated systems, that materials could flow into a factory or processing plant and finished goods move out at a rate of speed and volume and with the precise timing required to achieve substantial economies of throughput."[19] Howard Zinn provided a broader description of developments all of which required new bodies of information: "Between the Civil War and 1900, steam and electricity replaced human muscle, iron replaced wood, and steel replaced iron. . . . Machines could now drive steel tools. Oil could lubricate machines and light homes, streets, factories. People and goods could move by railroad, propelled by steam along steel rails; by 1900." Farmers also transformed: "Before the Civil War it took 61 hours of labor to produce an acre of wheat. By 1900, it took 3 hours, 19 minutes. Manufactured ice enabled the transport of food over long distances, and the industry of meatpacking was born."[20] James Beniger identified "control," as the necessary information about all aspects of railroading available to employees and their managers.[21]

Exaggerating the breadth of new information required to make possible the Second Industrial Revolution is difficult to do. That new information came from the development of steel, electrification, paper-making, petroleum, myriad chemicals, rubber, fertilizers, engines and turbines, larger and different machine tools (soon driven by electricity), creation of railroad rolling stock, bicycles, telecommunications, automobiles, trucks, airplanes, and many new business management practices. One should not forget, too, that electrical motors were some of the most important innovations of the century before the start of World War II.[22] Of course, as Howard Zinn observed, all this change also required "shrewd, efficient businessmen building empires, chocking out competition, maintaining high prices, keeping wages low, using government subsidies."[23]

A second feature of that era was the expanded literacy rates and resulting flow of information. By 1870 some 80 percent of the American population could read and write, although only 20 percent of African Americans. By 1940, the total literacy rate had climbed to 97 percent, nearly 99 percent for whites, and 80 percent for African Americans. Essentially, almost all children had attended elementary school, and in each decade the percentage of the population that had attended eight years, then graduated subsequently from high school, increased.[24] Today a third of the nation has attended post-secondary education. Increased sales of newspapers, magazines, and books were a by-product of all this education, resulting in more information being created, learned, and applied as one decade gave way to the next.[25]

Additional facets energizing information's life were two iconic applications: telegraph and telephone. Prior to the telegraph in the late 1830s, information could not move faster than at the speed of a horse; but with the telegraph, in seconds or minutes information moved across large expanses of nations. That made increased coordination of far-flung activities possible, such as train schedules and the avoidance of wrecks caused by two or more trains using the same track. Railroads compelled the nation to standardize time zones in many countries, too. In the 1870s, telephone conversations became possible, spreading quickly in business. Stock prices and new ways of selling increased, such as by mail order and with trained salesmen. All these activities were fueled by rapid infusion of information, often by the minute, as did diffusion of news both by telegraph and telephone. By the 1920s news services as an early version of telefax transmitted photographs over telephone lines. Meanwhile, by World War I radio had begun to spread and in the early 1920s became a popular way of transmitting (broadcasting) news, sports, music, lectures, and sermons across wide swaths of the United States and Western Europe. In short, information began moving at the speed of electricity.

As the cost of using electricity dropped, use of communications increased. While electrification of communications expanded, electrical motors made their way into factories, resulting in more distributed, efficient work, improving worker productivity. Little acknowledged, in large factories of the 1920s–1930s, telegraph and telephone systems within plants improved data collection, analysis, and adjustments in real-time to changing circumstances. But the key development was the telegraph, because it grew "up along the railroads in the new national market" for telegraphy.[26]

Creation and dissemination of information in both paper and electronic formats expanded simultaneously. Data piled up but also reached relevant parties. Information changed form as well. Information evolved from generalizations and prior experiences to what people increasingly called "scientific" knowledge. The accumulation of specific data could be obtained and decisions be made based on these, increasingly in near real time. Being more specific became possible, too. For instance, one could focus on the specifics of agricultural realities in individual southern or northern states of the United States and in other countries, with people confident in localized data and actions. Increasingly across all industries, professions, and disciplines, people expected information to be precise, specialized, numeric, and empirical.

Numeric data expanded massively between mid-century and World War II. While adjectives strapped to nouns were not dead, they came under siege. Little information was considered empirical or scientific by World War II unless grounded in numerical evidence. This reality applied to all industrializing economies. Statistics came into its own as a new branch of mathematics. Engineers, general management, and public officials applied statistical methods in business, government, science, and product development. By the end of the 1930s, the embryonic statistical practices that would become the centerpiece of Total Quality Management (TQM) (beginning in the 1950s) were being worked out inside British and American government agencies. W. Edwards Deming (1900–1993) worked at the U.S. Department of Agriculture, in one of the most "high-tech" "scientific" centers in the American government. Teachers began issuing standardized report cards in the 1920s with numerical grades, no longer just brief narratives of a student's performance. Churches began conducting statistical analyses of their own financial performance and studied rates and patterns of attendance at religious services. One scholar described the rise in the popularity of numbers as a "quantitative ethic."[27]

Finally, we need to consider the role of accounting. Without its expanded use large enterprises and government agencies would have struggled to exist. Even in prior centuries, large organizations relied on accounting of various sorts, including the Roman Empire and the East India Company. Accounting had several features attractive in the nineteenth and twentieth centuries. It was numeric, hence specific. It lent itself to increased automation, first, by using desktop adding machines, for example, later tabulators and computers. Its reports could be used to document the performance of a company in terms that could be standardized across companies and entire industries. While I discuss accounting later in this book, it is sufficient here to keep in mind that the Second Industrial Revolution would not have been able to give birth to large companies, as in the railroad industry, without accounting. As historian Chandler reminded us, accounting practices in wide use after the 1870s began to seep into the American economy at the same time as railroads were expanding.[28] That body of numeric information continues to be used, now universally.

After railroads, modern accounting appeared in steel manufacturing enterprises, moved to chemical firms (such as DuPont), to banks, later to insurance companies and large retail operations (such as department stores), and to government agencies, the latter for managing budgets. Accounting methods were developed to account for capital, such as depreciation, inventory valuation, cost calculations (the latter by the 1920s), operating expenses, budgets, salaries, and finally to calculate the effects of strategic options, such as the value of stock and productivity when building industrial oligopolies. Did it work? Just in the United States by the time the nation entered World War I in 1917 there existed 500 firms, each managing assets worth over $10 million, a task that would have been impossible without the accounting innovations just listed.[29] Accounting kept management focused on the essentials: budgets, cost controls, sales, revenues, and growth.[30]

One additional feature of the period has recently drawn the attention of historians: information-dense standards. Standards began to expand in scope and variety in everything from the size and shape of nuts and bolts to railroad gauges; to accounting practices; to measures of distance, quantities, and time; to even how professions were defined through the mechanism of discipline- and industry-centric associations. However, setting standards was never fully an empirical process, demonstrating that fact-based human activities were not as absolute as numbers might suggest. Practices that emerged during the Second Industrial Revolution "involved consensus-seeking committees of technical experts representing a range of stakeholders. Through iterative research, discussion, deliberation, and often voting, members of these committees attempted to reach consensus that had the buy-in necessary for voluntary adoption by all parties."[31] In other words, standard setting was at once a "social movement" and a process by which society created information and rationally deployed it in professions and industries.[32] That behavior continued right through the twentieth century, for instance, within such new disciplines as computer science.

ROLE OF GOVERNMENTS AS SUPPLIERS OF INFORMATION

Governments in industrializing economies have long played leading roles in creating and distributing information. These often funded research that resulted in new information used to improve agriculture, transportation, medical practices, and information technologies. Officials did this in four ways, beginning largely in the eighteenth century, intensifying in the second half of the next century, and continuing worldwide to the present. First, they established infrastructures for moving information in a society, such as postal systems and permitting the relatively free flow of facts and opinions, normally through a free press on both sides of the Atlantic. Second, various government agencies conducted research to promote the general welfare of a nation, such as about agricultural techniques, for instance, in mapping the American West, or in funding such work by others. Third, governments sponsored, staffed, and promoted education at all levels from elementary through graduate schools, including funding academic research. Already by the 1930s during the height of the Great Depression, the American Government was annually spending $100 million on such activities.[33] During the period of the Cold War, nearly 85 percent of all American university R&D funding came from public sources.[34] Fourth, governments disseminated information directly to their citizens through public libraries, free copies of publications, and experts educating and consulting with targeted audiences. These four initiatives proved so extensive that one can confidently conclude that the majority of the work done by most government agencies involved one or more of these information-centered activities.

There is debate about whether the public sector is too intrusive in national economies; too few people appreciated the role governments played in creating the information and supportive technologies. But the fact remains they have been at this for a long time.[35] A familiar example illustrates a long-standing interest of governments in improving practical information. British inventor Charles Babbage (1791–1871) considered a distant progenitor of the computer, experimented with mechanical means to perform mathematical functions for creating more accurate astronomical and mathematical tables. Mechanizing the process promised to reduce errors in navigation. In 1823, the British government commissioned Babbage to build such a machine, known as a "Difference Engine," awarding him a grant of £1,700.[36] While the project proved more expensive, difficult, and time consuming than anyone had anticipated, the initiative reflected the role of government to create information and data processing tools useful to society.

The four strategies can be illustrated briefly through the American experience from the Civil War to the start of World War II.[37] The first strategy was the creation of information infrastructures. The Second Continental Congress created a nationwide post office and put Benjamin Franklin in charge of it in 1775, the same media mogul who had run it for the British government before the American Revolution, and then made it permanent through legislation in 1792. Post offices were opened in all cities, and no town felt like a community until it had one, or at least a country store or hotel where one could pick up mail. In the beginning, Congress authorized free delivery of newspapers through the postal system. The national government and states built canals and roads, relied on ships and stagecoaches, and later used the railroad network and trucks to deliver mail to every corner of the nation. The cost of mailing letters, newspapers, and books was kept so low that the postal system never fully covered its expenses. By 1870, there were 28,492 post offices in the United States, thirty years later, 76,688 handling 7.1 million pieces of mail each year.[38] The volumes kept soaring right through the next century. The postal system appropriated every new infrastructure: all modes of transportation were used, including, briefly, horseback with the famed Pony Express, telegraph, telephone, radio, even the Internet to track packages with yet another government supported technology, UPC codes.

Local communities, and later state governments, created two other information infrastructures: schools and public libraries. Since we already discussed the spread of schools, we focus on libraries. In the second half of the nineteenth century many communities established free public libraries accessible by its citizens, and notably children, with nearly 80 percent established by women's organizations. Public libraries became as ubiquitous as churches, post offices, and country stores in American life.[39] Millions of Americans had a "library card" by 1950 and routinely used these, while librarians groused that too many people were reading novels and not enough non-fiction.[40] Remote communities and residents on farms also had access to information through bookmobiles, first wagons loaded with books that traveled the rural contours of the nation by the end of the 1880s; later trucks started providing an important service still today.

The second strategy—direct collection of information by government officials—became a constant effort from the earliest days of the new republic. A few examples illustrate how it was done. After concluding the Louisiana Purchase from France in 1803, which doubled the size of the nation by extending it to the Rocky Mountains, President Thomas Jefferson, himself a keen student of science and agriculture, commissioned army officers and civilians to explore, map, and document what the United States had just acquired. The expedition traveled west of the Mississippi River to the Pacific Ocean; collected massive quantities of new information about the geology, fauna, wildlife, and Indians of the North American continent; and prepared maps and sketches. By the 1840s, the army was the nation's largest collector of such information. After the Civil War, it was also charged with routinely gathering and sending weather information to Washington, D.C. The American government continued to collect such data; every weather report one sees today obtains its data from the American government, as it has done for over 150 years, all at taxpayers' expense.[41] In 1879 Congress reinforced these various initiatives by establishing the U.S. Geological Survey. Its scientists were responsible for studying the American landscape, natural resources, and effects of the environment on these. From its earliest days it created information drawn from biology, geography, geology, and hydrology.[42]

Another example concerns the creation and dissemination of information about agricultural best practices. Over 80 percent of all adults worked on farms at the start of the Second Industrial Revolution, so agriculture was both the nation's primary economic activity and bedrock of its culture. More than in most industrializing nations, in the United States, farmers relied on new technologies and scientific information in the post–Civil War period, which helped them become the most productive in the world. A crucial development was the passage of the Morrill Act in 1862 and subsequent laws later in the century that made land available to both homesteaders and—this is key—to state governments for establishing universities and agricultural experimentation stations (1883) to develop and diffuse information.[43]

Congress established the U.S. Department of Agriculture in 1862 to coordinate and promote the central idea of educating farmers in best practices and that involved research.[44] From its beginning this department conducted scientific research and established agricultural research and teaching at state universities all over the country. It created a network of agricultural agents in almost every county in the country through which it and local universities distributed information and advised farmers on all manner of agricultural issues.[45] These agents became trusted members of their communities and the nation's most important conduit of newly developed scientific information to farmers. By the end of the century, female "home economists" were beginning to do the same for women who were supported as homemakers, distributing information about sanitation; medical care for families; and how safely to can and cook vegetables, fruits, and meats.[46] In the next century, even children became involved through "Corn Clubs," better known today as 4-H programs.[47] All three activities expanded across the twentieth century and exist today. In the second half of the 1800s, the U.S. Department of Agriculture became one of the largest distributors of information in the nation, while state universities ran "short courses" (seminars) for farmers and later trained scientists in agricultural topics. By the end of the 1970s, farmers' having an "ag" degree from their local university proved fairly common across the nation.

The definition of agricultural information evolved too by crop; type of animal raised; new machine technology applied to farming; plant and animal diseases; new fertilizers; drugs and cures for animal and human illnesses; ecological topics such as sewage, water cleanliness, human and animal sanitation and weather; among others. A couple of data points suggest the amount. In 1880, 43 new books were published on agricultural themes, 76 in 1900 and 540 in 1916. To put those numbers in context, in those same three years other related materials appeared: in medicine and hygiene 114, 218, and 516, respectively; hundreds more on the "useful arts" and technology.[48]

The third strategy—expanded education from elementary school through university level—also involved federal, state, and local governments. While already briefly mentioned, we need to ask: what did they teach at the pre-college level, how many people were exposed to information in structured ways in school, and what were those bodies of information? "Book learning," as it was often called, had a history dating to the earliest colonies in the 1600s, was funded based on community in most towns and in all cities. By the end of the century, public school systems were ubiquitous across the nation. States passed laws mandating minimum number of days and years of school attendance for children funded through local and state taxes. By 1900 over 70 percent of all children were enrolled in some form of classroom-based instruction.[49] Curriculums and recruitment of teachers remained then, as now, largely a local responsibility.

Elementary schools transferred to students information, knowledge, values, and skills. They instructed children on religious and civic values, and instilled in them social norms and manners. Teachers taught them reading skills, writing, and basic mathematics. Increasingly by World War I schools introduced children to scientific knowledge. After that war, religious instruction declined in public schools, while training in vocational skills for boys and home economics for girls expanded; typing classes for both increased too. Boys needed to learn skills to find work, girls how to raise children and if they had to work, to do so as office and sales clerks, house keepers, nannies, secretaries, teachers, librarians, and home economists. Students were taught to obey, to understand the basics of American history (including much mythology, e.g., George Washington never told a lie) and how the government worked (called civics), piety and national and local duty, patriotism, and community involvement. To enhance the transmission of information, elementary and high schools established libraries or collaborated with local public libraries. In the area of science—the new broad subject of post-1870 America—by World War II children and high school students were exposed to basic concepts in physics, chemistry, and biology, and a few to such home economics issues as personal health and sanitation, how to prepare food safely, and elementary notions of nutrition and first aid.[50]

As the number of high school graduates increased, so too did enrollments in colleges and universities. The number of institutions increased too. The practice of colleges distributing information through classroom instruction and for graduate students through practicums augmented, paralleled, and often entwined with the diffusion of organized information through elementary schools and such student organizations as 4-H and Scouting.[51]

After 1870 people learned that information came in various topics, such as science, history, civics, and by profession (e.g., mechanics or agriculture), and that over time these categories (schema) of information became more specialized, such as scientific knowledge separated into physics or chemistry, mechanical arts (e.g., shop), and automotive repairs. They learned that each category of information had its own definitions of what constituted information and each their own vocabulary. For example, someone studying agriculture would learn about animals versus crops, and within crops about such categories as corn, wheat, and vegetables, while whole bodies of information and terms developed to discuss specific animals, notably horses, mules, cows of many breeds, pigs, chickens, and sheep. The categories of information that elementary and high schools taught became increasingly standardized across the nation. By the end of the 1920s, high school curriculums had settled into forms that remained largely unchanged through the century. These included instruction in mathematics (predominantly algebra and geometry), history (American), civics (how the federal and state governments were structured), science (biology, physics, chemistry), foreign languages (French and German, less so Spanish), physical education (known as "gym class" or "PE" for physical education, teaching baseball, football, basketball, volleyball, and exercises), vocational (typing, auto mechanics, how to work with wood and metal to make things—shop class—sewing, and cooking).

These broad classifications of information carried over to college curricula and to vocational schools at the post-secondary levels. Liberal arts colleges, for example, reflected the deepening of the high school agenda and added "majors" and "minors" in those fields, but at greater levels of detail.[52] Community colleges specialized in a growing number of vocations, including in such new topics as the work of electricians, plumbers, carpenters, machine operators, auto repair, nursing, and home economics. "Ag schools," often named such as Florida A&M University (Agricultural and Mechanical University), offered a four-year (or more) vocational training with a mixture, too, of liberal arts education and engineering. The extent of the entire educational infrastructure of the nation was as thick as any other societal structure one could imagine. It shaped profoundly how most people approached notions of information and knowledge, of their value in the work and play across the nation.[53]

Another feature of the period just being recognized as a feature of the times was the envelopment of people with information, ranging from mandating the creation of birth certificates at the dawn of the twentieth century to the assignment of some national identity number backed up by information collected for that effort (e.g., military during World War I, Social Security system in the United States beginning in the 1930s), employee identification information (e.g., height, weight, color of eyes and hair) by the end of the 1940s, more data for driver's and professional licenses, and finally the collection of information about people by data mining of our social media behavior on Facebook, for example.[54]

How Universities Disciplined Information

Colleges and universities became the largest organizations producing information by the Second World War. Production of information by professors in myriad academic disciplines, buttressed by studies and research conducted by their students, augmented through collaboration with government agencies for funding, and use of data and support from a growing number of foundations supporting similar initiatives, led nations on both sides of Atlantic Ocean to create massive quantities of facts. That production took off first in European universities and royal societies, largely in the eighteenth century.

By the first half of the next century, the bulk of the most innovative new information in the natural sciences (physics, chemistry, biology), economics, engineering, medicine, and proto-social sciences (anthropology, sociology, linguistics) was coming out of universities in England, Scotland, Italy, and Germany. Before the 1870s, American universities were small and did not have the capacity to compete with European institutions.[55]

That all changed in the century that followed the end of the American Civil War in 1865, with the result that already by World War II American universities were roughly on par with their European counterparts.[56] By the end of the 1950s, they led the world in the quantity and quality of their output. One can cite the number of Nobel Prizes awarded to Americans. From the early 1900s to the 1920s, people in the United States conducting research in the physical science, including economics, won one to three prizes per decade, but a total of nine in the 1930s, thirteen in the 1940s, twenty-seven in the 1950s, another twenty-eight in the 1960s, then forty-four in the 1970s. More telling, of the 876 laureates between 1901 and 2013, 350 resided in the United States.[57]

The number of PhD degrees issued in the United States in the post–World War I period went up year over year across disciplines. Just between 1920 and 1942—the interwar period—doctorates granted in economics went from 22 in 1920 to 138 in 1942.[58] If we look at the total number of PhDs conferred across all disciplines, again the evidence of increasing volumes of information creators is impressive: 54 conferred in 1880, 382 degrees in 1900, a decade later 443, and 615 in 1920. Lest one think that the production of information creators slowed in the 1930s, at the end of that decade in 1940, American universities had conferred 3,290 PhDs. And to state the obvious, degrees were granted in every year between the decennial ones just cited.[59] These degrees spread across all disciplines, from hard sciences to medicine, to agriculture to other biology subfields, psychology, even to accounting (first PhD awarded in 1939). Nearly a thousand were granted in the hard sciences (physics, astronomy, chemistry, earth sciences, mathematics, and engineering) in 1940 and 1942, reflecting the schooling undertaken in the late 1930s.[60]

As part of the training of creators of new information, American and European universities organized dozens of new subject areas into "disciplines," such as different types of engineering (e.g., civil, mechanical), chemistry from, say, natural philosophy, and different branches of medicine (internal, dentistry, psychology, among others). These many disciplines established national academic associations to reinforce identities for a specific discipline and to set standards for how research and publishing would be done, how individuals would be credentialed as experts, and how research agendas (i.e., creation of new information) would be shaped. Between 1880 and 1900 alone, sixteen of these scholarly societies were formed, another twenty-eight by the end of 1919, and in the following decade yet another twenty.[61] Such organizations carved out dozens of new specialties.[62] These became so strong and influential that by World War II it was not uncommon for an academic to be more loyal to their discipline than to the university that employed them.[63] These new disciplines were responding to society's demand for increased specialization and more specificity from information.[64] A great boom period for the identification of new bodies of information and their supporting departments within universities and societies occurred between the 1880s and the end of the 1930s.[65] As one historian noted, "Research became the handmaiden of teaching that we believe it is today."[66]

At the same time, while this exercise in professionalizing and disciplining the work of different fields of information was underway at universities, a similar parallel process was unfolding in public sector and business environments, often in collaboration with universities. For example, professional engineering societies and others for practicing medical doctors and accountants were established. By the end of the 1940s almost all professions dependent on documented bodies of information and certification had their national associations. These did more than just lobbying for licensing, tax benefits, and other market advantages. They hosted training and conferences where practitioners and academics shared information, published trade magazines—thousands of them—and books, later instructional movies and videos. Information exchange became the coin of the realm for these academic and professional associations.[67]

These PhDs and licensed professionals did not cluster just in universities. Many went to work in government; it took, after all, science-trained professionals to create weather reports, for example. Others found employment in the large corporations forming in the United States, particularly after 1900, as they established research centers to create new information that could be transformed into products and services. The most famous of these included Thomas Edison's Menlo Park research facility opened in 1876 in New Jersey, not far from the later established American Telephone & Telegraph (AT&T) Bell Laboratories (1925), DuPont (1902), and General Electric in 1900, the first industrial research laboratory organized in the United States.[68] Large manufacturers had theirs as well. Even the small high-tech company the Computing-Tabulating-Recording Company (CTR) established its first research center in 1922, when it had only 3,043 employees worldwide generating a gross income of $9 million. It would be two more years before it was renamed IBM.[69] Industrial research laboratories occasionally conducted basic research, such as in the 1930s and 1940s at Bell Labs on semiconductors, electronics, and communications. But these facilities did that with an eye toward solving operational problems, such as how to transmit long-distance telephone conversations effectively and inexpensively, which ultimately led to new products, most notably the transistor. They also did research to invent specific products, as IBM did when it conducted studies about card paper stock and electronics and in engineering to develop a wide range of data processing products in the 1920s–1940s, then its own computers, beginning in the mid-1940s.[70]

Academic researchers generally studied physical phenomenon through disciplines, such as physics, chemistry, and astronomy. They codified their findings in increasingly standardized ways using language specific to their discipline.[71] Their activities were then, as now, referred to as *basic research*. Researchers in government often did the same, such as those studying the economy, demographics, and weather. Some, however, also worked in what was called *applied research*, such as those who studied how to improve the quality of crops and fertilizers, cure crop and animal diseases, or improve the health of soldiers and sailors. Such pioneering work eradicated malaria and yellow fever in Cuba in the 1890s and at the Panama Canal in the 1910s.[72]

A virtuous circle developed during the Second Industrial Revolution is still functioning. Academics and industrial researchers would create (discover) new information, which then would be seen as of possible use in products, to solve a problem (i.e., discover penicillin to cure infections during World War II), or to help explain a natural phenomenon (i.e., the role of gravity). Despite copyrighting, patenting, and hiding some perceived findings of competitive value to a company that could slow diffusion of information through an economy, new bodies of information were shared among employees. Some of these individuals moved from one company, industry, or discipline to another, taking with them their knowledge and sharing it through presentations, work experience, job-hopping, and publishing. Their findings would encourage further funding by companies of their own labs and manufacturing sites, or subcontracting R&D to professors to further pursue and exploit these. Simultaneously, government agencies would provide financial support to academics who could develop new information that is too risky for a company to develop (i.e., early computing technologies, early-stage medications, or decades later DNA-based medical treatments). Such basic research morphed into applied research, which monetized information by converting findings into products, and increasingly after World War II into services as well.[73] These activities created an information ecosystem tightly entwined on both sides of the Atlantic throughout the nineteenth and twentieth centuries.[74]

Results were spectacular and, just as important, wide-ranging. For example, between 1870 and 1940, innovators and entrepreneurs discovered steel and learned how to make it, developed medicines and vaccines based on chemistry and biology, produced synthetic dies which took hard-to-make colors too expensive for the masses and made them widely available (e.g., purple), developed commercial air transportation, and invented the internal combustion engine used for cars, trucks, trains, factory machines, and tractors. New procedures in medical care, mass production in manufacturing, and cost accounting for companies, too, came into their own as continuously improving and expanding bodies of information. Physics, chemistry, astronomy, geology, and biology essentially were recreated as entirely new fields of information. It seemed few facets of society and work remained untouched by innovations of a fundamentally transformative nature.[75]

Spillover effects seemed endless. For instance, at DuPont Corporation chemists studied cellulose chemistry, then expanded their work in the 1920s to the new sub-disciplines of organic and chemical engineering. That latter work led to the development of improved rubber tires, later to synthetic rubber so essential in World War II, and to nylon, which the company applied immediately to the manufacture of highly popular lady's stockings.[76] Plastic, too, emerged out of parallel R&D, starting before World War I.

The academic world remained a major source of much new information. Their faculties behaved as "knowing through the exercise of reason," leading to a key twentieth-century information belief that "better knowledge will tend to displace inferior knowledge."[77] As that maxim proved true, governments, non-profit foundations, and corporations increased their investments in the development and use of new information.[78] It remains a practice still central in modern life, now in evidence around the world. On both sides of the Atlantic, academics and others competed for funding and prestige with the result that educational programs improved; corporate laboratories developed more sophisticated and relevant products; and governments acquired more advanced weapons, made possible medical cures, and nurtured infrastructures, most spectacularly roads and the Internet. The more than 175-year focus on infrastructures, in particular, included better, more scientifically based education, such as what the American government did to teach citizens about the importance of clean water, beginning in the 1880s, which resulted in statistically significant declines in mortality and extended life spans in the twentieth century.[79]

Using the term offered by historian Roger L. Geiger—"estates"—by the early 1900s on both sides of the Atlantic the hunt for new information helped to keep in mind that there were four, consisting of universities, government agencies, corporations, and non-profit foundations.[80] Analogous to fiefdoms, each estate had its own information ecosystems consisting of funding, clients, associations, specialized publications, and ways of interacting and sharing among themselves. People worked in one "estate" or another, moving back and forth, hiring each other, and contracting among themselves research and dissemination of new information. Each carefully guarded the boundaries of their disciplines through their definitions of what were in and out of their spheres of research and practice, while coordinating and collaborating with each other.[81]

One additional observation about these typologies of disciplines and disciplinary alliances suggest how varying perspectives and operational rivalries shaped how information evolved during the Second Industrial Revolution. It additionally needs introducing because these were evident throughout the period and influenced the work of protagonists discussed in future chapters. C. P. Snow (1905–1980), the British novelist who was also a chemist, captured the essence of a fundamental feature of information in the nineteenth and twentieth centuries when he pointed out that academics self-segregated into "two cultures"—one scientific (he meant engineering and medical too) and the other humanistic.[82] Both spheres competed for identity, and fought over issues of legitimacy, methodologies, and what constituted specificity of facts. They stood apart from each other, although episodically sought to collaborate in various interdisciplinary ways.[83] Let him explain:

> A good many times I have been present at gatherings of people who, by the standards of the traditional culture, are thought highly educated and who have with considerable gusto been expressing their incredulity at the illiteracy of scientists. Once or twice I have been provoked and have asked the company how many of them could describe the Second Law of Thermodynamics. The response was cold: it was also negative. Yet I was asking something which is the scientific equivalent of: *Have you read a work of Shakespeare's?* I now believe that if I had asked an even simpler question—such as, What do you mean by mass, or acceleration, which is the scientific equivalent of saying, *Can you read?*—not more than one in ten of the highly educated would have felt that I was speaking the same language. So the great edifice of modern physics goes up, and the majority of the cleverest people in the western world have about as much insight into it as their Neolithic ancestors would have had.[84]

The tension he identified appears throughout this book, even influencing which collections of knowledge workers I group together: scientists with engineers, political scientists with historians, among others. In a retrospective celebrating the fiftieth anniversary of his comments (originally his lecture was given in 1959), Lisa Jardine, a professor at Christ's College, observed that the debate over the two halves of Western civilization had not abated. Her point: "In the tradition of long-running disputes neither side has, then or now, been prepared to concede much ground, and the practitioners of the two intellectual spheres remain myopically as far apart as they were fifty years ago."[85] It remained a quiet, underground guerrilla war often hidden in the work of information creators, present but unseen. It permeated the thinking of many of the protagonists who appear in this book, even if they did not know about C. P. Snow.

Role of Early Data Processing and Communications Technologies

As industrializing economies mechanized manual tasks and documented processes for conducting work, these activities nurtured creative individuals to invent machines to collect and analyze information. As organizations became larger they needed to move information from one spot to another faster by stagecoach, ship, or any other possible way.[86] These various developments took off in the second half of the nineteenth century when society reached a tipping point in its use of information technology. As a by-product the necessary knowledge called for inventors and users to think through what data they wanted and how these should be formatted and handled. By the 1930s the groups discussed in subsequent chapters had more than a half-century of experience mechanizing information. They were essential to the evolution of information.

We do not spend much time in future chapters discussing the general trends in the underlying information technologies of the age, so I briefly introduce them here for context. Six classes of machinery emerged to process information prior to the arrival of the computer: typewriters, cash registers, adding machines, calculators, tabulators, and miscellaneous specialized equipment. All came in various models, styles, and functionality between the 1870s and World War II. Each class of machines was intended to facilitate the collection and manipulation of information, often specific types of data. So, a typewriter was good for writing letters and text (faster placing of information on paper than by handwriting); adding machines were used for summing or subtracting numbers (faster and often more accurately). As their use expanded rapidly, these devices helped their users to shape the nature of information. In some instances, these exercises involved simply creating and using existing data, such as sales and budget data, while in other cases, operators created new information, such as additional facts on a pre-printed form or to document scientific phenomenon. These machines contributed to the integration of paper files and other records with devices that could create, use, analyze, store, and distribute information for larger numbers of people.[87]

Such capabilities encouraged organizations to develop standard processes for working and managing information. These trends led to the standardization of information's form and format, making it possible to add to one's inventory of data. More data led to greater reliance on information with which to inform decision-making, particularly in how to control expenses, expand a business, or to formulate public policies. Such activities led to the creation of feedback loops that remain crucial in regularizing work activities. The most important new body of information created by these various activities involved statistics and narratives concerning the real-time performance of work (e.g., how many units or tasks were performed in a given period of time, number of failures or errors). By World War I efficiency experts were able to document productivity; to pinpoint bottlenecks in work practices; and to develop new designs for workflows, as in mass production assembly line operations. They began to call their efforts "scientific management," most notably Fredrick W. Taylor (1856–1915) and his disciples, whose methods spread from the United States to European factories.[88]

A second class of technologies was typewriters that made it possible to put more text on paper faster than by hand. That text could then be duplicated (e.g., using carbon paper) less expensively and more quickly than before. Lengthier descriptions of circumstances and processes became possible. U.S. diplomats at the Paris Peace Conference in 1919 settling World War I became the first national delegation to use typewriters to generate thousands of pages of position papers and other documents. Typewriting facilitated the development of manuals describing work procedures, making these ubiquitous publications by World War I. These ranged from one paragraph instructions to a railroad employee produced once or more daily all the way to book-length user manuals.[89] In short, typewriters facilitated the creation and use of sentence- and paragraph-length information.

A third technology, the cash register, was designed to collect and retain data on each sales transaction. These machines were small enough to sit on a table or counter and inexpensive enough for even small shops to use. Much has been made about the need to discourage sales clerks from stealing cash out of the "money box" by using these, but more importantly cash registers began informing store managers about what products sold and how many. The National Cash Register Corporation (NCR) became one of the largest, most high-tech, well-run corporations before the end of the 1800s, barely twenty years into its existence, supplying machines all over the world.[90] By the 1970s these were connected to computers to produce sales and cash reports, even to automatically generate reorders for goods sent directly to suppliers over telephone and private networks.

The fourth class of devices, adding and calculating machines, made it possible to manipulate numeric data accurately and more extensively, especially accounting and scientific information. That capability too expanded the uses of more frequent measures of performance, hence bureaucracies could inform employees and their managers about performance and facilitate enforced use of pre-determined business practices as routine activities. Such developments encouraged the creation of organizations much larger than those existed in earlier times.[91] By the end of the 1920s, these machines could integrate alphabetic data with numeric facts to produce printed reports of, say, named customers with their associated sales volumes or lists of employees with year-to-date salaries paid. For engineers that new functionality meant more accurate designs of bridges and buildings, because their analyses could include descriptions and instructions; for scientists more complicated mathematical calculations and narratives; for business accountants a broader range of numeric measures, such as cost accounting in the 1920s, timely and accurate customer billings even earlier, again with text for context and descriptors.[92]

Adding machines added and subtracted; calculators multiplied and divided; some performed all four functions. Accuracy became both prized and expected. As one executive in the "office appliance industry" recalled, "Bookkeeping, before the advent of the adding machines, was not an occupation for the flagging spirit or the wandering mind," as it called for "extraordinary" concentration at a time when businesses and governments needed more numeric data faster than could be provided by armies of "pen-and-ink accountants."[93] The machines could generate cost-effective information and, new in this era, statistical reports on such matters as number of products made in a given period of time, their cost, almost in real-time accounting of sales and expenditures, demographics, and information about the relative performance of one group as compared to another.[94] Middle management could now perform their primary functions of inspecting performance and setting objectives, relying on numerical and textual information.

The fifth class of tools concerned punched card tabulators, the most direct progenitor of the modern computer. Tabulators were the largest information-handling devices of their day, consisting of equipment that punched holes in cards to designate numeric and later alphabetic data, others to sort these by topic, then to perform mathematical calculations, and finally to produce reports or results. These were bigger than tabletop devices, occupying as much room and as tall as industrial machines or a kitchen stove. An early sales pitch offered, "Data appearing on order blanks, bills, time cards or forms of any kind, are transferred by means of the punching machines to cards, one card being used for each item of separate specifications," which then could be sorted or calculated to establish values.[95] These machines ultimately led to the creation of IBM and were the source of most of the revenues for this firm for the first six decades of the twentieth century.[96] Their attraction stemmed from the ability to use these to collate, sort, and organize vast quantities of data, beginning with national census statistics in the 1890s. Instead of taking a decade to do this work, for example, in the United States with its manual census of 1880, in the next decade for an even larger population, census takers completed the bulk of their work in eighteen months.[97] Business managers and public officials took note of this instance of spectacular improvement in data-handling productivity.

Insurance companies, city governments, armies, manufacturing firms, department stores, the National Census Bureau, banks, and other organizations quickly appropriated this technology, beginning in the 1890s. By the end of the 1930s, punched card tabulators had become essentially ubiquitous in large organizations.[98] These machines could mix and match numeric and alphabetic data based on literally millions of pieces of data to create facts, statistics, and narratives. They could do this quickly and less expensively than human "calculators."[99] Because these machines involved using multiple devices in a coordinated fashion, unlike typewriters and calculators, one needed to think in terms of *systems* for organizing and collecting information, thereby contributing to the routine collection and reliance on ever-broader sets of information in an organization.[100]

The variety of types of information one could collect expanded greatly. Popular uses included developing and using cost accounting analyses; tracking the purchases by an organization and the type of acquisition, shipping expenses, market forecasting, and sales projections; sizing uniforms needed by soldiers and sailors; generating medical statistics on diseases and medical procedures; creating actuarial tables for life insurance and worker compensation; and myriad trend analysis, among others. By World War I tabulators had made a possible wide application of a relatively new class of information—statistics—a type that continued to expand in popularity across the century.[101] By sorting and tabulating by topics, the technology justified its high costs.[102] Such machines could print reports with text and statistics by the mid-1920s, making these documents more "user friendly." So, control and standardization in work flows and information became normative, the same contribution was made by other classes of data processing equipment.

Tabulators facilitated the expanded use of standard forms in concert with the other classes of data processing devices. Forms are by their nature routinized ways of collecting standard information and have proven effective for centuries. However, with the ability to preprint these using inexpensive mechanical methods available after the 1860s, coupled with the calculating capabilities of the new data processing machines, one could acquire ever greater amounts of information on one form than before, often bringing together disparate pieces of data for the first time. For example, the City of New York began requiring registration of all local births at the dawn of the twentieth century and to include in that data collection effort information about where the child was born (not simply when), their name, and that of their parents. Over time, additional data accumulated as the process of using such forms became more widespread. The same occurred with death certificates and industrial injury reporting. By mid-century, it seemed every country on either side of the Atlantic had implemented such processes. That meant governments could understand more quickly changing demographics through analyses of data, hence plan for the provision of schooling, medical facilities, and other programs based on sufficiently accurate facts not available to them as recently as the 1880s.[103]

Then there was the spectacular case of the U.S. government convincing 400,000 businesses in 1927 to use a common purchase order, which saved both vendors and government agencies operating expenses. In the following decade, both could analyze and optimize purchasing/selling processes.[104] During World War II, the U.S. government became the world's largest purchaser of all manner of goods and services. It used these standard "P.O. forms" and their attendant processes to optimize the use of national resources, such as rubber tires for military vehicles, which the Allies considered one of a half-dozen most crucial war-related resources for prosecuting the war.[105] Similar progress in the use of such forms occurred elsewhere. By 1930 over 600 million sets of preprinted multiple forms were in use. Tabulators could print many of these almost as easily as a "dumb" printer." Post-war use continued to increase, and as scanners became available late in the Cold War era (1970s), computers could "read" data on forms, converting these into both digital files and calculate results, much as tabulators had done earlier with data "read" from cards.[106]

Tabulators and other machines reshaped information in another way: making possible continuous collection, processing, and production of data. Rather than episodically, say once a day, once a week, or once a month, data could be collected and reported out all day long, making it possible, for example, to adjust manufacturing steps on the shop floor or inform airplane pilots about changing weather conditions.[107]

Scientists, too, quickly and enthusiastically embraced every form of data processing equipment that came along. Desktop machines made their way into science classes and laboratories, while at Columbia University a collaboration with IBM led to the installation of tabulating equipment in the interwar period useful for astronomical and other calculations and as a learning exercise for IBM engineers. Data processing equipment eased the tedious nature of calculations and improved the accuracy—think quality—of the answers obtained by scientists, engineers, and mathematicians. They permitted comparative analysis of raw data. But, differences between scientific and engineering uses existed from those in commercial environments, variances that remained after the arrival of the computer. Generally, scientific users (scientists, engineers, and mathematicians) needed machines that had strong computational capabilities and most amounts of data. On the other hand, business users normally needed to process large volumes of data involving relatively less computation. Users increasingly understood these differences, so too did vendors developing data processing equipment of all types as early as the 1920s and built on that knowledge throughout the interwar years. Those different needs influenced the development of computers two decades later.[108]

Given the differences in calculating requirements, scientific data processing equipment that could work faster on complex calculations made tabulating equipment more attractive than desktop calculators or adding machines. Academics and students borrowed time on university, government, and private sector tabulators throughout the 1920s and 1930s to do more data-intensive work, such as in astronomy and physics.[109] Scientists, for example, calculated the movement of planets and moons using analogous calculations of paths.[110] Others attempting to calculate the trajectories of ballistics did the same.[111] Weather forecasters tried to use tabulators, which simply did not have software's computational horsepower; they had to await the arrival of computers.[112] British scientists, in particular, pushed the capabilities of tabulating and calculator applications, notably Leslie J. Comrie (1893–1950), a mathematician running the British Nautical Almanac Office during the interwar years. He encouraged other mathematicians and astronomers to use this technology to increase the amount of new scientific, numerically based data and resulting knowledge and insight about natural phenomenon.[113] To offer up a sense of the size of some of these projects, his calculations of moon positions required processing 500,000 cards using IBM tabulating equipment.[114]

Engineers, of course, had used mathematics for many centuries in their work. Tabulators and desktop calculators sped things up, making more calculations possible, such as applying formulas involving exponential and trigonometric terms. They began a long process of migrating away from published tables and use of slide rules, although they continued to rely on both for decades. (I used a K&E slide rule in high school in the early 1960s, with no computer in sight.) MIT had a differential analyzer in the interwar period, but that was only one experimental specialized machine. Engineers trained to use it went on to develop analog and digital computers over the next several decades.[115] Like scientists of their day, engineers still had to rely on slower desktop machines to quickly generate numeric answers to mathematical calculations.

HOW INFORMATION WENT GLOBAL

These data processing machines, from cash registers and typewriters to differential calculators and tabulating equipment, were in massive use on both sides of the Atlantic and in many corners of the world by the end of the 1930s. Their adoption by large organizations was so ubiquitous that literally hundreds of thousands of machines were all over the place. Here it is enough to recognize that with so many in use, the variety and quantity of numeric and alphanumeric data increased sharply within organizations.[116] An important by-product of the massive appropriation of such equipment was the proliferation of knowledge about how to design, build, and use these devices that, in combination with insights gained in electronics and in building radios, made it possible for thousands of individuals to participate in the invention and improvement of computers. Their work began in the 1930s and extended until these inventors retired by the end of the 1970s, only to be replaced by more populous new generations deeply steeped in computing technology.[117] Such practices in information creation and use were shared and copied around the world. "Knowledge workers"—a term that would not come into vogue until the 1960s—were everywhere, and they read the same journals and were called upon by salesmen selling books, magazines, adding machines, and other information-handling products.

A tiny piece of evidence hints at how early knowledge about tabulators and related peripheral equipment had gone global. A number of years ago I acquired the manual of an IBM field engineer responsible for repairing IBM tabulating equipment. It had his name on the title page and his address, as was the custom, along with the date of when he completed his training in installing and repairing equipment in Endicott, New York. It was dated 1932, and his address was in Shanghai, China. In the early 1990s while writing a history of the "Office Appliance Industry" as it was known until the 1950s, I came across photographs of a Chinese merchant using an NCR high-end cash register. For the same reasons and purposes in the United States, business people, scientists, engineers, and government employees collected, used, cataloged, analyzed, and made information available within their own societies.

The same collective attachment to the use of evolving forms of information created the massive knowledge base spread out among many diverse groups of people that made arrival of the computer possible after World War II. That circumstance proved so true that one could identify early computing projects underway for similar reasons and purposes in over two dozen countries within five years of the end of World War II.[118] That globalized collective behavior involving the use of information in homogenous forms was already in evidence by the start of World War I. The prosperity and rapid advances in education and uses of information in the 1920s reinforced such activities. The Great Depression slowed, but did not diminish the creation of new information. World War II led to the extended use of information total war, with new weapons, and in harnessing entire national economies to the effort.

WHAT OF THE THIRD INDUSTRIAL REVOLUTION?[119]

In 1971, Jeremy Rifkin, an author of books dealing with the effects of technological and scientific changes in today's society, published a volume entitled *The Third Industrial Revolution*. Here he argued that significant, fundamental changes in communications technologies were causing profound changes in economies functioned. It was widely accepted and read all over the world. Enthusiasts of computing and telecommunications technologies embraced the book, and its title became a new label for modern society's economy. As with all chronologies, when this new age ranges from the late 1960s to the 1980s it was to characterize a society intensely wired through "advanced" telecommunications. Diffusion of the widely available Internet beginning largely in the 1990s simply reinforced the notion that economic and social behavior had significantly changed sometime in that last quarter of the twentieth century.[120]

The notion seeped into discourses in various fields, such as media, corporate discussions, and in sociology and economics. Distinguished sociologists and historians participated, but often drawing, as I do, upon much longer chronologies to frame and assess the clearly increasing use of communications and computing than did Rifkin, coming to the discussion even before he did with his book.[121] Business historian Louis Galambos acknowledged that these technologies were (had) changed the way corporations and "our institutions" functioned, writing as early as 2005, more than a half decade before Rifkin.[122] It seemed everyone was networked and so the hunt was on for descriptions of that new way of living. The label proved convenient for aggregating much study and observation that had been underway since the 1970s.[123] The debate continues.

I have no disagreement with those who argued that technology furthered the evolution of societies—I make the same point in this chapter. However, the technology itself was and is a facilitator which made possible for its users to get to the heart of the matter—information—suggesting that technologies played a supportive role, not the main role in what people did. Computing was all about collecting and using information to do something, such as to run a business, make a profit, invent a new device, enjoy music and movies, arm up with medical information before engaging with a doctor, and so forth. Some readers may be more familiar with the variant label, "knowledge workers." It was such a line of thinking that led to such studies as the book you are reading. Also that thinking helps to explain why declaring some new rupture with the past as a Third Industrial Revolution seemed rational. While not necessarily wrong, such declarations need further buttressing that only more research and time can provide.[124]

CONCLUSIONS

Development of new scientific and engineering information accelerated in the first half of the nineteenth century, facilitating and shaping the emergence of large enterprises, government agencies, and universities, all with expanded missions. Much of the momentum in the creation and application of new information, however, percolated within the private sector in the nineteenth century, more so within the public sector and universities in the next century, although all three pillars of the Western world proved active. The constituent organizations generating new information influenced the kind of facts that were developed, motivated by an appetite to apply them for their own interests, such as development of new forms of accounting by large enterprises, manufacture of data processing equipment, and weapons by governments. Individual entrepreneurs, inventors, and scientists were a busy lot, too, in the century and a half since the 1840s.[125]

Useful accurate information begets more facts, often triggering acceleration in the development of new insights into a subject. Such circumstances existed in the 1800s and early 1900s. These existed, too, in the evolution of technology. We have only to think about what happened to computing with the development of the microprocessor and subsequent insight of Moore's Law since the 1960s. The "law" proved useful in understanding the continued evolution of computer chips. It motivated firms like Intel to develop new products in a prescribed time frame that conformed to Gordon Moore's observations as much as they were a response to the harsh realities of a highly competitive market. In short, across wide swaths of information, momentum built during the Second Industrial Revolution to create and use new facts, insights, and methods. Work done to understand the role of DNA in the past several decades is now translating into rapid development of programmable medicines targeting cancer, while efforts along those lines were slower to come thirty or forty years ago. The rapid development of vaccines to contain Covid-19 is yet another example of the process at work.

In turn, new and different information contributed mightily to the economic prosperity of the age, despite the punishing effects of World War I and a decade later of the Great Depression. The momentum created prior to 1914 was simply too great to slow the supply of information deemed useful by so many sectors of the world's economies and nations. Even colonies were not exempt from the introduction of new information deemed by their rulers, government agencies, and corporations useful to them. World War II had the effect of stimulating, not slowing, the creation and use of new information by Germany, the United Kingdom, and the United States. The Cold War did the same, adding the Soviet Union (especially Russia) into the mix. Today it is China as well.

That rise in global prosperity, in turn, funded new information everywhere. It is an important point to remember because scientific research and academic explorations in the humanities, social sciences, and in other disciplines (many of them new) became increasingly more expensive. Government-sponsored research, too, required more experts, such as in the U.S. Department of Agriculture. The latter's collective work led to the development of a large body of new information and practices that made it possible to correct many operational problems faced by farmers during the droughts of the 1930s, and that facilitated the global expansion of food supplies through the Green Revolution of the 1950s and 1960s. Without the economic wherewithal to create, invent, sponsor research, run R&D laboratories, to train, and educate across so many industries and populations, the pace of development of information would have been far slower and perhaps less practical and more limited. The most economically vibrant economies sponsored the largest amount of applied research and often were the quickest to convert this work into profitable products, as the German chemical industry demonstrated before World War I and by large enterprises in the United States in railroading, steel, and manufacturing.

To put a finer point on the magnitude of the changes that humanity experienced during the Second Industrial Revolution that resulted subsequently in their world being full of more information and activities dependent on facts, consider changes in the size of the population and the nature of work. In 1870, the world's population hovered at an estimated 1.3 billion people. In 1940 it had grown to 2.4 billion humans.[126] The U.S. population in 1870 was 38.6 million souls and in 1940 just over 132 million.[127] By any measure, both sets of growth were enormous. In 1870 in the United States, 47 percent of the workforce engaged in agriculture, only 32 percent in industry (largely manufacturing). In 1940, the agricultural workforce had declined to 15.4 percent, while the industrial labor pool remained roughly the same (37%). Because the overall population had increased, all these percentages represented more people (12.5 million workers in 1870 and 53.6 million in 1940).[128] One could cite the number of students and workers in offices handling documents, do the same by profession, and arrive at the same conclusion: the number of people dealing with specialized information had increased. The same held true for many European countries. So Daniel J. Boorstin was right, it was "an Age of Revolution," as also Robert J. Gordon who concluded that at the end of that revolution, "daily life had changed beyond recognition," and indeed had become "unique in human history."[129] I would add that the immediate foundation of that monumental transformation was the creation and use of information.

How information came to be identified and what it looked like was the result of the work done by communities within society often working independently of each other. Librarians are the first groups I studied to demonstrate this behavior, a result of their being forced to face the reality of so many new books and journals arriving at their doorsteps. Think of them as more than catalogers and creators of information typologies. What they thought about how information should be defined and be organized served as an important gateway for children and adults (along with how teachers thought of the topic) into the otherwise massive world of information. It is to their thinking and typologies during the Second Industrial Revolution that we turn to first.

Chapter 3

How Librarians Organized Information

> *Man learned to write. He became unbelievably inexpert at it. Confusion reigned in chaotic splendor. . . . The channels of information became clogged. Malignancy set in. Doctors were needed—Literature Doctors! The patient was—Analyzed and Synthesized, Classified and Codified, Catalogued and Analogued, Digitized, Anaesthetized. . . . And still the patient languished.*
>
> An anonymous librarian, 1962[1]

John Langdon Sibley (1804–1885) was the assistant librarian at Harvard College in the 1840s, and in 1856 the administration appointed him head librarian. Trained as a minister at Harvard, he had long been familiar with its holdings, which by 1841 consisted of some 41,000 volumes. Sibley recalled how in earlier times someone could walk into the library, ask for a book, and he typically knew where it was shelved.[2] That knowledge worked fine when the college had less than 20,000 volumes. Between keeping records of the growing inventory and serving as a scholar himself, he somehow kept up. His key problems—knowing what the college had and making these available to faculty and students—have been the central challenges faced by all librarians, even with the availability of online catalogs, Google, and increasingly AI-driven search algorithms.[3] This struggle to access information shaped how librarians viewed their definition of information and their efforts to develop means for organizing and accessing it. With the advent of the Second Industrial Revolution and its resultant massive increases in information, books, and journals, Sibley and his cohorts were losing control. But they fought back. Their initiatives set the stage for the first of the most important discussions about the nature of information held outside the purview of philosophers and theologians in response to the new age of industrialization, increasing literacy, and mass education. Every new profession and every academic discipline did the same, but because of the participation of librarians in all of these, their role proved foundational for the other information initiatives.[4] The majority of what they did took place in the United States in the nineteenth century, later spreading over across the world.[5] We will have occasion, however, to discuss European developments that came largely in the twentieth century. This chapter explains the activities of the librarians in two phases of their work: that of the nineteenth and early twentieth centuries when they took the initiative to catalog and organize information and that of the post–World War II period when they had to respond to the development of computers, a time when their earlier initiatives waned in the face of new classes of information experts ensconced in the world of computing. So, our account goes from the mid-nineteenth century to, in effect, the dawn of the twenty-first century.

Every person who could read or write since the late nineteenth century encountered librarians and libraries. In the United States alone in 2019, there were nearly 117,000 public libraries and nearly 240,000 in the rest of the world.[6] But, step back to see the arc of that large diffusion of libraries. In the mid-1870s there were over 400 American public libraries, each with a thousand books or more, even more additional libraries with less than 500 volumes. By the dawn of the new century, the number had increased to over 3,000 public libraries, each with 1,000 volumes or more. Collectively they had over 35 million books, a tally that did not include magazines or journals.[7] However, if one considered all libraries, then there were 10,000 as early as 1850.[8] Academic libraries also proliferated, some housing tens of thousands of volumes. No academic discipline of professors came close to such numbers; these were even outmatched by the number of people working as librarians. Yet the proverbial "everyone" expected librarians to acquire, organize, and make available vast quantities of information in quick, simple, and accurate ways across all disciplines.

This chapter focuses on librarians' views about information and how they could strategically and operationally address the massive increase in knowledge (their term). Theirs was a combination of intellectual debates and practical responses. In other chapters we see what "information" consisted of depended to a considerable extent on the professional worldviews of those engaged in the debate. I proceed, first, with a brief overview of the librarian's professional issues between the mid-1800s and the 1960s. I then discuss their solution: the mapping of all forms of knowledge. That is followed by how librarians viewed information in the post–World War II era when computing profoundly affected library operations.

OVERVIEW OF LIBRARIES AND LIBRARIANS

The American Library Association (ALA) describes four types of libraries: public, school, special, and academic. Public libraries are the overwhelmingly largest number in both the United States and around the world, the ones most people are familiar with. Their librarians nurture collections of books and other periodicals, run events, even shelter the homeless, and serve as safe havens for children and women. Most public librarians have a degree in library science. The second largest group consists of school libraries serving children in primary and secondary education. These are smaller than public libraries and have a combination of professionally trained librarians and volunteers. Third are specialized libraries, which are located in corporations, laboratories, government agencies, and nonprofit organizations. Their total number is not known; but librarians operating many of these have degrees in library science or backgrounds in the specialties of their holdings.

Fourth are academic libraries, those operating within colleges and universities, or run by library science schools (often termed "specialized libraries"). In addition to serving their users, librarians in academic libraries are often expected to conduct research and publish on their discipline. Finally, there are undergraduate and graduate schools of library science in which, as academic disciplines, faculty are expected to conduct research on their profession and about information or, to use their more widely applied term, *knowledge*. Much debate and research concerning librarians' views of information and information science comes out of library training programs. Public library employees have not engaged in such published conversations regarding information and their day-to-day operations, such as maintaining catalogs or about making materials available to readers. Professors in library schools and academic librarians have been prolific for over 150 years publishing on their field. There were nearly a dozen library journals before World War II, with the oldest established in 1876 by Melvil Dewey (1851–1931) as the *American Library Journal*, renamed *Library Journal* the following year. Today, there are over 225 journals dedicated to librarianship and information science.[9]

Public and school libraries exerted considerable influence on people from all walks of life. Users were exposed from very early ages to how librarians categorized information. The use of library catalogs, for example, introduced readers to types of information, topics, and authors. It became second nature to think that information existed about science, history, frogs, battles, flowers, cooking, and biographies, because of how these bodies of information were presented to people by librarians. Since their cataloging schema had remained essentially the same for over a century (Dewey or Library of Congress), that is the way the world of information became organized. The same applied to the vessels that held these bodies of information: books, journals, magazines, newspapers, pamphlets, microfilm, microfiche, video, TV, CDs, and now the Internet. How most people accessed information was largely learned initially from librarians long before high school teachers or professors had the opportunity to influence students with different approaches. Interviews of famous people routinely quoted them saying how wonderful these libraries and their librarians were, offering affectionate memoirs of childhood.[10] The public took no interest in discussions about information typologies and mapping, which were, however, of intense interest to those working in library schools and in related areas of information sciences. So, these debates remained partially masked, while those involving information conducted by computer scientists in the 1950s–1990s were more public, as were the worldviews of such social media behemoths as Facebook, Google, and Twitter, among others, in the 2010s.

From the beginning of the modern profession of librarianship in the 1870s, its members debated their identity and role. As women came to dominate the profession in the early decades of the twentieth century, much grousing occurred regarding their low salaries, whether they were "professionals" or simply caretakers of books, and what education they needed to qualify for their positions.[11] These conversations paralleled similar discussions underway about women in teaching and nursing. Many aspired to professional status, organized associations, and in the case of librarians, engaged in debates with academic disciplines regarding their own scholarly *bona fides*. Most of these debates occurred within academic communities where librarians were attempting to gain recognition as equals to the academics. They failed to gain that support, because they were unable to convince professors in other disciplines that they had the theory-based rigorous intellectual content and methods that scientists, for example, claimed.[12] The best they could do was grudgingly be thrown in with humanists, language and arts scholars, and even historians, but not with the hard scientists. Even changing their identity to "library science" in the mid-twentieth century and later into "Library and Information" schools and programs, never led to a solution to their image problem. As two economists describing the construct of the American information landscape noted about this profession:

> The eagerness with which library schools have moved to incorporate the word information into their titles is proof that their deans and faculties view the new technological developments in information handling as vital for their growth or even their survival. . . . Although library schools are quick to enlarge their curricula to include such aspects of information studies . . . often courses in information science consist merely of teaching students to use a new tool the computer.[13]

The identity issue had surfaced largely after librarians had made their greatest contribution to the definition of information. Historians of this profession speak of three eras. The first existed from the mid-nineteenth century to roughly World War I, when librarians mapped out what constituted the known knowledge field, developed the core cataloging processes still used today, and established associations and publications and implemented their original thinking. It was their Golden Age, and for this book the crucial one to understand. The second began between the two world wars and extended largely through the 1970s. It was an era when some discussion continued about the nature of information, led largely by the Documentalist movement. These participants attempted to expand the original mapping of information and leverage new tools, such as tabulating equipment, and more types of ephemera, such as film, photographs, other images, and microfilm.

The third began in the 1950s but came into full bloom in the 1980s when the crush of information technology on their profession fundamentally transformed it into "information science." It was now a subject area populated by experts from many disciplines and no longer dominated by librarians. This happened despite efforts by library school professors to rebrand themselves as working in "iSchools" and exploring information science. By then, computer scientists dominated thinking about information's typologies and organization; business professionals and academics in social media, sociology, and economics did too.

Some students of the profession are positing that a new era began when Google launched its initiative to digitize millions of books in the first decade of the new century. Google was offering to fulfill an age-old promise of building a universal library housing all knowledge. Regardless of whether one thinks it was an illusive pipe dream, millions of books were digitized, even more millions of people accessed these and in the process began to bypass brick-and-mortar libraries. It came to a halt when authors, publishers, and to some extent librarians were able to block this initiative over everyone's inability to overcome copyright concerns. But in this period in the twenty-first century one could see arguments marshaled by librarians that they were now widely in support of digital library holdings.[14]

Criticisms librarians aimed at each other could be brutal. For example, a leading light of mid-twentieth-century library studies Jesse H. Shera (1903–1982) leveled a serious volley at his colleagues in 1976 through their most widely read publication, *Library Journal*: "The librarians, too, have denied the importance of a philosophical frame of reference, and as a consequence have never developed a cohesive synthesis of their activities. As a result the movement has become fragmented, with the public, academic, and special librarians, along with the documentalists and information scientists, each group going its own way without any serious understanding of its relationship to the others."[15] Reflecting the criticisms leveled by other disciplines, he spoke about the librarians' "absence of synthesis which pervades every aspect of the librarian's practice" with many looking "to rhetoric and disputation rather than logic." The "term profession itself is suffering . . . because almost every human activity, in an effort to achieve prestige, calls itself a profession."[16] Librarians had made little progress. They failed to create "the rigorous discipline" they so wanted, while the attempt of the most important graduate school of library studies at the University of Chicago to create such rigor turned out to be "a complete disaster."[17] More specific to our interest about the nature of information, he called their research "unimpressive" with "much of it expended on problems that are relatively trivial, transitory, and hence inconsequential."[18] Yet that judgment did not stop librarians from conducting research using all the normal research methods of the day, such as history; surveys, qualitative, quantitative and statistical; case studies; citation analyses; and experiments.[19]

Shera thought the best work was done between the 1850s and later in the century with the creation of the Dewey cataloging system and establishment of the American Library Association, both in 1876. Shera concluded his attack on the hopeful note that perhaps the emergence of a new discipline called information science would provide librarians with the synthesis they needed to move forward. But in the meanwhile, "We must face the unpleasant fact [that] librarianship is basically much the same as it was in the days of Dewey, Cutter, Bowker, and their contemporaries."[20] Similar charges were leveled at the profession right into the twenty-first century. Such realities reinforce my observation that librarians made their most significant contributions in defining information, and how it could be made available to large audiences, during the roughly half-century beginning with the emergence of the Second Industrial Revolution.

Librarians made self-criticism a blood sport. Their problems became so bad that the greatest funder of libraries, the Carnegie Corporation, searching for understanding, commissioned a report on what was wrong with the profession and how it could be better prepared. It proved highly critical of the librarians. Its author, Charles C. Williamson, in 1923 enumerated reasons why library schools lacked the prestige enjoyed by professional schools in general. His list, which otherwise was reasonable and predictable (lack of sufficient assets to get the job done), added, "The total lack of anything recognized as productive scholarship."[21] Fifty years later, the outspoken Shera echoed such bluntness.

MAPPING THE WORLD OF KNOWLEDGE/ INFORMATION

The first significant contribution by librarians was to build on an old dream inherited from Europeans of somehow organizing all known knowledge in a way that made it accessible. The work of eighteenth-century French philosophes and their encyclopedia come quickly to mind along with the surge in bibliographies, anthologies, dictionaries, and indices in the eighteenth and early nineteenth centuries.[22] American librarians took the next step of proposing to describe the various types of information as reflected in publications—overwhelmingly books and journals—in such a way that these documents could physically be organized and easily accessed. Their objective was to create typologies of information and systems for organizing materials sufficiently open-ended to accommodate new topics and a rapidly growing body of publications. Their frameworks and approaches are still widely used.

Why they succeeded can be attributed to three factors. First, they sought to develop approaches that made it reasonably easy, indeed practical, for readers, researchers, librarians, and publishers to access information. So, they focused on the general notion of service to the end user. Second, they deployed their approaches so broadly and quickly that their users became comfortable with them.

One could walk into a school library that used the Dewey cataloging approach and quickly go to where all the books were about science or history, because that is how readers were raised. One could navigate the library's system. That leads to the third reason, one not scientifically understood then, but is now: that the human mind aspires to work with logical access points to information—mapping knowledge and having an understandable cataloging system facilitates—and that the mind wants to understand the structure of information. Cognitive scientists in the twentieth century developed mapping methods for identifying these relationships in methodical forms useful for the study of library services, information typologies, and cataloging systems.[23] One can see this mapping in action in the form of library classification systems and Internet directories. The librarians introduced the world to three classification methods that became widely embraced: Dewey Decimal Classification (DDC), Library of Congress Classification (LCC), and the Universal Decimal Classification (UDC).

Dewey Decimal Classification

Melvil Dewey (1851–1931) was both a librarian and college professor, born and raised in Adams Center, New York. While still in college he established the Library Bureau to sell index cards and file cabinets that in time resulted in the standardization of the library catalog card's size. Between 1883 and 1885 he served as the chief librarian at Columbia University, next holding the same position at the New York State Library (1888–1906). Meanwhile he became active in organizing librarians into a profession. So he had a perch and experience from which to consider how knowledge should be organized and a business to promote his ideas.[24]

Upon graduating from Amherst College in 1874, his alma mater hired him to reclassify its library holdings. He drew on ideas originally conceived by Sir Francis Bacon in 1605 as a way of categorizing knowledge. Dewey devised a decimal system for organizing information and linked it to a way to catalog publications that he intended be simple and concise.[25] In 1876, Dewey published his schema, *A Classification and Subject Index for Cataloging and Arranging the Books and Pamphlets of a Library*.[26] It included twelve pages of tables and an eighteen-page index for a total of forty-two pages. His second edition, published in 1885, expanded his concept to 486 pages.[27] He divided knowledge into ten classes, each with a family of numbers associated with them: General Works (000), Philosophy (100), Religion (200), Social Sciences (300), Language (400), Pure Science (500), Technology (600), Arts (700), Literature (800), and History (900). Each could be subdivided, so into 1 through 9 within, say, History for narrower historical topics, such as 901 or 907. Science—500—was subdivided into Mathematics (510), Algebra (512), and even more narrowly to Algebraic equations (512.2). To complete the description of his approach, a book could be cataloged as about Algebra, for example, by title, subject, and author, each with its own card. The three cards in the catalog list the book and with number 512.2 on its spine. Books and all other cataloged publications were physically arranged in numerical order. His schema and approach to the physical housing of materials remained essentially the same over the next nearly 150 years, albeit expanded.[28]

Lois Mai Chan, a prolific commentator about cataloging practices, pointed out another contribution to the concept of what constitutes information and how it could be accessed by emphasizing the power of standardization. That notion became a crucial feature of all subsequent information management schemas. It is easy to forget that it was not always so. She explained that standardization of descriptions of information made it possible for librarians to provide "some sort of topical labeling to help those who are trying to zero in on a subject," but too, "giving enough information about item at hand that a searcher reading its description can tell whether the item to which it pertains is a fair match to what he or she had in mind when formulating the search."[29]

Dewey was not alone in his hunt for typologies and standards. One student of Dewey's work, historian Colin B. Burke, pointed out that "Dewey's knowledge structure was not the most sophisticated of the era."[30] Other librarians in hot pursuit of "bibliographic control" included Sir Anthony Panizzi (1797–1879) working at the British Museum; Charles C. Jewett (1816–1868) at the Smithsonian Institution in Washington, D.C.; and Charles Ammi Cutter (1837–1903) at Harvard College and later at the Boston Athenaeum who produced a widely adopted cataloging schema, and at the start of the next century the U.S. Library of Congress. In the 1920s Williamson beat the drum in favor of standardization, devoting one chapter of his 165-page report to it.[31] Of growing concern to all these individuals was the exponential growth in the number of scientific papers that needed to be tracked and made available, and that in the twentieth century would lead to an extensive discussion among librarians (Documentalist movement), and not simply about books. In part, scientists themselves wanted to start tracking new information (discussed in chapter 6). Samuel C. Bradford (1878–1948), a leading commentator on the role of documents and cataloging in the early decades of the twentieth century argued that their papers, "needed cataloging just as much, or even more, than books, which only record a summary of original discovery, after the pioneers are many years ahead."[32] In other words, currency of information, too, had to be addressed. As of 1948, when Bradford published his comment, the problem had not yet been solved; it took scientists and software developers to proffer a solution, but that did not happen until the second half of the century.

Many hundreds of books and articles have been written describing Dewey's hierarchical schema, and it has had its critics, largely discussing his ten categories and how these needed to change or be expanded as the diversity of topics and their definitions evolved.[33] Over the next century, librarians periodically updated his classification system to accommodate new topics, such as about computers and atomic bombs. With publication of the twentieth edition in 1989, for example, the integrity of the hierarchical numbering system remained intact. That edition demonstrated, too, that the schema could evolve. Its description of the DDC required four volumes. The twenty-second edition (2003) continued the recent practice of incorporating into the description a classifier's user manual, because it had become so detailed.[34] Digital descriptions also became available.

The genius of the system consisted of the world of knowledge divided into ten (their contents varied over the next century, of course).[35] From an operational perspective, such schemes worked, even though librarians complained about its rigid categorization. However, it proved "good enough." Dewey demonstrated that the idea of "classification" of knowledge (i.e. information) made sense, and was flexible enough. He also linked it to publications. Dewey and others of the period thought more broadly than just how to organize books, beginning their work by thinking of how to organize knowledge, so that in the words of Jesse Shera, it would be "universal" and "that would be all things to all" people.[36]

Dewey promoted his classification and it spread rapidly in the United States, then to other countries. In 1988 the Online Computer Library Center (OCLC), located in Ohio, acquired the publishing rights to the DDC and publications related to it, and in the early 2000s the OCLC began posting descriptions of it on the Internet as WebDewey.[37] In 2020 over 200,000 libraries in nearly 140 countries used Dewey's classification to organize their collections, making it the most widely used cataloging system.[38]

Library of Congress Classification

The Library of Congress (LC) came into existence in 1800 and for nearly its first century primarily served the needs of the U.S. Congress. But at the dawn of the next century it was sharing its information with other libraries in the form of published catalog information, later bibliographies of its holdings. In the second half of the nineteenth century it had become one of the largest libraries in the United States, so its librarians inevitably engaged in knowledge categorization. By 1876, it had some 300,000 books, one million in 1901. To describe the arc of its growth, by 2019 it had over 38 million volumes and other printed material, some 14 million photographs, 5.5 million maps, and millions of other items for a total exceeding 167 million.[39] Almost all large research libraries in the United States use the Library of Congress cataloging system. So, LC's librarians became deeply involved in defining the scope of information and the library's physical legacies of books, other publications, and manuscripts. With the collection growing so rapidly and now being used by scholars and public officials, by the 1890s its old cataloging system no longer was practical. The Library of Congress Classification (LCC)[40] quickly became popular with large academic libraries that also faced problems of how to keep up with cataloging of expanding collections.[41] How to view the scope of information turned on the need to catalog materials quickly and cost effectively.[42] Melvil Dewey's approach was not an option, because he would not allow it to be modified to meet LC's needs, while European approaches were considered too philosophical.

So the LC librarians decided to build on the work of Charles Ammi Cutter (1837–1903), who had developed Harvard's card catalog system and during the 1890s had served as president of the American Library Association. Cutter described his categories in his publication, *Expansive Classification*.[43] An American librarian who had developed his cataloging approach roughly contemporaneously with Dewey, Cutter agreed to allow the LC to modify his system to reflect its own collection rather than have it structured to meet the definition of some universal concept of all knowledge.

Dewey and Cutter were rivals. As one librarian in the early decades of the twentieth century described their differences, Cutter "considered it erroneous to treat all fields of knowledge as though they were equal in scope; regardless of whether this was done according to decimals or according to letters," so between 1879 and 1886 he opted to assign capital letters "to some individual sciences."[44] Historian Wayne A. Wiegand observed that Cutter's approach "represented a watershed in cataloging history because it successfully established catalog codes in which entries were alphabetically interfiled under author, title, and subject."[45] These were reinforced in three subsequent editions introduced in 1889, 1891, and 1904 and peer-reviewed at the meetings of the American Library Association.

The rival Dewey–Cutter approaches were more than about dueling cataloging systems of interest just to librarians. Their views about knowledge—information—were on display, playing out in the operational context of cataloging. Wiegand makes clear these were "beliefs" that postulated:

> (1) it was possible to view the universe as a single cohesive whole; (2) elements of this universe had been revealed through intellectual discovery; (3) these elements existed in a hierarchical relationship; (4) listing these elements in their "natural" order would help define the essential characteristics of subject classes; (5) structuring this universe required that broadest subject classes reside at the top; and (6) to educate people and facilitate new knowledge, classificatory relationships had to give order to the universe of knowledge.[46]

Furthermore, they both believed that such schema—think cataloging discipline—would make it easier for a library to retrieve information while readers (users) would teach themselves how to find knowledge they wanted, thereby self-educating themselves about the world. No wonder such an underlying worldview of information would appeal to the librarians at the LC!

LC Librarian James C. M. Hanson (1864–1943) and his colleagues worked out details of a new cataloging approach based on Cutter's in the 1890s and early 1900s. Their schema combined mixed notations of letters and numbers. The librarians needed to define a wide scope of knowledge. Hanson introduced his initial description of knowledge in 1899 with each category a combination of letters and numbers. It was much longer than Dewey's original list. It included, in "A," for example, polygraphy, encyclopedias, general periodicals, and societies, philosophy, religion, theology, and church history. Biographies went into "C," while various discrete categories of history and geography into "D" through "G." Political science and the law lived in "H," sociology in "I," along with women; while sports, amusements, and music went into "J." Science, mathematics, astronomy, physics, and chemistry were housed with their own numbers in "N," while natural history in "O." Medicine went into "Q"; agriculture and the "useful arts" into "R"; "manufactures" into "S"; engineering into "T"; and all military, naval science, lifesaving and fire extinction, and light houses into "U." Bibliography gained its own section "Z."[47] In the LC categorization, science and engineering gained a larger space, reflecting the changing nature of information becoming available in the late 1800s. The letters were referred to as "classes," each defining what kind of information (knowledge) subjects were to be included in a catalog citation. All citations were letters and numbers, along with names and titles and subjects, echoes of the schemas of the 1800s. For example, my book, *All the Facts: A History of Information in the United States since 1870*, published in 2016, is listed in the LC as ZA3072.U6 C67 2016 and in the Dewey system as 020.973.

While it may appear a tad confusing to describe this cataloging approach, LC's scheme relied on the idea that information could be classified at a high level and then be divided into smaller portions in a hierarchical manner. It is a central idea shared by the influential nineteenth-century catalog designers that contributes to the definition and description of information. It constitutes an enormously important concept that emerged about the topic during the nineteenth century. Hanson and his colleagues redefined their notions to fit the needs of small libraries, then again to produce a more detailed one for larger ones in the early years of the next century. Now a small library could view the world of information as comprising works of reference, philosophy and religion, biography, history and geography (travels too), social sciences, natural sciences and arts, language and literature, and fiction, each with its own letter all called the "First Classification." Larger libraries had additional "top-level classes," such as Christianity and Judaism, and Ecclesiastical History, while "J" included Civics, Government, Political Science, and so forth. Recall, however, that its purpose was initially for the Library of Congress.

Because in 1901 the LC began distributing its catalog cards to other libraries—a cataloging initiative that continues to the present—it became a de facto typology for describing the great categories of information that future computer scientists and database developers encountered as university students. Like Dewey's classification, the LC's expanded and became more comprehensive as the types of information increased throughout the twentieth century. Like Dewey, it too had its subclasses (e.g., two Letters QA, QB) and uniform notations (e.g., QD146).

Work done in the United States in shaping how librarians defined the broad expanse of knowledge—information—did not go unnoticed in Europe, where librarians faced similar issues regarding cataloging and more fundamentally describing knowledge. One librarian from Germany, Georg Schneider (1876–1960), commented in the 1920s on the American experience:

> The work of developing bibliographical classification schemes began later in the United States than in other countries, but once begun it was carried on with great zeal. Interest in classification first arose in the United States in the seventies. It is now greater there than in any other country. The hope and belief in the possibility of obtaining a scheme that should prove applicable to all subjects in all countries for all time, a universal classification scheme such that every book

might find therein an unchanging and unchangeable place, and in which the classification and notation selected might be used to express the contents of a book by means of symbols, have led to many investigations.[48]

While the LC view of what constituted knowledge was broad, in its earliest incarnations it skewed to what the library had in its collections. However, because these increased so massively in the twentieth century, so did the LC's definition of what comprised bodies of information. At the same time and to the present it remained tethered to the types of materials in its collection. But, there were other librarians who sought an even more universal description of knowledge. In time these could be seen as linked to the thinking of such scientists, engineers, and mathematicians as Vannevar Bush, Alan Turing, and Claude E. Shannon in the 1930s and 1940s (see next chapter). But first we turn next to a young Belgian lawyer and his collaborators.

PAUL OTLET, THE UNIVERSAL DECIMAL CLASSIFICATION, AND THE DOCUMENTATION MOVEMENT

Cataloging books and other publications according to the rapidly adopted Dewey system in the 1890s, while practical and convenient, stopped at the information doorway of the publication. It did not get inside of these to catalog in detail their contents the way search engines do today through word searches. There was still that age-old aspiration of somehow collecting the entire world's knowledge—information—into one vast encyclopedia. To achieve that goal required a step beyond the cataloging schemes of the nineteenth century. Two Belgian lawyers dared to dream about that next step and to take important steps to implement it. Their actions proved effective enough that their schema is still used in the English-speaking world by specialized libraries and widely in French- and Spanish-speaking countries and in Central Europe. With their ideas developed, and enhanced by bibliographers and supported by librarians, there still remained before them what came to be their fundamental contribution to the world of librarianship prior to the arrival of the computer. In their work we glimpse early outlines of information technology's future influence on how information was seen and defined. From a practical perspective, too, as German librarian Schneider observed, the Belgians "formed the bridge between modern American bibliographic ideas and old Europe."[49]

The two lawyers, Paul Otlet (1868–1944) and Henri La Fontaine (1854–1943), had each been interested in improving bibliographies and were familiar with issues faced by nineteenth-century librarians in classifying book collections. La Fontaine was an expert in international law, and in the 1890s served as president of the International Peace Bureau. For his leadership he was awarded the Nobel Peace Prize in 1913. In 1895 he had been elected to the Belgian Senate, participated in the Paris Peace Conference in 1919, and subsequently served in the League of Nations. Interested in intellectual and educational matters, he joined with the younger Paul Otlet to establish the Union of International Associations in 1907 and in 1910 with him the *Institut International de Bibliographie* (later known as the International Federation for Information and Documentation, or FID). Paul Otlet became the senior member of this bibliographic duo, and he is today considered the father of information science, known in the early to mid-twentieth century by its more widely used name, "documentation."[50] He led the effort to create a new information schema called the Universal Decimal Classification, more commonly referred to as the UDC, and for facilitating its adoption in many countries before his death in 1944. In revised forms the UDC is still in use. He built it on the technological back of paper cards beginning in the 1890s, where it sat until the arrival of online cataloging in the 1960s.[51]

In 1895, the two lawyers created the Universal Bibliographic Repertory (*Réportoire Bibliographique Universal*, or RBU), which they intended to be a comprehensive index to all published knowledge and to be contributed to as a collaborative effort by librarians around the world. They thought to put information on cards, asking and getting from such libraries as the LC and the British Library paper copies of their catalog citations, cutting them to fit on those cards, and conceptualizing their organization using Dewey's Decimal Classification as a start. From the beginning Otlet wanted it to be a combination indexing and information retrieval system that could be accessed regardless of what language a user spoke by relying on a numeric scheme, thanks to Dewey.

With subjects already coded numerically, they envisioned using compounded numbers to link interrelated topics that could be used to identify relations between subjects, using symbols to represent these. Characteristics shared by subjects could be accumulated as separate lists, adding to all these features of their system as the variety and quantity of information increased and as required by users. They wanted to add detail on cards extracted from within the content of a publication, such as a book or other ephemera, including from the 1930s microfilm. Their original conception, published between 1902 and 1907, contained 33,000 subdivisions.[52] A second edition, published between 1927 and 1933, identified over 70,000 subdivisions, remaining essentially the primary version of the UDC until 1993, when it was replaced by an online database. The paper version had become unwieldy by the 1940s, but until the arrival of computers, could not be redesigned. Yet even in the 1930s librarians continued to enrich the system, with a German edition published between 1934 and 1951, which contained some 140,000 subdivisions.[53]

Otlet provided his fullest explanation of how to organize and think of information in 1934.[54] He introduced much new thinking and language, building on prior publications and user manuals he and his colleagues had prepared. A historian examining his thoughts likened these to "information technology, information retrieval, search strategies, information centers, fee-based information services, linked data bases, database management software, scholarly communication networks, multimedia and hypertext, even the modern, diffuse notion of 'information' itself."[55] In brief, Otlet had developed several ideas central to our study of the evolution of information. First, he demonstrated that information could be identified through bibliographic means, using rigorous methods, even scientific ones, a tip of the hat to the structure offered by Dewey. Second, he proffered that information about information could reside on cards arranged to reflect relationships among topics. Decks of cards could, thus, be continuously reshuffled, "interfiling" as subjects and content evolved. To do this one required a "detailed synoptic outline of knowledge" with which to arrange the cards and the novel idea of facilitating collaboration among scholars in the preparation of such a catalog. He anticipated a shift in responsibility for organizing materials from librarians to users, an old notion dating to the 1890s.[56] In other words, all human knowledge could be represented in one unified way. His was a proposal to do just that.[57]

The Belgian government financially supported his card-building activities. After World War II, the International Federation for Information and Documentation continued this work. It was never a trivial exercise. In 1897 he had 1.5 million entries, 9 million in 1912, 16 million in 1930.[58] The collection was called the Repertory and consisted of two broad files: author and extended subject. Other files were created to collect information on iconography and music, ballooning the collection of cards by an additional 250,000.[59] He next added text files to these various bibliographic cards, previewing his vision of the "Documentary Encyclopedia" in 1907. It came to include all manner of text from publications, including from inside books and journals across many topics. This encyclopedic project contained one million items under 10,000 subject files by the start of World War I in 1914.[60] The war interrupted further expansion of the project.

If this description of his projects seems eerily familiar, Wikipedia was similarly conceived as containing content from publications and about topics offered by volunteers from around the world. Google could flag and present text from inside a publication. Otlet just conceived of these capabilities a century earlier. In 1918 he described all of this as, "an immense map of the domains of knowledge."[61] It was all about linking together vast quantities of information.

His multifaceted classification system far exceeded Dewey's quickly as contributors kept working on it. Between 1904 and 1907, the first formal listing of all the tables and classifications required 2,000 pages; the second edition of the UDC did not appear until the 1930s. Its historian has characterized it as "a highly complex database management system," all paper-based![62] Colin B. Burke agreed with this assessment too, "It was a very complex scheme that was labor intensive and that required people highly skilled in both subject matter and the system."[63] It hinted at being a proto-hypertext information storage and retrieval system for managing such a database. Of course, it was enormously difficult to create, add to, and manage such a paper-based system. The UDC also required its keepers to be rigid and authoritarian in defining and enforcing standards. Such problems remained until the arrival of software search tools nearly a century later. Today the number compounding and synthesizing practices used by the software versions of the UDC make it possible to do what Otlet had originally envisioned as early as 1892.

He had other ideas, too. One historian described his thinking: "Recording 'analytically' single, separate pieces of information [on cards], be they bibliographical or substantive. Larger chunks of information could be recorded on separate sheets. Otlet called this identification and recording of 'bits' of information the 'Monographic Principle.'" *Monographic* was a precise term for Otlet, derived from the Greek, signifying "a single or individual piece or unit of writing."[64] In other words, he wanted to take apart, say a book, and absorb its contents into his system (or databases), his "repertories." He had in mind to develop the "Universal Book" as the "ultimate work of documentation," a work of "encyclopedic codification."[65]

Despite its physical limitations, and the interruption of World War I in Europe, his ideas sparked a sizeable movement of documentalists within the library community.[66] One of the most distinguished British librarians of the twentieth century, Samuel C. Bradford, published a description of the movement's ideas as late as 1948. Bradford's version: "the art of documentation is the art of collecting, classifying and making readily available the records of all kinds of intellectual activity. It is the process by which the documentalist is enabled to put before the creative specialist the existing literature, bearing on the subject of his investigation, in order that he may be made fully aware of previous achievements in his subject, and thus be saved from the dissipation of his genius upon work already done."[67] Despite the enormous increase in publications, notably in scientific journals requiring cataloging and classification, and the progress made by librarians to carry out these tasks through Dewey, the LC approach and Otlet's ideas, they were falling behind.

Bradford argued for more "abstracting services," itself an intellectually challenging task, since no one individual could understand all that was being produced, let alone create multiple abstracts for each published paper to take into account various perspectives. It was the challenge of cross-referencing multiple topics to meet the needs of a researcher. He cited the example of someone wanting information about the molecular structure of a frictionless surface. That individual would expect to find articles on that topic in journals devoted to general science, physics, molecular physics, colloids, chemistry, theoretical and physical chemistry, geophysics, and various types of engineering, metallurgy, and machining. There was much to be done in the 1940s to work out how to do this.[68]

In Otlet's and Bradford's thinking we see planted seeds of information science. The first generation of computer builders were attending classes and using libraries, while older scientists and mathematicians were witnessing some of the librarians' activities, such as Alan Turing (1912–1954) and Vannevar Bush (1890–1974), both of whom we meet in the next chapter. But with the start of World War II, the thinking that had started in the nineteenth century among librarians and bibliographers had played out. Their colleagues would spend the period from World War I until the arrival of computers in their libraries deploying systems charted earlier. Although some thinkers wanted to push forward, identifiable in the late 1930s, and in time forming what came to be known as information science, theirs was really a post–World War II phenomenon that also involved others outside the world of the librarians.

Before moving to that story, there is the matter of an undercurrent of thinking and bibliographic activities not to be ignored. It involved the notion of quality information. While the Documentalists were active, there was simultaneously yet a second activity underway that influenced them and librarians more broadly that needs to be understood to round out our understanding of events in the early decades of the twentieth century.

ONLY THE BEST BOOKS WILL DO

The centrality of the book is easy to find in the descriptions of librarians' role, in their textbooks, and in histories and analyses of what ailed their profession. In the nineteenth century most published information was sheltered inside books and journals (newspapers to a lesser degree). As time passed and to the end of the twentieth century other types of ephemera increased in abundance, also to be taken care of by librarians. The documentalists of the 1920s–1940s, for example, focused considerable attention on microfilming and incorporating photographs and other images into the broader world of what inventories librarians should protect. But the centrality of the book never diminished. For decades the American Library Association displayed as its bumper sticker motto, "The Best Books for the Most People at the Least Cost." Shera was blunt on the matter, writing in 1976 after a decade of extensive introduction of computers into library cataloging "that the librarian is, first of all, a bookman, and his primary responsibility is to place on his library's shelves only those books that contribute most to the intellectual growth of his clientele."[69] Dewey felt the same way a century earlier. To do this work, for hundreds of years librarians had developed bibliographies—inventories—of their holdings. It was the information contained in those bibliographies that morphed into card catalogs in the 1800s, but that also continued the tradition of book-formatted bibliographies. The hundreds of volumes of the LC's *National Union Catalog* became a monument to that practice.[70]

The library professionals debated furiously the role of books and bibliography for decades. It is widely believed that the reluctance of librarians to become more digitally oriented could be anchored to their older book-centered worldview.[71] The topic remains contested; nonetheless, developing bibliographic methods continued.[72] An ongoing concern was how to catalog one's own library's collection, but also librarians thought about how to organize bibliographic citations of materials, especially since often non-librarians created bibliographies on specific topics as well.[73] Over the course of nearly a half-century I prepared nearly a half dozen book-length bibliographies because (a) I was knowledgeable about the topic and so was aware of the extant literature on these topics and (b) recognized that others interested in similar subjects could use these as tools to get quickly to the relevant materials they then needed to have librarians make available to them.[74] Librarian's dominance over the development of bibliographies had started to shrink by the mid-twentieth century as experts published such lists of their domains. Nonetheless, librarians were told that the "bibliographical records of a library are only an inventory to its contents," as declared by Pierce Butler (1884–1953), professor of bibliographic history, in 1933 at the newly established Graduate Library School at the University of Chicago.[75]

Yet the dream of somehow encompassing all knowledge spilled over into their bibliographic work. As late as the mid-1960s manuals on compiling bibliographies still advised on how to be comprehensive. They did not discuss the use of computers to generate bibliographies, although such activities were already underway within large government agencies and corporations. The librarians' guides were still explained as manual book-centric tasks attempting to put together a universal guide that was now considered impractical as envisioned by Otlet and whose UDC had expanded to 12 million cards by then. One was being advised to have more narrowly focused lists. These included bibliographies of books in various languages, others on national publications (such as the LC's), and regions. Specialized bibliographies were encouraged, too, by subject, such as for chemistry or history; by nation, international linguistic; and by period, individual types of publications (e.g., Bible or Shakespeare), then even by physical format, such as large books or maps.[76]

Librarians serving the general public and students often worried about what were the "best books" to put in front of their clients. Librarians recognized there was much that had been published of questionable value. This mission led them directly to the concept that information had various degrees of quality. What is quality information? What is a good book? These questions were never answered with definitiveness. One librarian's poor book was another's quality publication. One historian noted that since Dewey's day, librarians had been told they needed to determine what quality was so that they could build book collections that made such materials available: "Thus, librarianship's structure and systems stressed useful knowledge, and the librarians functioned as cultural caretakers."[77]

One response in evidence long before Dewey's time that continues to the present was the preparation of bibliographies of best books, or those recommended for a particular audience, such as for children.[78] As the number of public libraries in the United States and in Europe increased by the end of the 1800s and certainly before World War II, recommended lists of best publications became widely available, indirectly through librarians introducing these to the public and by academic disciplines. Both promoted the notion that some information was "better" than others and that "better" was reflected in what appeared in these bibliographies. For example, in 1935 the Carnegie Corporation, which had funded the construction of over 2,500 libraries and purchases of books as part of the Carnegie family's library initiatives for many decades, published a list of books entitled *The Diffusion of Knowledge*, prepared by a librarian at the New York Public Library and the secretary of the Carnegie Corporation. It listed 5,000 books that the corporation had funded for libraries, all chosen by hundreds of librarians in many institutions as essential for their collections.[79] The bibliography was intended to guide other public libraries on what they, too, should acquire as good books. A librarian at Swarthmore College prepared a similar list aimed at what college libraries should acquire. Charles B. Shaw (1884–1962) published through the American Library Association in 1940, *A List of Books for College Libraries*, a follow-on to an earlier one appearing in 1931.[80]

Shaw's 1940 list included 3,600 titles recommended largely by Swarthmore's professors and other experts. Both the 1931 and 1940 lists organized citations by academic discipline. For example, his latter volume included astronomy, botany, chemistry, classics, economics, education, English, fine arts, geography, geology, German, history, mathematics, music, philosophy, hygiene, physics, political science, psychology, religion, Romance languages, sociology, and zoology. When I attended a liberal arts college in the 1960s—just twenty-five years after the publication of this bibliography—the table of contents of his book looked like the list of majors one could take up. Each department's professors continuously interacted with our college librarians to ensure that the small library budget included acquisition of what they, and such bibliographies, considered essential, the "best," or currently most useful publications.[81] This bibliography helped shape what was taught to students in many schools, because such bibliographies assisted small college librarians how best to support their faculties.

The idea of quality information as reflected in books became a permanent feature of modern life. Most academic societies award prizes for best books; leading newspapers annually rank the best books of the year; even professional and industry organizations do too, such as Bloomberg. Long before the Internet made available services to feed pre-selected materials to readers along the lines envisioned by the documentalists, printed anthologies of best books (or portions of their contents) proved successful business ventures. Generations of Americans, for example, read *Reader's Digest*, a commercial venture founded in 1922 as a monthly magazine published ten times a year aimed at the general public. It is still published with a global paid subscription of 10.5 million copies.[82] Book publishers did too, such as the *Encyclopedia Britannica* in 1952 with its fifty-four-volume set of Great Books of the Western world. Editors chose these because they were relevant to contemporary society, rewarding to read, and contributed to "the great conversation about the great ideas," which they had enumerated as consisting of exactly 102.[83] The notion of quality bubbled along all through the era of the computer. In the period of intensified political and public debates about fake facts in the 2000s, once again the issue of quality (i.e., accurate) facts surfaced as a massively discussed feature of information.[84]

Quality also meant getting to the "right," "best," more relevant materials. That quest was fundamentally a bibliographic one. Bradford, a documentalist, is less remembered for writing a textbook about the movement's thinking than for developing what came to be known as Bradford's Law, which he introduced in 1934.[85] It is an expression of geometric progression, related to Pareto's Law. It is an important mathematical and scientific finding that has been rigorously validated by information experts in multiple scientific fields. Librarians have a good right to claim it as a signal achievement.

His law quantifies the exponentially diminishing returns of looking for citations in scientific journals. It holds that looking for desired articles becomes less productive the more one searches increasing numbers of journals, that a few "core" publications yield the greatest return on the hunt for citations. So, if a scientist has a half-dozen core journals in his or her field generating, say, a dozen useful papers, the hunt for an additional dozen papers in other journals he or she would need to examine twelve journals, and so forth. He quantified this phenomenon. His observed pattern held true for scientific journals, less so for those in the humanities and social sciences.[86] I apply his law later in this chapter to explain what research librarians did in information science. The upshot is this: Go to a few core journals and you have all the key materials you are looking for. His insight made it possible for librarians to do fewer searches to yield a greater supply of relevant materials; scientists quickly learned to do the same. It is why, for example, to be taken seriously, an ambitious scientist must publish in *Nature* or *Science*, why a historian of information technology must publish in the *IEEE Annals of the History of Computing* or in *Technology & Culture*. Bradford was successful in uncovering this law in ways that could be measured. That fact was made possible because he was trained as a mathematician, while most librarian researchers were not.

Before moving to post–World War II events, note that over the course of a half-century, librarians had formed the habit of collaborating on all manner of issues, giving highly dispersed, under-funded, often little-trained librarians sufficient muscle to organize subjects and their publications, build libraries, and provide access to information. In the process they establish communal values, such as a commitment to serving readers, attributes that became woven into their profession and that would influence their activities down to the present.[87]

THE NEXT TRY: INFORMATION SCIENCE

Following World War II, the growing need to focus on the nature and role of information presented in electronic formats came so rapidly that one could argue librarians were simply outnumbered by people, technological developments, and the massive investments made in computing technology as one response to the exigencies of the Cold War.[88] I conclude this chapter by arguing that librarians bear considerable—but not all—responsibility for losing control over the discussion about the features and role of information. First a reminder: from the late 1800s to the 1960s, librarians remained wedded to notions of information and knowledge shaped by Dewey's generation and built out their collections of books and journals, cataloging, and other library practices that had essentially been defined by the start of World War I.[89] After World War II a resurgence of research debates regarding information erupted, largely in library schools, as some their staffs came back one more time to wrestle with the twin issues of academic legitimacy and now, too, in response to the surge of computing in their world.

Libraries were compelled by the benefits of computing to automate work they had done for decades. That activity reinforced aspirations of the documentalists of the early twentieth century. Unlike in earlier decades, however, this time participants included experts trained in other disciplines, including computing, psychology, and sociology.[90] During the Cold War years, librarian hegemony over the definition and shaping of information cracked, and in the process the conversation about the nature of information balkanized—a key point of the rest of this chapter. The notion that information should be the greater focus over the study of books and their use transitioned from the documentalists' interest to the greater library community essentially in the 1960s when, for example, library school professors began rebranding themselves as a new discipline: Library and Information Science (LIS). Although as the opening of professional library schools from the 1920s indicated, demand within that community for a rigorous research agenda had pushed them to emphasize information. Their focus began evolving from the 1950s toward "information retrieval," or more fashionably, *information science*.[91] This development was followed by the development of computerized bibliographic files and databases. An early computer scientist influential in the librarian's world, Calvin N. Mooers (1919–1994), signaled the need to use computing to distribute processing of information and retrieval through networks in the late 1940s and early 1950s. User-driven information retrieval, be they facts or citations, was now possible, and he called for mathematicians, computer scientists, and librarians to work out its implementation. Mooers argued that the easier such retrieval became, the more it would be used.[92]

Library issues and computing began merging into what came to be known as library and information science.[93] Training programs for librarians did not easily transform in a timely fashion to reflect that shift, although library schools changed their names to fashionably include information in their titles.[94] Research by librarians remained largely focused on operational issues, less on the nature of information, leaving academic boundaries fuzzy as psychologists, computer experts, and others began to think through the nature and role of information in a world moving to the use of computers.[95] By the end of the twentieth century, LIS could thus be described as multidisciplinary, with competition from computer science, and by the early 2000s, from those studying how brains work, and even from biology related to brains, nervous systems, and feedback loops and communications—an old notion dating to the 1940s, from Norbert Wiener and Claude Shannon, among others.

While librarians focused on giving people access to the documented knowledge accumulated by society, those working in information science studied the properties—features—of recorded symbols, how they were processed, and activities processed within an information system. I have commented elsewhere on the nature of information systems—information ecologies—to point out that they were far more pervasive than what librarians understood to be the case over the past half-century.[96]

The two fields began to merge slowly. American documentalists rebranded themselves in the 1970s into the American Society for Information Science and subsequently by other societies and journals.[97] Library schools began dropping the "L" word from their titles, rebranding themselves as Schools of Information (iSchools), and since the 2000s universities began folding these training programs into their larger computer science departments and colleges.[98]

What changes, then, occurred in how librarians defined and discussed information? An answer can be approached by tracing two of their publications that most focused on research related to information, *American Documentation* (launched in 1937) and through its successor the *Journal of the Association for Information Science* (beginning in 1968), examining every issue from 1937 through 2019—a demonstration of applying Bradford's Law. Many of the articles in both dealt with traditional issues involving cataloging and bibliography, and laboriously over the decades, the transition from card to online systems, with many case studies on how one technology or another was used. Twenty years into it—in 1958—one writer complained that his colleagues were still stuck in old conversations about classifications, hoping instead for more research on "mathematical logic" and in the "theory of numbers" as ways to understand "metalanguage" concepts. He acknowledged that librarians had to face the issue of the role of computers, "the threat of machines." Shannon and Weaver were complimented for "their quantification" of the "mathematical theory of communication," which held out "great promise for the theory and practice of documentation."[99] In the 1950s there was a renewed focus on coming up with ways of cataloging all written knowledge. It seemed everyone had a theory, a concept to promote that was logical, comprehensive, and could be implemented. Clearly, the old ways no longer could handle the growing volume (again) of information.[100] By the early 1960s, advocates for using computers were laying out their case.[101] This all represented a rather lengthy period of throat clearing and little substance on the matter of basic research about information.[102]

In the late 1960s the American Documentation Institute changed its name to American Society for Information Science. One technologist offered a positive definition: "*Information science* is that discipline that investigates the properties and behavior of information, the forces governing the flow of information, and the means of processing information for optimum accessibility and usability."[103] This quasi-definition provided something for everyone, including the tradition of being imprecise to make room for many in the librarian's tent. Perhaps it was a necessary step for a new generation. The same article carrying the definition cataloged 655 research projects across numerous disciplines. These included many familiar ones, such as information needs and uses, document creation and copying, language analysis, translations by machine, organization of libraries and information retrieval, and others involving modeling and other forms of data analysis common in non-library research, pattern recognition of images and speech, and "adaptive systems," better known then and now as artificial intelligence.[104] Meanwhile, explanations about what should be studied kept appearing.[105] Discussions about what computer scientists were doing, written by them, began appearing in this librarian's journal in the 1960s.[106]

Research on the behavior of information began to appear in these two journals in the 1960s, and by the early 1970s offered new insights into the subject. For example, Bruce J. Whittemore, a computer scientist at Ohio State University, and his colleagues explained notions of information flows to librarians that built nicely on Shannon's and Weaver's work of the 1940s, now in terms of interest to librarians. Information flow became a staple of computer science, librarians, and economists over the next half-century, while databases finally began to receive attention too, again explained largely by computer scientists.[107] Yet complaints from inside the tent continued. For example, James Williams and Chai Kim commented in their article from 1975: "Information science is at present a practice-oriented discipline somewhat analogous to nursing and that as a result information scientific theory is considered by many as idle speculation," arguing that "theory must be given equal emphasis with practice and empirical research." Until it had a theoretical basis, library science could not be considered a science.[108] Several months later, another commentator opined that "the enthusiasm and optimism have begun to wane. The prospect of fundamental theories of information phenomenon is not on the horizon"; too much remained unsettled with respect to theory. In short, there were no new developments at hand.[109]

In the 1970s and 1980s computing tutorials continued being written by computer scientists as librarians were now heavily engaged in implementing what computing's engineers had created in the previous twenty years.[110] Case studies of knowledge utilization continued to appear in the *Journal of the Association of Information Science* throughout the 1980s and 1990s.[111] As other disciplines developed ideas and practices, these represented new splits within the librarian's information research world, such as the development of medical informatics, an important new subfield of information studies that developed largely outside the world of library science. Simultaneously, computer scientists continued to find this journal useful for their reporting, often dominating conversations about research on information into the 1990s.[112]

Little progress was made, however, on the broader theme of studying the nature of information. Chaim Zins, a well-respected librarian, reported in

2007 an old problem that "there is not a uniform conception of information science. The field seems to follow different approaches and traditions; for example, objective approaches versus cognitive approaches, and the library tradition versus the documentation tradition versus the computation tradition." He added, "Nevertheless, all of them are represented by the same name, *information science*. No wonder that scholars, practitioners, and students are confused."[113] He put his finger on a great part of the problem facing library schools and their researchers: "Different knowledge domains imply different fields." Yet for over 150 years, librarians had claimed ownership of the field and defended it against discipline-based rivals, which he carefully defined in some ways in the tradition of Dewey and Cutter, with lists of topics/subjects.[114]

However, librarians were energized to study the role of the World Wide Web, because this technology facilitated the physical distribution of and access to information users outside libraries. That capability fundamentally challenged old notions of people showing up at libraries or accessing information at the book or journal level. Now they desired and were obtaining actual content. That was a world librarian researchers could appreciate, if armed with necessary, often computing, technical skills. They began to study the usage patterns of web-based catalogs, formed opinions about what Internet studies they should engage in, with searching practices a popular topic, while again proposing frameworks for future study.[115] Their activities represented moves into the world of computing after a half-century of reacting to and responding to work done by academic and commercial computer scientists and information technology vendors.

Such reports established two fundamental points. First, that research about computing, and most specifically about the role of the Internet, quickly drew the attention of researchers in the world of librarianship—Information Science—not just computer scientists. Second, they were beginning to report results affecting how one might view information in the new century. For example, a study from 2001 documented the use of "web spiders," a software to search on behalf of humans, a third of some 2.5 million searches in one case study alone.[116] This suggested that the old dream of the documentalists was possible, could be measured and tracked, and almost instantly involved massive quantities of samples. This information had to be digital. That data could be presented graphically representing an expanding form of information. It further suggested that an increasing manifestation of information was the statistic—numbers—to aggregate data that in earlier times might have been presented in textual, narrative form. I have long considered this feature of information as representing the decline of the adjective in favor of the perceived precision of a number in business circles, now evident too in the librarian's world.[117] Web searching became an early and popular process by which to understand digitized information, although in the new century many of the early studies still focused on user behavior, as over the previous century of research.

Librarians and others expanded their understanding about the growing quantities of information and how people sought it out. That behavior suggested information retrieval—search—was changing, driven by the capabilities of computing, making it possible for people to find more specific facts beyond what they and librarians could in the paper-only days or when computers did not provide online access to information.[118] This latter computing issue spoke to a growing interest in what scholars increasingly were labeling as "cognitive styles," defined as "tendencies displayed by individuals consistently to adopt a particular type of information processing strategy."[119] More than in any earlier period, it was becoming evident that the nature of a particular class of information affected search practices. For example, finding greater amounts of information helped searchers refine more precisely what problem, or issue, they wanted to investigate. That in turn changed a searcher's perception of the problem at hand. Researchers were able to document that search strategies changed, while improving the clarity of their thinking.[120]

One consequence reported by several library school professors in 2008 was that "information studies" (now a code term used by library school researchers) had become net exporters of new insights to other disciplines, notably computer science, engineering, business, and management. If their findings were later validated, it would represent a turn of events from the period 1930s–2000 when it was the library community that imported research findings regarding information from those disciplines.[121] "Citation analysis" had become a popular topic, and by 2008 over 275 information studies (IS) periodicals existed in which to report results of such research. Scholars in the humanities remained some of the most interested in information science studies, but an appetite for such materials also developed among computer scientists and business and management disciplines, which could be tracked and quantified as more information became available electronically that could be aggregated. Slightly over half of the 54,181 papers cited from 275 IS journals came from outside the IS community.[122] That interest encouraged interdisciplinary collaborative studies about information.[123]

Such developments bring us back to old questions long faced by librarians: What is information and what are its features? In the 2000s there was still no agreement on the definition and agreed-to list of its characteristics. One definition in 2006 held that "information is the pattern of organization of the *matter* of rocks, of the earth, of plants, of animal bodies, or of brain matter . . . also the pattern of organization of the *energy* of my speech as it moves the air . . . the only thing in the universe that does not contain information is total entropy; that alone is pattern-free."[124] In other words, information is "an objectively existing phenomenon in the universe."[125] An alternative older (1972) definition held that information is "a difference that makes a difference."[126] Students of the matter were formulating the idea that information could be observed as objective, something as independent, stand-alone, while others approached it as subjective or situational.[127] With echoes of Shannon of the 1940s, a third notion held that information is "a quality by a given signal relative to a certain mechanism," a reaction, say, of a person or animal releasing energy through thought and action, a signal.[128]

These various perspectives have not found unanimity of support from librarian and information science experts, because these are "frustrating" ways to view information.[129] People still sought a universal theory of information rather than a more narrowly one that makes the definition of information contextually situated. Perhaps looking for characterizations of "the nature of information" failed to lead to a theoretical foundation, the ultimate, yet illusive, prize librarians had sought for a century with which to make their field of study rigorous, theory-based, "scientific," and thus respected by other academic disciplines. So, old questions continued to be asked: What kind of science can information science be? (2012),[130] or What are the "boundary objects" in information science? (2017).[131] Context remained a popular battleground. In 2019, a flurry of articles reaffirmed interest in discussing what now was called "social informatics of knowledge," engaged by iSchool scholars from both North America and Europe.[132] As had been the case for over a century, older themes continued to draw attention as well, such as information retrieval in the age of computers and the Internet.[133]

But Silicon Valley operatives, including the founders of Google, were also doing the dreaming; it was no longer the purview of the librarians. Computer scientists and software programmers, however, in the 1960s took actions to make those realities. While the initiatives attempted by librarians to go digital came literally decades after other facets of society were well into it, their activities since 2000 suggested that in piecemeal fashion that had engaged fully in the transformation of their information holdings into increasingly digital formats. Library closing due to the Covid-19 pandemic simply reinforced the urgency to digitize access to their collections.[134]

CONCLUSIONS

Librarians, and those few within their ranks who led in pondering the nature of information have lived through three eras. The first, from the start of the Second Industrial Revolution to the start of World War II, saw development of such enduring typologies as Dewey's classification system, that of the U.S. Library of Congress, and the work of the European documentalists. It was in this long era that librarians contributed the most to our understanding of information. Because of the enormous expansion in the number of libraries and their use, it became comfortable to build on the innovations largely developed in the last third of the nineteenth century by expanding and building out libraries and their associated cataloging and bibliographic methods. As librarian Michael Buckland has argued, however, they experienced more growth than change and resisted embracing new technologies that had become available in the first half of the twentieth century, such as punched cards and microfilming. When these were proposed, librarians often viewed innovators as a threat to their way of life; they did not give in until the 1970s. He also pointed out that the leading professional library schools *resisted* embracing innovative technologies and research, blaming the leader of those institutions, the University of Chicago, as the worst and most influential offender.[135]

In the 1980s and early 1990s, fifteen library schools that followed Chicago's tradition-minded lead began closing in the United States. The University of Chicago's library school did so in 1989. Columbia University shuttered its pioneering library school, which Dewey had opened in 1887. Accreditation of these schools and their programs "legitimized mediocrity" at a time when demand for new methods and perspectives about information and computing technology proved urgent.[136]

Librarians and their thought leaders were aware of the changes. Some acknowledged the work of the documentalists and such technologists as Bush and Shannon. Some of the outsiders even wrote about the changing technologies, such as Joseph C. R. Licklider (1915–1990), who on behalf of the Council on Library Resources wrote a book published in 1965, *Libraries of the Future*.[137] If his name sounds familiar, it is because he was one of the more important computer scientists of the twentieth century. He articulated a vision for what would become known as "interactive computing." He was also an early pioneer in the development of conceptual features of the Internet in the 1960s, having worked with computers at the Massachusetts Institute of Technology (MIT) since 1950. It is nearly impossible to minimize his impact on the field of computer science. He was not the first to think about the study of information influenced by scientific and engineering precepts, for the term *information science* had circulated since the early 1950s in library schools, in their publications, and across the profession.[138]

By the time the library profession attempted to re-lead the information discourse, the opportunity had sped by them, the intellectual baton long having passed to computer scientists. But why that happened remains an open question, important because it could someday happen to computer scientists as biologists and cognitive studies communities ramp up their contributions. The answer is more than because librarians became comfortable with set ways in a period of fundamental growth in the number of libraries.

In 2018 two students of the problem published a paper examining the educational backgrounds of American librarians from 1950 to 2015. They discovered that by 1951—just as computers were becoming commercially available—58 percent of librarians had a college degree; that a one-third had majored in English and one-sixth in social sciences. These two majors represented a persistent pattern. In 1969, 72 percent of librarians had specialized in the humanities. That trend continued through the 1990s with history, English, and education majors dominating. Even librarians working in specialized libraries in engineering organizations reported 11 percent majoring in social science fields, 9 percent in liberal arts, and another 9 percent equally in education and fine arts, and 7 percent in history. Only 7 percent had engineering backgrounds, 7 percent in chemistry, and 4 percent in mathematics. Their findings reflected a continuing enormous imbalance of backgrounds to fill the paucity of needed skills. For over six decades librarians had studied English and history as undergraduates, in sharp contrast to the overall pattern of the nation's college students who trended far more toward biology, business, engineering, health, and the physical sciences—fields that provided much greater intellectual leadership in the general subject of information. Even doctoral degrees held by librarians skewed the same way (arts and humanities 59.9%, professions/applied sciences 24.4%, social sciences 8.8%, and natural sciences 5.4%).[139]

The authors politely understated the problem: "Humanistic disciplines seem to be overrepresented in librarianship."[140] They ended their study by pointing out that in recent years they could detect a slow decline in students earning undergraduate degrees in the humanities prior to becoming librarians, even though many majors were being positioned within the library community as social sciences. All of these backgrounds made sense when librarians focused predominantly on books decades earlier; however, as the disciplinary requirements of librarians changed, the education they received did not shift "at the same rate."[141] No wonder scientists had to develop their own information search tools, information maps, and databases. The authors pointed out that the number of people with STEM (science, technology, engineering, and mathematics) backgrounds was too few at a time when STEM research and work continued to expand, as it had for over 150 years.[142] The profession had relinquished leadership in shaping how people understood information in an Information Age.

The world had been transitioning to computing since at least the 1950s and in the wake of that fundamental change in how humans lived, worked, and played transformed their views of what constituted information and its role. The intellectual poverty of the librarian's profession had been masked by the enormous growth in the number of libraries, publications, and information that they experienced during these decades. That their profession was changing and that they were forced by transforming realities to evolve did not excuse the declining role of their profession in shaping modern perspective on information.[143]

Ultimately, many of the challenges faced by librarians remained unresolved, and still in flux: how to organize and access information. Physicist Niels Bohr lectured on that issue in the 1950s, arguing that humans synthesized information conceptually in their brains, increasingly understood to be heuristic behavior, and so librarians had to find a way to connect to that way of thinking.[144] That was a closed world constrained by experience, yet librarians never were able to escape the reality that information kept increasing, kept diversifying. That the culture and times in all three phases in the work of developing information schema kept evolving was not lost on some librarians. Jesse H. Shera reminded librarians of that reality in the late 1950s and 1960s: "The categories which man formulates, the terms of which he sorts out in responding to the world about it, are strongly conditioned by the culture into which he is born. Each formulates its own master plan, its structures of values, its own classification of knowledge."[145] His description is demonstrated by the actions of many other knowledge seekers who we meet in the rest of this book.

Students of contemporary library practices have documented a contextual problem that was real. Libraries, indeed the entire community of libraries in the United States and in Western Europe, simply did not have the financial wherewithal to step up to create their universal digital library; Google did and would have done so if not blocked by the courts. Their work was so labor-intensive that they could not dedicate resources to learning about computing and implementing even the mundane tasks of scanning texts. Economists backed up their poverty through their own analysis of the financial limitations of the discipline.[146] Two observers of the digital barriers faced by librarians included this conclusion for why library administrators had not made as much progress as they wished for by the early 2000s: "They simply needed infusions of cash, technology, and partnerships to allow them to move ahead."[147] It seems also a fair assessment, a partial balance to the arguments put forth in this chapter.

This chapter ends on a critical note about what otherwise were significant contributions made by librarians in shaping modern notions of information. It admittedly ends with a tinge of presentism brought about by the implication of my remarks that librarians should have taken the lead in shaping the management of facts at the dawn of the computer. Shera and others, however, in their own discipline had called them out on this problem. But more fairly to the librarians, they faced two problems that made it impossible for them to maintain their lead after the arrival of digital computing. First, they knew little about computers and even less about how to develop these technologies.

Second, to develop these technologies and the software needed to continue the disaggregation of information from books to paragraphs to sentences and then to their aggregation by topic from across sources required massive amounts of funding fabulously beyond the reach of librarians. So even if governments and corporations were willing to channel funding to them, they would not have been able to conduct the kind of research and development that, say, an IBM or U.S. Department of Defense could. To put a fine point on the matter, IBM alone spent some $5 billion in the first five years of the 1960s just to develop one important line of computers; it had been in the computer game since the 1940s and continued its R&D expenditures into the next century. The American government spent more.

I turn next to a discussion of the role played by those better-funded computer scientists; data processing and communications engineers; and users in shaping the definition, creation, and use of information. This collective community quickly became several orders of magnitude larger than the librarians, outnumbering them by any measure one chooses: number of people involved, users, publications, budgets for R&D and appropriation, degrees granted, or economic impact.

Chapter 4

Early Encounters by Computer Builders

There are databases everywhere; the world wouldn't know how to live without them.

Charles W. Bachman, 2004[1]

The development of electrified, digitized information became the next major transformation confronting the world's facts, data, and, increasingly, knowledge. Nothing like it had been so profoundly influential since the development of printed books in the 1400s. By the early years of the twenty-first century, more data existed in electronic forms than on paper. While paper-based storage and access to information actually increased in volume and use throughout the 1900s—electrification of data changed how these were developed, organized, used, and stored to an extent we are just beginning to understand, because this transformation is still unfolding.[2]

This chapter focuses on identifying the emerging features of electrified facts, most specifically those housed in and moved about by computers, the central conceptual and technological innovations that made this possible, and the effects of information's changed features on digitized information. It is a massive story, because developers of computers—and that is the essence of who I look at here—soon outnumbered librarians by an order of magnitude. By the end of the twentieth century, there were also more individuals using computers to work with information than people who were alive in the nineteenth century, when librarians went about defining the scope of information and how best to organize it.

Yet, creators of digital computing did not pop up as new wild seeds in some field of science. Their links to librarians and, more importantly, to nineteenth-century fact-managing technologies were long and strong. To understand how computing became such a tsunamic source of new types of information, it is useful to describe the contours of the new disciplines "computer science," "information technologies," and "data processing." Between the 1930s and the 1980s, digital computing developed, and by the last quarter of the century was ubiquitous. In this chapter I focus on the period into the 1980s. I look at the highly varied computer-based foundations of modern information. Their role was the most influential in the transformation of information in the twentieth century. It is also why this is the longest chapter in this book.

CONTOURS OF COMPUTER SCIENCE

What is computer science? Is computing an academic discipline? If not, why did it win academic credibility within a decade of it being proposed, while librarians still struggle for intellectual legitimacy? Ambiguity in identity and definition dogged the development of computers from its earliest days, when mathematicians, physicists, engineers, and others were trying to define their field, articulating their thoughts through complex mathematical and philosophical discussions (e.g., Alan Turing in the 1930s); game theorists and mathematicians trying to define machines and systems of computing (e.g., John von Neumann in the 1940s); telephone engineers pondering the flow of information (e.g., Claude E. Shannon in the 1940s and 1950s); and a string of cross-disciplinary thinkers describing brain activities (e.g., Marvin Minsky in the 1950s and 1970s). They lived in a world where technology and worldviews were conditioned by World War II, then the Cold War, and a sprawling community of scientists, mathematicians, scientists, and experts from other disciplines trespassing on each other's intellectual borders, to create a new definition of information.[3]

The ambiguity is compounded by the fact that basic technologies and thinking about the nature and use of information continues to evolve. But if we do not delve too deeply into definitions, instead hover slightly above the debates, we can arrive at a "good enough" description to inform our discussion about how information was electrified, endowing it with yet another layer of features. The nature of electrified information was transformed by who was doing the changing, and that is why understanding the major components of computer science is useful, even if there has never been a strong consensus on what it constituted.

While engineers, mathematicians, and scientists had studied automation of information processing and built computers in the 1940s, as a field of study, as an academic discipline, their efforts did not begin to coalesce until the second half of the 1950s. Members of professional associations were some of the earliest to define and shape the field, such as those in the ACM

(Association for Computing Machinery) and the IEEE's Computer Society, both in the United States. Faculty and graduate students, too, began creating and participating in interdisciplinary programs that led to the emergence of "computer science" as its own discipline.[4]

Today, one can see that the central feature of computer science is the study and use of activities—usually called processes—that interact with information, using programming languages to write instructions to computers on how to interact with data. Computer scientists and information technologists call such instructions *programs*, while users and vendors call them *applications*. Words matter, because for the rest of this book we encounter other terms developed by various disciplines and user communities to describe their engagement with computer-based information. Computer science—also called computation science—is the purview of scientists and engineers who develop algorithms and programming languages that we rely upon to incorporate computers into our work and play. These experts focus on the manipulation, storage, and communication of information, largely in digital formats. They study theories of information, electronics, and attendant physics and communications.[5] Computer science is rooted in a combination of mathematics, statistics, electrical engineering, physics, even chemistry, and increasingly too, biology—all subject areas far afield from the world of the librarians and most people.

To understand the historical evolution of computer science and digitized information, I engage in a short discussion of computing's typology for context. Think of computer science as falling into two broad categories of activities: theoretical considerations and design of software-centric systems. While the physics involved in the interactions between software and hardware are important, those are more the concern of product manufacturers, such as IBM with servers and Apple with smartphones. Here we are talking about the definition of electrified information. Those perspectives shaped how hardware and software evolved.

At its core, theoretical computer science is mathematical. Its purpose is to understand the characteristics of computation and to develop efficient methodologies for conducting such activities. It has essentially five aspects:

- Data structures and algorithms, which studies widely used methods of computation and measures of their efficiency.[6]
- Theories of computation, which addresses what can be computed and what resources are required to do so.[7]
- Quantification of information and coding theories, such as Shannon's work on communications. Coding is how information is converted from one code to another. This subject is crucial for understanding data compression,

cryptology, detection of errors and their correction, and the functioning of networks, such as the Internet.[8]
- Programming languages, which is about the creation and understanding of all aspects of writing and use of instructions humans give to computers. Widely used languages have included FORTRAN, Cobol, and C++. (Thousands of languages have been developed.) It is the study of the characteristics of computing languages, or to put another way, of digital linguistics.[9]
- Formal methods, which use mathematics to specify, develop, and verify the role of software.[10] This is about making formal "best practices" to improve both reliability and robustness of hardware and software designs.[11]

The second broad category—applied aspect—can be viewed as two distinct paths influencing the features of information: first, development of computer systems, and second, computer applications. Experts focus on conceptual designs of operational structures of a computer system, which combine various types of hardware and software working in tandem. For computer systems think of the following half-dozen pieces:

- Architectures, which involves computer and electrical engineers in the design of computer systems.[12] Practitioners work in universities and extensively in product development in IT companies.[13]
- Performance analysis, which looks at how information moves, usually referred to as *flows* through a computer *system*, comprising the combination of hardware and software. How throughput is sped up, how bottlenecks are identified and eliminated, and response times improved are among these activities. It is here where benchmarking is done.[14]
- Distributed systems, which is also thought of as concurrent and parallel processing, looks at how information can be used simultaneously—shared—in a system.[15]
- Networks, which is about moving data from one computer to another, such as from a personal computer (PC) through a corporate network, or over the Internet.[16]
- Security and cryptology, which studies how to preserve the privacy, accuracy, and physical security of data that travels through computers and networks. It was the study of security and cryptology that motivated some of the earliest development of computers in the 1930s and 1940s.
- Databases, which is the closest thing we have to libraries, is the study of how to create, organize, catalog, store, and access information in a computer. This activity includes exploring models of databases and the nature of query languages and tools, including information retrieval.[17]

Under the category of computer applications four subfields come quickly to mind:

- Graphics and visualization, which look at how to create visual images of data, such as charts and graphs, and involve image processing, integration of multiple digital files, and creation of one of rapidly expanding forms of data: images, pictures, video, and new forms of charts and graphs, all of which make possible video games and movies.[18]
- Human–machine interactions, which remains an old issue about how humans use computers, such as through nobs, wiring, keyboards, graphical images on screens (graphical user interface—GUI), and software, all to make computing more "user-friendly" and functional.[19]
- Scientific computing and simulations, which focus on creating mathematical models and quantitative studies and analytical techniques to answer scientific questions and to resolve scientific problems. This is largely done through simulations of issues in science, a massive application of computing that spills over into war games, optional business strategies, and development of new compounds for medicines, as examples.[20]
- Artificial intelligence (AI), which studies how computers can learn from experiences and prior calculations, make decisions based on accumulated data, adapt software to new conditions, and communicate and process data (i.e., think) by mimicking human and animal brain functions. It is one of the most exciting new areas of computational research and theorizing. Yet, the subject dates to the 1940s and so was one of the first areas of computational research.[21]

Another broad category of activities that shaped the nature of digitized information is often described as software engineering.[22] So, the notion of what constitutes computer science is diverse. Each has many tens of thousands of experts as a whole, dozens of professional societies and conferences, hundreds of journals worldwide, and many thousands of books and videos, and training and academic programs.

Before descending into the details of how all these theory-based mathematical, scientific, and engineering disciplines shaped information, a few statistics about how many people were involved gives one a sense of the magnitude of their activities. Just in the United States, where the largest amount of work was done to shape the nature of computerized data in the twentieth century, it became a massive activity. The first reliable comprehensive data on who worked with computers in the United States dates from 1960, when all information technology (IT) jobs totaled 12,000; in 2000, this population had reached 2.5 million. The U.S. Bureau of Labor Statistics

(BLS), which is the primary American agency collecting such information, reported in 2018 that there were 31,700 people conducting scientific and engineering studies as their fulltime employment. The BLS noted there were 117,000 database managers.[23] In 1990 almost one million workers manufactured and distributed computer parts; in 2018 that number hovered at 613,000, thanks to more efficient and improved products and their manufacture that led to greater productivity of human workers, machine automation, and robotic devices. Another million people made computers and other peripheral equipment. An additional 1.9 million in 1990 worked in the world of IT and 2.3 million in 2018, such as computer operators, programmers, and systems analysts.[24]

More dramatically today, all jobs in science, technology, engineering, and medicine (STEM) involve the use of computing. Putting a number on that, in 2015 in the United States there existed 8.6 million STEM jobs, occupying 8.6 percent of the workforce. Of the 8.6 million workers, some 45 percent were doing computer-related jobs, such as programmers, while an additional 19 percent were engineers, many lugging around laptops loaded with software essential to their work. Others bulked up their desks and cubicles with big-screen work stations. Another 4 percent were mathematicians, architects, surveyors, cartographers, and were in mathematically oriented science occupations. One BLS report declared that "seven out of the ten largest STEM occupations were computer related."[25] The same study noted 750,000 people were software developers. Even tiny professions were profoundly dependent on computers, such as astronomers and mathematical scientists, each with less than 2,000 professionals as of 2015.[26] I believe all these statistics understate the activity because of imprecise naming conventions.

To further link the major categories of computer science to the nature of the work force, again just looking at STEM professions, software developers were the largest community with the nearly 800,000 jobs referred to before, followed in descending order computer use support specialists (such as help desk engineers) with nearly 600,000, and slightly fewer computer systems analysts. Another nearly 400,000 focused on software development, while a similar number built and maintained networks (such as the Internet); less than 350,000 IT workers were computer and systems managers. The United States now only has some 300,000 full-time programmers; because programming has so evolved that many millions of individuals could write their own programs without having to know any programming languages. The recent surge in the development of smartphone apps approaches closely that reality. In the rapidly expanding area of information security analysts, in 2018 there were 112,300 employed in the United States.[27]

To put a final number to the theoretical work, in 1980 there were 218 individuals with PhDs in computer science in the United States, 705 in 1990, and in 2000 a total of 861. Most worked in universities or in industrial laboratories, such as those operated by IBM and Apple, later Google and Amazon.[28] There were many others working in computer science that held degrees in other fields, such as engineering and physics, so the total number of workers in this discipline were far more numerous.

UNFOLDING FEATURES OF INFORMATION IN DIGITAL FORMS

The central change in twentieth-century information was its increasing electrification. To be sure many new types of data and insights emerged too—more than in any other century of recorded human history—as did the continuing pileup of books, magazines, scholarly journals, and other paper ephemera. But it was electricity—more precisely over time in digital formats—that proved to be such a big change. That new condition clothed information with features different than when stored on paper. Many of the realities imposed on digitized information in the second half of the twentieth century, however, had begun to be its reality a century earlier.

The origins of electrification's link to information began with the development of the electrical telegraph in the 1830s. By 1865, Morse code—the transmission of dots and dashes through an electrical current in a wire from one point to another—began the standard format adopted around the world. That event signaled the disciplining of information in ways different from how facts were presented and moved on paper. The combination of electrical pulses within the interior of a line represented letters to the sender and receiver. It all sounds so simple, but work to get there had begun in the mid-1700s, because it proved complex and involved new concepts.[29] The telephone came next going into commercial use in the last quarter of the nineteenth century, also sending signals through electrified lines converted from sound into analog signals then back to sound at the other end.[30] A third transmission mechanism using electricity and radio waves led to the development of the radio. Initially it mimicked Morse code but soon voice. In the 1920s it took off as yet another commercially viable way to move about information in electrical formats.[31]

In the United States creation of a de facto telephone monopoly—the American Telephone and Telegraph Company (AT&T)—operated across most of the nation, endowing it with the financial and technical resources needed to establish a research facility to study the attributes of electronically communicated information. This was needed to improve the quality of transmitting data, to lower costs of operation and to increase the capacity of the network to handle larger volumes of messages.[32] We know the facility as the iconic Bell Telephone Labs (1925–1984) and later as AT&T Bell Laboratories (1984–1996).

Prior to the establishment of Bell Labs the phone company operated a research facility within its manufacturing division (Western Electric) in the late 1800s that in 1925 became "Bell Labs," funded by both Western Electric and AT&T.[33] Bell Labs is remembered for remarkable inventions, most notably radio astronomy, the transistor which became the heart of early computers, lasers, photovoltaic cells, charge-coupled devices, information theory (discussed later), a computer operating system known as Unix, and various computer programming languages, most significantly C and C++. Interest in telegraphy influenced the early development of computers a century later in important ways and also our understanding of electrified information.[34]

Just over a half-dozen features of electrified information evident over the course of that first century became more manifest in the subsequent decades following the arrival of the digital computer. Each conditioned the nature and definition of what constituted information throughout the second half of the twentieth century. It may be too early in their history to debate the relative importance (influence) of one over the other, but not too soon at least to identify them. They represent aspects of information and their ephemera related to what librarians engaged with that were profoundly different. For example, with both paper and electrically formatted information people explored how best to create, organize, catalog, and access facts. In the previous chapter we saw many citations of articles in endnotes written by electrical engineers and mathematicians published in library journals in the post–World War II era. They were tutoring readers about issues also faced by librarians in the prior century, but in the new context of electronics. These explained how computerized data was the same or different, how facts could be managed, information retrieved on demand by readers, and so forth. But electrified information was also different in many ways. It is important to understand these as they were themes that wove their way through the activities of engineers at Bell Labs and at other centers of interest in communications, later computers.

First, when in a telegraph or telephone network, later within a computer system, information could be moved "at electronic speed," to quote an IBM computer advertisement of the 1950s.[35] In IBM's case, this meant from when data entered the computer until it came out as a report. All occurred within the same room among multiple systems comprising a grand system of machines and software, housed in rooms called "data centers." Not until the next decade could that information be moved across telephone lines to other buildings, cities, or nations. On the other hand, at AT&T, moving data "at electronic speeds" had long meant exactly that, transporting information across short and vast distances faster than paper by wagons, trains, trucks, or airplanes.

Second, information could be broken down into little pieces, such as down to the letter, which is what a telegraph operator did when transmitting a fact; it had to be done one letter at a time. Put another way, electrification made it possible, indeed necessary, to disaggregate information, much as the Belgian librarians were trying to do by taking apart paragraphs and pages to break up information into smaller units into sentences and words. Telegraph operators went further by abbreviating words to save on the number of dots and dashes to transmit. A similar practice was adopted in computing to save space by concatenating data files, that is to say, combining text or data in a series without gaps.[36] The physical constraints of an article, chapter, or book were broken. Today one can even buy this book by the chapter, but not before e-books were published.

Third, the ability to disaggregate information made it possible to more easily and quickly reassemble facts in new ways. Today one often refers to that feature as "ease of use," especially in the world of marketing and computing. It is at the core of Apple's value proposition for why one should use their products over those of its competitors, for example. The collection and reorganization of statistical information, such as census data and corporate financial information, made it possible to create tables and visualizations of multiple collections of facts. That feature facilitated maturation of the sub-branch of mathematics known as statistics and to become widely used in the twentieth century.[37] In time hypertext emerged as a result of this feature of information handling. Even more important, perhaps, is what one librarian pointed out when online catalogs became the norm. He commented that one could not search a card catalog for all the pamphlets published in Paris in 1745, for example, but it is "easy to do that search with an online catalogue.... Therein lies the rub of any comparison between cards and computers: cards are only searchable using the strategies already put in place when the cards were typed." That meant "No new search strategy can be created, nor can multiple searches be combined," but can be routine with online systems. Not using digital files "renders any other option almost laughable."[38]

Fourth, technological advances made it possible and easier to connect people and bodies of information in ways impossible or impractical before electrification. This new capability was a consequence of developments in many hard sciences and electrical engineering. Physics, electrical engineering, mathematics, material sciences, construct of organizations such as AT&T and IBM, later of satellite manufacturers and NASA all proved essential in enhancing connectivity. The application of mathematics and increased understanding of how electronics (electricity too) worked proved essential to the process.

Fifth, and related closely to the second and third features, whole academic disciplines transformed as their adherents realized they could collect new types of information and organize them differently. Economics became highly mathematized by the 1960s; astronomy and statistical processing too, thanks to radio transmissions for the first and electricity for the second. Telescopes could be shipped to outer reaches of the known universe, look beyond, and send back to Earth radio signals that humans could convert into human words, images, and language. Increased ease in aggregating information did more than creating new fields of study, it also presented the ability to researchers to work with larger bodies of information. For example, for an historian of computing to interview ten to thirty early developers of computers was considered appropriate in the 1970s and 1980s. Today, that number of interviews would possibly be considered "light." Recently, two historians researching the history of FastLane, the primary online tool used by most scholars in the United States to apply for government funding for their research, talked to some 400 people.[39] When I wrote a history of how computers spread around the world, I consulted one order of magnitude more information than I had for a three-volume history I published a half-decade earlier on how computers spread across a dozen American industries.[40]

Sixth, electrified information, and most notably digitized forms, forced changes across society. Recall librarians having to surrender their card catalogs and embrace the centrality of more information housed in computers than in books. Other professions changed too, while new ones came along. The twentieth-century political economist Joseph Schumpeter (1883–1950), a proponent of mathematizing his discipline, spoke famously of "creative destruction," as new technologies forced older ones to decline (e.g., horse-drawn carriages displaced by automobiles) but also by creative innovations that opened new doors. As telegraphy began to spread in the 1840s, farming in the United States involved over 60 percent of the workforce (including unpaid wives and children); today's farmers produce so much food that their crops are major American exports, but only need 11 percent of the workforce to do so.[41] That is what Schumpeter meant, that is what could be enhanced in the late decades of the twentieth century with digitized information.[42] Today's farmers are extensive users of digitized information. Paper agricultural magazines of the nineteenth century are all but gone; the fabled *Farmer's Almanac*, continuously published since 1818, is more a nostalgic Christmas present than a weather guide for farmers.[43]

Seventh, more than in earlier centuries, combinations of differently formatted bodies of information could be integrated into reports and presentations of facts. For example, an online article in the *New York Times* (*NYT*) often includes video clips relevant to a story; graphs of information evolving over time shown in dynamic motion, such as changing demographics; hot terms that when one clicks on them takes the reader to another article or source of information housed inside or outside the confines of the *NYT*'s computers, such as to a video located on YouTube. Humans began receiving information in multiple formats made possible by electricity decades ago, such as from radio, later television, now tablets and smartphones, all ornamented with information in different formats combined to provide a multimedia presentation of what is now fashionably called "content." AT&T's engineers thought similarly as early as the 1910s and 1920s when they spoke of "signals," a very nineteenth-century telegraphic concept.[44] The most recent twist in the combinatory presentation of information using multimedia is that the reader could begin to retrieve facts this way, as access became possible to multiple digital files. They could do this through online systems, doing so in today's parlance "on demand," almost instantaneously without the intervention of an expert, such as a human librarian. The hypothesis expressed in the movie *Desk Set* (1957) had moved from cinematic fiction to reality.

BIRTH OF COMPUTERIZED DATA, DIGITAL COMMUNICATIONS, AND USES

A half-dozen ideas that surfaced in the twentieth century help us to understand the nature of computerized information. The seminal work of a few individuals, too, reinforce an appreciation of the new nature of data and facts, less so, however, of contextualized information and wisdom, the latter two not until the application of AI and machine learning began toward the end of the century. We can conveniently borrow from computer scientist Ken Steiglitz his list of key innovations. The first important idea is called "signal standardization and restoration," which explains how to protect data from being destroyed by "noise" (any disruption that interferes with the transmission of a message, think static in a radio broadcast to get a sense of the notion). Without such protections one cannot move data, say, from one's PC or smartphone to another device. Think of the word "signal" as a piece of information. A second concept is that of "valves," a mechanism for opening and closing access to communications of one datum, such as one signal (piece of data) controlling the flow of another. Steiglitz explains that these "have been realized with electromagnetic relays, then electrons moving in a vacuum (vacuum tubes), then electrons moving in a semiconductor (transistors)." He adds: "The idea of implementing logic with valves is founded on the mid-nineteenth-century mathematics of George Boole."[45] Two points are in order: again we see mathematics used and second another example of computing's origins deep in the nineteenth century. Valves—themselves a form of information—are seen as taking action, based on laws of physics and the nature of electronics, with their behavior described in the language of mathematics.

What about Moore's Law, which seems to be the most widely recognized observation about the nature of computing's foundation? Recall, the costs of semiconductors declines and capacity to hold more data increases at predictable rates. Steiglitz reminds us, however, that undergirding this notion is the fact that everything in the universe can be highly granular, that is to say, can be very tiny.[46] Most readers were probably taught in school that an atom was the smallest piece of any matter, also that an atom can be broken up into smaller units, specifically three: protons, neutrons, and electrons. The latter fly around and above a neutron in a cloud. Negative neutrons attract to positive nucleus, behaving like a magnet, keeping together an atom. So again, we see activity in play. Yet today, scientists believe that an electron itself can be subdivided—new thinking—into numerous parts, each controlling a portion of the electron's charge. The process is barely understood, but already has a useful name: fractionalization. For our purposes, the idea reinforces the notion that information, too, can be broken into ever more finite pieces if already electrified.

A fourth notion, called Nyquist's sampling principle holds that if a system "samples audio and video fast enough we can mirror any analog signal processing with digital signal processing."[47] In other words, a signal—piece of data—can flow back and forth as either a continuous stream or as discrete packages of signals, the latter a key concept behind the design of Internet communications. There is, too, another important idea, best known as Shannon's noisy coding theorem, which we soon explain in more detail, which illustrates one can transmit "noise-free digital communication, provided that one accepts the limitation of bandwidth and the delay and computational cost of encoding and decoding."[48] Our understanding of bandwidths and how they work are derived from Shannon's thinking of the mid-twentieth century.

Finally, there is the fundamental notion of the stored-program computer, best known as the Turing Machine. It holds that a machine can store data and instructions about what to do with that data, such as, "if this happens, then do such and such," and so forth, sometimes referred to as "conditional execution," or more simply, "features of a programming language." A programming language performs an action based on whether the situation it encounters is true or false, the idea of "on" or "off," positive or negative. For our purposes, we again reinforce the idea that data can be moved about, changed, and associated with other data in myriad ways after it has been created.

While all these ideas seem easy to catalog in a few paragraphs, they represent some of the most profound insights humans have uncovered about their physical world and information, so they warrant further examination. As done with librarians, I explore the work of several of the most important students of information. Since they were roughly contemporaries and knew of each other's work, the order of their introduction is less important than appreciating their thinking. They did their most important work in the early to mid-twentieth century, and in the second half of the period, their ideas were amplified and implemented. There are many others who could be added to the list, as table 4.1 suggests, but for our purpose of identifying the changing nature of information when it went electronic and digital, the work of these few individuals are sufficient to illustrate what happened. This table combines contributions of engineers, mathematicians, and contributors to what eventually came to be called *artificial intelligence*.

Table 4.1. Select Milestones in the Development of Modern Information Theories, 1924–1975

Year	Developer	Key Idea
1924	Harry Nyquist	Information (intelligence) can be quantified and the speed with which it can be communicated electronically measured
1928	Ralph Hartley	Demonstrates information as the logarithm of the possible number of messages with information being communicated when one can distinguish a sequence of symbols from others
1936	Alan Turing	Describes a hypothetical computer as a mathematical model which manipulates symbols per a set of rules
1940	Alan Turing	Introduces the concept of deciban—a unit of information—as a measure of data
1944	John von Neumann	Introduces a mathematical theory of games within the context of understanding economic and social organization
1945	John von Neumann	Describes an architecture for computers that remains the core organization of computers for the rest of the century. It has input, a processor, and external data storage for output
1948	Norbert Wiener	Credited with introducing the word *cybernetics* and the idea of feedback in information ecosystems
1948	Claude E. Shannon	Publishes "A Mathematical Theory of Communication"
1949	Claude E. Shannon	Publishes "Communication in the Presence of Noise"
1949	Robert M. Fano	Publishes *Transmission of Information* (MIT Press)
1950	Alan Turing	Proposes Turing Test to measure a machine's intelligence, an early AI event
1951	David A. Huffman	Introduces Huffman encoding as a method for identifying optimal prefix codes for lossless data compression
1953	August Albert Sardinas & George W. Patterson	Develop Sardinas–Patterson algorithm to decide if a given variable code can be decodable
1960s	Ray Solomonoff	Develops the mathematical theory of AI
1975	Marvin Minsky	Articulates the idea of frames as representations of information, with schemas and semantic links connected

Harry Nyquist (1889–1976) and His Sampling Principle

Harry Nyquist may be one of the least known important figures in the history of computing, and yet numerous developments of computing are attributed to him that space does not allow us to explore here.[49] Some are critical to understand within the context of information's evolution. He described the important features of electronic communications—the movement of signals (a.k.a. information)—that influenced other electrical engineers. Most importantly for our purpose, through sampling techniques pieces of information (again a.k.a. signals) messages sent through a network could be reconstructed in analog and digital formats.[50] His ideas contributed to the notions of how data behaved within a bandwidth and to the ability of technologists to transmit audio and visual information electronically late in the twentieth century.[51] Digitized information did not have to be just text or signals. He is also important because his ideas influenced designers of computers and communications methods and equipment. Remember, what makes digital information useful is the ability to move it accurately in a network from one machine to another, say, through many computers to one's smartphone. His work reflected the engineering culture at AT&T and Bell Labs. That especially held true for Shannon, for example, where at work he embraced and learned from "feedback cultures," a worldview we encounter, too, with mathematician Norbert Wiener (1894–1964) in the next chapter.[52] For historians of information and knowledge, he contributed to the idea that information theory was about activity, electrons symbolizing data in motion. Finally, for technical communities he developed ways to measure and recover signals passing through a network by applying compressed sampling methods, famously known as Sub-Nyquist Sampling or simply Nyquist's Sampling Principle.[53]

Like so many contributors to early-twentieth-century thinking about electrified information, Nyquist was an electronics engineer. Born and raised in Sweden, he was exposed to the subject at the University of North Dakota (B.S. 1914, M.S. 1915) and completed a PhD in physics at Yale University in 1917. Upon graduating, he went to work for AT&T in its R&D operations and stayed when Bell Telephone Laboratories was established. Nyquist is best remembered for his work in the 1920s and 1930s on telecommunications; although he helped to develop early facsimile machines in the 1920s. His research on the bandwidth requirements for transmitting information helped other engineers formulate theories of information, notably his colleague at Bell Labs, Claude E. Shannon.

We need to comprehend some of Nyquist's technical contributions, because some affected how scientists and engineers understand the behavior of digital and analog information. He worked out how to calculate the number of independent electrical pulses—signals—that could be pushed through a telegraphic network. His answer was that a network remained limited to twice the bandwidth of a channel. He published his explanations in 1924 and expanded his thinking in a paper published in 1928.[54] In that second one he quantified "the minimum band width required for unambiguous interpretation," declaring it to be "substantially equal, numerically, to the speed of signaling" and that "is substantially independent of the number of current values employed."[55] In other words, one could measure some of the activities of electrified information. He further refined his thinking to show that if one could sample audio fast enough to mirror analog and digital signals being processed by a network. One could begin to measure what was received compared to what was sent with a high degree of accuracy—today's Nyquist's Sampling Principle method.[56]

He was moving electrical engineering and telegraphy toward an ability to gain insight on what was going on in a network. That it was modeled on telegraphy was not so important, since many of its principles shaped telephony and later telecommunications among computers. As would influence subsequent conversations and growing understanding of electrified information, he explained his research overwhelmingly in mathematical language. While he was working out his sampling methods in the 1920s and 1930s, others were busy inside and outside his immediate community at Bells Labs; none proved so important than Alan Turing in England.

Alan M. Turing (1912–1954) and His Machine

While Nyquist has flown under the historian's radar, not so Alan M. Turing. In 2019 the British government announced that it was putting his image on a new £50 note; in 2012 it had issued a stamp featuring a cipher (code-breaking) machine he helped develop during World War II. A movie of his World War II activities, *The Imitation Game* (2014), starring Benedict Cumberbatch as Turing, grossed over $230 million. It may be impossible to find a history text or a technical survey of computing technology that has not discussed his work.[57] While he may be the most widely recognized computer developer of all time, his contributions are difficult to understand outside the confines of computer science, as these were largely articulated in the arcane language of mathematics.[58] He earlier helped to build the *bombe* machine, which Winston Churchill thought was one of the most important reasons for why the Allies were able to win World War II by deciphering German military communications. Turing developed a test in 1950 to see if people could differentiate between a machine in conversation and a live person (a progenitor of AI research).[59] Yet even earlier in the 1930s his thinking about computers before they were invented warrants understanding as his contribution to the history of modern information.[60]

At the time there were no computer machines. There were computers, however, young women who performed mathematical computations using desktop calculators. They were called *computers*. But thinking about automating mathematical calculations and even processing data by machine had long wafted like a gentle breeze through the eighteenth and nineteenth centuries. Born and raised in London, where he early on developed an interest in mathematics and science, at age sixteen Turing began to read Albert Einstein's work, demonstrating his understanding of the latter's concerns about Newton's laws of motion. He studied mathematics at King's College, Cambridge, graduating with honors in 1934, his PhD in mathematics and physics at Princeton University in 1938 at the age of twenty-five.[61]

While at Princeton he came to know mathematician John von Neumann further, having first met him at Cambridge in 1935. Before completing his studies Turing published an extraordinarily important mathematical paper, "On Computable Numbers, with an Application to the Entscheidungsproblem," in which he described hypothetical devices that later came to be known as Turing machines.[62] Entscheidungsproblem—meaning decision problem—was originally posed in 1928 by German David Hilbert (1862–1943), one of the most influential mathematicians of the past two centuries. In his paper Turing demonstrated that a universal computing machine would be able to perform any mathematical calculation if the problem could be posed as an algorithm. He further pointed out that anything computable could be calculated in a universal machine. In the following years, computer developers acknowledged the importance of Turing's notion, including von Neumann, who shaped thinking about what constituted computers for the rest of the twentieth century.[63] Like the engineers at Bell Labs, Turing envisioned an approach that processed symbols, in his case on tape based on a set of prescribed rules. It was a notion of proto-programming, with such a machine reading symbols on the tape with the tape moving right or left, reading these based on rules. It is enough, here, to acknowledge that he demonstrated mathematically that a machine could arbitrarily perform computations, while admitting there existed theoretical limitations.

His thought of such a machine as a central processing unit (CPU), in other words, a computer that controls the inflow and manipulation of any data (signals) coming into it, was novel at the time.[64] As he explained in 1948, he thought of his machine as comprising, "an unlimited memory capacity obtained in the form of an infinite tape marked out into squares, on each of which a symbol could be printed. At any moment there is one symbol in the machine; it is called the scanned symbol. The machine can alter the scanned symbol, and its behavior is in part determined by that symbol, but the symbols on the tape elsewhere do not affect the behavior of the machine. However, the tape can be moved back and forth through the machine, this being one of the elementary operations of the machine. Any symbol on the tape may therefore eventually have a meaning."[65] Here is an early description of a computer.

In Turing's thinking, information is used in discrete forms; you have to isolate control as a stored program within the machine; and the system has to be devised so that running—executing—a program is dependent on the results of prior calculations. To quote computer scientist Ken Steiglitz: "We now take the stored program for granted; what present-day all-digital computers do, step-by-step, is determined by a *program*, or sequence of *instructions*, written in some language that is convenient for the programmer, but translated into a more basic language that is directly interpretable by the machine's hardware."[66] This is what Turing conceived.[67] Turing also envisioned that data would be kept apart from the instructions about what to do with it, a core basis of what came to be known as databases decades later.

If Turing had done nothing else, he would still warrant inclusion in this chapter, but he went further, reinforcing links among anthropomorphic cognition, machines, and information in what came to be known as the Turing Test. In simple language, Turing wrote, "I propose to consider the question, 'Can machines think?'"[68] His goal: to determine if machines could behave in a way indistinguishable from a person. He proposed a test that a human observer could evaluate in which a machine and a person, kept separate from each other, could conduct a conversation by typing messages back and forth, thereby preventing the machine from responding directly with speech. If the evaluator could not differentiate between the machine's comments from those made by a person, then one concludes the machine had "passed" the test. It was important that machine's responses resembled those of a human, not that it got an answer right.[69] Turing named the test the "imitation game." The evaluator, often also called the interrogator, asks of a man and a woman located in a room apart from the machine to determine their sex. He argued the case for machines potentially having the ability to think, countering objections to that idea.[70] We care about the article because it became one of those seminal documents influencing the philosophy of AI.[71] A machine could be given a broad range of subjects to discuss, including presenting information. It was a simple test, and the results could be measured, even though definitions of intelligence remained illusive.

Turing's argument was, however, limited. For one thing, it really was not presented as a measure of intelligence, but more humbly as a statement by a young mathematician (remember he was still in his twenties) that one could have alternative ways of viewing thought within the context of machines. A second criticism is that Turing assumed the interrogator could determine if the machine could actually think, such as humans did. A third is that the test does not actually determine if a computer actually thinks, that is to say, behaves intelligently. There were many other objections, but his paper contributed to a more than half-century exploration of thinking connected to the creation and use of information beyond what humans do, to what computers could also. In short, he helped grease the wheels for the development of cognitive science as a field of study.[72]

Claude E. Shannon (1916–2001) and His Theory of Information

Turing's contemporary, just four years younger, working in the same state of New Jersey up the road from Princeton at Bells Labs, Claude Shannon, was busy working with colleagues on the behavior of signals (a.k.a. information) within telegraphy and, more specifically, telephony. One has to wonder if the researchers at Western Electric (Bell Labs), others at Princeton University, and at nearby RCA's facilities communicated with each other, since all were roughly a one-hour drive from Princeton to AT&T's facilities, or in New York City where such engineers also met to share their work. New Jersey had become an R&D hothouse on information. One should not forget that in the same period of the 1930s–1950s at the lower end of the state was nearby Philadelphia, another center of activity where electrical engineers and a small group of ham radio aficionados built the first generally recognized American digital computer in the 1940s called the ENIAC. They also constructed a sequel, while von Neumann was doing similar work at Princeton, also roughly a one-hour drive from Philadelphia. We also know that von Neumann interacted with those working in the Philadelphia region, at MIT and Harvard in Cambridge, Massachusetts; Bell Labs community; mathematicians and scientists in the Princeton area; others in England at Cambridge University and in Washington D.C.[73] Von Neumann was an expert networker and spreader of ideas.

Shannon looms so large in the history of information and computing that our challenge is to put him into perspective. Yet, it would also be misleading to diminish his contributions to our understanding of electrified information. They involved his work on communications theory, information theory, cryptology, computers, circuits, games, and even about population genetics (his PhD dissertation).[74] When someone presents a theory—a proposed way of looking at a topic—it is done largely through research with colleagues, which includes conversations with them; through formal presentations and lectures at discipline-specific conferences and meetings, such as those hosted by the IEEE and the ACM; and most effectively by publishing articles in the key academic journals in one's discipline. Shannon did all those things, although, as the editors of a massive published collection of his writings observed, "Much of Shannon's work was never published," their justification for a nearly 1,000-page anthology. In a word, he was prolific in thought and deed.[75]

While he gets much credit, he was also the product of the collective work of engineers and others at Bell Labs, a point not lost on historians.[76]

It is, thus, both a compliment to his performance and possible explanation of the importance of what he published that computer scientists around the world could point to one (or few) of his papers and say their world had now changed. Ken Steiglitz, for example, concluded that Shannon, "at one stroke founded a brand-new field, known as *information theory*."[77] Even behind the Iron Curtain of Cold War Soviet science, Russian mathematician Alexsandr Kninchin was able to similarly observe, "Rarely does it happen in mathematics that a new discipline achieves the character of a mature and developed scientific theory in the first investigation devoted to it."[78] We could quote similarly other scientists, engineers, and historians, all who were referring to a paper Shannon published in 1948.[79] With the passage of time, one could plausibly make the argument that his paper should rank with those Albert Einstein published in the early twentieth century, Turing's on his theoretical machine in the 1930s, or Thomas Kuhn's writings about the nature of scientific revolutions published in mid-century. So we must review what is arguably a very difficult paper to understand, if the reader is not a mathematician or electrical engineer, and that is often confusingly summarized (a risk I, too, run here). But recognize that he did not work in isolation, proof that others at Bell Labs were working on similar issues, some even two decades earlier, such as Ralph V. L. Hartley (1888–1970).[80] Also, Shannon was not without his critics, pointing out limitations in his thinking.[81]

Before diving into Shannon's work, and as an example of how Bell Labs was an information ecosystem populated with mathematicians and electrical engineers collaborating and influencing each other, consider Ralph Hartley's work as a buildup to Shannon's. Born in Nevada and graduated from the University of Utah in 1909, Hartley became a Rhodes scholar at Oxford University, where he studied mathematics, electrical engineering, and physics. Upon his return to the United States he went to work at Western Electric in research, where some of his early efforts involved developing radio receivers and radiotelephony before World War I. In this period Hartley built what he is often most remembered for—the Hartley Oscillator—but he had begun to understand signals and noise in transmissions.[82] He spent the rest of his career at Bell Labs where he studied electrical circuitry and transmission of signals and voices. He walked the same hallways as Nyquist and Shannon and shared their interests.

In 1928 Hartley published "Transmission of Information," in *Bell System Technical Journal*.[83] His article is widely considered a precursor to Shannon's own paper on information theory published two decades later; the latter was built clearly on some of Hartley's ideas about the transmission of signals (information). Unlike Shannon's work, Hartley's is more readable for the non-initiated. Before we summarize his thinking, keep in mind that much work done concerning the nature of information in the first half of the twentieth century was less about content itself (e.g., ideas and facts) and more about the conversion of those into electrical impulses and their transmission over various electronic mediums. Hartley worked at the epicenter of telecommunications in North America and for that matter, most of the world. Recall, Hartley had been doing research on communications for nearly fifteen years and was now forty years of age.

He reminded his readers in 1928 of one of the central research problems AT&T was addressing: "With the use of lines of increasing length and with increasingly severe standards of performance it is coming to be necessary to take account of the phase-frequency function as well."[84] By "phase-frequency" he was referring to the changes in modulation in which information (signals) was transmitted through discrete changes in the frequencies on a line. One of the challenges at the time was "to set up a quantitative measure whereby the capacities of various systems to transmit information may be compared."[85]

While he proposed protocols for doing that, it was his perspective on information that is of interest to us. He notes that in any normally operating line there is a "capacity of a system" which should be quantitatively measured and that the information is "a group of physical symbols, such as words, dots and dashes, or the like, which by general agreement convey certain meanings to the parties communicating."[86] As these are selected, the information passing through a communication line (telegraph, telephone, radio, or TV) becomes more precise. Thus, "Apples are red," would eliminate the consideration of all other types of fruits and the possibility of other colors. Many pages later he noted that the speed with which information moved through a line was affected by various forms of distortion (Shannon would use the word *noise*). These distortions limited the rate of messages with theoretically measurable certainty. He then began to lay down rules of behavior, such as that "a criterion for successful transmission" should various line interferences "exceed half the difference between the values of the wave at the receiving end which correspond to the selection of different values at the sending end."[87] In other words, what one sends as a message needed to be what is received at the other end of the line. For that the frequency of transmission and the rate at which signals traveled desirably needed to be done in some steady state.

All of this discussion led to his conclusion, the one that Shannon and others paid attention to: "The maximum rate at which information may be transmitted over a system whose transmission is limited to frequencies lying in a restricted range is proportional to the extent of this frequency-range."[88] Further: "From this it follows that the total amount of information which may be transmitted over such a system is proportional to the product of the frequency-range which it transmits by the time during which it is available for transmission."[89] In other words, there existed possible ranges for how much and how fast accurate information can be moved about given the condition of the line being used, wire or radio, for example. Important for future engineers of communications, he treated "symbol sequences" synonymously with the less technical term "messages."[90] A telephonic (or telegraphic or radio) system optimized message delivery by modulating frequencies of transmission to send more data down a line. His thinking applied to all manner of signals, including recorded symbols and images. Because he demonstrated all of this activity could be measured, he concluded that steady-state transmission could be done with sensible "uniform efficiency and during the time during which the system is available."[91] If this sounds like a conversation about uptime on the Internet or on some private corporate network, remember he wrote this in 1928, when Turing was still a teenager.[92] He ended his discourse by writing that one could even measure each message a system had to handle to understand the traffic and, by implication, to manage for optimization. As done by his colleagues, he underpinned his arguments with the credibility of mathematical proofs.

Hartley and others continued to do research on the behavior and measures of circuits through the 1930s and 1940s, while Shannon remained busy as well. Hartley retired from Bell Labs in 1950, as Shannon's star was rising. A new generation of experts on electronic information was stepping forward.

Back to Shannon and His Achievements

Shannon reflected a background similar to others at Bell Labs. He was a product of the American Midwest where he early on displayed a strong interest in mathematics, science, and electronics. In 1936 Shannon graduated from the University of Michigan with two degrees in mathematics and engineering, then went on to MIT to study electrical engineering.[93] His master's thesis in 1937 explored switching circuits and electromechanical relays used by AT&T to route calls. He relied on Boolean algebra to explore how such circuits could solve problems. Shannon might not have realized it at the time, but the idea that electrical switches could be used to implement logical instructions proved to be a foundational concept. He worked on his notions at the same time Turing was traveling through similar territory. In 1943 Shannon and Turing met and undoubtedly discussed each other's thinking, a point to keep in mind for what Shannon did after World War II, because during the war he too worked on cryptology. He came quickly to be seen as a leading expert on circuit design, in part because of his rigorous use of mathematics, influencing how engineers viewed their work on circuits shifting from informal, ad hoc approaches to more disciplined ones.[94] His ability to apply

Boolean algebra to construct any logical numerical relationship, in particular, positioned him well for what became his most well-known work.

In 1948 Shannon published a two-part article entitled "A Mathematical Theory of Communication" in Bell Labs' in-house journal, addressing the issue of how best to encode information someone can transmit.[95] His lengthy two-part publication relied on probability theory (based on the work of MIT mathematician Norbert Weiner) and on Shannon's thinking about the role of entropy as a way to measure characters in a message.[96] Remember our example of the red apple? It echoed in the background. His explanations, the extent and rigor of his mathematical application and demonstration of measures resulted in his paper being a fully developed scientifically vigorous theory of information. In the next several years he and his colleagues developed systematic ways of assigning codes and measures of probabilities, among other elements of managing and measuring information in a network, often called Shannon–Fano coding.[97] Shannon's paper became more widely known when in 1949 he and a fellow mathematician and scientist working at the University of Wisconsin, Warren Weaver (1894–1978), published a book length version of Shannon's article coupled with the Weaver's own work as well. It remains a classic in the field of telecommunications.[98]

So what did Shannon offer in 1948? He began by stating, "The fundamental problem of communication is that of reproducing at one point either exactly or approximately a message selected at another point." The engineering challenge was to select what message to deliver from a variety of options: "The system must be designed to operate for each possible selection, not just the one which will actually be chosen since this is unknown at the time of design."[99] He conceived of a communications system as comprising "an information source"; a "transmitter" that "operates on the message in some way to produce a signal suitable for transmission;" next a "channel," such as a wire, coaxial cable, or radio frequency; a "receiver," used to reconstruct the original message from the received signal; and finally, a "destination," such as a person or thing intended to receive the original message. Between the transmitter and the receiver, there is, of course "noise" that interferes with the message being sent, such as static, miscellaneous signals, even psychological or semantic interferences. Like others at Bell Labs, he discussed how to measure what was being sent and its quality, and the effects of noise on channel capacity. He was interested in quantifying the rate at which information could be transmitted through a channel. He argued that information reduced the amount of uncertainty on a line. The red apple is more certain than any apple, to return to Hardley's example. Shannon was starting to measure information more precisely. In the process he made use of probability analysis, a crucial tool for the development of communications theory, revealing that, in

Steiglitz's words, "Information is basically statistical in nature."[100] Information could be mathematically measured.

If the reader can take away only one idea from this chapter, let it be that information can be measured mathematically.

The creation, management, storage, and transmission of information in electronic forms could now be handled with a precision not possible before. An important component was Shannon's use of the word *entropy*, by which he meant the average information in a message stated as a logarithmic value. Knowing how much one could transmit included understanding how much noise (think errors because anything other than the desired message was noise) was on the line.[101]

His noisy coding theorem, which explained the role played by information theory in the development and management of communications and how to measure it, proved enormously useful to Bell's engineers. In the process Shannon created an information theory, "born in an exceptionally coherent form" while providing engineers the central result of his noisy coding idea that "channel capacity and the potential power of coding to achieve arbitrary small error rates" could be implemented.[102]

In collaboration with Warren Weaver, Shannon "defined information so that it would be calculated as the same value regardless of the contexts in which it was embedded, that is to say, they divorced it from meaning."[103] "Information must not be confused with meaning."[104] Shannon and Weaver witnessed that their ideas quickly embraced within the world of telecommunications. But the history of R&D at Bell Labs also demonstrated that Shannon and Weaver were building on the work of earlier engineers.[105] By the mid-1950s, one could conceive of telephony and computing as variants of each other, "kissin' cousins," to use AT&T's board chairman, Frederick Kappel's phrase in 1963.[106] Indeed, AT&T executives considered entering the computer business, but were blocked from doing so by the U.S. Department of Justice.

Historian Emily Goodman answered a question that perhaps may be on our minds by this point: Why all this discussion about telephony? Besides the obvious "kissin' cousins" connection, recall the conversation librarians had with respect to cataloging methods and books and journals more than a half-century earlier. Let Goodman explain: "The telephone system . . . was a primary technological platform that hosted a transparent debate between . . . contentious hardware and software issues regarding the definition of information, the use of data, and the future of networked access to information, broadly defined."[107] AT&T's work on networks, telephone directories, switching mechanism, and other technologies would eventually lead a future generation of engineers to develop what came to be known as the Internet and to development of search algorithms that used probability thinking to answer questions and to conduct language translations. These were all in response not necessarily guaranteed to be accurate, but that signals sent (statistically speaking) had a very high probability of being what we were searching for.[108]

Sergio Verdú, an IEEE Fellow, pointed to various fields that Shannon's information theory influenced, and the list is impressive. Just in computer science, this thinking about the nature of electrified information affected algorithmic complexity, data structures, cryptology, computational complexity, today's emerging quantum computing, and random number generation.[109] The same source of original thinking spilled into the study of probability, statistical inference, mathematics, physics, economics, biology, and chemistry.[110] For many of these fields, as well as regarding information itself, two computer scientists put it neatly: "Information theory can be viewed as the study of patterns and ways to exploit them."[111]

Because this book is a study of how information changed, one simple demonstration of how important conversations were changed by the increased use of mathematics, let's examine a sample page from Shannon's 1948 paper (figure 4.1). It illustrates what information increasingly began to look like in the twentieth century, a point reinforced in subsequent chapters. It is less important to discuss its content (here part of his explanation of choice, uncertainty, and entropy) than it is to see that mathematics and graphical representations express his findings about information. Many millions of scientific, economic, and social science papers published in the twentieth century looked like this page. Numeracy as a literacy was expanding rapidly across many disciplines.

Gerard ("Gerry") Salton (1927–1995) and Information Retrieval

Our discussion about the birth of computer-based information and its communication would be incomplete if the story ended before users of computing could access information online. It was the ability to retrieve electronic information in addition to computerized cataloging that brought librarians into the world of computing. Librarians did not develop digital information retrieval (IR) systems, computer scientists did that; none was more prominent in its development than mathematician and computer scientist Gerard Salton, whose major contributions to IR came furiously, beginning in the 1950s.

Gerard Salton was born in Nuremberg, Germany; his family moved to the United States in 1947. He graduated from Brooklyn College with a degree in mathematics in 1950, and became a U.S. citizen two years later.[112] He completed a PhD in applied mathematics at Harvard University under Howard Aiken, a giant in the early history of computing; Salton was his last student.

function of n. With equally likely events there is more choice, or uncertainty, when there are more possible events.

3. If a choice be broken down into two successive choices, the original H should be the weighted sum of the individual values of H. The meaning of this is illustrated in Fig. 6. At the left we have three possibilities $p_1 = \frac{1}{2}$, $p_2 = \frac{1}{3}$, $p_3 = \frac{1}{6}$. On the right we first choose between two possibilities each with probability $\frac{1}{2}$, and if the second occurs make another choice with probabilities $\frac{2}{3}$, $\frac{1}{3}$. The final results have the same probabilities as before. We require, in this special case, that

$$H(\tfrac{1}{2}, \tfrac{1}{3}, \tfrac{1}{6}) = H(\tfrac{1}{2}, \tfrac{1}{2}) + \tfrac{1}{2}H(\tfrac{2}{3}, \tfrac{1}{3})$$

The coefficient $\frac{1}{2}$ is because this second choice only occurs half the time.

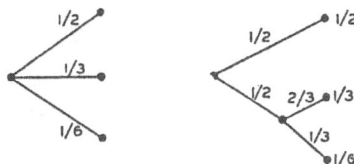

Fig. 6—Decomposition of a choice from three possibilities.

In Appendix II, the following result is established:

Theorem 2: The only H satisfying the three above assumptions is of the form:

$$H = -K \sum_{i=1}^{n} p_i \log p_i$$

where K is a positive constant.

This theorem, and the assumptions required for its proof, are in no way necessary for the present theory. It is given chiefly to lend a certain plausibility to some of our later definitions. The real justification of these definitions, however, will reside in their implications.

Quantities of the form $H = -\Sigma p_i \log p_i$ (the constant K merely amounts to a choice of a unit of measure) play a central role in information theory as measures of information, choice and uncertainty. The form of H will be recognized as that of entropy as defined in certain formulations of statistical mechanics[8] where p_i is the probability of a system being in cell i of its phase space. H is then, for example, the H in Boltzmann's famous H theorem. We shall call $H = -\Sigma p_i \log p_i$ the entropy of the set of probabilities

[8] See, for example, R. C. Tolman, "Principles of Statistical Mechanics," Oxford. Clarendon, 1938.

Figure 4.1. Page From Claude Shannon's 1948 article "A Mathematical Theory of Information." *Source*: "A Mathematical Theory of Communication" was published in two parts in the *Bell System Technical Journal*, Vol. 27, July 1948, pp. 379–423 and October 1948, pp. 623–656. (*Courtesy*: AT&T Archives and History Center, Warren, NJ).

In the 1960s at Cornell University Salton co-founded the Department of Computer Science. By then he was focusing his research on computing information retrieval, and in time, emerged as the most recognized expert on the subject. He became interested in IR in the 1950s, but in the 1960s and later, developed IR systems, most famously SMART (known either as "Salton's Magical Retrieval of Text" or more seriously, "System for the Manipulation and Retrieval of Text"). It was both an experimental IR software and a commercial product; Dow Jones Newswires used it. His work on IR facilitated the development of digital libraries, the concept that one can surf the Internet, navigate the World Wide Web, and to use keywords to retrieve desired information from digitized documents. He published 150 papers and five books on the subject.[113]

One of his technical contributions on understanding information was the idea that when mathematically scoring queries as term counts and finding the similarity between a document and a query, the score of a term in a document is represented as the ratio of the number of terms in that document divided by the frequency of the number of documents in which a particular term occurs.[114] Again, as with researchers at Bell Labs, mathematically expressed facts were posited as crucial for understanding how to create, move, and access information in electronic formats. Salton continued his work into the 1990s, exploring automated text summarization tools and digitized information analysis, even too, how to automate the generation of hypertext—all topics of growing interest to academic library and information science researchers at the time.

Because Salton was in the thick of the IR world, he had much to say about the evolution of IR systems and challenges. In the 1950s, at the start of his career, researchers focused on imagining how hardware could search stored files, using various indexing mechanisms in which key words attached to documents could replace the more widely deployed classification systems used by librarians. Topical words could be linked to specific documents as a possibility. Finding new search techniques became a priority too, including the use of "semantic code" to represent specific pieces of information.[115] Moving from indexing to key word searches represented an innovation, with key words assigned to documents. Experimentation led to the conclusion that the assignment of key words was an efficient way to find documents without the need to create librarians' *complex* structured vocabularies, as in earlier times. Results of such research were routinely reported to communities that included researchers in library and information sciences in the pages of *American Documentation*.[116]

In a retrospective look at the developments in IR, Salton saluted the work of Hans Peter Luhn (1896–1964), a computer scientist and specialist in library computing at IBM, who in the late 1950s introduced the idea of text processing, proposing that computers could theoretically do this, and not simply be deployed as number crunchers.[117] Luhn suggested that computers should conduct keyword matching and sorting tasks to find documents, hence automated indexing and term weighing. To use Salton's phrasing, "based on the frequency characteristics and on the location of the words in the texts under consideration."[118] In other words, Luhn proposed to use computers to do what the Belgian librarians attempted with millions of manually handled cards prior to World War II. Luhn's notions about automatic abstracting methods could rely on the frequency analysis of words appearing in a running text. As Salton put it, "The importance of a word was tied mainly to its occurrence frequency in particular text samples."[119] This became the soul of future computerized IR systems (see table 4.2). Over the next twenty years Salton and others strived to implement that vision.[120]

Table 4.2. Select Events in the Evolution of Information Retrieval, 1940s–1999

1940s	Corporations and government agencies expand IR research involving computers
1950	Calvin Mooers coins the term *information retrieval*
1959	Hans L. Luhn published a seminal paper on auto-encoding of documents for IR
1960s	Gerard Salton works on IR at Harvard University. IR models are developed in Europe and the United States for indexing systems
1963	Alvin Weinberg declares "crisis of scientific information"
1960s	First major machine-readable database and batch retrieval system Medical Literature Analysis and Retrieval System (MEDLARS) developed by the National Library of Medicine
1965	J. C. R. Licklider published his book *Libraries of the Future*
1968	Gerard Salton published his seminal textbook *Automatic Information Organization and Retrieval*
1970s	Commercial online search tools, such as MEDLINE, Dialog, ORBIT, and Hypertext, were introduced as a concept for use in IR
1979	C. J. van Rijsbergen published an extensive study on the probabilistic models of IR.
1982	Concept of ASK (Anomalous State of Knowledge) introduced
1980s	Additional end-user commercial IR systems introduced
1989	Tim Berners-Lee makes his initial proposals for the World Wide Web
1990s	Visualization schemas for IR gain attention
1990s	Late in the decade, first Internet search tools appear, launching a massive worldwide use by hundreds of millions of people in the new century
1998	Google founded as a search engine, developing algorithms for comparing relationships among websites, rather than the conventional use of ranking systems to count the number of time a search term appeared on a page.
1999	Ricardo Baeza-Yates and Berthier Ribeiro-Neto published their first comprehensive survey of all IR facets, *Modern Information Retrieval*

In 1987 Salton posited that the development of such search capabilities and automatic thesaurus constructions had far to go: "The problem is that when existing texts are used to derive word associations and to detect word similarities, the significance of these associations is often purely local, and thus not applicable to other new documents in related subject areas. This implies that the proposed inference mechanism is not likely to lead to generally valid term associations."[121] In other words, computer scientists had much to do before Google could be possible. However, it had already become evident that "when the topic area under consideration is narrowly specified and when the text processing task is of limited scope, useful knowledge structures can in fact be prepared intellectually for use in practical systems."[122] Over the next thirty years, much progress would be made. One of these involved the development of databases.

Just as Shannon lived in a world with other researchers focusing on concerns similar to his, the same can be said of Salton. One other contributor to the latter's world of IR was Calvin N. Mooers (1919–1994). Raised in Minneapolis, Minnesota, he graduated from the University of Minnesota with an undergraduate degree in mathematics in 1941. After wartime service at the Naval Ordnance Laboratory, where he was exposed to early computing, he completed a master's degree in mathematics and physics at MIT. In the late 1940s he developed a card-based IR system called Zatocoding and established a firm to sell it (Zator Company in 1947), while continuing the development of IR tools. He is often acknowledged as the creator of the term "information retrieval" while writing his master's thesis, and he presented it later as an article in 1950.[123] As a colleague described the concept, "Mooers had developed a clever method to store a large number of document descriptors on a single specially notched card, which he called Zatocoding" by "superimposing random, eight-digit descriptor codes." The concept made it into software IR tools, because his approach made sequential searches of large numbers of records quickly possible.[124]

THE CENTRAL ROLE OF DATABASES

Much of the work done by computer scientists and others in the field of information science extended lines of research launched by Turing, von Neumann, Shannon and Salton, among others. By the 1960s a new twist occurred in adding interest in how to organize information so that end users could access it. That development is largely about the emergence of databases, a construct that continues to dominate much organized information. The rest of us assumed that a well-written query could get us to any information we needed, à la Google, but changes in data storage technology made this shift possible.

When commercial computers were built in the early 1950s, there were two ways to store data: on punched cards that had been in use with tabulating equipment since the 1890s.[125] The second approach was to record data on magnetic tapes. That was a relatively new medium that became widely used during the second half of the 1950s.[126] In each instance, access to information occurred in the order in which it was stored. In other words, if you wanted the third piece of information on, say, a tape, you had to read the first two to get to the third.

Then in September 1956, IBM introduced a widely available commercial hard disk drive, called the IBM 305 RAMAC (Random Access Method of Accounting and Control).[127] For the first time, one could instruct a computer to go directly to a desired piece of information, speeding up access to data.[128] The new technologies crowded out punched cards and relegated magnetic tape to cheap backup storage for disk drives. By the early 1980s, computational devices smaller than a mainframe or a mini computer all relied on direct access files. From a data storage perspective, formulations of software and computing designs—often referred to as *data architectures* (*structures* too)—to manage the receipt and presentation of data to computers and end users were fundamentally transformed. One of those transformations involved the development of what came to be known as databases.[129] I will not engage in discussions about data standards, data integration, specific software packages, and so forth.[130] It is enough to realize much was going on that led to the development of databases, made possible, indeed attractive, when one could access specific pieces of information in a direct, fast, and reliable manner by the availability of the hard disk drive.

Since the evolving nature of information is the central issue of our book, we periodically need to pause to define terms. Databases (DBs) is one of those that kept changing over time. All notions involving information have long histories, so we should call out that databases began their digital lives in the 1960s, when even the term itself emerged, beginning with *data banks* morphing into *data base* then to *database*, and most frequently into its plural form of *databases*. The American National Standards Institute (ANSI) often defined technical terms subsequently embraced by scientists, engineers, and corporations. By the early 1960s, the ISO standard definition of *data* had not changed since the 1950s; it was still fundamentally, "a representation of facts, concepts, or instructions."[131] Then there was the new term—*data bank*—widely deployed at the start of the 1960s. The ANSI defined it as "a comprehensive collection of libraries of data. For example, one line of an invoice may form an item, a complete invoice may form a record, a complete set of such records may form a file, the collection of inventory control files may form a library, and the libraries used by an organization are known as its data bank."[132]

One other term that became enormously important is *data hierarchy*. ANSI defined it as "a data structure consisting of sets and subsets such that every subset of a set is of lower rank than the data of the set."[133] A *set* is a collection of data items, such as the word "Tuesday," as a member of a set that might be labeled "weekday." Because information can be broken down into ever smaller units, even to the sentence, word, letter, and number levels—we should add the definition of *data elements*: "The name for a class of category of data based on natural or assigned relationships that can be used to denote a set of data items. For example, the data item 'Tuesday' is a member of the set denoted by the data element 'weekday.'"[134]

How has the definition of database evolved into the early twenty-first century? A typical example: "A database is a data structure that stores organized information." Most databases contain multiple tables, which may each include several different fields. So, a company's database could include tables for products, employee information, and accounting and financial records. Each table had different fields relevant to data stored in a table.[135] Two other related terms are *hierarchical database* and *relational database*. The first organizes data in a tree structure that links disparate pieces of data to a single "owner," often also called a "parent," which serves as the primary record. Picture it as a corporate organization chart. A user gets to the database by going to the parent, then navigating "down" the tree to whatever specific data element they want, all done using software called *database manager*. The second term—*relational database*—"is a set of formally described tables from which data can be accessed or reassembled in many different ways without having to reorganize the database tables."[136] That requires an even more sophisticated database management software tool, such as the Structured Query Language (SQL). Access to a *piece* of data can be from a variety of entry points in a database.[137]

By the mid-1960s, databases were being created across many disciplines and industries. These files grew in size as the cost of hardware storage began its long and dramatic decline over the next half-century. In 1965, there were an estimated twenty significantly large databases known to exist in the United States, not including intelligence and military ones. By 1977, over 300; how many in private corporations and other institutions remains unknown, just that there were many more of those than the publicly available ones. Of the 300 databases, 50 became available to the public to access online via terminals connected to mainframes over telephone or private telephony networks. The size of these databases kept expanding. In the mid-1960s it was not uncommon for each database to annually increase its records by several thousand; by the mid-1970s by hundreds of thousands, in the next decade by millions.[138] For example, Chemical Abstracts Service (CAS) added annually nearly 400,000 new records to its database in the mid-1970s; BioScience

Information Service (BIOSIS) closer to a quarter of a million records at the time; while a giant in technical literature, the Institute for Scientific Information (ISI), was accumulating in excess of 400,000 records per year. All of these databases, of course, kept records accumulated in prior years, so the actual count of how much data they held became enormous. To bulk up matters even more, ISI, for instance, added ten citations per records, a throwback to the old librarian's penchant for having subject and author cards for each bibliographic citation. To have such massive files required computers.[139]

But what caused the greatest change in the nature of electrified information was less technological innovations, which would have been irrelevant to our history if they were not used, and more the number of people accessing these and their frequency of use. Usage proved so massive that one can point to databases as representing new facets of both the nature of information and how these were appropriated during the second half of the twentieth century. As evidence of the value of databases, in 1965 there were an estimated 10,000 individuals in the United States who used these. By 1970, their number had grown to 100,000, then to a million in 1975. These statistics did not include searches using library tools also coming online, such as the OCLC (originally Ohio College Library Center), which had begun with the early work of the U.S. Library of Congress.[140] I personally consider all these statistics woefully low. Today anyone operating a computer-like device is a database user, all five plus billion of us.

What kinds of information were in early publicly available databases? It is an important question, because the early ones set the pace for the massive use of such electronic files in subsequent years, particularly corporate and government databases. American government agencies created some of the earliest ones, such as the National Aeronautics and Space Administration (NASA), the Atomic Energy Commission (AEC), and the National Library of Medicine (NLM). Each accumulated technical and scientific information, expanded with others accumulating engineering data, and spilled over into all the hard sciences. Other disciplines followed quickly, such as psychology (Psychological Abstracts Tape Editions Lease and Licensing—PATELL); education (Research in Education—RIE and the Current Index to Journals in Education—CIJE); and myriad social sciences during the 1970s and 1980s, such as the popular Social Science Citation Index (SSCI). The SSCI included in its database citations from before the days of computers, while most other databases did not; these just added material that appeared after the creation of their databases. BIOSIS, too, was adding bibliographic records to its database, beginning in 1966. One of the earliest of the business databases appeared in the 1970s, ABI's INFORM. By the mid-1970s databases were targeted at both specific audiences, such as researchers, and increasingly the general public keen on seeking information about consumerism, advocacies, child care, medical advice, drugs, and politics.[141] All of this was happening for a good quarter-century or more before the Internet using the World Wide Web.[142]

But to continue answering our question, many of the early databases of the 1960s–1970s collected government reports, journal articles (or at least citations to these), and patent information. MARC (Machine Readable Cataloging) proved important because it collected monographic data. MARC relied on the information collected by the U.S. Library of Congress and from other sources, notably OCLC. One survey of trends as of 1975–1977 reported that "although the early data bases were largely bibliographic, we can now see a clear trend toward the inclusion of less permanent material . . . of very limited time value such as newspaper articles."[143] The same report anticipated electronic publishing as a capability that would come directly out of the existence of databases. Already the prediction was reality, because news services were offering online-based information. For example, Chemical Industry Notes (CIN) was already in operation, as was the news feed from the American Petroleum Institute, called the Petroleum/Energy Business News Index (P/E News). While most readers and even employees may think the *New York Times* entered the digital newspaper business only in 1995, it had created the *New York Times* Information Bank over twenty years earlier than the *L.A. Times*, *Milwaukee Journal*, *Chicago Tribune*, and the *Washington Post*. These news databases were loaded with earlier and current news stories for use by their staffs; it would be decades before these became available to the general public.[144] The existence of these databases created much of the justification and ease with which all major American news outlets moved quickly to the Internet.[145]

Individual professions began developing databases that had both bibliographic citations and actual texts. Some of the most iconic examples came out of the legal profession, such as LEXIS, the less known Selected Water Resources Abstracts (SWRA), the National Criminal Justice Reference Service (NCJRS), state statues (with Mississippi an early developer), and the Trademark Data Base, among others. Law enforcement agencies embraced data bases, and none more aggressively than the U.S. Federal Bureau of Investigation (FBI), which created various files accessible by all law enforcement agencies from local to federal; but police and other local law enforcement departments had to agree to feed these systems with information they collected, such as fingerprints and criminal records of individuals. This approach proved successful. By the early 1980s law enforcement had access to databases that collected information in two dozen categories, including about wanted and missing persons, stolen and recovered vehicles, firearms, boats, license plates, stocks and bonds, art, and an inventory of U.S. Secret Service protective files.[146]

Another class of information increasingly described in databases by the 1970s involved current projects. The Smithsonian Institution launched SSIE (Smithsonian Science Information Exchange). Others included the Current Research Information System (CRIS), Highway Research Information Services (HRIS), and the Register of Research Projects (CANCERPROJ). Most large U.S. government agencies launched similar databases in the 1970s and 1980s. These were largely filled with project descriptions and reports on results, including statistics. By about 2005, most Federal government reporting was disseminated electronically and its work was posted to databases accessible via the Internet.

Statistically filled databases also bloomed. These numerically intensive collections of information reflected the broader tendency in the twentieth century to gather and rely upon more numbers than in earlier times. Most important, in the mid-1970s the general public could begin to access large numeric databases for the purpose of downloading and manipulating the data. Predcasts, Inc. and Lockheed, for example, made their PATS databases available on DIALOG. PATS had about 100,000 statistical time series tagged so that one could retrieve a desired series, input their own data into it, and operate on this data applying standard statistical programs. Selling access to commercially available databases was now well on its way.[147] The arrival of spreadsheet and database management software on PCs by the start of the 1980s became "killer apps" that took the microcomputer market segment that sold tens of thousands of machines annually in the 1970s to tens of millions by the end of the 1980s.[148]

While development of databases and software to manage them were projects initiated by researchers and managers working in large private and public organizations, individuals made a difference too, by how they responded to and viewed information, and none looms so large for so many of these institutions than Charles W. Bachman.

Charles "Charlie" William Bachman, 1924–2017

I knew Charlie Bachman, beginning in the 1990s, when we served together on the board of the Charles Babbage Foundation. I was engaging with a kind, deferential computer expert. One might never know that he was an important early developer of database management software. He was never an academic and spent his professional career in the private sector. Raised in Kansas, the son of a football coach, he served in the American Army during World War II. He earned two degrees, one in mechanical engineering at Michigan State University in 1948 and a master's in mechanical engineering from the University of Pennsylvania (1950), but almost as important he completed the bulk of his classes for an MBA at the same university's Wharton School of Business. Of all the major early pioneers of computing from the 1950s, he was probably the only one with formal training in business management. He worked at Dow Chemical in the 1950s, serving as its first data processing manager. In 1960 General Electric hired him, where he soon developed one of the first database management tools, called the Integrated Data Store (IDS). During the 1960s he developed other tools, such as access software for IDS. In 1981 Cullinane Information Systems hired him to help sell IDS as a product, which it had acquired through a prior acquisition, now rebranded as IDMS.[149]

In 1983, Bachman founded Bachman Information Systems. One of the most important of its early products was the BACHMAN/Data Analyst, a software tool in support of another of his developments, the Bachman Diagrams. These were literally diagrams displaying data structures. Programmers used these to design data with a network in a relational model that separates data from the way data was stored in a computer. In his words, "The Data Structure Diagram is . . . a graphic technique . . . dealing with classes—specifically, with classes of entities and the classes of sets that relate them," which he illustrated by saying, "For example, individual people and automobiles are entities. When they are taken collectively, they make two quite different classes of entities. On the other hand, all of the automobiles belonging to a particular person constitute a set of entities that are subordinate to the owner entity." We need not linger on details, just keep in mind that he drew graphs to illustrate relationships. Figure 4.2 is a simple hypothetical representation, showing what a "set association of entities" might look like, reinforcing the growing use of a combination of graphics and text evident in the business community, beginning in the 1960s.[150]

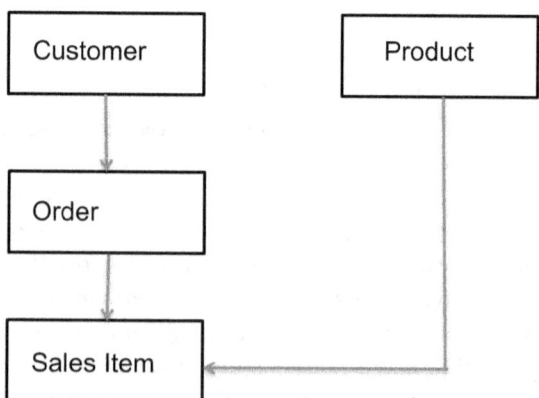

Figure 4.2. A Sample Bachman Figure, this one of a simple customer order

On the occasion of Bachman being given the prestigious ACM Turing Award in 1973, he delivered a lecture about databases. He noted that in his lifetime a shift had occurred "from a computer-centered to the database-centered point of view" followed by another conversion to where information was not seen as a stationery object but one that a person could "probe and traverse . . . at will," thanks to database tools and availability of DASD, of course.[151] Moving from sequential file accessing, as done with cards and tape, to direct access created the opening for databases. He noted that one responsibility for database software and associated staff was "the responsibility to maintain data between the time when it was stored and the time when it is subsequently required for retrieval. This retrieval activity is designed to produce the information necessary for decision making." It also is used to "update," just as "modification as things change, and ultimately, its deletion from the system when the data is no longer needed."[152] Here he tells us that software—automation—played a central role in the use of electrified information; today AI tools often do that and go the next steps of making decisions and taking action. As with other databases, even nineteenth- and early twentieth-century schemas of librarians, databases often had multiple types of information; recall his example of automobiles and car owners. But the big advantage for many organizations is that with databases multiple programs can tap into them, thus, "all redundant data can be eliminated, and in the process the costs of sustaining duplicate files and errors."[153]

Recalling his past achievements in 2004, he commented on the general subject of databases: "I think about relational systems as being report systems, a relational database is a way to generate reports, queries, or information that is in the database; they do that far more easily than IDS did."[154] The biggest problem a generation of database developers face "was really looking at how do you build a system that lets you access whatever you wanted to get, whenever you needed it."[155]

CONCLUSIONS

In the nineteenth and early twentieth centuries librarians organized and cataloged information, the story told in the previous chapter. The twentieth century involved other trends: development of an infrastructure to make information highly mobile and organizable in ever-granular and diverse forms, better understood as encoding of words into electronic (digital) formats.[156] These did not follow as many schemas dictated by librarians, rather more the will of end users who desired increasing amounts of specific and varied information impossible for paper-bound librarians and publishers to provide. The actors in this chapter were also influenced by wartime realities from the 1940s through the 1980s involving cryptanalysis, the genesis of AI, telecommunications, and massive funding by government and businesses. Here we focused on the technological infrastructure—computing and telecommunications—that made possible access to information from anywhere and to organize it as one pleased. Those developments were major developments in the history of information that can be set alongside such earlier ones as the invention of writing and publishing. In the next several chapters we explore some of the new bodies of information created in the past two centuries in mathematics, statistics, STEM subjects, and social sciences. I will not be comprehensive in describing these new facts, but as here and in the prior chapter, discuss broad changes in their features.

Information was converted into electrical signals; electrical engineers and computer scientists learned how to move it from one locality to another with accurate transfer of data (facts, information), and they acquired the capabilities required to store such messages efficiently and cost effectively. Otlet's idea that information could be autonomous by being moveable from its original home (e.g., a book's page) became practical reality by the 1950s. In 1962, fourteen years after publishing his seminal paper, Shannon reminded colleagues that the definition of information had changed. I would add its definition had done so more than it had in centuries. He said: "Information can be measured much as we measure energy or mass. The unit of measure is the bit. It corresponds to the information produced when a choice is made from two equally likely possibilities." He was essentially describing what computers really stored: "A computer with a million bits of storage" contains "a million independent yes-or-no decisions," the "0s" and "1s" so familiar in digital computing.[157] No librarians, philosophers, or priests needed to be present to explain. It was now how one was able to organize and use information in what Shannon called "arbitrarily small bits of matter or of energy."[158]

Shannon and millions of others accomplished practical results. Nothing seemed to reflect that reality more than the ability of people to sit in front of a terminal by the 1960s and download and read information organized as they wanted. "Online" may someday be seen as one of the most important technological concepts to originate in the twentieth century; it certainly is one of the most pervasive capabilities now used by billions of people. It would be difficult to exaggerate the importance of humankind's ability to look up "online" information. Without computers there would not have been software. Without software there would not have been databases. Without databases there would not have been online search tools. So we arrived at the late twentieth century with a near ultimate achievement: the ability of anyone to look up anything. Not until the dawn of the new century would that achievement be surpassed when automatic data collection, sortation, and searches could be routinely conducted with increasing use of AI (fashionably, too, called *cognitive computing*), sidestepping less efficient and slow mortals.

Like the early librarians, the computer science community shared the same dream of universal access to information. They had more resources than the librarians to convert that aspiration into reality. Their desire remained a fervent passion from the 1940s to the present. The technologists understood, too, the centrality of searching for information, and in the words of two students of the process, "freeing book content from the principles and practices of library science," hence not carrying for how libraries were organized nor how librarians thought and worked.[159]

The journey had been uncertain and rough, because in the early years of computer development it was seen as essentially a mathematical calculator, while another group viewed it as a communications device, notably Joseph Licklider (1915–1990) and Robert Taylor (1932–2017), both of whom played important roles in the development of the Internet. These two, aware of the work of Hartley and Shannon among others, however, observed that "information transmission and information processing have always been carried out separately and have become separately institutionalized." They called for and predicted a merger of the parallel developments thereby fundamentally changing the role of information.[160]

What, then, can one observe about online information? How information was organized became enormously varied from one software tool to another, from one discipline to another, from one individual to another. Most software interfaces between data and people were designed less to accommodate technological schema and more to make online access feasible by end users. Think about what a change that was. In the 1840s only telegraph operators could access and communicate information electronically, only telephone switchboard operators in the early next century could connect end users, the same with radio operators. In the 1950s military personnel could look at big screens to track incoming missiles, their civilian counterparts monitored airplane traffic, and weathermen observed environmental conditions. By the end of the 1960s, high school graduates working as clerks in accounting departments or in manufacturing plants could use online systems. Today a child can track Santa Clause's travel from the North Pole without the mitigation of military or weather experts, while the rest of us can resupply our homes with goods just as clerks did in factories. End users now dominate the informational landscape.

Databases that began as bibliographic collections of abstracts, blossomed into all manner of recorded information available to end users. Historians remind us that all this, too, became possible by the development of inexpensive communications networks.[161] Most development of early online systems occurred in the United States, which two scholars characterized as "an American phenomenon."[162] That merger is illustrated in how various disciplines and professions transformed information, which is described in the next five chapters. The work to make computing and online into realities took place in many countries.[163] In the American case, many of developers of electrified information infrastructures had highly diverse backgrounds: mathematics, electrical engineering, ham radio, psychology, later from computer science, business, social science, and library science. Some mutated into such disciplines as information science and computer science, while others retained distinct disciplinary purities, such as economists and specialized hardware and software experts. Early users were often librarians working in government and private sector organizations extracting information for others, but with the wide availability of PCs beginning in the 1980s, masses of workers bypassed these earlier intermediaries to do their own queries.

Students of the history of online services identified several patterns, which we can use to close our discussion of the role of information technologies to the end of the century. These patterns are briefly listed here:

- People needed more information with which to do their work and go about their lives than could be offered by colleagues, librarians, friends, or family.
- As the volume and diversity of information required for their work increased, the old manual, and even new "batch processing" methods proved too slow and inefficient, while online tools delivered speed and convenience.
- As using online systems became popular, these had to be expanded beyond, say, work hours or only used in offices and libraries, to where they could be used anywhere, anytime—what the Internet was able to deliver, but which became increasingly available by the late 1980s.
- End users continuously sought additional volumes of information, faster access, then full texts, images, online processing of data files such as those housed in digital spreadsheets, online publishing, e-mail, and all of these functions in combination with each other.[164]

All these transitions happened quickly but also slowly. It seemed fast because so much functionality and sheer volume of online information became available to so many people, particularly after the spread of Internet use—more essentially a twenty-first-century phenomenon, although the Internet had been around since the 1970s. With so much online accessing occurring through smartphones, this is a good time to remember that these handheld devices only became widely available largely after Apple introduced its products in 2007, essentially became ubiquitous within five years as much due to excellent marketing as to good product design and technology.[165] The transition to online was slow because earliest attempts to transmit information involving a combination of computers and telecommunications occurred in the 1950s, nearly three-quarters of a century ago, and if we add telegraphy to the chronology, nearly two centuries ago.

Circle back to the origins of computing, because additional observations provide necessary context for what is discussed in subsequent chapters. The received wisdom about the origins of computing places the 1940s, specifically 1948, when Norbert Weiner and Claude Shannon published their seminal works on telecommunications and feedback systems, as a central date in the history of the computer. The mathematized thinking about computing and communications that had been bubbling up over the previous century, raises the question of how avant-garde was computing in 1948? I have argued that computing was the next turn in the evolution of information. One might want to recall that in 1949 someone unfamiliar with computing wrote the third seminal work of the period about information: George Orwell (a.k.a. Eric Arthur Blair, 1903–1950), *Nineteen Eighty-Four*, a dystopian novel about modern society and information used by the state. All three writers shared a common interest in information that was both broadly extensive, because of its perceived value, and that there were accepted norms about how it should look and be used. To suggest otherwise is to trivialize the work of Weiner and Shannon, and their output possibly not to be recognized as seminal. The same holds true for Turing, and three decades later for Licklider.

Let a student of information's history and contemporary role suggest one additional implication: "Information theory was born not as a theory of information, but as a theory of communication that simply presupposed information as the material it would transmit."[166] The distinction is important, because changes made to information technology and communications were in the service of information, even if in the process these caused information to change. The innovators of the 1930s–1970s presupposed information rather than thought they were contributing to the formation of information. Without computing's existence as an available tool, Shannon and others would probably not have made their contributions.

We now turn our attention to communities that fundamentally changed what all these electronic infrastructures and other information mediums made possible: mathematicians, statisticians, and practitioners in the hard sciences.

Chapter 5

Mathematicians and Statisticians Create New Tools

So much of the mathematics of the last century has been absorbed by our culture, by us. It is very hard to imagine a time when people did not think in our terms.

Michael Atiyah, 2002[1]

Exchange between a modern Socrates and his follower: "How many birds are there in a flock?" "I cannot say." "How many bees in a swarm?" "I am uncertain." "How many dwarfs with Snow White?" "That I know, Sir, seven." "Ah, then you have firmer knowledge of fairies than of birds or bees?"

R. W. Gerard, 1961[2]

The first draft of chapter 5 took me six weeks to write. I wrote it in the first quarter of 2020 when the high temperature averaged 51 degrees Fahrenheit (10.6 Celsius). By the time I finished polishing it, I was able to reduce the chapter's size by 5 percent, although I had originally hoped for a range of between 7 and 10 percent. The final word count came in at 11,000 with seventy-two endnotes and two tables. It is now the third largest chapter in this book, but not a surprise since one of the subjects—mathematics—is central to our understanding of how information transformed in the twentieth century. Millions of scientific papers, others in economics and social science are dependent on mathematics, as we saw in chapter 4 with Claude E. Shannon's paper from 1948. His proved so long that it had to be published in two parts, both during the second half of that year.

Did you notice anything unusual about this first paragraph of this fifth chapter? Probably not, because in the early twenty-first century, it read like a normal report on an activity, one, however, laden with numbers the reader is familiar with: dates, various types of temperature, whole numbers, fractions, display of a range in prediction (good statistical practice), totals demonstrating that I can add (one of four basic functions in mathematics), and earlier use of tables presenting numeric data delivering a message. Had I written the first paragraph before the arrival of the Second Industrial Revolution, it would have read more like the diary entries of nineteenth-century authors. It might have started with: "It was in the spring, when the flowers were just blooming, that I turned my attention to the role of mathematics in our lives. It was a productive time for me, as I had seemingly worked out my ideas and needed to put quill to paper." An attractive text to read, delivering a similar positive message of accomplishment, but one relying on adjectives to describe the magnitude of the work, not numbers. This chapter explains how we became more reliant on numbers, a story continued in subsequent chapters, and about the kind of new information that shifted to an increased reliance on numbers, mathematics, and statistics. It was not, however, a smooth ride to that new style of information.

On the occasion of the Statistical Society of London's (a.k.a. Royal Statistical Society) establishment in 1834, its founders, including Charles Babbage (1791–1871), one of the early fathers of modern computing, let the world know that "The Statistical Society will consider it to be the first and most essential rule of its conduct to exclude carefully all opinions from its transactions and publications—to confine its attention rigorously to facts—and, as far as it may be found possible to facts which can be stated numerically and arranged in tables."[3] Over a century later, another president of the society commented that Babbage and his cohorts, "took no notice whatsoever of this stricture, and immediately started inserting their opinions about what their data on crime, health and the economy meant and what should be done in response to it."[4] Yet since 1834 statistics became a highly developed, widely applied body of mathematical practices respected and used worldwide in all facets of private, public, scientific, and business activities.[5]

Mathematics in all its variations became a growing part of the world's information infrastructure over the past two centuries. Its presence in people's thinking and work increased, driven by expanding levels of formal education, changing features of precision and standards at work, rising stocks of new knowledge, and the ability to collect vast quantities of data. That new information could be converted into useful forms. As with the previous chapters, this one focuses on another form of contemporary information infrastructures. I proceed with a brief discussion of terms, in this case, numeracy and various major branches of mathematics, including statistics. Statistics became widely used by non-mathematicians. This history begins in the early 1800s and extends to the end of the twentieth century.

Just as I introduced the thinking of Bell Labs' engineers and mathematicians at a level that gave the reader a view of the subject, as if peering down from a mountaintop into the valley of the subject, I do the same here. It is more important to understand the general intellectual landscape, the topography if you will of a topic, rather than its operational features. Readers were not required to know how to catalog books in chapter 3 nor how to transmit signals down a telephone line in chapter 4, so, too, here they do not need to know algebra to understand the contribution made by mathematicians to modern information.

WHAT IS NUMERACY?

The simple answer is the ability of an individual to use mathematics in their daily lives. If a person had any formal schooling since roughly the early eighteenth century in the Western world, they learned sufficient mathematics to use at work. Mathematical literacy expanded in the nineteenth century to include the majority of people on either side of the Atlantic, except around the Mediterranean (the latter largely in the twentieth century). Children counted marbles they won and kept score in myriad games, while their parents added up what they needed to acquire at stores subtracted from the amount of money they had to spend on such items. Butchers weighed meat and carpenters measured wood. Cooks measured flour and counted eggs for recipes standardized by the 1920s, instructing them how to calculate the amount of time needed to cook a dish and at what temperature. Other people had to learn how long it would take (time) to get from their office to the subway to get their train home. The list is nearly endless, spilling over into calculating sales, managing one's finances, assisting a child with her homework, monitoring our diets and weight, and sorting through statistics and other numeric data for work and politics. To state the obvious: numeracy is about using numbers to make sense of our actual world and to inform decisions. Numbers help one to create measurements, which in turn makes it possible to define operations—how to do something—that when performed yield desired results, which in turn are known to have been achieved through measurements of what happened. As one scientist explained, "The basic reason for such a requirement is to make the measurement process as objective as possible."[6] This belief in the power of numbers in augmenting precision was one of the most fundamental operational notions accepted by people in recent centuries.

Americans treated information as a tool, an object, and as one result by which they were able to enhance their quality of life.[7] A substantial amount of "information as a tool, an object" were numbers. That is numeracy at work. Beginning in the nineteenth century and increasing over the next two centuries, thinking numerically required mastering to varying degrees a half-dozen skills: the ability to read and interpret numbers presented as strings and tables, to comprehend numbers presented in charts and diagrams; in work often the ability to understand the performance of a process, frequently explained in statistical terms; to solve problems expressed in mathematical terms; to validate the accuracy of data, as not all spreadsheets provide correct answers if formulas used originally were faulty; to appreciate the context, calculations, and answers to understand or explain these; in giving people data—answers—that made it possible to make decisions they felt were rationale and to their advantage. It is about reasoning by relying on numbers.[8]

At its most basic level, numeracy was about the ability of individuals to perform the four basic arithmetic functions of adding, subtracting, multiplying, and dividing.[9] My use of the word *numeracy* is purposeful, here, because the ability to work at an elementary level with numbers was foundational to societies using statistics or mathematics at large. Historians who have studied statistics and mathematics usually have focused on the development and advanced uses of these by experts, such as accountants and scientists, even if these were small communities within larger populations. The work of such tiny cohorts, however, seeped out of their information ecosystems into the wider world, resulting in, to use historian Theodore M. Porter's phrase, "the rise in statistical thinking," beginning in roughly 1820 in Western Europe and the United States.[10]

Beyond these skills, one could include all other mathematical ones, of course, at least with sufficient skill with which to meet the demands of living and working. Some of the more advanced forms of understanding numeracy included the ability to appreciate real numbers, time, measures, and estimating, all considered fundamental. Even more advanced applications included understanding ratios, such as fractions and proportions, percentages, and probabilities. By the end of the 1800s, many office and technical workers required the ability to understand numeric information (e.g., charts, graphs) and statistics.

All of these activities were made possible by the fact that how numbers were expressed—notations—had already stabilized into the common use of Arabic numerals, the ten digits of 0s through 9s. As historians and others have reminded us, such notations were not always used, think of Roman numerals, such as someone is XXI years old. Our current way of expressing numbers has proven to be most effective for reckoning, that is to say, for enhancing one's ability to calculate. To put this system of notation, which is so basic to the evolution of modern mathematics in context, it was only one of about one hundred distinct ways of expressing numbers developed over the past 5,000 years.[11] As one student of numerals expressed it, the value of our current form of expressing numbers "to reckon is to evaluate, to assess, and to assign worth," what people have used in mathematics for centuries.[12] To say that the use of this numbering system is ubiquitous seems almost an understatement. The majority of all languages use a base of ten. One survey of 196 human languages documented that 125 were decimal, while 20 used a base of 20, another 22 a decimal vigesimal approach, and the rest various other formulations.[13]

WHAT IS MATHEMATICS?

Mathematics is a language. Galileo Galilei (1564–1642) spoke of mathematics as the language in which God has written the universe. Since the European, Western scientists have viewed mathematics as a useful way of describing it. The case for thinking of mathematics as a language is straightforward: it has vocabulary, grammar, and syntax, and is understandable by people who practice it. People all over the world can comprehend mathematics. Its symbols have precise universally accepted meanings (e.g., 2 +2 does not equal 5, only 4). Its syntax organizes its symbols into accepted linear structures. A mathematical proof can be used to create a narrative, telling a story. All users of mathematics in any discipline use it just as we follow rules for how we speak, for instance, Spanish or French. It is capable of both describing reality—real-world phenomenon—and to communicate abstract thoughts. It has nouns (e.g., Arabic numerals, fractions, variables, expressions, infinity, and Pi). It has verbs (action words), such as add (+), subtract (−), multiply (x), and divide (÷). Its grammar includes such rules as formulas are read left to right; Latin and Greek symbols have specific meanings; and parentheses and brackets have well-defined uses. This language can be mixed with traditional human languages to solve "word problems."[14]

Mathematics is also a collection of methods for viewing reality through the prism of numbers. Three broad categories are *quantities*, which involves number theory; *structures*, which uses algebra; and *space*, which applies geometry. There is a growing fourth pillar, known as *change*, which involves mathematical analysis.[15] Mathematics is used to identify patterns of action, of reality, by using mathematical proofs. Mathematics can help describe the behavior of a reality and offer predictability about its future performance, relying on a rigorous logic (its grammar). Beginning in the nineteenth century, mathematicians rapidly developed methods of rigorous deductions from axioms and definitions. Mathematicians at Bell Labs in the twentieth century did this; but, in more fundamental ways, earlier mathematicians, such as Giuseppe Peano (1858–1932) and David Hilbert (1862–1943), developed such methods. There is a great deal of it practiced to help discover, describe, and predict naturally existing realities, such as by physicists and biologists.[16]

Several branches of mathematics fundamentally shaped it. Its world can be thought of, however, as essentially divided into pure and applied mathematics.[17] Pure mathematics explores quantities, space, and change. Quantities are all about numbers and the operations one performs on these, such as adding and subtracting. Here is where we think of whole numbers, fractions, even infinity, natural numbers, integers, real numbers, complex numbers, and so forth. Algebra resides here. The study of space—the other side of pure mathematics—is about geometry, a combination of numbers and space calculated and expressed in graphical format, while algebra is expressed in formulas (the grammar of mathematics). Within geometry sits such well-known topics as the Pythagorean theorem (about the relationship of three sides of a triangle) and trigonometry (study of the relations between the sides and angles of triangles), non-Euclidean geometries, and the increasingly important subfield of topology.[18] The study of change has become important in the natural sciences and the tool of choice. Here resides calculus, which helps to calculate a changing quantity. This is where differential equations are applied as a body of mathematical practice that defines relationships between one quantity and its rate of change. Calculus is used to describe dynamic systems in nature and chaos theory to understand how unpredictable behavior occurs.[19] Apologies to mathematicians for oversimplifying pure mathematics, but for our purposes it is sufficient to draw a conceptual picture of this large body of information.

Applied mathematics—the second mega-collection of mathematical practices—is a collection of methods most applied in science, all branches of engineering, business, industry, space, and the military, among others. This is the side of mathematics where biologists and physicists look for ways to build arithmetic models to describe events. For example, when a government official opines that economic models indicate business is going to improve or not, or when a public health official explains why Covid-19 infections will increase or not, they are using mathematical models that have baked into them chosen assumptions which then are played out over time through calculations. Projecting a flight path for a rocket to the moon is another example. Models are used to predict future behavior. Since models require enormous amounts of calculation, they only became practical to define possibilities, multiple scenarios, and predictions once computers could be used to perform the mathematics involved.[20] Problems addressed by applied mathematics often then become subjects studied by pure mathematicians, such as engineering and transportation issues.[21]

The single most widely used sub-branch of applied mathematics is statistics, which I discuss more fully later, and related decision sciences. However, it is enough, here, to point out that statistics is formulated using mathematical terms and practices. In statistics much data (numbers, and numbers of signals in various patterns) are collected then analyzed to understand the behavior, say, of a process and to apply probability theory to anticipate its future performance. Statistics is concerned, too, with random sampling and experiments, with understanding observed data, making sense of the data, such as the trillions of signals that pass through the Internet or a telephone line that must be studied to understand the line's behavior, as we saw the Bell Labs engineers use in the 1920s–1940s.[22]

Computers have led to the creation of yet another sub-branch of applied mathematics, touched on in chapter 3, called *computational mathematics*. These are calculations too big or complex for humans to perform. We hear such stories as, "to calculate by hand such-and-such would take a billion years." It was a problem in the 1910s and 1920s, for example, in the study of the Moon's path before computers came along, despite heroic efforts using IBM tabulating equipment and desktop calculators manned by students and young women before World War II. In the development of compounds in chemistry and medicine, millions of various combinations of ingredients are modeled this way to get to the few that show (predictably) great promise as a cure. It is how, for example, scientists and doctors today can come up with a likely test for a new virus in weeks, rather than over many years.[23]

Circle back to topology as a growing source of new mathematically based information. It most often is associated with pure mathematics, not applied; we will not engage in the debate, because for our purposes it is more important to recognize it as a source of new information in the twentieth century. Topology studies the properties of space. There is the probably an urban myth that students in American high schools were asked by their English teachers to write an essay describing the inside of a ping-pong ball; however, in mathematics that is topology. French mathematician Henri Poincaré (1854–1912) was one of the leading lights at the dawn of the twentieth century because of his numerous contributions. He has long been considered one of the last mathematicians that had mastered all aspects of mathematics from pure to applied. He did much to introduce modern concepts of topology as a relative of geometry in the 1890s. Imagine being able to stretch a coffee mug into the shape of a doughnut, a square into a circle as if made out of rubber, and then be able to measure all of these surfaces, counting the number of holes or sides, and so forth. That is the work of topology. The key is to understand and document the properties of a geometric object as they change. In biology, for example, topology is used to study the effects of enzymes on DNA. Physicists use it to explore quantum field theory and physical cosmology, and in the development of robotics to understand what motions and spaces these devices would need.[24]

Even a cursory glance at any chronology of the history of mathematics leaves two accurate impressions: first, that much work had been underway by scientists and thinkers for centuries, and second, that the pace of innovations picked up in the nineteenth century and increased in volume during the twentieth century.[25] Table 5.1 briefly catalogs the milestones between the 1870s and the end of World War II. Note their features: new theorems, initial comprehensive explanations of subfields, formal construction of new ideas, and consolidated descriptions of otherwise fragmented accounts of subfields into more integrated explanations—all fundamental building blocks of the discipline. Observe, too, how quickly these came: many important events in almost every year from the dawn of the 1800s. Operational details and understandings underpinning the vast expanded use of mathematics proved substantial and complicated. Table 5.2 continues to memorialize the milestones since World War II, indicating that the momentum had not slowed.

Table 5.1. Milestone Events in the Development of Mathematics, 1872–1944

Year	Milestone Event
1872	Formal construction of real numbers described; rigorous definition of the integer is also published; "Erlanger program" in geometry introduced
1873	James C. Maxwell introduces four partial differential equations later known as "Maxwell's equations"
1879	Concept of time series introduced
1881	Venn diagrams introduced for use in set theory
1880s	Multiple texts published reflecting innovations in mathematics over the previous two decades, including on statistics, differential equations, and calculus
1890	Giuseppe Peano discovers space-filling curves
1892	Henri Poincaré publishes a detailed description of all motions of mechanical systems
1890s	Henri Poincaré studies and publishes on algebraic topology
1896	Prime number theorem proven; concept group characters introduced
1900	Theory of integral equations developed; theory of Fourier series introduced
1901	Theory of measures introduced
1902	Formal description of statistical mechanics published
1905	Albert Einstein publishes his special theory of relativity
1907	Albert Einstein publishes on general relativity
1909	First systematic presentation of analytic number theory
1913	First explanation of relations among analysis, geometry, and topology
1914	Theorem of distribution of zeros in the zeta function proved
1920	Class field theory explained
1921	John Maynard Keynes publishes his *Treatise on Probability*; concept of likelihood introduced into statistics
1928	John von Neumann proves minimax theorem in game theory
1935	Lambda calculus invented, proves a crucial tool for computer scientists
1936	Alan Turing publishes *On Computable Numbers*; Church's Theorem introduced
1944	John von Neumann publishes his seminal text on theory of games

Source: "A Mathematical Chronology," University of St. Andrews, http://mathshistory.st-andrews.ac.uk/Chronology/full.html (accessed June 25, 2020).

Table 5.2. Milestone Events in the Development of Mathematics, 1948–1998

Year	Milestone Event
1948	Norbert Wiener introduces *cybernetics* and feedback loops using mathematics to explain these concepts
1949	Proof offered for prime number theorem
1950s	Studies published or continued about probability, error-detecting and error-correcting codes, theory of partial differential equations, dynamical systems (the start of KAM theory)
1959	Marshall Hall publishes *Theory of Groups*
1961	Key findings reported on mathematical system with chaotic behavior, which leads to the development of chaos theory, one of the most important scientific ideas of the twentieth century
1962	Uses of functional analysis in mathematical physics are published
1965	Differential topology leads to Novikov Conjecture
1967	K-theory introduced
1969	New descriptions of simple groups
1972	Advances in catastrophic theory, demonstrating gradually changing forces can transform into catastrophes or abrupt changes, useful in biology and optics; advances in K-theory tools appear using geometric and topological methods
1976	Computers used to prove that the Four-Color Conjecture is true
1979	Non-commutative integration theory explained
1980	Classification of finite simple groups completed
1982	Expanded explanation of fractal geometry published
1984	Advances in differential geometry published
1998	Thomas Hales proves Kepler's problem on sphere packing.

Source: "A Mathematical Chronology," University of St. Andrews, http://mathshistory.st-andrews.ac.uk/Chronology/full.html (accessed June 25, 2020).

To assimilate a sense of what all these events accomplished that contributed so greatly to the development of new bodies of information expressed in numerical terms, turn to the distinguished British–Lebanese mathematician Michael Atiyah (1929–2019), who looked back on the achievements of this discipline during the twentieth century. He observed that mathematical problems grew over the century from focusing on narrow, local issues to global ones. For example, in the 1800s mathematicians studied complex analysis (a.k.a. function theory), exploring the role of one complex variable, a narrow enough topic for a mathematician to study and comment about.[26] By the end of the century, function theory had more properties, had become more nuanced and wide-ranging, and in his words, "by where their singularities were, where their domains of definition were, where they took their values." In other words, there were now many more ways to examine function theory. Differential geometry and number theory expanded in definition and functions too.[27] In physics that meant moving from just using, say, a differential equation to govern or understand a small-scale behavior to comprehend the features and functions of large-scale physical systems. In his words, "All physics is concerned really with predicting what will happen when you go from a small scale, where you understand what is happening, to a large scale, and follow through to the conclusions."[28]

Besides local (small, narrow) to broader scope, mathematicians and scientists shifted from studying, say, one variable to two or more during the 1900s. In differential geometries one might have studied curves and surfaces, but at the end of the century, "geometry of n-dimensional manifolds," moving from what one could see in space (such as curves and surfaces) to things one could imagine through use of mathematics, but could not actually see, but that these imagined things could be taken "seriously." Think of all the knowledge we have about faraway space and the behavior of stars and planets moving about before scientists had satellites and radio astronomy, the latter highly mathematized. In short, over the course of the century mathematicians made it possible to study more variables of innumerable problems. The move from finite to infinite variables, for which algebra was a useful tool to study such issues, increased their analytical capabilities.

He called a third trend—commutative to non-commutative—equally important. For the non-math reader, commutative is the idea that any group of quantities, when connected by mathematical operations generates the same result, regardless of the order of the numbers. So, $a \times b = b \times a$, or $2 \times 4 = 4 \times 2$. Non-commutative means that if you rearrange the order of the a and b here, you get a different answer. This second condition has been an important topic in the study of algebra, what he referred to as, "the bread and butter of 20th century algebraic machinery."[29]

A major transformation during the century was a move from linear to non-linear mathematics, where behavior was studied as, for one example, solitons and chaos. In his words: "They represent alternative extremes. Solitons [quantum or quasiparticle traveling as a wave without another before or after it and maintaining its shape, ed. note] represent unexpectedly organized behavior on non-linear differential equations, and chaos represents unexpectedly disorganized behavior. Both of them are present in different regimes."[30] It becomes easier to appreciate that by viewing the world in such a way, and with the development of appropriate mathematics to facilitate such studies, scientists could develop substantially large bodies of new information about realities. For example, linear partial differential equations are useful in the mathematics of electromagnetism, while the opposite (i.e., non-linear partial differential equations) are useful for exploring the structure of matter.

What about the great rivalry between the two fundamental pillars: geometry versus algebra, what Atiyah politely calls a "dichotomy," each with a long heritage: geometry the product of the ancient Greeks, the latter parented by Arabs and Indians. By 1900, Poincaré was a leading advocate of geometry (more specifically topology), while the other giant of the period, David

Hilbert (1862–1943) favored axioms, formal states, and structured presentations of mathematical evidence. Recall that geometry concerned the study of space, while algebra more with time. In algebra you calculate one sequence of operations one after another, hence over time. But in a hard science, say physics, one deals with both theory (concepts, ideas, laws) and "experimental apparatus," which favors algebra and that can be better used to understand motion and change.[31] With the arrival of computers and other scientific machines, algebra promised instructions, commands, feedback, and insights not quite possible with geometry. Algebra became enormously popular in the twentieth century. Both were increasingly used in tandem. Many techniques shared by both emerged, such as Homology theory, K-theory, lie groups, and finite groups. I will come back to these later.

His summary of the broad trends of the twentieth century suggested the kind of information mathematicians made possible. In the first half of the century, what Atiyah labeled an "era of specialization," much that was defined and formalized in mathematics (Hilbert's approach) proved influential. People learned much about what was possible from mathematics, specifically from algebra. In the second half of the century, what he called the "era of unification," mathematicians and scientists took techniques from one subfield and applied them to another, making mathematics "hybridized to an enormous extent."[32] The cross-border movement of practices and applications of more narrowly focused theories and techniques became evident in all disciplines in the hard and social sciences and across all manner of engineering and medicine in the same period. That trend helps to explain why so much new information and, indeed, different types of information, surfaced over the past century. It is why we discuss statistics later, because it was the poster child of that trend at work, a poster child because it was visible to hundreds of millions of people, not hidden behind the walls of laboratories, classrooms, or conference rooms. But first, we turn to all those people exposed to mathematics, beginning with the mathematicians themselves. The sidebar personalizes what I just discussed.

GETTING PERSONAL ABOUT MATHEMATICS

As a child in the 1950s, I was taught, as perhaps the vast majority of children then and now, the concept of counting, a recognition of the values of Arabic numbers, the four functions in arithmetic and, because there were no hand calculators available to children, we memorized the multiplication tables up through $12 \times 12 = 144$. Then in high school in the 1960s—still in Atiyah's first era—I studied in the following order a year of introductory algebra (required), a half year of introductory geometry (required), a second year of more advanced algebra (not required but recommended), and finally a half year of trigonometry (not required but available). A retired American Army officer-engineer taught these courses, and the sequence essentially followed that of all American and European high schools. One could see the sequential arc of the instruction from simple and narrow to the more complex but in order of practical application. Parallel to that set of classes, beginning in the period when taking the first algebra class, I also attended a course in carpentry in which we were taught to measure and where, if one had not mastered the concept of fractions before, they emphatically did now.

Calculus and vector analysis nearly ambushed me in my first year as a college student, not just because of their increased complexity for a young person more interested in history and humanistic studies, but because these represented a substantial leap into the second era Atiyah described, reinforced by every science course that I took in the 1960s. Not until the 1980s was I exposed to statistics, but when that happened, it seemed these prior classes in mathematics began to make sense, almost comfortable in understanding how this broad discipline could be used, providing someone else (or software) did the calculations for me.

THE EXPANDED USER POPULATION OF MATHEMATICAL INFORMATION

It took more than experts to develop new methods for acquiring and using information and even for presenting new information in new ways (e.g., highly quantitatively). It required people to use the new methods and formats of information, and so the adoption of mathematical approaches by ever-increasing numbers of people became part of the explanation for how information transformed over the past two centuries. In the 1900s population worldwide of people at least barely literate and exposed to some mathematics rose faster than in previous centuries, by 1820 to an estimated 12 percent of humanity. A century later (2016) some 86 percent were literate and had more years of formal education than the earlier population.[33] In 1900, there were worldwide 1.6 billion people, in 2000, 6 billion. The American population expanded from 38.6 million souls in 1870 to 76.2 million in 1900, then to 282.2 million in 2000.[34] Exposing children to mathematics in North America began early, if slowly, but by 1870 nearly 57 percent were obtaining some formal education; in 1900 72 percent. By the mid-twentieth century almost every child in America had been exposed to various amounts of mathematical education.[35] By the end of the 1920s, high school curriculums in the United States had become relatively uniform, remaining so into the next century, with classes on algebra and geometry core offerings. By the early years of the Cold War, high school attendance exceeded 90 percent.[36]

Higher education paralleled similar growth rates. By the end of the twentieth century over 25 percent of adult Americans had attended some form of post-secondary education. If they attended a four-year institution, they were exposed to more mathematics as an extension of their high school training, a great deal more if they majored in mathematics, a hard science, or engineering. If they attended a vocational institution, they were exposed to more mathematics than liberal arts students at a four-year institution, because they had to learn how to measure and calibrate in many disciplines and to understand the sizes of parts and products common to their professions.[37]

Several sets of American statistics suggest the size and breadth of the population deeply familiar with mathematics. In 1920 American universities granted 154 doctorates in the disciplines of physics, astronomy, chemistry, earth science, mathematics, and engineering—all extensive users and creators of mathematical information. The numbers rose each year, with nearly 1,000 (986) granted in 1942. Other doctorates in biology added to the population: 66 in 1920, but growing each year such that in 1942 it reached 297 diplomas. Many hundreds more were awarded in that period to medical doctors (50 in 1920, 331 in 1942) and close to a hundred per year in agriculture.[38]

Statistics for the second half of the century reinforced the fact that many people were deeply familiar with mathematics of all kinds. But several others reinforce the point. In the United States in 2015, universities awarded 4.7 million science degrees of all types, more than any other country, although in descending order of number others did too: China, Germany, United Kingdom, Japan, France, Canada, and Switzerland.[39] In 2013 there were over 7.8 million scientists worldwide, most deeply familiar with mathematics.[40] There were 80,000 full-time mathematicians in the world, of which 3,500 worked in the United States, while 1.6 million engineers and 5.8 million scientists for a total of 4.9 percent of the entire American workforce.[41] But these numbers do not seem as accurate as one would expect, because, for example, in the United States, there were 24,000 high schools in 2018, and as any American reader would probably attest, each had at least one mathematics teacher, and to teach that subject in the United States in a secondary school, they would have had to study the subject either as a major or minor in college or university to be licensed to teach. None of these statistics includes the computer science population, a profession also well versed in mathematics. One can add to these cohorts many tens of millions of accountants, business managers, shop floor and other blue-collar workers, students at many grade levels, religious officials, sociologists, government workers, teachers, and other educators. They all relied on statistics as part of their work activities.

STATISTICS COMES INTO ITS OWN

What is a statistic? What are statistics? What is statistical science? More than just collections of numbers, the discipline is a group of methods for understanding data by relying on mathematical ways useful for telling a story based on and with numbers, and for understanding natural phenomenon and other events.[42] In its most simple concept, a statistic is a number (datum, plural is data) extracted from a population of numbers, a piece of information, such as a fact about 25 percent of all the people who live in your community. If you knew 100 percent of the data (known as a parameter) your information would be definitive; however, since normally one never knows 100 percent of all information about a population (group of facts, numbers), you have to manage through the unknown to understand what is happening. Managing that gap in understanding is the role of statistics. It facilitates creating useful information and insights, leading to greater confidence in making decisions or predictions. Its leading historian Theodore M. Porter offered a useful perspective: "Statistics has become known in the twentieth century as the mathematical tool for analyzing experimental and observational data," although its foundations were laid over the course of one century, beginning in the 1830s.[43]

More formally, it is a set of methods to gather, review, analyze, and draw conclusions based on data, much of it numeric. The Royal Statistical Society president, quoted earlier, defined a statistic as "a number derived from a set of data," and statistical science as "the discipline of learning about the world from data," using a variety of techniques and analytical tools.[44] I think of statistics as he does—as the collection and analysis of data to learn something—but what also makes the discipline so attractive to millions of people is how findings are presented, in other words, all those tables, charts, and graphs that so populate the PowerPoint presentations, books, and academic articles. There is even a body of practices just on how best to present data visually.[45]

Statistical information comes in essentially two forms. The first is called *descriptive statistics*. These are summaries of data from samples drawn from indices, large population (amounts) of data, such as the distribution of points of view or behavior of human population. Figure 5.1 is a simple example. The second is called *inferential statistics*, which presents findings (conclusions) from data that is of a more random variation. In this second type, plots show the relationships between multiple variables. Figure 5.2 is an example.

2010 Demographic Profile Data: California		
	Number	Percentage
Asian Alone	**4,861,007**	**13.0**
Asian Indian	528,176	1.4
Chinese	1,253,102	3.4
Filipino	1,195,580	3.2
Japanese	272,528	0.7
Korean	451,892	1.2
Vietnamese	581,946	1.6
Other Asian	577,783	1.6
NHPI (Native Hawaiians and Pacific Islanders) Alone	**144,386**	**0.4**
Native Hawaiian	21,423	0.1
Guamanian or Chamorro	24,299	0.1
Samoan	40,900	0.1
Other Pacific Islander	57,764	0.2

Figure 5.1. Example of Descriptive Statistics. *Source*: U.S. Census Bureau
Note: **Data for Race Alone Population Only.**

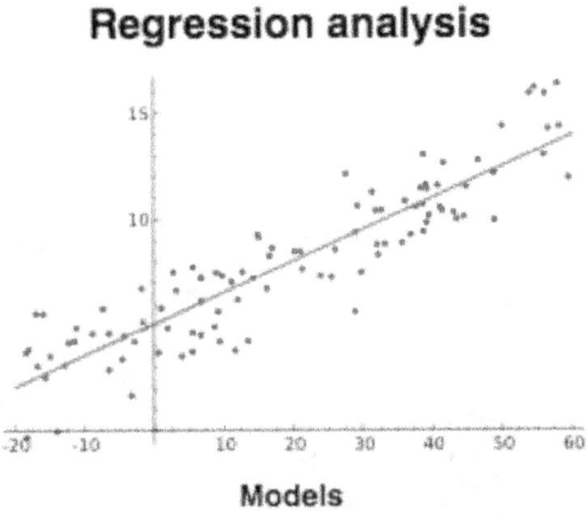

Regression analysis

Models

Figure 5.2. Example of Inferential Statistics. *Source*: Author's collection

In inferential statistics, hypotheses or models are created against which extant data is tested. I will not engage in a tutorial on how one conducts statistical studies; it can be quite complicated.[46] More important, here, is that descriptive statistics allows one to sort through a great deal of data to draw a picture of something, such as the percentage of voters who cast their ballots for one political candidate over another by age, ethnicity, political allegiance, or location. The second is to create new information, or fill in gaps, based on assumptions and other methods to provide findings with degrees

144 Chapter 5

of probability of being accurate or not.[47] In both instances, statisticians work with data within the context of uncertainty, seeking facts upon which to make decisions. Increasingly, since the 1960s, managers have become reliant on statistical data and modeling to assist in making decisions, because so many prior circumstances and experiences do not reflect current realities.[48] Figure 5.3 is an example of a trend analysis, a highly popular type of data representation, while figure 5.4 is a snapshot of information taken at one

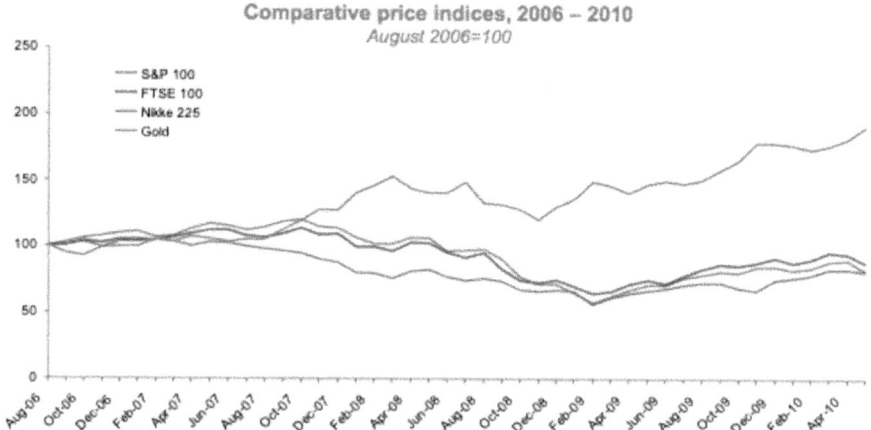

Figure 5.3. Example of Trend Analysis

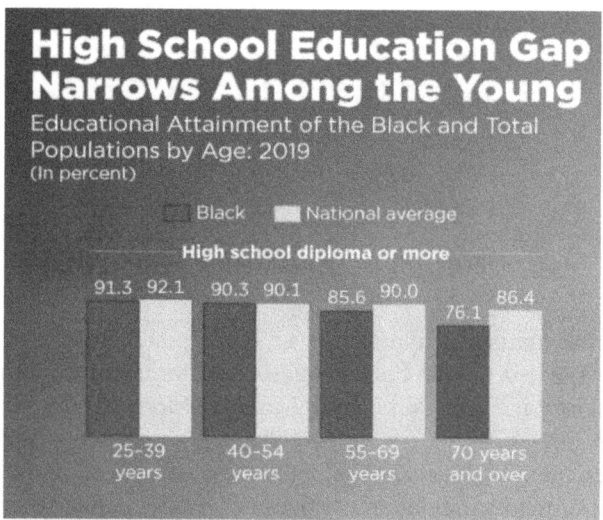

Figure 5.4. Example of Survey Data Presentation. *Source*: U.S. Bureau of the Census

time, in this case, survey data. The invention of such tools came as a result of information handlers in multiple disciplines needing specific yet widely applicable methods relying on mathematical probability for understanding mass phenomena. As one scholar pointed out, "Statistics was and continues to be seen as especially valuable for uncovering causal relationships where the individual events are either concealed from view or are highly variable and subject to a host of influences."[49]

What kinds of information have statisticians used, or made available, often from publicly available sources, such as government databases and corporate and academic research files, such as those generated by surveys and analysis of signals collected from software monitoring tools? When I worked at IBM's Institute for Business Value (2004–2012), we gathered vast sums of data from multi-question surveys and interviews conducted with thousands of people all over the world and by tapping into government census and economic databases. A PhD-trained statistician "crunched" the numbers, delivering insights that supported or invalidated hypotheses we had posited be tested.[50] Statistical data is some of the most widely collected, such as from existing files of numbers or facts and sample data reflecting larger populations. Another class of new information is experimental collections of data or of observations, usually used to understand the cause of some behavior or event, and to predict the effects of changes based on preselected (or discovered) variables. Conducting experiments became a far wider practice across many disciplines in the twentieth century than before, evident in medicine and in the development of new medications, such as testing one group with a potential drug and another giving them placebos to see the effects of a new treatment or medicine.

Finally, observational studies proliferated, often through surveys. Studies comparing the health of smokers to nonsmokers by gender and age to establish the effects on lung health and causality of lung cancer were widespread during the middle of the century, establishing the link between tobacco use and cancer.[51] To understand the practical uses of statistics requires a deeper understanding of how the subject evolved, because it was shaped into a series of mathematical tools, suggesting that their evolution has not ended. We are helped by the research of historians, such as that of Theodore M. Porter, who has done much to document the emergence of statistical tools. As with mathematics, he reminds us that one should "regard numbers, graphs, and formulas first of all [as] strategies of communications."[52] Yet imposing on any natural phenomenon rigorous rule-bound disciplines of mathematics and statistics is always difficult and subject to varying definitions of what constitutes objectivity. The good news is that statistical practices are, in his explanation, "extraordinarily flexible, so that almost any issue can be formulated in this language."[53] His study of mathematics and statistics, particularly with respect to descriptive statistics, argued that these new techniques made it possible for people "to use numbers casually and informally," with "quantification for public as well as scientific purposes" an ally "to a spirit of rigor."[54] Historians found such flexibility motivated mathematically skilled researchers in numerous academic disciplines to find ways to apply statistics in various ways, beginning in the eighteenth century. By the end of the nineteenth century, it was a fully developed discipline with multiple collections of tools relevant to hard and social sciences.[55]

Adolphe Quetelet (1796–1874), an early-nineteenth-century pioneer in the development of statistical tools, sought ways to show how disordered human activities could be understood at a high level as regular behavior, such as by documenting that certain aberrant behaviors were constant from one year to the next, for example, the incidence of mental diseases. Such insights appeared to him as "statistical laws."[56] Much work in the 1800s focused on documenting numerically various social ills, from crime to poverty, epidemics to political revolutions. Officials wanted to manage large populations, constrain and reduce crime, and control the expenses of public welfare programs. Statistics helped to define the shape and size of the problems they faced.[57]

A remarkable example came in the 1930s in the United States when the American government implemented its New Deal social programs to fight the Great Depression. To address those problems, its agencies had to develop measures of agricultural, labor, and social realities; numeric goals for addressing these with public policies; and yet other metrics to understand progress and success. Historian Emmanuel Didier documented how social needs shaped what statistical tools would be used and how their findings would affect public policies.[58] Porter's thinking aligned with his that statistics evolved as much as political history, one influenced by the other.[59] By the end of the 1800s—just one generation before the New Deal—statistics was recognized as a discipline, field, and body of knowledge and practice, and it had evolved, in Porter's words "in parallel with an array of human sciences," such as demography, economics, business, psychology, medicine, various social sciences as anthropology, political sciences, and sociology.[60] This represents a consensus opinion among historians of statistics and quantification.[61] One can put a finer point on the matter: statistics evolved as an entwined transformation of information across the past two centuries.

The first step in statistics was—and still is—the collection of data to study, involving sampling, experimental studies, and observations. In combination these sources tap into pre-existing data sets, such as those found in databases, or are accumulated (e.g., number and date of deaths from church records over many centuries), or are created through surveys and other data collection activities.

Humans had collected descriptive statistics for centuries, such as for tax rolls and economic information, but in the twentieth century it seemed no facet of human life was without its statistics. We do not even know how much was collected, just that their existence was ubiquitous.

So a summary: a descriptive statistic is simply a count, the number of your neighbors who drive sedans versus SUVs, the number of students in a school in various grade levels, all summarizing a sample of even larger sets of data. The second class of statistics, inferential statistics, is the result of using analytical methods to deduce (identify) the properties of the data being studied, even used to predict the behaviors of the data.[62] The first type of data is what can be observed, the second what can be inferred. For an example of the second, based on the academic performance of students reading development in the first year of school, one could predict what their academic achievements would probably be four years later, with a range of predictability. That sort of new information can be generated through the use of analytics.[63]

Like the librarians at the same time, developers of statistical tools had their luminaries who were just as fascinating, such as Quetelet, Francis Galton (1822–1911), and Karl Pearson (1857–1936), which space will not permit me to explore here, but who have been well studied by historians.[64] Many diverse sources account for the evolution of statistics. The use of probability to understand variation originated out of social sciences, such as in the work of Charles Gouraud (b. 1823–d. unknown);[65] for understanding the role of chance (in statistics, *randomness*) people turned to calculus, while even within probability studies mathematicians and others dived deeper to explore how to differentiate error from variation using frequency interpretation techniques, now standard in statistical work. Quetelet held the high ground for decades through his ability to show how to understand the distribution of traits in human populations, whether in health, economics, business, or other social and medical issues.[66]

Creating new information to explain *randomness*—today often also called *chance*—drew much attention. People in many disciplines sought out ways to predict behavior and until the nineteenth century that was mathematically impossible; by the end of the century the opposite was becoming increasingly possible, moving from need to hope. Charles S. Pierce (1839–1914), best known as the "father of pragmatism" but also a philosopher, mathematician, and logician, described a universe of chance, and his work led to the development of quantum physics in the 1920s where "the most fundamental particles of nature exhibit irreducible chance in their movements and interactions."[67] His work and that of physics established by the 1930s that chance was a fundamental feature of the world. Porter argued that the study of randomness—chance—came from the determination of scientists and their societies to use science to control nature, beginning by understanding it all, in this case with quantum physics, "a domain that had previously been seen "as "inscrutable whimsy."[68] His conclusion on the result: "The indeterminism of probability is so reliable and highly structured that randomness seems to disappear from the end result."[69] Another star of the statistical ecosystem, Ronald A. Fisher (1890–1962), concurred. In a 1953 speech he was not shy about the matter: "The effects of chance are the most accurately calculable, and therefore the least doubtful, of all the factors of an evolutionary situation."[70]

In the twentieth century, statistical analysis became prominently evident in many fields. Actuarial studies in the insurance and finance industries assessed risks of death by type of person, age, gender, and lifestyles, while in finance, the probabilities and possibilities of various natural disasters or human events affecting stock markets. Econometrics became a new field of study learning from all manner of economic data routinely collected by governments and academics around the world. Demographic studies evolved into data-intensive exercises and some of the largest collected bodies of data covering many hundreds of years.[71] Biostatistics, astrostatistics (about astronomical data), epidemiology (study of diseases), even about law (jurimetrics), medicine, political science, psychology, social statistics, chemometrics (about chemistry), and business statistics represented other types of information that expanded in volume were studied. All were made possible by the maturation of statistical methods.

From a practical perspective, such collections of data were used in most organizations to help shape what to do next. Figure 5.5 illustrates a model forecasting changing populations to inform government officials, while also explaining what causes these dynamics, in this (a positive feedback loop)

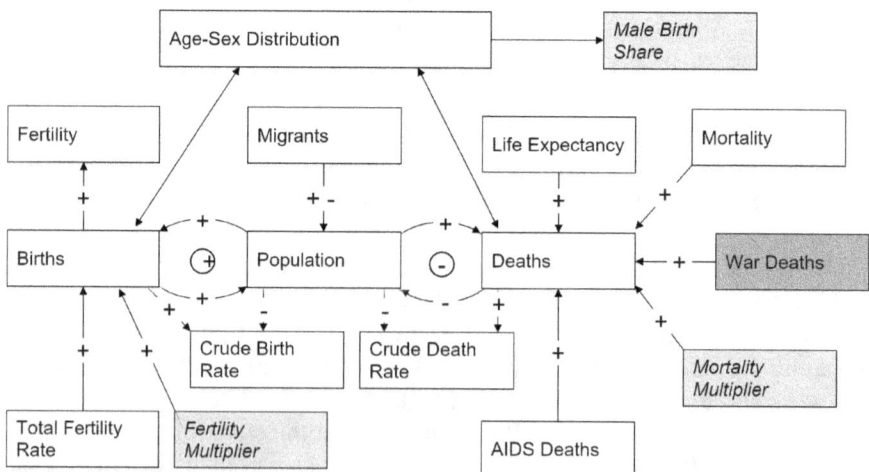

Figure 5.5. Example of a Forecast Model

fertility rates by linking population to births and a second (a negative feedback loop) the role of mortality linking deaths to population. Both are active regardless of the size of the population. Graphics prepared by the Imperial College London in March 2020 galvanized the British and American governments to impose aggressive measures to stop the Coronavirus from spreading, data that led tens of millions of people to understand the concept of "flattening the curve" so as to not overwhelm hospitals with a rush of new patients.

The processing power of desktop calculators, beginning in the early 1900s, and computers in the 1950s, facilitated rapid expansion in the use of statistics to such an extent that these have to be called out as a collective cause for the development of many different statistical tools and methods. This is a development apart from the normal intellectual process of studying a field, such as done by mathematicians in the nineteenth and early twentieth centuries using paper and pencils, blackboards, desktop calculators, and good brains. The availability of personal computers, spreadsheets, and other analytical software in the 1970s made computing the tool of choice for statisticians. This became especially so when they were able to access large data sets in government and mainframes in the 1980s. They could seek responses in minutes and hours that earlier would have taken days, weeks, or years to obtain. The cost of using a personal computer (PC) was infinitesimal in comparison, too, so they could iteratively revisit a research issue, doing "what if" analysis, changing variables and assumptions repeatedly and slightly, replacing thinking by "running the numbers" in various iterations.

Computers assisted in four ways. These could manipulate much larger data sets than a mere mortal, process more realistic models taking into account additional variables, study larger classes of models, and offer much improved visualization of data. An example of large datasets could include the entire population (census) of a nation for economists, or study all the genes in a species. Businesses collect vast quantities of data, think of what Google and Amazon do with their trillions of pieces of data. Computers can address problems of computational complexity better than humans, such as in the study of the behavior of billions or trillions of stars or germs, or in the study of thousands of regression analyses, offering insights of phenomenon impossible to gain before computing. It would be difficult to overstate the importance of statistical software, now used probably by nearly if not 100 percent of all statisticians and many hundreds of millions of non-statisticians searching for data and conducting their own analysis. Answers were not always perfect or accurate, as the media often reports, but far more helpful and reliable than one is led to believe.[72] Results could be presented using new and computer-generated visualizations.

Because the number of people conducting statistical analysis grew so much in the second half of the twentieth century, it became increasingly evident statistically, too, that common errors were evident in practice. Six problems and pitfalls complicated the use of statistics. First, the use of biased samples can skew conclusions toward more inaccurate ones; so much attention has to be paid to getting the samplings accurate. Second, overgeneralizing one group of data as if applied to all others is both a temptation and a weakness. Assuming that findings of how Ebola spread in Africa would apply to how an Asian bird flu would in North America is an example, because the population of data used for one study might not have the same characteristics as the population being generalized about. Third, understanding the dynamics of causality remains a common problem. Just because the stock market seems to go up at the same time as women's hemlines does not mean that the fashion industry is driving stock values up or down. Careful design of experiments is crucial here. Fourth, there are myriad incorrect analyses, such as those caused by bad mathematics, inaccurate arithmetic calculations, insufficient use of enough variables (or the wrong ones), or simply applying the wrong analytical tools or methods.[73] Fifth, some practitioners violate their own assumptions built into their models, perhaps introducing exceptions that circumstances lead to misleading (inaccurate) findings. One experienced statistician summed up the problems: "Deliberate fabrication of data appears to be fairly rare, but errors in statistical methods are frequent," and one seen all the time: "questionable research practices that tend to lead to exaggerated claims of statistical significance," which, for example, contributed mightily to the anti-vaccine movement at the dawn of the current century.[74] I would add a sixth encountered too frequently, particularly generated by those who build their own spreadsheets and models on their PCs and laptops: errors in data entry. The misplaced decimal point can be deadly, so too the lack of the common zero or more. For example, 10,000 is a lot different from 100,000.

While mathematics as both a language to communicate and a provider of new information became more complex, diverse and useful over the past two centuries, its offshoot of statistics did too. The ability to use statistics in all manner of subjects and disciplines demonstrated both its utility and flexibility. Without it, mathematics might not have become as important as it did, especially during the twentieth century. Mathematics and statistics combined made the power of numeracy an important feature of information by the end of the twentieth century. Porter's evidence that people thought increasingly in numbers as a language and their trust in that kind of data represents one of the major changes that occurred to information over time.

CONCLUSIONS

An editor of the leading science history journal, *Isis*, Harry Woolf, declared in 1961 that "measurement has long been considered a hallmark of science properly practiced, and once a new discipline has developed a mathematical discourse, it has almost immediately laid claim ... to the significant status—science!" Quantification—the use of numbers—added "precision" to the "dialogue between nature and the scholar," and facilitated the deployment of "increasingly higher levels of abstraction." Quantification—measurement—"in all science becomes of fundamental concern to theory and practice alike."[75] Historian Theodor M. Porter referred to "numbers, graphs, and formulas first of all [as] strategies of communication."[76] Numbers themselves are not laws of nature. As argued in this chapter, numbers are part of the languages of mathematics and statistics. Both are languages and so here the discourse focused on linguistics as much as about science-related issues and communications. Scientists increasingly communicated with numbers, and chemists mixed these with symbols to do the same in their disciplines.

No discussion about how scientists changed the form and content of information is possible without understanding the central role played by mathematics and statistics. That recognition justified the subject of this chapter. The use of these communications tools—I prefer more the analogy of languages—justified sandwiching an entire chapter between the engineers building computers, who also embraced numeracy and mathematics, and the large community of hard science professionals, who were largely an enthusiastic and early cohort of computing enthusiasts.

This move to mathematics and statistics is not a new gesture. Learned communities in Western Europe discoursed in Latin for over 1,500 years, in the eighteenth century largely in French, while German grew in fashion in the next century. In the twentieth century English predominated. Researchers and knowledge workers had long understood the need to use a universally accepted language with which to communicate with each other. Each language had its assumed and overt features, so too mathematics and statistics. In the previous chapter, we saw computer engineers develop "programming languages." The languages of numeracy included shared and accepted definitions of terms and values (e.g., the number 7 had the same value around the world), common uses understood by all (grammar, such as how to calculate an addition), and widely accepted norms for the presentation of evidence (e.g., format and outline for a journal article presentation).

However, mathematics was more than a language, it was, along with statistics, a way for creating new information, not just serving as an idiom to explain the known world. The disciplines and professions reviewed in subsequent chapters used these to define new ways to understand information, while working differently with their own concepts of information.

In the next chapter we see how scientists in several disciplines used the language of numbers to shape and communicate their new information that as early as the mid-twentieth century combined with human languages to become a lingua franca of modern times. To avoid getting ahead of ourselves, keep in mind that human languages and numbers dominated expressions of information, a practice that proved impossible to challenge until artificial intelligence (AI) reached a point where it could bypass humans and combine quantification with the electrical impulses Bell Labs engineers described a century ago. AI has not yet developed to that point of sophistication, so the languages of mathematics and statistics are still used to shape the forms of modern information.

Chapter 6

Scientists and Medical Experts Shape Information

> *The uniform character of mathematics is the essence of science, for mathematics is the foundation of all exact scientific knowledge.*
>
> David Hilbert (1862–1943)

The epigraph given here is perhaps one of the most widely quoted expressions of the role of mathematics; certainly it is the most widely attributed quote to mathematician David Hilbert. But, many scientists could just as easily have expressed it to describe their own reality. As this chapter demonstrates, scientists were practitioners of mathematics and its derivative, statistics, while medical doctors were largely the benefactors of new scientific information. Of all the broad fields of knowledge, none has received as much attention as the massive increases and diversity of information in the past two to three hundred years as in the general category of science. Rightfully so, that new collection of knowledge made possible a modern society with all its more positive than negative attributes, from a higher quality of life, longevity of life itself, improved medical practices, but too, development of nuclear bombs and chemically based pollution. However, as other chapters demonstrated, the emergence of a new understanding of how the world works was not completely dominated by the developments in the hard sciences, yet clearly predominant. Rather than add many more chapters to document that story, here we take a step toward synthesizing—identifying—the broad patterns in the creation of scientific information. There is value in looking less at trees and more at forests as the latter increase in size and diversity, thereby contributing a recent trend of the past three decades of consolidating, integrating, and leveraging the many fragmented bodies of scientific knowledge into more comprehensive syntheses—the current great promise of AI and myriad computing tools.

By definition, attempts to synthesize large bodies of information devolve into the subjective views of an author, and because of the diversity of scientific knowledge, the bias is here, if tempered by the experiences of other disciplines in the creation and transformation of information. But, as the distinguished French historian of biology's history, Michael Morange, explained for all who study science's past, we need to understand how scientific information evolved so as to appreciate current circumstances, such as how powerfully theories animate scientific research, while activities in the present can offer insights into past behaviors. More in this chapter than in others, we pick up on his notion that "building scientific knowledge depends above all on the techniques used and traditions of research that can persist over long periods of time"; the persistence of, in his word, "attitudes" toward knowledge creation.[1] His insight applies as well to computer scientists, economists, and engineers, among others.

I begin with a discussion of how scientists and information interacted by defining the broad trends evident across multiple disciplines. The role of information is explored in physics, chemistry, biology, and medicine from the mid-nineteenth century to the end of the twentieth century. I conclude with an introduction to recent trends in bioinformatics and medical informatics, straddling the late years of the past century and the start of the current one. This chapter rounds out our discussion of the natural sciences. These are clustered together in part because they are widely seen as related, also because they borrowed practices from one another, such as the use of numeracy, and shared views about how research should be done and results presented.

HOW SCIENCE AND INFORMATION SHAPED EACH OTHER

These are boom times for information in the world of science, and it has been so for over three centuries. Between 1665 and 2009, over 50 million scientific papers were published and since the latter year an additional 2.5 million more annually, bringing the total through 2020 to over 67 million. But, we really do not have a firm number, as these are estimates, despite the wonders of data mining to firm up the count. These do not include postings on the Internet, blogs, and other non-peer-reviewed reports.[2] But a key observation is that the curve of its trend line begins a slightly upward trajectory after 1870, next a massive hockey stick upturn by the late 1930s, after which the line shoots up like a rocket, beginning in the 1960s.[3] As the scientific community expanded after 1870, the number of researchers able to publish did too. The population of scientists continues to grow with some estimates putting it roughly 4 to 5 percent each year, although other calculations place the numbers at between

8 and 9 percent.[4] One consequence for all, however, is that scientists are complaining of "information overload," as each of their niche research spaces are flooded with papers and new information, often evermore narrowly conceived as specializations deepen with more data increasing in ever-narrower topics.[5]

The scientific fields we explore here share common features. First, these have always and today been driven by the hunt for information, its organization, and use. Think of new medicines, less dangerous modes of transportation, or saving Earth's environment. Second, scientists and engineers have developed numerous ways and devices for gathering, understanding, and extracting new insights from information. Statistical methods developed in the twentieth century have even created new information from studying the lack of information! Third, all these fields have disciplined its members' thinking and use of information by increasingly accepting two practices: reliance on mathematics to describe physical phenomenon and embrace of theory with its attendant rules of creation, acceptance, and revision.[6] Working with information the way Babbage did, by combining statistical data and a generous helping of reasoning and opining as a method, increasingly went by the wayside as scientists became more reliant on the tools of mathematics and statistics on the one hand, and on the other, expanding bodies of knowledge within their disciplines. As the mass of humanity increasingly gained access to the Internet at the dawn of the new century, the less-than-expert members of society did not as rigorously embrace those disciplines—mathematics, statistics, and scientific knowledge. That new circumstance resulted in substantial confusion as individuals sorted through fact and fiction.[7]

Another trend evident in the hard sciences and that increasingly appeared in other disciplines, explored in subsequent chapters, is the increasing role of information theories involving such topics as probability, statistical inference, computer science, and mathematics all translated (converted) into language and practices specific to one's discipline. One of many reasons to use science to inform humanity is to eliminate uncertainty and variability, so that one can anticipate and take advantage of opportunities while mitigating or resolving problems. Ancient Greek priests reading pigeon droppings to forecast the outcome of a battle for an anxious military leader has been replaced with statistical analysis, reducing chance to predictable behavior, and more recently chaos to a more ordered known phenomenon. Probability went from being driven either by intuition or misinformation to expected frequencies. In the process scholars have been learning that many physical and social phenomenon demonstrate a high degree of regularity in their patterns of activity. Researchers have also been learning that individual events were, in fact, unpredictable ones. Group wisdom seems on the ascendency.[8]

Into this stew pot of methods in the twentieth century one could add the Central Limit Theorem, Measure Concentration, Queuing Theory, and use of Large Deviation and Random Process Divergence analytical tools.[9] Statistical Inference has been strengthened, too, with Hypothesis Testing, Parameter Estimation, other estimating techniques, Bayesian statistics, predictive and discrete time-series analysis, and pattern recognition, among others.[10] We have already discussed the role of computing in processing complex algorithms, creating and managing data structures, processing of large bodies of data, and generating random numbers, among others, which were part of this large milieu of tools and techniques. In total, the majority of today's most widely used techniques were developed after 1893: correlation coefficient (1896), contingency analysis and chi-square test (1900), t-test (1908), analysis of variance (1918), and "degrees of freedom" (early 1900s).[11] All built on the earlier work of Francis Galton (1822–1911), Karl Pearson (1857–1936), and Ronald A. Fisher (1890–1962), among others. Statistics had become an applied field. Early-twentieth-century techniques continued to be used, too, alongside these, such as Fisher's analysis of variance, originally developed to study heredity, increasingly applied in many other fields.[12] The same can be said about the value of conducting small-sample analyses (today known as the t-statistic), developed by employees at the Guinness beer brewery.[13]

These uses and methods did not all appear at the same time, nor were they always adopted when introduced. An example of the ebb and flow of the introduction, resistance, then acceptance process that met almost every new theorem and technique is illustrated by probability analysis, a central concern in statistics, much of which had been worked out by the 1660s. It was never intuitive, which meant it ran into resistance for literally hundreds of years when people wanted to deal with the phenomenon of chance, but which makes sense if one accepts the idea that the expected frequencies of an event can be calculated, which takes us back to the idea that overall patterns have a regularity to them, while individual actions probably do not. In the first half of the twentieth century, mathematicians remained unimpressed, dismissing it as applied mathematics. It was a less fashionable topic to explore than, say, number theory, differential geometry, or even algebra. But in the second half of the century it became possible to use methods for determining probability to solve abstract problems. Now probability became a serious field of study that by the end of the century was viewed as central to mathematics.[14]

While the story told here may create an impression of one success built upon another, often using mathematics and statistics, reality proved messier. Historian William Aspray reminded us that scientists in different fields borrowed from each other in striving for a trans-disciplinarity of information, an ideal, even if it never quite happened.[15] Historians reminded us since the days of Norbert Wiener and Claude Shannon that scientists of many stripes helped to shape the definition of information as it transformed.[16] Shannon made it appear in his writings that information's evolution was a stable process, while Wiener saw his own work as confrontational against prior thinking, much of it dating from the seventeenth and eighteenth centuries. They were followed by those computer scientists discussed in chapter 4, and the subsequent work of scientists in multiple fields lent more evidence to Wiener's conceptualization of information than to Shannon's worldview, not the least of which was the work in cybernetics performed by individuals with a broad range of experiences drawn from the hard sciences, mathematics, and engineering, among others.[17]

Morange reminded us that scientists gathered up convergent observations, which they then used as evidence in support of new models. In his words, such exercises were "processes of coalescence," the way information changed over time and that continues today. To use his description of what happened, the process brings together evidence "to explain a phenomenon, of schemas that have recently been developed by different disciplines."[18] In all fields of the hard sciences, one could observe interdisciplinary transfers of methodologies, a pattern in evidence since the days of Galileo and Descartes. Biologists borrowed from models prepared by physicists to create new ones that illustrated human life as machine-like, more recently the nature of life, suggesting life functions as computer-like, with energy, too, being a form of information.

THE BOOM IN PHYSICS

No field of science benefited more from the increased volume of information, types, and tools to collect and apply these than physics. This was so much the case that while historians have found much to discuss about physics prior to the 1870s, most of what physicists know scientists uncovered during the past five generations. Lord Kelvin (1824–1907) belted out his dictum: "If you cannot measure, your knowledge is meager and unsatisfactory," although he was complaining about the "nihilism" of James Clerk Maxwell's (1831–1879) thinking about physical theory.[19] It may be the shortest statement ever made of what scientists did. Physics underwent a massive expansion and transformation in the volume of information and mankind's understanding of their physical world in the twentieth century. It may possibly be experiencing yet another round of growth and change, although critics are challenging that notion as published academic papers in the field continue to accumulate and evermore expensive complex projects are funded by governments.[20] Specifically, the Newtonian view of physics—that the world operated almost like a machine—is being challenged by discoveries in quantum mechanics and the work of biologists. Questions being asked that lead to new bodies of information include queries regarding whether everything in nature is networked, energy at work, information itself? As astronomer James Jeans suggested in 1983 about space but applies to our own earthly spaces, "The universe begins to look more like a great thought than like a great machine."[21] It has been nearly forty years since he made the comment; physicists seem to be migrating to his thought, So, much is happening with information. Regardless of how one views the subject of physics, it would be difficult to deny its achievements. One of its clearest defenders, Jim Al-Khalili, explained: "The grand scope and sweep of physics today are breathtaking. That we now know what (almost) everything we see in the world is made of and how it holds together; that we can trace back the evolution of the entire universe to fractions of a second after the birth of space and time themselves; that through our knowledge of the physical laws of nature we have developed, and continue to develop, technologies that have transformed our lives—this is all pretty staggering."[22]

Information in this discipline came in three forms. One type consisted of facts to explain facts in physics to the public, students, and colleagues. These came largely in the form of narratives using human language, nouns, and verbs. But, it could also be narratives understandable more by a technical community where, for instance, the writer assumed readers knew a great deal and so did not need to define every term and concept discussed. Often these descriptions were expressed in the form of theorems and principles, much as we saw with Claude E. Shannon's explanations in chapter 4. When the history of physics is studied, narratives move from articulation of one theorem to another, such as from Paul A. Dirac (1902–1984) replacing older ideas to today's Quantum Theory, or Erwin Schröedinger's (1887–1961) equation in physics.[23]

A second form was the by-product of the overwhelming reliance on mathematics to describe—and prove—that theorems, principles and narrative explanations were true, accurately describing reality. Why was this important? Much of what is known about how the universe and matter operate and their features are not discernable to the human eye. Have you ever seen a black hole in space? Yet, scientists say it exists and believe they have proven it does. Dirac expressed his insights as an equation to explain the connections between matter (originally a Newtonian perspective) and radiation (a Maxwellian interest). As one physicist explained, "The genesis of Quantum Field Theory, or QFT for short, whose applications in physics extend all the way from the theory of elementary particles to condensed matter physics, and now spreading even to the biological sciences" was articulated in mathematical terms.[24]

The third type of information were numerical expressions of physical phenomenon, such as the movement and behavior of electrons (e.g., notion of waves as offering insight into the likelihood of finding an object, using mathematics for guidance), radio waves, and temperatures, which so populated databases.[25]

These three forms of information appeared in such expanding corners of physics in the nineteenth and early twentieth centuries as in the study of special and general relativity and quantum mechanics, which for many remained the centerpiece of twentieth-century physics. As part of understanding that latter topic, scientists learned earlier that several fundamental interactions accounted for known forces. These included electromagnetism and weak interactions, discovering and understanding nuclear reactions (especially nuclear fusion) that made it possible to understand where solar energy came from. There was the development of radiocarbon dating that made it possible to know the age of a tree, ancient animal, or historic object. Later in the twentieth century, scientists developed a theory of electron waves, and learned how particles behaved with reliable rules (e.g., no two electrons circulating around one nucleus in an atom can simultaneously occupy the same quantum state). One German scientist, Werner Heisenberg (1901–1976), was able to describe quantum mechanics in the language of matrices (rectangular arrays of numbers, symbols, or expressions arranged in rows and columns), which could be used to plot graphs, apply statistics, and represent real-world data, such as demographic information.[26] Nuclear bombs, flight, space travel, what constitutes space and its galaxies, and roles of electricity and radio waves are examples of physics at work, with its insights and knowledge expressed in the three forms of information.

Practical considerations stimulated the creation of new information that went beyond the discovery of knowledge that mathematics led from one insight to another. For example, the study of thermodynamics—conversion of energy from one type to another and where it flowed, and even about its availability—was an enormously interesting topic as early as the nineteenth century.[27] The hunt for information on laws of thermodynamics was about describing physical phenomenon, often articulated in mathematical language. For example, Maxwell, who made many contributions to electromagnetic theory, thought frequently in statistical terms. That practice led to subsequent contributions to our understanding of how to use information to calculate when and how to cause energy to move or transform.[28] As one student of the process explained, "Information is a physical phenomenon, subject to the laws of thermodynamics."[29] Pause and re-read that quote. You have probably not seen that said before, but it is an insight into the nature of information that manifested itself in the twentieth century. It is a scientific affirmation that information is an object, not merely an intellectual construct of the mind.

At the risk of wading too far into the weeds nurtured by physics, there is quantum information to at least recognize. Recall that a bit of electronic information can only be in one state, the notion of "on" or "off," "positive" or "negative" at any time, hence a bit represents one value, no more. In quantum states an atomic particle "can be used to store data in a definable but still undetermined quantum superposition of two states at the same time."[30] If you have seen the illusionary picture of an old woman's profile then simultaneously that of a young woman, you understand what is happening (figure 6.1). It was first introduced in 1888, so the idea has been around a long time, but not until decades later could one connect it fully to science.[31]

Figure 6.1. Illusion of Old/Young Woman. *Source:* William Ely Hill, "My Wife and My Mother-in-Law," *Puck*, November 6, 1915.

As this chapter was being written in 2022, the word *quantum* was circulating widely and loosely and so should be better defined, because it is inextricably linked to scientific information and more specifically to physics. There are four uses of the word. First, there is *quantum physics*, an academic discipline with a rich history. It is the discipline that explains many features of the universe, such as the way to explain the behaviors of subatomic particles that make up electrons, protons, neutrons, and other items. Second, there is *quantum mechanics*, which comprise theory and mathematics used to solve problems, such as in wave equations.[32] Third, *quantum computing* has recently entered the lexicon, which refers to an emerging class of computers designed differently than those discussed in chapter 4. These new systems apply quantum mechanics' theories to build devices equipped with quantum circuits capable of massive amounts of simultaneous (parallel) computations.[33]

Finally, an even newer term is seeping into our vocabulary, *quantum information*. It refers to the information of the state of a quantum system, the basic unit (data) in the study of quantum information theory that can be worked with using mathematics and computing. In traditional computing one speaks of the basic unit of information as the *bit*, while in the quantum world it is the *qubit*. In computing one speaks of Shannon's entropy to measure information, while in quantum computing it is the von Neumann entropy, an extension of the earlier concept of entropy. In the former, each bit is a discrete piece of information (signal), while in quantum computing a qubit is a continuous value, but one that can still be measured as a discrete piece of information, although not as precisely as a bit (at least so far).[34]

Today, computer scientists are developing quantum computers that would increase dramatically their computational capabilities and speed, making it possible, for example, to have better encrypted systems and to perform far more complex mathematical calculations than currently possible.[35] Again, it is another conclusion demonstrating that in physics "the universe is fundamentally composed of data."[36] I do not discuss quantum information further because it lies beyond the chronological boundaries of this book, but is important enough to recognize as a possible next transformation of the nature of information.[37]

MATURING OF THE CHEMICAL INFORMATION ECOSYSTEM

Chemistry in its modern form emerged in the nineteenth century. Like physics, its practitioners studied physical realities, specifically how various compounds interacted with each other under myriad conditions. However, mention chemistry and people think immediately of chemical formulas. The use of formulas—and the concept of *formulas*—became widespread in the twentieth century and familiar to millions of students who did not become chemists. A formula is a way of expressing information using symbols; it also can mean more loosely the relationship between quantities. Mathematicians use it to identify what constitutes—equates—one mathematical statement to another, as used in mathematical theorems. Formulas have their own grammar. In chemistry, these expressions of information describe proportions and combinations of atoms that make up a specific chemical compound, the H_2O for water where two molecules of hydrogen when combined with one of oxygen become water. Chemical formulas are used to describe activity underway with molecules and serve as recipes for describing a solution to a physical problem.[38] Physicists use these too, such as $F=ma$ to express Newton's second law of motion, which describes quantitatively the measures of the forces acting upon a body (where "m" stands for mass, "a" for acceleration, and "F" for an object being equal to its mass multiplied by the acceleration of the object). Those who took an introductory course in chemistry remember little use of words but whiteboards covered with formulas. That is because the language and data of chemistry is overwhelmingly expressed with formulas.

Chemistry can claim to be one of the oldest fields of modern STEM fields. It began transforming into its modern form of using extensively scientific methods of observation and analysis and fact-based approaches by the mid-eighteenth century. But let a chemist describe his discipline: "Chemistry is universally classed among the exact sciences: that is, among those sciences making use of careful measurement, quantitative experiment, and indispensable precision equipment."[39] Chemists use empirical formulas to describe substances and empirical equations to explain exchanges and interactions among substances. They learn early in their careers how to conduct qualitative analysis, how to detect the presence of different chemical substances by their characteristic reactions, and how to perform quantitative analysis, which is the determination of how much there is of a substance in a given mixture or compound. To do these tasks requires specialized bodies of information expressed largely using formulas. For comparative perspective, physics did not start to work this way until the second half of the 1800s.

Chemistry's participants were some of the earliest and most prolific writers of scientific papers, as we conceive of that form of scholarly description of research results today. The volume of chemical information they created became one of the largest and fastest growing bodies of facts in all of science by the mid-1800s. While the librarians discussed in chapter 3 were codifying and organizing all manner of information, chemists were doing the same for their discipline for the same reason, because the amount becoming available to them was proving difficult to keep up with. So, it should be of no surprise that one of the first disciplines to start publishing abstracts of scientific articles was chemistry.[40] They needed such collections of secondary publications to summarize current academic articles and books.

These began to appear in the eighteenth century, but increased in quantity and variety in the nineteenth century. That trend continued to expand in number, size, and volume of abstracts throughout the twentieth century.[41] Because older research proved relevant even decades after publication, chemists consulted these, too, even ten-, thirty-, and sixty-year-old articles because they remained relevant. It was a practice clearly in evidence already during the first half of the twentieth century.[42] Chemists viewed articles as relevant if these described features of compounds and their interactions with each other. That is why, for example, a biologist or chemist can search for compounds and possible cures for, say, a new virus across the literature, perhaps finding a gem to pursue written decades before for some other intention. Computerized searches made such hunts extremely fast and precise, hence chemists embraced digital search tools as a convenient practice.[43]

What information did chemists want to keep up with? Since the dawn of the nineteenth century, with the work of John Dalton (1766–1844), Jöns Jacob Berzelius (1779–1848), the latter considered the father of modern chemistry, and others, they sought to study and work with chemical compounds, to understand their individual properties, to learn how to make specific ones, to identify compounds that had specific properties, and to find those with similar properties.[44] By the mid-1960s some 85 percent of entries in the largest index, *Chemical Abstracts* (*CA*), concerned compounds and materials and their chemical structures, which do not change over time.[45] Chemists shared common interests and basic information. These included studying the reactions and equations associated with compounds, the nature of chemical bonding, the three major states of all matter—gaseous, liquid, and solid—solutions, nuclear, organic, and biochemical. Other sub-disciplines emerged; each developed massive amounts of new information in the twentieth century and shared views about what to explore.

Focusing on compounds made it possible, for example, to develop ammonia used in fertilizers in agriculture, and also in munitions. Plastics originated out of chemistry (Bakelite).[46] During the first half of the twentieth century, physics and chemistry began overlapping, particularly with respect to the study of atoms.[47] The same happened with biology, and no better example exists than when James Watson (b. 1928) and Francis Crick (1916–2004) made their discoveries regarding DNA. They unveiled their findings in 1953, describing its double helical structure relying on their chemical research and use of X-ray diffraction patterns.[48] They changed their field as much as Shannon had his, each with one paper. Nearly instantly the new field of biochemistry was born, which today so profoundly influences medical practices and development of medicines across a wide swath of illnesses, not the least of which include cancers. As the amount of chemical information increased, the discipline began specializing, although earlier than in physics, astronomy, and biology. By the end of the twentieth century these new subfields included analytical chemistry, clinical chemistry, biochemistry, organic chemistry, theoretical chemistry, quantum chemistry, astrochemistry, environmental chemistry, organic chemistry, inorganic chemistry, and physical chemistry. Each launched journals, established organizations, held meetings, evolved their own language, and created indices, information ecosystems, and infrastructures.

The crown jewel of the entire discipline with respect to managing its chemical information ecosystem was the *Chemical Abstracts*, which began publication in 1907.[49] By the end of the century it was better known as the *Chemical Abstracts Service* (CAS). Its evolution mirrored what happened in many scientific disciplines, yet serving as a role model for others. For that reason alone one would be justified in declaring that it was a major source of change in the nature and use of information in the twentieth century, warranting discussion of its history. As one scientist explained, "Modern chemistry is unavoidably multidisciplinary" and, therefore, "the *CA* is used in medicine, engineering, and other disciplines, as well as in chemistry."[50] It is an important observation because, as described in the rest of this chapter, disciplines dealing with living matter had deep roots in chemistry and its information, including biology, medicine, and genetics.[51] But chemistry, too, had its own specific informational needs, such as about the structure and composition of molecules, a topic about which indexing information was collected into the *CA*, and the *Current Abstracts of Chemistry and Index Chemicus* (*CAC&IC*) and its earlier form, *Index Chemicus* (*IC*).

By the early 1800s it was becoming evident that chemistry consisted of a large diverse collection of organic compounds and that their number was growing, so any attempt to classify them had to take into account those twin realities. Various classification schemes came and went but by the end of the nineteenth century were stabilizing sufficiently such that *CA* could be launched in the United States to incorporate American chemistry into the then-predominantly European indices that had been associated in various ways with the American Chemical Society from its origin.[52] Hundreds of volunteer chemists prepared the first edition of *CA*, which appeared in 1907. It contained 11,847 abstracts drawn from 396 journals. Early editions mimicked the practice of libraries, including a heading with complete bibliographic information, such as article title, author, and his or her location, name of the journal, date, volume, issue, pagination, and language. These citations included an abstract of the paper or book. The number of indexed publications exceeded 1,000 by 1922, doubled in the next ten years, and by the end of the century to some 9,000 publications.[53] The number of categories in which these citations nested included as part of the file related ones from biology and medicine, expanding from seventy-three in 1962 to eighty in 1967. The number of categories continued to expand over the next half-century. In 2020, CAS included 160 million organic and inorganic substances drawn from the chemical literature, had 68 million protein and nucleic acid sequences, tapped 63 patent authorities, and included over 51 million records extracted from publications dating to the early 1800s in over fifty languages.[54] In other words, this had become a big database, has been used for more than a century, and built on abstracting needs and experiences for over 170 years.

It began as a publication, but today is an online operation; the paper version of *Chemical Abstracts* ceased paper publication at the end of 2009. CAS began using computers to catalog and store data in the mid-1960s, then through iterations of innovations as computing evolved, made its data available online in waves through the rest of the century. These waves included "Registry I" (1965), which made assessable information on compounds identified by name or molecular formula; "Registry II" (1968) that added inorganic substances, coordination compounds, polymers, mixtures, alloys, and other miscellaneous substances, computerized data collection (the latter for CAS staff), and files and descriptions further standardized and thus normalized for all users and data sets. "Registry III" (1973) brought more standardization and automation.[55] *Registry* refers to the assignment of a unique number to identify each substance in its discrete file. This number scheme is now the de facto standard worldwide.

In 1984 CAS began adding citations to its databases published prior to 1965, using optical scanning, and then converting these data into the norms followed by CAS in the 1980s.[56] These addressed long-standing issues in chemical information. In practice, researchers deal with chemical structures and reactions, both of which concern, too, chemical structures and physio-chemical entities, among other issues. Chemical structures were not always well defined, so across the twentieth century chemists and their information handlers expended enormous efforts to rectify that situation, often encountering great difficulty. But chemists developed lists of compounds and other topics, adding to these attributes of each subject. Addressing such issues remained the foundational motivation for registries.[57]

Across the entire twentieth century, estimates of how much data needed to be collected routinely underestimated the amount of information that could be collected, constantly challenging abstracting services. In its first five years of operation *CA* on average collected annually 262,000 citations; by 1996 over a million per year. In that latter year, it had 15.8 million substances and over 21 million names. As one student of its activities reported in 1997, "CAS Chemical Registry database is the largest collection of information on naturally occurring and synthetic chemical substances in the world."[58]

What information did CAS collect? Every substance is assigned a registry number, including all variations of a substance (i.e., different salts). Each is also given an index name (combination of letters and numbers), and lists all synonyms for that substance. The molecular formula and an image of its structure are also provided, in addition to other information. Figure 6.2

STNext

Transcript	2020_0002_Transcript
File **REGISTRY**	

CAS Registry Number:	50-78-2 REGISTRY
Entered STN: 16 Nov 1984	
CAS Registry Number Locator:	STN Files: ADISINSIGHT, ADISNEWS, ANABSTR, BIOSIS, BIOTECHNO, CA, CABA, View all
Deleted CAS Registry Number:	2349-94-2, 11126-35-5, 11126-37-7, 26914-13-6, 98201-60-6, 2087491-38-9

PROPERTY DATA AVAILABLE IN THE 'PROP' FORMAT

Chemical Name:	Benzoic acid, 2-(acetyloxy)- (CA INDEX NAME)	Adiro
		Albyl E
	OTHER CA INDEX NAMES:	Angettes 75
	2-(Acetyloxy)benzoic acid	Anopyrin
	OTHER NAMES:	ASA
	2-Acetoxybenzoic acid	Asaflow
	2-Carboxyphenyl acetate	Asagran
	A.S.A. Empirin	Asatard
	AC 5230	Ascoden 30
	Acenterine	Ascolong
	Acesal	Ascriptin
	Acesan	Aspalon
	Acetard	Aspergum
	Aceticyl	Aspirdrops
	Acetilum acidulatum	**Aspirin**
	Acetisal	Aspirin Protect 100
	Acetophen	Aspirin Protect 300
	Acetosal	Aspirin-Direkt
	Acetosalic acid	Aspirina
	Acetosalin	Aspirina 03
	Acetylin	Aspirine
	Acetylsal	Aspro
	Acetylsalicylic acid	Aspro Clear
	Acetyonyl	Aspropharm
	Acetysal	Asteric
	Acidum acetylsalicylicum	ADDITIONAL NAMES NOT AVAILABLE IN THIS FORMAT - Use FCN, FIDE, or ALL for DISPLAY
	Acimetten	
	Acisal	
	Acylpyrin	
Class Identifier:	COM	
Molecular Formula:	C9 H8 O4	

Figure 6.2. Example of CAS REGISTRY record for Benzoic Acid accessed via STNext on April 2, 2020 (*Courtesy*: CAS, a division of the American Chemical Society)

is a partial example of an entry, this one for Benzoic acid. It includes two-dimensional and three-dimensional information as well and cross-indexing. Because a third of its abstracts are biochemical, CAS is used extensively in pharmaceuticals, biology, genetics, and medicine, so a familiar format to many. By the 1990s, it included a large collection of chemically modified sequences and other groupings of large biomolecules consisting of sequence notations relying on codes for such things as amino acids and nucleotide base units to serve the needs of the biological ecosystem. That form of descriptor has been characterized as "a simple rearrangement of the words" in an index entry "to produce a phrase, corresponding to a near natural language sentence, that summarizes one aspect of the referenced study." While more difficult to produce than, say, a simple word index, "each entry conveys the needed information in a context that is not possible in keyword indexes, which lack syntax."[59] One sees in the example of Benzoic acid, another instance where the evolution of information was facilitated by the use of relevant language, not just the discovery of more information. Mathematics, statistics, chemical descriptors, and formulas ultimately came to grips with similar issues. Note the last word in the previous quote—syntax—the vocabulary of language and grammar at work.

Indexing evolved over time as the discipline (chemistry but other related fields, too) transformed and became more diverse and accumulated new information. That is how the *CA* became so complex and voluminous. Its publishers worked with various schemas to find ways to categorize information useful to its users. Some entries were alphabetical or by page number in the *CA* in the early years, while others were filled with descriptions (known as articulated indices).

Indexing policies proved to be another important evolving source of identity for chemical information. From the beginning of the *CA* standards for indexing were established and adhered to that resulted in the creation of indexing rules and standards. A boom period for such activities came in the late 1950s and early 1960s particularly relevant, driven by the *CA*'s editor, Charles L. Bernier, building on earlier practices.[60] These included, for instance, that only new information would be indexed. New index headings were to be created only after careful consideration, rather than because of immediate expediency. Index entries had to maximize specificity as their purpose. These all seem logical and obvious, but until the late 1950s had not formally been articulated and communicated to *CA*'s staff and users. They remained foundational rules to the present. In time hundreds of additional rules guiding this work appeared, certainly by the 1980s, many of which are operative today.[61]

CAS files became widely available digitally by the end of 1980, which meant a second generation of scientists always had online access to such information as part of their normal way of working. Lest we forget, the CAS

Source Index (CASSI) database lists publications since 1907, is kept current, and as over the previous century includes serial and non-serial scientific and technical literature. Thus, one can search by title of publications, abbreviation, and other normal bibliographic methods. It cross-links sources, and citations are curated.[62] For information of a substance itself, one accesses a file by matching the names of interested substances using typical database search tools as part of the CAS system.[63] Chemists were some of the first users of indices that required substantial alternative paths of entry to desired information regarding chemical structures. The normal practice then, as now, was to use a formulae or a chemical name to access desired information, although CAS has long also employed substance classification schemes to assist queries. Those needs led CAS's computing staffs to develop some of the most sophisticated information retrieval systems. That interest dated to the 1940s, facilitated by a chemist working at MIT, James W. Perry (1907–1971), who encouraged his computing students to test their IR ideas with chemists. He was himself a leading proponent of using computers for indexing, classifying, and searching for documents, thinking about such functions for queries that included "and," "or," and "not," which today seems elementary, but not so in the 1940s.[64]

CAS's early entwining with computers was replicated variously in other disciplines as information became more digitized, beginning in the mid-century.[65] In 1955 the CAS established an R&D department to explore the uses of technology and to improve operations to maintain the currency and accuracy of its content. The move to computers was a response to a growing problem: "It became evident that the traditional manual system for processing and publishing secondary chemical and chemical engineering information was too slow, too expensive, too rigid, and too wasteful in its use of highly trained manpower to be effective in the face of the ever growing volume of published information."[66] Streamlining data collection and cataloging was needed, so too only depositing one copy of the data into a system that could then display the data in various indices and publications. During the 1960s CAS installed its initial computer systems, much of these funded by the National Science Foundation.

The development of digital systems paralleled what was simultaneously underway in industry and government, so need not detain us here.[67] However, like other mainframe computer users in the 1960s and 1970s, CAS staff had to determine file layouts and formats, define fonts and rules for posting data. By the 1980s, as one report noted, "Online editing eliminated the several million sheets of paper that had to be handled, often times by as many as four people. And it was necessary to keep track of each piece of paper to ensure that no access paths to a given document were lost."[68] Once digitized, it became far easier and quicker to produce specialized indices. Additionally, the output from computers consisted of printed indices and online access. In the process, CAS became the world's largest abstracting service for all chemical subjects, transforming how the entire discipline collected, became dependent upon, and conducted much research with ever-growing massive amounts of information.

THE NEW INFORMATION ECOSYSTEM IN BIOLOGY (LIFE SCIENCES) AND MEDICINE

Biology and its variants are known as the natural sciences. It focuses on the study of living organisms. Under that broad definition one can include what they comprise, how they function, their chemistry, physiological mechanisms, even medicine. Like physics and chemistry, it has its numerous subfields, many of which were new to the twentieth century or expanded the variety and quantity of information these incorporated earlier. Some of the most obvious subfields include biology (life and living organisms), biotics (living creatures in an ecosystem), anatomy (structure of organs), physiology (how organs work), cytology (about cells), ecology (organisms in their environment), evolutionary biology (how life diversifies and evolves), genetics (heredity), molecular biology (DNA, proteins), biotechnology (manipulation and use of organisms to solve problems, e.g., manipulating DNA), paleontology (study of fossils), botany (plant life), and zoology (animal kingdom). Add medicine since it is the practice of addressing the problems of living organisms in humans and in animals (veterinarian).[69] Medicine, too, has many subfields, each with its own massive collections of information, publications, databases, and associations (known mostly as colleges).

The general field of biology acquired its single word identity in the nineteenth century. Two major developments in that period were finally the recognition of the existence of cells—germs—that helped launch the germ theory of disease, hence made possible much modern medical understanding, and the other—Charles Darwin's theory of evolution through natural selection. In the early 1900s genetics came into its own, leading to the growth of information about cellular and molecular biology. But each subfield flowered spectacularly in the twentieth century.[70] In the second half of the century so did additional subfields and topics, such as genetics and evolutionary theories, molecular biology, biochemistry, and microbiology. These subjects became complex, rested on large bodies of expanding knowledge, required increasingly larger staffs and funding to study and to publish findings, and that they pushed information to each other, while drawing from chemistry and mathematics. As a leading historian of biology has confessed, writing even a one-volume history of the topic (let alone this chapter as I do) displays an "excessive" ambition flying in the face of the more popular approach of "microhistories," but as argued at the start of this chapter, needed.[71]

Beginning in the nineteenth century, subfields created their own identities, organized their collections of information in ways that made sense to each and that practitioners embraced as canonical. Their behavior led to the same creation of niche journals, books, associations, and other accoutrements of academic information ecosystems as evident in other disciplines. The quantities of new information created just in the past 175 years are colossal. In the biomedical field alone, over one million papers are annually cataloged in the PubMed database that tracks one of the fastest-growing areas of STEM research.[72]

Luciano Floridi (b. 1964), Professor of Philosophy and Ethics of Information at Oxford University, reminds us of a reality appropriate for this broad subject area of biology: that information can be seen as describing a reality, such as tree rings or fingerprints; information for reality, such as algorithms and recipes; and information about reality, such as descriptions of organs or DNA.[73] All three aspects of information apply across biology.

The history of biology and its intimate relations with medical knowledge is a long and complicated one. Its first major new body of information—about germs—has been well documented, thus need not detain us here.[74] The second one—genetics—historians are still unraveling its evolution in information and medicine.[75] Its process of discovery has many features similar to what biologists did—still do—experience as they acquire new information and change its features. Both lines of information involve the use of observational tools, such as microscopes and now especially computers; both rely on mathematics, statistics, and chemical formulas; each requires the convenience and necessary perspectives offered by theories. Its realities are not always visible to the human eye, and so descriptions (information) of phenomenon must be visualized through artificial means, such as the illustrations used to describe a DNA double helix.

Because the study of genetics is one of the central areas of interest straddling biology and medicine, I look briefly at its emergence as a way to help illustrate how information changed in biology. The fundamental achievement of geneticists was their ability to acquire information about specific building blocks of life. It is a history that, as in other disciplines, reaches deep into the nineteenth century, then blossomed in the twentieth and even more so is evident in the twenty-first century. Like the idea of bits and electrons in communications and computing, so too in biology getting down to chromosomes in cells made it possible to understand much that was fundamental to life, to the actions and transformations of living creatures, potentially to cure illnesses, and to find protocols for correcting faults in living cells.

In the nineteenth century, much work had already been done to study the heredity of animals, people, and plants. By the 1830s, much of that conversation was expressed in mathematical terms—numbers. Regarding humans, a great deal of data was collected in the nineteenth century concerning mental diseases, with tabulations of observable data often the work of insane asylums. The cost of running these institutions and teaching "feebleminded" students were rising at levels that alarmed public officials. All the new tools of statistics were appropriated to understand these human conditions, including application of correlation tables, regressions, and cluster analyses resulting in new data and insights. In 1909 Wilhelm Johannsen (1857–1927), a Danish pharmacist and botanist among other roles, introduced to the world the words *gene*, *phenotype*, and *genotype*.[76] As one historian observed, now "the new genetics emphasized microscopy, agricultural breeding, and model organisms."[77]

In the nineteenth century humans were not the primary concern, but soon became so, as scientists applied hereditary evidence in medicine, to the organization of social institutions (e.g., mental hospital staffing), and to eugenics. Over the arc of the twentieth century further work led to the Human Genome Project, which reflected the hunt for those features of the human body's cells—genes—that affected the nature of talent, physical appearances, and diseases. It was a return to the origins of hereditary studies of an earlier time. Today, the study of genetics is considered one of the largest, most interesting of the public topics of Big Data research. Every little bit and pieces of new findings are routine headlines, even "breaking" news. Data mining was a concept already floating in the air as early as the 1850s and 1860s when researchers drew no distinctions between scientific statistics or commercial, bureaucratic numbers. Google and Amazon were the latest to be so ecumenical about data.

Historian Theodore M. Porter has documented the early history of genetics that followed an arc described in earlier and subsequent chapters in other disciplines in our book, in this instance in three phases. First came amassing numbers by asylums in lists of facts drawn from questionnaires of patients and their families, all for the purposes of understanding heredity and to defend the costs of running such institutions. From an information history perspective, this was the activity of acquiring new data, not necessarily transforming its forms. A second phase, coming in mid-nineteenth century on both sides of the Atlantic Ocean, involved the standardization (i.e., uniform data entry and tables) of these tables so that information could be compared from one year to the next within an institution and then to others. That effort led to the start in transforming information, specifically the use of correlation tables, which made possible placing a variable of concern on each axis to understand causal relationships. For instance, on one axis one might have a hereditary feature and on the other a type of illness. Risk of contracting an illness could now be explored. His third phase of hereditary research extended from the 1890s into the 1930s. Pedigree tables became popular at the turn of the century, and within thirty years, surveys of large local populations. In this era precursors of the modern post-1950 generation of researchers were already at work, including Francis Galton, Karl Pearson, and Charles Davenport (1866–1944). It was then that the eugenics movement thrived, the branch of genetics used by Nazi Germany to justify its anti-Jewish, anti-Slavic pogroms.[78] The tools used by scientists on both sides of the Atlantic were mathematics and statistics. While mental issues remained a focus, research broadened, although collecting and studying asylum statistics remained in wide practice. That specific focus led, in Porter's words, geneticists "to make common cause with biologists, statisticians, and social scientists."[79]

The resulting information began by describing—mapping—genetic code. To understand the relationship of such information for DNA, let a student of information explain: "DNA does contain genetic information, like a CD may contain some software. But the genetic code or, better, the genes, are the information itself. Genes do not send information," rather, "like a recipe for a cake, may only partly guarantee the end result, since the environment plays a crucial role." In other words, "genes do not contain information," nor do they describe information, rather, they promise to do something based on the recipe.[80] So, genes are instructions, biological algorithms. One can quickly begin to link thinking about worldviews and computing found in software and chemistry to the conversation about genetics. More specifically, it fits with what Shannon and others learned when they described theories of information. Scholars had reshaped genetics' information as an international project with exchanges of data and ideas, much as occurred, say, with computer engineers in the 1950s and 1960s.

The evidence demonstrates that James Watson's (b. 1928) explanation of the helix in the 1950s did not appear as if by magic. His work grew out of over a century of prior explorations of genetics. It involved the work of health experts, educators, social scientists, the negative additions of racists, the Nazis, and war, not to leave out the latter's stimulation in the development of computers.[81] Yet, let Porter explain today's efforts: "The study of human heredity continues to depend on mundane, routinized labor in places like asylums, hospitals, prisons, courtrooms, and schools. Our dazzling technologies for decoding and manipulating nucleic acids do not easily translate into practical solutions to medical and behavioral problems." His conclusion about the effects of such practices on information comes down to "the fruits of the postgenomic alliance of DNA Mystique with Data Deluge take the forms of probabilities, that is to say, measures of risk and uncertainty."[82] It all seems less confident in describing options for ills than the public might want. His observation is important because so much current medical research rests on expectations of new insights from genetics, when in reality the evolution of information in any discipline is slow with findings and insights hard to extract, despite the fact that good science always depends on what Porter calls "strategic simplification." Medicine, genetics, and science in general are complicated. That realization represents, in itself, a transformation in information. Thinking in computational terms, while assisting students of genetics and evolutionary biology understand their subjects, it was not the magic path to exact understanding.[83]

This line of discussion represents only one strand in the evolution of medical information. Another discussed in the following involves bioinformatics, but before focusing on its evolution, I pause briefly to offer context drawn from the evolution of medical information, because the convergence of medicine and biology is a long and complicated story that has been studied by many historians.[84] When science came into its own with its research methods, disciplines, and universities in the nineteenth century so too did medicine become scientific. To qualify as a doctor one needed scientific training—not so in earlier centuries—and with that new requirement the entire knowledge base of the profession transformed. Hospitals became central sites for the study of medical issues and laboratories too, where, for instance, microscopy made it possible to study cells. Microbiological research in the late 1800s by such individuals as Louis Pasteur (1822–1895) and Robert Koch (1843–1910), the latter often called the Father of Germ Theory, led to the emergence of a new field of study, immunology. Next came the study of nervous systems, leading to yet another new line of information that came to be known as neurophysiology. Biology and chemistry contributed to a growing understanding of the nervous system.[85] Finally, there was genetics to explore.

Hospitals and clinical practices added to the information load. Surgery kept improving, and insights documented, then taught to new doctors. Anesthesia and antisepsis came into their own and improved continuously. To surgery, too, came new technologies, notably X-rays at the dawn of the 1900s, but in the subsequent century new forms of scanning and surgery as well.[86] If surgery represented a fundamental improvement in medicine, more so was the development of drugs to treat illnesses and the entire information ecosystem of pharmacology. That last development's history demonstrated the blend of science, biology, chemistry, and clinical trials collaborating with doctors and hospitals, and myriad business start-ups and public health policies all beginning in the second half of the 1800s and running strong to this day.[87] Chemists learned how to purify compounds, biologists and doctors how drugs worked within the body, and the study of germs led to the birth of chemotherapy. Along the way, electricity came into the discussion.

It seems that in every chapter of this book, electricity and information are entwined. In the case of medicine, a medical historian explains: "Hormones are not the only way in which substances secreted by certain cells influence the activity of other cells." In the eighteenth century, "the main controlling part of the body, the nervous system, was recognized as working by some kind of electricity. But evidence accumulated that nerves acted on other cells, and even on each other, by chemical means, by substances bridging the tiny gaps between adjacent cells."[88] Chemical transmissions caused cells to react, but so did electricity. Readers may recall a high school biology experiment where a dead frog's leg was zapped with electricity and saw it twitch. As the twentieth century unfolded, biologists and medical researchers kept encountering electricity, which provided useful context for when they studied the role of genetics and how DNA communicated.

While statistics played an ever-growing role in all branches of medicine, it was not without struggle, as its first beachhead was in the area of public health and mental issues, not in mainstream medicine.[89] There were always advocates for using statistical methods in the 1800s, but many doctors did not accept the idea that statistics improved clinical judgments. Yet in time clinical trials were heavily influenced by statistics and as a consequence overall acceptance of statistically based information. For months in 2020 the world's media reported every twist and turn in clinical trials for Covid-19 vaccines, reporting on how many people were being tested and what the data was telling the pharmaceutical firms and regulators these meant, and in the process, millions of people were educated on statistics, Big Data, and the process for conducting clinical trials. By the mid-twentieth century the value of using statistics in such fields as agriculture, psychology, economics, and business (to mention a few) was becoming too obvious to ignore. Medical researchers began to integrate these tools into their work. As one historian of the process observed, "Statistics supported a research ideal of openness and public demonstration."[90]

But objectivity promised by statistics was difficult to reconcile with clinical judgment, a conundrum still evident. In time, however, inroads were made, medical schools hired statisticians to analyze experimental data and to help shape research methods. Regulatory authorities began insisting more frequently on the kinds of data rigors offered by statistics. Insurance companies began demanding numeric evidence for proposed therapeutics and protocols, which these businesses were being asked to pay for. The U.S. Food and Drug Administration would not approve new drugs without empirical (read, quantitative) evidence that these were effective and not harmful, thanks to legislative authorizations gained in the early 1960s. Demonstrating effectiveness of a proposed drug was done by conducting large trials of its use by giving one group the medication and another group the placebo. The results of both trials were explained quantitatively using statistical tools to determine how effective the new medication was. Drug testing protocols with statistical measures became standard for all clinical trials; the barriers of resistance had been breached. Now almost all medical research had to rely on statistical tests. As with so many other uses of statistical methods in other disciplines, as one historian explained, "The advances of statistics in medicine must be understood as responses to problems of trust," less due to the intrinsic features of the mathematics.[91] In other words, regulators, legislators, pharmaceutical firms, insurance companies, and patients had embraced the use of numerical information. Trust was no longer on the belief in God, the judgment of the old family doctor, or some patent medicine vendor. Trust lay in the numbers.[92]

Other new lines of information emerged, too, starting in the 1700s that space does not permit us to pursue, but are related to other fields of medicine and scientific practice. The most obvious is the study of mental health and the brain, the study of which with human behavior led to the original studies of genetics.[93] With these other lines of medical information in mind, we can turn to the current interest in bioinformatics.

BIOINFORMATICS AND THE EVOLUTION OF MEDICAL AND BIOLOGICAL INFORMATION

Against the background of new information emerging about a plethora of biological and medical issues, diseases, demographics, therapies, bodies of knowledge also from chemistry and public health policies was the emergence of a new way of branding with much of this work acquiring a name: bioinformatics. With acceptance of that label, our ability to track the evolution of biological and medical information made it clearer to see the convergence of data, how that data is cataloged and studied, and the role of computing (e.g., Big Data). By the end of the first decade of the twenty-first century, even a reasonably educated person who was not a scientist could recognize that something new was unfolding with bio-medical information portending new cures. The science sections of major newspapers and other media outlets chronicle almost daily developments in this subject of bioinformatics. So to complete our understanding of how biological disciplines changed information, we need to explore recent developments.

As information evolved it became more specialized, so definitions of types of knowledge changed. This activity occurred as categories of information, too, needed recalibration or replacement. All the information creators discussed in this book faced the constant need to redefine categories of data and reorganize them into new sub-disciplines or to align these to new professions. These actions took place within the broad fields of biology and medicine. It should be of no surprise that the term *bioinformatics* (BI) entered the vocabulary to reflect changing biological information. It came into use in the 1980s, emphasizing computational methods to perform comparative analysis of genomic data. It also reflected another trend: the merging of different disciplines into a new interdisciplinary specialty involving medical and biological research, medical education for doctors and nurses, clinical practices, information sciences (including the work of STEM librarians), and informatics. The term, too, evolved during its short life, because in the beginning it emphasized computing methods in biotechnology systems.[94] By the early 2000s, BI incorporated many informatics methodologies used to solve problems at the molecular and cellular levels. In the process it emerged as a discipline of its own.[95] One group of medical practitioners explained that BI was "widely recognized as an entire field that encompasses biology, medicine, computer science, mathematics, statistics, and information technology."[96] This conversion led to the development of new bodies of information concerning high throughput sequencing, Big Data, and use of the Internet. Since the early publications about the structure of DNA authored by James Watson and Francis Crick in 1953,[97] no significant breakthrough in either the study of genes or proteins failed to use computing. The most fundamental insight served up using computers was the realization about how complex biology really was, far outdistancing prior concepts.[98]

However, an earlier set of information that emerged in the 1950s transformed at the same time as BI, each affecting the other today known as *medical informatics* (MI). It brought together myriad computational techniques used in clinical and academic medicine, ranging from the use of instrumentation in clinical information programs to formal modeling of logic and uncertainty in medical decision-making. After the availability of the Internet, MI information became accessible essentially to everyone working in any aspect of medicine.[99] MI practitioners expanded their use of data and standardization of information, building on a long tradition from asylums in the early 1800s.[100] Both disciplines continue to debate their relationship to each other.[101]

The MI community focused on creating information that could be applied in clinical settings, tapping BI for insights, such as about how genetic information informs a doctor's understanding of a patient's condition. Briefly summed, MI had seven strands of new information: (1) statistical models for decision-making; (2) medical signal and image processing, and interpretation of that data using computing; (3) digitization of patient data for research; (4) normal administrative operations and patients' medical history; (5) digitized medical libraries, indexing, and information retrieval systems; (6) modeling and simulating biosystems; (7) medical education and patient simulations.[102] BI emerged out of computational studies of genetics as the most useful way to understand the coding, storage, and transfer of data among DNA, RNA, and proteins.[103] In fact, such activities were impossible and impractical to carry out without using computers and increasingly computerized visualization techniques, both beginning to be used in the 1960s.[104]

Across the broad spectrum of biology and medicine, practitioners dealt with two information challenges. The first, already identified, is the volume of increased amounts of information that people had to stay current with, especially after the advent of computers.[105] In the first decade of the 2000s, biological data increased from sets of hundreds of data entities to millions and billions.[106] It is an example of exponential growth in data, driving new definitions and categories of information just in what used to be simply called biology or medicine. A group of researchers living in the BI and MI world described the consequence of this growth in information as stimulating "the development of an ever-increasing number of bioinformatics tools" and the shift "in complexity, evolving from a gene-centric perspective to the systems level," with computers reducing large collections of data then converting these data sets "into usable knowledge."[107]

While I already discussed the challenges of growing bodies of information with researchers responding by using software, two other challenges shared by all STEM fields were the need to use new terms, nouns, and language, and wrestling with questions about whether older information classification systems of the nineteenth and first-half of the twentieth century were still relevant. Geoffrey C. Bowker, a leading authority on the history and use of information, has studied these issues. It is referred to as *reclassification*, and his exploration of the topic led him to several observations. First, doing so "is a long, slow process," with "no simple" path. Second, the discussion has been underway for two centuries, and evolved as pre-computer classifications and naming conventions were loaded into digital databases. Third, determining what those changes should be proved problematic (e.g., who first named a plant). Fourth, it is expensive to change a name, because all records would then have to be updated, assuming one could gain consensus for a name change.[108]

How did doctors and biologist/medical/genetic researchers behave? A brief jog through their experiences displayed several behaviors. Approaches similar to those of the geneticists, for example, proved beneficial in medicine and biology for understanding nervous systems and brain functions. As Floridi explained, "The nervous system, and the brain in particular, are studied from an informational perspective," applying in the past half-century "computational tools, methods, models, approaches, databases, and so forth, in order to analyze and integrate experimental data and to improve existing theories about the structure and function of the brain."[109] Computing provided tools for measuring and documenting biological phenomenon not evident to the human eye, just as such technologies have been used to measure and document other unseen realities as, for instance, what happens in space many light years away. Biologists began using computers in the 1960s, turning their interest into an information science as they became profoundly dependent on information technology. In the next decade they created an ocean of data about cloning, use of restriction enzymes, protein sequencing, and gene product amplification. In the process, they populated massive databases with genetic maps and atomic coordinates for protein and chemical structures, including protein sequences. A biologist from the 1950s would have been amazed, perhaps a bit lost and feeling underinformed about her field.[110] As one student of the transformation described the consequences, biology became "a data-bound science, a 'science' in which all the data of a domain—such as a genome—are available before the laws of the domain are understood."[111] To stay on top of such a tsunami of information, biologists turned to information science, AI, and information retrieval methods developed in other disciplines to mine their data (as in digging for coal or gems) for patterns and structures, beginning in the 1960s and widely since the 1970s.[112]

Adding new names and creating fresh identities for subjects to existing dictionaries of terms and lists of disciplines has been a common practice that is seen again with BI and MI. There are conventions for how new words and names are created in different disciplines, much like a grammar, to which one adheres, which the BI and MI world accepted.[113] The dream of each discipline having a common language lives eternal in the STEM world. Information-handling behaviors evident in other disciplines appeared in the BI/MI universe, most notably in the organization, cataloging, and description of the burgeoning corpus of new information. That effort mimics the experience of *Chemical Abstracts*.

The exemplar is the U.S. National Library of Medicine's (NML) equivalent, MEDLINE (Medical Literature and Retrieval System Online), which by 2020 contained in excess of 26 million bibliographic citations covering all manner of life sciences but concentrating on biomedicine. These citations are standardized, using the National Library of Medicine's (NML) Medical Subject Headings. MEDLINE has functioned since the 1960s, coming into existence early in the life of BI and MI disciplines. In 1964, a system was developed not accessible online (as is MEDLINE), called MEDLARS (MEDical Literature Analysis and Retrieval Systems). In 1971 MEDLINE became available to researchers and subsequently to the public over the years. The hosting organization, NLM, had been collecting medical bibliographic information since 1879 in a publication called *Index Medicus*, a monthly publication of articles appearing in thousands of journals.[114]

Citations in MEDLINE from over 5,600 journals around the world have routinely been collected, including citations back to 1950. Citations include normal bibliographic information and abstracts, the latter often written by article authors as part of their original publication. In all disciplines it is now common practice for articles to be preceded by an author-written abstract; these are reprinted in myriad bibliographic databases. The Belgian bibliographers of the early 1900s would have been pleased, as this was a long-term objective of theirs. Because of the availability of such citations and necessary search tools, researchers and clinicians developed many evidence-based protocols and research practices. Users became familiar with a standard set of terms called the *Medical Subject Headings* (*MeSH*), with retrieval software designed to respond to such terms. Use increased over the years to such a point that in 2017, for example, it was accessed 3.3 billion times, up from less than 400,000 searches annually in the late 1990s.[115] By the early 2000s, the database began providing access to the full texts of articles.[116] While others exist around the world, like the *CA*, MEDLINE became the largest consulted.

Finally—but briefly—it should be noted that artificial intelligence (AI) is increasingly being used to collect all manner of clinical data that can be used by software to detect medical conditions. AI, for example, is increasingly being portrayed as "cancer detectives" in the media because with growing bodies of data regarding specific cancers, software can compare information about an individual's condition to that of other people. For example, in the United States in 2021, the U.S. Food and Drug Administration (FDA) authorized the use of an AI tool to sort out prostate biopsy images that determined the odds of a suspected area of being cancerous, which then can be examined by a pathologist. That tool was a first. Radiologists have already started to use similar tools to analyze mammography and colonoscopy images, and CT scans, some of these three collections having been created as early as the 1990s.[117]

Conclusions

The world of science changed so profoundly in the twentieth century that a scientist from, say, the 1830s would feel lost. Certainly that poor soul would not understand most of today's scientific language and fundamentals, or how to use any of its tools with the exception of a pad of paper, a pencil, and a blackboard. This is not a weak attempt at literary hype; the world of science did change that much, and it was because of the new information and ways of handling it that surfaced post 1840. Rotate back to the thoughtful Luciano Floridi for a conclusion one can take from the experience of scientists and doctors: "Science has moved from being based on necessity and laws to being based on probability and constraints. Nowadays, the most accepted view in physics is that particles behave indeterministically and follow the uncertainty principle." He follows up: "Computational determinism is not an option."[118] In other words, the hunt was on for all information because with all of it, the implied expectation was that one could fully, or at least better, understand and predict.

This is heady thinking, if both naive and arrogant, but as computers become more powerful, it is too early to say if his pronouncement is anthropomorphic hype or an aspirational goal that can substantially move our knowledge base forward.[119] The usefulness of computing certainly affirms the expectation of more and new knowledge in all STEM disciplines. At a minimum, one can conclude with increasing probability of accuracy that scientists in all disciplines were moving to a rich information-based view of reality. Increasingly then, to come back to Floridi one more time, "the universe is fundamentally composed of data."[120] Physical matter then is a secondary manifestation of patterns and differences. The laws of thermodynamics become part of theories of information. Information are objects (Shannon) but now our world. Historian Morange acknowledged that understanding "the characteristics of living things and their evolution in informational terms are recurrent."[121]

Because in the twentieth century subfields in all sciences emerged, they generated so much information that spilled over and was relevant to other disciplines that scientists faced new issues. Historian Jürgen Renn identified one underpinning others, calling it a "borderline problem in classical physics," but it was more.[122] This was both a turf battle and a problem of how to embrace much new information from outside one's discipline across all of them, not just physics. The magic of that problem, however, is that of a mathematician at MIT (e.g., Norbert Wiener) identifying feedback loops, a communications expert at Bell Labs (e.g., Claude E. Shannon), explaining noise, and a biologist (e.g., James Watson) describing the very structure of life could so influence the next two generations of scientists. Each is doing it again to information scientists, life scientists, and those pan-disciplinary knowledge workers taking humankind through another round of AI. Observers of medical and pharmaceutical innovations speak in the language of information, such as how a new drug "interferes specifically with the chemical messages that would prompt the growth," say of a tumor, "thereby rendering it harmless" as its instructions on how to behave is altered.[123] They were not alone in creating disciplinary border problems; they were accompanied by thousands of colleagues doing the same.

Cross-disciplinary dependencies were not limited to one's reliance on mathematics and statistics. It occurred elsewhere, often in profound ways. Porter highlighted one: the dependency, indeed a foundational aspect of medicine, rested on chemical information, hence on this discipline's methods of research and explanations (e.g., use of formulas). Let him explain: "The isolation of active ingredients permitted the synthesis of drugs, which removed or greatly lessened the problem of natural variability."[124] Porter added that extant variability in drugs and compounds interacting with each other flew in the face of the urge to standardize treatments and medicines. That desire led to methods for testing for variability, for example, in vaccines, to control for side effects by controlling the chemical makeup of a drug or understanding the effects of various dosages.[125]

If patterns seem to be emerging from the experiences of so many figures tramping through the pages of these six chapters, then one begins to appreciate what happened to information in the twentieth century. But, we still remain near the starting gate, as we have more terrain to cover. In the next chapter I examine how the worlds of business and government, too, affected information since the 1870s. If anyone thought there were a great many scientists and engineers shaping information, we now meet two cohorts that massively outnumbered all the librarians, computer scientists, and STEM professionals combined. If you think we are living in the Information Age, we now meet the people whose behaviors could naively lead to such a conclusion.

Chapter 7

New Business and Government Information Ecosystems

> *In recent years record-keeping problems have multiplied because of the size of business, its competitive nature and the demands of management in wanting up-to-date facts with which to guide their business.*
>
> IBM, Early 1950s[1]

Businesses and governments shared three common features by World War I. As two components of the economies of the Western world combined, they employed more people than the earlier largest sector, agriculture, in the United States. These organizations often became very large, spread across massive geographic spaces, and maintained many layers of employees. In the late nineteenth century the largest had thousands of employees; a century later hundreds of thousands in business, millions in the U.S. government. All became massively reliant on all manner of information they needed with which to coordinate and collaborate within and across organizations and enterprises, and to direct their activities in support of measurable objectives.[2]

Both businesses and governments embraced new information, notably accounting—considered the language of business—statistics in all its forms, and a combination of standards and models of optional decisions. In the 1870s, both were pleased to be able to count people, things, and money, and to track their changes over time, thanks to the telegraph and then the telephone, to implement new accounting practices, and to the use of such data processing equipment as adding machines. These organizations ended the twentieth-century model alternative futures with such a degree of confidence about their accuracy that managements made investment and operational decisions based on these information fictions.[3] In the process of performing their work, these two large economic sectors created vast new bodies of data about all manner of human, animal, and physical activities, about the physical world, and shaped the research agendas of entire nations.[4] Nowhere was this so evident than in the United States where research across scores of disciplines provided rich bodies of ever-growing amounts of information that often influenced the information-handling practices evident in the functioning of both business and public sectors around the World.

To understand the scope of all these developments, I briefly review demographics and dollars. Then I examine the role of accounting information, models, and standards, and conclude with observations about Total Quality Management. The reader will quickly realize that information used to operate an organization is different than that of the scientist, even though like them and librarians, or computer scientists, managers and workers worried about how best to organize and access information. Protagonists of this chapter focused on the practicality of information, as opposed to what one historian insightfully described as the "detached and otherworldly outlook" fostered in mathematics and the hard sciences. Scientists used information to predict and control natural phenomenon, while businesses and governments focused on management and production, developing relations with information that can be characterized as a "quantitative practicality."[5] The pursuit of rigorous objectivity defined much of what these institutions pursued, both because of their acceptance of the usefulness of well-defined bodies of information and because subjective discretion increasingly was found either wanting or simply suspecting. In short, as we move from the nineteenth through the twentieth century, one can see the rising influence of the kinds of information advocated by mathematicians, scientists, and developers of computers and telecommunications.

THE WORLD OF AMERICAN BUSINESS AND GOVERNMENT BY THE NUMBERS

In 1870 a third of the American labor force worked in factories, another 16 percent in services. By 1940, a third still worked in the industrial sector, but now 22 percent in services.[6] The services sector included office workers, or what would be called knowledge workers by the end of the century.[7] The percentage of government workers in the American economy grew over the 150 years, usually hovering at between 15 and 17 percent of the total in the late 1900s, rising higher during wartimes.[8] Around 13 million people were in the labor force in 1870, over 150 million by the end of the 1990s.[9] In 1870 the U.S. population amounted to 38.6 million people; in 2000 it hovered at 282 million.[10]

The organizations that most drove the creation and use of information in the period 1870s–1940s were large corporations.[11] Governments competed for that accolade in the post–World War II period but with the private sector in close contention for that claim.[12] Large corporations represented the most important macro-business innovation of the period. By the end of the 1920s how these and large government agencies were structured and functioned had been established.[13] By then they had created and used more varied information than any other part of society.[14] In the second half of the twentieth century, these organizations embraced extensive use of computing. That adoption fundamentally increased the nation's reliance on information beyond anything imagined by previous generations of librarians, scientists, academics, business managers, or public officials.[15] In short, demand for information increased by many orders of magnitude between 1870 and the present.

We can briefly summarize the key issues facing business and government that sparked such an expanded use of information. The fundamental problem faced by large expanding companies in most industries and agencies, largely within the U.S. government, was that as they became big, the variety of tasks they needed to perform grew in number and complexity. Those circumstances required more information with which to manage and carry out their missions. As one historian summed it, "In the days before giant enterprises, businesses required very little in the way of administrative networks," because they employed so few people.[16] But with thousands of workers spread across entire states or the nation, complexity became a fundamental problem. Management—yes, now firms had increasingly professional managers—needed to know what was going on inside their enterprises. Complexity involved multiple tasks concurrently underway affecting each other, spreading across many departments, offices, manufacturing sites, and locations. Railroads became the poster child for the new work environment. The new reality led to a second issue: control.

Complexity required increased control so that management could allocate resources, understand how these were being used, and measure their effectiveness. For corporations that meant controlling expenses, making profit, fighting competitors, and growing their markets. For government it was about operating within budgets and legal mandates, while offering more and better services, especially in challenging times such as during the two world wars, the Great Depression, Cold War, and the Great Recession of 2008.[17] The solution to control was always the twin use of more bureaucracy and reliance on greater amounts of information. The tools of choice were enriched combinations of accounting and all manner of new types of information integrated into a thick information ecosystem that included administration and operational procedures.[18]

An additional response emerged: standardized work processes, embodied by Taylorism in the early 1900s and by the 1980s with quality management practices and process improvement initiatives.[19] Standards are just being studied by historians, but one finding already evident is how broadly these were implemented: standardized products, such as screws, nuts, and bolts; standardized training and certification in many professions, such as for electricians and medical doctors; regulatory requirements for firms and entire industries, such that all bank checks had to be of the same design; data standards, so that Social Security records could be maintained from 20,000 firms in the 1930s that would make it possible for the U.S. Department of the Treasury to pay seniors their pensions. In 1892 there were eight different measures for a U.S. gallon of gasoline, a generation earlier, seventy-five different time zones.[20] Such issues were mitigated. All these examples of standardization arrived before the technical rigors (standards) forced by the use of computing. The industrialized world addressed this problem of standardization, with the American experience one of the best documented. As one student of the response summed it, "The United States had become a world leader in techniques of testing, measuring, and standardizing."[21] Government agencies often led the way, such as the U.S. National Bureau of Standards, established early in the twentieth century, employing "the high priests of measurement." Historian Daniel J. Boorstin credited these officials with reinforcing, "the nation's faith in the language of numbers."[22]

Government officials had their own concerns as well, which they addressed in a similar manner as large commercial enterprises. For one thing, agencies were increasingly being called upon to engage in more social and economic issues than in earlier times. The U.S. Department of Agriculture was established during the Civil War to modernize farming and farm life through development and communication of science-based information.[23] The state university system was expanded to create new science and to help promote it.[24] The army was tasked with collecting weather data every day, until that responsibility was turned over to professional weather experts.[25] During World Wars I and II, entirely new agencies were required to run the American economy for war efforts.[26] Their tasks included determining what goods and services were needed, allocating scarce resources to meet those, compelling the private sector to do its bidding, and tracking everything. During the Cold War era, nuclear weapons, better intelligence, computing and communications technologies were needed with the result that, by the late 1950s, some 85 percent of all basic research and much applied R&D was funded by the American government through such organizations as the National Science Foundation, the Pentagon, and myriad agencies supporting research in all STEM fields, including medicine.[27] Government agencies collected almost all the economic, demographic, and social data available about the United States since the late 1800s.[28] Even the U.S. Census Bureau (made into a permanent agency in 1902) expanded to conduct various census studies across the twentieth century, not merely one every ten years.[29] The largest task carried out by government in the twentieth century was the collection, creation, and diffusion of information, even during wartime.[30]

Both business and public sectors turned to common tools to solve their problems, understand circumstances, and carry out their missions. These included accounting, statistics, planning, opinion and market polls and surveys, computing, standards, and theoretical models and theories. They increasingly embraced mathematical and scientific methods of analysis and decision-making, which rested on the growing mountains of new data. For example, such as what emerged in public health practices when by the 1880s officials understood that water-borne germs spread diseases, or that by the 1950s tobacco caused lung cancer, or most recently that airborne carbon dioxide from factories and vehicles deteriorated the Earth's environment.[31]

THE BIGGER ISSUE OF INNOVATION

Economists and economic historians paid less to the issues of control of the type just discussed, and the latter largely about accounting, which we turn to soon. Economists point out, however, that the fundamental role information served in much corporate and public administrative activity, explained in detail in the next chapter, involved enhancing innovation. Economists point to the enormous amount of that which occurred in development of new products and services. A great deal of this activity came in the form of new scientific knowledge. It is such a pervasive feature of the post-1870 world that we need to acknowledge its role.

Information that becomes useful is cumulative, that is to say, bits and pieces are uncovered, then eventually connected to create some new value. Proto-computer technologies percolated for nearly forty years before a corporation could order one from Univac or IBM; insights about DNA converted into medical procedures only over a half-century after it was understood; space travel did not go commercial for a half-century after the first human broke the bounds of earth. Because the formation of useful knowledge took a long time to create, while its end products remains unclear for so many decades, it became the practice of government agencies to fund early-stage R&D, as it did with computing, until the risks of converting such information into commercial products were known and could be controlled.[32] Investments in R&D by the private and public sectors led to innovations that made possible development of new business and entire industries.

Part of the innovation process was made possible by the availability of new information, which one can track through patents, copyrights, and trademarks. These played a duel role over the past two centuries. On one hand they provided monopoly protection to the creators of new products and publications for a period of time, which allowed them to enjoy the economic fruits of their efforts. That meant the diffusion of new protected information was limited—access to it controlled—by its creators for a while. The patent system worked in motivating the development of innovative products and services until well past World War II, but then became an inhibitor of innovations, although not in all industries at all times.

First, patents were extended beyond the original conception of inventing a new product to where one could obtain protection for new information and practices, such as databases, medical procedures, work and production processes, and analytical processes. These forms of patenting became a growing practice by the 1980s. Universities began patenting the research results of its professors and graduate students so as to sell rights to these bodies of information to corporations, most obviously to pharmaceutical firms. The University of Wisconsin, which "discovered" Vitamin D, did this for decades.[33] Second, laws changed to extend the years of patent protection through renewals of the monopolistic control over new information. This occurred at a time when competitive new collections of knowledge appeared, such as in optional medications to patented ones. Third, it became easier to acquire patents in the late twentieth century than in the nineteenth and most of the twentieth centuries.[34]

A fourth issue involved corporate strategies to collect (acquire, buy) patents around a broad general subject area to block competitors. Economists argue that this is a post–World War II phenomenon, often citing computer, software, and pharmaceutical companies as notorious examples of this practice.[35] However, the practice dated to the nineteenth century. NCR, for example, acquired patents related to cash registers or bought firms that held them to block their use by rivals. IBM and the companies that preceded its formation did the same in the 1890s through the 1920s, particularly as they related to tabulating equipment, and then from the 1920s through the 1960s, for typewriter technologies and keyboards.[36] Neither firm proved shy about hiding this strategy. IBM was obvious about its use in the 1950s and 1960s in the development of its computer products to such an extent that when the U.S. government launched its long antitrust suit against the firm in 1969, government lawyers spent the next decade documenting this practice.[37] Finally, collecting patents that could be used to extract royalties and penalty fees from others using them either legally or illegally—known as *patent trolling*—became an activity that mimicked managing the portfolios of financial investments.[38]

So, "patented value extraction," to quote an economist, had a long history affecting the speed with which new information appeared, was applied, or was held back from being shared or used.[39] Similar patterns of behavior were evident with copyrights across the entire period of the Second Industrial Revolution. Laws varied across countries. This is why, for example, it is more difficult to use European published materials without paying fees than to use American publications. Entire publishing strategies built on gate-keeping access to information, particularly that published in technical and scientific journals since the 1970s.[40] Underpinning the story told in the rest of this chapter, therefore, are the twin concerns of controlling the activities of an institution and creating economic opportunities driven by innovations. The latter required new information and led to controlling its access and use. Besides what engineers and scientists accomplished in shaping information, firms and governments needed tools to convert those into economic and socially attractive goods. This is where other information tools proved so important, beginning with accounting.

THE GROWTH AND DIVERSITY OF ACCOUNTING IN THE MODERN ERA

Accounting, the language of business, is the practice of keeping financial (numeric) records of an organization per a set of defined practices. It is one of the oldest bodies of information recorded in human history. With the emergence of large private and public sector agencies in the late 1800s, accounting practices expanded in type and scope, becoming more complex and varied throughout the twentieth century.[41] But many of its modern contours had been defined between the 1870s and the 1930s, which were subsequently augmented. For over a century, accounting encompassed financial information for use by investors, public, media, and regulatory agencies. Cash flows (money coming in minus expenses paid out, resulting in "closing cash balance" reports), profit and loss statements (money left over after expenses are subtracted from income), and income statements (variant of the profit and loss statement) were routine types of information gathered through such exercises.[42] Note the interest in the movement of information—hence the word *flow* appearing again in this chapter—and snapshots of the status of business information presented at prescribed times, such as monthly or quarterly.

Internal versions of such information, along with the specific accounting of the financial performance of a department or division, are known as management accounting. Data managers use this to understand the financial performance of their firm or agency, and it includes, for example, budgets for the current and next year, how one is spending in comparison to budget, including accounting for salaries and expenses for materials (often called cost accounting), which are used to manage the availability of cash and to track activities. Open a typical accounting textbook, and the major chapter topics include income statements, balance sheets and statements of cash flow, valuation of inventories, acquisition and disposal of property, factories and equipment, depreciation and depletions, intangible assets (the goodwill value of a company's name or moribund patents, business units), long- and short-term liabilities, stockholders' equity, earnings per share, investments, revenue recognition (think accounts receivable, money declared to be owed by the firm), income taxes, and cash flows.[43]

Such data made it possible for management to create large organizations, because they could answer questions crucial to controlling operations. Fundamental were answers to such questions as:

- How much debt does the firm have and what kind is it (e.g., short or long term)?
- Were sales higher or lower this quarter, this year than in the past quarter or past year?
- What assets are owned by the firm and what kind?
- What were our cash inflows and outflows this week, month, quarter, and year, and how do these compare with those of prior comparable periods?
- What profit (or loss) did we experience this month, quarter, or year?
- What products and services are profitable or not and by how much?
- What is the rate of return on net assets and what is the trend in those, increasing or decreasing?[44]

Reformulated another way, accounting helps firms understand demand and forecasting, production and costs, pricing and output decisions to inform strategies and tactics, to design and operate organizations, to regulate them, and to conform to government regulations.[45]

Long gone were the single journal entry scribes of the nineteenth century, replaced now with small armies of professionally trained accountants who, by the 1920s, were embedded in all departments in large companies and government agencies preparing similar charts of accounts by department that could be integrated into standardized formatted reports sent upward in the organization. These were consolidated until fully summarized at the "top of the house," normally in the form of summary documents, such as a corporate annual report or a government's budget summary and request for next year's funding.[46]

Those two broad areas—public reporting and internal management—of accounting are augmented by two other types of accounting information. The first is tax accounting, which is the preparation of financial data to determine and report what taxes are owed by a company that government agencies use to anticipate and track cash (income) into government, and that can be used to set budgets for agencies. Auditing is the practice of verifying the accuracy of accounting information provided by a firm or agency and to assist in preventing fraud.[47] Over time, standards for performing all manner of accounting became more formalized. For example, in the United States in 1934 the Congress created the U.S. Securities and Exchange Commission (SEC) to certify the accuracy of financial reports submitted to the government by publicly traded corporations. This is the data normally presented in annual reports.[48] In 1973, a non-profit standards organization came into existence, known as the Financial Accounting Standards Board (FASB) to set rules and provide guidelines for how accounting is done. Its rules are known as "Generally Accepted Accounting Principles" (more familiar as GAAP). Its standards are almost universally practiced by the more than 70,000 multinational corporations around the world, and by every publicly traded ones in the United States.[49]

Table 7.1 lists the kind of numeric information collected by American accountants between the end of the nineteenth century and World War II, with particular emphasis on the data used by corporations. These were shaped by GAAP rules late in the century but also by prior accounting practices. Three observations can be pulled from this table. First, standard formats for presenting results quickly became the norm, such as what data goes into specific columns on a table. Second, it became crucial to compare data from one period or type of information to another over time, for instance, the cost of salaries this month versus what they were last month or the same month a year ago. Third, since data was numeric it was but a small step to apply statistical analysis to these to understand trends, to provide insights for

Table 7.1. Accounting and Financial Information Collected by American Corporations, 1880s–1940s by Types

General ledger (summary costs, income)
Procedures (sales, purchases, cash receipts)
Auxiliary records (personnel, standards performance, expense analyses)
Financial data (assets, inventories, cost accounting, expense analyses)
Vouchers and expenditures by plants
Bankbook and cash transactions
Daily employee time cards
Trail cash spent by week
Customer payments (accounts Receivables)
Cost of ongoing production
Sales
Monthly financial reports
Maintenance and repair
Miscellaneous cash management recording

Sources: J. Brooks Heckert, *Accounting Systems Design and Installation* (New York: Ronald Press, 1936): 73–86; Margaret Levenstein, *Accounting for Growth: Information Systems and the Creation of the Large Corporation* (Stanford, CA: Stanford University Press, 1998): 62–39.

management, to plan based on expectations, and as we discuss later, to create mathematical models that described various operational futures.

Over time the frequency with which such information was collected and studied increased. If collecting and reporting such data was done, say, quarterly or monthly in the late 1800s, by the mid-twentieth century management wanted it as frequently as weekly; today it is not uncommon for some accounting systems to update data daily or in real time. Inventory counts and costs were the first to be collected and analyzed by computers in the 1950s.[50] Analyses of the costs of people (wages, training, offices, and benefits) versus automation, too, became subject to much study by the start of the 1960s.[51] Laws determined when reporting occurred. Government agencies had to prepare proposed budgets that legislatures adjusted and approved by certain dates. Corporations operated on similar time lines, although the start of their fiscal year could be any month they chose, not necessarily January 1; just as the U.S. government began its fiscal year on October 1st, many American state and local governments on July 1st.

No department was immune from collecting and living by the data collected in accounting. Factories had specialized accounting to track materials, inventories of different types (e.g., parts and finished goods), amount of labor and their costs, and so forth. Table 7.2 lists examples of accounting information that became standard by World War I, drawn largely from manufacturing industries.

Table 7.3 illustrates the kind of data collected by sales organizations. High-tech firms often led the way in methodically collecting accounting and other statistics related to sales, essentially co-mingling these to provide

Table 7.2. Sample American Accounting Data, circa 1914

Personnel (time punched in and out of work, daily)
Wages (hourly by job, by person, paid by week)
Inventory (by type, by part, number in warehouse, number and type delivered)
Transportation (number of train rolling stock box cars, cost to rent/maintain)
Factory budgets (for wages, materials, other expenses, energy, taxes)
Research (wages, supplies, building costs, patents)
Litigation and other administrative expenses (legal fees, government fees, accounting)
Machinery (purchase costs, energy costs, maintenance, replacement, depreciation)
Energy (cost of coal, later electricity, staffing)
Petty cash book, accounts payable, accounts receivable
Sales ledger
Daily receipts and disbursements

Sources: Alfred D. Chandler Jr., *The Visible Hand: The Managerial Revolution in American Business* (Cambridge, MA: Harvard University Press, 1977): 240–283; Margaret Levenstein, *Accounting for Growth: Information Systems and the Creation of the Large Corporation* (Stanford, CA: Stanford University Press, 1998): 87–139.

Table 7.3. Sales Accounting Data, circa 1890–1925

Number and type of sales calls on customers by salesman, weekly
Revenue by product, by salesman, by sales office, by geographic region, by country weekly and monthly, by product and totals by quarter
Profitability by product, salesman, geographic region
Cost of sales by office and region (includes rental of offices, salaries, energy, maintenance)
Salaries and commissions earned and paid by salesman, sales office, region, and product
Ranking of sales revenue by salesman, office, region, and division
Sales forecasting by salesman, product, sales office, region, country, by month, quarter, and year
Sales quotas by salesman, product, sales office, region, country by month, quarter, and year
Advertising budget and expenditures
Marketing and training literature budget and expenses
Sales training expenses by sales office, region, division, by quarter and year

Source: James W. Cortada, *IBM: The Rise and Fall and Reinvention of a Global Icon* (Cambridge, MA: MIT Press, 2019): 3–87.

a composite picture of sales activities. One of the leading innovators from the 1890s through to World War I was John H. Patterson (1844–1922) at NCR and subsequently his protégé, Thomas J. Watson Sr. (1874–1956), who went on to successfully run IBM for over four decades. As in other parts of an enterprise, senior management sought efficiencies and effectiveness in sales operations.[52] In the late nineteenth century, sales methods were more routinized and disciplined into a profession, what the leading innovator of that process, Patterson, called "scientific selling."[53] Watson, Sr., who spent nearly two decades working for Patterson as a salesman, manager, and executive, introduced these and additional enhancements to NCR's successful approaches to sales and measures of those activities while at NCR and later at IBM. He had the advantage, of course, of being able to use his own tabulating punched card equipment to collect accounting and operational statistics that could be analyzed for insights using the rapidly emerging field of statistics.[54]

For most readers, probably the most familiar set of accounting data is that which appears in an annual report. That reporting grew more complex and diverse over time. Looking at a long-established firm illustrates the evolution, in this case IBM which was established in 1911, beginning with its report for 1914, the first year of its long-term leader's rule (Thomas J. Watson, Sr.) and that continues to issue annual reports. The 1914 annual report was a small pamphlet eight pages in length; only three had accounting data. The major categories of such information included assets, capital and liabilities, and a consolidated statement of earnings for the year. Assets included cash on hand in banks, other investments, charges, value of plants and equipment, what the company owed (accounts payable), debts, and company stock. Everything was expressed in American dollars. The second report—consolidated earnings—included "deductions for obsolete material," net profits of subsidiary country firms, maintenance, expenses and other debts and obligations, and the all-important "surplus," in this case a total of $1.4 million.[55] The order in which the data was presented remained essentially unchanged over the next century.

IBM's annual report from 1955 was no longer a pamphlet. It was now an 8" × 11" sized twenty-two-page slick color publication. It had five full pages of accounting data, and several half-page trend charts drawn from that information scattered throughout the report. Notice what did not change, but also what IBM's accountants added. Leave aside the fact that the company was massively larger in 1955 than in 1914; all size did was make the numbers bigger (e.g., amount of revenue generated and costs paid out). The format and subject matter of IBM's annual reports were typical of thousands of other enterprises, less because of fashion and more because of regulatory requirements. The basic accounting topics had not fundamentally changed.[56] Then consider IBM's annual report for 2019. This edition was 144 pages in length, of which 116 pages were densely packed with accounting and statistical data and explanatory notes. In other words, more data was provided in this report than combined had been published in IBM's first fifteen annual reports. And that did not include the glossy marketing language touting the company's achievements or the Chairman's Letter, which added another twenty-three pages of text and photographs. Several things become quickly obvious. Much of the data was similar to what appeared in earlier annual reports and in the same manner, with similar definitions and formats. What made the document so long were alternative tables of similar information and deep dives into various parts of the business, not required to be reported on in the 1950s. Regulatory changes over the decades had required more detailed accounting information and explanations, such as how much senior executives were being paid, the amount of money set aside for pensions and financial performance results of those funds, levels of detail concerning the balance sheets and income statements by line of business (e.g., consulting, software, hardware, services, and so forth). So, while much remained the same, new information increased. Of particular note required by regulators was language to make it is easier for investors to understand, such as broad summary categories as "Revenue," "Net Income," and "Income from continuing operations," in addition to explanatory notes and other narrative texts.[57] Providing comparative data from one year to the next had now been standard in such reports for decades. As evident in other fields of information, diversity and quantity of information, and uses to which these were put, increased over time in business.

As in other disciplines, as the amount and variety of accounting data increased, so too did discussion about what further was needed, one we cannot engage with here. However, because so much of the kind of information collected by corporations remained so similar for many decades, it should be of no surprise that critics questioned the relevancy of some of this information. They suggested that some were no longer relevant or did not reflect the true fiscal health of a company or government agency. For example, two accounting professors accused corporations of not providing sufficiently useful information anymore for investors: "The amount of new or relevant information conveyed today by corporate financial reports is much less . . . more like 5 percent of what was deemed useful decades earlier."[58] They even cited Shannon's 1948 paper to say much of the financial data was "noise," not necessarily useful messages. They lamented the degree to which such information was useful, questioning its slow "timeliness, or newness."[59] By the time an annual report was published—usually about one hundred days into the next year—anyone who cared to know already has seen the previous year's accounting data, anywhere from a few days into the New Year or within a month or so.

Government agencies were not immune from ever-growing layers of accounting details. Each February the U.S. Office of Management and Budget (OMB) publishes an enormous, fat proposed budget running many hundreds of pages in length. In fact, it is always so physically big that the news media take photographs of it, while the U.S. government is always careful to only publish its cover such as not to hint at its page length. Recent editions organized data into seventeen sections that included an overview by department of proposed budgets, receipts by source, and outlays by function. Tables provide summary totals by type of expenditure, followed by more detailed tables for line items in the overall budget projects and proposals. These include comparisons in proportions, such as a receipt category as percentage of total tax receipts. Data is calculated both for prior years and proposed next year for revenues, expenses, deficits, and debt. Budgets passed by the Congress are then republished, organized by department then by agency, which become the data-driven documents that shape expenditures and programs of all, as required by laws.

Increasingly, in late-twentieth- and early-twenty-first-century editions these included models of optional scenarios and ranges of possible outcomes, demonstrating sound statistical practices. Summary historical tables provide data under such categories as "Revenues," as from individual income taxes, payroll taxes, corporate income taxes, excise taxes, estate and gift taxes, customs duties, and miscellaneous data. In a second category entitled "Mandatory Outlays," one can find Social Security, Medicare, Income Security, and various retirement programs. Under "Discretionary Outlays," data is housed on the defense budget and everything else. Budgets are presented for the current and proposed next full year, with dollar and percentage changes, as percentage of share of total revenues or outlays, and as percentages of GDP in dollars and changes. For each major category totals are expressed in dollars and as percentage of totals.[60] A similar story could be told about all fifty states and most national and provincial governments from the mid-nineteenth century to the present.

Accounting data was less useful if these did not appear in a report or a document. Not until the availability of online computer systems in the 1960s did individuals have an alternative way to look at the numbers. But even by law, internal regulation, and by auditor's preferences or habit, standard printed reports continued to be published. In the twenty-first century, annual reports and American 8-K and 10-K corporate filings are published on paper and digitally accessible forms. Formats for reports purposefully changed infrequently from one era to another. Accounting conventions dictated formats. Organizations wanted to compare data from one period to another, therefore, they needed both content and formats to remain the same, in other words, relatively stable. People became used to standard formats for reports, thus they could read them quickly, focusing on what was of concern to them (or different), confident that they understood the context from which these data emerged. Such patterns of reporting were as much in evidence in the 1980s as in the 1880s and some with barely any changes, such as the top line financial data on a balance sheet. In sum, accounting provided statistics, comparisons of data over time, documented activities and trends, setting up a growing capability to model scenarios, to increasingly do "what if" analysis based on growing amounts of information.

Like other classes of facts, accounting data could be molded to present a preferred narrative, leveraging the ever-increasing respect the public attributed to numbers that they were more objective than text. As the extent of accounting increased over time, the more discussions about the empirical value of numerical information extended beyond the walls of academia or professions. One historian has argued that local (read, non-numeric) knowledge had become increasingly inadequate to explain circumstances, the same problem scientists had before they embraced mathematics and statistics with which to explain realities. Theodor M. Porter, here, saw accounting thus transform into a "cult of impersonality."[61]

EXPANDING WORLD OF INFORMATION

A theme unfolding in each chapter is that the amount and diversity of information available over time kept increasing across all sectors of society.

A consequence of those two developments is that most jobs and all organizations either became more dependent on new bodies of information or seemed awash in too much of it. How history judges those two circumstances time will tell. But already clear is that the expanding ecosystems of information kept enlarging over the past century and a half to such an extent that the nature of work transformed for hundreds of millions of people. For one thing, we have seen that across many professions, workers and organizations became more reliant on statistics, trend analysis, measures of processes and performance, and written-down instructions for how to do their work.

For another, they increasingly learned how to analyze such information, thanks to the use of statistics, later spreadsheets with personal computers (PCs) and laptops. In the case of managerial practices in both government and business, their work evolved from relying on experiential ad hoc activities to codified formal "best practices," frequently encouraged by such highly respected business gurus as Peter F. Drucker (1909–2005).[62] Decision-making migrated downward from senior levels through the ranks as close as possible to where a decision directly affected productivity and work. This could be done because across the twentieth century workers at ever lower ends of an organization became better educated in the use of process management methods, measurements, models, and spreadsheets, and had sufficient data, thus could be trusted and be held accountable for results.[63]

That trend was facilitated, too, by the communications and data-handling capabilities of computers, because one could collect information at the point where these reflected action and could be quickly moved about inside an organization accurately and inexpensively.[64] The availability of databases relevant to government and business made information flows move horizontally as much as vertically in an organization. Communications and distributed processing facilitated movement of information, too, back and forth among suppliers, business partners, and customers. In other words, information came into and out of multiple organizations, crossing legal boundaries of corporations and government agencies. Thereby, were created information ecosystems combining statistics, standardized reports, financial and accounting information, procedures, contracts, and other texts.[65] Older notions of control from the nineteenth century evolved, as management weighed the "pros" and "cons" of centralized versus decentralized management of operations and how far inside or outside their organizations they permitted information to roam. These considerations devolved into discussions about coordination and collaboration. How to do it? Why to do it? How best to measure these?[66]

Such issues were not limited to the private sector. By the early 1990s, it had become evident across local and national governments that managerial practices were changing. A colleague and I asked both a mayor and Vice President Al Gore to explain these. Mayor of Madison, Wisconsin,

Joe Sensenbrenner, a leading reformer of public sector administration in the 1980s, observed improved operations when incentives to change began shifting from political pressure as a driver of more efficiency and coordination to more fact-based, citizen-oriented practices. Gore criticized the old "top-down, centralized bureaucracies" that were "patterned after the corporate structures of the age." He observed that by the late 1900s, public agencies were mimicking new information-rich, delegated distributed operations already evident in business enterprises.[67]

If permitted a personal observation, I could see the information-driven process unfold from the early 1970s and can trace it today by what managerial issues I wrote about.[68] While in the 1970s organizations were still figuring out how best to use computers, by the late 1980s managers were identifying and enhancing institutional "core competencies."[69] Their employees learned that information alone was insufficient. One management guru, James Brian Quinn (1928–2012), stated the obvious: "A large portion, but not all, of an organization's knowledge" resided "in three human reservoirs: (1) the cognitive understandings, (2) the learned skills, and (3) the deeply held beliefs of individuals."[70] While conducting research for a history of IBM, I found all three present in this data-rich company.[71]

Answers to the questions just raised often called for R&D of three types: *basic*, such as how electrons work so as to create new computer chips; *applied*, such as how to turn magnetized surfaces into memory, which could be plugged into a laptop; and *operational*, such as how to create a global supply chain. All three relied on Quinn's observation but also on the methods promoted by scientists, mathematicians, and statisticians. It is in this expanding environment of information that employees became "knowledge workers." Peter Drucker is credited as an early proponent of the phrase in the 1950s, but so too economist Fritz Machlup (1902–1983) at about the same time. Both saw that the basic capital resource of a nation was its knowledge and its educated, knowledgeable workers, not just the machines and decreasing manual work or muscle energy.[72]

I explore one example of the growing dependence on information to illustrate what was happening: inventory control. In manufacturing, retail and wholesale businesses, transportation, and users of supplies it is a crucial asset to manage. That had to be done with information. A university buys everything from pencils to trainloads of chemicals; Amazon.com is all about inventory management, so too UPS, Federal Express, and every postal service in the world; every organization has office supplies. The list for whom inventory control is important is essentially endless, even for those people who hoarded bathroom tissues during the Covid-19 pandemic in 2020 or are organizing a party at their homes this weekend.

If someone has a business that makes or sells a product, the optimal situation is to manufacture and sell it as quickly as possible, because the time it sits on the shelf or in the warehouse it is not generating revenue and it has already cost. So, a business wants to "turn" that inventory around, that is to say, build and then ship it to a customer as quickly as possible. If you have good data on what inventory is on hand, when it went into the warehouse, and how long it stayed there before being shipped out, you could measure its turn by product type by the 1950s (i.e., how many days or months it sat on the shelf) and by the 1980s, by individual product (i.e., by serial number per copy of product), and by 2010, where it was on its path from your warehouse to someone's front door. There have always been five ways to drive down the costs of inventory: (1) spend less for the materials that go into making it, (2) lower manufacturing costs by using new methods and for storage (e.g., mass production methods beginning in the 1910s, just-in-time manufacturing in the 1970s), (3) use less expensive employees (e.g., have the product manufactured in another country), (4) reduce the time from when it is made to when it is paid for, or the most obvious, (5) keep it for the least amount of time as possible.

None of these steps could be carried out without information, and the amount of detail had to increase over time, so too measures of performance of those strategies, such as inventory turns.[73] The more current the information the more workers could potentially optimize (i.e., lower) the costs of inventory. In the 1890s monthly reports might have been reasonably accurate; a century later they were quite accurate. By the 1950s one could lower costs of inventory between 1 and 15 percent, if armed with the right information to act upon.[74] With growing amounts of more granular information, one could formulate new actions for reducing inventory costs and run mathematical models to price various alternatives, often using data less than a few days old, thanks to the wide use of bar codes, beginning in the last quarter of the twentieth century. When linked to cost accounting, data management could assist in controlling costs, fraud, and inventory shrinkage. Then employees could continuously improve services to customers by increasingly having the right inventory to meet one's needs in a timely cost-effective manner.

Every industry expanded the diversity of useful information. Engineers late in the twentieth century had access to information concerning such topics as circuit designs, design analysis, facilities engineering, manufacturing specifications, mapping, piping, surveys, volume properties, and simulations—all new types of information by the 1960s.[75] Banks added to their collections of information to such an extent that, by mid-century, retail bankers routinely read accumulative transaction reports, others by auditors, billing records, delinquent notices, escrow analyses, late notices, loan profiles, credit reports, mortgage statements, and property tax data. Very little of that data was available to a bank in 1920; by the end of the century it was also in real time, or certainly not older in many cases than a week or two.[76]

Governments were in a similar situation. The Federal Bureau of Investigation (FBI), for instance, started creating manual, later digital, files on criminals and crimes in the 1930s that quickly became massive. As new bodies of information in one field became available, they were adopted. For example, when fingerprints and forensic evidence could be studied (thanks to the work of biologists and chemists), crime labs came into existence, and their work and data were collected and used. When people started stealing automobiles, the FBI set up a series of files (later digital) and databases to track these. Cities started tracking parking tickets to help plan better traffic flows.[77] Other law enforcement agencies enriched their information pools in many countries.[78]

The American armed services tracked every soldier in World War I down to the size of his or her uniform and skills; by the end of the century, the military also had DNA data on these too. The Pentagon began modeling warfare scenarios using mathematics and modeling algorithms to fight the Vietnam War in the 1960s. Today satellites and bar codes tell the military where everyone and almost everything is located.[79] Governments use the same kind of data as companies to track inventory, something crucial when there is a national crisis and supplies are needed to help citizens in a natural disaster, or when the President calls on military units to deploy to the Middle East, as happened during the Gulf War (1990–1991), which called for the movement of massive amounts of supplies to Kuwait and Iraq. Since the start of World War II, the American military has been the largest purchaser and manager of inventory in the United States.[80]

Tax management expanded and became highly mathematical as the variety of taxes and the complexity of American tax codes increased over the century, giving these the undesirable distinction of being some of the most complicated in the world. It is difficult to imagine the creation then management of evermore complex taxes and their ensuing returns and records without new bodies of information made possible by statistics, modeling software, and expanding bodies of tax knowledge. Tax collectors became some of the most sophisticated modelers of cash flows by the 1960s, able to tell a Congressman how much revenue a line item in a proposed bill would raise (or reduce) and to have that data be quite accurate.[81] When new subjects became interesting, government officials created new bodies of information. One of my favorites are nutrition facts about food. Officials dictated what to report on a can of soup, the definition of each factual item, and used that information to advise the nation on healthy eating habits.[82]

THE RISING POPULARITY OF MODELS

The twentieth century could arguably be labeled the "Century of the Mathematical Model," because in no prior one were so many developed or more applied by more people across more professions and industries. That is not to say models were new ways of looking at information. There is the Rule of 72, developed in 1494, the Bernouvilli Urn Model (1713), the Exponential Growth Model introduced in 1798 as an observation by Thomas Malthus (1766–1834) about growth patterns in population, and early variants of the Markov Decision Model of 1877. Some were called theorems (mathematical formulas), others simply *models*. Some were reinvented more than once, such as the Peron-Frabenius Theorem in 1907 and again in 1912, or the Half-Life Model in 1907 and rebranded in the 1950s. No matter what they were called, all shared one thing in common: each was a method based on mathematical calculations to describe a hypothetical view of a reality, such as the odds of someone winning or losing a coin toss, predicting tomorrow's temperature, or how many Europeans would die next month in 2020 because of Covid-19.

It is relevant to revisit the definition of a model to make sure we distinguish this class of information from others that could mislead how facts changed in the twentieth century. For a definition, listen to social scientist Scott E. Page: "Models are formal structures represented in mathematics and diagrams that help us to understand the world. Mastery of models improves your ability to reason, explain, communicate, act, predict and explore."[83] Models have been shown to improve reasoning and, in his words, to "make more robust decisions in your career, community activities, and personal life."[84] One can detect that models are applicable across many subject areas, disciplines, professions, and interests. We would be challenged to find many human activities that have not been modeled for one purpose or another. As Page explains, "We need models to make sense of the fire-hose like streams of data that cross our computer screens."[85] Add that this problem of large data sets had already troubled scientists and telecommunications engineers long before the arrival of the computer.

Models share common features proven to be useful for over a century. They help to clarify circumstances by presenting a situation in simple terms, by pulling away details that might otherwise obfuscate what one was looking at. That is done largely by using mathematics, rather than adjectives and verbs. Models force one to have a precise understanding of a situation, compelling one to a clearly understood definition, such as the probability that a belief is highly embraced or not. Models make it possible to create logic, posit hypotheses, formulate solutions, and apply data to a situation because of the simplification a model forces on us. These forced structures help to invigorate one's logical approach to a topic. It is the logic emanating from a model that makes it possible to understand, to believe, and to make decisions reinforced by having consulted data, context (one's assumptions about a given reality), and a formula. As noted earlier in this chapter, models are simplified abstractions as they cannot be real—they leave out the verbs, nouns, and adjectives that make situations concrete, specific. But, a model's logic can be used to help understand specific cases and situations.

Don't people have other ways of hypothetically envisioning options, causes, or realities? Experience is one of those: "Oh, I have seen this before, it happens all the time." Except that experience is individual, not necessarily universal or rooted in reality. Your experience could be unique, one diametrically different than someone else's. Therefore, it could be based on false facts. "Rules of thumb" is another closely related source of information about possible outcomes. "When the leaves turn brown, I know winter will always soon arrive." Not true, as winter can come later than normal or because the leaves could fall in August due to a hot summer rather than to a change in seasons. A theorem, or mathematical formula by itself could be too rigid, as we saw in chapter 5 with algebra, calculus, and geometry. These are useful but abstract, perhaps too arbitrary. But theorems come very close to models, so close that often models and theorems are titles used almost interchangeable. This is because a theorem is a general proposition that can be proven through the logic of a series of mathematical calculations or, to put it more elegantly, by means of accepted truth. The Pythagoras Theorem is a set of mathematical steps that proves every time what happens to a triangle. A theorem provides a major result. Theorems are always expressed in mathematical terms, where every term has a value, such as "a" = a number, "b" another, and so forth.

One can see that as mathematics and science became more widely used in the twentieth century, those facile in using numbers as their language, when coupled to the kinds of interests engaging to scientists and economists, for example, would be attracted to testing assumptions (hypotheses) using such tools, rather than untested assumptions, hunches, or rules of thumb. Having methods that increasingly turn out to be more true (hence useful) than not— the promise of a good model—became irresistible, particularly if decisions and insights emanating from one or more models turned out in hindsight to have been prescient or otherwise advantageous. Or to use Page's word, loaded with "wisdom."

So, mathematicians, scientists, economists, business management professors, engineers, social scientists, even historians and professors of literature not known for being extensive users of mathematically soaked models, increasingly embraced them. Many in STEM and business professions created them. To that latter point, consult the lengthy table 7.4. The list could

Table 7.4 Types of Models

Assembly	Predictive
Choice	Scale
Data	Simulations
Discrete	Software
Economic	Statistical
Ecosystem	Stochastic
Enterprise/business	System architecture
Future studies	Systems
Homology	Visualization
Information	Water quality
Mathematical	Discipline specific
Molecular	Profession specific
Multiscale	Government specific

have been doubled or tripled. Many of the models listed in this table exist with alternative names tailored to specific professions and disciplines. Most readers will recognize some, such as Six Sigma in business circles. While mathematicians and statisticians were prominent authors of models, these originated from many corners. Six Sigma, for example, was developed and embraced by businesses, Shannon's ideas about entropy from engineering researchers at Bell Labs. Physicists were active producers of models, so too computer scientists. Already people are able to create such tables drawn from the work of brain scientists and the AI community, two disciplines barely one generation old. Some are called theorems, others models, and normally whoever is given credit for first describing and demonstrating gets their name attached to it. Look more closely, because in every decade of the twentieth century important, widely embraced models became available, many more than from either the eighteenth or nineteenth centuries, even though in earlier times mathematicians and scientists developed models still used today. For our purposes, I do not need to describe individual ones, as it is more important to recognize that the kind of information that came out of their use became part of the library of humankind's understanding of their world, an extension of how they came to understand their growing collections of facts.[86]

STANDARDS AS A WAY OF LIFE, AS A WAY TO INFORM

Establishing standards is a theme running through the modern history of information, building momentum after the mid-nineteenth century, a point also made in this book.[87] Having common railroad tracks (size, design, gauges) made it possible to link together independent rail lines across entire nations.[88]

Having standard light bulbs made it possible to fill one's home with lamps; using a common format for electricity had the same effect of making it more accessible. There is hardly any aspect of human life and society that does not rely on common standards. These are norms for a product, process, behavior, quality, and so forth.

Standards also exist for information itself not just for the layout, say, of a book or as in information technology and computing. In the operation of large organizations, information standards proved crucial in insuring that the right data was collected and presented in a prescribed manner at an expected time and frequency—the idea of control linked to its underlying information infrastructure. A business expert from the 1920s explains: "The setting of standards of practice, the observation and measurement of capacity for output, the recording of experience as to expected costs, sales volumes, and so on, provides the management with facts which reduce uncertainties and permit the foreseeing and avoidance of many hazards."[89]

Information standards are established in order to conduct work in an orderly fashion in a "properly" run organization. An example replicated millions of times around the world since the 1950s is the installation of a computer system, as it involves the physical placement of equipment, loading it with software that runs effectively, training staff to ensure they operate both, and that documentation is clear, familiar, and useful. When IBM entered the computer business in the 1950s and by the end of the 1960s came to dominate it, its staffs used a process—a standard way—of installing computer systems. Installing computers is fraught with difficulty, many steps, and numerous decisions, even in the 2020s in large data centers. So, having a process that could be replicated to ensure hardware, software, and digitized data were installed in a timely and effective manner proved crucial. The process used since the 1950s grew out of experiences gained installing tabulating equipment between the early 1900s and the end of the 1950s.

IBM field personnel educated customers on the need to plan the installation of a data processing system by considering the following: "Data processing organization, selection and education of personnel, planning and progress control, systems design, program preparation, documentation, standardization, program testing, conversion, physical site preparation, and operating the installation."[90] The quoted document provided an overview of the process, running to over fifty pages in length, accompanied by a half-dozen even lengthier publications going through each of these points.[91] Text, followed by flow charts, forms, and tables displayed *the* standard way to install a system. These showed the sequence of steps, schedules, and when they had been met, and manpower scheduling using Gantt charts. Think of these guidebooks as a massive recipe for success that all parties were expected to follow and for which they were held accountable.[92]

IBM employees had been obsessive in documenting business procedures for decades. They transferred their discipline to millions of information processing (IT) workers in the twentieth century. Many tens of thousands of these technical employees went on to careers in business and government that extended into non-IT operations, ensuring that some of IBM's ways of working were applied to all manner of activities from sales to manufacturing, accounting to finance, to how senior managers ran organizations and entire companies.[93] So how they treated documentation offers a window into the role of standards across a broad array of operations in both the public and private sectors. A few excerpts on documenting work and information offers insights, a sense of standardization's messages, at least by mid-century:

- Significant information must be written down and kept clear and concise.
- Creation and maintenance of these records—documentation—is an essential and vital part of a computer installation.
- Information prepared for documentation should be reviewed and revised until it is sufficiently clear and complete to serve as the reference necessary.
- Preparing and maintaining complete, accurate, and timely records.[94]

Standardized information called for "clarity and intelligibility," "ease of alteration," and "organized filing."[95]

Standardized processes included creating a control book (a.k.a. "Application Manual" or "Master Run Book") that contained descriptions of data and operations, flowcharts of activities and software (programs and files), record layouts for data, sample forms, program listings, and program histories (e.g., progress in writing and testing software).[96] IBM and computing personnel were essentially ordered "to maintain a standards manual. This manual should contain a written record of all policies, procedures, and techniques that are to be standard throughout the data processing organization. The use of such a manual will contribute greatly to the success of the organization by improving communication and preventing the development of conflicting procedures." Even as to more specific tasks, "since standards are subject to change, it is convenient to maintain the standards manual in a loose-leaf binder."[97] Nearly a century earlier, such binders had come onto the market and were used by large enterprises and public agencies.[98]

Data processing personnel, business management, and STEM professionals were some of the most avid users of loose-leaf binders since before World War I.[99] The advice IBM doled out in the 1950s and 1960s remained essentially unchanged in the twenty-first century, except now these were published in hundreds of what the firm called Redbooks, and online.[100] Back to the advice IBM advanced in mid-century, there already existed lists of information that could "benefit from standardization." These included application and program documentation, operating procedures, and programming techniques.[101] Laying out the organization of files (data) was a crucial exercise in information standardization, and so IBM published a manual explaining how each piece of data should be organized and encoded.[102] Flowcharting, a quintessential way of presenting action steps popular throughout the twentieth century as a new way to communicate, had its own manual.[103]

IBM's auditing firm, Pricewaterhouse and Company, provided an explanation of what went into documenting a program, and it looked much like the kind of documentation produced in mid-century in defense and space travel.[104] These auditors wanted things written down in an organized manner to help people run computers and fix software, also to make it possible to train new users, give access to auditors to the data and its use, and to allow management to inspect. "The basic test in judging the adequacy of documentation is to ask whether a typical programmer can fairly readily read his way to an understanding of the system without supplementary information and discussions."[105] What information would be required? The answer: "A general written description of the overall system," with a "general system diagram," and "for each computer program, a description of the functions performed by the program," which includes "block diagrams showing the sequence of operations performed by the programs" and "record descriptions showing the form and content of all inputs and outputs and memory locations."[106] Lest the reader conclude that only software programmers and data center operators would be interested in such standardized information, the auditors explained that others would be using such material, including financial controllers, auditors, and government agencies (e.g., taxation authorities, military, procurement agencies, regulators).[107]

Another form of standardization of information was the use of forms. The subject has a long history, so we dwell only briefly on it. For many centuries in the West, governments, the Catholic Church, and later businesses used forms to collect standard pieces of information. Leaving a question or line blank would remind all involved not to overlook it. Having information in a standard format made it possible to collate and summarize many of the same types of information, such as census data involving millions of people, or reporting salaries to a government for calculating pension payments. Today, if one does not fill out all required fields in an online form, they cannot do something next, such as place an order. So, for a long time forms were also seen as a tool of business and government to control the activities of customers and citizens. Increasingly, since the early nineteenth century, people's growing paper trail consisted of forms: birth certificates, land titles, passports, driver's licenses, tax records, school report cards, online profiles, credit card applications, loan applications, criminal records, military records, and requests for municipal building permits. One's documentary identity began to be shaped by the content of forms, and almost universally they included one's name, often a number (e.g., social security, military identification, driver's license, employee number), and frequently one's home address and age. Datafication of one's identity became a near-universal feature of society after the mid-1800s. What information was collected and how it was used was long in place before George Orwell wrote *Nineteen Eighty-Four*. The ability of software and storage of such information in digital formats made it possible to construct new profiles of people by integrating together bits and pieces of data. As the twentieth century unfolded then, new configurations of information about people changed what we knew about an individual.[108]

HOW IT ALL CAME TOGETHER: THE DEMING EFFECT

By the 1960s it was becoming evident to some statisticians and business managers that all these various threads of information's evolution and uses across multiple disciplines were somehow merging into new ways of using facts. By the end of the 1980s, this convergence had a name, Total Quality Management (TQM). One of the high priests of the merger of these various strands who is considered one of the founders of the TQM movement (although he never embraced the label), needs introduction. J. Edwards Deming (1900–1993) was educated as an electrical engineer and in physics, worked as a U.S. government statistician, lectured extensively, and published on the merits of statistical process control. He persuaded a generation of Japanese managers on how to rebuild and improve industrial production in the post–World War II period using statistical analysis. His methods worked. He became highly revered in Japan due to the economic prosperity the nation experienced in the 1950s and 1960s. Deming advocated a fact-based, statistically understood way of measuring and managing work processes to improve them. Not until the 1980s did American and European management embrace his ideas, when the Ford Motor Company successfully applied them.

But the world is small. In 1927 Deming met Walter A. Shewhart (1891–1967), who worked at Bell Laboratories, at the same place as Claude E. Shannon.[109] Shewhart taught Deming how to apply statistical process control to work processes, which he began to do as a Federal employee at the U.S. Department of Agriculture in the 1930s. The 1940 U.S. Census applied his ideas about sampling, which came to be known as the Deming–Stephen algorithm for iterative proportional fitting. During World War II, Deming compiled war standards, which were published in 1942 by the American Standards Association.[110]

Deming spoke about the idea of "profound knowledge," as consisting of four components: (1) "appreciation of a system," which was about how an organization is structured and worked; (2) "knowledge of variation," which was the statistical notion that there were ranges and causes of variation in the quality of any process, understood through sampling metrics; (3) "theory of knowledge," which defined knowledge and its limitations; and (4) "knowledge of psychology," which was about understanding human nature. To apply these concepts he proposed what came to be known as his "14 Points."[111] He recommended that organizations stop inspecting products after they were made, instead measure statistically the performance of the processes by which a product was manufactured to catch failures and weaknesses earlier and to improve overall performance along the way. He argued that it should be a constant way of working.[112] Since all work varies, continuously measuring performance was crucial; technology and its sensors were increasingly making that possible, and today it is normal practice. He advocated for quantitative measures, which meant documenting processes, much as we saw in the IBM discussion about standards.[113] Visualizing activities using graphics drew upon his heritage in engineering, with emphasis on using flowcharts.[114] By the end of the 1990s it seemed all managers were speaking about processes and statistical measures of their effectiveness.[115] It is why today one would be hard-pressed to find a PowerPoint presentation without charts and graphs.

Part of the reason for Deming's success in persuading over two generations of management to embrace statistics and data-driven action is because he was able to communicate his ideas in non-technical terms. For example, when an organization focuses on improving quality he said, "Quality = Results of work efforts divided by Total costs, quality goes up, costs go down." If one focused just on cost, those rose and quality declines. Experience often proved him right. His Fourteen Points became a mixture—an integration and admonition—of new ways of using statistical information and managerial practices when adopted made organizations highly dependent on models, standards, statistics, and well-trained employees. Some of his best known points included: "Create constancy of purpose toward improvement," "Cease dependence on inspection to achieve quality," "Improve constantly and forever," "Institute Leadership," "Drive out fear," "Break down barriers between departments," and "Eliminate slogans, exhortations, and targets."[116] Numbers, nouns, and verbs had come together.

CONCLUSIONS

In the 1840s skilled workers were craftsmen, so they could, for example, individually build an entire product, such as a clock, and in the 1910s pretty much an entire automobile, or still a horse-drawn carriage. By the 1920s with mass production they were still skilled, but at doing a piece of the total job, and by the end of the 1980s were instructing robots what to do using computerized systems. In the 1840s small shops and factories were the norm; by the end of the 1920s some plants had thousands of employees. By the end of the 1960s multiple factories around the world coordinated the manufacture of a product, such as an automobile with thousands of parts from several countries. In the 1870s there were few office clerks, barely any secretaries, and hardly anyone knew how to type. By 1910 office workers were some of the fastest-growing professions on both sides of the Atlantic; by the end of the 1900s they and the services sector of the economy dominated nearly 80 percent of the U.S. gross domestic product (GDP). A soldier in the 1860s wore an ill-fitting suit; by World War I the U.S. Army could issue him a uniform that fit based on his size, with "size" being a number. In the 1870s Americans and Europeans had a modicum of education; by World War II over 25 percent of the U.S. population had graduated from high school. By the end of the century over 25 percent of all residents in America had postsecondary education. In each of those circumstances, the transformative underpinnings of the changes in how they worked were the presence of new information. In all those situations, the amount and variety of information they worked with had evolved.

Put in counterfactual terms, without the changes in information described in this and in earlier chapters, people's work practices would probably not have changed that much. We know that to be the case because historians of earlier centuries, when information transformed less quickly, life styles and work practices evolved far slower than later. It is why historian Robert J. Gordon, for example, when writing his history of the United States of the Second Industrial Revolution could look back from the twenty-first century and declare that "daily life had changed beyond recognition," further declaring the period "unique in human history." He did not exaggerate, he chose his words carefully.[117]

Governments and businesses grew in size and diversity of work because they could depend on more detailed and variegated information—data and facts—in myriad forms: narratives, statistics, charts and graphs, columns of numbers, trend analysis, modeling, and massive quantities of statistics. All of this information became available more frequently, from monthly or quarterly to many instances daily or in real time. Manually calculated accounting and other limited statistical data gave way to partial automation with the use of desktop calculators, then tabulators, next large computers, followed by desktop computing and computing embedded in all manner of machines, and now to handheld smart devices, and sensors that collect more information that they push into the Internet than all humans combined do. Hand in glove with the emergence of more and varied information were ways and tools with which to engage with it.

Activities became numerically intense; personal experience began to count for less, particularly after the 1960s as the amount of "hard" data washed over all enterprises in the West and increasingly everywhere else too. As the amount of formal education one acquired increased, the more these individuals relied on formal bodies of information: books, manuals, journals, later computers, PCs, and spreadsheets and modeling software. Work became more cerebral, reliant more on data and far less on brawn. I have said it before and it bears repeating again: numbers ascended and adjectives descended in practice. It was no accident that people began to speak of living in an Information Age or of being "knowledge workers." More information made it possible to reduce errors by increasing rigor. Originally in the nineteenth century management wanted to train and manage unprofessional workers, but in time the workers became more professional, and thus their productivity increased in part because of the greater use of more useful information. How to accomplish the former—reduce errors—even came to have its own "error theory." Precision became a design point of measurements and processes, in other words, of new bodies of information.[118]

Literally on the floor of an office or factory, the cultivation of relevant information influenced the most humble of work tasks. Historian Craig Robertson recently pointed out the example of the filing clerk and their file cabinets doing, in effect, what librarians a century earlier had strived for: the organization of information into units small enough to be relevant and accessible. A filing clerk disassembled or standardized information through the act of filing it in folders. He explains: "The reconfiguration of information and labor through a process of 'taking apart' was intended to create something small that could be apprehended, understood, and connected to something else (and, if need be, exchanged). In organizing paper, file clerks learned to handle information in a way that prioritized reducing it to a size as small as efficiency demanded and technology allowed."[119] In other words, that behavior foreshadowed seeing information as physical objects, as discrete objects, later as computer bits. Electrification of information did not eliminate the fundamental purpose of filing; it actually increased the need for it.

Business and government had their own specific information needs, but they borrowed quickly and continuously from the new collections of facts generated by scientists, engineers, mathematicians, and statisticians. Workers and managers, academics and experts applied scientific approaches to much that they did. It seemed most large enterprises with complex products had set up laboratories and research centers by the start of World War II; finding exceptions to that practice became difficult to do by the end of the twentieth century. IBM, AT&T, Phillips, GE, Ford, General Motors, Google, and Microsoft, and so many other large enterprises had multiple research centers, most populated with larger numbers of PhDs than many small universities.

Business and management in public and private sectors professionalized in the 1900s. In the process they consumed vast quantities of information. Book publishing boomed as a result, for example. One publisher observed that "by 1990 sales of professional books were seventy times what they had been in 1960, having grown more than three times as fast as trade and textbook sales."[120] I know this was true, because I had been writing business books since the 1970s, and every editor I wrote for wanted more material quicker.[121]

Historian Alfred D. Chandler Jr. had been right when he argued that professional management had put together the large enterprises so characteristic of American business—governments too—in the twentieth century.[122] A key path for understanding what happened with information is to watch the evolution of management practices since those are the people who cause change, invest in new processes and information, and ultimately are held accountable for results. Throughout the twentieth century, as a group they embraced every form of new information that became available.[123] But to sum up, they began to see the world as a collection of systems and processes—what I think of as the Deming Effect—but it was always broader than that; even Deming was swept up by the rising tide of data perspectives of work. In the process it became difficult for most managers to make decisions without first consulting the data oracles. Often these were accountants, statisticians, data scientists, data processing personnel, and STEM professionals. By the end of the century no self-respecting manager would be far from his or her spreadsheets and data-crowded PowerPoint slides. Tacit knowledge did not go away: there was Steve Jobs and Jeff Bezos famously consulting less data and more their own insights for what products and services they wanted to offer the world; but once launched they hugged their data just as much as the rest of management. Google's managers built a massive business on the backs of such behavior.

There are functions that could not exist without such a reliance on the variety of data explored in this chapter. Recall supply chains, but today, were global. They include such information-rich capabilities as planning, sourcing of products and services, delivery, selling, and services. Every industry marches to some variant of this model of how one builds and operates a supply chain.[124]

Coupled to supply chain management is a skill essential for any manager viewing the world through the lens of processes and models: project management. The central skill required of a good project manager is the ability to keep track of all the activities underway, making sure these are done in the correct order in a timely fashion, and that their results are documented, compared, analyzed, and studied to ensure everything stays on track. Since the 1970s, managers have been taught to manage processes, to do, in effect, what IBM's computer installation people were instructed to do. In short, business and government changed because information had too. The new forms of information developed since the 1870s had escaped the confines of the librarians, scientists, mathematicians, and statisticians. Their insights and collections of data had become commonplace.

One could be tempted at this point to ask for a more detailed explanation of how the information created and transformed in business and government was used, how the work was done. Space would not permit me to satisfy that urge, but I have explained elsewhere in considerable detail industry by industry how that happened, focusing largely on the use of computing as the immediate tool compelling changes in information. I found few work processes that had not changed in the twentieth century, especially after the availability of computing in ever less expensive forms.[125]

With so many hundreds of millions of people using so many new facts, experts in information began to reflect on these developments, reverting to a practice of the STEM community of specializing. In the process they too created new forms of information about old interests, most notably economics and politics. In the next chapter we begin to explore their findings.

Chapter 8

What Information Economists Created

> *Even that amount of information which we have been able to derive so far was as much due to the application of our common-sense understanding of the modus operandi of our facts as it was to the facts themselves. The consequence of this is that we must now try, with a view of acquiring a more powerful apparatus of analysis, to refine upon our common-sense methods exactly as we must try to increase our stock of facts and to improve upon our statistical methods.*
>
> Joseph A. Schumpeter, 1939[1]

When following economic or business news, one is exposed to economists opining on all manner of topics. This has been the case for over a century. But the public has heard the old joke that starts with the question: What happens when you put ten economists in a room? You get eleven opinions. Or, did you know that economists have predicted nine of the last five recessions? For the public at large, it seemed so difficult to understand economics, even though physics, chemistry, and biology are arguably equally (or more) complex. Fewer people were exposed to formal economics training than to STEM topics, which is a possible explanation for the difference in perceptions. Economists are defensive and contend, as did John Maynard Keynes as early as 1922, that his discipline "does not furnish a body of settled conclusions immediately applicable to policy. It is a method rather than a doctrine" called "a technique of thinking, which helps its possessor to draw correct conclusions."[2] Nearly a century later, the answer was: "We have very little idea of how little we know."[3] Today economists and psychologists admit that economics is difficult, due to "the constraints of the human cognitive system."[4] That last remark may be an elegant way of saying people are not smart enough. Regardless, the topic is of sufficient interest to warrant this chapter.

But there is, too, another interpretation that affected directly the creation and use of information. Let an economist explain: "Individual researchers choose to work on one, or at most a few, among an astonishing variety of questions presented by the full range and diversity of modern economic life," as "each chooses to frame whatever is the chosen question in a particular way," such as picking assumptions, while "what evidence to bring to bear, among all the potentially relevant aspects of observable economic activity, is likewise a matter of choice." In other words, "economic analysis is a highly individualistic endeavor."[5] Another described the same process as "strategic selection designed to distil from the chaos of ordinary observation the kind of assumptions and variables which would, when deductively connected, shed a penetrating light on the main causal factors at work in a situation."[6] It was the plethora of economic data that encouraged such behavior over the past several centuries and now more evident in other social sciences in the twentieth century.

This chapter is necessary because economics has drawn lessons from science and management, extended the corpus of information and influenced how to study it, often funded or motivated by the agents discussed in the previous one. There is operations research (OR) and how it grew out of the necessities of World War II management. OR also came out of what scientists and economists had been studying since at least the days of Adam Smith in the eighteenth century. OR, economics, political science, and most recently, behavioral economics (which includes studying psychology) are stimulating a multi-disciplinary use of information. This practice is drawn from the more separated disciplines of old to form composite views of reality based on massive quantities of data and computer-driven analyses through the construct of models. Laced through all this work is that of economics.[7]

Our approach is similar to that in earlier chapters. I explore economics by introducing briefly the major topics of interest to many of the constituencies within the discipline, since these are the sources of information and how it was shaped since the nineteenth century. We introduce the work of representative stars of their profession and some of their informational milestones. Similar themes appear as well, such as increased amounts and diversity of data and insights, growing use of mathematics, reliance on computer-driven modeling, and attempts to apply scientific principles to decisions that in earlier times would have been made based on prior poorly articulated experience, rules of thumb, or ignorance. It also wrestles with the real problem in growing evidence in many disciplines—specialized jargon less known to those not working in the discipline. We could have discussed this issue in earlier chapters, particularly in the last one, but the problem can be explained more lucidly using economics as the example.

WHAT IS ECONOMICS?

Leaving aside the clever quotes from famous economists, at its most fundamental core, it is the study of how people and entire economies function. Economics is divided into two major subfields: macroeconomics and microeconomics. The first concentrates on the behavior of entire national, regional, or global economies, understanding such issues as the role of manufacturing, consumption of goods and services, investments, employment and unemployment, inflation, growth, savings, public policies, role of capital and such assets as land, buildings, machinery, and money, exploring how these behave, change, and why.[8] Within macroeconomics are located studies of economic growth of entire economies and nations, business cycles, the roles of unemployment, inflation, monetary policies, international economics, international trade, national economic development practices, and even labor practices (although also in microeconomics). Since the eighteenth century days of Adam Smith, the father of modern economics, the role of market competition has sat supreme as the discipline's "central conceptual apparatus." As one student of the process observed, "Much of the field's development since then has involved working out in greater depth and sophistication just how market competition work, and what consequences ensue when it fails to do so."[9]

Microeconomics looks at the narrower pieces of an economy, such as markets, industries, companies, individuals, households, professions, buyers, and sellers. This subfield also tries to understand how these behave, change, and why.[10] There are many specialized areas within each of these two, ranging from finance to health care, role of education and schools, family, politics, religion, science, war, environment, and social values. Within microeconomics one finds studies regarding production, costs, effectiveness, efficiencies, specialization, supply and demand, role of companies, game theory, market failures and successes, and activities of the public sector. Studies are also conducted that combine both subfields, borrowing from each other.

Economists explore entire economic systems and/or individual situations, but tend to favor studies of aggregate conditions, such as the role of information or effects of information technology on an economy, while non-economists might be more interested in, say, the role of IBM or Amazon. Aggregation is about rising above the role of individuals to understand in broader terms their behavior, such as that of entire or multiple high-technology industries, rather than the role of Apple and Google, for instance. They prefer to look at entire markets, or what drives the evolution of prices. They try, like scientists, to identify laws, such as the law of supply and demand, in this case, the hidden hand that the father of modern economics Adam Smith

(1723–1790) wrote about in the 1770s.[11] They look for cause and effects, which is where statistical analysis plays an important role.

Economists are extensive users of models and work diligently to include in them all or as many variables as possible that might influence economic behavior. They call these endogenous variables, whereas things that happen to any economic activity not accounted for are called exogenous variables, like the unpredicted tornado or more recently, the global pandemic.[12] This is an important point, because economists have published many thousands of papers showing what happens when variables are defined and acted upon. That is also a criticism often leveled that these are not "realistic," because in real life it is impossible to factor in all variables.[13] Ultimately, like scientists they look for theories and laws of behavior that are replicable or usable in understanding familiar situations. Practitioners in the physical sciences criticize economists for not being able to reach the level of certainties that they think scientists do when describing the physical realities found in physics, chemistry, and biology.[14] Economists use large data sets housed in digitized databases, running experiments and tests against them to explore the effects of hypotheses. They rely extensively on mathematics, even more so on statistics and such tools as regression analysis to quantify relative influences of specific attributes. In the process they create new information based on combinations of extant data, or create and test new collections of statistics. They build input–output models and rely on linear programming methods to push a great deal of data through a software model, say, to identify and quantify the effects—impact—of a government policy or market strategy.[15]

Let us return to criticisms because these can influence the kinds of information economists create. For example, their extensive use of mathematical models, long criticized outside their discipline, has led some economists to back off on their use and to look at actual historical realities, or to include in their analysis findings from information science and phycology since the 1980s that are now gaining currency.[16] Economic theories are often co-opted by political figures to justify their actions. Economists have long tried to influence national policies, such as John Maynard Keynes (1883–1946), in encouraging governments to take more proactive roles in governing an economy.[17] No national government in industrial economies would dare avoid appointing teams of economists to inform senior officials. While such actions are no different than when a scientist attempts to persuade national leaders to implement policies to alter the Earth's environmental condition or earlier in the 1950s and 1960s to reduce the public's consumption of tobacco, economists are criticized even within their ranks. One of my favorite economists, Deirdre McCloskey (b. 1942), has accused her profession of performing poor economics; others agreed.[18] The International Monetary Fund (IMF) examined the role of economists in predicting sixty recessions, and found they had only accurately predicted two of them one year in advance.[19] Such critiques brought into question the discipline's use of data and the quality of its findings that it proliferated through refereed articles and books intended for the general public.[20] However, economics remained highly mathematical, complex, and to the untrained, obtuse. In short, its informational foundations continued to be largely defined by theories and models for organizing facts for over a century.[21]

Other disciplines observed how economists worked as tests of their own practices. For our purposes, it is more important to call out the problems seen as a caution not a condemnation: use of unrealistic or unverifiable data, overly simple assumptions, and hypotheses that are stacked in favor of a desired outcome. These issues even have names: perfect information, profit maximization, rational choices, and so forth.[22] There has long been a debate about the balance between the use of qualitative factors and hard data (numbers).[23] One response has been the flourishing of psychologically influenced behavioral economics, often popularly known as Freakonomics, discussed more fully in the following, that integrated new collections of data and disciplines into economics, again altering the nature of its information.[24] So, we have the odd situation where the public and other disciplines want economic insights, but without all the details that economists are wont to wallow in, and yet be able to read their work too. For most people this is a challenge, even when an economist makes a sincere effort to speak to the "rest of us" in non-technical language.

EVOLUTION IN ECONOMIC THEORY AND INFORMATION

Economists have a long history of individual members of their discipline and later groups of them adhering to the ideas of one or more economists as to how to develop, exercise, and promote ways of understanding economic behavior. That is why so many theories or "schools of thought" are tied to the work of an individual. Economic history is often presented as a history of successive introductions of new theories, such as Marxian Economics, Marshallian Economics, or Neoclassical Economics, and within each are celebrity economists, ranging from Adam Smith to Karl Marx (1818–1883), from Keynes to today's luminaries. Along the way a remarkably large number of economists shaped their discipline, with the majority crowding history's pages since the mid-1800s.

While this is not the book in which to tell their story (others have done that), it is the place to make two observations. First, when a new economic theory and convincing evidence in support of it surfaced, those insights and data could be scaled up and distributed quickly through publications, later by training economists, and even later by using computers. That portability of ideas and data made it possible for economic thinking to spread widely, often uniformly and at the same time across the discipline. It is a pattern evident in STEM disciplines too. That did not mean uniform acceptance of new information, but it did imply that strongly held beliefs formed about how information should be received and be dealt with.[25]

Second, some economists and schools of thought stimulated changes to the information one used in economics and, thus, to the way one used and studied it. To help shed light on how economics affected information since the start of the Second Industrial Revolution I look at several developments: evolution of classical economics in the nineteenth century, by briefly examining the thinking of Alfred Marshall (1842–1924) and William S. Jevons (1835–1882); expansion in the use of econometrics (mathematics) in economics in the twentieth century through the work of Joseph A. Schumpeter (1883–1950) and his colleagues; rise of informational economics, and end with a short discussion of behavioral economics. Our approach leaves out much about such topics as the specifics of prices, values, finances, role of innovation and technology, games, such classroom themes as product and resource markets, role of government, growth strategies, money and banking, and so forth.

But, recognize that every theme added to the overall pool of economic information in the form of theories of how things worked, raw data and analyzed information in vast quantities, and in ways that ranged from narrative text (the nineteenth-century manner of communicating) to today's often highly mathematized jargon-riddled papers. Findings had a cumulative effect on the discipline because as one student of its history, Mark Blaug, pointed out, "Contemporary theory wears the scars of yesterday's problems now resolved, yesterday's blunders now corrected, and [sic] cannot be fully understood except as a legacy handed down from the past." He reminded us that "there is a mutual interaction between past and present economic thinking."[26] Long before the mid-nineteenth century, where I start our discussion, what information should be included in economic discussions came from such luminaries as John Locke, David Hume, Adam Smith, Edmund Burke, David Ricardo, John Stuart Mill, Karl Marx, and Henry George. That is an impressive list that includes some of the most important thinkers about all manner of information and disciplines in Western society since the eighteenth century.

Neoclassical Economics' Influence on Economic Information

As European and American economies were transforming into industrializing forms in the 1800s, new perspectives regarding economics were needed. A large coterie of economists emerged that in time articulated variations of earlier economic theories, their work becoming known as "neoclassical economics." They began their efforts in the 1860s and extended their work deep into the next century. Sub-schools appeared too, such as the Austrian school of economics and Anglo-American neoclassical economics. These narrower perspectives later identified with specific academic departments, most spectacularly the "University of Chicago School," which referred to its Department of Economics. Its members garnered more Nobel Prizes in Economics in the twentieth century than any other.[27] Recipients were well known to scholars in other disciplines, also to public officials and business management, and their awards were always front page news in the media. The reason for dwelling on their celebrity is that they increasingly attracted public and professional attention. As that happened, people who were not economists encountered their work, if ever so superficially, sensitizing them to the existence of economic information and to topics they might not have considered exploring. In the second half of the twentieth century some economists became best-selling authors, such as Milton Friedman, John K. Galbraith, and most recently the *New York Times* columnist Paul Krugman.

The new generation of post-1860 Europe and America followed earlier colleagues in exploring the implications of the changing economy as nations industrialized and appropriated new technologies and science, increasingly describing new sources of economic value. Early leaders in that effort included French mathematician turned economist Léon Walras (1834–1910) and the most publicly recognized William Stanley Jevons (1835–1882), an English economist and "logician." Walras argued that economics was a science, much like physics or chemistry, hence more precise in its findings and subject to the disciplines of scientific methods of research. He sought "pure truths" in economics, in what later came to be known as theoretical economics.[28] Jevons did the same, arguing if economics is to be a hard science, it had to be mathematical. Only then could it focus on its true concern: quantities. Historians give Jevons the greater nod over Walrus and other early advocates for starting the mathematical methods phase of economics, because in 1862 he published his study, *A General Mathematical Theory of Political Economy*.[29] Such an approach required understanding "the mechanics of utility and self-interest," new topics for a new age. These economists began to nudge economic information into more abstract forms expressed in mathematical terms (equations), giving their conversations what economist Mariana Mazzucato characterized as "based on Newtonian physics."[30]

Their notions focused on the reproduction, exchange, and income distribution that occur in an economy. They introduced such new concepts as "marginal utility," which continued as a more than a century-long discussion about how economies created value. Marginal utility explains how income was the reward for economically productive activities. Most influential by the dawn of the twentieth century, British economist Alfred Marshall applied his training as mathematician to describe how economics worked. He was the giant of his age, and his 1890 text, *Principles of Economics*, in its first edition was 750 pages in length, and subsequent editions 870 pages. His work shaped the thinking of several generations of economists.[31]

He relied on calculus, for example, to understand how marginal change in one variable affected changes in others, such as how a price change influenced demand for a product.[32] Prices became attractive to study; how these behaved spun off a large body of new information in the next century. He and his cohorts launched what came to be known as the neoclassical school of economics. A twenty-first-century economist explains: "Microeconomic theory, the theory of how firms, workers and consumers make choices, is based on the neoclassical theory of production and consumption which rests on the maximization of profits (firms), and utility (consumers and workers)."[33] Even in her language one sees demonstrated a second attribute of the new economic information of the age: different vocabulary that is standard fair in economics—firms and utility.

Marshall demonstrated through use of mathematics a convincing case—theory—that when money was worth more (or the same) to a consumer than a commodity, then an economy could be characterized as in "equilibrium," much like Newton thought that gravity held together the Earth. Systems could be in balance along the peaceful curves of equilibrium and evolution. As Marshall advised a student, "Use mathematics as shorthand language, rather than as an engine of inquiry." He also advised that explanations be enhanced with examples "important in real life," then "burn the mathematics."[34] While Marshall used mathematics to study the economics of supply and demand, marginal utility, and costs of production as an integrated whole, he did not want his calculations to dominate the conversation. We can consider him, therefore, a transitional figure in the use of economic information, because when econometrics became fashionable, any reticence he had on the matter was swept aside by others, although not appreciation for his contributions.

It seemed that almost every economics paper published in the twentieth century had to include a section on methodology, that is to say, how authors did their mathematical and statistical calculations and to discuss the numerical sources of their data that they analyzed. It was not uncommon, and contrary to Marshall's advice, that more than half of a paper was devoted to these two topics. That behavior encouraged the use of discipline-specific language. It spilled over also into shorthand for aligning a paper with a specific school of economics.

His intellectual legacy remained rock solid and passed on to two other great economists of the next century, Arthur Cecil Pigou (1877–1959) and

John Maynard Keynes. Marshall's legacy was less about the use of mathematics anyway and more about continuing the exploration of how economics could be understood and appropriated to improve material conditions through social and political means. He had trained as a philosopher, excelled in mathematics, and always maintained an interest in improving the lot of people. More than any of his contemporaries, he moved economics into the realm of a respected scholarly discipline.

The most influential economists of the next century followed his lead; many others however, never burned their mathematics. Many were able to add to the body of information about how to measure utility.[35] Economists injected tables and calculations into their publications and lectures, hypotheses, and theories. More narrative explanations of how an economy worked so common in the eighteenth and early nineteenth centuries gave way to new forms of communicating and bodies of numeric data and graphs.[36]

We take it for granted that graphs help to communicate complex ideas. Marshall understood this and is remembered for one in particular: the first supply and demand graph used by an economist (figure 8.1). His comment next to the graph spoke of it as "this may be taken as the typical diagram for stable equilibrium for a commodity that obeys the law of diminished returns."[37] It became a graph used by economists over the next century to illustrate the basic features of both demand and supply by using curves to discuss market equilibriums, relationships between quantities and prices, even his law of marginal utility, another law of diminishing returns, and the

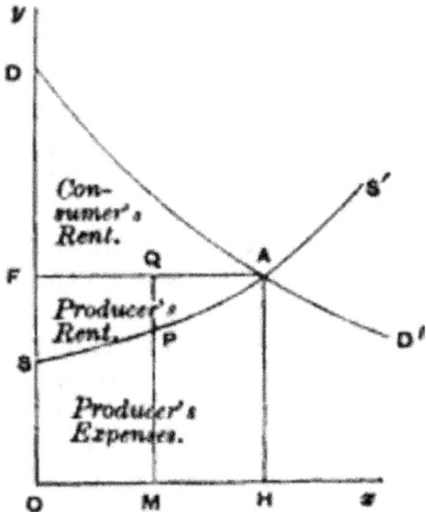

Figure 8.1. Alfred Marshall's Supply and Demand Graph, 1895. *Source:* Alfred Marshall, *Principles of Economics* (London: Macmillan, 1895).

222   Chapter 8

role of consumer and producer surpluses. These were ideas whose relationships to each other were—are—complex. Graphs helped to clarify issues. He also practiced what he preached. In his opus Marshall segregated his calculations to an appendix at the end of the book, devoting the body of his text to explanatory narrative.[38] His graph encouraged generations of future economists to do the same.

An Economic View of Information

Before proceeding further, I offer a brief interlude to summarize how an economist describes data. To begin with, they use terms such as data, information, and knowledge. More often the last term was in evidence during the 1800s and early 1900s; today both data and information dominate their vocabulary. Information—data—have several economic features. First, it is non-rival, which means many individuals can use the same data without that supply of information declining. Who owns it is irrelevant to the idea. Second, data varies in whether it is excludable, which is what makes it a *public good* about which we will discuss later. This feature means anyone can use it, especially if it is easy to get it, such as from the Internet, a database, or by checking a book out of their library. Third, in the language of the economist, information involves externalities, which usually means its usefulness (value) increases when it is combined with other data. Fourth, information can have increasing or decreasing returns, which means that sometimes having more makes it all more useful (valuable), while at other times more does not make it more valuable. Fifth, again in the language of the economist, information has a large option value, which means it is difficult to predict how its value might change, when new issues, data, technologies, or circumstances intervene. Sixth, collecting information is expensive if you have upfront costs, such as computers or point-of-sale terminals in a store, but then is subsequently far less expensive to collect, and for that matter, to distribute, such as when I copy you on a digital file that I already owned. Seventh, using information calls for investments that cost more, such as computers, software, or trained users.[39] These seven features would have held in the mid-twentieth century as much as in the 2020s.

Additionally, there are other characteristics of interest to economists that bubble up from other disciplines, such as data science. These include knowing what the information is about, how general purpose it is, what temporal value it possesses, what is its quality and sensitivity, and how easy it is to work with.[40] All were issues economists began thinking about when they turned to mathematics and statistics to work through how best to deal with these features of information.

Econometrics and Mathematizing Economic Information

The history of how information was shaped involved people in pivotal situations invariably with unusual backgrounds. John Dewey promoted his library cataloging system as a business entrepreneur, not knowing that it would become the de facto way to organize vast quantities of information and entire libraries all over the world. Claude E. Shannon wrote a paper that he probably thought only a telecommunications engineer could love, let alone understand. Yet today it is recognized as one of the foundational documents of twentieth-century science, even cited by media people when they talk about data "noise" and "signals." In each instance—and there are many more one could call out—all the incremental activities, new types of information, different ways to organize it, and then use it required someone to pull it together into some structure that lent itself to wide acceptance. The variety of ways that happened—often the subject of diffusion conversations in most disciplines—need not detain us here, except when it concerns the specifics of a subject we are studying.

Economists had many seminal people, we meet two more of them now, one a visionary who shaped economic research practices for decades, Ragnar Frisch (1895–1973), and the far more colorful promoter who many economists think did his best intellectual work before the age of forty but today is considered an inspired economist by technologists of all stripes, Joseph A. Schumpeter (1883–1950). The first was Norwegian-born, the second a socially upper-class Austrian; both ended up teaching in the United States before World War II.[41] Since it is virtually impossible to think of twentieth-century economics without conjuring the images of algebraic equations and statistical acrobatics, and since, too, mathematical practices in economics spilled into social science disciplines, including recently history and languages, we need to probe deeper into this story. It is the confluence of mathematics, statistics, and economic theory on the information side and on the other a few leaders that set the entire discipline on this course. This behavior was similarly replicated in other disciplines of their day and in subsequent decades in new fields. Essentially, this behavior involved individuals creating new types of information, gaining and embracing a disciplinary identity (as physicists did and librarians tried to do), formed professional and academic associations, then published discipline-specific scholarly journals. In the process they embraced common research strategies, theories, and ways of working.[42]

In the late 1800s and early 1900s numerous economists increasingly turned to mathematics to buttress and confirm their theories and observations.[43] In the process they began to appreciate that mathematics and statistics were improving their skills in applying logic in their thinking. Irving Fisher

(1867–1947) was one of the first American neoclassical economists and in his day a giant in his field, led[44] him in 1941 to acknowledge that "Edgeworth and Pareto, more than any other writers, by linking the three subjects of economics, statistics, and mathematics virtually founded what is now called econometrics."[45] Before that merger a movement was underway to create what was called "synthetic economics," which involved the application of simultaneous equations to reflect consensus in the exchange, production, capitulation, and distribution activities in an economy; use of mathematics to understand the dynamics of a series of variables in a problem dealt with as functions of time; and buttressing equations with specific statistical forms. Henry L. Moore (1869–1958), who was involved in that movement, characterized it as "both deductive and inductive; dynamic, positive, and concrete."[46]

But such activities were not enough. Calls for further integration of methods floated in the air, and Fisher was breathing that new oxygen. A handful of economists banded together to form The Econometric Society in 1930, largely through the leadership of Irving Fisher and Ragnar Frisch (1895–1973), and their launch of a journal, *Econometrica*, in 1933, which continues to publish today. This organization and its journal became focal points for promoting what came to be known then as now as econometrics. By the end of the 1990s, the journal appeared six times annually in some 1600 pages. In 1933 it launched with four annual issues and barely 112 pages in total that year for an initial membership of less than 200 souls. It had 3,000 subscriptions by 1960.[47] We must plow deeper into its activities because, as one economist/historian proclaimed: "The Econometric Society is the most prestigious learned society in the field of economics." Its first editor for many years (Frisch from 1933 to 1954) joined with Jan Tinbergen (1903–1994) to become the first recipients of the Nobel Prize in economics in 1969. Fourteen of this society's presidents were so recognized by the end of the century, including such well-known figures as Kenneth J. Arrow, Lawrence Klein, Paul Samuelson, and Robert Solow, among others, while a recent editor of *Econometrica*, Angus Deaton, too, in 2015. In the prior year, the society's president from 1998, Jean Tirole, received the Nobel Prize.

Establishment of this society and its journal opens a window into how information evolved in the modern era. Irving Fisher, acknowledged as the key founder of the society and journal, which he established in his living room with colleagues in 1930, looked back on his many decades as an economist in 1941. He observed that in 1890, while a graduate student at Yale University, he was already interested in the role of mathematics in economics—referred to at the time as "mathematical economics"—when few even had considered the concept. Fisher argued that it "was almost as much on the defensive as it had been for the two proceeding decades since Jevons and Walrus pled for it."[48] Few economists even had a working knowledge of mathematics. By

1941, Fisher was able to opine that "mathematical economics is no longer cold-shouldered; and no longer needs defense."[49] Yet he still felt the need to argue the case for mathematizing economics, especially for the study of supply and demand, determination of prices, about the effects of taxes and tariffs on prices, and the intricate theory of income. "Familiarity with mathematics will save many confusions of thought," pointing out that "it is just as important in economics to distinguish between a high price and a rising price as it is in physics to distinguish between velocity and acceleration."[50] As other earlier users of numbers also liked to point out, statistics, too, were needed, such as in the study of correlations. Fisher declared that the correlation coefficient has "become almost a standard procedure in economic statistics as well as in other sciences, including biology."[51] He added that the study of probability, prediction (forecast in business), and population studies needed statistics too. Establishment of the Econometric Society forced economics and statistics into a "mated team working in harness."[52]

He ended his recollections citing examples of statistics and mathematics used in sociology and political science, among various social sciences as corroborating evidence of the value of mathematical/statistical approaches. This was early evidence, too, for students of information's history that disciplines peeked over their back fences to learn new ways to do their work.

He summed up the problem of getting the field to adopt these two numerical sets of skills: "I have already referred to the resistance of old-fashioned economists to the intrusion of mathematicians. I think it is also true that the old-fashioned statistician opposed the mathematical invasion of his domain as did the old-fashioned biologist his. Conversely, perhaps strangely, mathematicians have often rebelled against their clan going far afield into the realms of thought," with some advocating for their field to remain "pure."[53] As cautioned in earlier chapters, the move from one form of information to another met resistance. Change did not occur without effort. So, what was the move?

In the first issue of *Econometrica* the question was answered, and then re-answered repeatedly over the years, usually in anniversary articles on the history of the journal.[54] The lead article in the first issue was written by Joseph Schumpeter. He was a successful, if controversial, economist who in the 1930s had taken a position teaching at Harvard University. Socially affable, in today's terms we would describe him as a great networker, because he knew "everyone" in his field, was charming, and could persuade people to come together. He joined Fisher and Frisch to put together their society in Fisher's living room. In describing the purpose of the journal, Schumpeter said their credo was simply "that economics is a science," and "that this science has one very important quantitative aspect." This aspect was not a "school" of thinking: "Much of what we want to know about economic phenomena can be discovered and stated without any technical, let alone mathematical, refinements upon ordinary modes of thought, and without elaborate treatment of statistical figures."[55] But he then pointed out that "some of the most fundamental economic facts," contrary to some other disciplines, "present themselves to our observation as quantities made numerical by life itself. They carry meaning by virtue of their numerical character."[56] That meant "econometrics is nothing but the explicit recognition of this rather obvious fact, and the attempt to face the consequences of it."[57]

He observed the best economists displayed "a remarkably mathematical turn of mind," although it is curious that Schumpeter himself, while always interested in promoting the use of mathematics in economics, did not practice what he preached.[58] He quoted Jevons from an 1871 publication—from over fifty years earlier—that "it is clear that Economics, if it is to be a science at all, must be a mathematical one."[59] As of the 1930s, Schumpeter therefore observed that "reasoning on economic facts means, and always meant, within a very important sector, quantitative reasoning."[60] The journal was established to facilitate the "discussions of concrete problems of a quantitative and, as far as may be, numerical character."[61] "Our aims are first and last scientific," because "for as long as we are unable to put our arguments into figures, the voice of our science, although occasionally it may help to dispel gross errors, will never be heard by practical men. They are, by instinct, econometricians all of them, in their distrust of anything not amenable to exact proof."[62] As in so many other disciplines, a new era had already dawned in the nature of information.[63]

From the beginning and periodically thereafter, the journal discussed the methodology for the preparations of refereed articles. These statements, simple and short as they were, give us other signposts of how a discipline became increasingly the producers of quantitatively oriented papers, following long-standing practices established in the hard sciences. For one thing, the original mission and purpose of the journal did not change. Here is its statement from 1980, fifty years after the founding of the society: "The Econometric Society is an international society for the advancement of economy theory in its relation to statistics and mathematics," and "its main object is to promote studies that aim at the unification of the theoretical-quantitative and the empirical-quantitative approach to economic problems and that are penetrated by constructive and rigorous thinking."[64] While it insisted that papers be readable across the entire discipline, an objective one might question whether it was always achieved if being judged by a non-economist, nonetheless the journal called for the reader being told why the results reported were important.

Clearly, tension had lingered for a long time between economists with mathematical skills and those without. As early as 1931, Fisher had suggested that the early issues of the journal be short but also provide "enough non-technical and non-mathematical connective tissue to sustain the interest of our non-mathematical members," many of whom would "gradually begin to read more technical material and, once interested, they can be led to put in more and more time upon technical articles."[65] In time his insight paid off and the journal grew in page length, number of issues, and influence. By the 1960s, most economists were facile with mathematics; by the end of the 1970s it was even difficult to find an economic history professor in any history department unable to deal with numbers.[66]

But even from its earliest days, the journal's organizers needed to do more than plead for good writing; there seemed a need to also explain when and where to apply mathematics. Writing in 1947, one economist from Columbia University, John M. Clark (1884–1963), explained that there were three areas in which mathematics could prove useful:

> The first is the study of relations between tangible aggregates in the economy at large. Here mathematics is at its best, verification is the most nearly practicable, and the difficulties of other methods are at their greatest. The second is the analysis of business reactions, assumed to be directed to maximizing profits. Here the assumption is indefinite in meaning, involving arbitrary limitations on the business man's expectations of consequences, which involve logical dilemmas, and involving also simplification of the environmental conditions. It is also seriously incomplete as an explanation of actual business behavior. The third is the analysis of individuals' choices between qualitatively different values, typically via indifference curves. Here the attempt to avoid psychology excludes major parts of the essential problem, while the remaining psychological implications, minimal as they attempt to be, are sufficient to do violence to the character of economic choices.[67]

Clark had a reputation for conducting rigorous economic analysis so the right person to lecture colleagues on the role and way of using mathematics in economics. But he did not stop with the three problems, he went to the heart of the matter: "The essence of mathematics, as a logical process, consisted in rigorous definition of terms and a deliberately pedestrian inclusion of all the steps. And this is necessary to one who would verify the results of particular studies, without having followed the entire development of them in the literature, during which the initiated have become accustomed to taking many things for granted."[68]

Any competent scholar would also remind us that exogenous forces were at work, followed consequentially by endogenous ones, too. What might those have been? Joseph J. Spengler (1902–1991), an economist, also a statistician and historian, may have provided the answer in 1961, at a time when not only had econometrics become well established, but was actually coming to dominate research and explanatory styles in economics with its emphasis on the use of mathematics and statistics. Let him explain: "The progress in quantification in economics, as in other social sciences, was conditioned by the availability of data and hence by the magnitude of the economic role assumed by the state, together with the amount of data purportedly required to fulfill this role."[69] Until recently, he noted, the social sciences did not have much data to work with, so had to do so with whatever was available. Availability of numeric data, thus, helped shape the nature of how researchers in multiple fields worked and the nature of their studies.[70]

Economic Information Goes Public

The world learned about the benefits and dangers of more active government involvement in national economies beginning in World War I and through both the Great Depression and World War II. All three major events drew officials into greater involvement in guiding their national economies. Right behind them came the economists to advise them on how best this should be done.[71] So, it should be of no surprise that leading economists opined on the role of data—information—in informing public economic policy. That role provides additional insights into the changing nature of economic information in the post-war period. Kenneth J. Arrow (1921–2017) provides a window into these discussions in his presidential address delivered to the Econometric Society in 1956.[72] An American who did his graduate work in economics at Columbia University, Arrow was an economist in the neoclassical heritage and a long-serving professor at Stanford University, later at Harvard University. His undergraduate degree was in mathematics from the City College of New York. A few years after making his presidential speech he had the opportunity to help implement his ideas when he served on the staff of the Council of Economic Advisors in the 1960s with Robert Solow.[73]

In his speech in 1956, Arrow stressed the importance of economic policy being linked to the use of economic statistics, because "the marginal productivity of investment in statistical information is very high in all countries," especially for those governments that have assumed "primary responsibility for economic growth."[74] He was talking about decision problems faced by officials, each possessing four features: "(a) an *objective function* which indicates the relative desirability of different possible outcomes; (b) a range of policy alternatives, or *instruments* . . . among which the decision-maker (the government in this case) must choose; (c) the *model*, which specifies the empirical relations connecting the instruments, the variables entering the objective function, and other relevant variables; and (d) the *computational methods* by which the decision-maker chooses the values of the instruments so as to maximize the objective function subject to the conditions implied by the model."[75] Arrow's own work on how all this applied led him to argue that public policies had two characteristics: they were sequential and uncertain.

The first refers to actions and consequences that unfold over time and the second to the fact that predictions of outcomes remain imperfect, in other words, inaccurate, unknowable. After a discourse on the nature of sequential time, data is needed, arguing that if one had "sufficiently detailed" information, one could "make a reasonably good forecast of the effects of alternative policies in the short run."[76] Today one assumes that the most major public policy decisions in the "advanced economies" are made based on using models and data, but not so in 1956.

With respect to computational information we see the introduction of practices in the use of data in later years: "Because of the impossibility of giving explicit solutions to any computational problem above the trivial level, we need a system of signals for correcting mistakes. We may have to assume that the government will guess at a policy . . . and watch some observed variable for suggestions for change." Economic analysis could allow for such behavior, with signals including how supply and demand unfolded, the same with monetary and fiscal policies, for example. Computing can help to speed up the analysis and that requires accumulating economic enumerations that can "serve as benchmarks."[77]

However, "too much energy has gone into squeezing the last bit of juice out of old data collected for different purposes relative to the design of new types of data." Arrow suggested that officials "start new time series even though it may be many years before enough observations accumulate to make analysis worthwhile." In the meanwhile, cross-sectional studies could be conducted, such as engineering studies to understand the "structure of production" or "panel studies of income" (about people's income over time).[78] But his conclusion reflected why so many governments invested in data collection agencies for over a century: "In view of an economic system, it would take only a very small percentage of improvement in economic stability or growth to make almost any conceivable data collection worthwhile. The situation is analogous to the reported results of the use of linear programming in industry; the gains are small in proportion to previous profit levels but still very much larger than the cost of the programming." But at the moment, "No country is adequate in respect to its data."[79] Over six decades later, economists were still defending the value of governments affecting economies based on sound economic information.[80]

Beyond academic discussions, such as that took place within the pages of *Econometrica*, economists and statisticians were applying their new information in business and government, and no place did this seem to generate more economic data than in countries like Great Britain, France, and the United States, particularly in the post–World War I era. In chapter 7 we saw that government agencies created vast quantities of new economic data, much of it statistical, such as counting populations, number of businesses by type, and revenue flowing through an economy.[81] But that is not the same as the kind of information added to those collections during the twentieth century when governments employed economists who plied their trade to inform citizens, companies, and public officials. Obvious cases from the United States, for example, include the Federal Reserve regional banks, each specialized in specific aspects of economic behavior, published white papers; and the U.S. Departments of Commerce, Labor, and Agriculture that also did similar work. Within these departments economists were embedded for decades, and in some instances, for over a century.

These economists, statisticians, and their agencies shared common features. Those plying the economist's trade were trained by the professors doing the types of research that appeared in such journals as *Econometrica*. Many American Nobel Prize winners taught generations of government economists and served in government roles themselves, as on the Council of Economic Advisors within the Executive Office of the American president since 1946. Its most widely known deliverable was empirical research results published annually as the *Economic Report of the President*.[82]

Government economists became some of the most relied-upon sources for economic data and analysis for some now over a century. To set aside a possible confusion, the Bureau of the Census, one of the oldest data collection agencies in the American government, was a statistics-gathering enterprise, not the producer of economic analysis. Agencies that did economics included the Bureau of Labor Statistics (BLS) and the Bureau of Economic Analysis (BEA), among others. We will visit both.

The missions of various bureaus and departments called for them to publish their findings, which they did through in-house journals, such as the widely circulated *Monthly Labor Review* published by the BLS since 1915, which had a circulation of some 20,000 by 1920, far more today.[83] These agencies served as intellectually rigorous sources of economics, normally reflecting the academic standards of the profession. Their contributions to the shaping of information in modern times lay in their extensive application of new economic principles and sources of statistics and methods to such an extent that the use of such information by others across industries, firms, and government became routine, habitual, and codified. Without these agencies and their practices, economic insights might have remained corralled within the economists' discipline unknown outside their circle, let alone comprehensible.

The BLS focuses largely on labor economics. It assembles statistics on this topic for use by academic, business economists, and other government agencies (including the U.S. Congress).[84] It is one of the oldest such agencies, established in 1880 as the Bureau of Labor, then restructured as the BLS in 1884. The BLS focused its attention on the collection and statistical analysis of data concerning jobs, employment, and such other family dynamics as marriage, divorce, and, for a while, temperance. Later its staff studied the economic dynamics of wages, cost of living, hours worked, prices for goods and services, and union activities. Much as the quantitative economists, BLS's cohort applied quantitative methods in their studies of social and economic problems. They became a major source of information on price indices, beginning in 1902, launching its move into the realm of tracking and analyzing current economic trends.[85]

By the turn of the twenty-first century, BLS was publishing a series of statistics often in tandem with research findings based on two dozen topics. Some of the most widely known included the Consumer Expenditure Survey (CE), Consumer Price Index (CPI), Current Employment Statistics (CES), and the Producer Price Index (PPI). Almost echoing the concerns of nineteenth- and early-twentieth-century librarians and academics, BLS developed various classification systems for its data that shaped its statistical and economic practices. It established consistent data that could be compared to each other and to those of different periods. Its most widely appreciated classification system involved the agency's industry classification, which evolved over time as new industries emerged, dropping old ones (e.g., chewing gum industry) and adding new ones (e.g., satellite telecommunication industry). Originally created in the 1930s, it became known as the Standard Industrial Classification (SIC) system, around which massive bodies of data and studies were subsequently conducted inside and outside of BLS.[86] Another included an international version called NAICS (North American Industry Classification System), others for occupation, workplace injuries and illnesses, and expenditures on goods and services, among others. The BLS created an appetite for multi-year multi-decade trend analyses drawn from these consistent collections of information, now considered routine and common in economics.[87]

To illustrate the link between data and analysis, look at any issue of the *Monthly Labor Review*.[88] I did that while writing the first draft of this chapter, examining the April 2020 issue. It contained rigorously prepared data-rich articles on "Consumer Expenditure Survey Methods," "Estimating Variances for Modeled Wage Estimates," "Fatal Occupational Injuries to Older Workers," and testimonial evidence of its long-term participation in the economics ecosystem with an article on "70 Years of the Occupational Outlook Handbook." This last article is about the primary source used by the media, politicians, or business leaders when they want to opine on future jobs.[89]

Then there is the Bureau of Economic Analysis (BEA), which can be thought of as an economist's dream gift shop full of useful data and analysis. Like similar agencies within the World Bank, the International Monetary Fund (IMF), and the Organization for Economic Co-operation and Development (OECD), it gathers data, applies statistical analysis to these, and conducts rigorous economic research, making results available to the public.[90] The American government had been collecting information about commerce as early as 1820 and, long story short, in 1866 formed the Bureau of Statistics to collect information about commerce and trade, and so forth. More reorganizations later, it had added additional streams of data related to the nation's economy, including statistics and analyses on national income in the early 1930s. Such later efforts informed New Deal economic recovery programs and assisted companies and their industry associations conduct routine but better-informed business planning and forecasting.[91]

BEA made important, although not glamorous, contributions to twentieth-century information. It conditioned its constituents to accept data in standardized layouts, such as tables that it consistently produced and updated. It created appetites for specific types of information, most famously the GDP (gross domestic product), which quickly became one of the most valued sources of information about the economy.[92] Before we turn our attention to further discussion of the GDP, note that the BEA in its current form (as of 1972) was seen as part of the American government's economic ecosystem, reporting into the Economics and Statistical Administration within the U.S. Department of Commerce. While its primary mission is to gather statistics on the national economy, how BEA organized and presented these helped shape what economists knew about modern economics.

Central to the organization of economic information is its organization of national accounts that presents data on production, consumption, investment, exports and imports, and incomes and savings. From this data its staff creates summary information, such as the GDP, and other summaries of corporate profits, personal income and spending, savings by individuals, government expenditures, value of fixed assets, and data on the net worth of the American economy. When one reads that the U.S. economy is, say, $22.32 trillion in size (just prior to the start of the pandemic in 2020), that figure originated in the BEA, so too that this economy was the largest in the world.[93] In addition to a set of National Economic Accounts, it produces similar data sets for industries (Industry Economic Accounts), for International Economic Accounts, and yet another called Regional Economic Accounts.[94] Thus, it produces GDP by industry and by state and metropolitan areas. Its international data includes such key items as balance of payments, trade statistics, investment positions, and activities of multinational enterprises. While some of these classes of information date to the early 1800s (e.g., trade with foreign countries) others were new to the twentieth century, such as the GDP.[95]

As did its sister statistical agencies, BEA embraced economic practices to express its worldviews. It developed skills for expressing its points of view and finding in clear non-technical language aimed at audiences not trained in economics. For example, in 2015, in terms aimed at the larger public that one could understand without a grounding in economics, it explained that if one thought of an economy as solely consisting of businesses and individuals, then "individuals provide the labor that enables businesses to produce products and services," but, "alternatively, one can think of these transactions in terms of monetary flows that occur. Businesses provide individuals with income (in the form of compensation) in exchange for their labor. That labor, in turn, spent on the goods and services businesses produce."[96] While Fisher, Solow, and others might find such statements incredibly elementary, they set the context for what data the BEA collected and organized and why sufficiently intelligible to audiences bigger than Fisher and his contemporaries could otherwise reach.

Notions of "input" and "output" were crucial to the thinking of its economists and statisticians. These led to such practices, say with GDP data, that "includes market production and some nonmarket production," that "whenever possible, GDP is valued at market prices," that "is equal to the value of goods and services for 'final' users, and that GDP should be measured in multiple ways (e.g., sum of expenditures or purchases by final users, sum of all these charges, total sales less value of intermediate inputs or totals of "value added" at each stage of production)." Other criteria shaping GDP data also existed, such as the requirement that it "captures output produced in the United States," and that it be considered a "gross measure."[97] BEA published studies dealing with its economic and statistical practices and frameworks, others on its statistical estimating methods and sources of data, a series of publications on chained-dollar indexes, quantities, pricing, and on the reliability of its data sets and methods.[98]

GDP as Emblematic of Widely Distributed Economic Information

Because GDP provides an additional window into how economic data was shaped and used, it deserves additional attention here. To quote an economist, "GDP is the way we measure and compare how well or badly countries are doing." But too, "GDP is a made-up entry."[99] Another pointed out, "It is crucial to remember that all types of accounting methods are evolving social conventions, defined not by physical laws and definite 'realities' but reflecting the ideas, theories and ideologies of the age in which they are devised."[100] GDP fits into this circumstance. It was created in the 1940s during World War II, built out of the harsh economic experiences of the 1930s. By the twenty-first century, its formulation and use was the subject of political controversy, because officials used it to inform national and international economic policies that affected the lives of individuals and whole groups. While here is not the place to engage with such issues, it is to offer up that the subject of distinguishing between productive and unproductive economic activities has been of concern to economists since Adam Smith, affecting the nature of economic information. Until the neoclassical economists came into prominence, economists thought of a national economy as comprising its material production. Then, the thinking evolved. Alfred Marshall, for example, in 1890, set aside that productive/unproductive model in favor of one that combined material and "personal non-material wealth," in other words, services as part of what constituted national income. The definition of "national income," hence was not a fixed formula. Economists picked up from where Marshall left off and filled in details, such as the effects of inflation and distribution of income across groups. The demand for hard economic data during the Great Depression of the 1930s had increased interest in such activities.

Simon Kuznets (1901–1985) meticulously created new bodies of statistics, publishing his first figures in 1934, which demonstrated that the national economy had shrunk by half between 1929 and 1932.[101] Kuznets would eventually be recognized for this work with a Nobel Prize in economics. But more immediately, the American government used that data to craft recovery strategies. The call for broader sets of data increased during the 1930s and to a debate that one economist, Dine Coyle, described as boiling down to, "What was the meaning of economic growth and why were statisticians measuring it?"[102] The short answer was so that governments could use economic insight to devise fiscal policies. In 1942, American GDP statistics went public. It distinguished between types of expenditures, business taxes and depreciation, and crucially added government's economic role (expenditures) into the equation, which "made Keynesian macroeconomic theory the fundamental basis of how governments ran their economies in the postwar era."[103]

Coyle described the accounting in crafting the GDP as "the sum of all spending in the economy" and that had to "add up to all incomes in the economy," so had to include "income from employment, from self-employment, from dividends and interest, business profits, income from overseas, and so on."[104] Since these pieces of information were collected from various data sets, in practice they did not always fit neatly together, but to use an old American phrase, were "good enough for government work." The perceived fuzziness of the measure encouraged debate about its meaning and relevance just as the winds of change and priorities in the world of economics did too, such as with the growing interest in the value of information or the perception that we now worked in a "knowledge economy."

So, what does the GDP look like today? Figures 8.2 and 8.3 come directly from the BEA, in this instance from 2019 to 2020. The reason for presenting several figures from just one set of the many thousands of measures assembled by government agencies around the world is to illustrate several changes that occurred to information in the twentieth century. Each represents an aggregate of many collections of statistics, which, in turn, were

What Information Economists Created   235

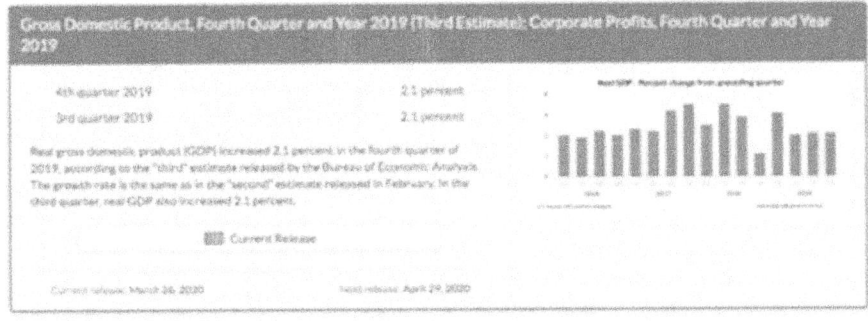

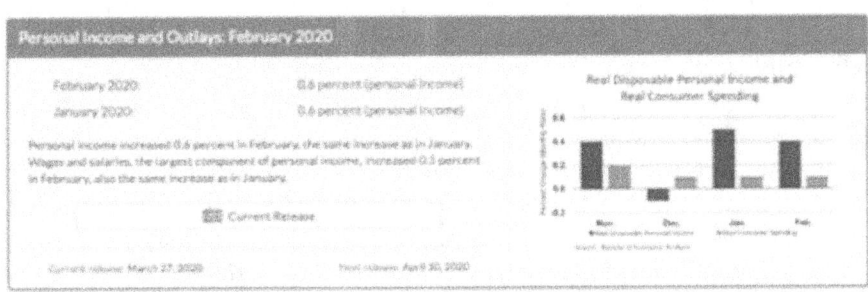

Figure 8.2. Example of Gross Domestic Product, 2019 and Personal Income and Outlays, 2020. *Source*: U.S. Bureau of Economic Analysis (accessed September 26, 2022)

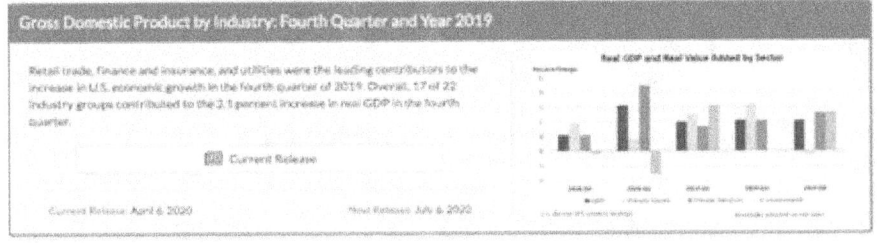

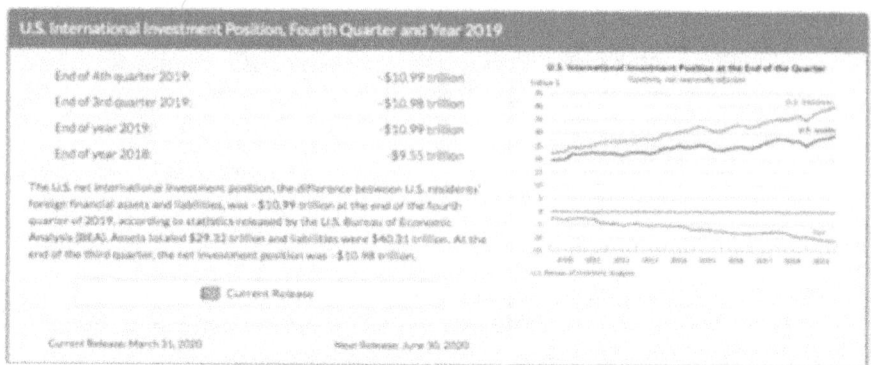

Figure 8.3. GDP by Industry and U.S. International Investment Position. *Source*: U.S. Bureau of Economic Analysis (accessed September 26, 2022)

further summed to evermore macro-statistics. Over time, people in all walks of life wanted more but simpler, fewer numbers—the "elevator answer"—to such questions as, "How big is the American economy?" But, they were conflicted. On the one hand, policy makers and economists wanted the underlying detail, yet on the other, many less-engaged individuals wanted fewer numbers, so the answer to the question was and is, "Well, it depends. It's complicated." These materials are presented in both tabular and graphical forms, with an increasing appetite for charts and graphs over long lists of numbers. Those who worked in large enterprises in the second half of the century undoubtedly noticed how PowerPoint presentations evolved from text and numerically intensive formats to more graphically filled versions. While these GDP figures are numerous, at one time summary data would possibly have fitted on one sheet of paper, as they certainly still do if just tabular.[105] But, while one impulse was to drive toward the simple "elevator answer," a countercurrent held, "No, you need to see at least several layers" or variety of data to understand current reality. In the instance of these examples, on the day I collected these figures, BEA actually had twelve in the set; but I did not need to present all of them to explain our observations. The tension wormed its way through similar paths in the presentation of new and diverse bodies of information in other parts of economics and across all STEM disciplines.

Information Economics Introduces Information as an Economic Topic

As economies changed, or new insights emerged in various parts of society's activities, economists demonstrated a willingness to explore these, and nowhere did this seem more so than in the basic activity of buying and selling of goods and services. Through their actions economists contributed new information in the form of theories, models, insights about human behavior, and vast quantities of data. Adam Smith studied manufacturing when it was becoming a mainstream economic activity, then over a century and a half later, Joseph Schumpeter studied the role of technology in shaping economic activities. So, it should be of no surprise that as information itself came to be seen as an active agent in the lives of humans, and biologists too of all living matter, economists would turn their attention to understanding the role of facts in economic terms. This happened simultaneously as engineers, scientists, biologists, and business professionals were doing the same within the context of their types of information. It should also not be a surprise that when economists turned their attention to information they wanted to understand it as a tangible object, a "thing," or in their parlance a "good," as in goods.

While the history of how economists dealt with the new topic of information awaits thorough explication, that account may well begin with the work of Fritz Machlup (1902–1983) who, in the 1950s, began documenting the presence of knowledge (his word for information) in the American economy, as reflected in professions and industries (e.g., librarians and publishers), and in products (e.g., books, newspapers, radios). As with so many of his academic cohorts, he was born and raised in Austria. In the 1930s he came to the United States, after having already established himself as a distinguished academic economist.[106] We encountered Machlup in earlier chapters, notably regarding his work to create an awareness that modern economies were becoming information societies, a line of research that he pursued until his death.[107] While other economists participated in shaping information as an economic topic, his ideas gained considerable early attention due to the activities of yet another Austrian émigré to the United States, Peter F. Drucker (1909–2005), who more assiduously than Machlup promoted to the wider world of business the idea of the "knowledge worker," drawing on the good work of his fellow countryman. We do not know if they met, but I would think so, because both worked in the United States since the 1930s.[108]

Economists turned their attention to information. Friedrich Hayek (1899–1992) studied pricing mechanisms and the effects of information on these in the 1940s,[109] George Stigler (1911–1991) explored the economics of information,[110] A. Michael Spence (b. 1942) introduced notions of signaling, that is to say how people telegraph information about themselves to others,[111] George Akerlof (b. 1940), on adverse selection of decisions based on what someone did or did not know,[112] and later Joseph E. Stiglitz (b. 1943), on how people reveal information to an under-informed second party.[113] All were exploring how information asymmetry played out in an economy, that is to say, how people with different levels and types of information were affected in their economic behavior.[114] Many studies, models, and cases were published over the past seventy-five years exploring such issues.

Machlup's interest in information as goods originally motivated my own studies as an historian of the role of information as an object, a thing, and most important, as tools.[115] More economists than historians, however, probed this issue.[116] Building on his ideas, the scope of the conversation expanded, beginning with definitions. For example, one of the early information economists, Marc Uri Porat, conducted a massive study similar to Machlup's, which the U.S. Department of Commerce published in 1977. It went beyond earlier definitions, positing that the information economy encompassed "all the workers, machinery, goods and services that are employed in processing, manipulating or transmitting information. The telephone, the computer, the printing press, the calculator, the manager, the secretary and the programmer—these are all essential members of the information activity. It would be almost impossible to handle information without resorting to these resources."[117] He argued that all human activity contained cognitive activities, hence used information, unknowingly coming close to the idea ventured in previous chapters that some engineers and STEM workers were positing: that all matter and activity were informational. Porat's definition joined those of other economists entwining the traditional concerns of the discipline with those raised by the new topic of information.

Economists discovered that the economics of information goods were different than for others, such as automobiles and houses. If someone uses a specific piece of information, that act does not prevent another person from doing the same. Economists say that a collection of information has nearly no marginal (additional) cost for a second copy. I can write a book, which is the expensive part of the process, but then send it electronically to all my friends at essentially no additional expense to me, or, one can download a piece of music from Apple at essentially no additional cost to Apple other than to pay the copyright holder a royalty, which comes out of what you paid Apple for the song. Economists learned that one could not make information exclusionary, that is to say, to deny a copy to anyone else. Once it exists it is difficult to keep others away from it, so it quickly becomes a "public good," even though one can think of it as a product, a thing.[118]

Finally, and only so far, information markets are not highly transparent. By that economists mean one has to know it to evaluate its value, its potential use. For example, you or I have to see a movie to evaluate it, we have to learn to use a software package before we can appreciate its value, let alone understand how to use it. In other words, to participate in the market for a specific piece of information, we have to invest time in it, just as you are doing by reading this chapter to learn about information in economics. By the end of the twentieth century these features were well understood and, indeed, represented new bodies of information unknown prior to World War II.[119]

The role of information fits neatly into preexisting paradigms, for example, the overarching categorization of economic activity as either macroeconomic or microeconomic. At a microlevel there are products, such as books, movies, software, theater, arts, CDs, DVDs, telephone services, even consulting and research—Machlup's terrain. Organizing the distribution of its products—goods—is prized as is the ability to measure the movement and demand for these, because such collections of information are paid for by consumers. These products are in some ways similar to more traditional goods as well, such as that they can be reused. One can read a book many times but also use a home coffee maker. But, many of these information products can be duplicated and distributed easily, not so a coffee maker. One can download an article from the *New York Time*s and then send it at no expense to someone or to all their colleagues. In theory, and often in practice too, one would have to pay for that right of replication, thanks to copyright laws that are more enforced in some countries than in others.[120] The behavior of individuals using information represents a large area of study for economists, media analysts, and businesses. Much work has begun to explain the behavior of consumers (demand issues) and how they use it.[121]

Economists asked what value did information provide.[122] Until they engaged in this conversation, priests, philosophers, educators, and parents had opined and waxed on the question for centuries. But that was not the way of the modern quantitatively oriented economists who were influenced by scientific research behaviors.[123] Reaching back to Schumpeter of nearly a century ago, then extending right to Robert Solow who explained that up to 80 percent of the innovations in an economy come from technology, one could see the value of information and technology entwined. Innovations based on the application of new information were the by-product of incremental accumulations of prior facts that, when applied differently or merged with others, offered new information, hence new opportunities to create economic value.[124] As economist James Bessen describes the cycle while thinking about technological evolutions, "Each module is complementary to the rest, so that improvements in one module increase the payoff to an invention that improves the performance of another module."[125] Almost any modern medicine one can think of came about this way, so too, for that matter, the blow hair dryer of the 1980s that had its roots in a steam-driven French bonnet dryer in the 1890s. Innovation is the by-product of accumulated innovations, which themselves are the accumulations of prior information.[126]

That most innovations fail is also a finding made by economists, which tells us that not all information converts into valued products or services. Economists learned a great deal about the value of collaborative innovation, such as the role played by the American government in funding the research and development of digital computers in the 1940s and 1950s, the Internet from the 1970s to the 1990s, and most recently cyber security.[127] Economists understand that innovations and the information underpinning these accumulate value over time as one leads to yet another innovation valued by an economy.

In the wake of all these various insights, economists populated hundreds of journals and books with examples, theories, rules of thumb, mathematical proofs, and practical advice on capturing the value of information and increasingly after the availability of the Internet as an economic agent.[128] The vast field of study concerning the role of copyrights and patents is a case in point.[129] There has long permeated, too, the notion that information can be seen as the flow of signals, without differentiating value, an idea more in evidence in the 1950s–1960s than later and that had an affinity with the Shannon–Weaver's ideas of the 1940s.[130] Recall from chapter 4 that signals can be accurate or wrong; hence messages can be valuable or useless. An example of an inaccurate message is if down a wire the wrong voltage is sent that cannot be used at the receiving end, or if it is $2 \times 2 = 5$ or 17. Economists are interested in the quality of information, because of its effects on decision-making. Work has been underway on that issue for decades.[131] In recent years the likes of Google, Amazon, Apple, and eBay demonstrated how massive quantities of "signals" (i.e., data about our daily activities) could be translated into revenue-generating data, such as what products to sell. They spun off considerable amounts of new information about economic, physiological, and communications networks and their effects on economics, business, and social interactions.[132]

BEHAVIORAL ECONOMICS ENTWINES WITH BIOLOGICAL AND SOCIOLOGICAL DISCIPLINES

In an intellectually less diverse world, our story about economics and its data could have ended here, with the discussion about the economic value of information. But that could not happen because, as when looking at STEM activities, scholars and researchers were intellectually promiscuous. They borrowed ideas and information from each other's disciplines with the result that the volume and nature of information increased and diversified. A large-scale example of that behavior can be found in economics where interest in behavioral economics is integrating a growing understanding about the functioning of the human brain with what biologists are learning about animals and plants, communications and ecosystems into microeconomics (so far). This book is also an example, because it discusses what was happening in multiple disciplines, while it was often necessary to hold onto one's own—albeit the former a risky endeavor since no one author can reasonably be expected to understand everyone else's information ecosystem. It is why almost every chapter has to include an apology to the residents of that topic if we are to try and view the overall landscape of information's transformation.

For example, writing on the role of business in modern society and on the history of IBM and other firms would have been impossible without paying attention to what economists and sociologists had to say. IBM is seen today as a nerve center of hundreds of thousands of employees operating in their various information ecosystems, while individual executives always (as now) imposed their values, thinking, and personalities on the work of the firm. IBM no longer can be portrayed as a monolithic organization operating in some efficient Newtonian fashion. Rather, it is like a bustling city of self-absorbed individuals going about their affairs, but sharing common values who collectively somehow moved from one success (or failure) to another over thirteen decades.[133]

Information theories from various disciplines, economic thinking about how people and organizations interact with information, more traditional economic concerns such as decision making, psychology, and biology are now in some sort of furious conversion. This appears to be the next major transformation in the nature of information offered up by economists. While very much a story of the twenty-first century, it began in the past several decades of the previous one, and so needs to be included in our discussion.

A proper economic definition of this kind of information would state that it is the study of how psychological, cognitive, cultural, emotional, social, and professional attitudes and behaviors affect the economic decisions of both individuals and organizations. It is the consideration of such variables when dealing with the traditional issues in economics as decision-making that gives behavioral economics its raison d'être. A formal economic definition would further explain that it concerns the role of rationality in human behavior and its limits (hence the word *bounds* often used by economists), integrating into economic analysis psychology, insights from neuroscience, and of course, microeconomic theory.[134] So, it must seem an anomaly if we turn to two academic psychologists who write clearly for a more understandable definition of the field: "Behavioral economics uses insights from the social sciences (e.g., sociology) in general, and psychology in particular, to inform economic thinking and theorizing. It takes knowledge from judgment and decision-making research to inform *realistic* assumptions about how people think, feel and act."[135] Such research makes it possible, for instance, to test predictions in laboratory settings through controlled studies or in the field, such as in observing how farming communities organize themselves for economic purposes.

Two economists writing for a general audience pointed out that "people navigate this field using intuitive theories and various cognitive devices such as naïve theories, metaphors, and heuristics that imbue them with a false confidence."[136] A psychologist who is also a cognitive scientist put it this way: "Intuitive theories are our untutored explanations for how the world works."[137] This is an important observation, because for some two hundred years it has been canonical in classical and neoclassical economics that people made rational decisions that were in their best economic interests. It is a point of view modified in the second half of the twentieth century by the effects of imperfect information, the discussion about asymmetric information. Behavioral economics suggests that not all human economic activity is rational, challenging long-standing beliefs nurtured by generations of economists.

Back to the same psychologists quoted earlier, they point out that the aim of these new economists is to "provide a scientific account of real economic behavior," through the traditional development of theories, hypotheses, predictions, and testing these against actual real-world decision-making.[138] Scientists know today that the mind consists of various subsystems specializing in various cognitive activities, such as to acquire and use language, memory, learning, reasoning, and so forth, and that they interact with each other. These activities are seen as "software" of biological and psychological forms—borrowing ideas from computing while computer scientists did the same from them in AI—all lodged in the physical brain, analogously thought of as the "hardware" of the human.[139] So, the poor economist of the pre-behavioral world is confronted with a growing body of empirical evidence presented in rigorous scientific academic fashion that we mortals "do not always, or typically, behave to maximize our immediate financial self-interest."[140] Even more complicating to economists then, "Our social behavior seems to be governed by considerations of fairness, cooperation and the 'warm glow' we feel when we help other people—although, getting along and cooperating with others may well be a selfish strategy in the longer-run when the economic games we are playing allow for punishment and reciprocity."[141]

In addition to upsetting much long-standing economic thinking, the new research began again to cause economists to change and add to their store of information. They now have to study the heuristics of how people make decisions, which evidently are overwhelmingly done using such cognitive shortcuts as rules of thumb. They have to identify and describe the mental models of people's worldviews and behaviors, academically referred to as *framing*.[142] Economists, however, can return to more familiar territory using insights from psychology and brain biology to make sense of how markets work, the role of non-rational decision-making, and inefficiencies in such market behavior as non-optimized pricing, or how best to craft messaging in advertisements.[143]

But it actually gets worse for them, because they face the potential of losing intellectual control over their discipline, which is what happened to librarians when the computer community muscled its way into their sphere. In 2002 Daniel Kahneman (b. 1934), a psychologist, received a Nobel Prize in economics for his work entwining psychology and economics to help explain how people made decisions in uncertain circumstances. He was one of the first researchers to demonstrate empirically that people were not as rationale in decision-making as economists had believed for two centuries.[144] However, in subsequent years economists did win Nobel Prizes for their work in behavioral economics, which is important, because such events sanctified these new lines of study within the economic discipline.[145] But, as with prior shifts in economic thinking, some in the old guard pushed back, a debate one can set aside, pointing out that the discussion back and forth generated new information about the general subject and how it fit (or did not) within the confines of earlier economic judgments.[146]

Entirely new bodies of information were created that combined psychology, biology, and economics around such issues as nudge theories (positive reinforcement of behavior),[147] behavioral finance,[148] myriad quantitative behavioral themes,[149] a renewal of interest in game theories,[150] and even economic-style reasoning among animals.[151] Wading into these subjects came the artificial intelligence community now interacting with economists and psychologists.[152] Interdisciplinary boundaries had been breached, with ever new subfields emerging, such as "neuroeconomics."[153] We saw in the world of STEM researchers and business management similar boundary-breaking activities; economists were not immune from this overarching trend in the evolution of information.

One could demonstrate this as done with earlier disciplines by walking through the pages of some academic journals, but that will not be necessary. We can tell this all happened by asking if specialized journals came into existence in which economists and others were willing to publish their research, in addition to doing so in their more traditional mainline journals. These exist. For example, there is the *Journal of Applied Behavioral Science* (psychology), *Brain and Behavior* (neuroscience and psychology), and *Journal of Business and Psychology.* Closer to home, there is the *Journal of Economic Psychology,* established in 1981 for the International Association for Research in Economic Psychology, the even older journal *Organizational Behavior and Human Decision Processes* (established in 1966 as *Organizational Behavior and Human Performance,* renamed in 1985), *Marketing Science,* and for taking the pulse of the entire field, including behavioral economics, *Annual*

Review of Economics. A glance at the notes for this chapter demonstrates the cross-polarization that occurred, such as an early article on "animal consumers" in the *Quarterly Journal of Economics* demonstrated.[154]

IS BIG DATA NOW AFFECTING ECONOMIC PRACTICES?

The jokes about economists never agreeing on an issue and having more opinions than the number of economists expressing them, while amusing, reflect a long-standing issue in the discipline of perhaps not always having enough of the right information to establish certainty. This circumstance exists despite the massive increase in the amount of economic data described in this chapter. But in the past decade raw economic data has been increasing at even greater amounts and, just as important, at near-instant (what computer scientists call "real-time") speeds. It is the same phenomenon that Big Data is now bringing to most disciplines and areas of computer use. Businesses collect real-time data about what customers are buying, making that available to management and to software constantly during the day. Card payments and bank transactions are being tracked that way. Physical and software sensors are beginning to make collecting such data possible. It is widely believed in business, government, and economic circles that such real-time data can improve policies and operations. That is why banks, for example, are tracking transactions conducted with cell phones. They and others are analyzing this data far quicker, not over months and years, as in earlier times. In October 2021 *The Economist* presented a lengthy discussion of this evolution in economic data, cautioning that "instant economics" will not necessarily lead to better economics. Rather, it noted that more was now being collected, studied, and used, but also that it was not "about clairvoyance or omniscience. Instead its promise is prosaic but transformative: better, timelier and more rational decision-making."[155]

But the new data meanwhile has begun framing economic debates, as had new supplies of information in earlier decades—GDP being one of the major examples featured in this chapter. As in other disciplines, all the new data is not always welcomed, with critics accusing some of their economist colleagues of becoming data scientists. Macroeconomics, long under attack for being too theory based has to give some way to its micro brother, which is fertile ground for Big Data. Such data has invigorated economic theory over the past several decades, despite the genuine concern about the quality of the data being collected. In answer to our question, yes Big Data is changing the nature of much economic information, paralleling similar developments in other industries and academic disciplines.

CONCLUSIONS

To draw upon a boxing analogy, economists have punched above their weight class since at least the 1860s. Collectively they did three things that influenced profoundly the type, quality, and quantity of information that ballooned over the next century and a half. In this chapter, we explored their activities from the mid-1800s to essentially the end of the twentieth century; it represented their most formative period in their history.

First, they aligned their interests and work to the scientific research style that became more disciplined (i.e., "scientific") in this period. In other words, economists were influenced by the milieu and trends evident in their day in the hard sciences. It is easy to imagine how this could happen. Most economists worked in universities where they would have rubbed elbows with scientists physically co-located with them. Economists were exposed to non-economic literature and lectures, too. They were trained in a similar manner: seminars, lecture courses, projects, and common research methodologies. In short, they saw themselves more like scientists than as humanists, aligning more with physicists, mathematicians, and biologists before "social science" became a new no man's land situated between the humanists (i.e., philosophers, historians, literature professors) and the hard scientists. It was also an era with less specialization so the borders between one area of study and another were less defined. In fact, in the 1800s and early 1900s it was not uncommon to think of economics as the study of "political economy." In this no man's land, one found, for example, sociologists and anthropologists for a while until the latter drifted toward the hard sciences.

Second, they embraced the use of mathematics and statistical methods for collecting, analyzing, and presenting the results of their research and thinking. They did this to such a degree that one could claim they were as mathematically focused as mathematicians, perhaps an exaggeration but not an inaccurate characterization of their image in other disciplines and in the eyes of the public. Spengler asked the provocative question: "Did quantification transform economics, or did it merely render economics more exact?"[156] He thought quantification made the discipline more exact, at least in 1961. Six decades on, we know that more than many other disciplines the move to quantification invigorated his field and resulted in better logic, more hard data, and new credible insights about human economic activity. Yet economists paid a price: such practices kept much of their work insulated from wider audiences. It took the likes of John Maynard Keynes and Paul Krugman to translate for the general public and government officials what their colleagues were doing, in addition to conducting their own research on matters of interest to them.

In recent years, a coterie of economists around the world have stepped in to translate their discipline's parochial language (e.g., mathematically intense discourses and stiff jargon-filled style of writing) for wider audiences, and with good results. That behavior raises the interesting question: Are economists returning to the eighteenth- and nineteenth-century practices of using narrative (e.g., adjectives) to describe economic behavior? They still include their charts, graphs, and tables, which are based on statistical data. They still write about short- and long-term trends, but then explain what these mean in more detail than they might in an academic paper. They state laws currently accepted as truth without exposing their readers to discussions of underlying mathematical rationalizations. They can then opine on interesting questions relevant to larger audiences. For one small example, a group of French economists recently devoted a chapter to answering the question, "Can we bypass industrialization?" if any national economy wants to move from agricultural to modern. It is an important question for political and business leaders across India and Southeast Asia, and increasingly in Africa. They concluded yes, explaining the economic activities involved in making such a leap, drawing largely on prior economic thinking by many economists but also from other disciplines.[157] It is the act of writing in non-technical language that allows economists to continue punching above their weight.

I admit to having sublimely chastised economists for introducing complexity into information that prevented others outside their confraternity from fully able to understand their data. But, to be fair, their cohorts in the hard sciences did the same, so collectively they complicated access to information for all. The problem seems wide enough that it has even been discussed in mainstream media, such as in the *New York Times*. One study reported that the more obfuscating and jargon-filled a paper was, the less likely it would be either read or cited.[158] Both the academic study and the newspaper reporting are a plea to improve accessibility to the good work of researchers.

Economists' embrace of mathematical analysis and extensive use of models encouraged other, less scientific and more humanistic disciplines to become more quantitative, particularly in the second half of the twentieth century. Included in that cohort one could put political science (thanks to polling and statistics, for example), historians (due to their use of cliometrics), sociology, and most spectacularly, anthropology. Anthropologists did more than just embrace mathematical and statistical practices, they also appropriated practices and information drawn from myriad other hard sciences, notably a wide range of subfields in biology and climate studies.

Third, economists massed vast bodies of new facts—data—that led to much new information about all manner of human activities. Think of all the statistical data sets governments and businesses use today that they also "mine" for insights. Their methods often originated in those used by economists. Government economists in many countries were advocates for collecting much new data and eager consumers of those, as Arrow called for in the 1950s and 1960s. GDP is an example of the results of their collecting so much new information. Their appetite went through a couple of phases. Initially in the nineteenth century, Jevons and others advocated for more data-driven economics. By World War I, they, governments, and large enterprises were beginning to enjoy buffets of new data sets. By the end of the 1930s most had become addicted to massive uses of information, enjoying the experience of new insights, as a consequence. The behavior of economists meant that today in most disciplines, a researcher will look at more facts than they might have needed a century earlier. In fact, they *must* consult more information to meet today's criteria for credible research, which helps to explain why in the second half of the century ever-narrower subdisciplines emerged, as a response to managing the scope of their own capabilities. Economists contributed directly to these circumstances.

These three actions constituted the fundamental donations made by economists to the world's collection of information and to some of its transformation. Their energetic behavior made this all possible, contributing to the shaping of modern information. A remarkable number of mathematicians and others trained extensively in *both* mathematics and statistics gravitated toward the economics profession, particularly in the several decades before it became highly defined and structured by the end of the 1930s. These were smart people, but more important—I think—they were very productive. When one examines the bibliographies and curriculum vitae of both well-known and minor economists, it is striking how prolific they were. They published articles—the normative format for their work—and books, and still found time to have day jobs in government, academia, and business. They found time to establish and sustain hundreds of journals, many of which published more pages of content than less scientific disciplines. While quantity is not always a good measure of quality, when combined with normal academic practices of peer reviews and engaging in dialogues through discipline-specific norms, they were a busy lot.

So, they had something of value to say about how economies function, what government officials should do to continue the momentum of prosperity enjoyed by humanity during the Second Industrial Revolution, how better corporations could run, and in explaining how *homo economicus* thought, bought, and sold. These were not monolithic progressions in the evolution in the behavior by the economists. There were some practitioners in the late 1800s and early 1900s that thought the profession should not rush too quickly into mathematics or into using experimental models. As the joke at the start of this chapter about the ten economists having eleven points of view suggested, no economic fact was always as "hard," as absolute, as factual as a physicist or chemist would claim for their own findings. But ultimately, economists became a gateway for social scientists and those working in the humanities to shape their bodies of information in ways different than what was more normal prior to the twentieth century.

But we give the second to the last word to Francis Y. Edgeworth (1845–1926), Irish philosopher, statistician, and political economist, whom the Irish historian Theodore M. Porter called "the poet of statisticians," who in the 1880s and 1890s advocated for the use of mathematics. He captured the essence of what economists would in time do with their creation of new information: "As the wise slave in the ancient comedy says, when his master begins to reason about love, a thing which is in its nature irregular and irrational, cannot possibly be governed by reason. It would be like going mad according to method. Natural philosophy has however triumphed over this paradox. Mathematicians have constructed an apparatus for reducing to rule errors."[159] Edgeworth's thoughts about the slave appeared in 1890; nearly a century later, Porter concluded his own study with "statistics, indeed, remains a basic form of social knowledge."[160] That this became possible was due to a considerable degree to the work of economists.

While there are many disciplines one can consult to see how such influence unfolded, I look next at the activities of political scientists and historians and at what they did to shape information in modern times, because they represented disciplines immediately beyond the pale of economists and closer to the world of the social sciences and the humanists.

Chapter 9

Contributions of Political Scientists and Historians to Modern Information

> *A historian must not merely get the facts right. He must get the right facts right. . . . Historical evidence must be a direct answer to the question asked and not to some other question. . . . The best relevant evidence, all things being equal, is evidence which is most nearly immediate to the event itself.*
>
> Historian David Hackett Fischer, 1970[1]

> *Statistics, like veal pie, are good if you know the person that made them, and are sure of the ingredients. By themselves they are strangely likely to mislead.*
>
> Political Scientist A. Lawrence Lowell, 1910[2]

We now enter the world of social sciences, often derisively called the "soft sciences," as these disciplines are accused of lacking the "hard" precision so valued by physicists, chemists, computer scientists, and others who live in the STEM world, or next door to this, such as the economists. The world of social sciences is vast, populated by a wide diversity of disciplines, each stock piled with massive quantities of information packaged in the usual forms of articles and books, blogs and digital files, stone carvings, artifacts, and, in the case of history, billions of pages of archival materials, the latter accounting for nearly 10,000 years of human experience. The disciplines that come to mind include anthropology, archaeology, sociology, history, and political science. One could easily add to that list many others, but the point is that a massive amount of information has been accumulated, and since the mid-nineteenth century, transformed by these disciplines to accommodate their needs. Their information behaviors are very similar to what we have reviewed in prior chapters: development of their own vocabularies, research agendas, journals, associations, books, certification programs, training, academic degrees, and prizes that combined helped change information. Most of these engaged in such activities at roughly the same time as the scientists, engineers, and economists, borrowing practices from each other. But unlike some of the STEM disciplines, they have long pedigrees. History as we know it predates the ancient Greeks; political science may have been the first discipline along with astronomy (probably began as either agricultural or religious).

Because of the similarity in both how social and hard sciences evolved and the shape of their information too, I focus less attention on the specifics of these disciplines. They embraced greater use of mathematics, more so, statistics, and most recently digital sensors to collect data. They also had their unique challenges, such as historians having to focus on observing what happened in the past as opposed to experimenting to understand the present, as might a biologist or physicist. The social sciences and, even more, the humanities used modeling less, but slowly embraced hypothesizing methods then proving/disproving assumptions, but again, less definitively than in the hard sciences. I discuss those differences with the two disciplines chosen to review more briefly than we did the economists: political science and history. As one reads this chapter and begins to feel that political scientists and historians bore a close resemblance to pre-1960s librarians, they would be right. As noted in our discussion of librarians, many were trained in history, social sciences, or in the humanities such as art or literature. So their sense of what information was all about and how it should be put together was empathetic.

With these two disciplines I discuss a couple of emblematic examples of where they influenced the shape of information, rather than the whole assemblage of their respective disciplines. This allows us to spill over into other non-STEM areas, showing links. In the case of political scientists I explore the roll of polls, which to be more precise, was the contribution of statisticians, such as George H. Gallup (1901–1984) who was not trained as a political scientist, but whose expertise and that of others about polling became perhaps the most visible tool in a political scientist's kit bag when they appeared on television commenting on an election's results, for example. Polling became a widely used method to create new information across all the social sciences. After I describe what historians do, and in particular, the special role of archival materials, we also explore the role of cliometrics, which is as close as historians have reached in their use of mathematics. Like political scientists and others in the social sciences, historians embraced statistics, just not so extensively as in STEM fields; nonetheless, statistics became increasingly important to them too.[3]

In prior chapters one reason presented for why disciplines came into being is because there was so much specialized information being created that required focus and specialization. With political science and history becoming distinct disciplines begs the question of why did they split into two? After all, much history written prior to the nineteenth century was about politics. As noticed with science splintering into narrower fields, and later the social sciences and humanities doing the same, the question comes up again. A more nuanced explanation would hold that as the community of practitioners in a field increased, their worldviews and communities of like-minded colleagues would fragment, naturally creating both intellectual and social sub-tribes. One of those most remarkable observers of a discipline that comes along at rare moments helps us understand what happened with the actors in this chapter. The late Peter Novick observed that "most modern academic disciplines emerged through secession—as physics, chemistry, biology and the rest emerged from undifferentiated 'natural philosophy,' or as political science, economics, sociology, and history broke with the omnibus American Social Science Association in the late nineteenth century. In the majority of cases the establishment of an autonomous discipline was grounded in claims to exclusive sovereignty over a distinctive subject matter." He added that these "secessions" were "the result of contingent circumstances and political struggles," eventually compelling old and new disciplines to define what constituted their information ecosystems, credibility, and so forth, what the librarians faced throughout the twentieth century.[4] Any shared assumptions about common practices, definitions of objectivity and ethics established by World War II, experienced another round of serious fragmentation, beginning in the 1980s, particularly in history. Their fragmentation and intellectual discord paralleled the behavior evident in physics at the same time. So information changed for sociological reasons, too, not simply because there was so much of it.

So that there is no confusion, while the title of this chapter might imply that I am arguing for the existence of an overall form of well-defined information in some modern paradigm, information creators in the social sciences and humanities experienced the same circumstances as in other disciplines in the creation, transformation, and use of information. While they came into the nineteenth century confident in the structure of their information's "look and feel," that changed, too, in the nineteenth and twentieth centuries. In the process they contributed to the ever-expanding volume and type of information that now is part of our contemporary information ecosystem. To reiterate, too, the choices of political science and history—fields I consider close cousins—these often spill over into so many other social sciences in both topics of study and intellectual behavior that they serve as exemplars of a much larger community of information transformers.

WHAT IS POLITICAL SCIENCE?

As an historian I have long viewed political science as a close relative to history. Both have long traditions of focusing on the history of politics and government. Political scientists have not hesitated to dip into history to identify behaviors, such as to document voting patterns and even earlier, role of kings, presidents, and legislatures. Untrained aficionados and practitioners capable of doing excellent work rival both disciplines. In the case of political science, journalists are prominent and often more widely read than their academic cohorts; the same holds for historians. Those practicing political science or history "without a license" (i.e., without credentialing of a PhD in the discipline) find reading the research findings of political scientists and historians not to be a problem. Neither have extremely obfuscating vocabulary or such elegant theories and models that would require extra attention to understand, as encountered, say, in economics. Everyone in these disciplines uses vocabulary that even high school students would understand. Unlike in economics, too, most people have been exposed to some history, even as children and many to what in the United States is called "civics"—classes on how local and national governments are organized and operate. For over two centuries in the United States educating people on how to be good citizens was a central objective of primary education, so that meant introducing many hundreds of millions of people to information about the constitution, how government works, and the responsibilities of citizenship.[5]

But to the point, what is political science? It is the study of how governments operate. It involves the analysis of political activities (such as of political parties and candidates running for office), documentation and history of political thinking, and observations of the public's political behavior. Like history and other social sciences, in practice it is more observational than experimental, although in the past several decades those seeking to apply psychology and cognitive neuroscience to the discipline have attempted some experimentation. Those activities are largely twenty-first-century developments. Like historians, however, political scientists conduct archival research (e.g., in government records, private papers of politicians). They note contemporary commentary, study activities of politicians, and observe the public's behavior and political views reported in such contemporary media as newspapers, television, and Internet sources. They conduct polls, write case studies, do statistical analysis, and create models.[6] They sit closer to the hard scientists and economists than do historians.

As the discipline increased its membership, it too underwent similar experiences evident in other fields, two in particular. First, it subdivided into narrower areas of interest. These included comparative politics, political economy (a label from the eighteenth century), international relations (i.e., too, diplomacy), political theory, public administration, public policies, and methodologies.[7] These subdivisions further divided by nations, such as political science in the United States, or topics focused on China or Germany. Large subdivisions included the study of constitutions (one's own national or compared to those of different countries), and the role of politicians, say, in legislatures. Some political scientists specialized in types of government. For example, in the twentieth century Robert A. Dahl and Arend Lijphart did brilliant work explaining the rise and nature of democratic forms of government.[8] Juan Linz did the same for dictatorships.[9] Barrington Moore Jr. taught a generation of "poli sci" cohorts how to blend history and politics to conduct comparative political science.[10]

A second experience involved participation in political science by individuals not trained in the subject per se, notably historians and journalists. Most history prior to the mid-nineteenth century focused largely on the political behavior of nations, with a modicum of social or economic confectionary added into the mix. Early newspapers and pamphleteering in the West began largely in the seventeenth century and were overwhelmingly about domestic politics and international relations. Many of these publications eventually made possible the emergence of what today one fashionably calls the media, but more specifically the rise of professional newspaper reporting. Many reporters and commentators of contemporary events wrote books about the nature of politics, while individuals who became politicians later turned their hand to writing about politics too. By the last quarter of the twentieth century it had become customary for politicians and reporters to flood book markets with publications reminiscing or opining about contemporary political issues of the day.

After the 1840s, and continuing through the next century, the world saw the rise of large industrial-based democracies, authoritarian regimes and, of course, communist models of government. Totalitarianism came into vogue as both phrase and concept.[11] The two world wars of the twentieth century knocked out the earlier European governmental model of royal governing with the one notable exception of Great Britain's, although it too became subject to a greater will of prime ministers. All the others were gone by 1918. Dictatorships, however, came and went, as they still do. All of these developments were fair game for political scientists and their rivals in other disciplines who were also keen to study such governments. Interest concentrated on the nature of decision-making, exercise of power, integration or displacement of the interests of various groups in a society in how they were governed, distribution of wealth and justice, and implementation of such social needs as education, health, income and social safety nets, and military security.[12]

So, political science sits somewhere between social sciences (such as sociology and economics) and the humanities (more like history and communications). In the United States it is characterized as liberal arts. The word *science* in the discipline's title is more of an American affectation, while in other parts of the world the concept is perceived more as political studies, or simply government or politics. The Americans imply the use of scientific methods of research and discourse. Europeans, Latin Americans, and Asians lean more toward historical and philosophical methods of study; but even the latter have increasingly appropriated the North American style of doing political research.[13] Research, which becomes the source of information contributed by political scientists, therefore, parallels what is generated in other social sciences: hypotheses, measures of the effectiveness and results of performance of specific government policies (usually called policy analysis), the economic and psychological costs and results of public sector activities, roles of participants (e.g., voters, politicians, lobbyists), descriptions of historic events (e.g., such as specific wars and programs), and observational analyses of behaviors of institutions, groups, and individuals.

The mindset of what information can be collected and shaped may have best been explained and encouraged by an early president of the American Political Science Association, A. Lawrence Lowell, who, in 1910, dismissed experimentation methods, because "politics is an observational, not an experimental science." He added that political scientists were "inclined to regard a library as the laboratory of political science, the storehouse of original sources, the collection of ultimate material. To some extent this is true, but for most purposes books are no more original sources for the physiology of politics than they are for geology or astronomy."[14] He put the discipline on a trajectory for the next century with his final thought that the main source of information his colleagues had to collect came from "the outside world of public life. It is there that the phenomena must be sought," if the discipline was to make a contribution to their "science."[15] To put a fine point on the matter, like so many other disciplines, part of how political scientists changed information was by adding new types to those they otherwise used and, too, combining both into new forms.

If the subject of political science appears less specific than STEM topics, one would be right to reach such a conclusion. However, as a convenience, table 9.1 lists many of the topics that tend to constitute a consensus view of the field's categories. It is not a definitive list; however, such categorizations are helpful in sorting out what information a discipline develops, as the nineteenth-century librarians taught us to do.

Table 9.1. Sub-fields of Political Science

Comparative politics	Development studies
Geopolitics & political geography	Institutional theory
International relations	Security studies
Nationalism studies	Political behavior
Political economy	Political fiction
Political theory & philosophy	Political sociology
Electoral systems & voting	Policy analysis & studies
Foreign policy analysis	Public administration
Local government	Strategic studies
Area studies	International organizations
Constitutions & constitutional law	Political philosophy
Forms of government	Political behavior
Ideologies	Political decision-making

Source: Modified from the list "Outline of Political Science," *Wikipedia* https://en.wikipedia.org/wiki/Outline_of_political_science#Fields_of_study_of_political_science (accessed October 26, 2020).

Emergence of Opinion Polling Information

What President Lowell might have suspected was happening, collecting opinions regarding American political elections had been underway for years, largely as an amateur affair until the decade he opined on statistics. These were not being assembled and analyzed methodically by statisticians or political scientists—that came later. But, opinion polling was such a part of the American political landscape that it cannot be ignored. It represents such a new injection of political information into American, and later European and Japanese affairs, that by the end of the twentieth century, political scientists had appropriated opinion polling as new sources of information, while waxing on local television news programs and in more national podiums about what these meant. These had become a central component of their information ecosystem.

However, opinion polling's features and how these evolved lay clearly in the hands of professional pollsters who were deeply skilled in the use of statistical methods, had learned how to turn their knowledge into lucrative careers that for celebrity pollsters far exceeded those of academic political scientists. These had become a vital tool used by public officials to operate agencies or to run for political offices from city council and mayoral elections to state and national campaigns. By the 1940s, American politicians campaigning for national offices had become data-driven, shaping their strategies and their commentary based on what opinion pollsters were telling them.[16] The American experience serves as a dramatically large and widespread case study of the role of polling information, particularly in the second half of the twentieth century.

Political polling in the United States dates from at least the 1824 presidential election, when reporters questioned people in ad hoc ways, asking who they were going to vote for, with no statistical methodology involved, just talking with folks in bars, hotels, and restaurants. That casual approach continued for most of the nineteenth century, making for good copy.[17] Newspapers reprinted such results and the public found these stories interesting. The U.S. Department of Agriculture did some polling of farmers about their quality of life prior to World War I.[18] By then the effects of people wanting more scientifically arrived-at data, in combination with the growing use of statistical methods, led to more structured surveying by the start of that war. The public had been sufficiently conditioned to consider numbers as more accurate (truthful) than narratives; so political opinion polls became more popular.

The *Literary Digest* magazine, a popular general interest periodical, pioneered many statistical methods used to forecast the results of presidential elections, and from 1916 through 1932 had correctly predicted their outcomes. Then, in 1936, it predicted incorrectly, with the result that this national publication, already suffering from Great Depression declines in subscriptions, went out of business two years later. The Republican candidate Alf Landon lost, Franklin D. Roosevelt won by a substantial margin. The miss by this magazine became a national news story. Consensus thinking of political scientists, historians, and statisticians held that the magazine made errors in who they polled: financially well-off readers who owned telephones (telephones were luxury items), while the majority of potential voters were less prosperous and voted in larger numbers. The second problem the surveyors faced was that the return rate for mailed surveys proved low, despite their huge mailing to some 10 million readers, of which only 2.3 million responded. Roosevelt won by a landslide, with 60 percent of the popular vote; his opponent carried only two states.[19] As these issues were publicly aired, with debates about the accuracy of polls swirling for decades, Americans underwent a tutorial on polling techniques and in the process came to appreciate the value of proven statistical methodologies.[20]

But that year one pollster got it right, George H. Gallup (1901–1984). Developer of the Gallup Poll, for the next three-quarters of a century his was one of the most respected national polling organizations on political sentiment. Gallup's undergraduate and graduate studies at the University of Iowa were in journalism, but later he taught classes on advertising. Gallup built a business around political and commercial polling, beginning in the 1930s. Crucial to his success was not mailing 10 million surveys, rather to select carefully the survey group, unlike the case of 1936. He reached out to only 50,000 people, who represented all manner of economic and social classes.[21] In 1948 he failed to predict Harry S. Truman's election, which he concluded was due to running the survey too early. Nonetheless, his organization went on to conduct useful political and advertising surveys into the next century.[22] Other pollsters increasingly relied on statistical methods, too, such as Elmo Roper (1900–1971), who pioneered market research and opinion polling techniques.[23] His organization, the Roper Research Company, continues to conduct surveys.[24]

Before moving on with our discussion, linger momentarily with polling examples from the 1930s to gain a sense of what new information was being collected. Table 9.2 recreates one of Gallup's early polling results, this one concerning the public's attitude toward the consumption of alcoholic beverages. It is about as simple as one could get. Table 9.3 is designed the same way but asks about a foreign policy issue, taken during the first week of World War II in Europe. This survey caught the attention of the White House. Now look at Table 9.4, which Gallup conducted within a month of

Table 9.2. Americans' Perception of Local Drinking Situation, 1935, Pre- vs. Post-Prohibition

In your locality, is the situation in respect to the use of alcoholic beverages better, about the same, or worse than it was during the last few years of Prohibition?	U.S. Adults (%)
Better	36
About the same	31
Worse	33

Modified from the original table, Gallup survey taken October 8–13, 1935, https://news.gallup.com/vault/267830/gallup-vault-little-thirst-restoring-prohibition-1935.aspx (accessed October 28, 2020).

Table 9.3. Americans' Support for Assisting England, France, and Poland

"How far should we go in helping England, France and Poland?"	Yes (%)	No (%)
Should we sell them food supplies?	74	27
Should we sell airplanes and other war materials to England And France?	58	42
Should we send our Army and Navy abroad to fight against Germany?	16	84

Modified from the original table, Gallup survey taken September 1–6, 1939, https://news.gallup.com/vault/265865/gallup-vault-opinion-start-world-war.aspx (accessed October 28, 2020).

Table 9.4. Americans' Views on the Republican Party

Do you think the Republican Party is dead?	U.S. Adults (%)	Republicans (%)	Democrats (%)
Yes	27	8	39
No	73	92	61

Modified from the original table, Gallup survey taken December 2–7, 1936, https://news.gallup.com/vault/189884/gallup-vault-1936-gallup-asked-gop-dead.aspx (accessed October 28, 2020).

the infamous publication of the *Literary Digest*'s faulty forecast. It is an early example of a follow-up issue-oriented survey. All three are simple, but their genius lay in the kind of information sought and how questions were designed to get at that kind of insight. Here we do not have forecasting, or for that matter, extensive statistical gymnastics, simply four functions of mathematics, but these kinds of reports taught a nation to look at polls.

The number of people surveyed and the quantity and variety of polls increased steadily throughout the century. Early polling focused on measuring opinions, as with Gallup's, which remains a genre of polls. But by World War I some pollsters were shifting to using such data to forecast election outcomes and in advertising surveys to predict consumer behavior, such as their anticipated responses to the introduction of a product.[25] In politics the purpose of polling was to understand how potential voters might vote and how to influence them through appealing messages. So a vast body of new information about opinions was created rooted in several disciplines.

First, there was the creation of statistics and measures of their relevance (i.e., accuracy and effectiveness) that could be used to persuade the public on a point of view, or that would lead a candidate to tailor a more attractive message. A great deal of information was thus generated that identified the strengths and weaknesses of candidates and political parties. Such data was obviously of enormous interest to political scientists too. Salience—the importance of one problem or issue as compared to others—became a useful body of information in politics. Since partisanship plays a crucial role in political discourse, that too was monitored. Much of the data for these kinds of issues were in the form of percentages of respondents who were "for" or "against" a candidate or in support (or not) of an issue or proposed action, often cataloged by a respondent's party affiliation. So, a survey about social security reforms might indicate that 75 percent of Democrats were for changes, while 43 percent of Republicans did not want to consider this option.[26]

Polling question writing became a fine art, as practitioners realized quickly that wording could skew responses.[27] Any issue could be surveyed. For example, keeping Social Security pensions financially sound could lead to the question: Who had the best ideas for doing that? Republicans? Democrats? Neither? Or Independents?[28] The performance of presidents is now routinely surveyed with results presented in statistical forms measuring results over time, compared to each data set, and to other presidents. Normally these are featured as percentiles of the public that approves the president's performance on the economy, foreign affairs, or handling of a particular crisis.[29] Presidential approval ratings date to the 1940s and are normally presented in comparison to other presidents, usually as averages, maximum and minimum approval ratings, and with standard deviations. The public learned increasingly what margins of error mean, a result of the increased application of statistical methods to the data collected.[30]

Social and economic issues evolved into political issues, folding into the concerns political scientists had as their own sub-disciplines expanded. In the United States political scientists, professional pollsters, public officials, and interest groups (e.g., lobbyists) polled and studied major issues. The most obvious issues included abortion, largely because of the national debate over the Supreme Court's ruling in *Roe v. Wade* in 1973; affirmative action, which grew out of the American Civil Rights Movement of the 1960s; alienation from politics, as a measure of how people were in support and engaged in the political processes of the nation; taxation and public sector budgets; wars, such as about support for or against the Vietnam conflict, later those in the Middle East; political campaign financial reforms; civil liberties and racism; death penalty; terrorism; all manner of economic issues, education, the environment, health care, and the United Nations.[31] There was something to appeal to any political scientist.

Information was initially presented in small and large tables, soon too as comparative percentages and line graphs. Information settled into three types in political science, shaping much information as comparative over time. This kind of data lent itself to supporting rules of thumb or to specific statistical correlations that could be buttressed by statistical analysis then converted into models of political behavior using mathematics. The first were *benchmark polls*, often used in political campaigns, giving candidates an idea of how voters were responding to them, identifying strengths and weaknesses among different classes of voters, and how people were reacting to different messages.[32] The second type are called *brushfire polls*. These are conducted after benchmark polls during a campaign or national dialogue on an issue, but are largely used by political candidates. These kick up information on what progress a candidate is making, which groups of potential voters are "for" or "against" their messages so that a campaign team can optimize their positions on issues. These polls are normally used to persuade rivals to drop out of a race, by demonstrating that they cannot possibly win and were fracturing voting blocks. The third type are *tracking polls*. These are used to prepare moving averages of responses collected daily or weekly to see how a candidate is performing. These are all about understanding trends, providing a continuous moving picture of a candidate's performance. In national elections these are conducted daily.

Political scientists endorsed polling as these became statistically disciplined. By the 1960s, they understood such concepts as margin of errors caused by bad sampling or poorly written questions; the role of nonresponse bias, which was a problem for the *Literary Digest*; response biases; false correlations; and coverage biases. Rigorous use of polling in the second half of the century made it possible for political scientists and other observers to formulate theories and to gain insights about voter behaviors. For instance, they learned that just by participating in polls could influence voter behavior.[33] Voters have been shown to support a candidate who was "winning in the polls," known as the *bandwagon effect*. There is even an *underdog effect* as well, which is the reverse of bandwagoning.[34] In recent years a theory called "cognitive response" emerged to explain how a respondent to a poll reacts to why a party or candidate won or lost, or went up or down in polls, if presented with polling questions that did not align with their original thinking.[35] As appeared in other social science disciplines, behavioral responses are now subjects of research, in which a potential voter seeks out information to add to their "mental list" of facts and criteria for affecting their voting decision.[36]

So, polling influenced both politicians and voters, while political scientists observed their respective behaviors. In sum, by the late 1900s political scientists were shaping information in ways similar to other disciplines relying on statistics, behavioral, and other cognitive inputs, less mathematics than applied by economists, and significantly embraced polling and surveying of contemporary issues.

WHAT INFORMATION DID NOT CHANGE MUCH: DIPLOMACY

Perhaps the three oldest government professions have been rulers, military, and diplomats. Diplomacy, or international relations, is squarely part of political science. It is also specialized, with academic departments and schools within universities devoted to the topic, such as the Institute for the Study of Diplomacy, established in 1978 at Georgetown University in Washington D.C. There, diplomats, political scientists, and others explore and teach about the craft of diplomacy. Just a few miles away in Northern Virginia is the Foreign Service Institute (established 1947), which is the U.S. Department of State's training center for American diplomats that teaches the craft but also other needed bread-and-butter skills such as foreign languages, area studies, economics, management and computing. France, Germany, Spain, and dozens of other national governments have similar training centers. They all share with each other and the entire diplomatic profession practices that have essentially been codified and made routine for several hundred years.[37]

The U.S. Department of State alone has some 280 offices staffed with over 13,000 diplomatic personnel (called Foreign Service Officers), not to mention employees from other American government agencies. The United States is only one of some 200 countries that maintain a diplomatic corps, not including such international agencies as the United Nations and the European Union. Collectively they constitute a large cohort, outnumbering political scientists, the vast majority of the former trained in history and political science. Back to the American experience, there are less than 6,000 full-time political scientists, over twice as many Foreign Service Officers.[38]

While today's diplomats use e-mail, host all manner of other government employees in their embassies, their role and the information they need with which to perform their duties have not changed fundamentally in centuries.[39] They collect and use bodies of information that have worked for them, so they represent a possible counter-case to all those discussed in this book in that they did not change substantially the nature of their information since the 1870s. The roles had not changed fundamentally, which contributes to the more static nature of their information than that of many other professions. A diplomat has three roles to play that remained essentially the same for several thousand years. They represent their nation (or ruler) at the capital of another country to explain the views and actions of their home country to another government. They gather information about what the country they are assigned to is involved with, attitudes, alliances, wars, economic practices, and so forth. They negotiate agreements (treaties) between their home government and the one to which they are assigned over such matters as trade, economic exchanges, political and military alliances, and how local officials deal with their own citizens.[40] They work out of consulates, embassies, and at home in their foreign offices, the latter led by cabinet-level officials. Consulates are located in large cities for the purposes of promoting trade between their two countries, to issue visas and passports, promote cultural exchanges, and explain the home government's policies and points of view. Embassies are situated in national capitals led by ambassadors. In addition to consular work, staffs at embassies negotiate treaties; meet with senior national leaders; and consolidate reporting on local political, diplomatic, economic, and cultural activities for their home office.[41] Some of these "missions" (as they are called), have existed for over a half-millennium, such as the French embassy in Spain, others for a couple of centuries, such as the U.S. Consulate in Barcelona, established in 1797.[42]

What kinds of information did diplomats collect for centuries that they still work with today? They gathered information on politics, economics, cultural, and intellectual activities. Diplomats gathered this information from newspapers and books, thought leaders, officials, business executives, and academics. Much of this information is about the activities and points of view of various political parties, the military, the social and political elites, and of senior leaders. These are reported in dispatches and e-mails sent on a regular basis to the home foreign office. Included are analyses providing historical and current contextual information about what they are reporting for the government to which they work with. They prepare statements representing their own government's perspectives used to explain these to local officials. The themes broadly concern economic and political relations, military affairs, and international relations among the two and all other parties, such as, say, the United States and France and between those two countries and the European Union. Such reporting is heavily annotated with historical perspectives and doses of economics and political science.[43]

Routine specialized reports include collections of the kinds of economic data discussed in the previous chapter produced by the U.S. Bureau of Economic Analysis and the U.S. Department of Labor. Consulates monitor imports and exports of goods out of their cities and surrounding provinces. They track the number and types of passports issued, and other permits. Copies of treaties between two nations are kept as references. Treaties are simply contracts between nations and like commercial agreements they prescribe what each party agreed to do and are considered subfields of political science and law called *international law*.[44] One can read treaties from the 1600s and others from the European Union of the 2000s and notice that they have the same kind of content.[45]

These bodies of information are routinely published in anthologies distributed to embassy and consular libraries (also too in internal databases), which are also stocked with publications on diplomatic history, economics, and contemporary political affairs.[46] Foreign Offices maintain libraries with similar materials, some of which were established several hundred years ago.[47] They collect and use materials published by local foreign offices and other national government agencies. They mirror each other's classes of information: diplomatic history, polemical publications of the day, foreign policy statements, press releases, economic reports, budget data, biographical information on officials, and diplomatic regulations, among others. For centuries they also collected newspaper clippings and entire runs of newspapers and relevant journals; today much of that material is available online.

Other government agencies involved in diplomatic matters also collected and communicated information to each other. For example, over the past three centuries national legislatures routinely asked their foreign offices to transmit to them copies of diplomatic correspondence related to some issue, say the lead-up to a war, such as the U.S. Congress did relative to the Spanish–American War of 1898.[48] These were often published as part of the legislative record of the nation.[49] The United Nations and the European Union have done the same since their founding. Such bodies of information are largely about the various negotiating positions of each government, minutes of meetings, analyses of what such events meant for specific groups and people, and recommendations for next steps.

It is important to re-emphasize that the types of diplomatic information is that their features and subjects had essentially not changed for centuries. The one exception one can call out is that over time, diplomats dealt with more data, publications, mail and e-mail, but the themes and the types of information had not. This is because much as in the practice of law, their purposes did not evolve as much as had, for instance, STEM-based professions, technical positions in the military (e.g., flight by World War I, counter-insurgency management), or work in businesses due to the appropriation of information technologies. How diplomats went about their work evolved, such by their use of telegraph, telephones, e-mail, air travel, and so forth, but less so the information they used. The new dynamic was increased speed (i.e., shorter turnaround time for back-and-forth dialogue and exchange of facts), which encouraged more flow of information.

Political scientists studied international affairs, adding large bodies of new information to their storehouses of how nations dealt with one another. They modeled negotiating strategies and described power politics, warfare, economics, and so forth. Diplomats-in-training or in the course of their work were exposed to this body of work, but these topics were sidebars because most diplomats, like lawyers, practiced very narrowly based work dictated by specific instructions from their home office. Foreign policy has always been dictated either by officials at the headquarters of a foreign ministry or more realistically by the king, dictator, or president from their own offices, such as by an American president with his personal staff housed in the White House in the Office of the President, not at the U.S. Department of State. This reality meant that all the well-meaning insights developed by political scientists about international affairs would be considered through the filter of local or national political realities. There were partial exceptions, of course, such as President Richard Nixon or President George H. W. Bush, both with diplomatic experience, the former assisted by the exceptionally experienced political scientist turned diplomat, Dr. Henry Kissinger.[50]

One can conclude that in the world of political science, the body of information ranged from the innovation of polling to the other extreme of diplomatic topics relatively unchanged. The field grew in diversity, and it was that expanded scope, thus variety of work that made possible the co-existence of traditional and transformed information. These were not mutually exclusive bodies of information. Rather they exemplified a co-habitation sufficiently close to the broader changes in society's total collection of information. Those engaged in any manner of political science were products of their times, aware of many of the changes in information underway in other professions and disciplines. As such, their times and practices led to changes in the information that they developed and used.

HOW HISTORICAL EVIDENCE EVOLVED: ARCHIVAL SOURCES, FOOTNOTES, AND TRUTH

It is quite possible that every university student in the Western world who took a course in historiography or historical methods in the twentieth century has heard of Leopold von Ranke (1795–1886). A history professor for nearly fifty years at the University of Berlin, beginning in 1825, he urged historians to consult original documents as the bases of their research. He pioneered the use of the seminar method of teaching to assist students learn how to evaluate the usefulness of archival materials. Ranke believed that by relying on primary source materials (e.g., contemporary manuscripts, diplomatic reports, and diaries), as opposed to the more widely embraced strategy of using secondary ones (e.g., history books), he could encourage colleagues and students to describe past events the way documents evidenced events transpired.[51]

In other words, he injected into the profession practices that called for critical analysis of information, asking that people understand what the documents told, why they were written the way they were, who were the intended audiences, and so forth, all standard practices in history by the dawn of the twentieth century. He and his colleagues were said to be practicing "scientific history." Jacques Barzun and Henry F. Graff, two distinguished American historians in the mid-twentieth century, summed up what Ranke and his German cohorts were doing: "They analyzed sources, criticized authorities, compared parallel documents, and when they had finished, they were ready to maintain that they knew what had happened in History."[52] The Germans almost exclusively focused on political history. The two historians just quoted pointed out a pattern encountered in earlier chapters: "A byproduct of the 'scientific' method was that historians were writing for one another rather than for the large public," making the historian a "professional."[53] Ranke was a prolific author, practiced what he advocated, and demonstrated how to do archival-based research. Historian Peter Novick made the point that American scholars in all fields embraced scientific methods in the late 1800s almost as a cult, and that "no group was more prone to scientific imagery, and the assumption of the mantle of science, than the historians."[54] This did not mean creating theories, rather applying "the scientific method" was what von Ranke had proposed: rigid factual and empirical research, yet avoiding hypotheses, remaining neutral on big questions, searching for "definitive" history, von Ranke's mantra of *wissenschaftliche Objecktivität*.[55]

To use historian G. R. Elton's famous expression, nineteenth-century historians launched the creation and use of information as a "controlled reconstruction of the past," what other scholars more warmly bringing the past to life. The British historian/observer of contemporary events Raphael

Samuel argued that the connective activity of past to present "was arguably the hinge of the nineteenth century revolution in historical scholarship and rise of archive-based research." That exercise caused a massive expansion in the kind of information historians sought after and the insights they extracted from extant records.[56]

It is in part because of von Ranke when one reads, say, a biography, that the author will quote from correspondence, diaries, and so forth written by the subject or by others of his or her era. Although criticized for his dismissal of philosophies of history in favor of telling stories based on the hard paper evidence, his approach—"how things actually were" (*wie es eigentlich gewesen*)—became the core guiding light for historians.[57] If this sounds as if paralleling new ways of handling evidence emerging in the mid- to late nineteenth century, that sentiment would fit because facts mattered. Such grand historians as Fernand Braudel and E. H. Carr replaced many of his other historiographical ideas with new ones during the course of the twentieth century, but not the practical matter of how to handle information. As a British historian in the 1960s echoing von Ranke's call for accuracy snarked, "Do not guess, try to count, and if you cannot count, admit that you are guessing;" in other words, generalizing was dangerous business.[58] That is why we still discuss the German historian.[59]

The second practice he advocated for, already reflected in the works of other historians and those working in economics and hard sciences, was the use of citations—footnotes. He and others advocated for these to make it possible for a reader to locate and see for themselves the same sources the author had consulted. It may seem trivial, but his students and then scholars in all fields embraced this practice, not just historians. Over time the use of notes evolved, which is why today, for example, if I quote a letter written by, say, President Abraham Lincoln, I would be expected to have a note that told you to whom he wrote the letter and its date, what collection of manuscripts it came from, even from which box, and within that box even which folder.[60] That practice has now been codified in numerous guides, most often learned from *The Chicago Manual of Style*, which even prescribes the format of the citation to be used by both authors and publishers.[61] The book you are reading has endnotes because of what the German historian demanded. The vast majority of doctoral dissertations in history written since the late 1800s have had as a requirement that students demonstrate their ability to (a) consult and use archival ephemera, (b) cite specifically those sources, and (c) tell the story (history) based on these materials by critically analyzing documents, while piecing together a narrative that makes sense of all this information and defends a point of view about the materials' evidence.[62]

The singular most obvious by-product of Ranke's thinking that fundamentally affected information in the twentieth century was his penchant for consulting primary source materials. Although archival collections were being built and expanded in his day, as the world became wealthier in the twentieth century, it could afford to create massive archival collections, which historians were drawn to for all manner of topics.[63] Collections holding millions of pages of primary materials became commonplace. In the United States, there is, for example, a network of presidential libraries, which house the papers of public officials of individual presidential administrations, including the office papers of the president himself. Thus, there is a presidential library for John F. Kennedy in Boston, one for Lyndon B. Johnson in Austin, and others for the presidents since the late 1920s.[64] For earlier presidents there are collections housed in such places as the U.S. Library of Congress and in various state universities and associations. Some collections are thematic, such as those at the Charles Babbage Institute at the University of Minnesota (your author's home base), which has a large and diverse archival collection devoted to the history of information technology.[65] There are many thousands of such archives around the world that keep adding to their collections.[66]

If there was a downside to the way historians demanded more primary materials, it is that they got their wish: they often now encounter a situation where the number of documents they must consult far exceeds what would have been expected of historians working on similar topics even a half-century earlier. Von Ranke would have been pleased because in his day collections were few and quite manageable. A recent example of how daunting it had all become is the case of Robert A. Cato, who has published (so far) four lengthy volumes on the life of President Lyndon Johnson. The first volume came out in 2002, the fourth in 2012, for a total (so far) of over 3,000 pages.[67] Cato even wrote a short book describing the magnitude of the project, and he was not even an historian, more an outstanding journalist/biographer.[68]

Archivists and historians responded to the growing quantities of materials the same way as librarians did in the 1800s: they organized materials into logical groupings, created finding aids to describe what an archive had, and employed archivists who were intimately familiar with the documents themselves. Beginning in the 1990s, a massive wave of digitizing materials ensued, which has not slowed. So, the productivity of a researcher improved, because in the comfort of one's home office a historian could increasingly consult collections without always having to physically show up at an archive. The majority of archival materials have yet to be digitized, however, so realistically both physical research and virtual research are required. But the key is that many thousands of students and historians brought into the general swirl of information massive amounts of new facts by publishing and writing based on manuscripts and other unpublished ephemera. Those new collections of information became increasingly integrated into already published bodies of facts. In the process, archivists and historians fundamentally changed the content of historical information. Anne Frank's (1929–1945) diary of life in Amsterdam during the World War II is now joined by thousands of other diaries and additionally many millions of pages of personal letters written, say, by families to each other during every major war that the United States has participated in since the 1810s.

Von Ranke and others wrestled with a central issue still evident in today's handling of information by billions of people accessing these over the Internet. What is true, false, misleading, or genuine? Since historians are asked to be objective, what does being objective mean? How do you do it?[69] Historians still struggle with these questions. With the surge of inaccurate and misleading information easily posted onto the Internet, "fake news" is now a major source of "false facts" that can trip up a scholar as much as an ordinary user simply looking for some data, such as the truth of what is Covid-19, a topic that became a boom business for conspiracy peddlers in a matter of weeks in 2020. Historians studying the assassinations of both Abraham Lincoln (1865) and John F. Kennedy (1963) have struggled over similar issues since Ranke's day in the case of Lincoln. In neither instance are historians satisfied that they have properly established all the key details of these events.[70] They are again engaged, as are other experts in multiple academic disciplines, in dealing with similar issues involving the Internet, as they strive to "fact-check" more than simply President Donald Trump's penchant for not telling the truth. Information on both events evolved as new interpretations of prior facts evolved.

WHAT ELSE DID HISTORIANS DO TO INFORMATION: ORAL AND QUANTITATIVE HISTORIES

In addition to injecting archival content into humanity's pool of information and discourse, historians added oral histories, which became an important new class of information, and they dabbled with quantitative history, called *cliometrics*, which too became new forms of information. Of the two additional types, oral histories were the most significant, so far.

Oral history involves the collection of information through interviews, somewhat like a journalist or a lawyer does when gathering facts not available in documents or to enhance understanding of what they contained. Oral histories are typically recorded and later transcribed, and eventually many end up in libraries and archives. These have become possible thanks to the ability to record voices inexpensively since the 1950s. As historians increasingly studied recent history, in which many of the protagonists of a research project were still alive, they interviewed them. The range of interviewees is vast: World War II veterans; surviving Holocaust victims; participants in the American Civil Rights Movement; early developers of computers, satellites, and other technologies; founders of important companies; heads of government agencies; presidents and prime ministers; retired diplomats and military officers; housewives; scientists; rural farmers; and movie stars and musicians, to mention a few. So many have been interviewed that there is even an organization focused on this type of research, the Oral History Association, which has published *The Oral History Review* since 1973.[71]

A leading authority on how to conduct oral histories, Donald Richie, explains: "Oral History collects memories and personal commentaries of historical significance through recorded interviews. An oral history interview generally consists of a well-prepared interviewer questioning an interviewee and recording their exchange in audio or video format."[72] Historians collect this kind of information to fill gaps where traditional documentation is silent, to understand the context in which events occurred, to gain biographical details otherwise unavailable, to gain insights on the motivations of various people for actions they took and for documents they wrote, to understand how a technology functioned or why something was created, to learn what it was like to live and work in a particular circumstance.[73] In short, it is about filling in information gaps and to improve understanding why things happened. But let a practitioner put a finer point on the matter: "It is a creative, interactive methodology that forces us to get to grips with many layers of meaning and interpretations contained within people's memories. It is the combination of oral history as an interactive process (the doing), and the engagement of the historian with the meanings that people ascribe to the past (the interpretation), that marks it out as a peculiar historical practice."[74]

Oral histories are different than legal depositions or interviews conducted by reporters. Lawyers attempt to uncover facts of a circumstance to gather evidence in defense of a position they have already chosen to defend. Not all of their interviews are made public. Journalists too have an agenda, a topic they want to understand and to gain corroborative evidence in support of, such as three people saying that they saw the same thing happen. Their interviews are highly focused and much shorter than those conducted by historians. The latter may conduct one or multiple interviews that run one to several hours a session, so far more in depth. Historians are less focused on finding evidence in support of a specific point of view, such as done by lawyers. They are more interested in uncovering facts they had not considered or known about before.[75]

A historian examines the documented record and reads the secondary literature about a topic or person. Armed with this detail the historian decides what information he or she needs, so what questions to ask. They have developed many effective practices to improve the quality of their interviews. It is not uncommon today for a historian to spend several hours or more preparing for every hour of interview, generating a considerable amount of new information in short order. Some types of history are almost impossible to uncover without recourse to a few or dozens of interviews. Recently for a history of an American government agency, two historians interviewed some 400 people, which by oral history standards is a large number, particularly considering that each interview required hours of preparation, the interviews themselves, and then transcriptions.[76] In some areas of history, it is nearly impossible to conduct research without recourse to oral history interviews, notably about the computer's history or nearly contemporary events. In the case of computing, literally hundreds or interviews have been deposited in libraries, such as at the Charles Babbage Institute and at the Smithsonian Institution.[77] Family historians and local historical societies around the world conduct these too.[78] It is not uncommon while conducting these that the subject of the interview makes available to the interviewer and to libraries and archives paper records and photographs related to the subject of the conversation in their possession.

A second class of new information generated by historians parallels what other disciplines were also creating during the twentieth century: use of statistics, largely applied in the study of economic, demographic (such as census data, parish and military records), social, and business history. This body of information is called cliometrics, and essentially is the application of statistics, as practiced by economists, except these are for events that have already occurred (history), hence no modeling of the future by historians. They rely on using whatever extant numeric and other data are available to them. In short, it is quantitative history.[79] Its practice came into vogue after World War II and gained momentum after it acquired its name in 1960.[80] In 1993 the name gained even more cache when historians Robert William Fogel and Douglass Cecil North were awarded Nobel Prizes in economic sciences for applying economic practices to the study of such topics as slavery and railroads.[81] As with every new form of information, and as mathematical advocates in economics encountered early in their advocacy, economic historians faced critics to such an extent that cliometrics has been less practiced than other forms of historical research.[82] Historians have also suffered from the same problem as librarians: insufficient training in mathematics and statistics.

Cliometrics is also known as *quantitative history*. Its historians use large data sets; use computer modeling; conduct content analysis; and focus primarily on economic, social, ethnographic, and political history. Today there are at least four journals dedicated to this kind of history: *Journal of Interdisciplinary History* (established in 1968), *Historical Methods* (1967), *Cliodynamics: The Journal of Quantitative History and Cultural Evolution* (2010), and the venerable *Social Science History* (1973).[83] Historians tend to think of this subfield as young, but its small band of practitioners have plied their trade for nearly seventy-five years. Through their practices they paralleled work done by political scientists and other social science scholars by introducing more statistical content into their collections of information.

Its practice is opening up new vistas in historical research, while affecting the tone of conversations among historians at large. Ian Morris is an important practitioner of quantitative history in addition to being a clear-thinking writer. Let him explain what this kind of history does to his discipline: "Quantification does not necessarily make debates more objective, but it does normally make them more explicit, forcing rivals to spell out exactly what they mean by the terms they use and to explain why they assign specific numerical values to these differences. Anyone who disagrees with another scholar's judgments will then be able to focus on the evidence and methods being used to calculate the scores, instead of trading vague, undertheorized generalizations."[84] While one could chide him for being too harsh on those who do not quantify, because not all history lends itself to quantification (e.g., a biography), tacit knowledge and deep contextual knowledge of a highly experienced historian is enormously important. Nonetheless, his explanation differentiating this new class of historical information is valid. He points out that quantification was now "well established" in such other social sciences as anthropology, archaeology, economics, public administration, and sociology, so why not in history.[85]

Advocates for quantification can be enthusiastic in their support within various disciplines, which can persuade historians to embrace their methods as a new way to sift through historical evidence. The growing primacy of quantification in the social sciences is, as Morris notes, a growing way to research and present evidence and arguments. Three enthusiastic social scientists give us a sense of the mood today and, perhaps, with a tinge of hubris: "Quantitative data now commonly are presumed to be better, clearer, and more reliable representations of reality than any other form of evidence. The preponderance and ubiquity of quantitative data, coupled with dramatic advances in computational technology and the sheer maturation of quantitative methods, have steadily raised the baselines of mathematical skill required to produce capable quantitative scholarship in the social sciences."[86] While historians are caught up in that milieu, like Morris they are testing its limits and may find as economists did late in the twentieth century that some in their profession had been too exuberant in their use of numbers, which made way for the appropriation of psychological analyses of economic behavior.

WHAT HISTORIANS HAVE LEARNED ABOUT INFORMATION

Over 12,000 members of the American Historical Association are historians or historians-in-training. Most members live in the United States. More than that number work in Europe, and by the time one includes those in Latin America, Asia, and Africa, the number probably exceeds 50,000. That figure does not include journalists and amateur historians, which clearly outnumber the professional ones, that is to say, those with master's or PhD degrees in the discipline. The professionals share in common that each has a point of view about what is information in all its variants: knowledge, data, facts, evidence, primary materials, and so forth.[87] Historians have been commenting on the nature of information for a long time; however, in the past several decades they have started to explore the history of information as a discrete topic per se, just as they see economic history or military history as distinct sub-fields of inquiry.[88] The book you are reading is an example of this new kind of history.

The introductory chapter to this book is a demonstration of how a historian deals with the history of information. They are still formulating definitions, identifying features, and working out the issues, even phrasing for the topic. For example, we have used the word *information* as both an adjective and noun, both in the singular and the plural. In some disciplines data and datum are still being sorted out. The grammarians would point out that *datum* is one piece of information, *data* the plural, but the reader knows everyone ignores that dictum until confronted by a publisher's copyeditor, then we fight over our phrasing. But one trend apparently growing is interest in the topic of information. The *American Historical Review* published a conversation hosted by its editor with a half-dozen historians expert in the subject in 2011.[89] At that time, they (I too) were more wedded to conversations about the ephemera of information, such as books and newspapers, and the tight link with information technologies, specifically computers, than historians were a decade later. These experts in 2011 were still debating differences in meaning of such words as *information* and *knowledge*. As one historian in that earlier conversation declared, "Nowadays information is seen as part of a scale of complexity where data are the raw phenomena and the information is the processing of those phenomena into higher-order meanings."[90] The imprint of information theory is evident here, certainly in this comment. Information theory shifted focus from semantics closer to how information was transmitted. Claude E. Shannon would have been pleased, because today's historians have moved further and speak about networks and ecosystems too. That all happened in less than fifteen years. Knowledge transformed from being about information to various hierarchies of quality, more ill-defined notions of societies and cultures. Knowledge was becoming old school thinking about facts, data, and information. Then there is your author who also likes to think of information as tools.

Nearly a decade later, we could take a tentative pulse of the subject by reading what the editorial team at *Information & Culture* published in a curated issue devoted to celebrating the milestone conversations of recent years about the history of information.[91] Much as we did with other disciplines by looking at their journals of record, here we can quickly summarize common themes. Its editor, Ciaran B. Trace, pointed out that archival history was becoming more about literacy, writing, and social memories; that traditional histories of "The Book" were being reshaped into a subfield of information science for a new "intellectual cross-fertilization"; that information had a history outside of institutions too, such as in homes and other "social spaces"; that scholars could draw from the history of computing, social informatics, business, and economics; and that "information history is situated in a space that transcends academic and disciplinary boundaries."[92] She noted that historians of information were defining new contours of information, showing these "to be allied to the study of artifacts (physical and digital), organizations, workers, institutions, business activities, and the communication practices of everyday life."[93] Definitions and issues to discuss remained in flux, as always happens in new subfields. She concluded that these historians were "challenged to define the full nature and expanse of the domain of information history and to think about how to foster stronger connections between its disciplinary subfields."[94]

One fundamental perspective embraced by historians of information is that in all ages of recorded human history people lived in social environments densely laden with information, so there were earlier "information ages" before ours.[95] Long before computers, people used organized bodies of information housed in newspapers, pamphlets, and books. Before these, people had handwritten books, and even earlier, scrolls were written on papyrus, animal skins, or parchment. Handwritten books were called *codices*, the tomes monks spent years writing and copying by hand before invention of the European printing press in the mid-1400s. Once that innovation came, its use set off a massive increase in organized information much as we are seeing today with an even greater upsurge in information on the Internet.[96]

The Internet stimulated thinking about what information circulates in a society, how people obtain, use, and shape it. It has been a quick stimulus for the subfield. Historians like William Aspray, Paul Ceruzzi, and myself began as students of computing's past and so observed up close the emergence of the Internet. But, after it began diffusing, we began migrating to studies of information, first information and the Internet, and then Aspray and myself to information partially separated from the technology.[97] Aspray succeeded the most in distancing information per se from the technology, but aware they remained linked. The book you are reading reflects that continuing effort by historians to give information its own space while acknowledging its ties to information technologies (paper, electrical, and digital) and its roots in intellectual disciplines and institutions. That is a contribution historians are using to shape their view of information in the twenty-first century.

CONCLUSIONS

If there is a broad historical generalization to make here, rather than wait for some finale in the last chapter, it is that across all fields of information, facts became more "scientific" over the past fifteen decades. The evidence was everywhere: in scientific research methods, in the thirst for empirical data, and in the use of statistics and mathematics. Historians were swept up by such realities. And why not? These approaches worked to help researchers and users of facts to flush out vast quantities of useful information. But, that megatrend also put some residents of the information ecosystem on the defensive, such as those who worked in the fine arts, literature, and some social sciences; students of politics; and historians. Historian Parson E. Tillinghast, commenting on the relationship between historians and their readers at the start of the 1970s did not hesitate to openly plant the problem: "The question whether history can properly be labeled a science or whether it is really a branch of literature has provoked a great deal too much attention."[98] The concern is that historians share attributes of both, each overlapping in their work, and for that matter, that of other disciplines in the humanities and social sciences. There is no neat, clean division of duties and disciplinary boundaries. Ambiguity weaves through their disciplines like a chronic condition in an age that demands increasing specificity, clarity of scope, and more sharply delineated intellectual boundaries. When measured against the benchmark of hard science and mathematics, some of these disciplines are seen as within the veil, others outside the walls of accuracy and science. The more one moves away from current reality (the home of science) the more one engages with historical reality, such as what historians, anthropologists, and even poets and novelists deal with, a point made several times in this book. But what disciplines beyond the pale did largely in the twentieth century was to gain partial entrance into the scientific ecosystem with mixed results. Both sides weaponized information, what we have politely been referring to as *shaping information*.

Lest I create the impression that historians have gone all in on new information history, historian Adam Crymble reminds us that despite using personal computers and making accessible online vast quantities of historical information, they remain "resolutely tied to scholarly traditions—dust in the archives rather than bytes in the computer's memory."[99] This has the tone of what economists were experiencing vis-à-vis mathematics in the

1920s–1940s. Yet, we agree that as historians become more reliant, hence familiar with computing, these experiences will shape what information they use and how they collect and handle it. In turn, that will cause transformations in the historical data (facts) themselves. Crymble points to the sources of historian's evolving engagement with technologies that I contend are affecting information itself. His short list applies to social scientists, humanists, and STEM academics: archives, classrooms, self-learning ecosystems (e.g., a colleague showing you how to download an app), and scholarly communications (e.g., growing use of blogs and individual websites to transmit their research and insights).[100]

While we have occasion later to discuss implications, here one can recognize that social sciences and the humanities have produced ideas and perspectives that, too, can be considered forms of information, not just necessarily fashionable scientific-formatted types. Let Tillinghast comment further, because his stance continues to be widely supported a half-century later by well-intentioned, even brilliant, scholars and writers, so there is merit to be considered as part of the humanistic *weltanschauung*, or worldview: "Some of us to (*sic*) recreate for our readers a way of life long past, different enough from ours to have interest and excitement; others stress the factors in a more statistically treated analysis of societal pressures."[101] He points out that most historians are humanistic:

> They present a portrait of a personality or an era. Social scientist-historians insist on the usefulness of history in solving certain kinds of problems, and they base intelligent political and social action on an understanding of the implications of these problems. The humanists offer a selection of past experience to form some kind of unity, and they hope to gain from it a deeper insight into "human nature in general," a term they carefully avoid defining. The social scientists enlarge on a properly analyzed past as a possibly quantifiable guide for future policies. Most historians, in their sensible way, have one foot in each camp.[102]

But as a distinguished historian, Carl Becker, expressed for the vast majority of academic historians and many who were not but practiced the craft well over seven decades ago, "History prepares men to live more humanely in the present, and to meet, rather than foretell, the future."[103] Whatever it is that helps one confront the future is obviously information, tacit knowledge, insight, or whatever one wishes to call it. I see it as yet-hard-to-define information tools.

But it is an idea that attracted attention from inside and outside the pale of scientific information. Social scientists, political scientists, and historians long thrived here, now being joined by psychologists and biologists. We know it is a hunch or intuition. Either way, it is about laboring with ambiguity, or to put it more precisely, the acquisition of information without having to reason consciously to arrive at it.[104] Philosophers have fed off this phenomenon for a long time; famous twentieth-century psychologists have too, including Sigmund Freud (1856–1939), yes another Austrian, and Carl Jung (1875–1961), but he was Swiss.[105]

Like the librarians, historians, political "scientists," and those living in the humanities, all sought the respectability that scientists were gaining over these many decades.[106] In the twentieth century they were mildly suffering from a collective case of inferiority complex and so seemed slightly defensive when describing the value of what they studied and about their methods. At the conclusion of discussions about the information, social scientists and the humanistic traditions offered up did not just lack the specificity of a number or some provable fact in science, these were not clearly precise enough for our second or third industrial age, especially in the face of such magnificent achievements as curing diseases, sending humans to the Moon, or peering trillions of light years into the universe.

So historians, and to varying degrees, their cohorts in the humanities (less so in the social sciences), do not organize information as hypotheses to be tested, rather they confront facts of events having already taken place. A president was elected, a war was fought, a society enjoyed greater or lesser health, and so forth. That reality of their craft is, however, what helped them to shape information. They never made it to the promised land of the hard sciences, although they loaded massive amounts of new information onto their disciplinary wagons.[107] I have always found it fascinating that so many American presidents and European prime ministers, including Winston Churchill, read a great deal of history. Their behavior has been evident for over a century. They were always busy people, and history articles and books were never short, pithy briefing documents; they required large blocks of time to digest, let alone read. Why did they do this? It comes back to how this chapter started, by recognizing that people who work outside the pale of hard science had to deal with forms of information that in the modern age people wanted to avoid: the imprecise, the tacit, what philosophers, priests, poets, artists, and one's old wise grandmother knew to be wisdom. Our diplomats lived with this reality. As the adage goes, everyone knows it when they see it, but nobody can define it. Wisdom remained at the frontier of information as one worked through the first 20 percent of the twenty-first century: it was there, valuable, but still difficult to define, let alone acquire in some industrially organized (a.k.a. scientific) manner.

Political scientists aligned with social scientists and their methods of working with and structuring information. By the end of the century, a political scientist could shout from the rooftops that "political science is one of the *social sciences*."[108] But, of course, not all political scientists grabbed their calculators and pulled up spreadsheets. They were about also understanding "common sense, folk traditions, and craft and practical knowledge mediated through everyday life experience."[109] But let us be clear, their approach in how they shaped the forms of their information parallel to those of other social scientists. As a political scientist observed, "The methodologies that underlie political science research also direct inquiry in its sister social sciences." We know from the behavior of others described in earlier chapters that one's approach to information influenced how they shaped it.[110]

Why have this discussion here? If there is an innate "wisdom of the crowds," as business journalist James Surowiecki argued compellingly was so, then this may mean we are moving in the direction of the humanists, increasingly joined by psychologists and students of how humans make decisions.[111] If crowds are smarter than the experts, and if the case is increasingly being proven that they for certain matter, can we observe a collective acceptance of information crafted by all the cohorts we have studied in this book? Can we do this observing altered behavior clearly influenced by the changing nature of information in recent times? Surowiecki pointed out what our cohorts from this chapter already knew: diversity of information and opinions about that when brought to bear on a problem or issue is an important part of the answer for why crowds are generally smarter than our shapers of information.[112] And for certain, they force continuous transformation of information.

Chapter 10

How Information Evolved

We need to know—and, of course, we must also understand how to make productive use of—a great many truths.

Harry G. Frankfurt[1]

Harry G. Frankfurt is a philosopher, and in the epigraph above states a fundamental belief shared by societies for at least as long as people have kept records, for as long as they have had priests and philosophers: truth is essential to living successfully. His use of the word *productive* is a suitable adjective with which to describe the intent and value of information. Nowhere does this seem so true as in the profound economic, social, technological, and scientific transformations people experienced over the past two centuries. The enormous changes humankind experienced in the previous several centuries were made possible by having a rapidly growing body of information—truths to use Frankfurt's word—that could be used to solve a growing portfolio of old and new problems and to pursue opportunities. The accumulation of accurate and useful information increased in volume and speed in its creation and distribution since the mid-nineteenth century. We are still living in a period where the volume and diversity of information continues to increase and intensify, today thanks to such features of modern society as the Internet, artificial intelligence (AI), and the oldest of these technologies, computing.

So this book has no logical ending. It is written as the story continues to unfold. Therefore, I propose that we treat as tentative any conclusions drawn on modern experience with information, except for the multi-thousand-year belief that accurate information—truth—is useful, regardless of what technologies and media platforms are in use. Cave drawings accurately depicting bison, horses, and elephants in France and Spain were of use to the artists and their constituencies, so too computerized models informing officials about effective public health policies to implement during a pandemic.

This chapter pulls together broad findings and conclusions learned in earlier chapters. I first explain how information evolved in broad terms across time, disciplines, and formats. My intent is not to provide a formal theory of how information changes, rather to describe some of its obvious patterns as an assist in understanding the role of information in modern times. Then I discuss the consequences of information's transformation and, frankly, its diversity. A third section presents a discussion of the implications of these changes for the future of information. In defense of an historian speculating about the future—normally a very bad practice in that discipline—I am continuing research on the current evolution of information, focusing on trends since the 1990s, so in support of some of the observations made in this last chapter.

HOW INFORMATION EVOLVED

I begin by summarizing why it evolved. While several distinct reasons can be offered up, all increasingly were present with one or another more or less important, depending on when. Computers were an important influence, but that is a post-1950 one, while the role of new professions more so since at least the mid-1800s. Once an influence came into play, it remained active, entwining with others. Nineteenth-century historian Leopold von Ranke, credited with developing many of the practices of the modern historian, would have understood that causal analyses are thus complicated by the milieu of events and new influences. Second, while the story told in this book is largely about events in the United States, the evolution of information was largely a global one. To think it involved only both sides of the Atlantic is to ignore events in South America and Asia and even in Africa, the latter particularly during its colonial phases. Any history of modern information and its disciplines largely tell the story of European professors, universities, and their research activities as dominant in the evolution of information. North American dominance in that behavior did not begin to become evident until at least the 1920s–1930s and most obvious after World War II. That we know less about such activities outside the Atlantic community does not signal inactivity. Yet, we know the most about European and North American transformers of information, so we began by studying their activities. Librarians on both sides of the Atlantic worked, émigré scientists from Nazi Europe did too in the United States and elsewhere, and computing became quickly a global affair. Because I focused largely on events in the United States there is work to be done to study the developments in other countries.[2] With these caveats in mind, there is a combination of five behaviors and factors to summarize.

First, a great deal of new information was produced during the period of the Second Industrial Revolution. At its core, much of it was demographic, scientific, economic, or otherwise—often called *objects*—that required understanding. That production of new information, in turn, led to new fields of specialization—I have used the word *disciplines* to describe that development—that expanded the domain of broad subjects, but most formidably in science. As Jürgen Renn observed, this development led to "a handful of abstract concepts," yielding a vast array of scientific knowledge. "The concepts of space, time, force, motion, matter, and a few others played the role for classical physics, the concept of chemical compounds assumed a similarly foundational role for chemistry; and the concepts of species, gene, selection, variation, and adaptation structured classical evolutionary biology."[3] These are the objects that served as the basis for much new information.

Second, the emergence of all this new information energized, but also worried, increasing numbers of those creating it and those charged with assisting. All wanted to be able to access and master the scope of these rising mountains of facts. That is how the librarians entered our narrative, working to organize this content, then to make it available to humanity. Melvil Dewey's work is emblematic of these efforts, but they remain a continuing process. Lest anyone think the librarians were slackers, a literature review of such issues as informetrics, webometrics, data mapping, and visualization studies covering just developments between 2000 and 2007 yielded nearly 14,000 citations of articles and other publications about projects and measures core to the work of the librarians organizing information. Recall, they had been at this activity since the early 1800s.[4] Librarians, too, similarly experienced what affected scientists. The author of the literature survey explains: "At the beginning of the 21st century, besides the 'traditional' major informetric topics, citation analysis, theory and productivity measures that continue to thrive, we witness the emergence of new topics, like webometrics, the h-index and open and electronic access and the strengthening of previously existing topics."[5]

A third factor was the expanding role of electrification of information, beginning with the telegraph and continuing to various forms of data storage made possible by tabulating equipment, magnetic tape, later disk drives, and other forms of computer-related storage facilities. When combined with computers and telecommunications the ability to cost-effectively collect, store, analyze, and learn from information expanded exponentially. That growth in capability to store and process information—users called it *data processing*—increased at double-digit rates of percentages for three-quarters of a century (so far). Like what the physical scientists and librarians face, computer scientists and users of their technology still do not see an end in sight for slowdown in the expansion of digitized—electrified—information. Computer scientists and IT business executives see very soon, the ability to collect information on the activities of almost every human on Earth; already thousands of pieces of data about you are collected each day. For over a century, mechanical aids to data processing have been useful tools to assist in the collection, organization, and use of information. In the process of doing so, these became entwined work methods of a discipline with the capabilities of computers.[6] The future promises entirely new collections of facts to work with, such as that of the several billion people using Facebook.

Earlier I discussed the role of statistics as a new branch of mathematics that began emerging in a formal manner in the nineteenth century. By the early years of the twenty-first century statisticians were thinking similarly as computer scientists, echoing Claude E. Shannon and his telegraphic/telephonic constructs, which he had worked out in the 1930s and 1940s, most famously his notions of signals and noise. One expert on teaching statistics promulgated as one of his core rules of behavior using language that computer scientists would recognize stipulated that "signals always come with noise: It is trying to separate out the two that makes the subject interesting. Variability is inevitable, and probability models are useful as an abstraction."[7]

The continued evolution of computing created a fourth reason for why information evolved. Essentially to the end of the twentieth century and, too, with the wide availability of the Internet, humans controlled how computers collected information. Millions of people manually injected information into computers, first busily typing in data as "data entry clerks" since the 1890s with tabulating equipment and punched cards, later into computers. Only in the 1960s did the technology evolve sufficiently that some data entry could be partially automated, allowing software and hardware to accept information through scanning and moving it about from one program or file to another. That trend has continued to the present, growing exponentially in practice. However, we now have two situations shifting how this is done. First, the development of sensors, both big and small, built with computing into them, have taken over a great deal of the data collection done earlier by humans, while also acquiring the capability of accumulating vast quantities that no person could possibly do. Stock transactions on Wall Street are collected and analyzed in fractions of a second, satellites measure temperatures of the oceans at many localities every second; examples are endless. Today, more data flows through the Internet contributed by sensors than by humans. These sensors do not put into the Internet data in human language, rather as those signals and noises referred to by Shannon. Only when humans want to insert themselves into this body of information do computers convert it into anthropomorphic objects. A century earlier, almost all information was anthropomorphic; now these are exceptions.

An additional new aspect is the growing role of AI, specifically the expanding capability of these technologies to do analytical and decision-making work of humans. AI can be instructed to interact with sensors in the language of sensors—not human—to understand, make decisions, and take action. In a very primitive way this started with expert systems in the 1970s, today sensors and AI guide flight into space. Almost every weather report you read on a website or newspaper is no longer written by a human; an expert system using grammar and data-handling rules does it very well. The list of examples is not endless, as in data processing, but rapidly growing in number. The central command and control of humans shaping what information is collected, how it is collected and used continues to shift to computing, although people are currently still in charge.[8] This is not the place to debate the rivalry of "man versus machine," but it is for pointing out the obvious: computing can do many things with information that people cannot, and the need to do so remains vital. César Hidalgo of MIT's Media Lab explained: "The universe is made of energy, matter, and information, but information is what makes the universe interesting. Without information, the universe would be an amorphous soup. It would lack the shapes, structures, aperiodic orders, and fractal arrangements that give the universe both its beauty and its complexity."[9] He made the point librarians had 150 years earlier, that "information is physical" and should no longer be viewed as, "a synonym for the ethereal, the unphysical, the digital, the weightless, the immaterial."[10] It is the reordering of physical items, such as one sees when shuffling a deck of playing cards, each with a fact (number or value). Hidalgo proposed an answer to the question of why information continues to grow in quantity and types: "So in the word of atoms and economies the growth of information hinges on the eternal dance between information and computation. This dance is powered by the flow of energy, the existence of solids, and the computational abilities of matter."[11]

A fifth source for why information evolved is economic. Simply put, the world could afford to acquire, change, and use more information. That ability made it possible to create new wealth, improve standards of living, and so forth. This symbiotic back-and-forth co-dependency between economic prosperity and the application of new information is nothing less than a spectacular feature of human activity that we so boringly refer to as the *Second Industrial Revolution*. It is the story told in chapter 2. To be sure, it is not a perfect world, because humans are not masters of everything, as the pandemic of the 2020s brutally demonstrated. However, humankind is wealthier, safer, and healthier today than in 1860. Information is also far less expensive, more useful, and better than in 1860. Charles Babbage was commissioned by the British Government in the early 1800s to build what today we loosely could, and do, call a *computer*. The project was expensive enough that only one of the wealthiest nations on Earth could afford to support the project, and while technological limits frustrated his attempts, these limitations did not hide the confidence of this era in its ability to fund and attempt to build such a system.

A century and a half later, the government of the United States still continued that tradition with its various military, scientific, and medical investments through grants and contracts. Babbage would have understood the importance of DARPA, NASA, and the NIH.

Now we need to ask: What changed? It helps to begin by acknowledging that many students of the nature and history of information debate its definition; we engaged in that at the start of this book. That ongoing exercise suggests definitions and descriptions remain in flux. It seems that every time I write about information, I, too, am compelled to engage in similar exercises.[12] But it seems those who study the topic almost invariably come to the point where they describe the existence of data, which are seen as components of information that, when multiple collections of information are aggregated, result in knowledge, and that ultimately leads to wisdom. Figure 10.1 captures the essence of that notion. The journey is hierarchical from the lowly explicit piece of datum (e.g., signals, a fact, a number) to less specific but more actionable and relevant insights (i.e., knowledge, rules of thumb) to the ultimate tacit form of information, wisdom (e.g., "You will know when it is time to retire"). Datum is a humble reality, wisdom the highest form of abstract findings. Humans handle this hierarchy well, perhaps AI will too. So the depiction in figure 10.1 represents the most widely conceived model coming into the twentieth century and that survived relatively intact. The language changed over time, such as from the nineteenth-century use of knowledge to the greater preference for information, to the expanded application of facts for information by the end of the century, so too descriptions of their features. For the most part it remains a familiar construct in the third decade of the twenty-first century.

While it remains a useful model, I present a modestly different one that reflects changing circumstances in the concept of information, building on the earlier one, because both are simultaneously useful. One of the reasons

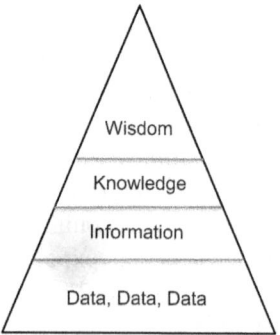

Figure 10.1. Evolution of Information: Traditional View

that the traditional model works is because it is demonstrably true, a solid reflection of different types of facts, insights, and so forth. It has also allowed students of information to conveniently organize features and commentary, even alternative models. For example, with respect to the category of Information, one can point out that its material is less disaggregated than in the category labeled Data. In other words, information requires multiple data that somehow are related and that specific information is dependent on that intimacy among the data. Another involves the category marked Knowledge. It is here that one looks for multiple collections of information translating into patterns, into the ability to recognize those, and to apply experience (e.g., personal or learned from others). Within the category of Wisdom, one looks for more tacit, ill-defined but relevant insights that also require solid pattern recognition skills. They want results of which that can be applied, or at least formulated into specific recommendations for actions and opinions. All were subject to change as one affected the other in dynamic fashion.

The traditional view makes possible more explicit cataloging of activities involved in the collection and transformation of information. Under the category of Data, where there are many collections of facts that may or may not be related to each other, the key activities involve that actual accumulation of these facts and organizing them into collections, which is what the librarians and database administrators always did. Much work has been done to study the activities and features of data.[13] Under the category of Information, the key activity is the aggregation of the most useful (e.g., right) data sets, so a broader, perhaps more sophisticated, form of organizing information into sufficient groups to allow someone to embrace a point of view and to take action. In the category of Knowledge, one describes mastery of a larger body of information, the ability to apply this without necessarily having to examine specific narrower instances (cases) that can prove influential. One often crudely thinks of this as the "elevator answer" to a problem or question. Wisdom extends that exercise.

The four categories make it possible to discuss the messy issue of a collection of information straddling more than just one neat category. Those engaged since the 1970s with what came to be known as *knowledge management* frequently believed they straddled at least information and knowledge, hence their self-imposed descriptor Knowledge Management (KM).[14] I was involved in KM between the 1980s and the end of the century and felt that straddling.[15] If figure 10.1 feels like a supply chain and not simply a hierarchy, that would be a fair categorization of the discussion. One could just as easily imagine a figure with four boxes read from left to right of data, information, knowledge, and wisdom, with arrows directing one from one box to next.

However, not all data eventually ends up being part of someone's information (e.g., an address file), nor does wisdom track back its genealogy directly to specific data sets, let alone a datum, but it could. Information changes faster than knowledge, so presumptions underpinning knowledge could be faulty when there is a disconnect between newer or different information than what undergirded someone's knowledge. That gets back to earlier discussions in this book about how as circumstances changed, one's prior experience could be less valuable than what new evidence, including models and predictions, suggested or represented current reality.[16] The widely held belief that wisdom transcends that problem has yet to be empirically proven (or at least that finding widely disseminated), although if observational and anecdotal evidence is believed, such as what emerges from religious beliefs, or out of the mouths of people with gray hair, its acceptance endures.

Now look at figure 10.2, which suggests that during the twentieth century a new paradigm began to emerge in parallel with what was depicted in the earlier figure. The cases examined in prior chapters hinted at this development. First, there was the presentation made by Claude E. Shannon, later by experts in the computer sciences and telecommunications, that data or information was electronic signals or, to use my earlier term, electrified information. Clusters of data formed the basis of well-defined, highly structured, even hierarchically formed databases, which served either as surrogates or replacements for the notion of information. Databases became necessary when facts were electrified, or if one prefers more precision, magnetized to store on tape and disks. It was required by the nature of the physical technology to be organized in such ways that software and hardware could be used to house and display what otherwise would be anthropomorphically called facts, data, or simply information. In other words, physical features of computers compelled the need for databases to be conceived as forms of information.

From that collection of facts one needed a way to gain insights based on multiple groups of data. For that a new form of information evolved, conveniently called models, largely after the 1950s. With models people applied mathematics (e.g., statistics) to glean probabilities. Models, which I have referred to as "fictions," are suppositions of what reality looks like, or could. I am not alone in that supposition.[17] Scott E. Page, a clear-thinking expert on

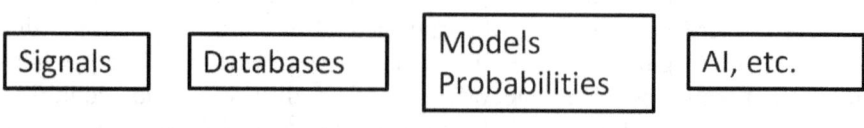

Figure 10.2.   Evolution of Information: Emerging View

how to use models, thinks of them as "analogies," or as "fictional worlds," both "mined for ideas and insights."[18] When combined with visualization techniques, it is how, for example, we understand the existence of black holes in space and recently, even images of what they look like.[19] Finally, there is the growing addition of AI, artificially created intelligence (i.e., mechanical and software-based thought) that holds the potential of being more capable than humans to collect and process information and to take actions on the physical world through its own cognitive functions. If we can learn more about how humans change information, these lessons can be applied by AI to do the same.

Two facets of this emerging new view of information became apparent in the course of conducting research for this book. First, interactions with signals moving about in this paradigm can occur simultaneously, which is a difficult task for humans to perform. We think about one thing at a time, so if we have multiple issues to ponder, we do it one after the other.[20] One may do that many times in some iterative fashion, but we are challenged to run multiple mental models at the same time or in parallel as independent exercises. If we could do otherwise, I would want you to simultaneously read and digest all the chapters in this book. When we ask a super computer to compare, contrast, and document the interactions of millions of compounds to find a vaccine that might prevent a disease, we ask that system to run those models at the same time. That means they must dialogue back and forth with other models in real time, or that they run independently of each other at the same time. There is less respect for the formality of hierarchy from a processing perspective, because, as with Big Data practices, that behavior changes information. For example, a person who knew how to speak a half-dozen languages in the early 1900s could translate a phrase either because they had acquired specific information about what that looked like in the language to which it must be converted or had acquired other information that gave him or her the knowledge, or wisdom, to construct a workable translation. People who studied Latin often say it proves valuable in navigating Romance languages. That human act of translation could reasonably be said to require a hierarchy of information management activities. But in the emerging new, more horizontal paradigm, one does not need knowledge or wisdom.

Rather, the one required is the ability to construct probabilities, not to know two languages. Take all the vocabulary in the two languages and ask a computer to search for all possible combinations of words based on its massive databases of the two, such as looking for whole sentences drawn from publications using the words presented to it in the order in which they were offered (e.g., a specific sentence). Then ask it to come back and say, in effect, "Based on the phrase you want translated, there is a 98.4 percent probability that it looks like." We see it on a screen simply presented as the translated text without the qualifying statement that the odds are pretty high that the translation is x, y, and z. Again, no knowledge of the language is required. That is an epic change from what a human translator does. The act of translation is then the action of comparing and contrasting similar sets of electronic signals (e.g., the configuration of the pulses, like in telegraphy or in more modern forms, the combination of zeroes and ones in bits and bytes). The same concept of probability is increasingly applied to all manner of information handling, which is why modeling and statistics are caused to collaborate.

During the Second Industrial Revolution, use of graphical representations of concepts (e.g., knowledge and wisdom) proved increasingly useful for communicating abstract notions, or at least ambiguous data, and to explain their relationships to each other over space and time. We are all familiar with organization charts and how convenient they are; undoubtedly the reader has also seen PowerPoint presentations using graphical representations of complex ideas. That is what we do with figure 10.3, a very twentieth-century form of information display. Its new vision suggests several features of information as it evolved over time. From the nineteenth century to our time, anecdotal information, which was the result of observing specific situations, began being replaced or forced to co-exist with increasingly more experimental (e.g., scientific or mathematical) information. Anecdotal and observational information never went away; it just no longer dominated descriptions of information.

Second, small quantities of information displayed different features than higher volumes of data, facts, or information (use the term you are most comfortable with). Those features are listed to the left of the chart. As information increases in volumes, so do its characteristics change. Again, as in the

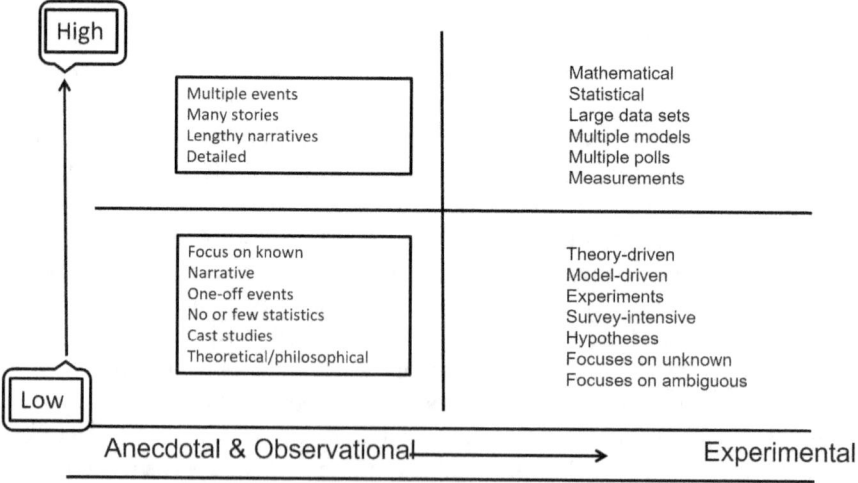

Figure 10.3. Types of Information Model

instance of type of information, these features are present today as they were a century ago, when looking at anecdotal and observational information. As information became more experimental, low volumes displayed certain characteristics, and those volumes increased or acquired additional or different features. Those are displayed to the right in figure 10.3. The features to the left are contained in the two boxes to suggest that they are far more clearly defined and specific because of their narrow scope, while those on the right have less defined informational boundaries and so may expand or contract based on changing circumstances more than would those on the left. All four quadrants' catalog descriptors discussed in earlier chapters are now brought together into this one composite figure.

We use the model presented in figure 10.3 to depict briefly the arc of historical changes that occurred to information over the past two centuries. Figures 10.4 and 10.5 impose on our model types of information and where the originators of new information fit in roughly 1870, and again a century later. It is at best a rough estimation that one could accuse of presenting a view only as anecdotal and observational—fair enough. In their defense where a particular topic or creator of information is positioned grew out of the more detailed presentation about these various types of facts that came out of the research presented in earlier chapters. For our purpose, we need a high-level reasonable conceptual framework—tacit knowledge—to typify classes of information, one that highlights contrasts and similarities between the distances of a century, or that can inform future research on the subject, all situated in some contextual form. These figures allow us to stand back from the detail embedded in individual chapters to see how content in one relate to another.

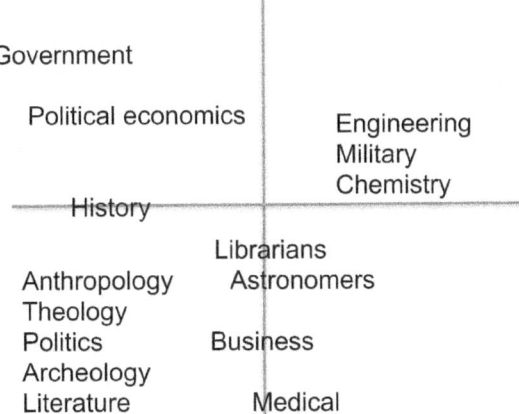

Figure 10.4. Sample Types of Information by Subject and Profession, 1870

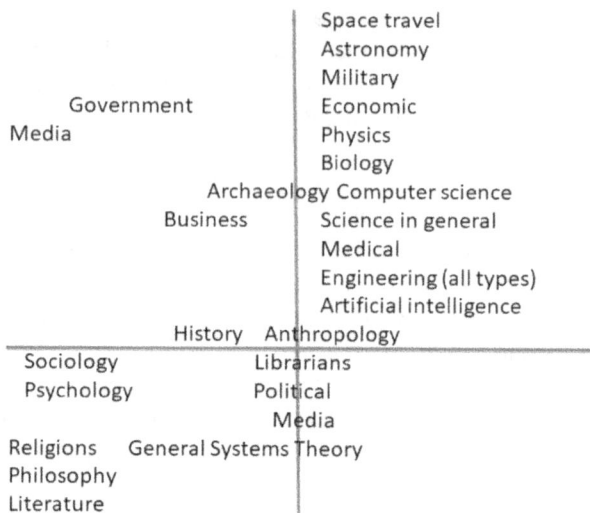

Figure 10.5. Sample Types of Information by Subject and Profession, 1970

These two figures suggest several facts. First, between 1870 and 1970, the number of new topics and their features increased and became increasingly more scientific, explicit, theory-based, and numeric. Second, these topics and their creators displayed behaviors and offered up new bodies of information that older ones had occupied in the 1870s as well as in the 1970s. Governments and the humanities are examples. We can see that some subjects shifted more than others. For instance, librarians were in the lower-left-hand corner in the 1870s, trying to move toward the lower-right-hand side to which a century later they had made some progress, having also inched closer to the upper-right-hand quadrant. If one were to create a figure based on 2020, the librarians might be pleased to know I would squarely put them in the lower end of the upper right quadrant, because they had moved substantially from the 1980s in their use of computing. Because agriculture has become such a science-based profession, where farmers use satellites, Big Data, analytics, scientific and managerial information, and other modern data-handling tools in 2020, I would place them just a tad below biology in the upper right-hand corner.

Notice in Figure 10.5 that the crosshairs in the chart are not perfectly centered. That is to signal the majority of the subjects and creators had migrated to the upper right-hand quadrant over time, a process still underway. That is to say, using the template from Figure 10.3, many subjects and their creators developed and relied upon information that was more mathematical and statistical, based on larger data sets, models, polling, and measures than a century ago.

A secondary issue weaving its way through this book has been about the diffusion of information through society. We have commented on facilitative events, such as rising rates of literacy and formal education, credentialing, and licensing of professions. But those are not all the influences affecting the spread of information through society. The literature on diffusion is now substantial, and in earlier projects I learned a great deal about how that happens, as have other historians, particularly with respect to computing.[21] Here one can ask the question of the research underpinning this book: Are there patterns of transformation in information that facilitated diffusion, that is to say, new or greater uses of data, facts, and knowledge?

To answer that question, students of diffusion often use analogies of either ocean waves crashing on shores which, while never exactly the same, do the job of bringing ocean waters to a beach on a continuous basis. Others think in terms of what happens when one throws stones into a lake and sees waves spread out in a 360-degree manner. The latter analogy works comfortably with what information spread through society. The idea is simple. Every time a new form of information emerged, think of that as a stone tossed into the still lake. A still lake can be thought of as a useful paradigm of accepted beliefs, practices, and data. It is somewhat analogous to what Thomas S. Khun famously argued happened in science, and what we saw with librarians comfortable with their own worldviews until the computer community disturbed their universe.[22] Instead of waves, he thought in terms of extant paradigms, which collapsed under the weight of new information. Once a stone was tossed in, a new form of information forever changed the surface of the lake, the same in a profession or in the nature of information. Think of new forms of information as the pebbles, and accept, as I argue, that the pebble throwers had an agenda, a reason for tossing stones. Reasons tied their professional development and careers in support of those institutions that supported their jobs, statures, and professional ecosystems.

Think also of each tossed pebble as larger than previous ones, while waves created by earlier ones were still pushing forward. With each toss the next stone has to be larger if it is to overcome, or least push along, the effects of the previous wave, otherwise it has no effect as no new wave is launched or is blocked from proceeding. Figure 10.6 begins to capture the essence of this idea. It is also a way of stating an obvious conclusion drawn from earlier chapters: That there was a sequence of types of changed information that subsumed disciplines and professions to one degree or another. Nobody operated in isolation from each other. Of course, each new wave influenced the nature of information in different professions and disciplines at varying rates and speeds of adoption, which make graphical representations of the phenomenon admittedly contrived. But that can always be adjusted if one looks at specific disciplines, topics, or professions.

I can quickly summarize the findings. In the mid-1800s narrative facts (qualitative facts) dominated the world of information. That was followed by the growing use of numbers with subsequent expanded development and application of mathematics and statistics (data). Then theory-based and modeling by discipline became the norm, and which could not have been done without the language of mathematics. This was particularly so in the hard sciences, later increasingly in the social sciences. Models should be included in this wave, since so many were based on the use of mathematics. Thank the economists for helping us to understand the rationale for this observation. Then most recently there are general systems theories, now slowly working their way through the world of information as the latest attempt to bring together these separations of data and information that our pebble analogy suggests are occurring. This chapter discusses general systems thinking later, but for now think of it as if an attempt to create a Big Bang theory that explains how all the universe (all information) was created and works. The hunt is on for such a theory to explain information and humanity's involvement with it. More or less, information transformed into these types of information through five phases. Each overlapped and, like the water in the lake, never went away; they simply mixed with other information.

Did a similar process unfold with respect to institutions and professions that emerged in the same period? In other words, were there waves of organizations and professions formed that could be tied to the patterns outlined in figure 10.6? The answer is yes. Thinking in terms of institutions and professions in our pebble waves help here, too. In the early 1800s core residences of information were in people's beliefs and experiences, their published supplies of facts largely in history, agriculture, and some medicine. To be sure this is

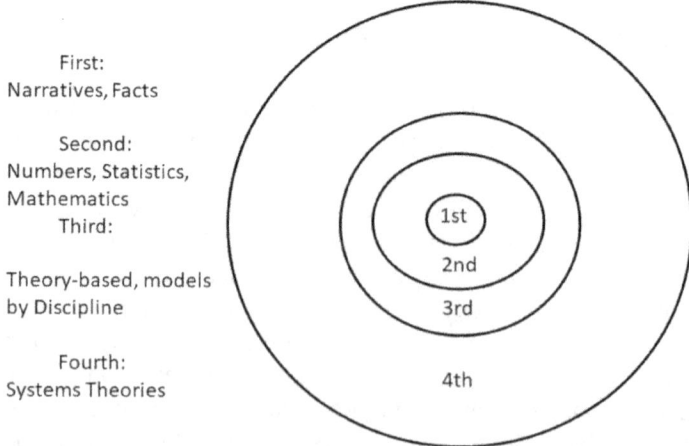

Figure 10.6. Waves and Patterns of Information Transformations, Waves 1860s–2000s

a broad generalization, however, it quickly began changing by mid-century as mathematicians, engineers, political economists, and librarians created a second wave, which by the end of the century included statisticians, doctors, and scientists. A third wave could be imagined by 1900 pushing out in all disciplinary and professional directions as new jobs, specializations, academic disciplines, professional societies, and publishers increased in number and diversity. Disciplines clearly dominated this third wave, these being defined largely by academics as a long process taking the entire twentieth century to spread out.

We may now be seeing the start of a fourth wave spreading out. This one is facilitated by the use of communications and computing—the *digital plumbing* referred to in earlier chapters—which is sufficiently installed around the world to almost dare us to use the adjective ubiquitous with which to describe it. I dare to suggest this because as the first draft of this chapter was being written, thousands of satellites had been launched in just one payload into space to provide global access to the Internet.[23] With Earth increasingly being "wired," and no longer an exaggeration promoted by enthusiastic technophiles, humankind worldwide is experiencing simultaneously the spread of information.

That circumstance stands in contrast to earlier waves. In the nineteenth century, only the most economically prosperous nations dotted with large population centers were creators or recipients of new information, established new institutions, and developed new professions. That was essentially a story of U.S. East Coast and Western European developments during the first wave. These then seeped inland westward in the United States and into a few parts of Latin America (e.g., Argentina), eastward in Western Europe, particularly into the northern half of the continent, and sporadically into Asia, largely Japan and later South Korea and Taiwan. As communications and transportation infrastructures improved and dropped significantly in cost during the course of the Second Industrial Revolution, new information and its social and professional manifestations developed more rapidly and spread increasingly in more uniform fashion. One could track that increased velocity by counting the number of publications that appeared by topics, subscription rates, birth dates of academic and professional organizations and their number of members, and later work licenses issued by country. Much of the work to document such activity has yet to be done, but some has been. When I wrote *All the Facts*, which focused on U.S. developments since the 1870s, I felt nearly overwhelmed by the amount of rich statistical and observational evidence supporting the sweeping comments made in this paragraph. The many thousands of history books published on the economic development of the world since the 1840s confirm similar generalizations about the second and third waves of information's diffusion.

Finally, we can reinforce the observation that the chronologies line up. For example, when the major academic disciplines began emerging and its agents started establishing their societies, many of them were doing so at the same time, routinely during the second wave. That initial wave activity set a pattern of behavior that carried forward to the present. As a new discipline emerges, its adherents form organizations to promote the creation and sharing of information about their chosen subject area, publish journals and magazines, offer training programs, and host regional and national conventions to disseminate information and foster networks among its members. In turn, those actions promote their waves to continue pushing out geographically, carrying new generations of experts with it. As computer science came into existence in the 1940s and 1950s, again a new interdisciplinary wave of journals appeared and associations formed, followed by yet newer ones for evermore narrowly defined specializations within the broad category of computing.[24]

One example illustrates the process, using historians. They had been around for centuries, but during the Second Industrial Revolution in the United States, colleges and universities hired a growing number of full-time professors to teach American history. In 1884, a group of these academics and gentleman historians "of leisure" formed the American Historical Association (AHA). In 1889 the U.S. Congress recognized the AHA as a quasi-official organization by granting it a charter. In 1895 it began publication of its flagship journal, *American Historical Review*. Its editors followed the practices of European history journals, some of which were also launched in the nineteenth century. As a salute to the European model of scholarship, the AHA made von Ranke its first honorary member. By World War II, professional historians—yes, they were recognized as a profession with all the requirements of shared values and common behaviors—were members of the AHA. That meant a second and third generation participated.[25] When I entered graduate school to study history in 1969, I was *ordered* by my academic advisor to join the AHA, to read its journal, expect to attend its conventions, and to embrace the professional values it promoted. I am still a member. When I attend its conferences I still see people in their twenties and thirties—paid-up members—reading papers, networking in the hallways of the convention center, and discussing article and book ideas with editors. This is the same story for other disciplines and professions.

Still not convinced that this behavior is ubiquitous? Then one more short case involving a body of factual, observational, and anecdotal information is evident in every household in the world since the emergence of the human species: food preparation. We are only learning about how events of the past two centuries affected information about cooking and when uncovered mirrors the behavior of all the cohorts discussed in this book. In the early

1900s a new collection of information began emerging—food science—created by academics and home economists, the latter a new profession since the 1880s. Early academic research involved agricultural themes, such as plant and animal diseases and their healthy development. In 1905 one could count ten dairy science schools in North America, all located at universities. Three years later the American Chemical Society established a division for yet another sub-discipline: Division of Agricultural and Food Chemistry. Ten years later the University of Massachusetts established the first department of food science. The new discipline established its first journal in 1936, *Food Research*, which was acquired after the establishment, in 1939, of the Institute of Food Technologies, and renamed as the *Journal of Food Science*. The sub-discipline took off, borrowing from biology, chemistry, medicine, agriculture, and other disciplines. By 2017 some forty-five American departments of food science were teaching new ways of dealing with food and cooking, and conducting research that changed the body of information about the subject.[26] So today's cookbooks include much about the biological and chemical effects of food preparation. Many of these were "best-sellers."[27] The protagonists here participated in at least the second and subsequent waves at essentially the same time as so many other groups.

So the first wave, building on a large body of experience and qualitative knowledge and a few specialties, and even fewer journals and disciplinary associations, proved sufficient to toss the first pebble into our information lake. The first wave pushed out, taking less than a third of a century to, in turn, make way for a second, bigger one, to spread its influence and information, certainly in most disciplines by late 1800s. By a bigger wave I mean more members of the discipline or profession, larger number of publications and events, more numerous audiences, and impact. The third was well in motion in the early 1900s and a fourth by the last quarter of the twentieth century.

This fourth turn of using society's digital plumbing predated the wide availability of the Internet. The latter turbo-charged the diffusion of all manner of information by experts, amateurs, and both well-meaning and malicious actors already underway. Three mid-career professors surveying the landscape of their world and its future in 2018 may have provided as much of an observation about what happened in the prior two centuries as of their own time: "Fresh capacity is built alongside established units, new functions are layered on top of inherited ones, and universities overall become more complicated mechanisms for producing knowledge as they move through time."[28] One could add to their term universities, professions, professional associations, enterprises, and government agencies, as they also tossed pebbles into lakes. In fact, as those professors impugned, so many other professions doing the same things were outgunning the academics.

In sum: all of the activities described in this book began and remained rooted in research, which created new information, which in turn could be applied while motivating additional hunts for new knowledge. As a science historian explained, we have now reached a point where modern research is done differently: "Current approaches often consist in accumulating data, from which information is then extracted, in particular through comparisons with earlier data, rather than in forming hypotheses that one then seeks patiently to confirm."[29] Research becomes an act of comparing data, or collaborating with teams with diverse skills.

CONSEQUENCES OF THE EVOLUTION

Over the course of nearly two centuries people changed much of their activities and many of their views, thanks to their access to new or profoundly transformed information. Historians and economists explained how the physical face of cities, towns, products, and things changed. Wood and leather gave way to metal and plastic, steam to oil and electricity, horses to cars and airplanes. They documented changes in attitudes, as religious beliefs partially gave way to secularism, royal governments to more representative republics with side shoots of communism and socialism. Small organizations relinquished economic dominance to ever-larger ones. Wars became bigger, more lethal, and destructive, while medical treatments and public health policies improved life and longevity. Inaccurate beliefs increasingly gave way to scientific realities.

Less obvious consequences emanated from these dynamic activities. For one, we thought our world had come to be dominated by a worldview described in the language of statistics. It had, of course, but is it now retreating because humans can measure everything—the Big Data issue. Are data and statistics becoming mutually exclusive? Do vast amounts of data tell a story or do we need statistics with which to conduct the conversation? Perhaps, probably, or at least for the foreseeable future because statistics will remain a ubiquitous presence in information gathering and use. At a minimum one can be certain that any "Age of Simplicity" was killed off by the availability of so much new information, and at no time was this more the case than in the nearly eight decades following World War II. Evidence-based decision-making became widespread, as reflected in the use of statistics, computerized models, massive quantities of data, discipline-based rules and studies, and scientific findings. The shift to such practices increased confidence in the certainty of information, which consequently encouraged more projections and forecasts. This occurred regardless of the persistence of uncertainties, acknowledgment of our ignorance of some subjects such as some medical features of Covid-19, or the lack of effective action to contain it after experts had forecasted its arrival months before nations took action.

Uncertainties still roamed the land; only now there were increasingly more people documenting these as time passed. Despite the initiative to stamp these out, they remained. Economist John Kenneth Galbraith (1908–2006) in a widely read but also criticized book entitled *The Age of Uncertainty* (1977) pointed out that instabilities lingered, so too inefficiencies and social and economic inequities. Arguing largely from the perch of economics, Galbraith saw contrasts between the confident assurances, he used the word *certainties*, of the 1800s and the more tentative varied perspectives of economists in the twentieth century.[30] I would add that his position could be true because of the availability of so much new information by the 1950s. Recessions and wars were going to come and go regardless of what information existed, so too social dynamics and problems, but the availability of so much new data made it increasingly obvious that no circumstance could be viewed in simple black-and-white terms. Every topic was subtle, and to use a casual phrase of the late 1900s, every situation was, "well, it depends." Galbraith reaffirmed indirectly the rising tide of information shaping the thinking and actions of entire societies: "The ideas that made the revolutions of the nineteenth century did not originate with the masses, (*sic*) with the people who, by any reasonable calculation, had the most reason to revolt; they came from intellectuals. In similar fashion, the ideas that saved the reputation of capitalism in the years before and after World War II came not from businessmen, bankers or owners of shares but again from intellectuals," people who traded in information.[31] Experts had evolved from providing simple to far more nuanced explanations. As a consequence, their explanations became more qualified and uncertain, in other words, less absolute, less confident. "Well, it depends," was frequently replaced with a new answer: "It's complicated," but explainable.

Did we have too much information? Or, was what we had too fragmented, meaning too many disciplines had different or more varied answers to the same questions? Was our comprehension of a topic much like a bag of children's Lego building blocks of different colors and shapes, all waiting to be pieced together? Scientists studying how the human mind works, and now interacting with both AI experts and librarians (information retrieval experts), could argue that people would prefer the simple composite answer based on a mountain of certainty, a confident "elevator answer," as opposed to the detail. Perhaps the recent flood of conspiracy theories, "fake facts," and potentially sinister intentions in the promulgation of questionable "elevator answers" may cause people to push back on glib responses, both factual and not. One can suspect that people's heuristic processing of information makes speculating on what they will do a risky enterprise.

Yet, one should still ask: has a backlash begun against complexity? Are there too many disciplines, professions, and sub-fields of information? Are people losing focus and direction? The physicists encountered in chapter 6 may be going through such an experience as some hunt for a general theory to knit together the disparate pieces of their discipline. If so, any attempt to unite information would be a consequence of historic significance. That may actually be happening, although quietly, almost imperceptibly at the moment. But that tiny initiative already has a confident name: General Systems Theory (GST).

Like all concepts, it also has a history. Credit for its origin traditionally goes to Ludwig von Bertalanffy (1901–1972), an Austrian biologist who trained at the University of Vienna, began teaching in Austria, eventually arriving at the University of California in 1955. He taught, too, in Canada, concluding his career at the State University of New York at Buffalo.[32] His work on GST originated in the 1950s, focusing on the idea that complex systems share organizing principles. These principles could be identified and be modeled mathematically, a theme that should by now resonate as it existed in many disciplines described in earlier chapters. Bertalanffy searched for a general theory to explain all systems, regardless in which scientific disciplines they originated. In academic terms, he sought interdisciplinary study of systems. For those outside of the academy his quest held out the promise of making sense of far more, such as about how to organize a company, a project, or a society and for any of that to happen, how to organize and understand information.

To work, his theory had to reflect reality—nature—and be anthropomorphically centered and understood.[33] One can anticipate that someday his thinking might appeal to AI systems, but not possible in the early 2020s. As with any systems' perspective, it had to account for a system's purpose, structure and environmental realities. It also had to be explainable by describing its functions. Systems transform, that is to say, they learn and adapt, so a systems theory would need to account for those realities as well. To understand how a system functioned, one should be able to measure its activities and effects. To comprehend and then apply such a theory requires taking into consideration what individual disciplines learned about systems, recognizing that no one offered sufficient insight to describe a system in its entirety and the organization of its activities. We care about such ideas because by the end of the century they offered insight to those conducting systems thinking research, others trying to understand and develop machine logic and systems engineering in computer science, and increasingly in AI.[34] GST incorporated concepts encountered in this book, such as systems, feedback loops, throughput or flow, and data. For his ideas he drew from mathematics, psychology, biology, game theory, and social network analyses.[35]

One student of GST made its case: "The more science becomes divided into specialized disciplines, the more important it becomes to find unifying principles. What we need to understand is not the behavior of individual parts but rather their orchestration."[36] With the emergence of large-scale problems in the 1950s and 1960s, such as those regarding space travel, nuclear bombs and war or mitigating environmental problems, earlier smaller collections of information and understanding were proving inadequate to addressing these, hence the emergence of systems thinking on a scale not seen before. In other words, holistic approaches were desired, piecemeal efforts were failing.

GST emerged because it was based on an assumption increasingly buttressed by scientific data and modeling that indicated perhaps all manner of systems shared common features. If a theory could be developed describing such features, it would (a) transcend extant disciplines and thus not become yet another one and (b) point the way to reorganize and use information to solve complex problems, many of which were newly defined in the late twentieth century. Critics, however, accused its defenders of drifting into discipline-specific language by calling it a "systems science," while GST's proponents called for it to be described as a *metadiscipline*.[37] Its destiny remains yet to be realized; meanwhile it is in play.

Consult any general text on the subject and, as with other theories, there are various ones to select.[38] They all include extensive consideration of the roles of communication and information theories. They discuss such topics as the interrelationships among time, place, and channels, Shannon's ideas (of course), information theories, roles of entropy (Shannon again), redundancy, noise, and coding. As understanding about how the human brain worked grew in the last quarter of the twentieth century, those findings too seeped into GST. Now it is AI's contemporary form making the same journey into GST.

The structures of networks—a subject attracting much attention in the new century—are turning out to be a crucial element of GST, because these are being described with language increasingly similar to how students of AI, communications, and computing do. For example, here is how Scott E. Page, who we encountered in earlier discussions about models (also a component of GST thinking), explained the structure of networks: "A network consists of *nodes* and *edges* that connect them. We refer to nodes connected by an edge as *neighbors* and to a network as *connected* if it is possible to get from any one node to any other along edges. Networks can be represented as graphs, as lists of edges, or as matrices of zeros and ones, where a one in row A and column B denotes an edge between node A and node B."[39] Edges can be pointed in some direction in an information network. One could easily descend into lengthy Shannon-like discussions about path lengths and features, but we get the idea. So far, the node is considered the unit of study, of analysis.

Where one sits in an organization can affect their influence on the affairs of that information ecosystem, just as the ability of a stockbroker to have sub-second response times to affect trades can be economically influential. A combination lawyer and political scientist, Anne-Marie Slaughter, explained that networking theory combined much science that emerged in the past twenty to thirty years so people have not "had a chance to take all that theory out of the universities and apply it to ask: 'What kinds of networks should we build, and for what purposes?'"[40] Interest in applying at least pieces of GST is an emerging if impatient one nurtured in an era when science and information are recognized as critical tools. Lars Skyttner, an authority on GST, summed up what it represented: "Science of today."[41]

THE POWER OF BEING IN THE RIGHT PART OF A NETWORK: A PERSONAL WAR STORY

In the mid-1990s, IBM appointed a general manager to run its management consulting business in North America and gave him authority to corral existing consulting practices under his authority. These practices employed many thousands of consultants led by divisional directors and vice presidents who initially controlled budgets and size of staffs. I was one of several people the GM recruited to help carry out his mission. We were middle managers in a company that valued hierarchy and rank, so in theory, with no authority with respect to these practice leaders. My value lay in the fact that I knew how to navigate IBM's organization, procedures, rules, and politics. Because I reported directly to the GM, it became obvious to the practice leaders who outranked me in a traditional organization chart that I had his ear. So my opinions and good graces were essential if they were to keep or expand their budgets, gain approvals for hiring additional staff, and be assigned financial and billable targets that optimized their professional and financial success. They cultivated me, as if I was their peer in rank, supplicating me for their needs and wants that I helped translate into plans and recommendations for the GM with which to take action. I was also a conduit back to them about things going on higher up in IBM and perspectives held by the GM. Collaborating with the rest of the staff we worked up budgets, achieved financial targets, settled arguments, established managerial practices, wrote hundreds of pages of PowerPoint slides, and established processes for validating the expertise of consultants. I wielded power derived from where I sat in the network,

> how I collected quantitative and qualitative information, which I and others molded into an organizational construct. That worked to make the "IBM Consulting Group" a powerful organization within IBM's sales division. That is what networking looks like in practice.

In earlier chapters I noted that critics always accompanied new notions of information, such as the librarians initially resisting online systems. In GST this is the role played early by Robert Lilienfeld, for example, who in the 1970s thought it had several problems:

- That it was a universal myth relying on the prestige of science. In earlier times prestige came from philosophy and theology.
- That GST experts lingered too long on vague concepts and definitions, not on specifics.
- That it engaged in too much speculation although with some empirical data.
- That as theory it has not been empirically tested.
- That it is neither science nor philosophy, perhaps more an ideology.[42]

There is no need to engage in a debate on the merits of GST, because the subject is still embryonic. It is enough to know that with fragmentation of information, motivated constituencies are at work to reintegrate facts into broad-based knowledge, as it seemed had existed prior to the dawn of the Second Industrial Revolution, but in fact had not.[43]

Embedded in these various influences and theories extending across disciplines was a less appreciated influence on how information changed over time. The influence brought about interactions of old with constantly new disciplines, for example, in biology the emergence of new disciplines, such as genetics and biochemistry with all their academic and intellectual accoutrements, in competition for attention and acceptance with older disciplines. One historian spoke of the rise and fall of these as a "complex dance of disciplines." He illustrated the idea with examples, for instance, genetics: "Genetics developed all the more quickly as it was isolated from the other biological disciplines, and it defined a research program that was all its own." Over time its dominant position it now has derived from the perception of many biologists that it had the look and feel, the appearance of being the "physics" discipline of biology, because it had emerged as "the only branch of biology that was experimental, had established laws, and analyzed results with the use of mathematical tools."[44] The same observer noted that genetics had an object, the gene, which in biology served the same purpose, as did the atom in physics. Borrowings of analogies, techniques, and world views could be found across other disciplines. Even some historians tried to come up with rules and apply econometric tools, so too political scientists and social scientists. In short, disciplines played an enormous role in the evolution of information and shared many interdisciplinary aspirations. Historians and philosophers, too, were some of the first to think of synthetic grand theories for how everything worked; now the physicists are attempting to do the same.

One additional effect and consequence of the growth in all manner of information was the reengagement of the well-meaning amateur, the person on the street, the mischievous and the malicious rumormonger and conspirator, neighbors who want to share interesting data, others who cannot distinguish between truth and nonsense, activists, and self-promoters. They outnumbered vetted experts who at one time or another dominated the creation and presentation of information. Only electronic sensors outnumber and out-produce "everyman."

Not everyone is convinced as I that there is so much going on, so in fairness to balance let me quote one expert (with apologies for his language, which is purposeful), the retired distinguished philosopher from Princeton University, from his erudite discourse *On Bullshit*. He asks why is there so much of it? He hypothesizes that "there is more communication of all kinds in our time than ever before, but the proportion that is bullshit may not have increased."[45] Then he argues why there is so much: "Bullshit is unavoidable whenever circumstances require someone to talk without knowing what he is talking about. The production of bullshit is stimulated whenever a person's obligations or opportunities to speak about some topic exceed his knowledge of the facts that are relevant to that topic. This discrepancy is common in public life, where people are frequently impelled—whether by their own propensities or by the demands of others to speak extensively about matters of which they are to some degree ignorant."[46]

A possible consequence of having so much available information could be that people feel they must now be seen as having mastery of some of it, an implication of the philosopher. An American TV comedian, Jimmy Kimmel, has a standard sketch where he sends an actor pretending to be a reporter onto a street to ask strangers to answer questions on live television about something the audience knows the answer for, or realizes the interviewee does not, exemplifying the philosopher's point that rather than admit ignorance, the individual will BS their way through it. The reporter might announce that something happened, which did not, then ask had the individual seen the news about it, asking what they thought about it. The interviewee waxes eloquently on the matter as if he had seen the reports. The other type of question he uses is to establish the ignorance of people, such as asking them to identify countries or entire continents on a map, including states in the United States of citizens interviewed in, say, California. In some instances people "wing it," faking their way through their ignorance. Of the two sketches, Jimmy Kimmel's "Lie Witness News" is the better case for our point, when the reporter announces a fake piece of news communicated by the media and then asks people to react to it, finding many pretending they were familiar with it. Kimmel called it lying; the Princeton philosopher would have called it not wanting to appear ignorant.[47] In either case, people are caught in the act of creating (or changing) information.

How people deal with fake facts should lead us to conclude that "it is complicated." Such people lived in other times too, but today they appear on television, blog, Facebook, and visit websites filled with inaccurate or malicious materials. Occasionally, someone acts in a dangerous way, such as attacking an ethnic minority or a pizza parlor that Hillary Clinton supposedly used for human trafficking and to run a child sex ring in the same year she was the Democratic Party's presidential candidate.[48] One wonders where she found the time to participate in Pizzagate.

But we can inject a bit of empirical insight without having to rely solely on Princeton philosophers and late night television comedians to add perspectives to the discussion of expertise versus espoused opinions. Several scholars have studied discourses by tracking language used by the public at large in books. They documented the decline in collective discussions and the increased shift to individual ones, from reliance on rationality toward emotion, with the shift occurring over the previous forty years. Language that demonstrated reasoning rose from the 1850s, such as the application of such words as "determine" or "conclusion." However, since the 1980s, commentators have been shifting to a greater personal reliance, using such words as "feel" and "believe." Use of these two words, for instance, declined between the 1850s and the end of the 1980s, then began an ascendency. They noticed the same occurring in articles published by the *New York Times*, so was not limited to books. They speculated on the causes of these trends: "One possibility when it comes to the trends from 1850 to 1980 is that the rapid developments in science and technology and their socio-economic benefits drove a rise in status of the scientific approach, which gradually permeated culture, society, and its institutions ranging from education to politics. As argued early on by Max Weber, this may have led to a process of 'disenchantment' as the role of spiritualism dwindled in modernized, bureaucratic, and secularized societies." With so many social and economic benefits of modern society explained in rational scientific terms not well explained, it could be, they speculate, that it was the reason for the shift away from rational (i.e., scientific, authoritative) explanations. They further observed about the shift to sentiment to explain phenomenon accelerated in 2007 as hundreds of millions of people waded into myriad discussions through the public's wide use of social media, relying less on rational data and arguments and more on "emotion-laden language" worldwide. What they may have uncovered is a seesawing of two basic modes of thinking: "reasoning versus intuition."[49] Their findings remind us that all the agents discussed in this book who shaped the type and form of information constituted a small (if influential) percentage of the general population, that the larger cohort operated in some cognitive space between the rationale and the emotional, and that the larger world progressed slower along the lines described in this book. In short, there is much more study needed to understand the transformation of information as it moved from its creation to its wider use in societies all over the world.

When one steps back even farther from all of these various issues and discussions about how information changed, we see two processes at work: first, and the most obvious, is the discovery of information about how the world works and is, such as what scientists do all the time, and that has been the subject of considerable attention in this book. However, there is a second one, and that is the creation of new information in vast quantities, such as what was collected on application forms for birth certificates, entrance to college, identification for pensions, military service and employment, and to obtain a driver's or fishing license. Physiological personality tests and records, too, were new creations. All of these activities ensured that by the 1930s, individuals were as much identified by information attached to them as by their personalities and behaviors. Lose your identification cards or have your tax and bank records hacked and you will realize how much of you consists of data and not just bones and muscles. Much of what constitutes Big Data today are creations of new information, not necessarily discoveries.[50]

IMPLICATIONS FOR THE FUTURE OF INFORMATION

Discussions about implications inevitably lead to the risky business of forecasting, considered a mortal sin when engaged in by historians, less so by pollsters, and almost fashionably attractive by scientists and political scientists. In the hard sciences one relies on theory laced with solid provable evidence that patterns of behavior can lead to expectations, even predictions. Thanks to the enormous progress made in their handling of information in the past century, statisticians egg them on. Weathermen do it all the time with some impunity, but with high rates of accuracy for the next three to four days then with declining reliability the further out in time they project. But if we are to answer the question "So what?" one should expect a forecast. It is not enough to say that more and different information will come in this new century. AI, additional innovations in computing, massive abilities to collect data, even someday potentially about every living creature on Earth, and that new science will cure cancer, extend our lives, and transform our bodies increasingly into new forms beyond today's heart pacers, prosthetic limbs, and organs are obvious expectations. One did not need to read this book to know that. But several other thoughts are worth laying before the reader.

The first is the power of national statistics, which have been increasing in variety, volume, and accuracy since the eighteenth century and exponentially since World War II. There will be more such facts and measures and reliance on them by government officials and other institutions to craft public policies and draw insights. In recent years, nations have even begun to measure the happiness of its citizens, because scientists had discovered one's happiness makes them healthier, economically more productive, and less prone to criminal behavior.[51] As scientists and others learn about how to cure the Earth of its environmental woes, progress will be measured; indeed it has already started.[52] Economists complain that many collections of statistics need improvement and new data sets. They will create new ones.[53] The Soviets in the 1930s tried to model their entire economy, but could not because the technology to do so did not exist; humans were not up to the task either. Today every transaction conducted by 100 percent of the population could potentially be tracked with existing information technology, should the appetite be there to do so. Based on past experience, one could expect that to happen. Privacy issues may or may not be addressed, although the technology exists to anonymize one's data, should a society wish to do so.

Second, systems of information, theories, visualization, and models are just possibly hitting their stride. Certainly the media coverage of Covid-19 using all three features of modern information handling created dramatic reporting, also an enhanced appetite for such information. It will be difficult to revert to earlier forms of reportage after the pandemic is gone. This second collection of expectations will affect the kind of information collected, indeed too their content and form.

Third, because codification of practical knowledge benefited societies profoundly during the Second Industrial Age, one can reasonably expect that practice to continue for both extant bodies of knowledge and practices, also for as yet undeveloped new ones. To take a wild guess, medical protocols that will be needed for doctors practicing their profession on Mars or the Moon come to mind. Ridiculous you say? China, United States, other countries, and even billionaires are investing in systems to colonize Mars. Whole new bodies of information about space will pour forth. Quite probably, some of this new information will reflect unforeseen transformations in its structure, form, and accessibility. Humans might not even have access, or need to it, either.

Fourth, computer scientists are in universal agreement that their technologies have not stopped transforming. Hyperbole aside, one is challenged to find anyone in the field who thinks they are done. There are literally millions of people still transforming computing. A director at the Max Planck Institute explains the implication: "Science is subjected to it, it tries to understand it, and it all contributes to shaping it. For many sciences, digitization creates great opportunities because it fills a gap between experimentization, modeling, and theory."[54] The evidence presented in this book affirms his observation. Furthermore, he is not forecasting something; he is describing a circumstance in many disciplines and professions already underway that are core to their activities.

These four forecasts are quite normal in how they are unfolding. Like weather reporting that is so accurate in the short term, because the meteorological activities that will shape tomorrow's weather are already in motion, so too these four points. At the end of each of our chapters these kinds of discussion suggested conclusions one could draw from the evidence presented. But history teaches us that disruptive events occur all the time that upset learned and thoughtful projections, even in the near term. We have to remember only how 9/11 changed so much so quickly, how Covid-19 did too, while breakthroughs in various disciplines spur renewed surges in the creation and transformation of information.

So, how is one to think about information's evolution in the longer term? It is not enough to just say AI will change everything, even if it does a great deal. But, we are not helpless. We know, for example, that in business thinking about how technological innovation and the influence of one's industry affect an individual's potential future. That works.[55] Such considerations apply to how information might evolve, which is one reason why this book adopted an historical tact, bringing into discussion a combination of technological innovations and industry/academic disciplines. With increased ability to massage larger bodies of data, the greater the opportunity exists to define more accurately potential optional futures, just as more data made it possible for weathermen to accurately forecast weather two days out, then three days out, and now more confidently for an entire week.

Futurists—yes, there is such a profession, Alvin Toffler was one—favor using processes linking together strategic and operational issues, identifying driving forces, while being open to both conducting contingency planning and anticipating the inevitable unexpected. Can that be done with information? Librarians are barely really doing this, even information scientists, but futurists could. The best one gets today about information is the identification of underlying forces. I did it when writing *All the Facts*, library science professors often do too when offering yet more frameworks. Because so much change in information surfaces from science-based industries, influences on the shape of future facts can be cataloged. This is made possible when based largely on the work of futurists and what was discussed in earlier chapters:

- shifts in underlying science and technology
- continuing innovations in science and technologies

- changes in regulatory practices
- changes in business models and their inputs
- emergence of new participants, such as competitors
- changing demographics (e.g., getting older)
- changing geopolitical environments
- pressure to bring out new products (e.g., Covid-19 vaccines)
- declining duration of patent exclusivity
- public opinion and political and social pressures.[56]

Each can be documented to lead to assumptions and hypothesis, the former essential for models, the latter for research.

One can then take the first step of mapping what kind of information is anticipated to emerge, or is desired, based on considering these ten driving factors. In classic managerial consulting fashion, one identifies the information they have today and devises a vision for what is needed or anticipated beyond the normal one to three-year planning horizons; try for a vision ten to fifteen years out. That latter horizon forces one to break away from the mentality of forecasting a continuation of today's trends. That also leads to a discussion of what is needed, and that may be, for example, where requirements for future AI research are formulated as marching orders for AI researchers and others participating in that broad area of information's future. These steps are being taken today.

Over a decade ago, a colleague, Heather Fraser, and I observed these steps underway in the pharmaceutical industry, when that experience existed at a time while the basic science undergirding the industry was transforming from chemically based to biologically based. Industry participants found the exercise easy to describe, challenging to implement, but confidence building, because it caused them to take actions to realize expectations. They controlled the information.[57] Because of the long-term view, it departs from more traditional scenario planning processes. For information scientists, business leaders, and officials, it requires funding mechanisms that sponsor projects that might not lead to results for well over a decade. NASA is comfortable with this approach, especially, when it has to build a satellite that will not send back images from space for many years. The model for thinking and funding this way exists. Corporations and foundations should consider embracing this mindset more than they do today.

Finally, it bears repeating that it is time for both children and adults to gain a new information literacy suitable for their world that delivers so much content to them via the Internet and concurrently through media and academic (e.g., scientific-styled) publications. One could begin by learning how to read scientific papers, which journalists now quote with increasing regularity, and for which they include pointers to in their texts. Journalists are often as weak in their understanding of statistics and scientific language as is the general public. Yet, we live in a world where increasingly experts in one field want to engage with or be seen as facile with the data of another. They want to avoid the possibly naughty behavior—bullshit—that the Princeton philosopher had the courage to dignify with scholarly gravitas. People's recent desire across so many walks of life to understand Covid-19 brought home this point.[58]

A *New York Times* reporter took a step to educate his readers on how to read scientific papers. Scientific papers from the physical and social sciences have a prescribed ritual, an organizational style that is far from what journalists use. The latter begin their articles with the most important fact, "A man bit a dog." Scholars begin with a summary of what they are going to discuss, ritualistic throat clearing. Scholars use their own language, touched upon in this book, which may not be understood by an "outsider." Baked into that language are assumptions that a learned reader understands certain bodies of information, such as what a specific theory means, or a phrase. Today, a paper begins with a briefing on prior research on a topic, often plowing through relevant literature to demonstrate mastery of extant issues. Then comes the obligatory justification for why this new paper's research is needed by mankind, or at least a few colleagues. A carefully written description of the methods used to gather and analyze data comes next, often the most painful part of the paper to read, sometimes surpassed only by the subsequent section that contains the data, statistics, mathematics, and analysis in language often challenging to appreciate, but crucial to the process. It ends with an analysis of what this all means, observations about the limits of their methods and findings, which are not necessarily fake humility, and recommendations for further research.

Leaving aside that too few outside the social sciences or humanities are blessed with training on how to write engagingly, few stories or narratives are presented. Instead of saying, "The virus is spread by sneezing on someone," the scientist will write, "A correlation exists between sternutation, the convulsive expulsion of air and proximity of the infected subject." It, too, does not help that there is a massive literature. After Covid-19 had been recognized for a mere six months, the National Library of Medicine reported it had accumulated a list of over 17,000 published papers about it.[59] So which one are you going to read, especially since the summary at the beginning may not tell you what you want, probably too the title, and the "Discussion" section at the end may be only one paragraph long after slogging through ten, twenty, or fifty pages? It gets worse, as the reporter cautioned, "When you read through a scientific paper, it's important to maintain a healthy skepticism. The ongoing flood of papers that have yet to be peer-reviewed—known as preprints—includes a lot of weak research and misleading claims."[60] Authors retract some papers from consideration before final publication, while others are thoroughly reworked.[61] Just because a title screams out a headline drawing one's attention, such as that young people do not get the virus (not true, they do, and some die) beware, just as one would be with a bogus website.

This reporter understood the core issue of any literacy: how to read the paper. His advice was spot on: "When you read a scientific paper, try to think about it the way other scientists do. Ask some basic questions to judge its merit. Is it based on a few patients or thousands? Is it mixing up correlations and causation? Do the authors present the evidence required to come to their conclusions?" He concludes, correctly I think, "It's never a revelation of absolute truth. At best, it's a status report on our best understanding of nature's mysteries."[62] Given all the transformation in information over the past two centuries still underway, his advice applies to this vast landscape.

We end where we began, taking interest in how information changed over time. It changed for the many reasons stated in this book, but also for one other: because information was important in supporting the activities of people. But, there is more. Philosophy professor Colin Koopman documented how people left a paper trail of their lives that grew in increasing size the closer we came to the present to such an extent that we mortals began to observe and manage our personal brands, even seeing our immortality shaped by the legacy of our records. He may have a point: "Our data do not simply point at who we already were before information systems were constructed. Rather, our information composes significant parts of our very selves. Data are active participants in our making. The formats structuring data help shape who we are."[63] His answer to the question "So what?" may strike at the heart of why people change information: "Our information is today so deeply woven into who we are that were we to be deprived of it, we could no longer be the persons we once so effortlessly were."[64] If there is a lesson to draw from this book and from a philosopher's musings, it is that information is not always certain, that it keeps changing because we need it to do so for which no end is in sight. Did Koopman and Shannon suggest that Information Theory became stripped of its semantics, even too in common parlance? What effects might such an assumption have had on how different disciplines and professions understood theirs and others' information? If, even apparently it did not, how interesting is that? We have much yet to learn. So what? Relevant information always holds out the promise of a better life, of progress, of enhancing society and delivering peace and health. It can possibly save our planet; priests and philosophers would add our souls too. That is why So what.

We care because we need more information with which to conduct our lives. The *New York Times*, in late 2022, carried on its front page the sorts of lead articles that major newspapers had for two hundred years: that hurricane Ian had battered Florida and was about to do the same to other American states, and right below that story as its second lead, an account of Russia announcing its annexation of four Ukrainian provinces. These are—were—quite normal pieces for the past two centuries. But the newspaper included on its front page an article that twenty or thirty years earlier would have been printed many pages later in the paper, and much shorter: "What Is a 'Healthy' Food? The F.D.A. Wants to Change the Definition."[65] The editors had concluded that news about new nutritional labels on food packages and cans was worthy of discussing at the same time as a massive hurricane and a war in Central Europe. In fact, this information was essential to those many readers who wanted to base their eating habits and health practices on empirical facts. The world had changed a great deal in two centuries because of new and different information. Humankind had become more dependent on it than before.

Endnotes

PREFACE NOTE

1. In particular, birds: Betsy Mason, "Do Birds Have Language? It Depends on How You Define It," *Knowable Magazine*, February 15, 2022, https://knowablemagazine.org/article/mind/2022/do-birds-have-language?utm_source=newsletter&utm_medium=email&utm_campaign=newsletter_axiosscience&stream=science (accessed February 16, 2022).

1. DEFINING INFORMATION IN MODERN TIMES

1. For examples, Horace Cooper, *How Trump Is Making Black America Great Again: The Untold Story of Black Advancement in the Era of Trump* (New York: Bombardier Books, 2020); Steven Buser and Leonard Cruz (eds.), *A Clear and Present Danger: Narcissism in the Era of Donald Trump* (Asheville, NC: Chiron Publications, 2016); O. Wesley Allen, *Preaching in the Era of Trump* (St. Louis, MO: Chalice Press, 2017); Ethan Porter and Thomas J. Wood, *False Alarm: The Truth about Political Mistruths in the Trump Era* (Cambridge, MA: Cambridge University Press, 2019); Timothy Zick, *The First Amendment in the Trump Era* (New York: Oxford University Press, 2019).

2. Thomas Kuhn, *The Structure of Scientific Revolutions* (Chicago, IL: University Chicago Press, 1962).

3. Tom Wheeler, *From Gutenberg to Google: The History of Our Future* (Washington, D.C.: Brookings Institution Press, 2019): first quote, 187–188, second quote, 189.

4. Quoted in M. G. Siegler, "Eric Schmidt: Every 2 Days We Create as Much Information as We Did Up to 2003," *TechCrunch* (August 4, 2010).

5. Ibid.

6. Wheeler, *From Gutenberg to Google*, 187.

7. Peter Wohlleben, *The Hidden Life of Trees: What They Feel, How They Communicate—Discoveries from a Secret World* (Vancouver: Greystone Books, 2016).

8. Michael Pollan, *Cooked: A Natural History of Transformation* (New York: Penguin Books, 2013): 322–327.

9. Jacques Ellul, *The Technological Society* (New York: Alfred A. Knopf, 1964, but originally published as, *La Technique ou l'enjeu* [Paris: Armand Colin, 1954]).

10. John Wilkinson, "Translator's Introduction," in Jacques Ellul, *The Technological Society* (New York: Vintage Books, 1964): xvii.

11. For a brief but useful history of the term, see Ronald R. Kline, "Cybernetics, Management Science, and Technology Policy: The Emergence of 'Information Technology' as a Keyword, 1948–1985," *Technology and Culture* 47, no. 3 (July 2006): 513–535.

12. Quotes drawn from Jean-Baptiste le Rond, "Preliminary Discourse," in *The Encyclopedia of Diderot & d'Alembert Collaborative Translation Project*. Translated by Richard N. Schwab and Walter E. Rex (Ann Arbor: Michigan Publishing, University of Michigan Library, 2009). http://hdl.handle.net/2027/spo.did2222.0001.083 (accessed November 30, 2019). Originally published as "Discourse Préliminaire," in *Encyclopédie ou Dictionnaire raisonné des sciences, des arts et des métiers*, 1: i–xlv (Paris, 1751).

13. Andy Oppel, *SQL Demystified* (New York: McGraw-Hill, 2005): 7.

14. Neil Safier quoted in "AHR Conversation: Historical Perspectives on the Circulation of Information," *The American Historical Review* 116, no. 5 (December 2011): 1428.

15. Jack W. Bradbury and Sandra L. Vehrencamp, *Principles of Animal Communication*, 2nd ed. (Oxford: Oxford University Press, 2011); Wohlleben, *The Hidden Life of Trees*.

16. Toni Weller (ed.), *Information History in the Modern World: Histories of the Information Age* (London: Palgrave Macmillan, 2011); Trevor Haywood, *Info-Rich Info-Poor: Access and Exchange in the Global Information Society* (London: Bowker-Saur, 1995); Geoffrey C. Bowker and Susan Leigh Star, *Sorting Things Out: Classification and Its Consequences* (Cambridge, MA: MIT Press, 1999); James W. Cortada, *The Digital Flood: The Diffusion of Information Technology across the U.S., Europe, and Asia* (New York: Oxford University Press, 2012); and for an extensive bibliography that includes much about information, see Henry Lowood, "Current Bibliography in the History of Technology 1999," *Technology and Culture* 43 Supplement (April 2002), entire issue.

17. James R. Beniger, *The Control Revolution: Technological and Economic Origins of the Information Society* (Cambridge, MA: Harvard University Press, 1986): 293.

18. Toni Weller, *Information History—An Introduction: Exploring an Emerging Field* (New York: Neal-Schuman, 2008); Peter Burke, *What Is the History of Knowledge?* (Cambridge, MA: Polity Press, 2016); Jeremy Black, *The Power of Knowledge: How Information and Technology Made the Modern World* (New Haven, CT: Yale University Press, 2014).

19. The classic in the field is Andrew Abbott, *The System of Professions: An Essay on the Division of Expert Labor* (Chicago, IL: University of Chicago Press, 1988); see

also Eliot Freidson, *Professional Powers: A Study of Institutionalization of Formal Knowledge* (Chicago, IL: University of Chicago Press, 1986); Keith M. Macdonald, *The Sociology of the Professions* (London: Sage, 1995).

20. Robert J. Gordon, *The Rise and Fall of American Growth: The U.S. Standard of Living Since the Civil War* (Princeton, NJ: Princeton University Press, 2016) documents this progress, but concludes negatively that it is over, 566–652; for an opposite conclusion and the case for how information changes human achievements, see psychologist Steven Pinker, *Enlightenment Now: The Case for Reason, Science, Humanism, and Progress* (New York: Viking, 2018); for an economist's perspective, see Michael Lind, *Land of Promise: An Economic History of the United States* (New York: HarperCollins, 2012); see also David Warsh, *Knowledge and the Wealth of Nations: A Story of Economic Discovery* (New York: W. W. Norton, 2006).

21. Ken Steiglitz, *The Discrete Charm of the Machine: Why the World Became Digital* (Princeton, NJ: Princeton University Press, 2019): 187.

22. Luciano Floridi, *Information: A Very Short Introduction* (New York: Oxford University Press, 2010); R. Vigo, "Representational Information: A New General Notion and Measure of Information," *Information Sciences* 181, no. 21 (2011): 4847–4859; a bit more challenging to understand, but useful here, James Gleick, *The Information: A History, a Theory, a Flood* (New York: Pantheon, 2011); Paul Young, *The Nature of Information* (Westport, CT: Greenwood Press, 1987).

23. Burke, *What Is the History of Knowledge?*, 15–43; and for examples of knowledge and context, see Matthew Daniel Eddy, "The Shape of Knowledge: Children and the Visual Culture of Literacy and Numeracy," *Science in Context* 26, no. 2 (2013): 215–245, and Donna Haraway, "Situated Knowledge: The Science Question in Feminism and the Privilege of Partial Perspective," *Feminist Studies* 14, no. 3 (1988): 575–599.

24. Paul Boghossian, *Fear of Knowledge: Against Relativism and Constructivism* (Oxford: Clarendon Press, 2007).

25. Daniel J. Boorstin, *Gresham's Law: Knowledge or Information?* (Washington, D.C.: Library of Congress): 1–3.

26. To dip into the subject, see Simon Blackburn and Keith Simmons (eds.), *Truth* (Oxford: Oxford University Press, 1999); Hartry Field, *Truth and the Absence of Fact* (Oxford: Oxford University Press, 2001); Richard L. Kirkham, *Theories of Truth: A Critical Introduction* (Cambridge: MIT Press, 1992).

27. For a brief introduction to the concept, David Brock, *Understanding Moore's Law: Four Decades of Innovation* (Philadelphia, PA: Chemical Heritage Foundation, 2006); R. R. Schaller, "Moore's Law: Past, Present and Future," *IEEE Spectrum* 34, no. 6 (June 1997): 52–59; William Aspray (ed.), *Chasing Moore's Law: Information Technology Policy in the United States* (London: SciTech Publishing, 2004).

28. "Wisdom," *Oxford English Dictionary*, http://www.oed.com (accessed December 3, 2019).

29. The argument is essentially about gaining insight that can be applied, for example, "to understand market conditions," "as a driver of innovations," and about "how a company utilizes the collected data," *What Is Big Data?*, Research Data Alliance, https://www.rd-alliance.org/group/big-data-ig-data-development-ig/

wiki/big-data-definition-importance-examples-tools#:~:targetText=Big%20Data%20 helps%20the%20organizations,can%20be%20captured%20and%20analyzed (accessed December 3, 2019). See also Dawn E. Holmes, *Big Data: A Very Short Introduction* (New York: Oxford University Press, 2014): 14–25.

30. R. David Lankes, *The New Librarianship Field Guide* (Cambridge, MA: MIT Press, 2016): 25.

31. "Fact," *Oxford English Dictionary*, http://www.oed.com (accessed December 3, 2019).

32. A *bit* is a computer science term and is a short term for *binary digit*, which in turn is the smallest unit of data one can have in a computer. Each of the 0s and 1s computer scientists speak about is a bit. A combination of 8 bits equals a *byte*, which in turn is enough information to express an ASCII character, such as the letter "b." A string of bytes formed from bits can be assembled to express a full word, such as "James."

33. Lankes, *The New Librarianship Field Guide*, 25.

34. "Data," *Oxford English Dictionary*, http://www.oed.com (accessed December 3, 2019). It came into vogue with computers in the 1940s, although it had existed in English since the 1640s. See also Peter Checkland and Sue Holwell, *Information, Systems, and Information Systems: Making Sense of the Field* (Chichester, West Sussex: John Wiley & Sons, 1998).

35. Michael Buckland, *Information and Society* (Cambridge, MA: MIT Press, 2017): 111.

36. Claude E. Shannon, "A Mathematical Theory of Communication," *The Bell System Technical Journal* 27 (July–October 1948): 379–423, 623–656.

37. For example, Burke, *What Is the History of Knowledge?*, 1–14.

38. Accounting is the most obvious example of the age, Margaret Levenstein, *Accounting for Growth: Information Systems and the Creation of the Large Corporation* (Stanford, CA: Stanford University Press, 1998); Peter Temin (ed.), *Inside the Business Enterprise: Historical Perspectives on the Use of Information* (Chicago, IL: University of Chicago Press, 1991); H. T. Johnson and R. S. Kaplan, *The Rise and Fall of Management Accounting* (Boston, MA: Harvard Business School Press, 1987). For a useful introduction to scientific encounters with specialized language, see Robert A. Day and Nancy Sakaduski, *Scientific English: A Guide for Scientists and Other Professionals*, 3rd ed. (Westport, CT: Greenwood Press, 2011); John Henry, *A Short History of Scientific Thought* (New York: Palgrave Macmillan, 2012): 231–294.

39. Particularly in American political life since the election of 2016; William Aspray and James W. Cortada, *From Urban Legends to Political Fact-Checking: Online Scrutiny in America, 1990–2015* (Berlin: Springer-Verlag, 2019): 107–133; Seth Ashley, Jessica Roberts, and Adam Maksi, *American Journalism and "Fake News": Examining the Facts* (Santa Barbara, CA: ABC-CLIO, 2018).

40. James W. Cortada, *All the Facts: A History of Information in the United States since 1870* (New York: Oxford University Press, 2016): 4; for a description of that massive investment in the digital plumbing of modern organizations, see James W. Cortada, *Information and the Modern Corporation* (Cambridge, MA: MIT Press, 2011).

41. Colin Koopman, *How We Became Our Data: A Genealogy of the Informational Person* (Chicago, IL: University of Chicago Press, 2019): 178. The observation on how data changed in the 1700s originated with Daniel Rosenberg, "Data before the Fact," in L. Gitelman (ed.), *"Raw Data" Is an Oxymoron* (Cambridge, MA: MIT Press, 2013): 15–40.

42. Koopman, *How We Became Our Data*, 178.

43. Lisa Gitelman and Virginia Jackson, "Introduction," in Lisa Gitelman (ed.), *"Raw Data" Is an Oxymoron* (Cambridge, MA: MIT Press, 2013): 2–3.

44. The study of the paper/digital paradigm has a long history; see Evegeny Morozov, *To Save Everything, Click Here* (New York: Public Affairs Press, 2013); Jorge Reina Schement and Terry Curtis, *Tendencies and Tensions in the Information Age: The Production and Distribution of Information in the United States* (New Brunswick, NJ: Transaction Publishers, 1995); Fritz Machlup published half a dozen books on the subject, most influential of which was *Knowledge: Its Creation, Distribution, and Economic Significance* (Princeton, NJ: Princeton University Press, 1980). I discussed the volume of printed materials, radio, and TV in James W. Cortada, *The Digital Hand: How Computers Changed the Work of American Financial, Telecommunications, Media, and Entertainment Industries* (New York: Oxford University Press, 2006). This book also contains an extensive bibliographic essay on these topics.

45. William H. Walters, "Journal Prices, Book Acquisitions and Sustainable College Library Collections," *College & Research Libraries* 69, no. 6 (November 2008): 576–586; Ellen Safley, "Demand for E-Books in an Academic Library," *Journal of Library Administration* 45, nos. 3–4 (2006): 445–457; Katherine Daniel, Joseph Esposito, and Roger C. Schonfeld, *Library Acquisition Patterns* (New York: ITHAKA S+R, January 29, 2019).

46. Lester K. Born, "History of Microform Activity" (1960), https://www.ideals.illinois.edu/items/5842 (accessed December 4, 2019); Nicholson Baker, *Double Fold: Libraries and the Assault on Paper* (New York: Vintage Books, 2001): 22–46.

47. For example, Kayte Korwitts, "Print Books vs. E-Books: What Is the Future of Reading," *Curiosity at Work*, https://www.surveymonkey.com/curiosity/print-books-vs-e-books-whats-the-future-of-reading/ (accessed December 4, 2019); Lucy Handley, "Physical Books Still Outsell e-Books—and Here's Why," *CNBC*, September 19, 2019, https://www.cnbc.com/2019/09/19/physical-books-still-outsell-e-books-and-heres-why.html (accessed December 4, 2019); Michael Kozlowski, "Our Love Affair with ebooks Is Over," *GoodEreader*, March 11, 2019, https://goodereader.com/blog/e-book-news/our-love-affair-with-ebooks-is-over (accessed December 4, 2019); Jim Milliot, "The Bad News about E-Books," *Publisher's Weekly*, January 20, 2017, https://www.publishersweekly.com/pw/by-topic/digital/retailing/article/72563-the-bad-news-about-e-books.html (accessed December 4, 2019).

48. "ImageNet: Where Have We Been? Where Are We Going," Association for Computing Machinery (ACM) TechTalk Series, https://www.acm.org/education/ai-ml-techtalks (accessed December 4, 2019); John Brockman, *Possible Minds: Twenty-Five Ways of Looking at AI* (New York: Penguin Books, 2019).

49. Amy Sue Bix, *Inventing Ourselves Out of Jobs? America's Debate over Technological Unemployment 1929–1981* (Baltimore, MD: Johns Hopkins University Press, 2000); Martin Ford, *Rise of the Robot: Technology and the Threat of a Jobless Future* (New York: Basic Books, 2015); and widely consulted, Erik Brynjolfsson and Andrew McAfee, *The Second Machine Age: Work, Progress, and Prosperity in a Time of Brilliant Technologies* (New York: W. W. Norton, 2014).

50. Richard Carr, *Charlie Chaplin: A Political Biography from Victorian England to Modern America* (New York: Routledge, 2017): 156–171.

51. Seth Lloyd, "Learning How to Control Complex Systems," in David C. Krakauer (ed.), *Worlds Hidden in Plain Sight: The Evolving Idea of Complexity at the Santa Fe Institute, 1984–2019* (Santa Fe, NM: SFI Press, 2019): 61.

52. David Edgerton, *The Shock of the Old: Technology and Global History since 1900* (Oxford: Oxford University Press, 2011).

53. Ibid., 8.

54. Ibid.

55. Abigail J. Sellen and Richard H. R. Harper, *The Myth of the Paperless Office* (Cambridge, MA: MIT Press, 2001).

56. It has already started. The first bookless library in the United States opened in San Antonio, Texas, in 2013; it looks like an Apple Store with rows of Apple computers, and no books: Josh Sanburn, "A Bookless Library Opens in San Antonio," *Time.com*, September 13, 2013, http://nation.time.com/2013/09/13/a-bookless-library-opens-in-san-antonio/ (accessed December 4, 2019).

57. A key finding in Cortada, *All the Facts*.

58. Max Roser and Esteban Ortiz-Ospina, "Literacy." Published online at OurWorldInData.org, 2019, https://ourworldindata.org/literacy (accessed December 7, 2019).

59. Richard Lipsey, Kenneth I. Carlaw, and Clifford T. Bekhar, *Economic Transformations: General Purpose Technologies and Long Term Economic Growth* (New York: Oxford University Press, 2005), especially pp. 131–218.

60. The literature on this topic is vast, however, widely consulted discussions include David S. Landes, *The Unbound Prometheus: Technological Change and Industrial Development in Western Europe from 1750 to the Present* (Cambridge, UK: Cambridge University Press, 1976); Nathan Rosenberg, *Inside the Black Box: Technology and Economics* (Cambridge, UK: Cambridge University Press, 1982); Eric Schatzberg for a broader discussion of the nature of modern technologies in *Technology: Critical History of a Concept* (Chicago, IL: University of Chicago Press, 2018).

61. David A. Hounshell, *From the American System to Mad Production, 1800–1932: The Development of Manufacturing Technology in the United States* (Baltimore, MD: Johns Hopkins University Press, 1984); Bernard C. Breaudreau, *Mass Production, the Stock Mark Crash and the Great Depression* (New York: Author's Choice Press, 1996); Satoshi Hino, *Inside the Mind of Toyota: Management Principles for Enduring Growth* (New York: Productivity Press, 2005).

62. An idea clearly recognized within a decade of its invention within the computer industry: Adam Osborne, *An Introduction to Microcomputers*, vol. 1, *Basic Concepts*

(Berkeley, CA: Osborne-McGraw Hill, 1980); and Michael S. Malone, *The Microprocessor: A Biography* (Berlin: Springer-Verlag, 1995); later by historians: Joel N. Shurkin, *Engines of the Mind: The Evolution of the Computer from Mainframes to Microprocessors* (Hoboken, NJ: W. W. Norton, 1996); Paul E. Ceruzzi, *A History of Modern Computing*, 2nd ed. (Cambridge, MA: MIT Press, 2003): 217–224, although he made similar comments in the first edition in 1998.

63. Brockman, *Possible Minds*.

64. Joel Mokyr, *A Culture of Growth: The Origins of the Modern Economy* (Princeton, NJ: Princeton University Press, 2016); *The Lever of Riches: Technological Creativity and Economic Progress* (New York: Oxford University Press, 1990); and most importantly, *The Gifts of Athena: Historical Origins of the Knowledge Economy* (Princeton, NJ: Princeton University Press, 2002).

65. Margaret J. Wheatley, *Leadership and the New Science: Discovering Order in a Chaotic World* (San Francisco, CA: Berrett-Koehler, 2006): 94–95.

66. Ibid., 97.

67. Cecilia Zirn, Vivi Nastase, and Michael Strube, "Distinguishing between Instances and Classes in the Wikipedia Taxonomy," Conference paper, 2008, https://link.springer.com/chapter/10.1007%2F978-3-540-68234-9_29 (accessed May 18, 2020).

68. S. Vegas, "Maturing Software Engineering Knowledge through Classifications: A Case Study on Unit Testing Techniques," *IEEE Transactions on Software Engineering* 35, no. 4 (2009): 551–565; S. Ore, "Critical Success Factors Taxonomy for Software Process Deployment," *Software Quality Journal* 22, no. 1 (2014): 21–48.

69. Scott Atran, *Cognitive Foundations of Natural History: Towards an Anthropology of Science* (Cambridge, UK: Cambridge University Press, 1990, 1996): 1–46.

70. David G. Luenberger, *Information Science* (Princeton, NJ: Princeton University Press, 2006): 1–2.

71. Ibid., 2–4.

72. When engaged in one of my disciplines or careers, I too waded into schema wars, for example, James W. Cortada, *Information and the Modern Corporation* (Cambridge, MA: MIT Press, 2011) and *Best Practices in Information Technology* (Upper Saddle River, NJ: Prentice Hall PTR, 1997), wearing my "business profession" hat.

73. James W. Cortada, "New Approaches to the History of Information: Ecosystems, Infrastructures, and Graphical Representations of Information," *Library & Information History* 32, no. 3 (August 2016): 179–202.

74. James W. Cortada, "The Case for the Long Book," *Journal of Scholarly Publishing* 46, no. 4 (July 2015): 355–365.

75. Moving to a next step, see James W. Cortada and William Aspray, *Fake News Nation* (Lanham, MD: Rowman & Littlefield, 2019); Aspray and Cortada, *From Urban Legends to Political Fact-Checking* (Cham, Switzerland: Springer-Verlag, 2019) and Cortada, "Building Blocks of Modern Society" (forthcoming). Each study migrated to extensive case studies that illustrate how information was used and consequences for specific groups. Many of the articles published in *Information & Culture* are case studies too.

76. I subsequently began to fill in these gaps with subsequent research, including in *Birth of Modern Facts*.

77. Cortada and Aspray, *Fake News Nation*, and James W. Cortada, *Building Blocks of Society: History, Information Ecosystems, and Infrastructures* (Lantham, MD: Rowman & Littlefield, 2021).

78. James W. Cortada, *The Digital Hand*, 3 vols. (New York: Oxford University Press, 2004–2008).

79. Not to be confused with the national historical societies, which in Europe were routinely established in the eighteenth century as royal societies that published journals devoted to the history of one entire country.

2. SECOND INDUSTRIAL REVOLUTION ENCOUNTERS INFORMATION

1. For decades, students and historians were schooled in these ideas by the book *The Robber Baron: The Great American Capitalists, 1861–1901*, by Matthew Josephson (New York: Harcourt, Brace & World, 1962).

2. Quote from Robert J. Gordon, *The Rise and Fall of American Growth: The U.S. Standard of Living since the Civil War* (Princeton, NJ: Princeton University Press, 2016): 1.

3. Quote from ibid.

4. For example, the work of distinguished historian Norman Davies, *Europe: A History* (Oxford: Oxford University Press, 1996): 759–896.

5. Ian Morris, *Why the West Rules—For Now: The Patterns of History and What They Reveal about the Future* (New York: Farrar, Straus and Giroux, 2010): 490–521; and with a good nod to science and innovation, Richard J. Evans, *The Pursuit of Power: Europe, 1815–1914* (New York: Viking, 2016): 355–443; Edmund Phelps, *Mass Flourishing: How Grassroots Innovation Created Jobs, Challenge, and Change* (Princeton, NJ: Princeton University Press, 2013): 77–110. For more traditional, "Old School" thinking by an outstanding historian, see Jill Lepore, *These Truths: A History of the United States* (New York: W. W. Norton, 2018)

6. James W. Cortada, *All the Facts: A History of Information in the United States since 1870* (New York: Oxford University Press, 2016). I was one of those students who took a course entitled "The Gilded Age," the content of which barely showed up in my history of the period, written nearly fifty years later. Yet, it was probably my favorite course taken as an undergraduate or graduate student. For a smattering of a growing emphasis on the role of information across broad sweeps of history, see Emily S. Rosenberg (ed.), *A World Connecting, 1870–1945* (Cambridge, MA: Harvard University Press, 2012); and for most useful facts about information, see Jürgen Osterhammel, *The Transformation of the World: A Global History of the Nineteenth Century* (Princeton, NJ: Princeton University Press, 2014): 3–44, 710–723, 779–814.

7. Historians of science long led the charge exploring the role of new information. One of the best studies of scientific and technological developments is James McClellan III and Harold Dorn, *Science and Technology in World History: An Introduction*,

3rd ed. (Baltimore, MD: Johns Hopkins University Press, 2015). These historians began putting this story together in the 1990s, publishing their first edition in 1999.

8. The modern conversation began with a discussion of the First Industrial Revolution with the scholarship of David S. Landes, *The Unbound Prometheus: Technological Change and Industrial Development in Western Europe from 1750 to the Present* (Cambridge: Cambridge University Press, 1969) and continued in the second edition, 2003, and also continued in his *The Wealth and Poverty of Nations: Why Some Nations Are So Rich and Some So Poor* (New York: W. W. Norton, 1998), especially 186–309.

9. Landes devoted an entire chapter to the influence of knowledge, calling it a form of wealth, *The Wealth and Poverty of Nations*, 276–291.

10. Andy Clark, *Mindware: An Introduction to the Philosophy of Cognitive Science* (New York: Oxford University Press, 2001): ix.

11. Quoted in Evans, *The Pursuit of Power*, 716. Sir Grey (1862–1933) died twelve years before the end of World War II when one could consider as the time (1945) that Europe began turning the lights of civilization and peace back on.

12. It was not a perfectly healthy economy, but compared to those of Europe's it was far better off. While we need to generalize a great deal in this chapter to stay focused on information, much work has yet to be done to understand the role of information in the lives of various groups in the United States that either benefited spectacularly from all the innovation or where profoundly oppressed and denied access to the new wonders of their age: Howard Zinn, *A People's History of the United States* (New York: HarperPerennial, 2003): 253.

13. Mitchell L. Stevens, Cynthia Miller-Idriss, and Seteney Shami, *Seeing the World: How US Universities Make Knowledge in a Global Era* (Princeton, NJ: Princeton University Press, 2018): 8–26.

14. For carbon's and graphite's fascinating story, Mark Miodownik, *Stuff Matters: Exploring the Marvelous Materials that Shape Our Man-Made World* (Boston: Houghton Mifflin, 2013): 159–178. The author also traces the long evolution in scientific and technological information of other substances, such as steel, concrete, paper, plastic, and glass, among others. While most had been the source of new information for literally thousands of years, a huge increase about each occurred beginning in the nineteenth century and continuing to the present.

15. Alfred D. Chandler, Jr., *Scale and Scope: Dynamics of Industrial Capitalism* (Cambridge, MA: Harvard University Press, 1990): 1.

16. Conveniently presented as "U.S. Railroad Route Miles and Revenue," https://www.railserve.com/stats_records/railroad_route_miles.html (accessed December 10, 2020).

17. Statistics on rail mileage, pp. 723, 727, number of employees, pp. 439–741 in U.S. Bureau of the Census *Historical Statistics of the United States, Colonial Times to 1957* (Washington, D.C.: U.S. Department of Commerce, 1975), pt. 2.

18. Conveniently described by Margaret Levenstein, *Accounting for Growth: Information Systems and the Creation of the Large Corporation* (Stanford, CA: Stanford University Press, 1998); Chandler, *Scale and Scope*, 53–58, and in Great Britain, ibid., 252–255.

19. Chandler, *Scale and Scope*, 26.

20. Zinn, *A People's History of the United States*, 253.

21. James R. Beniger, *The Control Revolution: Technological and Economic Origins of the Information Society* (Cambridge, MA: Harvard University Press, 1986).

22. Vaclav Smil, *Creating the Twentieth Century: Technological Innovations of 1867–1914 and Their Lasting Impact* (Oxford: Oxford University Press, 2005); David S. Landes, *The Unbound Prometheus: Technological Change and Industrial Development in Western Europe from 1750 to the Present* (Cambridge, UK: Cambridge University Press, 1969); Thomas J. Misa, *A Nation of Steel: The Making of Modern America, 1865–1925* (Baltimore, MD: John Hopkins University Press, 1995); Robert W. Fogel, *Railroads and American Economic Growth: Essays in Econometric History* (Baltimore, MD: Johns Hopkins University Press, 1964); David E. Nye, *Electrifying America: Social Meanings of a New Technology* (Cambridge, MA: MIT Press, 1990).

23. Zinn, *A People's History of the United States*, 257.

24. Gordon, *The Rise and Fall of American Growth* for a useful table showing its rise, 174.

25. I discuss these developments more fully in Cortada, *All the Facts*, 44–46, 58–62.

26. Michael Lind, *Land of Promise: An Economic History of the United States* (New York: Harper, 2012): 159.

27. Robert H. Wiebe, *The Search for Order, 1877–1920* (New York: Hill and Wang, 1967): 40.

28. Alfred D. Chandler, Jr., *The Visible Hand: The Managerial Revolution in American Business* (Cambridge, MA: Harvard University Press, 1977): 115.

29. Thomas R. Navin, "The 500 Largest American Industrials in 1917," *Business History Review* 44 (1970): 369–383.

30. Levenstein, *Accounting for Growth*, 191; Richard K. Fleischman and Vaughan S. Radcliffe, "The Roaring Nineties: Accounting History Comes of Age," *Accounting Historians Journal* 32, no. 1 (June 2005): 61–109.

31. JoAnne Yates and Craig N. Murphy, *Engineering Rules: Global Standard Setting since 1880* (Baltimore, MD: Johns Hopkins University Press, 2019): 3.

32. The quoted phrase captures a key finding of ibid., 11.

33. Geiger, *To Advance Knowledge*, 255.

34. National Science Foundation, *Scientific Research and Development in Colleges and Universities: Expenditures and Manpower* (Washington, D.C.: National Science Foundation, various years); W. Richards Adrion, "1950–1974: Science Information, Computing Facilities, Education, and Basic Research," in Peter A. Freeman, W. Richards Adrion, and William Aspray (eds.), *Computing and the National Science Foundation, 1950–2016: Building a Foundation for Modern Computing* (No City: ACM Press, 2019): 4–9.

35. Part of the problem is that governments have done a poor job educating their publics about the role agencies played in the creation and support of new information. For an introduction to the issue, see Mariana Mazzucato, *The Value of Everything: Making and Taking in the Global Economy* (New York: Public Affairs, 2018).

36. For a brief account, see Martin Campbell-Kelly, William Aspray, Nathan Ensmenger, and Jeffrey R. Yost, four leading historians of computing, *Computer: A History of the Information Machine* (Boulder, CO: Westview Press, 2014): 4–8; the book contains a useful bibliography.

37. James Schwoch, *Wired into Nature: The Telegraph and the North American Frontier* (Urbana: University of Illinois Press, 2018): 83–106.

38. Bureau of the Census, *Historical Statistics*, part 2, 805.

39. Paula Watson, "Founding Mothers: The Contribution of Women's Organizations to Public Library Development in the United States," *Library Quarterly* 64, no. 3 (1994): 234–236.

40. Angus Campbell and Charles A. Metzner, *Public Use of the Library and of Other Sources of Information* (Ann Arbor: University of Michigan Institute for Social Research, 1952): 22, 51–52.

41. Kristine C. Harper, *Weather by the Numbers: The Genesis of Modern Meteorology* (Cambridge, MA: MIT Press, 2008); Robert Henson, *Weather on the Air: A History of Broadcast Meteorology* (Boston, MA: American Meteorological Society, 2010): 1–23; Schwoch, *Wired into Nature*, 83–106.

42. Mary C. Rabbitt, *A Brief History of the U.S. Geological Survey: USGS General Information Product* (Washington, D.C.: U.S. Government Printing Office, 2013).

43. Less appreciated but also part of the legislation was the promotion of education and development of new techniques for use in industrial settings, in what often was called the "mechanical arts," which too resulted in new types of industrial information over the next century.

44. Paul K. Conklin, *A Revolution Down on the Farm: The Transformation of American Agriculture since 1929* (Lexington: University Press of Kentucky, 2009): 19–20, 29; Alan L. Olmstead and Paul W. Rhode, *Creating Abundance: Biological Innovation and American Agricultural Development* (Cambridge, UK: Cambridge University Press, 2008); Peter D. McClelland, *Sowing Modernity: America's First Agricultural Revolution* (Ithaca, NY: Cornell University Press, 1997); Gladys L. Baker et al., *Century of Service: The First Hundred Years of the United States Department of Agriculture* (Washington, D.C.: Government Printing Office, 1963); Wayne Rasmussen, *Taking the University to the People: Seventy-Five Years of Cooperative Extension* (Ames: Iowa State University Press, 1989).

45. Roy V. Scott, *Reluctant Farmer: The Rise of the Agricultural Extension to 1914* (Urbana: University of Illinois Press, 1914).

46. Kathleen Rebecca Babbitt, "Producers and Consumers: Women of the Countryside and Cooperative Extension Service Home Economists, New York State, 1870–1935" (Unpublished PhD dissertation, Binghamton, NY: SUNY, 1995). For a deep dive into the flow of information among farm wives and home economists in the twentieth century, see James W. Cortada, *Building Blocks of Society: History, Information Ecosystems, and Infrastructures* (Lanham, MD: Rowman & Littlefield, 2021): 131–179.

47. Franklin M. Reck, *The 4-H Story: A History of 4-H Club Work* (Ames: Iowa State University Press, 1951).

48. Michael Winship, "The Rise of a National Book Trade System in the United States," in *A History of the Book in America*, eds. Carl F. Kaestle and Janice A. Radway, vol. 4, *Print in Motion: The Expansion of Publishing and Reading in the United States, 1880–1940* (Chapel Hill: University of North Carolina Press, 2009): 60–61.

49. William J. Reese, *America's Public Schools: From the Common School to "No Child Left Behind"* (Baltimore, MD: Johns Hopkins University press, 2005): 71–78.

50. Cortada, *All the Facts*, 64–65.

51. Stevens, Miller-Idriss, and Shami, *Seeing the World*, 11–16.

52. Ibid., 40–60.

53. The central thesis of Cortada, *All the Facts*.

54. Colin Koopman, *How We Became Our Data: A Genealogy of the Informational Person* (Chicago, IL: University of Chicago Press, 2019): 35–65.

55. Roger L. Geiger, *The American College in the Nineteenth Century* (Nashville, TN: Vanderbilt University Press, 2000); see also his *To Advance Knowledge: The Growth of American Research Universities, 1900–1940* (New York: Oxford University Press, 1986).

56. Stevens, Miller-Idriss, and Shami, *Seeing the World*, 40–45.

57. http://www.nobelprize.org/nobel_prizes (accessed December 14, 2020).

58. *Historical Statistics of the United States: Colonial Times to 1970*, part 1, p. 388.

59. Ibid., 382–386, for a number of other PhDs by discipline as well.

60. Ibid.

61. Claudia Goldin and Lawrence F. Katz, *The Race between Education and Technology* (Cambridge, MA: Harvard University Press, 2008): 263–266.

62. Ibid., 265.

63. Ralph Bate, *Scientific Societies in the United States* (Cambridge, MA: MIT Press, 1965).

64. Stevens, Miller-Idriss, and Shami, *Seeing the World*, 83–86.

65. Goldin and Katz, *The Race between Education and Technology*, 263–266.

66. Ibid., 265.

67. Bruce A. Kimball, *The "True Professional Ideal" in America: A History* (Cambridge, MA: Blackwell, 1992); Cortada, *All the Facts*, 178.

68. For the example of transistors out of Bell Labs, see Ernest Braum and Stuart Macdonald, *Revolution in Miniature: The History and Impact of Semiconductor Electronics* (Cambridge, UK: Cambridge University Press, 182): 33–72. On DuPont, see David A. Hounshell and John Kenley Smith, *Science and Corporate Strategy: DuPont R&D, 1902–1980* (New York: Cambridge University Press, 1988).

69. James W. Cortada, *IBM: The Rise and Fall and Reinvention of a Global Icon* (Cambridge, MA: MIT Press, 2019): 41–42; Pugh, *Building IBM*, 60, 65.

70. Described in considerable detail by Charles J. Bashe, Lyle R. Johnson, John H. Palmer, and Emerson W. Pugh, *IBM's Early Computers* (Cambridge, MA: MIT Press, 1985); Pugh, *Building IBM*, 37–55, and passim.

71. Stevens, Miller-Idriss, and Shami, *Seeing the World*, 83–103.

72. In particular, the work of Dr. Walter Reed, US Army, William B. Bean, "Walter Reed and Yellow Fever," *Journal of the American Medical Association* 250,

no. 5 (August, 1983): 659–662; J. R. Pierce, *Yellow Jack: How Yellow Fever Ravaged America and Walter Reed Discovered Its Deadly Secrets* (Hoboken, NJ: John Wiley & Sons, 2005); Matthew Parker, *Panama Fever: The Epic Story of the Building of the Panama Canal* (New York: Anchor Books, 2009): 284–303; David McCullough, *The Path between the Seas: The Creation of the Panama Canal, 1870–1914* (New York: Simon & Schuster, 2004): 140–145, 409–419, 464–468.

73. For clearly written description of the process by an economist, see Mariana Mazzucato, *The Value of Everything: Making and Taking in the Global Economy* (New York: Public Affairs, 2018: 189–238.

74. I explored how this worked with the spread of information about computing in the 1950s–1970s, in James W. Cortada, "When Knowledge Transfer Goes Global: How People and Organizations Learned about Information Technology, 1945–1970," *Enterprise and Society* 14, no. 1 (2014): 68–102. But even diplomats and non-research-oriented groups did the same, James W. Cortada, "The Information Ecosystems of National Diplomacy: The Case of Spain, 1815–1936," *Information and Culture: A Journal of History* 48, no. 2 (2013): 222–259.

75. The central narrative of Gordon, *The Rise and Fall of American Growth*.

76. David A. Hounshell and John Kenly Smith, *Science and Corporate Strategy: DuPont R&D, 1902–1980* (New York: Cambridge University Press, 1988); Stephen Fenichell, *Plastic: The Making of a Synthetic Century* (New York: HarperBusiness, 1996). Plastic has a history dating back to the late nineteenth century with the development of protoplastic substances, then celluloids for early movies, followed by the development of Bakelite, cellophane, nylon, and vinyl plastic.

77. Geiger, *To Advance Knowledge*, 9.

78. Stevens, Miller-Idriss, and Shami, *Seeing the World*, 104–118.

79. Gordon, *The Rise and Fall of American Growth*, 533–565.

80. Geiger, *To Advance Knowledge*, 255.

81. Ibid. If the term "estates" sound familiar, it is because the term is used by historians to describe the three social classes in pre-Revolutionary France: clergy, nobility, and commoners. Each was a distinct social class with its own rules of behavior, rights, and standing in society.

82. Charles Percy better known as C. P. Snow, *The Two Cultures and the Scientific Revolution* (Cambridge, UK: Cambridge University Press, 1959, reprinted 2018). His key point was that "the intellectual life of the whole of western society" is divided into the humanities and sciences, posing a real problem to solving many of the world's problems. He followed up with a second book on the same topic, *The Two Cultures: And a Second Look* (Cambridge, UK: Cambridge University Press, 1965).

83. Stevens, Miller-Idriss, and Shami, *Seeing the World*, 83. For an explanation of how the humanists, and specifically sociologists, embraced and dealt with their sphere as explanations of how models of innovation functioned, see Benoit Godin, *Models of Innovation: The History of an Idea* (Cambridge, MA: MIT Press, 2017).

84. "Across the Great Divide," *Nature* 5, no. 5 (2009): 309.

85. Lisa Jardine, "C. P. Snow's Two Cultures Revisited," *Christ's College Magazine* (2010): 49.

86. The literature is now substantial; early studies included Beniger, *Control Revolution*; JoAnne Yates, *Control through Communication: The Rise of System in American Management* (Baltimore, MD: Johns Hopkins University Press, 1989); and James W. Cortada, *Before the Computer: IBM, NCR, Burroughs, and Remington Rand and the Industry They Created, 1865–1956* (Princeton, NJ: Princeton University Press, 1993).

87. Documented with examples by Beniger, *Control Revolution* and Yates, *Control through Communication*.

88. Most notably associated with Frederick W. Taylor. For his most important explication of how this worked, *The Principles of Scientific Management* (New York: Harper, 1911); Daniel Nelson, *Frederick W. Taylor and the Rise of Scientific Management* (Madison: University of Wisconsin Press, 1980).

89. While operational manuals await their historians, for perspectives on how they were used, see Christopher Roser, *Faster, Better, Cheaper in the History of Manufacturing: From the Stone Age to Lean Manufacturing and Beyond* (Boca Raton, FL: CRC Press, 2017): 217–285.

90. Cortada, *Before the Computer*, 64–78.

91. A central point made by Chandler, *The Visible Hand*. For a brief introduction to where information on performance diffused across corporations by the early 2000s, see James W. Cortada, *Information and the Modern Corporation* (Cambridge, MA: MIT Press, 2011); for historical perspective, see Thomas K. McCraw, *American Business since 1920: How It Worked* (Wheeling, IL: Harlan Davidson, 2009); Levenstein, *Accounting for Growth*; Peter Temin (ed.), *Inside the Business Enterprise: Historical Perspectives on the Use of Information* (Chicago, IL: University of Chicago Press, 1991) for case studies.

92. I discuss these developments more expansively in Cortada, *All the Facts*, 92–131.

93. John S. Coleman, *The Business Machine* (New York: Newcomen Society, 1949): 8.

94. Cortada, *Before the Computer*, 29.

95. Tabulating Machine Company, *Salesmen's Catalog* (New York: Tabulating Machine Company, n.d. [1910–1915]): 1.

96. Pugh, *Building IBM*, 1–66.

97. Geoffrey D. Austrian, *Herman Hollerith: Forgotten Giant of Information Processing* (New York: Columbia University Press, 1982): 58–73.

98. For quantitative evidence, Cortada, *Before the Computer,* 44–63, 128–143.

99. The first calculators were humans, people who did mathematical calculations, Paul E. Ceruzzi, "When Computers Were Human," *Annals of the History of Computing* 13, no. 3 (July–September 1991): 237–244.

100. For a broader consideration of the notion, see JoAnne Yates, "Evolving Information Use in Firms, 1850–1920: Ideology and Information Techniques and Technologies," in Lisa Bud-Frierman (ed.), *Information Acumen: The Understanding and Use of Knowledge in Modern Business* (London: Routledge,1994): 41–46.

101. David Alan Grier, "The Origins of Statistical Computing," *AMSTATNEWS*, September 1, 2005, https://magazine.amstat.org/blog/2006/09/01/origins-of-statistical-computing/ (accessed December 19, 2020).

102. Austrian, *Hollerith*, 203; George Jordan, "A Survey of Punched Card Development" (M.S. thesis, Massachusetts Institute of Technology, 1956): 15–16.

103. The history of forms is a neglected topic, but for some useful thinking about how to explore this class of documentation, see Matthew S. Hull, an anthropologist, "Documents and Bureaucracy," *Annual Review of Anthropology* 41 (2012): 251–267.

104. Perley Morse, *Business Machines* (London: n.p., 1932): 6–18.

105. Fenichell, *Plastic*, 181–186.

106. Morse, *Business Machines*, 67, 71.

107. Over the course of the century, enterprises in multiple industries learned not just to automate the collection and use of information but also that work processes could work better if reformed to optimize the technical and operational characteristics of the data processing hardware, especially computers, see Thomas H. Davenport, *Process Innovation: Re-engineering Work through Information Technology* (Boston, MA: Harvard Business School Press, 1993).

108. G. W. Baehne, *Practical Applications of Punched Card Method in Colleges and Universities* (New York: Columbia University Press, 1935); V. Johns, "On the Mechanical Handling of Statistics," *American Mathematical Monthly* 33 (1926): 494–502; Wendell A. Milliman, "Mechanical Multiplication by the Use of Tabulating Machines," *Transactions of the Actuarial Society of America*, part 2, 35 (October 1934): 253–264.

109. Cortada, *Before the Computer*, 133–136.

110. L. J. Comrie, "The Application of the Hollerith Tabulating Machine to Brown's Tables of the Moon," *Monthly Notices*, Royal Astronomical Society 92, no. 7 (1932): 694–707.

111. Herman Goldstine, *The Computer from Pascal to von Neumann* (Princeton, NJ: Princeton University Press, 1972): 72–83, 127–139.

112. The history of weather forecasting is increasingly drawing the attention of historians, Kristine C. Harper, *Weather by the Numbers: The Genesis of Modern Meteorology* (Cambridge, MA: MIT Press, 2008).

113. For lists of contemporary academic papers discussing the scientific uses of tabulating equipment, see Cortada, *Before the Computer*, endnotes 37 and 38, pp. 312–313.

114. B. V. Bowden (eds.), *Faster than Thought* (London: Sir Isaac Pitman, 1953): 24–26.

115. Goldstine, *Computer*; Bashe, Johnson, Palmer, and Pugh, *IBM's Early Computers*, 25.

116. For extensive discussion of how many machines and where they were sold, see Cortada, *Before the Computer*.

117. Paul E. Ceruzzi, *A History of Modern Computing*, 2nd ed. (Cambridge, MA: MIT Press, 2003): 1–176. Although a U.S.-centric story as he tells it, much work was done outside the United States. I have described that in considerable detail in James W. Cortada, *The Digital Flood: The Diffusion of Information Technology across the U.S., Europe, and Asia* (New York: Oxford University Press, 2012).

118. A key finding in ibid.

119. Jeremy Rifkin, *The Third Industrial Revolution: How Lateral Power Is Transforming Energy, the Economy, and the World* (New York: Palgrave Macmillan, 2011).

120. To avoid confusion on dates of diffusion, limited use of the Internet among government, academic, and military suppliers began in the 1970s, but it was not until the introduction of the World Wide Web in the 1990s did the Internet become practical to use by the public and companies.

121. For examples, see sociologist Manuel Castells, *The Rise of the Network Society* (London: Blackwell, 1996); historian George Galambos, "Recasting the Organizational Synthesis: Structure and Process in the Twentieth and Twenty-First Centuries," *Business History Review* 79 (2005): 1–38; and economists Erik Brynjolfsson and Lorin M. Hitt, "Beyond Computation: Information Technology, Organizational Transformation and Business Performance," *Journal of Economic Perspective* 14, no. 4 (2000): 23–48. The go-to one volume for varying views of changes in society in these years remains Frank Webster, *Theories of the Information Society* (London: Psychological Press, 2002) and subsequent updated editions.

122. Giovanni Dosi and Louis Galambos (eds.), *The Third Industrial Revolution in Global Business* (Cambridge. UK: Cambridge University Press, 2013): 1.

123. For a discussion of the historiographical and sociological discussion, ibid., 1–19.

124. On knowledge workers there is an anthology of writings by different observers, James W. Cortada (ed.), *Rise of the Knowledge Worker* (Boston, MA: Butterworth-Heinemann, 1998); James W. Cortada, *21st Century Business: Managing and Working in the New Digital Economy* (Upper Saddle River, NJ: Financial Times/ PTR, 2001), *How Societies Embrace Information Technology: Lessons for Management and the Rest of Us* (Hoboken, NJ: John Wiley & Sons, 2009), and *Living with Computers: The Digital World of Today and Tomorrow* (Cham, Switzerland: Springer Verlag, 2020).

125. Godin, *The History of an Idea*.

126. The standard source for this kind of data is Angus Maddison, *The World Economy: Historical Statistics* (Paris: OECD, 2003).

127. U.S. Census Bureau.

128. U.S. Bureau of Labor Statistics.

129. Gordon, *The Rise and Fall of American Growth*, 1.

3. HOW LIBRARIANS ORGANIZED INFORMATION

1. "The Information Problem," *American Documentation* 13, no. 4 (October 1962): 377.

2. Alfred C. Potter and Charles K. Bolton, *The Librarians of Harvard College, 1667–1877* (Cambridge, MA: Library of Harvard University, 1897): 40–41.

3. Elisabeth Jones, "The Public Library Movement, the Digital Library Movement, and the Large-Scale Digitization Initiative: Assumptions, Intentions, and the Role of the Public," *Information & Culture* 52, no. 2 (2017): 229–263.

4. For discussion of the various information ecologies, see James W. Cortada, *All the Facts: A History of Information in the United States since 1870* (New York: Oxford University Press, 2016).

5. For the global story, Pamela Spence Richards, Wayne A. Wiegand, and Marija Dalbello (eds.), *A History of Modern Librarianship: Constructing the Heritage of Western Cultures* (Santa Barbara, CA: Libraries Unlimited, 2015).

6. American Library Association, "Number of Libraries in the United States," https://libguides.ala.org/numberoflibraries (accessed January 13, 2020); Ilovelibraries, "Public Libraries around the World," http://www.ilovelibraries.org/article/public-libraries-around-world (accessed January 13, 2020). These statistics do not include academic or specialized libraries (e.g., corporate and government), which if included would increase the totals by several tens of thousands.

7. Michael Kevane and William A. Sundstrom, "The Development of Public Libraries in the United States, 1870–1930: A Quantitative Assessment," *Santa Clara University Scholar Commons*, 2014, https://scholarcommons.scu.edu/cgi/viewcontent.cgi?article=1039&context=econ (accessed January 13, 2020).

8. Cited by Wayne A. Wiegand, *Part of Our Lives: A People's History of the American Public Library* (New York: Oxford University Press, 2015): 25.

9. Scimago Journal & Country Rank, https://www.scimagojr.com/journalrank.php?category=3309&page=2&total_size=227 (accessed January 13, 2020).

10. For example, see Wiegand, *Part of Our Lives*, 221–224. One historian noted, however, that visits to the public library often were for reasons other than to obtain information, because they also served as social centers. Wayne A. Wiegand, "Falling Short of Their Profession's Needs: Education and Research in Library and Information Studies," *Journal for Library and Information Science* 58, no. 1 (Winter 2017): 41.

11. Charles C. Williamson, *Training for Library Service: A Report Prepared for the Carnegie Corporation of New York* (New York: Carnegie Corporation, 1923): 1–9.

12. Ostler, Dahlin, and Willarson, *The Closing of American Library Schools*, 31–36.

13. Fritz Machlup and Una Mansfield, "Cultural Diversity in Studies of Information," *The Study of Information: Interdisciplinary Messages* (New York: John Wiley & Sons, 1983): 21.

14. It is a position that this chapter demonstrates was not as positively inclined toward computing as some would argue. For a pro-computing argument, especially for the past 2000 years, see Deanna Marcum and Roger C. Schonfeld, *Along Came Google: A History of Library Digitization* (Princeton, NJ: Princeton University Press, 2021).

15. Jesse H. Shera, "Failure and Success: Assessing a Century," *Library Journal* 101, no. 1 (January 1, 1976): 281.

16. Ibid., 282.

17. Ibid., 283.

18. Ibid., 285.

19. Kalervo Järvelin and Pertti Vakkari, "LIS Research Across 50 Years: Content Analysis of Journal Articles," *Journal of Documentation* 78, no. 7 (2022): 65–88.

20. Shera, "Failure and Success: Assessing a Century," 287.

21. Williamson, *Training for Library Service,* 142.

22. Daniel R. Headrick, *When Information Came of Age: Technologies of Knowledge in the Age of Reason and Revolution, 1700–1850* (New York: Oxford University Press, 2000): 15–58.

23. Chaim Zins, "Knowledge Mapping: An Epistemological Perspective," *Knowledge Organization* 31, no. 1 (2004): 49–54; see also Chaim Zins and Plácida L.V.A.C. Santos, "Mapping the Knowledge Covered by Library Classification Systems," *Journal of the American Society for Information Technology* 62, no. 5 (2011): 877–901.

24. Wayne A. Wiegand, *Irrepressible Reformer: A Biography of Melvil Dewey* (Chicago, IL: American Library Association, 1996); Wiegand, "The 'Amherst Method': The Origins of the Dewey Decimal Classification Scheme," *Libraries & Culture* 33, no. 2 (Spring 1998): 175–194.

25. Wiegand, "The 'Amherst Method': The Origins of the Dewey Decimal Classification Scheme," 175–194; Amanda J. Tinker, A. Steven Pollitt, Ann O'Brien, and Patrick A. Braekevelt, "The Dewey Decimal Classification and the Transition from Physical to Electronic Knowledge Organization," *Knowledge Organization* 26, no. 2 (1999): 80–96.

26. Melvil Dewey, *A Classification and Subject Index for Cataloging and Arranging the Books and Pamphlets of a Library* (Amherst, MA: Privately printed, 1876).

27. Melvil Dewey, *Decimal Classification and Relative Index for Arranging, Cataloging, and Indexing Public and Private Libraries and for Pamphlets, Clippings, Notes, Scrap Books, Index Rerums, Etc.* (Boston, MA: Library Bureau, 1885).

28. A standard textbook on cataloging and classification that has gone through many editions explains the schema as it has evolved over time: Lois Mai Chan, *Cataloging and Classification: An Introduction*, 3rd ed. (Lanham, MD: Scarecrow Press, 2007): 320–340.

29. Ibid., 4.

30. Colin B. Burke, *Information and Intrigue: From Index Cards to Dewey Decimals to Alger Hiss* (Cambridge, MA: MIT Press, 2014: 21.

31. Williamson, *Training for Library Service*, 120–135.

32. Samuel C. Bradford, *Documentation* (London: Crosby Lockwood & Son Ltd., 1948): 16.

33. For a history of how the Dewey Classification System evolved over time, see M. P. Satija, *The Theory and Practice of the Dewey Decimal Classification System* (Oxford: Chandos Publishing, 2007); Arlene G. Taylor and Daniel N. Joudrey, *The Organization of Information*, 3rd ed. (Westport, CT: Libraries Unlimited, 2009): 384–390; and Jesse H, Shera, *Introduction to Library Science: Basic Elements of Library Service* (CO: Libraries Unlimited, 1976): 70.

34. Lois Mai Chain and Joan S. Mitchell, *Dewey Decimal Classification* (Dublin, OH: OCLC, 2003). For online materials about the Dewey system, see https://www.oclc.org (accessed January 14, 2020).

35. Satija, *The Theory and Practice of the Dewey Decimal Classification System*, 42–44.

36. Shera, *Introduction to Library Science*, 70.

37. OCLC, *Dewey Decimal Classification* 4 vols (Dublin, Ohio: OCLC, 2022).

38. "Dewey Decimal Classification," *Wikipedia*, https://en.wikipedia.org/wiki/Dewey_Decimal_Classification (accessed January 14, 2020).

39. Library of Congress, "Fascinating Facts," https://www.loc.gov/about/fascinating-facts/ (accessed January 14, 2020).

40. Burke, *Information and Intrigue*, 49–50.

41. Marcum and Schonfeld, *Along Came Google*, 27–32.

42. Lois Mai Chan, *A Guide to the Library of Congress Classification* (Englewood, CO: Libraries Unlimited, 1999): 6–9); to know more about problem that continued into the 1940s, see Martha M. Yee, "Attempts to Deal with the 'Crisis in Cataloging' at the Library of Congress in the 1940s," *The Library Quarterly* 57, no. 1 (January 1987): 1–31.

43. Francis L. Miksa, *Charles Ammi Cutter: Library Systematizer* (Littleton, CO: Libraries Unlimited, 1977); Charles A. Cutter, *Expansive Classification* (Boston, MA: Self Published, 1890). He expanded his classification and published additional versions throughout the 1890s and first years of the 1900s.

44. George Schneider with translation by Ralph Robert Shaw, *Theory and History of Bibliography* (New York: Columbia University Press, 1934): 227.

45. Wayne A. Wiegand, "United States and Canada," in Richards, Wiegand, and Dalbello (eds.), *A History of Modern Librarianship*, 87.

46. Ibid., 87.

47. Chan, *A Guide to the Library of Congress Classification* is considered the standard source on the classification system and includes a discussion of its evolution over time. For a brief summary of the LC classification system, see Richard E. Rubin, *Foundations of Library and Information Science*, 4th ed. (Chicago, IL: Neal-Schuman, 2016): 309–310.

48. Quoted from the English translation of his seminal work, Georg Schneider, *Handbuch der Bibliographie*, 2nd ed. (1926); two additional expanded editions appeared in the 1930s. The quotes in English appeared in Shaw, *Theory and History of Bibliography*, 210.

49. Georg Schneider, *Theory and History of Bibliography* (New York: Columbia University Press, 1934): 283.

50. W. Boyd Rayward, "The Origins of Information Science and the International Institute of Bibliography/International Federation for Information and Documentation (FID)," *Journal of the American Society for Information Science* 48, no. 4 (1997): 289–300.

51. Ibid., for citations of Otlet's publications; Ron Day, "Paul Otlet's Book and the Writing of Social Space," ibid., 310–317; Isabelle Rieusset-Lemarié, "P. Otlet's Mundaneum and the International Perspective in the History of Documentation and Information Science," ibid., 301–309; and for a detailed bibliography, see Aida Slavic-Overfield, "Classification Management and Use in a Networked Environment: The Case of the Universal Decimal Classification," Unpublished PhD diss., University College London (April 2005): 295–375.

52. *Manuel du répertoire bibliographique universal*, IIB Publications No. 63 (Brussels, Belgium: Institut International de Bibliographie, 1904–1907).

53. Rayward, "The Origins of Information Science and the International Institute of Bibliography/International Federation for Information and Documentation (FID)," 293.

54. Paul Otlet, *Traité de Documentation. Le livre sur le livre: Théorie et practique* (Liege, Belgium: Centre de Lecture publique de la Communauté française, 1989, reprint).

55. Rayward, "The Origins of Information Science and the International Institute of Bibliography/International Federation for Information and Documentation (FID)," 290.

56. His seminal publications are conveniently anthologized in W. Boyd Rayward (ed. and trans.), *The International Organization and Dissemination of Knowledge: Selected Essays by Paul Otlet* (Amsterdam: Elsevier, 1990).

57. R. David Lankes, *The New Librarianship Field Guide* (Cambridge, MA: MIT Press, 2016): 23–24.

58. Otlet, *Traité de documentation*, 405.

59. Rayward, "The Origins of Information Science and the International Institute of Bibliography/International Federation for Information and Documentation (FID)," 291–292.

60. Ibid., 292.

61. Quoted in ibid.

62. Ibid., 293.

63. Burke, *Information and Intrigue*, 53.

64. Ibid., 295.

65. Otlet, *Traité de Documentation*, 409.

66. On the decline of Otlet's crusade, Burke, *Information and Intrigue*, 237–238.

67. Bradford, *Documentation*, 11.

68. Ibid., 122–123. Ultimately, the Library of Congress prevailed. As Burke explained in *Information and Intrigue*, 238, its rivals could not "overcome all the economic and psychological hurdles to the application of a universal classification system. One reason was that too much had already been invested in the Dewey and Library of Congress schemes."

69. Shera, *Introduction to Library Science*, 51.

70. The Library of Congress began publishing a catalog to capture the book publishing output of a nation, in this case the United States and Canada. One series documented pre-1956 publications, a second post-1956. The pre-1956 series when completed consisted of 754 volumes with over 528,000 pages, published as *National Union Catalog, Pre-1956 Imprints: A Cumulative Author List Representing Library of Congress Printed Cards and Titles Reported by Other American* Libraries; Verner W. Clapp, "The Role of Bibliographic Organization in Contemporary Civilization," in Jesse H. Shera and Margaret E. Egan (eds.), *Bibliographic Organization: Papers Presented before the Fifteenth Annual Conference of the Graduate Library School, July 24–29, 1950* (Chicago, IL: University of Chicago Press, 1951): 3–23.

71. George E. Bennett, *Librarians in Search of Science and Identity: The Elusive Profession* (Metuchen, NJ: Scarecrow Press, 1988): 179.

72. Rubin, *Foundations of Library and Information Science*, 318–325; Chan, *Cataloging and Classification*, 12–19 and passim; Larry J. Ostler, Therrin C. Dahlin, and J. D. Willardson, *The Closing of American Library Schools: Problems and Opportunities* (Westport, CT: Greenwood Press, 1995): 31–36.

73. A. M. Lewin Robinson, *Systematic Bibliography* (London: Clive Bingley, 1966): 17.

74. James W. Cortada, *A Select Bibliography of Materials Published Outside of Spain on the Franco Period of Spanish History, 1939–1971* (Barcelona: Instituto

Municipal de Historia de Barcelona, 1971); *A Bibliographic Guide to Spanish Diplomatic History, 1460–1977* (Westport, CT: Greenwood Press, 1977); *An Annotated Bibliography on the History of Data Processing* (Westport, CT: Greenwood Press, 1983), which won a *Choice* magazine award for best bibliography; *A Bibliographic Guide to the History of Computing, Computers, and the Information Processing Industry* (Westport, CT: Greenwood Press, 1990), published in the press's library series on bibliographies and indexes; *Second Bibliographic Guide to the History of Computing, Computers, and the Information Processing Industry* (Westport, CT: Greenwood Press, 1996); *A Bibliographic Guide to the History of Computer Applications, 1950–1990* (Westport, CT: Greenwood Press, 1996). Greenwood Press was the primary publishing source for bibliographies used by American librarians at the time.

75. Pierce Butler, *An Introduction to Library Science* (Chicago, IL: University of Chicago Press, 1933): 100.

76. Robinson, *Systematic Bibliography*, 14–15.

77. Wiegand, *Part of Our Lives*, 55.

78. Ibid., 17.

79. James E. Gourley and Robert M. Lester, *The Diffusion of Knowledge: A List of Books* (Philadelphia, PA: Carnegie Centenary, 1935).

80. Charles B. Shaw, *A List of Books for College Libraries, 1931–38* (Chicago, IL: American Library Association, 1940); the earlier volume, *A List of Books for College Libraries* (Chicago, IL: American Library Association, 1931).

81. James Edward Scanlon, *Randolph-Macon College: Traditions and New Directions* (Ashland, VA: Randolph-Macon College, 2013): 381.

82. John Heidenry, *Theirs Was the Kingdom: Lila and DeWitt Wallace and the Story of the Reader's Digest* (New York: W. W. Norton, 1993).

83. In 1960 a second round of editions appeared, this time increased to sixty volumes, "Great Books of the Western World," *Wikipedia,* https://en.wikipedia.org/wiki/Great_Books_of_the_Western_World (accessed January 22, 2020).

84. However, the quality of information (facts) has been a concern in the United States since the 1700s across many parts of society, a conversation hardly involving librarians, James W. Cortada and William Aspray, *Fake News Nation: The Long History of Lies and Misinformation in America* (Lanham, MD: Rowman & Littlefield, 2019). That many facets of society are engaged in confirming the truthfulness of facts and in exposing poor or faulty facts in the age of the Internet can be seen through a series of case studies, William Aspray and James W. Cortada, *From Urban Legends to Political Fact-Checking: Online Scrutiny in America, 1990–2015* (Cham, Switzerland: Springer Verlag, 2019).

85. Samuel C. Bradford, "Sources of Information on Specific Subjects," *Engineering: An Illustrated Weekly Journal* 26 (January 26, 1934): 85–86; reprinted under the same title in *Journal of Information Science* 10, no. 4 (October 1985): 173–180.

86. V. A. Yatsko, "The Interpretation of Bradford's Law in Terms of Geometric Progression," *Automatic Documentation and Mathematical Linguistics* 46, no. 2 (2012): 112–117.

87. Marcum and Schonfeld, *Along Came Google*, 14–36.

88. This observation should not be confused with the widely discussed notion of technological determinism, often seen as "path dependency," an economic concept, because computers did not force the librarians to use them in certain ways; librarians were motivated by their attractive functions. That so many libraries waited for decades to use the technology does more than suggest that technological determinism was not realistically in play.

89. Richards, Wiegand, and Dalbello, *A History of Modern Librarianship*; George Bobinski, *Libraries and Librarianship: Sixty Years of Challenge and Change, 1945–2005* (Lanham, MD: Scarecrow Press, 2007): 113–125; Rubin, *Foundations of Library and Information Science*, 239–304; Ostler, Dahlin, and Willardson, *The Closing of American Library Schools*; Bennett, *Librarians in Search of Science and Identity*, 165–170; Fredrik Åström, "The Social and Intellectual Development of Library and Information Science," Unpublished PhD Diss., Umeå University, 2006, pp. 42–58; and his article, "Changes in the LIS Research Front: Time-Sliced Cocitation Analyses of LIS Journal Articles, 1990–2004," *Journal of the American Society for Information Science and Technology* 58, no. 7 (2007): 947–957.

90. Bennett, *Librarians in Search of Science and Identity*, 46–172; Bobinski, *Libraries and Librarianship*, 113–120.

91. Bobinski, *Libraries and Librarianship*, 119–120. The shift is normally dated to the publication by Calvin Mooers (1919–1994), "Zatocoding Applied to Mechanical Organization of Knowledge," *American Documentation* 2 (1951): 20–32.

92. Eugene Garfield, "A Tribute to Calvin N. Mooers, A Pioneer of Information Retrieval," *The Scientist* 11, no. 6 (March 17, 1997): 9.

93. M. K. Buckland, "Documentation, Information Science, and Library Science in the U.S.A.," *Information Processing & Management* 32, no. 1 (1996): 63–76.

94. Ostler, Dahlin, and Willardson, *The Closing of American Library Schools*, 25, 35, passim.

95. M. K. Buckland and Z. M. Liu, "History of Information Science," *Annual Review of Information Science and Technology* 30 (1995): 385–416; W. Boyd Rayward, "The Origin of Information Science and the International Institute of Bibliography/International Federation for Information and Documentation," *Journal of the American Society for Information Science* 48, no. 4 (1997): 289–300; Järvelin and Vakkari, "LIS Research across 50 Years: Content Analysis of Journal Articles," 65–88.

96. See, for example, James W. Cortada, "Exploring How ICTs and Administration Are Entwined: The Promise of Information Ecosystems," *Administration & Society* 50, no. 9 (October 2018): 1213–1237; and "New Approaches to the History of Information: Ecosystems, Infrastructures, and Graphical Representations of Information," *Library & Information History* 32, no. 3 (August 2016): 179–202.

97. Bobinski, *Libraries and Librarianship*, 119–120.

98. Librarians were in a minority. As of 2019, of the 101 institutional members of the iSchools membership directory, only 40 had ALA-accredited programs, and an even smaller cohort among the 900 information-related master's degrees at 468 institutions. Half were located in business schools, and among the other half, programs were in biological and health science, library science, public administration,

communications, and education, Samantha Becker and Bo Kinney, "Graduate Information Programs and Accreditation: Landscape Survey and Analysis," *Researchgate* 2016, citeseerx.ist.psu.edu/voewdoc/download?doi=10.1.1.372.6915&rep=rep 1&type-pdr (accessed September 29, 2022); Terry Weech, "Trends in Accreditation: New Definitions and Distinctions," *American Libraries*, May 20, 2019, https://americanlibrariesmagazine.org/2019/05/20/trends-in-library-school-accreditation/ (accessed January 16, 2020).

99. Emmett R. McGeever, "Documentum Ad Absurdum: An Essay on the Directions of Documentation Research," *American Documentation* 9, no. 2 (April 1958): 73–76. Readers were finally introduced to Shannon's ideas, but by experts outside the field of library studies, for example, by Clifford J. Maloney with a background in biology and chemistry, "Semantic Information," ibid., 13, no. 3 (July 1962): 276–287.

100. For example, Layman E. Allen, "Toward a Procedure for Logically Cataloguing Knowledge," ibid., 10, no. 4 (October 1959): 296–315; L. B. Heilprin, "On the Information Problem Ahead," ibid., 12, no. 1 (January 1961): 6–14; Yehoshua Bar-Hillel, "Is Information Retrieval Approaching a Crisis?" ibid., 14, no. 2 (April 1963): 95–98; Joseph C. Donohue and N. E. Karioth, "Coming of Age in Academe—Information Science at 21," ibid., 17, no. 3 (July 1966): 117–119.

101. Verner W. Clapp, "Research in Problems of Scientific Information—Retrospect and Prospect," ibid., 14, no. 1 (January 1963): 1–9.

102. Claire K. Schultz and Paul L. Garwig, "History of the American Documentation Institute—A Sketch," ibid., 20, no. 2 (April 1969): 152–160.

103. H. Borko, "Information Science: What Is It?" ibid., 19, no. 1 (January 1968): 3–5.

104. Ibid., 4.

105. Manfred Kochen, "Stability in the Growth of Knowledge," ibid., 20, no. 3 (July 1969): 186–197.

106. For an early, useful example that linked nicely to the interest of librarians, see B. Mittman, R. Chalice, and D. Dillaman, "Mixed Data Structures in a Multi-Purpose Retrieval System," *Journal of the American Society for Information Science* 24, no. 2 (March–April 1973): 135–141.

107. Bruce J. Whittmore, "A Generalized Conceptual Development for the Analysis and Flow of Information," ibid., 24, no. 3 (May–June 1973): 221–231; Jacques F. Vallee and Gerald L. Askevold, "Information Organization for Interactive Use: Design Implications in Data-Base Systems," ibid., 24, no. 4 (July–August 1973): 287–299.

108. James G. Williams and Chai Kim, "On Theory Development in Information Science," ibid., 26, no. 1 (January–February 1975): 7.

109. Vladimir Slamecka, "Pragmatic Observations on Theoretical Research on Information Science," ibid., 26, no. 6 (November–December 1975): 318.

110. For example, Martha E. Williams, "Networks for On-Line Data Base Access," ibid., 28, no. 5 (September 1977): 247–258; Hank Epstein, "The Technology of Library and Information Networks," ibid., 31, no. 6 (November 1980): 425–444; M. C. Yovitts, C. R. Foulk, and L. L. Rose in a series of articles, the most relevant for

librarians, "Information Flow and Analysis: Theory, Simulation, and Experiments," ibid., 32, no. 3 (May 1981): 187–202; and ibid., 32, no. 4 (July 1981): 243–248; Joseph Becker, "An Information Scientist's View on Evolving Information Technology," ibid., 35, no. 3 (1984): 164–169. For the first discussion about AI in this journal, see "Introduction and Overview," ibid., 35 (September 1984), a nearly dedicated issue to the topic. On the role of PCs, see Donald Case, "The Personal Computer: Missing Link to the Electronic Journal?" ibid., 36, no. 5 (1985): 309–313.

111. Thomas E. Backer, "Information Alchemy: Transforming Information through Knowledge Utilization," ibid., 44, no. 4 (1993): 217–221; William Paisley, "Knowledge Utilization: The Role of New Communication Technologies," ibid., 44, no. 4 (1993): 222–234.

112. Lois F. Lunin and William R. Hersh, "Medical Informatics: Information Technology in Health Care," ibid., 46, no. 10 (1995): 726–728; Paul N. Gorman, "Information Needs of Physicians," ibid., 729–738; Bradley M. Hemminger, "Introduction to the Special Issue on Bioinformatics," ibid., 56, no. 5 (2005): 437–439, the bulk of this issue is devoted to the subject; Peter van den Besselaar and Loet Leydesdorff, "Mapping Change in Scientific Specialties: A Scientometric Reconstruction of the Development of Artificial Intelligence," ibid., 47, no. 6 (1996): 415–436.

113. Chaim Zins, "Conceptions of Information Science," ibid., 58, no. 3 (2007): 335.

114. Ibid; but see his "Classification Schemes of Information Science: Twenty-Eight Scholars Map the Field," ibid., 58, no. 5 (2007): 645–672.

115. Michael D. Cooper, "Usage Patterns of a Web-Based Library Catalog," ibid., 52, no. 2 (2001): 137–148; Bernard J. Jansen and Udo Pooch, "A Review of Web Searching Studies and a Framework for Future Research," ibid., 52, no. 3 (2001): 235–246; and in a series of articles by Amanda Spink, T. D. Wilson, Nigel Ford, Allen Foster, and David Ellis, "Information-Seeking and Mediated Searching: Part 1. Theoretical Framework and Research Design," ibid., 53, no. 9 (2002): 695–702; "Part 2. Uncertainty and Its Correlates," ibid., 704–715; "Part 3. Successive Searching," ibid., 716–727; "Part 4. Cognitive Styles in Information Seeking," ibid., 728–735.

116. Cooper, "Usage Patterns of a Web-Based Library Catalog," ibid., 52, no. 2 (2001): 137–148.

117. James W. Cortada, *The Essential Manager: How to Thrive in the Global Information Jungle* (Hoboken, NJ: John Wiley & Sons, 2015): 16.

118. Bernard J. Jansen and Udo Pooch, "A Review of Web Searching Studies and Framework for Future Research," ibid., 52, no. 3 (2001): 235–246; Spink et al., "Information-Seeking and Mediated Searching," series of four articles, ibid., 52, no. 9 (2002): 695–735.

119. Nigel Ford, T.D. Wilson, Allen Foster, David Ellis, and Amanda Spink, "Information Seeking and Mediated Searching. Part 4. Cognitive Styles in Information Seeking," ibid., 53, no. 9 (2002): 728.

120. Ibid., 728–735.

121. Blaise Cronin and Lokman J. Meho, "The Shifting Balance of Intellectual Trade in Information Studies," ibid., 59, no. 4 (2008): 551–564.

122. Ibid.

123. Steve Sawyer and Haiyan Huang, "Conceptualizing Information, Technology, and People: Comparing Information Science and Information Systems Literatures," ibid., 58, no. 10 (2007): 1436–1447.

124. M. J. Bates, "Fundamental Forms of Information," ibid., 57, no. 8 (2006): 1033.

125. Ibid., 1034.

126. Bateson, G., *Steps to an Ecology of the Mind* (New York: Ballantine, 1972): 453.

127. For summary of these notions, Birger Hjørland, "Information: Objective or Subjective Situational?" ibid., 58, no. 10 (2007): 1149, but see entire article too, 1448–1456.

128. Quoted in ibid., 1451.

129. Ibid., 1455.

130. Michael Buckland, "What Kind of Science *Can* Information Science Be?" ibid., 63, no. 1 (2012): 1–7; Lai Ma, "Meanings of Information: The Assumptions and Research Consequence of Three Foundational LIS Theories," ibid., 63, no. 4 (2012): 716–723; Jens-Erik Mai, "The Quality and Qualities of Information," ibid., 64, no. 4 (20013): 675–688.

131. Isto Huvila, Theresa Dirndorfer Andeson, Eva Hourihan Jansen, and Adam Worrall, "Boundary Objects in Information Science," ibid., 68, no. 8 (2017): 1807–1822.

132. Eric T. Meyer, Kalpana Shanker, Matthew Willis, Sarika Sharma, and Steve Sawyer, "The Social Informatics of Knowledge," ibid., 70, no. 4 (2019): 307–312 and the entire issue of this journal dedicated to this subject; Paul J. Graham and Harley D. Dickinson, "Knowledge-System Theory in Society: Charting the Growth of Knowledge-System Models over a Decade, 1994–2003," ibid., 58, no. 14 (2007): 2372–2381.

133. Diane Kelly and Cassidy R. Sugimoto, "A Systematic Review of Interactive Informational Retrieval Evaluation Studies, 1967–2006," ibid., 64, no. 4 (2013): 745–770; Otto Tuomaala, Kalervo Järvelin, and Pertti Vakkari, "Evolution of Library and Information Science, 1965–2005: Content Analysis of Journal Articles," ibid., 65, no. 7 (2014): 1446–1462.

134. Marcum and Schonfeld, *Along Came Google*, 37–71.

135. Michael Buckland, "Documentation, Information Science, and Library Science in the USA," *Information Processing and Management* 32, no. 1 (1996): 63–76.

136. Ostler, Dahlin, and Willardson, *The Closing of American Library Schools*, 69.

137. J. C. R. Licklider, *Libraries of the Future* (Cambridge, MA: MIT Press, 1965).

138. F. R. Shapiro, "Coinage of the Term Information Science," *Journal of the American Society for Information Science* 46, no. 5 (1995): 384–386.

139. Rachel Ivy Clarke and Young-In Kim, "The More Things Change, the More They Stay the Same: Educational and Disciplinary Backgrounds of American Librarians, 1950–2015," *Journal of Education for Library and Information Science* 59, no. 4 (2018): 179–205.

140. Ibid., 188. I used the word "politely" because the authors are librarians and one also a professor at a library school and their study was published by a library journal.

141. Ibid., 194.

142. Confirmatory evidence of the intellectual misdirection of the profession had been coming in for some time, but with little effect on the training and skills of librarians. See, for example, Stephen E. Atkins, "Subject Trends in Library and Information Science Research, 1975–1984," *Library Trends* (Spring 1988): 633–658; W. Boyd Rayward, "The History and Historiography of Information Science: Some Reflections," *Information Processing & Management* 32, no. 1 (1996): 3–17; Gary P. Radford, "Trapped in Our Own Discursive Formations: Toward an Archaeology of Library and Information Science," *The Library Quarterly* 73, no. 1 (January 2003): 1–18; Kelly Blessinger and Michele Frasier, "Analysis of a Decade in Library Literature: 1994–2004," *College & Research Libraries* 58, no. 2 (March 2007): 155–169.

143. Bobinski, *Libraries and Librarianship*.

144. Niels Bohr, *Atomic Physics and Human Knowledge* (New York: John Wiley & Sons, 1958): 67–82.

145. Jesse H. Shera, *Libraries and the Organization of Knowledge* (London: Crosby Lockwood & Son, 1965): 131–132.

146. William J. Baumol and Matityahu Marcus, *Economics of Academic Libraries* (Washington, D.C.: American Council on Education, 1967); Marcum and Schonfeld, *Along Came Google*, 65.

147. Marcum and Schonfeld, *Along Came Google*, 70.

4. EARLY ENCOUNTERS BY COMPUTER BUILDERS

1. "An Interview with Charles W. Bachman," with Thomas Haigh, September 25–26, 2004, p. 101, Charles Babbage Institute, University of Minnesota.

2. My use of the term *electrified information* was inspired by the use of the phrase "electronic information" by archivist David Bearman, "Diplomatics, Weberian Bureaucracy, and the Management of Electronic Records in Europe and America," *American Archivist* 55 (Winter 1992): 169–170.

3. This milieu was first presented by William Aspray, "The Scientific Conceptualization of Information," *Annals of the History of Computing* 7, no. 2 (1985): 117–140; Bernard Dionysius Geoghegan, "The Historiographic Conceptualization of Information: A Critical Survey," *IEEE Annals of the History of Computing* 30, no. 1 (January–March 2008): 66–81.

4. A useful way to track its identification is through the debates held within universities and funding organizations. See, for example, William Aspray, Andrew Goldstein, and Bernard Williams, "The Social and Intellectual Shaping of a New Mathematical Discipline: The Role of the National Science Foundation in the Rise of Theoretical Computer Science and Engineering," in Ronald Colinger (ed.), *Vita Mathematica: Historical Research and Integration with Teaching* (Washington, D.C.: Mathematical Association of America, 1996): 209–230; Peter A. Freeman, W. Richards Adrion, and William Aspray, *Computing and the National Science Foundation, 1950–2016: Building a Foundation for Modern Computing* (No City: Association for Computing Machinery, 2019): 4–26; Jesse T. Quatse, "Hardware Design in the Founding of Computer Science at CMU," *IEEE Annals of the History of Computing*

28, no. 3 (July–September 2006): 76–80; Jack Minker, "Forming a Computer Science Center at the University of Maryland," ibid., 29, no. 1 (January–March 2007): 49–64; Gopal K. Gupta, "Computer Science Curriculum Developments in the 1960s," ibid., 29, no. 2 (April–June 2007): 40–54.

5. For understanding all facets of the new discipline, see Allen B. Tucker (ed.), *Computer Science Handbook*, 2nd ed. (Boca Raton, FL: CRC Press, 2004). This volume divides the discipline into "Algorithms and Complexity," "Architecture and Organization," "Computational Science," "Graphics and Visual Computing," "Human–Computer Interaction," "Information Management," "Intelligent Systems," "Net-Centric Computing," "Operating Systems," "Programming Languages," and "Software Engineering" through 110 contributed chapters; Jan van Leeuwen, *Handbook of Theoretical Computer Science* (Cambridge, MA: MIT Press, 1994); and the many editions of Anthony Ralston, Edwin D. Reilly, and David Hemmendinger (eds.), *Encyclopedia of Computer Science*, especially 4th ed. (Hoboken, NJ: John Wiley & Sons, 2003). For short course in its history, see Edwin D. Reilly, *Milestones in Computer Science and Information Technology* (Westport, CT: Greenwood Press, 2003); Matti Tedre, *The Science of Computing: Shaping a Discipline* (Boca Raton, FL: CRC Press, 2014).

6. Donald Knuth, *The Art of Computer Programming*, vol. 1, 3rd ed. (Boston, MA: Addison-Wesley, 1997); Peter Brass, *Advanced Data Structures* (Cambridge, UK: Cambridge University Press, 2008), and one of the earliest studies, Niklaus Wirth, *Algorithms and Data Structures* (Englewood Cliffs, NJ: Prentice-Hall, 1985).

7. Peter J. Denning, "Computer Science: The Discipline," 1999, http://denninginstitute.com/pjd/PUBS/ENC/cs99.pdf (accessed February 11, 2020).

8. Edwin D. Reilly (ed.), *Concise Encyclopedia of Computer Science* (Hoboken, NJ: John Wiley & Sons, 2004): 120–121, 437. In computing the word *code* refers to instructions given to computers; another word for programs.

9. The most comprehensive study is by Donald E. Knuth, *The Art of Computer Programming*, published in four volumes beginning in the 1990s, but see the latest printing (Boston, MA: Addison-Wesley, 2011); on early developments, see Jean E. Sammet, *Programming Languages: History and Fundamentals* (Englewood Cliffs, NJ: Prentice-Hall, 1969); Robert Balzer, "A 15 Year Perspective on Automatic Programming," *IEEE Transactions on Software Engineering* SE-11 (November 1985): 1257–1268; for a bibliography, James W. Cortada, *A Bibliographic Guide to the History of Computing, Computers, and the Information Processing Industry* (Westport, CT: Greenwood Press, 1990): 344–395.

10. Jean François Monin and Michael G. Hinchey, *Understanding Formal Methods* (Berlin: Springer-Verlag, 2003).

11. In this category many discussions are held regarding standards—I liken these to grammar or writing styles, but more rigorous—also a major development that began in the late 1800s and continues to this day as an influence on the nature of information, Martha Lampland and Susan Leigh Star, *Standards and Their Stories: How Quantifying, Classifying, and Formalizing Practices Shape Everyday Life* (Ithaca, NY: Cornell University Press, 2009); Andrew L. Russell, *Open Standards and the Digital Age: History, Ideology, and Networks* (Cambridge, UK: Cambridge University Press, 2014).

12. Thomas C. Bartree, Irwin L. Lebow, and Irving S. Reed, *Theory and Design of Digital Machines* (New York: McGraw-Hill, 1962); Bill Moggridge, *Designing Interactions* (Cambridge, MA: MIT Press, 2007); Robert Latham and Saskia Sassen (eds.), *Digital Formations: IT and New Architectures in the Global Realm* (Princeton, NJ: Princeton University Press, 2005).

13. Charles J. Bashe, Lyle R. Johnson, John H. Palmer, and Emerson W. Pugh, *IBM's Early Computers* (Cambridge, MA: MIT Press, 1985; Emerson W. Pugh, Lyle R. Johnson, John H. Palmer, *IBM's 360 and Early 370 Systems* (Cambridge, MA: MIT Press, 2003).

14. Bob Wescott, *The Every Computer Performance Book* (No City: CreateSpace, 2013); Jim Gray (ed.), *The Benchmark Handbook for Database and Transaction Systems*, 2nd ed. (Burlington, MA: Morgan Kaufmann, 1993); Raghunath Nambiar and Meikel Poess (eds.), *Performance Evaluation and Benchmarking* (Berlin: Springer-Verlag, 2009). Your author engaged in some of this activity in the 1970s and early 1980s, James W. Cortada, *Managing DP Hardware: Capacity Planning, Cost Justification, Availability, and Energy Management* (Englewood Cliffs, NJ: Prentice-Hall, 1983): 79–80.

15. For an introduction, see Jiacun Wang, *Real-Time Embedded Systems* (Hoboken, NJ: John Wiley & Sons, 2017); Hagit Attiya and Jennifer Welch, *Distributed Computing: Fundamentals, Simulations, and Advanced Topics* (Hoboken, NJ: John Wiley & Sons, 2004); Gerard Tel, *Introduction to Distributed Algorithms* (Cambridge, UK: Cambridge University Press, 1994).

16. For an introduction, see Andrew S. Tanenbaum, *Computer Networks* (Englewood Cliffs, NJ: Prentice-Hall, 1989; Richard W. Watson, *Timesharing System Design Concept* (New York: McGraw-Hill, 1970); John Bellamy, *Digital Telephony*, 2nd ed. (New York: John Wiley & Sons, 1991); Eli M. Noam, *Interconnecting the Network of Networks* (Cambridge, MA: MIT Press, 2001); and on the specifics of information theory, see John R. Pierce, *Signals: The Telephone and Beyond* (San Francisco, CA: W. H. Freeman & Co., 1981). There is a growing body of historical literature on the pre-Internet. Examples include Elaine B. Kerr and Starr Roxanne Hiltz, *Computer-Mediated Communication Systems: Status and Evaluation* (New York: Academic Press, 1982); Patrice Flichy, *Dynamics of Modern Communications: The Shaping and Impact of New Communication Technologies* (London: SAGE Publications, 1995); John Bray, *The Communications Miracle: The Telecommunications Pioneers from Morse to the Information Highway* (New York: Plenum, 1995); David E. Nye, "Shaping Communication Networks: Telegraph, Telephone, Computer," *Social Research* 64 (Fall 1997): 1067–1091; Philip L. Frana, "Telematics and the Early History of International Information Flows," *IEEE Annals of the History of Computing* 40, no. 2 (April–June 2018): 32–47.

17. The topic has a massive literature. For an introduction, see David M. Kroenke and David J. Auer, *Database Concepts*, 3rd ed. (Upper Saddle River, NJ: Prentice-Hall, 2007); for bibliographies of historically relevant materials, see James W. Cortada, *A Bibliographic Guide to the History of Computing, Computers, and the Information Processing Industry*, 446–448; and *Second Bibliographic Guide to the*

History of Computing, Computers, and the Information Processing Industry (Westport, CT: Greenwood Press, 1996): 345–348.

18. On graphics, see Manuel Lima, *Visual Complexity: Mapping Patterns of Information* (New York: Princeton Architectural Press, 2011); on games, see Casey O'Donnell, *Developer's Dilemma: The Secret World of Videogame Creators* (Cambridge, MA: MIT Press, 2014); Henry Lowood and Raiford Guins (eds.), *Debugging Games History: A Critical Lexicon* (Cambridge, MA: MIT Press, 2016); Keith Burgun, *Games Design Theory: AA New Philosophy for Understanding Games* (Boca Raton, FL: CRC Press, 2013); Nick Montfort and Ian Bogost, "Random and Raster: Display Technologies and the Development of Videogames," *IEEE Annals of the History of Computing* 31, no. 3 (July–September 2009): 34–43.

19. For two historical introductions, see Susan B. Barnes, "Computer Interfaces," in Atsushi Akera and Frederik Nebeker (eds.), *From 0 to 1: An Authoritative History of Modern Computing* (New York: Oxford University Press, 2002): 133–147; Jonathan Grudin, "Three Faces of Human-Computer Interaction," *IEEE Annals of the History of Computing* 27, no. 4 (October–December 2005): 46–62.

20. For historical perspective, see Mary Ellen Bowden, Trudi Bellardo Hahn, and Robert V. Williams (eds.), *Proceedings of the 1998 Conference on the History and Heritage of Scientific Information Systems* (Medford, NJ: Information Today, Inc. for American Society for Information Science and the Chemical Heritage Foundation, 1999); Douglas S. Robertson, *Phase Change: The Computer Revolution in Science and Mathematics* (Oxford: Oxford University Press, 2003).

21. On current thinking, see John Brockman (ed.), *Possible Minds: 25 Ways of Looking at AI* (New York: Penguin Press, 2019).

22. Andreas Brennecke and Reinhard Keil-Slawick (eds.), "Position Papers for Dagstuhl Seminar 9635 on History of Software Engineering," August 26–30, 1996, http://citeseerx.ist.psu.edu/viewdoc/download?doi=10.1.1.89.2506&rep=rep1&type=pdf (accessed February 12, 2020).

23. Ian D. Wyatt and Daniel E. Hecker, "Occupational Changes during the 20th Century," *Monthly Labor Review* (March 2006): 39.

24. Data from various tables, U.S. Bureau of Labor Statistics.

25. Stella Fayer, Alan Lacey, and Audrey Watson, "STEM Occupations: Past, Present, and Future," *Occupational Outlook Quarterly* (Winter 2002–2003): 1–4, 24, 31.

26. Ibid.

27. Ibid.

28. This data is routinely collected by the National Science Foundation. A personal example: in the summer of 2018 my two grandsons, aged eight and ten, respectively, took a one-week afternoon course in writing apps for a total of fifteen hours, and at the end of it had (a) learned basic Java programming language, (b) wrote a functioning online game, and (c) converted their work from laptops to installation as a smartphone app. Prior to the course they had no experience with programming, but had played online games on tablets and smartphones. I think that the number of PhDs is undercounted since they came out of multiple disciplines, but we will not debate the issue here, because it is out of scope with the history of information.

29. An historian wrote about the long development of the technology, David Hochfelder, *The Telegraph in America, 1832–1920* (Baltimore, MD: Johns Hopkins University Press, 2012).

30. Robert V. Bruce, *Alexander Graham Bell and the Conquest of Solitude* (Ithaca, NY: Cornell University Press, 1990); Andrew Wheen, *Dot-Dash to Dot.com: How Modern Telecommunications Evolved from the Telegraph to the Internet* (Berlin: Springer-Verlag, 2011).

31. Hugh G. J. Aitkin, *The Continuous Wave: Technology and the American Radio, 1900–1932* (Princeton, NJ: Princeton University Press, 1985); G. R. M. Garratt, *The Early History of Radio: From Faraday to Marconi* (London: Institution of Electrical Engineers in association with the Science Museum, 1994).

32. For an introduction, see Jon Gertner, *The Idea Factory: Bell Labs and the Great Age of American Innovation* (New York: Penguin, 2012).

33. M. D. Fagen (ed.), *A History of Engineering and Science in the Bell System: Volume 1 The Early Years (1875–1925)* (New York: The Bell Telephone Laboratories, 1975). *Volume 2, National Service in War and Peace (1925–1975)* (Murray Hill, NJ: Bell Telephone Laboratories, 1978) should also be consulted.

34. E. G. Andrews, "Telephone Switching and the Early Bell Laboratories Computers," *Bell System Technical Journal* 42 (1963): 341–353; Lillian H. Hoddeson, "The Emergence of Basic research in the Bell Telephone System, 1875–1915," *Technology and Culture* 22 (July 1981): 512–544, and Lillian H. Hoddeson, "The Entry of the Quantum Theory of Solids into the Bell Telephone Laboratories, 1925–40: A Case Study of the Industrial Application of Fundamental Science," *Minerva* 18 (Autumn 1980): 422–447; B. D. Holbrook and W. Stanley Brown, *A History of Computing Research at Bell Laboratories (1937–1975)* (Murray Hill, NJ: Bell Telephone laboratories, 1982).

35. IBM advertisement page, "Getting Your Answers . . . *at Electronic Speed!*" (Copy in author's collection).

36. MS-DOS users combining contents of multiple files use a "copy command," while Linux and Unix users do the same by using "cat command."

37. Statistical activities enhanced by the use of computing include functions that require working with large bodies of data to conduct, for example, bootstraps, smoothing, image analysis, and apply EM algorithms. These are intended to work with larger datasets, develop more realistic models, analyze larger classes of models and analyze existing simple models more diversely, and to visualize data.

38. Stephen J. Greenberg, "Card Tricks: The Decline & Fall of a Bibliographic Tool," *Circulating Now*, February 6, 2020, http://www.circulatingnow.nim.nih.gov/2020/02/06/card-tricks-the-decline-and-fall-of-a-bibliographic-tool/ (accessed February 11, 2020).

39. Thomas J. Misa and Jeffrey R. Yost, *FastLane: Managing Science in the Internet World* (Baltimore, MD: Johns Hopkins University Press, 2016).

40. This was not by choice, but by the necessity that so much additional material was conveniently available in digital form that simply in good conscious could not be ignored, James W. Cortada, *The Digital Flood: The Diffusion of Information Technology across the U.S., Europe, and Asia* (New York: Oxford University Press, 2016) and *The Digital Hand*, 3 vols. (New York: Oxford University Press, 2004–2008).

41. U.S. Bureau of the Census.

42. James W. Cortada, *All the Facts: A History of Information in the United States Since 1870* (New York: Oxford University Press, 2016): 117–118, 123–127.

43. Earlier versions date to 1792. Forecasts are made eighteen months in advance and historically have been approximately 80 percent accurate. For decades now the publisher has relied on modern meteorological professionals and their vast supply of digitized weather data and computerized models of weather forecasting, John E. Walsh and David Allen, "Testing the Farmer's Almanac," *Weatherwise* 34, no. 5 (1981): 212–215.

44. Such as by Ralph Hartley (1888–1970) who studied radio and telephone communications. See, for example, his article, "Transmission of Information," *Bell System Technical Journal* 7, no. 3 (July 1928): 535–563.

45. Ken Steiglitz, *The Discrete Charm of the Machine: Why the World Became Digital* (Princeton, NJ: Princeton University Press, 2019): 186.

46. Ibid., 186.

47. Ibid., 186.

48. Ibid., 186.

49. For example, the highly regarded historian of computing, Paul E. Ceruzzi, does not mention him in his classic text, *A History of Modern Computing*, 2nd ed. (Cambridge, MA: MIT Press, 2003).

50. Analog information is continuous or "more-or-less" such as when a watch displays the large hand slightly to the right of the second bar from the top, suggesting it is just past two o'clock. Digital information is specific, such as when an electronic watch displays "2:05," which means five seconds after two o'clock.

51. Steiglitz, *The Discrete Charm of the Machine*, 83–90.

52. D. A. Mindell, *Between Human and Machine: Feedback, Control, and Computing before Cybernetics* (Baltimore, MD: Johns Hopkins University Press, 2002): 320; Geoghegan, "The Historiographic Conceptualization of Information: A Critical Survey," 73–74.

53. As one student of his work defined it, "To capture faithfully the frequencies in a signal, we must sample at a rate at least twice the highest frequency present in the signal"; ibid., 85.

54. Harry Nyquist, "Certain Factor Affecting Telegraphic Speed," *Bell System Technical Journal* 3 (1924): 324–346; and "Certain Topics in Telegraph Transmission Theory," *Transactions of the AIEE* 47 (February 1928): 617–644, reprinted in *Proceedings of the IEEE* 90, no. 2 (February 2002).

55. Nyquist, "Certain Topics in Telegraph Transmission Theory," 280.

56. He argued that the principle was a necessary condition, that is to say, one has to sample at a rate twice the speed as the highest frequency of a signal in order to understand it, but that this measure does not necessarily guarantee an accurate representation of the original analog message, but that it normally can establish perfectly what was the original signal. Hence theoretically, we have confidence that a signal—data—sent down the line is what the original sender intended and that it could be measured, Steiglitz, *The Discrete Charm of the Machine*, 86.

57. Matti Tedre, *The Science of Computing: Shaping a Discipline* (Boca Raton, FL: Chapman and Hall, 2017); Jack W. Copeland, Carl J. Posy, and Oron Shagrir

(eds.), *Computability: Turing, Gödel, Church, and Beyond* (Cambridge, MA: MIT Press, 2015).

58. The movie was based on a solid early biography. Andrew Hodges, *Alan Turing: The Enigma* (New York: Simon & Schuster, 1983); Chris Bernhardt, *Turing's Vision: The Birth of Computer Science* (Cambridge, MA: MIT Press, 2016).

59. For his thinking and work from the 1930s into the 1950s, see Jack B. Copeland (ed.), *The Essential Turing* (New York: Oxford University Press, 2004), also Jack B. Copeland "Alan Turing's Forgotten Ideas in Computer Science," *Scientific American* 280, no. 4 (1999): 99–103; and Jack B. Copeland et al., *The Turing Guide* (New York: Oxford University Press, 2017); and for a biography by Copeland, see *Turing: Pioneer of the Information Age* (Oxford: Oxford University Press, 2012). On the Turing Test, see Stuart M. Shieber, *The Turing Test: Verbal Behavior as the Hallmark of Intelligence* (Cambridge, MA: Bradford Books, 2004).

60. His life ended early, at almost the age of forty-two. Turing was gay at a time when it was illegal to be so in England, and he is believed to have committed suicide because of his sexual orientation.

61. An intriguing fact: scientist and future novelist C. P. Snow was a graduate student at Cambridge in the same college while Turing was an undergraduate there.

62. Alan M. Turing, "On Computable Numbers, with an Application to the Entscheidungsproblem," *Proceedings of the London Mathematical Society* 2, no. 42 (1937): 250–265, and a correction to his original paper, ibid., 43 (1937): 544–546.

63. Copeland, *The Essential Turing*, 22. See also, Jon Agar, *Turing and the Universal Machine* (Duxford, UK: Icon, 2001).

64. Although in the interwar years Vannevar Bush (1890–1974) had his analog differential analyzer at MIT, which would have been known to all the protagonists described in our chapter.

65. Alan M. Turing, "Intelligent Machinery," written in 1948, published in 1968; C. R. Evans and A. D. J. Robertson (eds.), *Cybernetics: Key Papers* (Baltimore, MD.: University Park Press, 1968) and more widely available in the 1969 reprint, *Machine Intelligence* 5 (1969): 3–23.

66. Steiglitz, *The Discrete Charm of the Machine*, 132.

67. Bernhardt, *Turing's Vision*, 25–68, 87–106; Rolf Herken (ed.), *The Universal Turing Machine: A Half-Century Survey* (New York: Springer-Verlag, 1995); Rod Downey (ed.), *Turing's Legacy: Developments from Turing's Ideas in Logic* (Cambridge, UK: Cambridge University Press, 2014).

68. Alan M. Turing, "Computer Machinery and Intelligence," *Mind* LIX (1950): 433, full article, 433–460.

69. Over a half-century later, AI developers wanted the machine to provide accurate answers to questions, as demonstrated, for example, by IBM's computer *Watson* on the highly popular TV program *Jeopardy* in 2011, John Markoff, "Computer Wins on 'Jeopardy!': Trivial, It's Not," *New York Times*, February 1, 2011, Section A, p. 1.

70. Turing, "Computer Machinery and Intelligence," 433–460.

71. Stuart Russell and Peter Norvig, *Artificial Intelligence: A Modern Approach*, 4th ed. (Upper Saddle River, NJ: Prentice Hall, 2020).

72. Robert M. French, "Moving beyond the Turing Test," *Communications of the Association for Computing Machinery* 55, no. 12 (2012): 74–77 and his earlier, "The Turing Test: The First 50 Years," *Trends in Cognitive Sciences* 4, no. 3 (2000): 115–121.

73. William Aspray, "The Mathematical Reception of the Modern Computer: John von Neumann and the Institute for Advanced Study Computer," *MAA Studies in Mathematics* 26 (1987): 166–194 also his, "The Mathematical Reception of the Modern Computer: John von Neumann and the Institute for Advanced Study Computer," in Esther R. Phillips (ed.), *Studies in the History of Mathematics* 26 of Studies in Mathematics (Washington, D.C.: Mathematical Association of America, 1987): 166–194; Julian Bigelow, "Computer Development at the Institute for Advanced Study," in N. Metropolis et al. (eds.), *History of Computing in the Twentieth Century: A Collection of Essays* (New York: Academic Press, 1980): 291–310; Nancy Stern, "John von Neumann's Influence on Electronic Digital Computing, 1944–1946," *Annals of the History of Computing* 2, no. 4 (October 1980): 349–362. For an understanding of the breadth of his research interests, see A. H. Taub (ed.), *John von Neumann: Collected Works*, 6 vols. (Oxford: Pergamon Press, 1961–1963), but see also Neumann, *Papers of John von Neumann on Computing and Computer Theory* edited by William Aspray and Arthur Burks (Cambridge, MA: MIT Press, 1987).

74. Claude E. Shannon, "An Algebra for Theoretical Genetics" (unpublished PhD dissertation, Massachusetts Institute of Technology, April 15, 1940). It was eventually published in 1993. Von Neumann, too, published a seminal paper on computing ranked with the publishing by Shannon of his in 1948 on information theory: John von Neumann, "The Principles of Large-Scale Computing Machines," *Annals of the History of Computing* 3, no. 3 (July 1981): 263–273 and republished in ibid., 10, no. 4 (1989): 243–256. The paper was originally released as a mimeographed document dated May 15, 1946.

75. N. J. A. Sloane and Aaron D. Wyner (eds.), *Claude Elwood Shannon: Collected Papers* (Piscataway, NJ: IEEE Press, 1993): ix.

76. Geoghegan, "The Historiographic Conceptualization of Information: A Critical Survey," 66–81.

77. Steiglitz, *The Discrete Charm of the Machine*, 90.

78. Quoted in ibid.

79. He articulated his key idea several times, initially in 1948 within Bell Lab's internal publication, *Bell System Technical Journal*, the next year in a collaborative book on the same subject with Warren Weaver, *A Mathematical Theory of Communication*, and subsequently summarized in other papers and speeches.

80. "Ralph Hartley," *Engineering and Technology Wiki*, https://ethw.org/Ralph_Hartley (accessed March 3, 2020).

81. Charles Cole, "Shannon Revisited: Information in Terms of Uncertainty," *Journal of the American Society for Information Science* 44, no. 4 (May 1993): 204–211.

82. Such a device produces an oscillating (moving) electrical signal, often also referred to as "waves." The device converts direct current into an alternating current, hence in the language of telephony, into signals, which we call messages.

83. R. V. L. Hartley, "Transmission of Information," *Bell System Technical Journal* 7, no. 3 (July 1928): 535–563.

84. Ibid., 552.

85. Ibid., 535.

86. Ibid., 536.

87. Ibid., 544.

88. Ibid., 555.

89. Ibid.

90. Ibid., 556.

91. Ibid., 564.

92. I cannot help myself, but Paul Baran, a key developer, was two years old, Donald Davies four years old, Charles M. Herzfeld three years of age, and Bob Taylor and Larry Roberts were not even born. Vinton G. "Vint" Cerf was born in 1943 and the Rock Star baby of them all, developer of the World Wide Web, Sir Tim Berners-Lee, was born in 1955, five years after Hartley died.

93. For a short biography, see Sloane and Wyner, *Claude Elwood Shannon*, xi–xvii, but see also Anthony Liversidge, "Profile of Claude Shannon," ibid., xix–xxxiii, and for a complete list of his publications, ibid., xxxv–xliv.

94. Howard Gardner, a leading expert in developmental psychology and author of numerous books on human intelligence, opined that Shannon's graduate work at MIT was "possibly the most important, and also the most noted, master's thesis of the century," Gardner, *The Mind's New Science: A History of the Cognitive Revolution* (New York: Basic Books, 1987): 144.

95. Claude E. Shannon, "A Mathematical Theory of Communication," *Bell System Technical Journal* 27 (July and October 1948), 379–423, 623–656; reprinted in Sloane and Wyner, *Claude Elwood Shannon*, 5–83.

96. For a technical/mathematical explanation of entropy, Luenberger, *Information Science*, 12–13.

97. Robert Fano, "The Transmission of Information," *Technical Report No. 65* (Cambridge, MA: Massachusetts Institute of Technology, Research Laboratory of Electronics, March 17, 1949), available at https://archive.org/details/fano-tr65.7z/page/n1/mode/2up (accessed March 7, 2020).

98. Claude E. Shannon and Warren Weaver, *The Mathematical Theory of Communication* (Urbana: University of Illinois Press, 1949), reprinted for years by the press; for example, the seventeenth printing appeared in 1998.

99. Shannon, "A Mathematical Theory of Communication," 379.

100. Steiglitz, *The Discrete Charm of the Machine*, 95.

101. For a clear explanation of Shannon's ideas, see ibid., 90–102.

102. Ibid., 102.

103. Quoted in Emily Goodmann, "A Tale of Two Networks: The Bell Telephone System and the Meaning of 'Information,' 1947–1968," *Information & Culture* 54, no. 3 (2019): 281–310, quoted in p. 295.

104. Shannon and Weaver, *Mathematical Theory*, 4, but see entire book because Weaver's writing clarified much of Shannon's ideas for a larger audience.

105. Goodmann, "A Tale of Two Networks: The Bell Telephone System and the Meaning of 'Information,' 1947–1968," 295–299.

106. Quoted in ibid., 302.
107. Ibid., 305.
108. Sergio Verdú, "Guest Editorial," in Verdú and McLaughlin, *Information Theory: 50 Years of Discovery*, ix.
109. Verdú, "Fifty Years of Shannon Theory," ibid., 27.
110. Ibid., 26–27.
111. János Körner and Alon Orlitsky, "Zero-Error Information Theory," Ibid., 163.
112. To clarify his name, he was born Gerhard Anton Sahimann, and his family changed its name to Salton and Americanized the boy's too. His work on IR was published under his Americanized name.
113. See, for example, G. Salton, A. Wong, and C. S. Yang, "A Vector Space Model for Automatic Indexing," *Communications of the ACM* 18, no. 11 (1975): 613–620; Gerard Salton, *Introduction to Modern Information Retrieval* (New York: McGraw-Hill, 1983), his textbook on the subject of IR, *Automatic Information Organization and Retrieval* (New York: McGraw-Hill, 1968), and *A Theory of Indexing* (Philadelphia, PA: Society for Industrial and Applied Mathematics, 1987) in which he proposed a method for ranking indexing terms. He continued to study IR almost to the end of his life; see, for example, Gerard Salton and Chris Buckley, "Improving Retrieval Performance by Relevance Feedback," *Journal of the American Society for Information Science* 41, no. 4 (June 1990): 288–297.
114. A similar idea was enhanced by British computer scientist Karen Spärck Jones (1935–1971) at Cambridge University in the early 1970s with her concept of the inverse document frequency, used in modern search engines, J. I. Tait, "Karen Spärck Jones," *Computational Linguistics* 33, no. 3 (2008): 289–291.
115. R. Rees and A. Kent, "Mechanized Searching Experiments Using the WRU Searching Selector," *American Documentation* 9, no. 4 (1958): 277–287.
116. See, for example, C. D. Gull, "Seven Years of Work on the Organization of Materials in the Special Library," ibid., 7, no. 4 (1956): 320–329; H. P. Luhn, "A New Method of Recording and Searching Information," ibid., 4, no. 1 (1953): 14–16; M. Taube and I. S. Wachtel, "The Logical Structure of Coordinate Indexing," Ibid., 3, no. 4 (1952): 213–218; M. Taube and Associates, "Storage and Retrieval of Information by Means of the Association of Ideas," ibid., 6, no. 1 (1955): 1–18; J. W. Perry, "Information Analysis for Machine Searching," ibid., 1, no. 3 (1950): 133–139.
117. Raised in Germany, he worked in Switzerland in the textile industry, then came to the United States to pursue patents in that industry before joining IBM in 1941, where he took over research on IR. In the late 1940s he engaged in documentation research at the behest of a customer. He soon advocated putting data into "buckets" to speed up searches for their contents, today called *hashing algorithms*. He is also credited for the development of KWIC method of indexing, which is what largely drew Salton's attention and admiration, Claire K. Schultz, *H. P. Luhn: Pioneer of Information Science: Selected Works* (New York: Spartan Books, 1968); Hallam Stevens, "Hans Peter Luhn and the Birth of the Hashing Algorithm" *IEEE Spectrum* 30 (January 2018): 42–47, and for his own words, see Luhn, "Keyword-in-Context Index for Technical Literature," *American Documentation* 11, no. 4 (1960): 288–295.

118. Gerard Salton, "Historical Note: The Past Thirty Years in Information Retrieval," *Journal of the American Society for Information Science* 38, no. 5 (September 1987): 376.

119. Ibid.

120. Salton, "Historical Note: The Past Thirty Years in Information Retrieval," 375–380; Stephen Robertson, "A Brief History of Search Results Ranking," *IEEE Annals of the History of Computing* 41, no. 2 (April–June 2019): 22–28.

121. Salton, "Historical Note: The Past Thirty Years in Information Retrieval," 377.

122. Ibid., 379.

123. Calvin N. Mooers, "Information Retrieval Viewed as Temporal Signaling," *Proceedings of the International Congress of Mathematicians, Cambridge, Massachusetts* (September 1950): 572–573; "Zatocoding Applied to Mechanical Organization of Knowledge," *American Documentation* 2, no. 1 (January 1952): 20–32; and his description of a software tool implementing his ideas called TRAC, see "TRAC, a Procedure-Describing Language for the Reactive Typewriter," *Communications of the ACM* 9, no. 3 (March 1966): 215–219.

124. Eugene Garfield, "A Tribute to Calvin N. Mooers, a Pioneer of Information Retrieval," *The Scientist* 11, no. 6 (1997): 9–10.

125. For introductions to the technology, see Geoffrey Austrian, *Herman Hollerith: The Forgotten Giant of Information Processing* (New York: Columbia University Press, 1982); Harry P. Cemach, *The Elements of Punched Card Accounting* (London: Sir Isaac Pitman, 1951); Francis J. Murray, *Mathematical Machines*, vol. 1, *Digital Computers* (New York: Columbia University Press, 1961), especially early chapters that help explain the technological transition from tabulating to digital computers using cards.

126. There was enormous controversy regarding the move to tape since a human could not see the data as on cards, and there were concerns about the accuracy of electronic movement of information: Committee on the New Recording Means and Computing Devices, Society of Actuaries, *Current Status of Magnetic Tapes As A Recording and a Data Processing Medium* (Chicago, IL: Society of Actuaries, 1955); "Digital Magnetic Tape Recorders—A Survey," *Datamation* 6, no. 2 (March/April 1960): 19–22; James W. Cortada, "Tape Drives, IBM," in James W. Cortada, *Historical Dictionary of Data Processing: Technology* (Westport, CN: Greenwood Press, 1987): 355–359.

127. Paul E. Ceruzzi, *A History of Modern Computing* 2nd ed. (Cambridge, MA: MIT Press, 2003): 69–70; James W. Cortada, "RAMAC," in James W. Cortada, *Historical Dictionary of Data Processing: Technology*, 327–329; for bibliography, James W. Cortada, *Second Bibliographic Guide to the History of Computing, Computers, and the Information Processing Industry* (Westport, CT: Greenwood Press, 1996): 78–79.

128. I have described each generation of these software tools, James W. Cortada, "Database Management Systems," *Historical Dictionary of Data Processing: Technology*, 123–138; C. J. Date, *An Introduction to Database Systems*, 6th ed. (Reading, MA: Addison-Wesley, 1995); Thomas Haigh, "'A Veritable Bucket of Facts': Origins of the Data Base Management System, 1960–1980," in W. Boyd Rayward and

Mary Ellen Bowden (eds.), *The History and Heritage of Scientific and Technological Information Systems* (New Medford, NJ: Information Today, 2004): 73–88 and his, "How Data Got Its Base: Information Storage Software in the 1950s and 1960s," *IEEE Annals of the History of Computing* 31, no. 4 (October–December 2009): 6–25. An entire issue of this journal was devoted to the subject: 31, no. 4 (October–December, 2009). It should be noted that the Univac File Computer (1951) also had a random access storage, or drum memory, but did not gain the visibility and acceptance to the degree of IBM's RAMAC, *An Introduction to the UNIVAC File-Computer System* (Toronto: Remington Rand, 1951).

129. Standard texts on the subject, John B. Bass and J. Kates, *Achieving Usability through Software Architecture* (Pittsburgh, PA: Carnegie Mellon University, 2001); G. Lewis, S. Comella-Dorda, P. Place, D. Plakosh, and R. Seacord, *Enterprise Information System Data Architecture Guide* (Pittsburg, PA: Carnegie Mellon University, 2001). Sometimes the subject is linked to discussions about data warehousing, a development beginning in the 1960s, actualized in the 1980s, William Inmon, *Building the Data Warehouse* (New York: John Wiley & Sons, 1992) and subsequent editions.

130. For an excellent overview of database systems, Luenberger, *Information Science*, 264–283; but see also J. L. Harrington, *Relational Database Design Clearly Explained* (London: Academic Press, 1998).

131. IBM, *Data Processing Techniques: A Data Processing Glossary* (White Plains, NY: IBM Corporation, undated [1960–1962]): 15.

132. Ibid.

133. Ibid.

134. Ibid.

135. "Database," *TechTerms*, https://techterms.com/definition/database (accessed March 7, 2020).

136. "What Is a Relational Database," Oracle, https://techterms.com/definition/database (accessed March 7, 2020).

137. "Piece of data" was a conventional slang phrase used in computing circles in the late twentieth century, a descendent from a similar earlier notion that a datum could be broken into ever-small units, such as into a byte or even more narrowly into a bit. These ideas date from the mid-1950s. Werner Buchholz, of IBM, is usually credited with introducing the term *byte* in June, 1956. "The Word 'Byte' Comes of Age," *Byte Magazine* 2, no. 2 (February 1977): 144; first use of the term in print, G. A. Blauw, F. P. Brooks, Jr., and W. Buchholtz, "Processing Data in Bits and Pieces," *IRE Transactions on Electronic Computers* EC-8, no. 2 (June 1959): 118–124.

138. Martha E. Williams, "Data Bases—A History of Developments and Trends from 1966 through 1975," *Journal of the American Society for Information Science* 28, no. 2 (March 1977): 71.

139. Ibid.; M. C. Gechman, "Generation and Use of Machine-Readable Bibliographic Data Bases," in *Annual Review of Information Science and technology* 7 (Washington, D.C.: American Society for Information Science, 1972): 323–378.

140. Williams, "Data Bases—A History of Developments and Trends from 1966 through 1975, 71–72.

141. Ibid., 72.

142. S. Keenan, "Abstracting and Indexing Services in Science and Technology," *Annual Review of Information Science and Technology* 4 (Chicago, IL: Encyclopedia Britannica for American Society for Information Science, 1969): 273–304.

143. Ibid., 72.

144. I have discussed these trends down into the early 2000s in more detail in James W. Cortada, *The Digital Hand* vol. 2, *How Computers Changed the Work of American Financial, Telecommunications, Media, and Entertainment Industries* (New York: Oxford University Press, 2006): 314–325.

145. John V. Pavlik and Shawn McIntosh, *Converging Media: An Introduction to Mass Communication* (Boston, MA: Pearson, 2004): 89–90.

146. J. Van Duyn, *Automated Crime Information Systems* (Blue Ridge, PA: TAB Professional and Reference Books, 1991): 5–16; see also James W. Cortada, *The Digital Hand* vol. 3, *How Computers Changed the Work of American Public Sector Industries* (New York: Oxford University Press, 2008): 102–139.

147. R. Finer, *A Guide to Selected Computer-Based Information Services* (London: Aslib, 1972). It was 113 pages in length, an indicator that many services listed.

148. Martin Campbell-Kelly and Daniel D. Garcia-Swartz, *From Mainframes to Smartphones: A History of the International Computer Industry* (Cambridge, MA: Harvard University Press, 2015): 105–123.

149. Andrew L. Russell, "Oral-History Charles Bachman," April 9, 2011, *IEEE Oral History Network*, https://ethw.org/Oral-History:Charles_Bachman (accessed March 9, 2020).

150. Charles W. Bachman, "Data Structure Diagrams," *DataBase: A Quarterly Newsletter of SIGBDP* 1, no. 2 (Summer 1969): 4. This article includes citations to earlier writings by Bachman.

151. Charles W. Bachman, "The Programmer as Navigator," *Communications of the ACM* 16, no. 11 (November 1973): 654.

152. Ibid., 655.

153. Ibid.

154. "An Interview with Charles W. Bachman Conducted by Thomas Haigh on 25–26 September, 2004, Tucson, Arizona," ACM Digital Library, https://dl.acm.org/doi/10.1145/1141880.1141882 (accessed March 9, 2020). Other oral histories are available at the Charles Babbage Institute and also the Charles W. Bachman Papers, collection CBI 125.

155. Ibid., 53.

156. For a brief summary that also argues historians played a role in this conversion, see Adam Crymble, *Technology and the Historian: Transformations in the Digital Age* (Urbana: University of Illinois, 2021): 46–47.

157. Claude Elwood Shannon, "Computers and Automation—Progress and Promise in the Twentieth Century" (1962), Sloane and Wyner, *Claude Elwood Shannon Collected Papers*, 837.

158. Ibid., 839.

159. Deanna Marcum and Roger C. Schonfeld, *Along Came Google: A History of Library Digitization* (Princeton, NJ: Princeton University Press, 2021): 39.

160. Quoted by Paul Duguid, "Communication, Computation, and Information," in Ann Blair, Paul Duguid, Anja-Silvia Goeing, and Anthony Grafton (eds.), *Information: A Historical Companion* (Princeton, NJ: Princeton University Press, 2021): 249.

161. Bourne and Hahn, *A History of Online Information Services*, 406.

162. Ibid., 408.

163. A key finding of James W. Cortada, *The Digital Flood: The Diffusion of Information Technology across the U.S., Europe, and Asia* (New York: Oxford University Press, 2012).

164. List prepared by Bourne and Hahn, *A History of Online Information Services*, 410.

165. To be more precise, IBM is credited with developing the first smartphone in 1992 and introduceing it as a product in 1994 called the Simon Personal Communicator (SPC). An excellent description of this product can be found at "IBM Simon," *Wikipedia* https://en.wikipedia.org/wiki/IBM_Simon#Features (accessed March 20, 2020).

166. Colin Koopman, *How We Became Our Data: A Genealogy of the Informational Person* (Chicago, IL: University of Chicago Press, 2019): 183.

5. MATHEMATICIANS AND STATISTICIANS CREATE NEW TOOLS

1. Michael Atiyah, "Mathematics in the 20th Century," *Bulletin of the London Mathematical Society* 34, no. 1 (January 2002): 1–15, quote p. 1.

2. R. W. Gerard, "Quantification in Biology," in Harry Woolf (ed.), *Quantification: A History of the Meaning of Measurement in the Natural and Social Sciences* (Indianapolis, IN: Bobbs-Merrill, 1961): 206.

3. Quoted in I. D. Hill, "Statistical Society of London—Royal Statistical Society: The First 100 Years: 1834–1934," *Journal of the Royal Statistical Society: Series A (General)* 147, no. 2 (1984): 130–139.

4. Spiegelhalter, *The Art of Statistics*, 68.

5. A classic study on the early history of statistics is Stephen M. Stigler, *The History of Statistics: The Measurement of Uncertainty before 1900* (Cambridge, MA: Harvard University Press; 1986); also his *Statistics on the Table: The History of Statistical Concepts and Methods* (Cambridge, MA: Harvard University Press, 2002); for continuation of the story deep into the twentieth century, see Prakash Gorroochurn, *Classic Topics on the History of Modern Mathematical Statistics: From Laplace to More Recent Times* (Hoboken, NJ: John Wiley & Sons, 2016). The most detailed study is by Anders Hald in three volumes, *A History of Mathematical Statistics from 1750 to 1930* (Hoboken, NJ: John Wiley & Sons, 1998); and *History of Probability and Statistics and Their Application before 1750* (Hoboken, NJ: John Wiley & Sons, 1990); and *A History of Parametric Statistical Inference from Bernoulli to Fisher, 1713–1935* (Berlin: Springer-Verlag, 2007).

6. S. S. Wilks, "Some Aspects of Quantification in Science," in Woolf, *Quantification*, 5.

7. James W. Cortada, *All the Facts: A History of Information in the United States since 1870* (New York: Oxford University Press, 2016).

8. M. E. Brooks and S. Y. Pui, "Are Individual Differences in Numeracy Unique from General Mental Ability? A Closer Look at a Common Measure of Numeracy," *Individual Differences Research* 4, no. 8 (2010): 257–265; Isaac M. Lipkus, Greg Samsa, and Barbara K. Rimer, "General Performance on a Numeracy Scale among Highly Educated Samples," *Medical Decision Making* 21, No. 1 (February 2001): 37–44.

9. Historians argued that such skills were needed many centuries earlier, but that was for experts and scientists, while not so for the general public until the early 1800s, Harry Woolf (ed.), *Quantification: A History of the Meaning of Measurement in the Natural and Social Sciences* (Indianapolis, IN: Bobbs-Merrill, 1961).

10. Theodor M. Porter, *The Rise of Statistical Thinking, 1820–1900* (Princeton, NJ: Princeton University Press, 1986, reprinted with a new preface, 2020).

11. Stephen Chrisomalis, *Reckonings: Numerals, Cognition, and History* (Cambridge, MA: MIT Press, 2020): xii.

12. Ibid., xiii.

13. Bernard Comrie and David Gil, *The World Atlas of Language Structures*, vol. 1 (Oxford: Oxford University Press, 2005), and for an analysis of these patterns of usage, see Chrisomalis, *Reckonings*, 184–186.

14. Paul J. Riccomini et al., "The Language of Mathematics: The Importance of Teaching and Learning Mathematical Vocabulary," *Reading & Writing Quarterly* 31, no. 3 (2015): 235–252; Edward S. Klima and Ursula Bellugi, *The Signs of Language* (Cambridge, MA: Harvard University Press, 1979), although this book does not discuss mathematics specifically, it is an essential source on language structures and role of symbols.

15. Calculus is often viewed as the tool of choice for studying change in mathematics. It can help measure rates of change in a number (value) and at a specific time, Leonard Susskind and George Hrabovsky, *The Theoretical Minimum: What You Need to Know to Start Doing Physics* (New York: Basic Books, 2013): 50–53, 110; Ron Larson and Bruce H. Edwards, *Calculus: Early Transcendental Functions*, 6th ed. (Boston, MA: Cengage Learning, 2014).

16. By 2006, there were over 1.9 million books and articles in mathematics focused largely on mathematical concepts; while 75,000 books were being added annually since then. These do not include the many more millions of publications that use mathematical principles to describe the activities and insights in other disciplines, such as those in science, Mikhail B. Sevryuk, "Arnold's Problems," *Bulletin of the American Mathematical Society* 43 (January 2006): 101–109.

17. John Stillwell, *Mathematics and Its History*, 3rd ed. (London: Springer-Verlag. 2010).

18. Understanding the Pythagorean theorem is a fruitful way of understanding the kind of new mathematical information that increasingly became available since the mid-nineteenth century. Eli Maor, *The Pythagorean Theorem: A 4,000 Year History* (Princeton, NJ: Princeton University Press, 2007); Stillwell, *Mathematics and Its History*, 1–16.

19. Steven Strogatz, *Infinite Powers: How Calculus Reveals the Secrets of the Universe* (New York: Houghton Mifflin Harcourt, 2019): 141–166.

20. For an excellent introduction to modeling in multiple fields, see Scott E. Page, *The Model Thinker: What You Need to Know to Make Data Work for You* (New York: Basic Books, 2018).

21. Pure mathematics is a recent development, essentially since about 1900, A. S. Hathaway, "Pure Mathematics for Engineering Students," *Bulletin of the American Mathematical Society* 7, no. 6 (1901): 266–271.

22. Spiegelhalter, *The Art of Statistics*, 39–72.

23. For a simple example, see Nina Bai, "How Computers Are Searching for Drugs of the Future," *PHYSORG*, April 6, 2017, https://phys.org/news/2017-04-drugs-future.html (accessed March 25, 2020).

24. David S. Richeson, *Euler's Gem: The Polyhedron Formula and the Birth of Topography* (Princeton, NJ: Princeton University Press, 2008): 156–172, 202–230.

25. "A Mathematical Chronology," University of St. Andrew, http://mathshistory.st-andrews.ac.uk/Chronology/full.html (accessed March 25, 2020).

26. It is in mathematics, and more precisely in physics, a process (often called a *mathematical machine*) of accepting numbers into a process and providing number(s) as output; in sociology, it is a point of view that society is made of different but related parts, each with its own purpose.

27. Atiyah, "Mathematics in the 20th Century," drawn from the version in *NTM* N.S. 10 (2022): 26.

28. Ibid., 27.

29. Ibid., 28.

30. Ibid.

31. His words quoted, ibid., 30–31.

32. Ibid., 38.

33. Max Roser and Esteban Ortiz-Ospina, "Literacy." Published online at *OurWorldInData.org*, 2020. Retrieved from https://ourworldindata.org/literacy (accessed March 25, 2020).

34. U.S. Bureau of the Census.

35. William J. Reese, *America's Public Schools: From the Common School to "No Child Left Behind"* (Baltimore, MD: Johns Hopkins University Press, 2005): 77–78.

36. Ibid., 211–214.

37. Discussed by profession and types of education and training in Cortada, *All the Facts*, passim.

38. U.S. Bureau of the Census, *Historical Statistics of the United States: Colonial Times to 1970* (Washington, D.C.: U.S. Government Printing Office, 1975): part 1, p. 387.

39. UNESCO, En.unesco.org/node/252277 (accessed March 25, 2020).

40. Ibid.

41. U.S. Bureau of Labor Statistics. The variance can be attributed to job titles. High school mathematics teachers would have been counted as teachers, not as mathematicians.

42. One of the most accessible texts and clearly written explanations of the entire field is Spiegelhalter, *The Art of Statistics*.

43. Porter, *The Rise of Statistical Thinking*, 3.

44. Ibid., 404.

45. The leading authority on displaying information is Yale University statistics professor Edward R. Tufte who self-published a series of books that are seminal, *Envisioning Information: Narratives of Space and Time* (Cheshire, CT: Graphics Press, 1990); *Visual Explanations: Images and Quantities, Evidence and Narrative* (Cheshire, CT: Graphics Press, 1997); *The Visual Display of Quantitative Information*, 2nd ed. (Cheshire, CT: Graphics Press, 2001); but see two other of his publications, the first a pamphlet with two case studies, *Visual and Statistical Thinking: Visual and Statistical Thinking: Displays of Evidence for Making Decisions* (Cheshire, CT: Graphics Press, 1997) and his criticism of PowerPoint presentations, *The Cognitive Style of PowerPoint: Pitching Out Corrupts Within* (Cheshire, CT: Graphics Press, 2006, 2011). Most recently, Tufte has expanded his studies to further demonstrate the blend of statistics and graphical representations of data, *Seeing with Fresh Eyes: Meaning, Space, Data Truth* (Cheshire, CT: Graphics Press, 2020).

46. Textbooks have become more understandable and focused on specific audiences over the decades; see, for example, Russell T. Warne, *Statistics for the Social Sciences: A General Linear Model Approach* (Cambridge, UK: Cambridge University Press, 2018); for a standard text, see Mario F. Triola, *Elementary Statistics* 13th ed. (London: Pearson, 2017).

47. Spiegelhalter, *The Art of Statistics*.

48. James W. Cortada, *The Essential Manager: How to Thrive in the Global Information Jungle* (Hoboken, NJ: IEEE Press/John Wiley & Sons, 2015): 1–39; Chris Wood, "Science in a Complex World—Big Data Opportunity or Threat?" *Santa Fe New Mexican*, December 2, 2013, https://www.santafe.edu/news-center/news/sfnm-wood-big-data (accessed March 26, 2020).

49. Theodore M. Porter, *Trust in Numbers: The Pursuit of Objectivity in Science and Public Life* (Princeton, NJ: Princeton University Press, 1995): 3.

50. For a continuing supply of these kinds of studies from IBM, see https://www.ibm.com/thought-leadership/institute-business-value/ (accessed March 27, 2020).

51. Philip J. Hilts, *Smoke Screen: The Truth behind the Tobacco Industry Cover-Up* (Boston, MA: Addison-Wesley, 1996); Naomi Oreskes and Erick M. Conway, *Merchants of Doubt: How a Handful of Scientists Obscured the Truth on Issues from Tobacco Smoke to Global Warming* (New York: Bloomsbury, 2010); for a short version of the issue from the perspective of two historians of information, see James W. Cortada and William Aspray, *Fake News Nation: The Long History of Lies and Misinterpretations in America* (Lanham, MD: Rowman & Littlefield, 2019): 159–173.

52. Porter, *Trust in Numbers*, viii.

53. Ibid., 5.

54. Ibid., 75.

55. Porter, *The Rise of Statistical Thinking*; Thomas S. Kuhn, "The Function of Measurement in Modern Physical Science," *Isis* (1961): 161–193; Stephen Stigler,

The History of Statistics: The Measurement of Uncertainty before 1900 (Cambridge, MA: Harvard University Press, 1987).

56. Porter, *The Rise in Statistical Thinking*, xiii; Kevin Donnelly, *Adolphe Quetelet, Social Physics and the Average Men of Science, 1796–1874* (Pittsburgh, PA: University of Pittsburgh Press, 2015); Ian Hacking, *The Taming of Chance* (Cambridge, UK: Cambridge University Press, 1990); Alain Desrosières, *The Politics of Large Numbers: A History of Statistical Thinking* (Cambridge, MA: Harvard University Press, 1998, reprinted 2010).

57. Porter, *The Rise in Statistical Thinking*, xvi.

58. Emmanuel Didier, *America by the Numbers: Quantification, Democracy, and the Birth of National Statistics* (Cambridge, MA: MIT Press, 2020): 119–121, 341–348.

59. Porter, *The Rise in Statistical Thinking*, xvi.

60. Ibid., xviii.

61. Donald MacKenzie, *Statistics in Britain, 1865–1930: The Social Construction of Scientific Knowledge* (Edinburgh, UK: Edinburgh University Press, 1981) for an example of how statistics and its methods were socially constructed; Theodore M. Porter, *Karl Pearson: The Scientific Life in a Statistical Age* (Princeton, NJ: Princeton University Press, 2004), the standard biography; and not to be overlooked, Gerd Gigerenzer et al., *The Empire of Chance: How Probability Shaped Science and Everyday Life* (Cambridge, UK: Cambridge University Press, 1989).

62. Graham G. Upton and Ian Cook, *Oxford Dictionary of Statistics* (New York: Oxford University Press, 2008).

63. Sergio Verdú, "Fifty Years of Shannon Theory," in Sergio Verdú and Steven McLaughlin (eds.), *Information Theory: 50 Years of Discovery* (New York: IEEE Press, 2000): 26–27.

64. See, for example, on Quetelet, Donnelly, *Quetelet*; on Galton, Martin Brookes, *Extreme Measures: The Dark Visions and Bright Ideas of Francis Galton* (London: Bloomsbury, 2004); on Pearson, Porter, *Karl Pearson*.

65. In one publication especially, Charles Gouraud, *Histoire du calcul des probabilités depuis son origine jusqu'à nos jours: avec une thèse sur la légitimité des principes et des applications de cette analyse* (Paris: Auguste Durand, 1848).

66. Porter, *The Rise of Statistical Thinking*, 91.

67. Ibid., 150.

68. Ibid.

69. Ibid.

70. Quoted in ibid., 319.

71. Angus Maddison, *Development Centre Studies the World Economy: Historical Statistics* (Paris: OECD, 2004), but see also his *Contours of the World Economy: 1–2030 AD: Essays in Macro-Economic History* (Oxford: Oxford University Press, 2007).

72. Brady T. West, Kathleen B. Welch, and Andrzj T. Galecki, *Linear Mixed Models: A Practical Guide Using Statistical Software*, 2nd ed. (Boca Raton, FL: CRC Press, 2015); Gareth James, Daniela Witten, Trevor Hastie, and Robert Tibshirani, *An Introduction to Statistical Learning* (New York: Springer-Verlag, 2017): 15–58; Richard M. Heiberger and Burt Holland, *Statistical Analysis and Data Display* (New

York: Springer-Verlag, 2015): ix–xi, 13–28. Springer-Verlag publishes one of the largest collections of "how to" texts in statistics, keeping them current. On the problems involving bad statistical practices with examples, see Spiegelhalter, *The Art of Statistics*, 341–360.

73. A major point made by Spiegelhalter, *The Art of Statistics*.
74. For both quotes, Ibid., 360.
75. Quoted in Woolf, *Quantification*, 3.
76. Theodor M. Porter, *Trust in Numbers: The Pursuit of Objectivity in Science and Public Life* (Princeton, NJ: Princeton University Press, 1995): viii.

6. SCIENTISTS AND MEDICAL EXPERTS SHAPE INFORMATION

1. Michael Morange, *A History of Biology* (Princeton, NJ: Princeton University Press, 2021): 149.

2. Arif E. Jinha, "Article 50 Million: An Estimate of the Number of Scholarly Articles in Existence," *Learned Publishing* 23, no. 3 (July 2010): 258–263. It is not fully clear if these include non-scientific papers as well.

3. Ibid., 262.

4. Mark Ware and Michael Mabe, *The STM Report: An Overview of Scientific and Scholarly Journal Publishing* (The Hague, Netherlands: International Association of Scientific, Technical and Medical Publishers, 2015). The same report stated that as of 2015, there were over 28,600 peer-reviewed scholarly journals worldwide, Ibid., 6; Sarah Boon, "21st Century Science Overload," *Canadian Science Publishing*, January 7, 2017, http://blog.cdnsciencepub.com/21st-century-science-overload/ (accessed March 26, 2021).

5. The complaints are legion; two sources will suffice to introduce the issues, Philip G. Altbach and Hans de Wit, "Too Much Academic Research Is Being Published," *University World News*, September 7, 2018, https://www.universityworldnews.com/post.php?story=20180905095203579 (accessed March 26, 2020); Esther Landhuis, "Scientific Literature: Information Overload," *Nature*, July 20, 2016, https://www.nature.com/articles/nj7612-457a (accessed March 26, 2021).

6. Peter Burke, *A Social History of Knowledge*, vol. 2: *From Encyclopédie to Wikipedia* (Cambridge: Polity Press, 2012): 81–84.

7. For examples of the issue, see William Aspray and James W. Cortada, *From Urban Legends to Political Fact-Checking: Online Scrutiny in America, 1990–2015* (Cham, Switzerland: Springer-Verlag, 2019).

8. David Spiegelhalter, *The Art of Statistics: How to Learn from Data* (New York: Basic Books, 2019): 205–252.

9. A. R. Barron, "Entropy and the Central Limit Theorem," *Annals of Probability* 14 (1986): 336–342; A. Dembo, "Information Inequalities and Concentration of Measure," ibid. 25 (1997): 927–939; V. Anantharam and S. Verdú, "Bits through Queues," *IEEE Transactions on Information Theory* 42, no. 1 (1996): 4–18; A. Dembo and O. Zeitouni, *Large Deviations Techniques and Applications* (Boston,

MA: Jones and Bartlett, 1993); S. Kullback, J. C. Keegel, and J. H. Kullback, *Topics in Statistical Information Theory* (Berlin: Springer, 1987).

10. S. Kullback, *Information Theory and Statistics* (New York: Dover, 1968), a minor classic; I. Vajda, *Theory of Statistical Inference and Information* (Dordrecht: Kluwer, 1989; R.E. Blahut, *Principles and Practices of Information Theory* (Reading, MA: Addison-Wesley, 1987); A. R. Barron, "Information-Theoretic Characterization of Bayes Performance and Choice of Priors in Parametric and Nonparametric Problems," *Bayesian Statistics 6: Proceedings of the Sixth Valencia International Meeting* (June 1998); Spiegelhalter, *The Art of Statistics*, 307, 313–316.

11. Theodor M. Porter, *The Rise of Statistical Thinking, 1820–1900* (Princeton, NJ: Princeton University Press, 2020): 315–316.

12. Ronald A. Fisher, *The Genetical Theory of Natural Selection* (Oxford: Oxford University Press, 1930); Joan Fisher Box, *R. A. Fisher: The Life of a Scientist* (Hoboken, NJ: John Wiley & Sons, 1978).

13. Joan Fisher Box, "Guinness, Gosset, Fisher, and Small Samples," *Statistical Science* 2, no. 1 (1987): 45–52. She was Fisher's daughter.

14. Two mathematicians, Hillel Furstenberg and Gregory Margulis, were awarded the most prestigious award in mathematics, the Abel Prize, in 2020, for the fundamental work on probability in the twentieth century. Kenneth Chang, "Abel Prize in Mathematics Shared by 2 Trailblazers of Probability and Dynamics," *New York Times*, March 18, 2020 https://nyti.ms/3ddcLSS (accessed March 18, 2021).

15. William Aspray, "The Scientific Conceptualization of Information," *Annals of the History of Computing* 7, no. 2 (1985): 117–140.

16. Bernard Dionysius Geoghegan, "The Historiographic Conceptualization of Information: A Critical Survey," *IEEE Annals of the History of Computing* 30, no. 1 (January–March 2008): 66–81.

17. Steve J. Heims, *Constructing a Social Science for Postwar America: The Cybernetics Group (1946–1953)* (Cambridge, MA: MIT Press, 1993); J. P. Dupuy, *The Mechanization of the Mind: On the Origins of Cognitive Science* (Princeton, NJ: Princeton University Press,2000).

18. Morange, *A History of Biology*, 376.

19. For as close to the original quote attributed to Kelvin, see Sir William Thomson, "Electrical Units of Measurement," *Popular Lectures and Addresses* (London: Macmillan, 1889): vol. 1, p. 73. Regarding his motivation for the expression, see Theodore M. Porter, *Trust in Numbers: The Pursuit of Objectivity in Science and Public Life* (Princeton, NJ: Princeton University Press, 1995): 71–72.

20. Jim Al-Khalili, "Has Physics Lost Its Way?" *New York Times*, March 17, 2020 https://nyt.ms/2QkAYwo (accessed March 18, 2021); David Lindley, *The Dream Universe: How Fundamental Physics Lost Its Way* (New York: Doubleday, 2020): 145–201.

21. Quoted in Fritjof Capra, *The Turning Point: Science, Society, and the Rising Culture* (New York: Bantam, 1983): 86.

22. Jim Al-Khalili, *The World According to Physics* (Princeton, NJ: Princeton University Press, 2020): ix.

23. James E. McClellan III and Harold Dorn, *Science and Technology in World History: An Introduction*, 3rd ed. (Baltimore, MD: Johns Hopkins University Press,

2015): 403–413. Dirac is best known for the "Dirac Equation," which describes massive particles such as electrons and quarks, accounting for their special relativity within quantum mechanics, hinting at the existence, for instance, of antimatter. His key work included, P. A. M. Dirac, "The Quantum Theory of the Electron," *Proceedings of the Royal Society A: Mathematical, Physical and Engineering Sciences* 117, no. 778 (1928): 610–624, and "A Theory of Electrons and Protons," ibid. 126, no. 801 (1930): 360–365; Bernd Thaller, *The Dirac Equation* (Berlin: Springer-Verlag, 1993).

24. A. N. Mitra, "Mathematics: The Language of Science," *Current Science* 102, no. 9 (2012): 7.

25. McClellan and Dorn, *Science and Technology in World History*, 403–410.

26. Werner Heisenberg actually published three papers that year, but for an exposure to his thinking, see Edward MacKinnon, "Heisenberg, Models, and the Rise of Quantum Mechanics," *Historical Studies in the Physical Sciences* 8 (1977): 137–188; Jagdish Mehra and Helmut Rechenberg, *The Formulation of Matrix Mechanics and Its Modifications, 1925–1926: The Historical Development of Quantum Theory* (Berlin: Springer-Verlag, 2001).

27. Luciano Floridi, *Information: A Very Short Introduction* (New York: Oxford University Press, 2010): 61.

28. Ibid., 64–66.

29. Ibid., 66.

30. Ibid.

31. First appeared in 1888 as a German postcard, but more widely known for the version published by William Ely Hill, "My Wife and My Mother-in-Law," *Puck*, November 6, 1915.

32. John Maston, "What Is Quantum Mechanics Good For?" *Scientific American*, November 2, 2010, https://www.scientificamerican.com/article/everyday-quantum-physics/ (accessed November 1, 2021).

33. Michael Nielsen and Isaac Chuang, *Quantum Computation and Quantum Information* (Cambridge, UK: Cambridge University Press, 2000); Seiki Akama, *Elements of Quantum Computing: History, Theories and Engineering Applications* (Berlin: Springer International, 2014); Gregg Jaeger, *Quantum Information: An Overview* (Berlin: Springer-Verlag, 2006).

34. Charles H. Bennett and Peter W. Shor, "Quantum Information Theory," *IEEE Transactions on Information Theory* 44 (October 1998): 2724–2742; Mark. M. Wilde, *Quantum Information Theory* (Cambridge, UK: Cambridge University Press, 2017)

35. Juan Zhang et al., "Study on Worldwide Development and Trends of Quantum Technologies Based on Patent Data," *International Journal of Information and Education Technology* 10, no. 3 (March 2020): 239–244; David Roe, "Quantum Computing: Challenges, Trends, and the Road Ahead," *CMS Wire*, November 19, 2019, https://www.cmswire.com/information-management/quantum-computing-challenges-trends-and-the-road-ahead/ (accessed April, 2021).

36. Floridi, *Information*, 70.

37. Physicists have experienced considerable uncertainty and problems with its various recent theories of "everything," despite being richly funded over the past

half-century to do their work. They appear to have more theories than data in support of these. For an introduction to the issues, see "Physics Seeks the Future," *The Economist*, August 28, 2021, pp. 68–70.

38. For an introduction, consult a textbook, such as Rich Baur, James Birk, and Pamela Marks, *Introduction to Chemistry*, 5th ed. (New York: McGraw-Hill 2019): 171–213; M. P. Crosland, *Historical Studies in the Language of Chemistry* (London: Heinemann, 1962); on the history of its notations; William J. Wiswesser, "Historic Development of Chemical Notation," *Journal of Chemical Computer Science* 25 (1985): 258–263.

39. Henry Guerlac, "Quantification in Chemistry," in Harry Woolf (ed.), *Quantification: A History of the Meaning of Measurement in the Natural and Social Sciences* (Indianapolis, IN: Bobbs-Merrill, 1961): 64.

40. M. P. Crosland, *In the Shadow of Lavoisier: The Annales de Chimie and the Establishment of a New Science* (London: British Society for the History of Science, 1994).

41. Helen Schofield, "The Evolution of the Secondary Literature in Chemistry," in Mary Ellen Bowden, Trudi Bellargo Hahn, and Robert V. Williams (eds.), *Science Information Systems: Proceedings of the 1998 Conference on the History and Heritage of Science Information Systems* (Medford, NJ: American Society for Information Science and Chemical Heritage Foundation, 1999).

42. F. A. Tate, "Handling Chemical Compounds in Information Systems," *Annual Review of Information Science and Technology* 2 (1967): 285–309.

43. D. J. Whittingham, F. R. Wetsel, and H. L. Morgan, "The Computer Based Subject Support System at Chemical Abstracts Services," *Journal of Chemical Documentation* 6, no. 4 (1966): 230–234.

44. C. M. Bowman, "The Development of Chemical Information Systems," in J. E. Ash and E. Hyde (eds.), *Chemical Information Systems* (Chichester, UK: John Wiley & Sons, 1974); Schofield, "The Evolution of the Secondary Literature in Chemistry," 96; Aaron J. Ihde, *The Development of Modern Chemistry* (Garden City, NY: Dover edition, 1984, original ed. 1964): 57–258; William H. Brock, *The Chemical Tree: A History of Chemistry* (New York: W. W. Norton, 1992): 128–209.

45. Tate, "Handling Chemical Compounds in Information Systems," 285–309.

46. Stephen Fenichell, *Plastic: The Making of a Synthetic Century* (New York: HarperBusiness, 1996): 79–104.

47. Although there is a belief that this trend was a by-product of the Internet, not so; it had started much earlier. For a discussion of current trends, Christine L. Borgman, *Scholarship in the Digital Age: Information, Infrastructure, and the Internet* (Cambridge, MA: MIT Press, 2007).

48. James D. Watson and Francis H. C. Crick, "Molecular Structure of Nucleic Acids: A Structure for Deoxyribose Nucleic Acid," *Nature* 171 (1953): 737–738.

49. Evelyn Constance, "A History of Chemical Abstracts Service, 1907–1998," *Science & Technology Libraries* 18, no. 4 (2000): 93–110.

50. Eugene Garfield, "History of Citation Indexes for Chemistry: A Brief Review," *Journal of Chemical Information Computing Science* 25 (1985): 170–174, quote p. 170.

51. Historians of these various disciplines discuss chemistry; see, for a recent example, Theodore M. Porter, *Genetics in the Madhouse: The Unknown History of Human Heredity* (Princeton, NJ: Princeton University Press, 2018).

52. Evelyn Constance Powell, "A History of Chemical Abstracts Service, 1907–1998," *Science & Technology Libraries* 18, no. 4 (2000): 93–110; David W. Weisgerber, "Chemical Abstracts Service Chemical Registry System: History, Scope, and Impacts," *Journal of the American Society for Information Science* 48, no. 4 (1997): 349–360; Schofield, "The Evolution of the Secondary Literature in Chemistry," 94–106; Colin B. Burke, *Information and Intrigue: From Index Cards to Dewey Decimals to Alger Hiss* (Cambridge, MA: MIT Press, 2014): 231–232.

53. Ibid., 101–102.

54. "CAS Content," American Chemical Society, https://www.cas.org/about/cas-content (accessed April 2, 2021).

55. Weisgerber, "Chemical Abstracts Service Chemical Registry System: History, Scope, and Impact," 352–353.

56. K. A. Hamill, R. D. Nelson, G. G. Stouw Vander, and R. E. Stobaugh, "Chemical Abstract Service Chemical Registry System: 10. Registration of Chemical Substances from pre-1965 Indices of Chemical Abstracts," *Journal of Chemical Information and Computer Science* 28, no. 4 (1988): 175–179, Robert E. Bunstrock, "Chemical Registries—In the Fourth Decade of Service," Ibid., 41 (2001): 259–263.

57. Ibid.

58. Weisgerber, "Chemical Abstracts Service Chemical Registry System: History, Scope, and Impact," 354.

59. Both quotes, D. F. Zaye, W. V. Metanomski, and A. J. Beach, "A History of General Subject Indexing at Chemical Abstracts Services," *Journal of Chemical Information and Computer Science* 25 (1985): 392.

60. Powell, "A History of Chemical Abstract Service," 97–98.

61. Ibid., 394.

62. CAS/American Chemical Society, "CAS Source Index (CASSI) Search Tool," https://cassi.cas.org/about.jsp (accessed April 2, 2021).

63. Weisgerber, "Chemical Abstracts Service Chemical Registry System: History, Scope, and Impact," 358; C. H. Davis and J. E. Rush, *Information Retrieval and Documentation in Chemistry* (Westport, CT: Greenwood Press, 1974); K. J. Lipscomb, M. F. Lynch, and P. Willett, "Chemical Structure Processing," *Annual Review of Information Science and Technology* 24 (1989): 189–238; J. Rush, "Handling Chemical Structure in Information," Ibid., 13 (1978): 209–262.

64. Charlotte Davis Mooers and Calvin N. Mooers, 1993 "Oral History Interview with Calvin N. Mooers and Charlotte D. Mooers," Charles Babbage Institute, Retrieved from the University of Minnesota Digital Conservatory, https://hdl.handle.net/11299/107510 (accessed February 5, 2020). On Perry's ideas, see James W. Perry, "Defining the Query Spectrum—The Basis for Developing and Evaluating Information-Retrieval Methods," *IEEE Transactions on Engineering Writing and Speech* 6, no. 1 (1963): 20–27.

65. Powell, "A History of Chemical Abstract Service," 98, 101–105.

66. Quoted in Zaye, Metanomski, and Beach, "A History of General Subject Indexing at Chemical Abstracts Services," 397.

67. I explore many of these issues in James W. Cortada, *The Digital Hand*, 3 vols. (New York: Oxford University Press, 2004–2008).

68. Ibid., 398.

69. Eliot Freidson, *Profession of Medicine: A Study of the Sociology of Applied Knowledge* (New York: Harper & Row, 1970): 327–330.

70. Jon Agar, *Science in the Twentieth Century and Beyond* (Cambridge, UK: Polity Press, 2012); Garland E. Allen, *Life Science in the Twentieth Century* (Cambridge, UK: Cambridge University Press, 1975); Peter J. Bowler, *Evolution: The History of an Idea* (Berkeley: University of California Press, 2003); Robert Bud, *The Uses of Life: A History of Biotechnology* (Cambridge, UK: Cambridge University Press, 1993); Kevin Davies, *Cracking the Genome: Inside the Race to Unlock Human DNA* (New York: Free Press, 2001); Stephen Jay Gould, *The Structure of Evolutionary Theory* (Cambridge, MA: Belknap Press of Harvard University Press, 2002); Lois M. Magner, *A History of the Life Sciences*, 3rd ed. (New York: Marcel Dekker, 2002); Jan Sapp, *Genesis: The Evolution of Biology* (New York: Oxford University Press, 2003).

71. Morange, *A History of Biology*, xvi.

72. Landhuis, "Scientific Literature: Information Overload." In 1926 Erwin Schrödinger described the probability of finding an electron in a specific position, leading to his model known better as the quantum mechanical model of the atom, in "Über das Verhältnis der Heisenberg-Born-Jordanschen Quantnmechanik zu der meinem," *Annalen de physic* 384, no. 8 (1926): 734–756. He published three papers that year; this is the critical one. For a biography, see Walter J. Moore, *Schrodinger: Life and Thought* (Cambridge, UK: Cambridge University Press, 1989, 2015).

73. Floridi, *Information*, 74.

74. Begin with Robert P. Gaynes, *Germ Theory: Medical Pioneers in Infectious Diseases* (Herndon, VA: ASM Press, 2011); John Waller, *Discovery of the Germ: Twenty Years That Transformed the Way We Think about Disease* (New York: Columbia University Press, 2003). On the public's awareness, see Nancy Tomes, *The Gospel of Germs: Men, Women, and the Microbe in American Life* (Cambridge, MA: Harvard University Press, 1998).

75. However, Morange has done a superb job in linking the long history of genetics to current trends, providing an essential source on the topic, Morange, *A History of Biology*, 297–307, 352–363.

76. Frederick B. Churchill, "William Johannsen and the Genotype Concept," *Journal of the History of Biology* 7, no. 1 (Spring 1974): 5–30.

77. Porter, *Genetics in the Madhouse*, 2.

78. A subject that Nazi Germany learned about from American experiences; Stefan Kuhl, *The Nazi Connection: Eugenics, American Racism, and German National Socialism* (New York: Oxford University Press, 1994): 13–26, 37–76; on the American experience, see Wendy Kline, *Building a Better Race: Gender, Sexuality, and Eugenics from the Turn of the Century to the Baby Boom* (Berkeley: University of California Press, 2011).

79. Ibid., 12, and for his three-phase approach, see ibid., 8–12.

80. Ibid., 79.

81. The history of new information is not always a settled matter. After decades of acceptance as to who made the "breakthroughs" in DNA, evidence has recently surfaced that at least one other individual's data became the basis of Watson's explanations, Howard Markel, *The Secret of Life: Rosalind Franklin, James Watson, Francis Crick, and the Discovery of DNA's Double Helix* (New York: W.W. Norton, 2021).

82. Both quotes, Porter, *Genetics in the Madhouse*, 343.

83. Timothy Lenoir, "Shaping Biomedicine as an Information Science," in Bowden, Hahn, and Williams, *Science Information Systems*, 27–45.

84. For a collection of such studies and citations to many others, see Roy Porter (ed.), *The Cambridge History of Medicine* (Cambridge, UK: Cambridge University Press, 2006).

85. W. F. Bynum, *Science and the Practice of Medicine in the Nineteenth Century* (Cambridge, UK: Cambridge University Press, 1994).

86. Mark M. Ravitch, *A Century of Surgery: 1880–1980*, 2 vols. (Philadelphia, PA: J. B. Lipincott, 1982); Own H. Wangensteen and Sarah D. Wagensteen, *The Rise of Surgery: From Empiric Craft to Scientific Discipline* (Minneapolis, MN: University of Minnesota Press, 1978).

87. J. Parascandola, *The Development of American Pharmacology: John J. Abel and the Shaping of a Discipline* (Baltimore, MD: Johns Hopkins University Press, 1992); M. Weatherall, *In Search of a Cure: A History of Pharmaceutical Discovery* (Oxford: Oxford University Press, 1990).

88. Miles Weatherall, "Drug Treatment and the Rise of Pharmacology," in Porter (ed.), *The Cambridge History of Medicine*, 226.

89. Richard H. Shryock, "The History of Quantification in Medical Science," in Woolf, *Quantification*, 101–104.

90. Theodor M. Porter, *Trust in Numbers: The Pursuit of Objectivity in Science and Public Life* (Princeton, NJ: Princeton University Press, 1995): 204.

91. Ibid., 208–209.

92. Account of the past two chapters are drawn from ibid., 202–209.

93. Roy Porter, "Mental Illness," ibid., 238–259.

94. Paullen Hogweg, "The Roots of Bioinformatics in Theoretical Biology," *PLOS Computational*, March 31, 2011, https://journals.plos.org/ploscompbiol/article?id=10.1371/journal.pcbi.1002021 (accessed November 1, 2020).

95. V. Maojo and C. Kulikowski, "Medical Informatics and Bioinformatics: Integration or Evolution through Scientific Crises?" *Methods of Information Medicine* 45, no. 5 (2006): 474–482.

96. Clément Levin et al., "A Data-Supported History of Bioinformatics Tools," Cornell University Digital Libraries, July 18, 2018, p. 2, https://arxiv.org/abs/1807.06808 (accessed November 2, 2020).

97. Their seminal paper, James Watson and Francis Crick, "Molecular Structure of Nucleic Acids," *Nature* 171 (1953): 737–738.

98. H. Gerola and R. E. Gomory, "Computers in Science and Technology: Early Indications," *Science* 225 (1984): 11–18.

99. Maojo and Kulikowski, "Medical Informatics and Bioinformatics," 477–479.

100. Porter, *Trust in Numbers*, 29–32.

101. V. Maojo and C. A. Kulikowski, "Bioinformatics and Medical Informatics: Collaboration on the Road to Genomic Medicine," *JAMIA* 10, no. 6 (2003): 515–522.

102. This source counts six streams; my count is seven from their evidence, V. Maojo and C. Kulikowski, "Medical Informatics and Bioinformatics: Integration or Evolution through Scientific Crises?" 477.

103. Ibid.

104. Morris F. Collin and Marion J. Ball, *A History of Medical Informatics in the United States* (Berlin: Springer-Verlag, 2015).

105. For details, Levin et al., "A Data-Supported History of Bioinformatics Tools," 2.

106. Z. D. Stephens et al., "Big Data: Astronomical or Genomical?" *PLOS Biology* 13 (July 7, 2015), https://journals.plos.org/plosbiology/article?id=10.1371/journal.pbio.1002195 (accessed November 1, 2020).

107. Levin et al., "A Data-Supported History of Bioinformatics Tools," 2.

108. Geoffrey C. Bowker, "The Game of the Name: Nomenclatural Instability in the History of Botanical Informatics," in Bowden, Hahn, and Williams (eds.), *Science Information Systems*, 74–83.

109. Floridi, *Information*, 86.

110. Lenoir, "Shaping Biomedicine as an Information Science," 27.

111. Ibid.

112. Early accounts of the growing use of computing include, A. G. Oettinger, "The Uses of Computers in Science," *Scientific American* 215, no. 3 (1966): 161–172; F. C. Bernstein et al., "The Protein Data Bank: A Computer Based Archival File for Macromolecular Structure," *Journal of Molecular Biology* (1977): 535–542; P. Bork and T. J. Gibson, "Applying Motif and Profile Searches," in R. F. Doolittle (ed.), *Computer Methods for Macromolecular Sequence Analysis* (San Diego, CA: Academic Press, 1996): 162–184; R. M. Friedhoff and W. Benzon, *The Second Computer Revolution: Visualization* (New York: W. H. Freeman, 1989); L. Hunter (ed.), *Artificial Intelligence and Molecular Biology* (Menlo Park, CA: AAAI Press, 1993); L. Katz and C. Levinthal, "Interactive Computer Graphics and the Representation of Complex Biological Structures," *Annual Reviews in Biophysics and Bioengineering* 1 (1972): 465–504; R. S. Ledley, *Use of Computers in Biology and Medicine* (New York: McGraw-Hill, 1965).

113. Adrienne Rich, "Cartographies of Silence," in Adrienne Rich (ed.), *The Dream of a Common Language: Poems, 1974–1977* (New York: W. W. Norton, 1993): 16–21; Michael Ohl, *The Art of Naming* (Cambridge, MA: MIT Press, 2018): 37–72.

114. On the nineteenth-and twentieth-century roots, see Wyndham D. Miles, *A History of the National Library of Medicine: The Nation's Treasury of Medical Knowledge* (Washington, D.C.: U.S. Department of Health & Human Services, 1982).

115. "Key Medline Indicators," National Library of Medicine, https://wayback.archive-it.org/org-350/20200416170941/https://www.nlm.nih.gov/bsd/bsd_key.html (accessed November 1, 2020).

116. For a description of the structured abstracts with an example, see "Structured Abstracts," https://www.nlm.nih.gov/bsd/policy/structured_abstracts.html (accessed November 1, 2020).

117. Conor Hale, "FDA Clears Paige's AI as First Program to Spot Prostate Cancer in Tissue Slides," *Fierce Biotech*, September 22, 2021, https://www.fiercebiotech.com/medtech/fda-clears-paige-s-ai-as-first-program-to-spot-prostate-cancer-amid-tissue-slides (accessed March 30, 2022); Mike Allen,"Meet the New AI Cancer Detectives," *Axios AM Deep Dive*, April 2, 2022, www.axios.com/2022/04/02/artificial-intelligence-cancer-screening (accessed September 29, 2022).

118. Floridi, *Information*, 71.

119. Some would argue that it is the Internet that is causing such changes, Eric T. Meyer and Ralph Schroeder, *Knowledge Machines: Digital Transformation of the Sciences and Humanities* (Cambridge, MA: MIT Press, 2015): 23–67.

120. Ibid., 70.

121. Morange, *A History of Biology*, 326.

122. Jürgen Renn, *The Evolution of Knowledge: Rethinking Science for the Anthropocene* (Princeton, NJ: Princeton University Press, 2020): 126–127, 221–224.

123. Geoff Watts, "Looking to the Future Revised," in Porter (ed.), *The Cambridge History of Medicine*, 334.

124. Theodor M. Porter, *Trust in Numbers: The Pursuit of Objectivity in Science and Public Life* (Princeton, NJ: Princeton University Press, 1995): 29.

125. Ibid., 29–32.

7. NEW BUSINESS AND GOVERNMENT INFORMATION ECOSYSTEMS

1. IBM Corporation, *An Introduction to IBM Punched Card Data Processing* (White Plains, NY: IBM Technical Publications Department, undated [circa 1950s–early 1960s]): 2.

2. Points made by many students of the period, for example, by Robert J. Gordon, *The Rise and Fall of American Growth* (Princeton, NJ: Princeton University Press, 2016): 27–61; Alfred D. Chandler, Jr., *The Visible Hand: The Managerial Revolution in American Business* (Cambridge, MA: Harvard University Press, 1977): 484–498; Charles S. Maier, "Leviathan 2.0: Inventing Modern Statehood," in Emily S. Rosenberg (ed.), *A World Connecting, 1870–1945* (Cambridge, MA: Harvard University Press, 2012): 39–195; Robert J. Gordon, *The Rise and Fall of American Growth* (Princeton, NJ: Princeton University Press, 2016); James W. Cortada, *The Digital Hand*, 3 vols. (New York: Oxford University Press, 2004–2008).

3. Models improve how one understands the world and improves the reasoning behind good decision-making. I use the word *fiction* because they can never be absolutely true. As one expert on models explained, "All models are wrong because they simplify. They omit details," Scott E. Page, *The Model Thinker: What You Need to Know to Make Data Work for You* (New York: Basic Books, 2018): 6.

4. James W. Cortada, *All the Facts: A History of Information in the United States since 1870* (New York: Oxford University Press, 2016); Cesar Hidalgo, *Why Information Grows: The Evolution of Order, from Atoms to Economies* (New York: Basic Books, 2015): 127–171. I use the word *sector* to mean all employment in government, non-agricultural, and agricultural industries. Economists use the same word to organize labor into agriculture, manufacturing, and public sector. I use the term in both ways.

5. Both quotes from Theodore M. Porter, *Trust in Numbers: The Pursuit of Objectivity in Science and Public Life* (Princeton, NJ: Princeton University Press, 1995): 89.

6. U.S. Bureau of Labor Statistics. This agency is a textbook example of the expanding role of government in collecting new information, Cortada, *All the Facts*, 152–157; Joseph P. Goldberg and William T. Moye, *The First Hundred Years of the Bureau of Labor Statistics* (Washington, D.C.: Government Printing Office, 1985); and on a related agency, see U.S. Bureau of Economic Analysis, ibid., 157–159.

7. For a collection of seminal sources on the history of knowledge workers, see James W. Cortada (ed.), *Rise of the Knowledge Worker* (Boston, MA: Butterworth-Heinemann, 1998).

8. U.S. Bureau of Labor Statistics.

9. Ibid.

10. U.S. Bureau of the Census.

11. For an introduction to many of the issues involved, see JoAnne Yates, "Investing in Information: Supply and Demand Forces in the Use of Information in American Firms, 1850–1920," in Peter Temin (ed.), *Inside the Business Enterprise: Historical Perspectives on the Use of Information* (Chicago, IL: University of Chicago Press,1991): 117–154.

12. Cortada, *The Digital Hand*, vol. 3: *How Computers Changed the Work of American Public Sector Industries*, 184–210.

13. A central finding of Chandler, *The Visible Hand*.

14. For a growing body of evidence in support of this statement, see Lisa Bud-Frierman (ed.), *Information Acumen: The Understanding and Use of Knowledge in Modern Business* (London: Routledge, 1994); Margaret Levenstein, *Accounting Growth Information Systems and the Creation of the Large Corporation* (Stanford, CA: Stanford University Press, 1998); Cortada, *All the Facts*, 92–117, 281–325.

15. I explore this growing dependence in two studies, *The Digital Flood* in three volumes covering over a dozen industries including government, and in James W. Cortada, *Information and the Modern Corporation* (Cambridge, MA: MIT Press, 2011).

16. Glenn Porter, *The Rise of Big Business, 1860–1920* (Wheeling, IL: Harlan Davidson, 1992): 18.

17. James E. Beniger, *The Control Revolution: Technological and Economic Origins of the Information Society* (Cambridge, MA: Harvard University Press, 1986).

18. I discuss this in further detail, James W. Cortada, "Exploring How ICTs and Administration Are Entwined: The Promise of Information Ecosystems,"

Administration & Society 50, no. 9 (October 2018): 1213–1237, and "A Framework for Understanding Information Ecosystems in Firms and Industries," *Information & Culture* 51, no. 2 (2016): 133–163; see also Porter, *Trust in Numbers*, 90–98.

19. Robert E. Cole, *Managing Quality Fads: How American Business Learned to Play the Quality Game* (New York: Oxford University Press, 1999); David A. Hounshell, *From the American System to Mass Production, 1800–1932* (Baltimore, MD: Johns Hopkins University Press, 1984).

20. Daniel J. Boorstin, *The Americans: The Democratic Experience* (New York: Viking Books, 1973): 190; R. R. Blake and J. S. Mouton, *The Managerial Grid* (Houston, TX: Gulf Publishing, 1964); G. Hamel, "The Concept of Core Competence," in G. Hamel and A. Heene (eds.), *Competence-based Competition* (Chichester, UK: John Wiley & Sons, 1994): 11–33; J. Pfeffer and G. R. Salancik, *The External Control of Organizations: A Resource Dependence Perspective* (San Francisco, CA: Harper & Row, 1978).

21. Ibid., 192.

22. Ibid., 192, 193.

23. Gladys L. Baker, Wayne D. Rasmussen, Vivian Wiser, and Jane M. Porter, *Century of Service: The First Hundred Years of the United States Department of Agriculture* (Washington, D.C.: Government Printing Office, 1963); Roy V. Scott, *The Reluctant Farmer: The Rise of Agricultural Extension to 1914* (Urbana: University of Illinois Press, 1970).

24. Wayne Rasmussen, *Taking the University to the People: Seventy-Five Years of Cooperative Extension* (Ames: Iowa State University Press, 1989); Roger L. Geiger, *To Advance Knowledge: The Growth of American Research Universities, 1900–1940* (New York: Oxford University Press, 1986).

25. James Schwoch, *Wired into Nature: The Telegraph and the North American Frontier* (Urbana: University of Illinois Press, 2018): 7–8, 39–40, 84–85, 151–158.

26. I have explored events during World War II as part of a study I conducted on IBM's role, James W. Cortada, *Before the Computer: IBM, NCR, Burroughs and Remington Rand and the Industry They Created, 1865–1956* (Princeton, NJ: Princeton University Press, 1993): 189–205.

27. Paul N. Edwards, *The Closed World: Computers and the Politics of Discourse in Cold War America* (Cambridge, MA: MIT Press, 1996): 43–74; Elena Aronova, "Big Science and 'Big Science Studies' in the United States and the Soviet Union during the Cold War," in Naomi Oreskes and John Krige (eds.), *Science and Technology in the Global Cold War* (Cambridge, MA: MIT Press, 2014): 393–442.

28. So much was created that it is not uncommon for major research university libraries to employ a full-time dedicated librarian focused on managing this body of information sources.

29. Cortada, *All the Facts*, 148–152.

30. Cortada, *The Digital Hand*, vol. 3.

31. The last two issues has been the subject of research by William Aspray and myself as part of a larger effort to understand the role of misinformation and conspiracies in the United States, James W. Cortada and William Aspray, *Fake News Nation:*

The Long History of Lies and Misinformation in America (Lanham, MD: Rowman & Littlefield, 2019): 159–210.

32. Mariana Mazzucato, *The Value of Everything: Making and Taking in the Global Economy* (New York: PublicAffairs, 2018): 191–202.

33. University of Wisconsin took control of a patent to increase the concentration of Vitamin D in food filed for by two of its professors (Harry Steenbock and James Cockwell) in 1923. Their patent did not expire until 1945. Their discoveries led to the virtual eradication of rickets by the end of World War II. For details, Rima D. Apple, "Patenting University Research: Harry Steenbock and the Wisconsin Alumni Research Foundation," *ISIS* 80, no. 3 (1989): 374–394.

34. Mazzucato, *The Value of Everything*, 204–206.

35. Ibid., 205.

36. I discuss these variously in *Before the Computer* and in *IBM*.

37. Cortada, *IBM*, 325–352.

38. Mazzucato, *The Value of Everything*, 205.

39. Ibid., 202.

40. Since gaining access to a scholarly article, for example, could cost $30 in 2020, researchers in corporations and in universities gain access through subscriptions to bundles of databases of such materials that publishers sell to institutions. Thus, for example, it is not uncommon for a major university to be subscribed to 600 or more databases of this type.

41. Bud-Frierman, *Information Acumen*, 7–25; Levenstein, *Accounting for Growth*, 1–19; Temin, *Inside the Business Enterprise*, 1–6.

42. As with statistics with long-standing practices, accounting textbooks reveal through multiple editions both long-standing practices but also nuanced constant changes. See, as one yet typical example, Donald E. Kieso, Jerry J. Weygandt, and Terry D. Warfield, *Intermediate Accounting*, 17th ed. (Hoboken, NJ: John Wiley & Sons, 2019). It runs into the many hundreds of pages in length in each edition.

43. Ibid., v.

44. Ibid., 3–3.

45. R. C. Moyer, F. H. deB. Harris, and J. R. McGuigan, *Managerial Economics*, 11th ed. (Mason, OH: Thomson Higher Education, 2007): iv.

46. For example, in the United States the U.S. Bureau of the Budget and the Office of Management and Budget (OMB) annually produces such reports for the national government. For an example, see OMB, *An American Budget: Historical Tables: Budget of the U.S. Government* (Washington, D.C.: Government Printing Office, 2018).

47. C. A. Moyer, "Early Developments in American Auditing," *Accounting Review* 26, no. 1 (1951): 3–8; modern auditing practices came largely from Great Britain, Derek Matthews, *A History of Auditing: The Changing Audit Process in Britain from the Nineteenth Century to the Present Day* (London: Routledge, 2006); Lai Balkaran, *The Rise of Accounting, Auditing, and Finance: Key Issues and Events That Shaped These Professions for over 200 Years* (Hauppauge, NY: Nova Science, 2019).

48. Joel Seligman, *The Transformation of Wall Street: A History of the Securities and Exchange Commission and Modern Corporate Finance*, 3rd ed. (New York: Aspen Publishers, 2003): 1–38.

49. Kees Camfferman and Stephen A. Zeff, *Financial Reporting and Global Capital Markets: A History of the International Accounting Standards Committee, 1973–2000* (Oxford: Oxford University Press, 2006): 61–89, on U.S. developments, 155–163; Kalin Kolev, Carol A. Marquardt, and Sarah E. McVay, "SEC Scrutiny and the Evolution of Non-GAAP Reporting," *The Accounting Review* 83, no. 1 (January 2008): 157–184.

50. This information was considered so valuable that the first generation of commercially available computers were cost-justified largely on the savings in costs for inventory that could be achieved by using this digitized information. Reductions in inventory costs of 5 to 15 percent were normal for American corporations across numerous industries, Cortada, *The Digital Hand*, vol. 3: *How Computers Changed the Work of American Manufacturing, Transportation, and Retail Industries*, 92–97.

51. A major area of concern I found across all industries, Cortada, *The Digital Hand*, 3 vols.

52. Walter A. Friedman, *Birth of a Salesman: The Transformation of Selling in America* (Cambridge, MA: Harvard University Press, 2004): 117–150.

53. Samuel Crowther, *John H. Patterson: Pioneer in Industrial Welfare* (Garden City, NY: Doubleday, Page & Company, 1924): 152–167.

54. James W. Cortada, *IBM: The Rise and Fall and Reinvention of a Global Icon* (Cambridge, MA: MIT Press, 2019): 27–90.

55. Computing-Tabulating-Recording-Co. (C-T-R), *Annual Report of the Computing-Tabulating-Recording-Co. For the Year Ending December Thirty-First Nineteen Fourteen* (New York: C-T-R, 1015). C-T-R was renamed International Business Machines Corporation (IBM) in 1924.

56. IBM Corporation, *IBM Annual Report 1955* (Armonk, NY: IBM Corporation, 1956).

57. Ibid., 24.

58. Baruch Lev and Feng Gu, *The End of Accounting and the Path Forward for Investors and Managers* (Hoboken, NJ: John Wiley & Sons, 2016): 42.

59. Ibid., 43; for a summary of their ideas, Ibid., xiii–xx.

60. Congressional Budget Office, "Budget and Economic Data—Congressional Budget Office," https://www.cbo.gov/about/products/budget-economic-data#2 (accessed April 7, 2020).

61. Porter, *Trust in Numbers*, 90–94.

62. Jack Beatty, *The World According to Peter Drucker* (New York: Free Press, 1998): 101–132; but see his most widely consulted study, Peter F. Drucker, *Management: Tasks, Responsibilities, Practices* (New York: Harper & Row, 1973).

63. H. James Harrington, *Business Process Improvement* (New York: McGraw-Hill, 1991); Jack D. Orsburn et al., *Self-Directed Work Teams: The New American Challenge* (Burr Ridge, IL: Irwin Professional Publishing, 1990); W. Edwards Deming, *Out of the Crisis* (Cambridge, MA: MIT Center for Advanced Engineering Study,

1986); Armand V. Feigenbaum, *Total Quality Control*, 3rd ed. (New York: McGraw-Hill, 1991).

64. A key finding in Cortada, *The Digital Hand*, 3 vols.; Thomas K. McCraw, *American Business since 1920: How It Worked* (Wheeling, IL: Harlan Davidson, 2009); James Brian Quinn, *Intelligent Enterprise: A Knowledge and Service Based Paradigm for Industry* (New York: Free Press, 1992).

65. I describe such information ecosystems in "Building Blocks of Modern Society: Information Ecosystems, and Infrastructures" (forthcoming, Rowman & Littlefield).

66. Cortada, *All the Facts*, 287–290.

67. Both essays were commissioned for James W. Cortada and John A. Woods (eds.), *The Quality Yearbook 1995* (New York: McGraw-Hill, 1995): Joe Sensenbrenner, "The Big Picture: The Third Revolution in Government Change," 151–154, Al Gore, "Introduction to the National Performance Review," 155–165.

68. James W. Cortada, on what to use computers for, *EDP Costs and Charges* (Englewood Cliffs, NJ: Prentice-Hall, 1980) and in *Strategic Data Processing: Considerations for Management* (Englewood Cliffs, NJ: Prentice Hall, 1984), on empowered workers and distributed control and authority facilitated by computing, *21st Century Business* (Upper Saddle River, NJ: Financial Times, 2001) and in *How Societies Embrace Information Technology* (Hoboken, NJ: John Wiley & Sons and IEEE Press, 2009).

69. Quinn, *Intelligent Enterprise*, 60–64.

70. Ibid., 253–254.

71. Cortada, *IBM*.

72. Drucker, *Management*, 32; Fritz Machlup, *The Production and Distribution of Knowledge in the United States* (Princeton, NJ: Princeton University Press, 1962).

73. Having information did not always lead to savings. In 1975 I toured Mack Trucks' parts division warehouse in New Jersey where the inventory manager bragged about how he knew what he had in stock for dealers and repair shops all over the nation. I saw a mountain of radiators and asked what they were. He responded that these were radiators for trucks manufactured in the 1920s and 1930s and was proud of the fact that he had seventy-two years' worth of supply for the entire nation! In other words, the company had held on to the inventory already for over forty years and based on his reckoning, some of it would be around for another seventy-two years!

74. The example from GE stimulated the move to computer-facilitated inventory management, Roddy F. Osborn, "GE and UNIVAC: Harnessing the High-Speed Computer," *Harvard Business Review* 32, no. 4 (July–August 1954): 99–107; J. Buchan, *Scientific Inventory Management* (Englewood Cliffs, NJ: Prentice-Hall, 1963); Thomas E. Vollmann, William L. Berry, and D. Clay Whybark, *Manufacturing Planning and Control Systems* (Homewood, IL: Irwin, 1988); and for historical perspective, David F. Noble, *Forces of Production: A Social History of Industrial Automation* (New York: Oxford University Press, 1986).

75. John MacKrell and Betram Herzog, "Computer-Aided Engineering (CAE)," in Anthony Ralston, Edwin D. Reilly, and David Hemmendinger (eds.), *Encyclopedia*

of Computer Science, 4th ed. (London: Nature Publishing Group, 2000): 274–278; "The Impact of Automation on Engineering/Manufacturing Productivity," *Impact* (November 1980): 15; Arthur D. Little internal newsletter, "Market Research," CBI 55, Box 8, Folder 19, Archives of the Charles Babbage Institute, University of Minnesota, Minneapolis.

76. Banking Files, "Application Briefs," IBM Corporate Archives, Poughkeepsie, New York.

77. U.S. Department of Justice Programs, Bureau of Justice Statistics, *Directory of Automated Criminal Justice Information Systems 1993*, vol. 1, *Law Enforcement* (Washington, D.C.: Government Printing Office, 1993): 809–831; J. Van Duyn, *Automated Crime Information Systems* (Blue Ridge Summit, PA: TAB Professional and Reference Books, 1991): 5–16; Cortada, *All the Facts*, 254–261.

78. Josh Ellenbogen and Alison Landmead, "Forms of Equivalence: Bertillonnage and the History of Information Management," *Technology and Culture* 61, no. 1 (January 2020): 207–238.

79. Cortada, *The Digital Hand*, vol. 3, 49–101.

80. Ibid.

81. I discuss this in more detail in ibid., 16–48, and in *All the Facts*, 261–264.

82. For sample labels, see U.S. Food and Drug Administration; for an early example of similar information made available to the American public, see Eleanora Sense, *America's Nutrition Primer: What to Eat and Why* (New York: M. Barrows and Company, 1941): 48–55.

83. Page, *The Model Thinker*, 1.

84. Ibid.

85. Ibid., 4.

86. Most of the models in this table are defined, with examples, in ibid.

87. Increasingly studied by historians, JoAnne Yates and Craig N. Murphy, *Engineering Rules: Global Standard Setting since 1880* (Baltimore, MD: Johns Hopkins University Press, 2019); Andrew L. Russell, *Open Standards and the Digital Age: History, Ideology And Networks* (Cambridge, UK: Cambridge University Press, 2014).

88. Chandler, *The Visible Hand*, 159–175.

89. Henry P. Dutton, *Business Organization and Management* (Chicago, IL: A. W. Shaw Company, 1927): 55.

90. IBM Corporation, *Planning for an IBM Data Processing System* (White Plains, NY: International Business Machines Corporation, 1960, 1967): title page.

91. IBM Corporation, *IBM Study Organization Plan: The Method Phase I* (1963), *IBM Study Organization Plan: The Method Phase II* (1963), *IBM Study Organization Plan: The Method Phase III* (1963), *Organizing the Data Processing Installation* (undated, circa 1950s), *Management Control of Electronic Data Processing* (1965), *A Data Processing Glossary* (undated, circa early 1960s), *IBM Study Organization Plan: The Approach* (1961), *Basic System Study Guide* (1963).

92. While at IBM, I was responsible for similar installations all through the 1970s and 1980s, and in each instance, we used updated versions of essentially the same processes and documentation practices. Process reengineering consultants in the 1990s to the present have used virtually the same approach as well.

93. Cortada, *IBM*, 177–324.
94. IBM, *Planning for an IBM Data Processing System*, 25.
95. Ibid.
96. Ibid., 26–29.
97. Ibid., 30.
98. JoAnne Yates, *Control through Communication: The Rise of System in American Management* (Baltimore, MD: Johns Hopkins University Press, 1989): 72, 199, 242, 262.
99. They also used 3 × 5 cards, folders, file cabinets, and other standardized documents, ibid.
100. "IBM Redbooks," *Wikipedia*, https://en.wikipedia.org/wiki/IBM_Redbooks (accessed April 8, 2020).
101. IBM, *Planning for an IBM Data Processing System*, 30.
102. IBM Corporation, *IBM Study Organization Plan: The Method Phase I* (1963).
103. IBM, *Flowcharting Techniques* (White Plains, NY: IBM Technical Publications Department, 1969, but had been published in earlier editions in the 1950s); Thomas McInerney, *A Student's Guide to Flowcharting* (Englewood Cliffs, NJ: Prentice-Hall, 1973); Jerry L. Jones, *Structured Programming Logic: A Flowcharting Approach* (Englewood Cliffs, NJ: Prentice-Hall, 1986); Peggy Aldrich Kidwell, "Flowcharting Templates," *IEEE Annals of the History of Computing* 41, no. 1 (January–March 2019): 55–57; Gerardo Con Diaz, "Embodied Software: Patents and the History of Software Development, 1946–1970," ibid. 37, no. 3 (July–September, 2015): 8–19.
104. W. E. Hurt et al., *Ground Support Requirements for Selected Shuttle Payloads* (Houston, TX: IBM Federal Systems Division, August 1975); IBM, *DOD STS Data Systems Integration: DOD/STS Payload Data Communications Basics* (Houston, TX: Federal Systems Division, July 20, 1984).
105. IBM, *Management Control of Electronic Data Processing*, 11.
106. Ibid.
107. Ibid., 23–24; issues I focused on as well over a decade later, James W. Cortada, *EDP Costs and Charges: Finance, Budgets, and Cost Control in Data Processing* (Englewood Cliffs, NJ: Prentice-Hall, 1980) and *Managing DP Hardware: Capacity Planning, Cost Justification, Availability, and Energy Management* (Englewood Cliffs, NJ: Prentice-Hall, 1983).
108. A point articulated in detail with case studies by Colin Koopman, *How We Became Our Data: A Genealogy of the Informational Person* (Chicago, IL: University of Chicago Press, 2019).
109. They could not have met in 1927 because Shannon was only eleven years old, but they could have in the 1940s when Deming and Shewhart were collaborating.
110. Rafael Aguayo, *Dr. Deming: The American Who Taught the Japanese about Quality* (New York: Fireside, 1990): 3–82; Cecelia S. Kilian and W. Edward Deming, *The World of W. Edwards Deming*, 2nd ed. (Boca Raton, FL: SPC Press, 1992); W. Edwards Deming, *Out of the Crisis* (Cambridge, MA: Massachusetts Institute of Technology, Center for Advanced Educational Services, 1982, 1986), especially 1–16, 237–254, 265–316; Mary Walton, *The Deming Management Method* (New York: Dodd, Mead & Co., 1986).

111. Deming, *Out of the Crisis*.

112. Andrea Gabor, *The Man Who Discovered Quality: How W. Edwards Deming Brought the Quality Revolution to America* (New York: Penguin, 1992).

113. IBM employees met with Deming over the years, conversation between W. Edwards Deming and James W. Cortada, 1990–1991. Personal note: He was incredibly hard of hearing, and his assistant ordered me to yell at him if I wanted him to hear my questions.

114. For a brief discussion of his ideas, James W. Cortada and John Woods (eds.), *McGraw-Hill Encyclopedia of Quality Terms and Concepts* (New York: McGraw-Hill 1995): 354.

115. Cole, *Managing Quality Fads*, but also on Deming specifically, 8, 56, 72–74, 82–83.

116. Deming, *Out of the Crisis*.

117. Gordon, *The Rise and Fall of American Growth*, 1. I simultaneously drew a similar conclusion when looking at the same period, Cortada, *All the Facts*.

118. Porter, *Trust in Numbers*, 200–201.

119. Craig Robertson, "Learning to File: Reconfiguring Information and Information Work in the Early Twentieth Century," *Technology and Culture* 58, no. 4 (October 2017): 976.

120. Beth Luey, "The Organization of the Book Publishing Industry," in Paul Nord, Joan Shelley Rubin, and Michael Schudson (eds.), *A History of the Book in America*, vol. 5, *The Enduring Book: Print Culture in Postwar America* (Chapel Hill: University of North Carolina Press, 2009): 40.

121. Personal note: When my two daughters went to college, to pay for all their expenses, I simply wrote books on the use of information, and they sold so well that I do not recall even one dollar of education expense coming out of my salary or savings.

122. Argued most forcefully in Chandler, *The Visible Hand*.

123. James W. Cortada, *The Essential Manager: How to Thrive in the Global Information Jungle* (Hoboken, NJ: John Wiley & Sons, 2015): 1–39.

124. Andrew McAfee, "Mastering the Three Worlds of Information Technology," *Harvard Business Review* 84, no. 11 (November 2006): 141–149.

125. Cortada, *The Digital Hand*, three volumes; but for convenience, my findings are summarized in James W. Cortada, "*The Digital Hand*: How Information Technology Changed the Way Industries Worked in the United States," *Business History Review* 80 (Winter 2006): 755–766.

8. WHAT INFORMATION ECONOMISTS CREATED

1. Joseph A. Schumpeter, *Business Cycles: A Theoretical, Historical, and Statistical Analysis of the Capitalist Process* (New York: McGraw-Hill, 1939): vol. 1, p. 30.

2. John M. Keynes, "Introduction to the Series," in D. H. Robertson (ed.), *Cambridge Economic Handbooks*, vol. 2 (Cambridge, UK: Harcourt, Brace, 1922): v.

3. Daniel Kahneman, *Thinking, Fast and Slow* (New York: Farrar, Straus and Giroux, 2011): 24.

4. David Leiser and Yhonatan Shemesh, *How We Misunderstand Economics and Why It Matters* (London: Routledge, 2018): 11.

5. Benjamin M. Friedman, *Religion and the Rise of Capitalism* (New York: Knopf, 2021): 9.

6. Donald Winch, "Introduction," in David Ricardo, *The Principles of Political Economy and Taxation*. With an introduction by Donald Winch (London: Dent, 1973): xviii.

7. Increasingly, however, economists have begun to form greater consensus on some issues. For evidence, see D. Geide-Stevenson and A. La Parra Perez, "Consensus among Economists 2020—A Sharpening of the Picture," Working Paper, researchgate.net/publication/35752661_Concensus_among-economists-2020-A-sharpenin-of-the-picture (accessed January 9, 2022), summarized in "The New Consensus," *The Economist*, January 8, 2022, p. 64.

8. For a standard text, see Olivier Blanchard, *Macroeconomics Updated*, 5th ed. (Upper Saddle River, NJ: Prentice Hall, 2011); Ben Heijdra and Frederick van der Ploeg, *Foundations of Modern Macroeconomics* (New York: Oxford University Press, 2002).

9. Friedman, *Religion and the Rise of Capitalism*, 107.

10. For a standard text, see Robin Bade and Michael Parkin, *Foundations of Microeconomics* (Boston, MA: Addison Wesley, 2001); and on how it is conducted, see, for example, Timothy Dunne and Mark J. Roberts, *Producer Dynamics: New Evidence from Micro Data* (Chicago, IL: University of Chicago Press, 2009); and a classic in the subfield is Milton Friedman, *Price Theory* (New Brunswick, NJ: Aldine Transaction, 1976).

11. Adam Smith, *An Inquiry into the Nature and Causes of the Wealth of Nations* (1776), considered the foundational text of modern economics. The Law of Supply and Demand is actually a theory used to explain how prices are set in an economy. It essentially says the prices for a good (thing), labor, or other assets varies until the amount demanded by the market equals the quantity available, resulting in an economic equilibrium; J. E. King, "Aggregate Supply and Demand Analysis since Keynes: A Partial History," *Journal of Post Keynesian Economics* 17, no. 1 (1994): 3–31; Mark Blaug, *Economic Theory in Retrospect*, 4th ed. (Cambridge, UK: Cambridge University Press, 1985): 39–43.

12. Steven G. Medema and Warren J. Samuels, *Foundations of Research in Economics: How Do Economists Do Economics?* (Cheltenham, UK: Edward Elgar, 1996). More formally, an endogenous variable is a statistical variable that changes or is determined by its relationship to other variables within a model, thus it correlates with other factors (data) in a model. Exogenous variables are independent variables (forces) that are outside of a model but can influence an endogenous factor. With causal modeling, economists explain outcomes such as in supply and demand; Philippe Aghion and Peter W. Howitt, *Endogenous Growth Theory* (Cambridge, MA: MIT Press, 1997): 11–52, although the entire volume explores variations of these concepts as applied by economists since the nineteenth century.

13. William Milberg, *The Crisis of Vision in Modern Economic Thought* (Cambridge, UK: Cambridge University Press, 2005); John Cassidy, "The Decline of Economics," *New Yorker*, December 2, 1996, pp. 50–64 and with Edward Nik-Khah, *The Knowledge We Have Lost in Information: The History of Information in Modern Economics* (New York: Oxford University Press, 2017): 1–30.

14. But more interesting is that economists themselves have found fault with their discipline's approaches. See, for example, Philip Mirowski, *More Heat than Light: Economics as Social Physics, Physics as Nature's Economics* (Cambridge, UK: Cambridge University Press, 1989): 377–378.

15. Hugo A. Keuzenkamp, *Probability, Econometrics and Truth: The Methodology of Econometrics* (Cambridge, UK: Cambridge University Press, 2000): 13; Peter Kennedy, *A Guide to Econometrics*, 5th ed. (Cambridge, MA: MIT Press, 2003): 390–396; Stephen T. Ziliak, "The Standard Error of Regressions," *Journal of Economic Literature* 34, no. 1 (1996): 97–114.

16. A discussion evident for decades, Albert Fishlow and Robert W. Fogel, "Quantitative Economic History: An Interim Evaluation Past Trends and Present Tendencies," *The Journal of Economic History* 31, no. 1 (March 1971): 15–42; J. Morgan Kousser, "The Revivalism of Narrative: A Response to Recent Criticisms of Quantitative History," Social Science Working Paper 453, Division of the Humanities and Social Sciences, California Institute of Technology, November 1982, https://authors.library.caltech.edu/81855/1/sswp453.pdf (accessed April 13, 2020); Douglas C. North, John Joseph Wallis, and Barry R. Weingast, *Violence and Social Orders: A Conceptual Framework for Interpreting Recorded Human History* (Cambridge, UK: Cambridge University Press, 2009): 1–29; Douglas C. North, *Structure and Change in Economic History* (New York: W. W. Norton, 1982). North is a Nobel laureate in economics.

17. Widely credited with doing this more than any other economist in the twentieth century, Peter Clarke, *The Twentieth Century's Most Influential Economist* (New York: Bloomsbury, 2009); Donald Markwell, *John Maynard Keynes and International Relations: Economic Paths to War and Peace* (Oxford: Oxford University Press, 2006).

18. For example, Stephen T. Ziliak, Deirdre N. McCloskey, "Size Matters: The Standard Error of Regressions in the *American Economic Review*," *Economic Journal Watch* 1, no. 2 (April 2004): 331–358; but see also her books, *The Rhetoric of Economics* (Madison: University of Wisconsin Press, 1985) and *If You're So Smart: The Narrative of Economic Expertise* (Chicago: University of Chicago Press, 1990). To clear potential confusion, these two books were published under her first name, Donald; she later changed it to Deirdre.

19. Prakash Loungani, "How Accurate Are Private Sector Forecasts? Cross-Country Evidence from Consensus Forecasts of Output Growth," *IMF Working Paper No. 77* (Washington, D.C.: International Monetary Fund, April 2000). https://www.imf.org/external/pubs/ft/wp/2000/wp0077.pdf (accessed April 13, 2020). The paper provides empirical evidence in support of the joke presented at the start of this chapter. The key finding: "This predictive failure could arise either because forecasters lack the requisite *information* (in terms of reliable real-time data or reliable models) or because they lack the *incentives* to predict recessions" (p. 29).

20. Adam Cox, "Blame Nobel for Crisis, Says Author of '"Black Swan,"' *Reuters*, September 28, 2010, https://www.reuters.com/article/us-nobel-crisis-interview/blame-nobel-for-crisis-says-author-of-black-swan-idUSTRE68R2SK20100928 (accessed April 13, 2020).

21. Mariana Mazzucato, *The Value of Everything* (New York: Public Affairs, 2018); and see any textbook, such as Campbell R. McConnell, Stanley L. Brue, and Sean M. Flynn, *Economics: Principles, Problems, and Policies*, 18th ed. (Boston, MA: McGraw-Hill Irwin, 2009); Steven Rappaport, *Models and Reality in Economics* (Cheltenham, UK: Edward Elgar, 1998).

22. Steven Rappaport, "Abstraction and Unrealistic Assumptions in Economics," *Journal of Economic Methodology* 3, no. 2 (1996): 215–236.

23. Mirowski, *More Heat than Light*.

24. The phrase originated with Stephen J. Dubner and Steven Levitt, *Freakonomics: A Rogue Economist Explores the Hidden Side of Everything* (New York: William Morrow and Company, 2005). Levitt is an economist at the University of Chicago, Dubner a journalist at the *New York Times*.

25. Thomas S. Kuhn, *The Structure of Scientific Revolutions* (Chicago, IL: University of Chicago Press, 1962); Everett M. Rogers, *Diffusion of Innovations*, 5th ed. (New York: Free Press, 2003), originally published 1962.

26. Blaug, *Economic Theory in Retrospect*, vii.

27. Since the institution of the Nobel Prize in economics in 1969, twenty-eight out of the seventy-four Laureates had an association with the University of Chicago, with the majority in the Economics Department. The list reads like a Who's Who of highly influential economists, such as Paul A. Samuelson (1970), Kenneth J. Arrow (1972), Friedrich August von Hayek (1974), Tjalling C. Koopmans (1975), Milton Friedman (1976), Herbert A. Simon (1978), Theodore W. Schultz (1979), Lawrence R. Klein (1980), George J. Stigler (1982), Gerard Debreu (1983), Franco Modigliani (1985), James M. Buchanan Jr. (1986). Trygve Haavelmo (1989), Harry M. Markowitz and Merton H. Miller (1990), Ronald H. Coase (1991), Gary S. Becker (1992), Robert W. Fogel (1993), among others.

28. Michio Morishima, *Walras' Economics: A Pure Theory of Capital and Money* (Cambridge, UK: Cambridge University Press, 1977).

29. Bert Mosselmans, *William Stanley Jevons and the Cutting Edge of Economics* (London: Routledge. 2007): 1–51. Jevons' *Theory of Political Economy* has been republished many times and remains in print.

30. Mazzucato, *The Value of Everything*, 60.

31. Blaug, *Economic Theory in Retrospect*, 328–424; Peter Groenewegan, *A Soaring Eagle: Alfred Marshall: 1842–1924* (Cheltenham, UK: Edward Elgar, 1995) is the near definitive biography, but see his shorter biography, *Alfred Marshall: Economist, 1842–1924* (London: Palgrave, Macmillan 2007); Jha Narmadeshwar, *The Age of Marshall: Aspects of British Economic Thought, 1880–1915* (London: F. Cass, 1973); and a fascinating piece by John Maynard Keynes, "Alfred Marshall, 1842–1924," *The Economic Journal* 34, no. 135 (September 1924): 311–372.

32. Mazzucato, *The Value of Everything*, 62.

33. Ibid., 63.

34. Quoted in Robert W. Dimand, "Keynes, IS-LM, and the Marshallian Tradition," *History of Political Economy* 39, no. 1 (2007): 81–95.

35. Blaug, *Economic Theory in Retrospect*, 328–497.

36. Ibid.

37. Alfred Marshall, *Principles of Economics*, 3rd ed. (London: Macmillan, 1895), vol. 1, p. 425. Marshall pointed out with respect to the ideas in the graph evidence of his borrowing from physics: "When demand and supply are in stable equilibrium, if any accident should move the scale of production from its equilibrium position, there will be instantly brought into play forces tending to bring it back to that position; just as, if a stone hanging by a string is displaced from its equilibrium position, the force of gravity will at once tend to bring it back to its equilibrium position. The movements of the scale of production about its position of equilibrium will be of a somewhat similar kind," ibid.

38. Ibid., 791–811.

39. For a succinct summary of these concepts, Diane Coyle, Stephanie Diepeveen, and Julia Wdowin, "The Value of Data—Summary Report 2020" (Cambridge, UK: Bennett Institute for Public Policy, Cambridge University, February 2020): 4, https://www.bennettinstitute.cam.ac.uk/media/uploads/files/Value_of_data_summary_report_26_Feb.pdf (accessed April 22, 2020).

40. Ibid., 5.

41. Schumpeter's name may sound familiar to technologists and business experts because some of his research, which he conducted during the first half of the 1900s, concerned the role technology played in shaping modern economies. He argued the case that technology's evolution was a "gale of creative destruction," whereby an old technology and its products gave way to new ones. He described the "process of industrial mutation that incessantly revolutionizes the economic structure from within, incessantly destroying the old one, incessantly creating a new one," Joseph A. Schumpeter, *Capitalism, Socialism and Democracy* (London: Routledge, 1994 ed., original published 1942): 82–83. His idea became of enormous interest in the industrialized world after the arrival of the computer and other technologies. See also, Aghion Philippe and Peter Howitt, "A Model of Growth through Creative Destruction," *Econometrica* 60, no. 2 (1992): 323–351 and their book, *Endogenous Growth Theory* (Cambridge, MA: MIT Press, 1997). A trade book popularized his ideas in business circles at the end of the century, Richard Foster and Sarah Kaplan, *Creative Destruction: Why Companies that Are Built to Last Underperform the Market—And How to Successfully Transform* (New York: Currency, 2001).

42. Andrew Abbott, *The System of Professions: An Essay on the Division of Expert Labor* (Chicago, IL: University of Chicago Press, 1988) and his *Chaos of Disciplines* (Chicago, IL: University of Chicago Press, 2001); R. Fagan, J. Y. Halpern, Y. Moses, and M. Y. Vardi, *Reasoning about Knowledge* (Cambridge, MA: MIT Press, 1995); Diana Hicks, "The Four Literatures of Social Science," in Henk Moed (ed.), *Handbook of Quantitative Science and Technology Research* (Dordrecht, Netherlands: Kluwer Academic, 2004); M. Gibbons, C. Limoges, H. Nowotny, S. Schwartzman, P. Scott, and M. Trow, *The New Production of Knowledge: The Dynamics of Science and Research in Contemporary Societies* (London: Sage, 1994); F. Morillo,

M. Bordons, and I. Gomez, "Interdisciplinarity in Science: A Tentative Typology of Disciplines and Research Areas," *Journal of the American Society of Information Science and Technology* 54, no. 13 (2003): 1237–1249; S. J. Pierce, "Subject Areas, Disciplines and the Concept of Authority," *Library and Information Science Research* 13 (1991): 21–35.

43. For an acknowledgment of early contributors, see Gerhard Tintner, "The Definition of Econometrics," *Econometrica* 21, no. 1 (January 1953): 3.

44. Robert W. Dimand and John Geanakoplos, "Celebrating Irving Fisher: The Legacy of a Great Economist," *American Journal of Economics and Sociology* 64, no. 1 (January 2005): 3–18; Robert Loring Allen, *Irving Fisher: A Biography* (London: Wiley-Blackwell, 1993): 1–19.

45. Irving Fisher, "Mathematical Method in the Social Sciences," ibid. 9 no. 3 (July 1941): 187. Francis Ysidro Edgeworth (1845–1926) was both a philosopher and political economist who developed numerous statistical methods, largely in the 1880s and was a founding editor of *The Economic Journal*. Vilfredo Pareto (1848–1923) trained as an engineer and was an early sociologist, political scientist, and economist with a strong interest in income distribution, microeconomics using statistics in his studies, and most famously the Pareto principle, known to most people the 80/10 Rule.

46. Henry L. Moore, *Synthetic Economics* (New York: Macmillan, 1929): 6.

47. Robert J. Gordon, "What is the Econometric Society? History, Organization, and Basic Procedures," *Econometrica* 65, no. 6 (November 1997): 1443. Some additional statistics on this journal: Between 1928 and 2020, it published 2957 articles, which amounted to 76,515 pages; it had 5812 individual subscribers in 2020, e-mail from Mary Beth Bellando-Zaniboni (Publication Relations Manager, Econometric Society) to James W. Cortada, April 24, 2020.

48. Irving Fisher, "Mathematical Method in the Social Sciences," *Econometrica* 9, nos. 3–4 (July–October 1941): 185.

49. Ibid., 187.

50. Ibid., 188–189.

51. Ibid., 191.

52. Ibid., 192.

53. Ibid., 197.

54. Joseph Schumpeter, "The Common Sense of Econometrics," *Econometrica* 1, no. 1 (January 1933): 5–12; Trygve Havelmo, "The Role of the Econometrician in the Advancement of Economic Theory," Ibid., 26, no. 3 (July 1958): 351–357; Hugo Sonnenschein and Dorothy Hodges, "Manual for Econometrica Authors," Ibid., 48, no. 5 (July 1980): 1073–1082; The Editor, "Editorial," Ibid., 51, no. 1 (January 1983): unpaginated; Carl F. Christ, "The Founding of the Econometric Society and Econometrics," Ibid., 51, no. 1 (January 1983): 3–6; Olav Bjerkholt, "Ragnar Frisch, Editor of Econometrica 1933–1954," Ibid., 63, no. 4 (July 1995): 755–765.

55. Schumpeter, "The Common Sense of Econometrics," 5.

56. Ibid.

57. Ibid., 6.

58. Ibid.

59. Ibid., 8.; referring to William S. Stanley, *Theory of Political Economy* (London: Macmillan, 1871). A reading of this book makes it clear why Schumpeter quoted him; Jevons was not shy in providing mathematical evidence in defense of his ideas that in a book of less than 270 pages he presents a wide range of theories: "Theory of Pleasure and Pain," "Theory of Utility," "Theory of Exchange," "Theory of Labor," "Theory of Rent," and "Theory of Capital," all topics that would become massive bodies of new information over the next century and a half.

60. Schumpeter, "The Common Sense of Econometrics," 10.

61. Ibid., 11.

62. Ibid., 12.

63. Wassily Leontief, "Joseph A. Schumpeter (1883–1950)," *Econometrica* 18, no. 2 (April 1950): 103–110; Kenneth J. Arrow, "The Work of Ragnar Frisch, Econometrician," Ibid., 28, no. 2 (April 1960): 175–192; Blaug, *Economic Theory in Retrospect*, 425–653; Mazzucato, *The Value of Everything*, 57–74.

64. Sonnenschein and Hodges, "Manual for Econometrica Authors," 1073.

65. Quoted in Bjerkholt, "Ragnar Frisch, Editor of Econometrica, 1933–1954," p. 759.

66. A new generation of economic historians began emerging in the late 1960s. For example, Edward E. Malefakis, who saw himself as a historian of Spanish history, not economic history, published *Agrarian Reform and Peasant Revolution in Spain: Origins of the Civil War* (New Haven, CT: Yale University Press, 1970), which contained some—not a lot—of statistical analysis, but when published was seen as quite innovative in a subfield of history not known for using much mathematics or statistics. Of course, all of that changed over the next half-century in economic history, but not to the extent a modern economist would reasonably acknowledge as applying intensively mathematical or statistical tools.

67. John M. Clark, "Mathematical Economists and Others: A Plea for Communicability," *Econometrica* 15, no. 2 (April 1947): 75–78.

68. Ibid., 77.

69. Joseph J. Spengler, "On the Progress of Quantification in Economics," in Harry Woolf (ed.), *Quantification: A History of the Meaning of Measurement in the Natural and Social Sciences* (Indianapolis, IN: Bobbs-Merrill, 1961): 133–134.

70. Ibid., 134–138.

71. They had been learning already from business practices, "Charles F. Roos, "Business Planning and Statistical Analysis," Ibid., 17 (Supplement: Report of the Washington Meeting, July 1949): 69–72.

72. On his scholarly role, see Eric S. Maskin, "The Economics of Kenneth J. Arrow: A Selective Review," *Annual Review of Economics* 11 (August 2019): 1–26.

73. Kenneth J. Arrow, "Statistics and Economic Policy," *Econometrica* 25, no. 4 (October 1957): 523–531,

74. Ibid., 523.

75. Ibid.

76. Ibid., 527.

77. Both quotes, Ibid., 528.

78. Ibid., 529.

79. Ibid., 530.
80. Mazzucato, *The Value of Everything*, 229–269.
81. Joseph W. Duncan and William C. Shelton, *Revolution in United States Statistics: 1926–1976* (Washington, D.C.: U.S. Department of Commerce, 1978).
82. Thomas S. McCaleb, "The Council of Economic Advisers after Forty Years," *Cato Journal* 6, no. 2 (1986): 685–693; Hugh S. Norton, *The Employment Act and the Council of Economic Advisors, 1946–1976* (Columbia: University of South Carolina Press, 1977); James Tobin and Murray Weidenbaum (eds.), *Two Revolutions in Economic Policy: The First Economic Reports of Presidents Kennedy and Reagan* (Cambridge, MA: MIT Press, 1988); and for an example of explicit application of economic information, see Saul Engelbourg, "The Council of Economic Advisors and the Recession of 1953–1954," *Business History Review* 54, no. 2 (1980): 192–214.
83. Joseph Goldberg and William Moye, *First Hundred Years of the Bureau of Labor Statistics*, BLS Bulletin 2235 (Washington, D.C.: Government Printing Office, 1985): 110.
84. William J. Wiatrowski, "BLS at 125: Using Historic principles to Track the 21st Century Economy," *Monthly Labor Review* (June 2009): 3–25.
85. On the history of BLS, see James W. Cortada, *All the Facts: A History of Information in the United States Since 1870* (New York: Oxford University Press, 2016): 152–157.
86. When selecting the more than one dozen industries to study for my history of computing by industry (*The Digital Hand*), I began as other historians did, by consulting this classification. The suggestion to do this was given to me by none other than Alfred D. Chandler Jr. who had done the same thing when researching his magisterial *The Visible Hand*. How actual collections of data were assembled is a complex, yet fascinating, story. For how this was done within the American government in the 1920s–1940s, see Emmanuel Didier, *America by the Numbers: Quantification, Democracy, and the Birth of National Statistics* (Cambridge, MA: MIT Press, 2020).
87. Wiatrowski, "BLS at 125: Using Historic Principles to Track the 21st-Century Economy," 3–25.
88. I have regularly read this publication for over forty years to stay informed largely about the nature of American work and its economic impact.
89. https://www.bls.gov/mlr/ (accessed April 20, 2020).
90. For a brief history of BEA, see Cortada, *All the Facts*, 157–159.
91. Didier, *America by the Numbers*.
92. Mazzucato, *The Value of Everything*, 75–100.
93. "BEA, "National Economic Accounts," https://www.bls.gov/mlr/ (accessed April 20, 2020).
94. Ibid.
95. BEA, *Measuring the Economy: A Primer on GDP and the National Income and Product Accounts* (Washington, D.C.: U.S. Department of Commerce, December 2015), available at https://www.bea.gov/sites/default/files/methodologies/nipa_primer.pdf (accessed April 20, 2020).
96. Ibid., 2.
97. Ibid., 3–4.
98. Ibid., 16.

99. Diane Coyle, *GDP: A Brief But Affectionate History* (Princeton, NJ: Princeton University Press, 2014): 4.

100. Mazzucato, *The Value of Everything*, 76.

101. Doyle, *GDP*, 13.

102. Ibid., 15.

103. Ibid., 19.

104. Ibid., 30.

105. See, for example, a sample list of GDP data format, ibid., 26, and while at it, GDP can be expressed mathematically as an equation: $GDP = C + I + G + (X - M)$, which translates into English as consumer spending plus investment spending plus government spending plus exports minus imports (trade surplus or deficit), explained in ibid., 27–28.

106. Gottfried Haberler, "Fritz Machlup: In Memoriam," *Cato Journal* 3, no. 1 (1983): 11–14.

107. He was a prolific author; for our purposes, his key works are Fritz Machlup, *The Production and Distribution of Knowledge in the United States* (1962); and *Knowledge: Its Creation, Distribution, and Economic Significance*, 3 vols. (Princeton, NJ: Princeton University Press, 1980–1984). He intended to publish additional volumes, but died before he could complete the project.

108. He published over thirty articles in the *Harvard Business Review*; see also Peter Drucker, *Managing for Results* (New York: Harper & Brothers, 1964); *The Age of Discontinuity* (New York: Harper & Row, 1969); and *Managing in Turbulent Times* (New York: Harper & Row, 1980). He wrote thirty-nine books, all of which were also issued in foreign language translations. For a useful biography, Jack Beatty, *The World According to Peter Drucker* (New York: Free Press, 1998).

109. Friedrich A. Hayek, "The Use of Knowledge in Society," *American Economic Review* 35, no. 4 (1945): 519–530; and *Individualism and Economic Order* (Chicago, IL: University of Chicago Press, 1948).

110. George Stigler, "The Economics of Information," *Journal of Political Economy* 69, no. 3 (1961): 213–225; "Information in the Labor Market," ibid., 70, no. 5, Part 2 (1962): 94–105.

111. A. Michael Spence, "Signaling in Retrospect and the Informational Structure of Markets, [Nobel] Prize Lecture," December 8, 2001, https://www.nobelprize.org/prizes/economic-sciences/2001/spence/lecture/ (accessed April 20, 2020).

112. George Akerlof, "The Market for 'Lemons': Quality Uncertainty and the Market Mechanism," *Quarterly Journal of Economics* 84, no. 3 (1970): 488–500. This paper became a classic almost as quickly as it was published on asymmetric information for which he was awarded the Nobel Prize in economics. He demonstrated how the quality of products (goods) can degrade if information asymmetry existed between sellers and buyers, hence leaving only lemons (i.e., a defective automobile discovered to have problems after it had been purchased). The price to an uninformed buyer leads to a bad decision, causing high-quality products to leave the market (e.g., properly operating automobiles). Such a circumstance can destroy a market.

113. Joseph E. Stiglitz, "The Theory of 'Screening,' Education, and the Distribution of Income," *The American Economic Review* 65, no. 3 (June 1975): 283–300; and

with Andrew Weiss, "Credit Rationing in Markets with Imperfect Information," Ibid., 71, no. 3 (1981): 393–410.

114. It continues, see Marcin Pęski and Juuso Toikka, "Value of Persistent Information," *Econometrica* 85, no. 6 (November 2017): 1921–1948.

115. Echoed most forcefully in the way I organized and discussed information in American society from the 1870s to the present, James W. Cortada, *All the Facts*.

116. For example, Diane Cozel, *The Weightless World* (Cambridge, MA: MIT Press, 1997); Carl Shapiro and Hal R. Varian, *Information Rules: A Strategic Guide to the Network Economy* (Boston, MA: Harvard Business School Press, 1999). Non-economists gained large audiences, too, particularly in business circles, for example, James McGee and Lawrence Prusak, *Managing Information Strategically* (New York: Random House, 1993); Donald Tapscott, *The Digital Economy* (New York: McGraw-Hill, 1996).

117. Marc Uri Porat, *The Information Economy: Definition and Measurement* (Washington, D.C.: U.S. Department of Commerce, Office of Telecommunications, May 1977): 2. See also Ibid., 104–134; also available in James W. Cortada (ed.), *Rise of the Knowledge Worker* (Boston, MA: Butterworth-Heinemann, 1998): 101–131.

118. Joseph E. Stiglitz, "Knowledge as a Global Public Good," in Inge Kaul (ed.), *Global Public Goods: International Cooperation in the 21st Century* (New York: Oxford University Press, 1999): 308–324; Michael L. Katz. and Carl Shapiro, "Network Externalities, Competition, and Compatibility," *American Economic Review* 75, no. 3 (June 1985): 424–440.

119. For a spectacular example of the growing appreciation of the role of information, in 2001 The Royal Swedish Academy of Sciences awarded the Nobel Prize in economics to three economists who had done considerable research into information economics: George A. Akerlof, who was working at the University of California at Berkeley, A. Michael Spence then at Stanford University, and Joseph E. Stiglitz at Columbia University. As the press release explained succinctly, "for their analyses of markets with asymmetric information." As for further explanation: "During the 1970s, this year's Laureates laid the foundation for a general theory of markets with asymmetric information. . . . The Laureates' contributions form the core of modern information economics," The Nobel Prize Press Release, October 10, 2001, https://www.nobelprize.org/prizes/economic-sciences/2001/press-release/ (accessed April 20, 2020).

120. For example, Gerardo Con Diaz, *Software Rights: How Patent Law Transformed Software Development in America* (New Haven, CT: Yale University Press, 2019): 1–10.

121. The topic has been explored for decades, Alan R. Andreasen and Brian T. Ratchford, "Factors Affecting Consumers' Use of Information Sources," *Journal of Business Research* 4, no. 3 (August 1976): 197–212; there are even textbooks on the topic, such as Michael R. Solomon, *Consumer Behavior: Buying, Having, and Being*, 12th ed. (Essex, UK: Pearson Education, 2018). See also for more focused examples, Gordon Moore, John A. Quelch, and Emily Boudreau, *Choice Matters: How Healthcare Consumers Make Decisions* (New York: Oxford University Press, 2018); Richard H. Thaler and Cass R. Sunstein, *Nudge: Improving Decisions about Health, Wealth, and Happiness* (New Haven, CT: Yale University Press, 2008).

122. For a useful and detailed review of the literature, Diane Coyle, Stephanie Diepeveen, and Julia Wdowin, *The Value of Data: Literature Review* (Cambridge, UK: Bennett Institute for Public Policy, Cambridge University, February 2020), https://www.bennettinstitute.cam.ac.uk/research/research-projects/valuing-data/ (accessed April 22, 2020).

123. One Oxford University professor specializing in information studies snarked that "information-theoretical approaches to economic topics have become so popular and persuasive that one may be forgiven for mistaking economics for a branch of information science," Floridi, *Information*, 91.

124. One could see interest in information and economics, in all its mathematically intense forms, increase through the pages of *Econometrica*, for examples, Glenn M. MacDonald, "Information in Production," *Econometrica* 50, no. 5 (September 1982): 1143–1162; Vincent P. Crawford and Joel Sobel, "Strategic Information Transmission," ibid., 50, no. 6 (November 1982): 1431–1451; Richard D. McKelvey and Talbot Page, "Common Knowledge, Consensus, and Aggregate Information," Ibid., 54, no. 1 (January 1986): 109–127; Richard D. McKelvey and Talbot Page, "Public and Private Information: An Experimental Study of Information Pooling," Ibid., 58, no. 6 (November 1990): 1321–1339; Nicola Persico, "Information Acquisition in Auctions," ibid., 68, no. 1 (January 2000): 135–148.

125. James Bessen, *Learning by Doing: The Real Connection between Innovation, Wages, and Wealth* (New Haven, CT: Yale University Press, 2015): 46. His bibliography is excellent on the economic literature of innovation.

126. Mazzucato, *The Value of Everything*, 191–192.

127. The literature on this issue is extensive, but the point is made in Ibid., 229–269. In particular, the Cold War period spurred considerable private–public sector innovations, Stuart W. Leslie, *The Cold War and American Science: The Military-Industrial-Academic Complex at MIT and Stanford* (New York: Columbia University Press, 1993): 203–231; Margaret Pugh O'Mara, *Cities of Knowledge: Cold War Science and the Search for the Next Silicon Valley* (Princeton, NJ: Princeton University Press, 2004); Sharon Weinberger, *The Imagineers of War: The Untold Story of DARPA, the Pentagon Agency That Changed theWorld* (New York: Knopf, 2017); Annie Jacobson, *The Pentagon's Brain: An Uncensored History of DARPA, America's Top-Secret Military Research Agency* (New York: Little, Brown, 2015).

128. Shapiro and Varian, *Information Rules*; Shane Greenstein, *How the Internet Became Commercial: Innovation, Privatization, and the Birth of a New Network* (Princeton, NJ: Princeton University Press, 215).

129. Mazzucato, *The Value of Everything*, 202–206.

130. Claude E. Shannon and Warren Weaver, *The Mathematical Theory of Communication* (Urbana: University of Illinois Press, 1949).

131. Richard N. Langlois, "Systems Theory and the Meaning of Information," *Journal of the American Society for Information Science* 33, no. 6 (November 1982): 395–399; David G. Luenberger, *Information Science* (Princeton, NJ: Princeton University Press, 2006): 130–140.

132. Mazzucato, *The Value of Everything*, 213–239; César Hidalgo, *Why Information Grows: The Evolution of Order, from Atoms to Economies* (New York: Basic Books, 2015): 73–126; I too have commented on these issues, James W. Cortada,

"Building Blocks of Modern Society: History, Information Ecosystems, and Infrastructures" (forthcoming).

133. Cortada, *IBM*.

134. Peter Diamond and Hannu Vartiainen (eds.), *Behavioral Economics and Its Applications* (Princeton, NJ: Princeton University Press, 2007); Robin M. Hogarth and Melvin W. Reder (eds.), *Rational Choice: The Contrast between Economics and Psychology* (Chicago, IL: University of Chicago Press, 1987): 1–24; Richard H. Thaler, "Behavioral Economics: Past, Present, and Future," *American Economic Review* 106, no. 7 (2016): 1577–1600.

135. Philip Corr and Anke Plagnol, *Behavioral Economics: The Basics* (London: Routledge, 2019): 3.

136. Leiser and Shemesh, *How We Misunderstand Economics and Why It Matters*, 123.

137. Andrew Shtulman, *Scienceblind: Why Our Intuitive Theories about the World Are so Often Wrong* (New York: Basic Books, 2017): 4.

138. Corr and Plagnol, *Behavioral Economics*, 4.

139. Ibid., 113.

140. Ibid., 120.

141. Ibid.

142. For example, K. Daniel, D. Hirshleifer, and A. Subrahmanyam, "Investor Psychology and Security Market Under- and Overreactions," *Journal of Finance* 53, no. 6 (1998): 1839–1885; David Genesove and Christopher Mayer, "Loss Aversion and Seller Behavior: Evidence from the Housing Market," *Quarterly Journal of Economics* 116, no. 4 (March 2001): 1233–1260.

143. Matthew Rabin, "Psychology and Economics," *Journal of Economic Literature* 36, no. 1 (1998): 11–46; consult the extensive bibliographies in Corr and Plagnol, *Behavior Economics*, 229–241; and in Leiser and Shemesh, *How We Misunderstand Economics and Why It Matters*, 137–159.

144. Press Release, Nobel Foundation, "The Sveriges Riksbank Prize in Economic Sciences in Memory of Alfred Nobel 2002," October 2002, https://www.nobelprize.org/prizes/economic-sciences/2002/summary/ (accessed April 22, 2020).

145. In 2013 Robert J. Shiller for his studies of asset pricing as a contribution to behavior science, ibid.; in 2017 Richard Thaler for demonstrating that people behaved in irrational ways contrary to existing economic theory, ibid. (both accessed April 22, 2020).

146. Richard F. Kitchener, "Against Behaviorism: A Critique of Behavioral Science," *Philosophy of the Social Sciences* 12, no. 4 (December 1, 1982): 445–448; "Criticisms of Behavioral Theory," *Economicsonline*, undated, https://www.economicsonline.co.uk/Behavioural_economics/Criticisms_of_behavioural_economics.html (accessed April 22, 2020).

147. The now seminal work on the subject, Richard H. Thaler and Cass R. Sunstein, *Nudge: Improving Decisions about Health, Wealth, and Happiness* (New Haven, CT: Yale University Press, 2008).

148. For examples, Tom C. W. Lin, "A Behavioral Framework for Securities Risk," *UF Law Scholarship Repository* (January 1, 2011), https://scholarship.law.ufl.edu/cgi/viewcontent.cgi?article=1144&context=facultypub (accessed April 20, 2020); Charles

D. Kirkpatrick and Julie R. Dahiquist, *Technical Analysis: The Complete Resource for Financial Market Technicians* (Upper Saddle River, NJ: Financial Times Press, 2007); Shiomp Benartzi and Richard H. Thaler, "Myopic Loss Aversion and the Equity Premium Puzzle," *Quarterly Journal of Economics* 110, no. 1 (1995): 73–92.

149. For examples, J. Scott Armstrong, Nicole Covielo and Barbara Safranek, "Escalation Bias: Does It Extend to Marketing?" *Journal of the Academy of Marketing Science* 21, no. 3 (1993): 247–352; Gunduz Caginalp and A. Duran, "Overreaction Diamonds: Precursors and Aftershocks for Significant Price Changes," *Quantitative Finance* 7, no. 3 (2007): 321–342 (he was the editor of *Journal of Behavioral Finance* and is a mathematician by training).

150. Now fashionably called "behavioral game theory" by Colin Camerer, *Behavioral Game Theory: Experiments in Strategic Interaction* (Princeton, NJ: Princeton University Press, 2003).

151. Although to be accurate, this kind of work is being done by psychologists and biologists, borrowing ideas and methods from economists to understand economic reasoning among animals, such as pigeons. See, for example, Raymond C. Battalio et al., "Income-Leisure Tradeoffs of Animal Workers," *American Economic Review* 71, no. 4 (1981): 621–632; John H. Kagel, Raymond C. Battalio, and Leonard Green, *Economic Choice Theory: An Experimental Analysis of Animal Behavior* (Cambridge, UK: Cambridge University Press, 1995).

152. For an introduction to this growing topic, see Tshilidzi Marwala and Evan Hurwitz, *Artificial Intelligence and Economic Theory: Skynet in the Market* (Berlin: Springer-Verlag, 2017); John H. Holland and John H. Miller, "Artificial Adaptive Agents in Economic Theory," *The American Economic Review* 81, no. 2 (May 1991): 365–370; Scott J. Moss and John Rae (eds.), *Artificial Intelligence and Economic Analysis: Prospects and Problems* (Aldershot, UK: Edward Elgar Publishing, 1992).

153. Clement Levallois et al., "Translating Upwards: Linking the Neural and Social Sciences via Neuroeconomics," *Nature Reviews Neuroscience* 13, no. 11 (2012): 789–797.

154. John H. Kagel et al., "Demand Curves for Animal Consumers," *Quarterly Journal of Economics* 96, no. 1 (1981): 1–16.

155. "Instant Economics," *The Economist*, October 23, 2021, p. 13.

156. Spengler, "On the Progress of Quantification in Economics," 142.

157. Philippe Aghion, Céline Antonin, and Simon Bunel, *The Power of Creative Destruction: Economic Upheaval and the Wealth of Nations* (Cambridge, MA: Harvard University Press, 2021): 149–172.

158. Katherine Kornei, "Are You Confused by Scientific Jargon? So Are Scientists," *New York Times*, April 9, 2021; the original study is Alejandro Martinez and Stefano Mammola, "Specialized Terminology Reduces the Number of Citations of Scientific Papers," *Proceedings Royal Society B*, 288 (2021): 1–6.

159. For Edgeworth's quote, see Theodor M. Porter, *The Rise of Statistical Thinking, 1820–1900* (Princeton. NJ: Princeton University Press, 1986): 260, and on Edgeworth's work, see ibid., 255–269.

160. Ibid., xxi (a new preface published in 2020 to his 1986 reprinted book).

9. CONTRIBUTIONS OF POLITICAL SCIENTISTS AND HISTORIANS TO MODERN INFORMATION

1. David Hackett Fischer, *Historians' Fallacies: Toward a Logic of Historical Thought* (New York: Harper Torchbooks, 1970): 62.

2. A. Lawrence Lowell, "The Physiology of Politics," *The American Science Review* 4, no. 1 (February 1910): 10. He was the incoming president of the American Political Science Association when he made this remark.

3. On mistakes historians make using statistics, see Fischer, *Historians' Fallacies*, 110–118, 153–154; but a subject considered part of the historical discipline since at least the mid-twentieth century, R. G. Collingwood, *The Idea of History* (New York: Galaxy Book, 1946, but consulted 1956 ed.): 94, 228; but not by the venerable, frequently consulted G. R. Elton, *The Practice of History* (New York: Thomas Y. Crowell, 1967).

4. For both quotes, Peter Novick, *That Noble Dream: The "Objectivity Question" and the American Historical Profession* (Cambridge, UK: Cambridge University Press, 1998): 577–578.

5. William J. Reese, *America's Public Schools: From Common School to "No Child Left Behind"* (Baltimore, Md.: Johns Hopkins University Press, 2005).

6. Consulting an introductory textbook on the subject is a practical way to gain a sense of the scope of the subject, for example, see Michael G. Roskin, Robert L. Cord, James A. Medeiros, and Walter S. Jones, *Political Science: An Introduction*, 13th ed. (Upper Saddle River, NJ: Prentice Hall, 2013). Oxford University Press has published over a dozen large anthologies on politics by subject, similar to the topics listed in table 7.1.

7. For an overview, Leonardo A. Morlino, Dirk Berg-Schlosser, and Bertrand Badie, *Political Science: A Global Perspective* (Thousand Oaks, CA: SAGE, 2017); Robert E. Goodin (ed.), *The Oxford Handbook of Political Science* (New York: Oxford University Press, 2009): 3–60.

8. Robert A. Dahl, *Democracy and Its Critics* (New Haven, CT: Yale University Press, 1989), one of a series of books he published with this press, and my favorite by him, *Polyarchy: Participation and Opposition* (New Haven, CT: Yale University Press, 1971) for its analytical presentation; Arend Lijphart, *Democracy in Plural Societies: A Comparative Exploration* (New Haven, CT: Yale University Press, 1977); see also Gabriel A. Almond and Sidney Verba (eds.), *The Civic Culture Revisited* (Boston, MA: Little Brown, 1980).

9. Juan J. Linz, *Totalitarian and Authoritarian Regimes* (London: Lynne Rienner, 2000), joining a long list of works by political scientists on this theme.

10. For example, Barrington Moore Jr., *Injustice: The Social Bases of Obedience and Revolt* (London: Routledge, 1978); *Social Origins of Dictatorship and Democracy: Lord and Peasant in the Making of the Modern World* (Boston, MA: Beacon Press, 1966); and *Political Power and Social Theory: Seven Studies* (New York: Harper Torchbooks, 1965); on his work, see Dennis Smith, *Barrington Moore, Jr.: A Critical Appraisal* (New York: Routledge, 2018, original edition Armonk, NY M. E. Sharpe, 1983).

11. Beginning most decisively with Hannah Arendt, *The Origins of Totalitarianism* (New York: Schocken, 2004, originally published in 1948).

12. Hans-Dieter Kingermann (ed.), *The State of Political Science in Western Europe* (Opladen, Germany: Barbara Budrich Publishers, 2007); S. F. Schramm and B. Caterino (eds.), *Making Political Science Matter: Debating Knowledge, Research, and Methods* (New York: New York University Press, 2006); as with other disciplines, a review of prior issues of leading journals in the field exposes the trends, and with political science it is the *American Political Science Review*, published since 1906. Volume 100, no. 4 (November 2006), which is devoted to a history of the discipline. In particular, see "John S. Dryzek, "Revolutions without Enemies: Key Transformations in Political Science," ibid., 487–492, James N. Druckman, Donald P. Green, James H. Kuklinski, and Arthur Lupia, "The Growth and Development of Experimental Research in Political Science," ibid., 627–635. This same issue listed the most cited articles of all times.

13. Publications on political issues remains extensive in most of these countries, but for sensing trends in the kinds of information collected and assessed, see *European Political Science*, published since 2001.

14. Lowell, "The Psychology of Politics," 7.

15. Ibid., 8.

16. Paul Brace and Barbara Hinckley, *Follow the Leader: Opinion Polls and the Modern Presidents* (New York: Basic Books, 1992); Richard E. Neustadt, *Presidential Power and the Modern Presidents* (New York: Free Press, 1990); Seymour Sudman, "The Presidents and the Polls," *Public Opinion Quarterly* 46, no. 3 (Fall 1982): 301–310.

17. Tom W. Smith, "The First Straw: A Study of the Origins of Election Polls," ibid. 54, no. 1 (Spring 1990): 21–36.

18. On early polling, see Claude E. Robinson, *Straw Votes: A Study of Political Predictions* (New York: Columbia University Press, 1932); Adam J. Berinsky, Eleanor Neff Powell, Eric Schnickler, and Ian Brett Yohai, "Revisiting Public Opinion in the 1930s and 1940s," *Political Science & Politics* 44, no. 3 (July 2011): 516–520.

19. Peverill Squire, "Why the 1936 Literary Digest Poll Failed," *Public Opinion Quarterly* 52, no. 1 (Spring 1988): 125–133; Sharon L. Lohr and J. Michael Brick, "Roosevelt Predicted to Win: Revisiting the 1936 *Literary Digest* Poll," *Statistics, Politics and Policy* 8, no. 1 (2017): 65–84, and for a contemporary analysis, Archibald M. Crossley, "Straw Polls in 1936," *Public Opinion Quarterly* 1, no. 1 (January 1937): 24–35.

20. Harold F. Gosnell, "Technical Research: How Accurate Were the Polls?" ibid. 1, no. 1 (January 1937): 97–105; see also Floyd H. Allport, "Toward a Science of Public Opinion," ibid., 7–23.

21. George Horace Gallup (ed.), *The Gallup Poll: Public Opinion, 1935–1971*, 3 vols. (New York: Random House, 1972); there is no book-length biography of George Gallup, but for a useful short overview, see Alec Gallup and George H. Gallup Jr., "Gallup, George H.," in John G. Geer (ed.), *Public Opinion and Polling around the World: A Historical Encyclopedia* (Santa Barbara, CA: ABC-CLIO, 2004): Vol. 1, pp. 407–411.

22. Cortada, *All the Facts*, 168, 170–171.
23. Carl W. Brown Jr., "Roper, Elmo," in Geer, *Public Opinion and Polling around the World*, 447–451.
24. Jean M. Converse, *Survey Research in the United States: Roots and Emergence 1890–1960* (New York: Routledge, 2017): 113–124, *passim*.
25. Cortada, *All the Facts*, 168–171.
26. For bibliography on these methodological issues, Geer, *Public Opinion and Polling around the World*.
27. Howard Schuman, *Method and Meaning in Polls and Surveys* (Cambridge, MA: Harvard University Press, 2008): 10–138; Herbert F. Weisberg, "Total Survey Error," in Lonna Rae Atkeson and R. Michael Alvarez (eds.), *The Oxford Handbook of Polling and Survey Methods* (New York: Oxford University Press, 2018): 13–27; the entire volume is a superb source on all aspects of polling.
28. For example, see http://people-press.org/dataarchive (accessed October 28, 2020).
29. David J. Barber, *The Presidential Character: Predicting Performance in the White House* (Englewood Cliffs, NJ: Prentice-Hall, 1972); Paul Brace and Barbara Hinckley, *Follow the Leader: Opinion Polls and the Modern Presidents* (New York: Basic Books, 1992); Jeffrey E. Cohen, "The Polls: The Dynamics of Presidential Favorability, 1991–1998," *Presidential Studies Quarterly* 29 (1999): 896–902; John Mueller, "Presidential Popularity from Truman to Johnson," *American Political Science Review* 65 (1970): 18–34.
30. David Spiegelhalter, *The Art of Statistics: How to Learn From Data* (New York: Basic Books, 2019): 244–247.
31. For discussion of each and with useful bibliographies, see Geer, *Public Opinion and Polling around the World*.
32. Kenneth F. Warren, *In Defense of Public Opinion Polling* (Boulder, CO: Westview Press, 1992): 200–201.
33. "Response Rates—An Overview," *American Association for Public Opinion Research*, https://www.aapor.org/Education-Resources/For-Researchers/Poll-Survey-FAQ/Response-Rates-An-Overview.aspx (accessed October 28, 2020).
34. Galen A. Irwin and Joop J. M. Van Holsteyn, "Bandwagons, Underdogs, the Titanic and the Red Cross: The Influence of Public Opinion Polls on Voters," *Communications Presented at the 18th Congress of the International Political Science Association, Quebec* (2000): 1–5.
35. John T. Cacioppo and Richard E. Petty, *Attitudes and Persuasion: Classic and Contemporary Approaches* (London: Routledge, 1996, 2018): 125–162, 238–250.
36. For example, John C. Wahike, "Pre-Behavioralism in Political Science," *American Political Science Review* 73, no. 1 (March 1979): 9–31; Benjamin R. Knoll, Tyler J. O'Daniel, and Brian Cusato, "Physiological Responses and Political Behavior: Three Reproductions Using a Novel Dataset," *Research & Politics* 2, no. 4 (October 2015), available at https://journals.sagepub.com/doi/10.1177/2053168015621328# (accessed October 28, 2020).
37. In the spirit of transparency, my graduate training in modern history was heavily skewed toward diplomatic history, with both my MA thesis and PhD dissertation

dealing with Spanish and U.S. diplomatic history. I went on to write a half-dozen books on diplomatic history, and my father (James N. Cortada) was a U.S. Foreign Service Officer for thirty-two years. I continue to publish on the topic; see, for example, James W. Cortada, "The Information Ecosystems of National Diplomacy: The Case of Spain, 1815–1936," *Information and Culture: A Journal of History* 48, no. 2 (2013): 222–259. Much work was done in the 1800s to codify practices to such an extent that standard works often remained in print for over seventy-five years and appeared in multiple languages. See, for example, M. De Hoffmann, *Guide Diplomatique de Traite . . .*, 3 vols. (Brussels: Meline, Cans et Compagnie, 1838), and that was not even the first edition. On treaties, see P. Soler y Guardioloa, *Apuntes de Historia Politica y de los Tratados, 1490–1815* (Madrid: Librearia de Victoriano Suarez, 1895); F. S. Northedge and M. J. Grieve, *A Hundred Years of International Relations* (New York: Praeger, 1971).

38. U.S. Bureau of Labor Statistics, https://www.bls.gov/oes/2018/may/oes193094.htm (accessed October 28, 2020). The American Political Science Association claims to have 11,000 members from around the world from 100 countries, https://apsanet.org/ABOUT/About-APSA (accessed October 28, 2020).

39. William James Roosen, *The Age of Louis XIV: The Rise of Modern Diplomacy* (Cambridge, MA: Schenkman, 1976); Corneliu Bjola and Markus Komprobst, *Understanding International Diplomacy: Theory, Practice and Ethics*, 2nd ed. (London: Routledge, 2018); Joseph M. Siracusa, *Diplomacy: A Very Short Introduction* (New York: Oxford University Press, 2010).

40. Paul Sharp and Geoffrey Wiseman, *The Diplomatic Corps as an Institution of International Society* (New York: Palgrave Macmillan, 2007).

41. François De Callières, *The Practice of Diplomacy* (London: Constable & Co.,1919, originally published in 1716 as *De maniè de négocier avec les Souverains* [Amsterdam: La Compagnie]); Matthew S. Anderson, *The Rise of Modern Diplomacy, 1450–1919* London: Longman, 1993); Sir Harold George Nicolson, *The Evolution of Diplomatic Method* (New York: Praeger reprint, 1977, London: Constable, 1954); Abraham de Wicquefort, *The Ambassador and His Functions* (multiple editions in the 1700s in French) and a classic for over a century, Ernest Satow, *A Guide to Diplomatic Practice* (New York: Longmans, Green & Co., 1917).

42. Eula McDonald, "Highlights in the History of the United States Post at Barcelona, Spain, 1797–1959," *Cuadernos de la Historia Económica de Cataluña* (1969–1970): 21–63; James W. Cortada (ed.), *A City in War: American Views on Barcelona and the Spanish Civil War, 1936–39* (Wilmington, DE: Scholarly Resources, 1985).

43. A widely consulted "user manual" by diplomats, R. P. Barston, *Modern Diplomacy*, 5th ed. (New York: Routledge, 2019).

44. A classic short text, Harold Nicolson, *Diplomacy* (Oxford: Oxford University Press, 1936) was still in print late in the twentieth century; James Crawford, *Brownlie's Principles of Public International Law*, 9th ed. (Oxford: Oxford University Press, 2019), especially Section 6, beginning on p. 353.

45. Examples drawn from the private collection of James W. Cortada, *Tratado para la continuacion y renovacion de paz y amistad entre las Corinas de España y la*

Gran Bretaña (Madrid: Imprenta de Domingue Garcia Morras, 1667), *The Treaty of Peace, Union, Friendship and Mutual Defense between the Crowns of Great-Britain, France, and Spain* (Dublin: S. Powell, 1729); *A Treaty of Peace between the United States and Spain* (Washington, D.C.: Government Printing Office, 1899), but signed December 10, 1898; *Tratado CEE y Acta Unica Europea* (Madrid: Closas-Orcoyyen, 1992).

46. Some of these libraries are magnificent. For example, the American Embassy in Teheran, Iran, had developed what reputedly was one of the finest collections on Iran (Persian) history during the early twentieth century, only to have it destroyed when Iranian radicals occupied the facility in November 1979.

47. For example, the British Foreign Office was established in 1782, the Spanish Ministerio de Estado earlier in the century, and the Quai d'Orsay in France in 1547, each with a library. Each also maintained large archives of diplomatic correspondence, most of which were transferred to national archives after World War II, Daniel H. Thomas and Lynn Marshall Case (eds.), *The New Guide to Diplomatic Archives of Western Europe* (Philadelphia: University of Pennsylvania Press, 1975). A series of guides were published in the 1990s by country, "Guides to European Diplomatic History and Research" by Rowman & Littlefield.

48. The U.S. Congress made such requests on Spanish relations over three dozen times in the nineteenth century. On the war with Spain in 1898, see *Message of the President of the United States Communicated to the Two Houses of Congress on the Relations of the United States to Spain by Reason of Warfare in the Island of Cuba*, 55th Congress, ed. Session, Document No. 405 (Washington, D.C.: Government Printing Office, 1895).

49. They can represent an extraordinarily valuable source of information to public officials. In the early 1970s I discovered a collection of documents sent to the Spanish parliament (Cortes) explaining how Spain became involved in transporting and supporting militarily France's invasion in the late 1850s of what eventually became known as Vietnam, an action lost to history until the discovery of these papers, James W. Cortada, "Spain and the French Invasion of Cochinchina," *Journal of Politics and History* 20, no. 3 (December 1974): 335–345; and "Spain and Cochinchina, 1858–1863," *Rivista Di Studi Politici Internazionali* 42, no. 3 (August–September 1975): 392–398.

50. Like so many great scholars working in the United States in the twentieth century, he was Jewish, German-born, and moved to the United States in the 1930s. His AB, MA, and PhDs were in political science from Harvard University (College for the AB). His many publications on international affairs were largely histories, and his teaching at Harvard focused on international affairs within the Department of Government. While many books and articles have been written about him, his own publications add to our understanding of the craft of diplomacy and the information diplomats used, Henry Kissinger, *Diplomacy* (New York: Simon & Schuster, 1994); and with Winston Lord, *Kissinger on Kissinger: Reflections on Diplomacy, Grand Strategy, and Leadership* (New York: Allpointsbooks, 2019), especially 1–12, 101–138.

51. Andreas D. Boldt, *The Life and Work of the German Historian Leopold von Ranke (1795–1886): An Assessment of His Achievements* (Lewiston, NY: Edwin

Mellen Press, 2015); and his, *Leopold von Ranke: A Biography* (London: Routledge, 2019); Felix Gilbert, "Historiography: What Ranke Meant," *The American Scholar* 56, no. 3 (1987): 393–397; Georg Iggers, "The Image of Ranke in American and German Historical Thought," *History and Theory* 2, no. 1 (1962): 17–40; Iggers and J. M. Powell (eds.), *Leopold von Ranke and the Shaping of the Historical Discipline* (Syracuse, NY: Syracuse University Press, 1990); Leonard Krieger, *Ranke: The Meaning of History* (Chicago, IL: University of Chicago Press, 1977). Ranke never published a monograph on how to conduct historical research. On his cult-like influence on American historians, see Novick, *That Noble Dream*, 21–31.

52. Jacques Barzun and Henry F. Graff, *The Modern Researcher* (New York: Harcourt, Brace & World, 1957): 187. This was a standard text that many thousands of graduate students in history were required to study in the United States. In my own copy from an undergraduate course in history, I scribbled on the title page in 1967: "Well written, excellent, practical!"

53. Ibid.

54. Novick, *The Noble Dream*, 33.

55. The term, crucial to understand for its centrality in the belief systems of historians, is difficult to translate, but Novick has explained it better I believe than any other English-writing scholar, Novick, *The Noble Dream*, 24–26.

56. Raphael Samuel, *Theatres of Memory: Past and Present in Contemporary Culture* (London: Verso, 1994, 2012): 197.

57. Richard Evans, *In Defense of History* (London: Granta Books, 2000): 17.

58. G. Kitson Clark, *The Making of Victorian England* (London: Routledge, 1962): 14.

59. Michael J. Salevouris and Conal Furay, *The Methods and Skills of History: A Practical Guide*, 4th ed. (Oxford: John Wiley & Sons, 2015): 13–26, 169–178; Simon Gunn and Lucy Faire (eds.), *Research Methods for History* (Edinburgh University Press, 2012); William H. McDowell, *Historical Research: A Guide for Writers of Dissertations, Theses, Articles and Books* (New York: Routledge, 2013): 1–26, 39–76, 109–125, 155–169; Martha Howell and Walter Prevenier, *From Reliable Sources: An Introduction to Historical Methods* (Ithaca, NY: Cornell University Press, 2001): 17–42, 69–87, 146–150.

60. For example, James M. McPherson, *Abraham Lincoln* (New York: Oxford University Press, 2009).

61. University of Chicago Press Editorial Staff, *The Chicago Manual of Style*, 17th ed. (Chicago, IL: University of Chicago Press, 2017).

62. Years after writing my dissertation, I wrote a history of that project that demonstrates the role of documents, citations, filtering and analyzing information, James W. Cortada, *History Hunting: A Guide for Fellow Adventurers* (Armonk, NY: M. E. Sharpe, 2012): 27–56; see also John Lewis Gaddis, *The Landscape of History: How Historians Map the Past* (New York: Oxford University Press, 2002).

63. As a bit of context, in the nineteenth century the most influential scholars in the West trained in England, Italy, France, and at various German universities across all disciplines of the day, from science and medicine to philosophy and history. An American wanting a fine graduate education studied in Europe, especially in

Germany, where many scholarly innovations were being developed that they brought back to the United States.

64. National Archives, "Presidential Libraries," https://www.archives.gov/presidential-libraries/about/history.html (accessed October 28, 2020); Christian A. Nappo, *Presidential Libraries and Museums* (Lanham, MD: Rowman & Littlefield, 2018), which includes the descriptions of other presidential collections not housed in formal presidential libraries.

65. "Charles Babbage Institute Collections," http://www.cbi.umn.edu/collections/index.html (accessed October 28, 2020).

66. "List of Archives in the United States," *Wikipedia*, https://en.wikipedia.org/wiki/List_of_archives_in_the_United_States (accessed April 28, 2020); Michael Duchein, "The History of European Archives and the Development of the Archival Profession in Europe," *The American Archivist* 55, no. 1, Special International Issue (Winter 1992): 14–25.

67. Robert A. Caro, *The Years of Lyndon Johnson: The Path to Power* (New York: Alfred A. Knopf, 1982), *Means of Ascent* (New York: Alfred A. Knopf, 1990), *Master of the Senate* (New York: Alfred A. Knopf, 2002), and *The Passage of Power* (New York: Alfred A. Knopf, 2012).

68. He also added extensively to the corpus of new information—oral histories, which he discusses in his short volume, Robert A. Caro, *Working: Researching, Interviewing, Writing* (New York: Alfred A. Knopf, 2019). The LBJ Library, Cato's primary source of archival materials, houses 45 million pages of documents, 650,000 photographs, 5,000 hours of recordings, and some 2,000 oral history interviews, LBJ Presidential Library, http://www.lbjlibrary.org/research (accessed October 28, 2020).

69. Peter Novick, *That Noble Dream: The "Objectivity" Question and the American Historical Profession* (Cambridge, UK: Cambridge University Press, 1988): 281–319.

70. William Aspray and I have studied the general problem and specifically the cases of both presidential assassinations, James W. Cortada and William Aspray, *Fake News Nation: The Long History of Lies and Misinterpretations in America* (Lanham, MD: Rowman & Littlefield, 2019): 53–88; and on the problem of false information on the Internet, see William Aspray and James W. Cortada, *From Urban Legends to Political Fact-Checking: Online Scrutiny in America, 1990–2015* (Cham, Switzerland: Springer-Verlag, 2019).

71. For details, https://www.oralhistory.org/about/do-oral-history/ (accessed October 29, 2020).

72. Quoted at ibid.

73. The standard work in the field is by Donald A. Ritchie, *Doing Oral History* (New York: Oxford University Press, 2002, 2015); but see also Barbara Sommer, *The Oral History Manual*, 3rd ed. (Lanham, MD: Rowman & Littlefield, 2018); Thomas L. Charlton (ed.), *History of Oral History: Foundations and Methodology* (Lanham, MD: Rowman & Littlefield, 2007): 95–124; Lynn Abrams, *Oral History Theory*, 2nd ed. (New York: Routledge, 2016): 18–32; Ronald E. Doel, "Oral History of American Science: A Forty-Year Review," *History of Science* 41, no. 4 (2003):

349–378: Patricia Leavy, *Oral History: Understanding Qualitative Research* (New York: Oxford University Press, 2011).

74. Abrams, *Oral History Theory*, 18.

75. Sommer, *The Oral History Manual*, 11–30; Ronald J. Grele et al., *Envelopes of Sound: The Art of Oral History* (Westport, CT: Praeger, 1991).

76. Thomas J. Misa and Jeffrey R. Yost, *FastLane: Managing Science in the Internet World* (Baltimore, MD: Johns Hopkins University Press, 2016).

77. "Search CBI Oral Histories," http://www.cbi.umn.edu/oh/, "Oral and Videohistory Collections," http://siarchives.si.edu/research/oralvidhistory_intro.html (both accessed October 29, 2020); but other major collections can be found in the United States at the Library of Congress and at most major research universities.

78. Akemi Kikimura, "Family Life Histories, a Collaborative Venture," in Robert Perks and Alistar Thomson (eds.), *The Oral History Reader* (London: Routledge, 1998): 140–144); Linda Barnickel, *Oral History for the Family Historian: A Basic Guide* (No City: Oral History Association, 2010); Laurie Mercier and Madeline Buckendorf, *Using Oral History in Community History Projects* (No City: Oral History Association, 2007).

79. Francesco Boldizzoni, *The Poverty of Clio: Resurrecting Economic History* (Princeton, NJ: Princeton University Press, 2011); Giovanni Federico Martina Cioni, and Michelngelo Vasta, "The Long-term Evolution of Economic History: Evidence from the Top Five Field Journals (1927–2017)," *Cliometrica* 14 (2020): 1–39; John S. Lyons, Louis P. Cain, and Samuel H. Williamson (eds.), *Reflections on the Cliometrics Revolution: Conversations with Economic Historians* (London: Routledge, 2008).

80. Traditionally attributed to Douglas North and William Parker after they took over the editorship of the *Journal of Economic History*.

81. For the press release announcing the award on October 12, 1993, see https://www.nobelprize.org/prizes/economic-sciences/1993/press-release/ (accessed October 29, 2020). It specifically cited their work in "having renewed research in economic history by applying economic theory and quantitative methods in order to explain economic and institutional change." Further, "They were pioneers in the branch of economic history that has been called the 'new economic history," or cliometrics, i.e., research that combines economic theory, quantitative methods, hypothesis testing, counterfactual alternatives and traditional techniques of economic history, to explain economic growth and decline," ibid.

82. For a discussion of the criticisms and defense of cliometrics, see Arthur M. Diamond Jr., "Age and Acceptance of Cliometrics," *The Journal of Economic History* 40, no. 4 (December 1980): 838–841; Claude Diebolt, "The Cliometric Framework," *Historical Social Research/Historische Sozialforschung* 26, nos. 2/3 (1996–97): 250–254; John R. Meyer, "Notes on Cliometrics' Fortieth," *The American Economic Review* 87, no. 2, Papers and Proceedings of the Hundred and Fourth Annual Meeting of the American Economic Association (May 1997): 409–411.

83. *Historical Methods* is a useful journal to monitor to gauge changes in how historians work and what new types of information they produce.

84. Ian Morris, *The Measure of Civilization: How Social Development Decides the Fate of Nations* (Princeton, NJ: Princeton University Press, 2013): 3.

85. Ibid.

86. Stevens, Mille-Idriss, and Shami, *Seeing the World*, 93.

87. "AHR Conversation," Historical Perspectives on the Circulation of Information," *American Historical Review* 116, no. 5 (December 2011): 1393–1435; for a collection of seminal articles on this topic, *Information & Culture: A Journal of History* 54, no. 1 (2019).

88. I have participated in that discussion, James W. Cortada, "Shaping Information History as an Intellectual Discipline," *Information & Culture,* 47, no. 2 (2012): 119–144.

89. "AHR Conversation."

90. Ibid., 1429.

91. *Information & Culture: A Journal of History* 54, no. 1 (2019).

92. Ciaran B. Trace, "Curated Issue of *Information & Culture: A Journal of History*," ibid., 2.

93. Ibid., 3.

94. Ibid.

95. Many examples of this realization could be cited, but I settle for one to make the point, Michael E. Hobart and Zachary S. Schiffman, *Information Ages: Literacy, Numeracy, and the Computer Revolution* (Baltimore, MD: Johns Hopkins University Press, 1998).

96. The explosion of new information and its diffusion resulted in some one million books being published during the second half of the 1400s, Lucien Febvre and Henri-Jean Martin, *The Coming of the Book: The Impact of Printing 1450–1800* (London: Verso, 1997), a history that includes information about subject matters and that has been in continuous print for decades as a popular history written by two of the most respected French historians of the twentieth century.

97. William Aspray (ed.), *Chasing Moore's Law: Information Technology Policy in the United States* (Raleigh, NC: SciTech Publishing, 2004); and with Paul Ceruzzi (eds.), *The Internet and American Business* (Cambridge, MA: MIT Press, 2008); Aspray and Cortada, *From Urban Legends to Political Fact-Checking*; Aspray (ed.), *Historical Studies in Computing, Information, and Society* (Berlin: Springer-Verlag, 2020). This last volume combines papers on information and computing, all prepared by historians who spent the bulk of their careers studying the history of information technologies.

98. Parson E. Tillinghast, *The Specious Past: Historians and Others* (Reading, MA: Addison-Wesley, 1972): 61.

99. Adam Crymble, *Technology and the Historian: Transformations in the Digital Age* (Urbana: University of Illinois Press, 2021): 1.

100. Ibid., 9.

101. Ibid., 62.

102. Ibid., 62–63.

103. Quoted in C. W. Smith, *Carl Becker: On History and the Climate of Opinion* (Ithaca, NY: Cornell University Press, 1956): 117.

104. Matthew D. Lieberman, "Intuition: A Social Cognitive Neuroscience Approach," *Psychological Bulletin* 126, no. 1 (2000): 109–137; defined, J. Bruner, *The Process of Education* (Cambridge, MA: Harvard University Press, 1960): 57.

105. Helen Walker Puner, *Sigmund Freud: His Life and Mind* (New York: Dell Publishers, 1961); 197–20; see also Gary Klein, *Intuition at Work* (New York: Random House, 2003).

106. On the experience of the historians, Novick, *That Noble Dream*, 47–85.

107. Elton, *The Practice of History*, 73–83. The subsequent few pages on imagination are thought-provoking too with respect to shaping information and are worth the time to read, 83–87.

108. Italics in original quote, McNabb, *Research Methods for Political Science*, 13. For a useful survey of the status of research and information in political science, see ibid., 34–46, and for an update on the growing influence of behavioralist research and information, see the second edition (New York: Routledge, 2016): 3–14.

109. Harry C. Boyte, "The Struggle against Positivism," *Academe* 86 (July–August 2000): 49.

110. For the quote, McNabb, *Research Methods for Political Science*, 31.

111. James Surowiecki, *The Wisdom of Crowds: Why the Many Are Smarter than the Few and How Collective Wisdom Shapes Business, Economies, Societies and Nations* (New York: Doubleday, 2004).

112. Ibid., explained by just reading his first chapter. The bulk of the book comprises interesting case studies.

10. HOW INFORMATION EVOLVED

1. Harry G. Frankfurt, *On Truth* (Princeton, NJ: Princeton University Press, 2017): 34.

2. For an excellent example based on biology, beginning with European developments and eventually included North American ones, see Michael Morange, *A History of Biology* (Princeton, NJ: Princeton University Press, 2021).

3. Jürgen Renn, *The Evolution of Knowledge: Rethinking Science for the Anthropocene* (Princeton, NJ: Princeton University Press, 2020): 221.

4. Judit Bar-Ilan, "Informetrics at the Beginning of the 21st Century—A Review," *Journal of Informetrics* 2 (2008): 1–52.

5. Ibid., 34.

6. I expand on this phenomenon elsewhere, so no need to do so again here, James W. Cortada, *Living with Computers: The Digital World of Today and Tomorrow* (Cham, Switzerland: Springer, 2020).

7. David Spiegelhalter, *The Art of Statistics: How to Learn From Data* (New York: Basic Books, 2019): 379.

8. On people still in charge and what they are doing about managing information, Alex Pentland, *Social Physics: How Good Ideas Spread—The Lessons from a New Science* (New York: Penguin, 2014).

9. César Hidalgo, *Why Information Grows: The Evolution of Order, From Atoms to Economies* (New York: Basic Books, 2015): ix.

10. Ibid., xv.

11. Ibid., 181.

12. For my most extensive discussion of this issue, see James W. Cortada, *All the Facts: A History of Information in the United States since 1870* (New York: Oxford University Press, 2016): 1–47.

13. Peter Burke, *What Is the History of Knowledge?* (Cambridge, UK: Polity Press, 2016): 46.

14. For an introduction to its concepts, Kimiz Dalkir, *Knowledge Management in Theory and Practice* (Cambridge, MA: MIT Press, 2017): 1–36; Donald Hislop, Rachelle Bosua, and Remko Helms, *Knowledge Management in Organizations: A Critical Introduction*, 4th ed. (New York: Oxford University Press, 2013): 49–67. There are well over 7,000 books on this topic as of 2020.

15. For examples, James W. Cortada and John A. Woods (eds.), *The Knowledge Management Yearbook, 1999–2000* (Boston, MA: Butterworth-Heinemann, 1999) and their *Knowledge Management Yearbook, 2000–2001* (Boston, MA: Butterworth-Heinemann, 2000).

16. There is a massive literature on how to manage institutional change, but far less about the problems associated with one's personal experience becoming outdated with respect to the management of and personal use of information emanating from prior experience.

17. Not sure if this observation has meaning, but I came to this same idea years before reading Page's description.

18. Scott E. Page, *The Model Thinker: What You Need to Know to Make Data Work for You* (New York: Basic Books, 2018): 13.

19. It combined multiple images into databases that were then reconfigured—collated—into one image, Ota Luz, "How Scientists Capture the First Image of a Black Hole," *Teachable Moments*, April 19, 2019 (Jet Propulsion Laboratory, California Institute of Technology), https://www.jpl.nasa.gov/edu/news/2019/4/19/how-scientists-captured-the-first-image-of-a-black-hole/; Dennis Overbye, "Darkness Visible, Finally: Astronomers Capture First Ever Image of A Black Hole," *New York Times*, April 10, 2019, https://www.nytimes.com/2019/04/10/science/black-hole-picture.html (both accessed June 15, 2020).

20. This is a slight variation of a well-known ideas attributed to American novelist F. Scott Fitzgerald, who wrote in 1936, but republished in a collection of essays by him, *The Crack-Up*, that it required a smart person "to hold two opposed ideas in the mind at the same time, and still retain the ability to function." For this quote, see Matt Blumberg, "First Rate Intelligence," *Business Insider*, April 28, 2011, https://www.businessinsider.com/first-rate-intelligence-2011-4 (accessed June 15, 2020). The full quote is: "The test of a first-rate intelligence is the ability to hold two opposed ideas in the mind at the same time, and still retain the ability to function," published in "The Crackup," *Esquire* (February 1936).

21. I include an extensive bibliography on this topic in James W. Cortada, *Digital Flood: The Diffusion of Information Technology Across the U.S., Europe, and Asia* (New York: Oxford University Press, 2012): 733–768, and the classic historians always begin with Everett M. Rogers, *Diffusion of Innovations*, 5th ed. (New York: Oxford University Press, 2003).

22. Thomas S. Kuhn, *The Structure of Scientific Revolutions* (Chicago, IL: University of Chicago Press, 1962, 4th ed. 2012).

23. Daniel Clery, "Tens of Thousands of Communications Satellites Could Spoil View of Giant Sky Telescope," *Science*, February 27, 2020, https://www.sciencemag.org/news/2020/02/tens-thousands-communications-satellites-could-spoil-view-giant-sky-telescope; Alan Boyle, "5 Trillion Bytes a Day: SpaceX Engineers Flash Some Facts about Starlink Satellites," *GeekWire*, June 8, 2020, https://www.geekwire.com/2020/5-trillion-bytes-day-spacex-engineers-flash-facts-starlink-satellites/ (both accessed June 15, 2020).

24. Using computer science as an example, instances of founding dates of its societies demonstrate the links with the emergence of the field: Association for Computing Machinery (1947), Data Processing Management Association (1949), IEEE Computer Society (1951), Society for Computer Simulation (1952), SHARE (1955), GUIDE (1956), Joint Users Group (late 1950s), and International Federation for Information Processing (1960). As new subfields of computing formed in subsequent decades, the pattern continued to the present.

25. Robert B. Townsend, *History's Babel: Scholarship, Professionalization, and the Historical Enterprise in the United States, 1880–1940* (Chicago, IL: University of Chicago Press, 2013); Ian Tyrell, *The Practice of American History, 1890–1970* (Chicago, IL: University Press of Chicago, 2005); James W. Cortada, "A Perspective on *Perspectives*," *AHA Perspectives* (December 2012): 1–4.

26. Guy Crosby, *Cook, Taste, Learn: How the Evolution of Science Transformed the Art of Cooking* (New York: Columbia University Press, 2009): 103.

27. For examples, see America's Test Kitchen, which has published extensively this genre of books, such as *Just Add Sauce: A Revolutionary Guide to Boosting the Flavor of Everything You Cook* (Boston, MA: America's Test Kitchen, 2018) and its *What Good Cooks Know* (Boston, MA: America's Test Kitchen, 2016); J. Kenji López-Alt, *The Food Lab: Better Home Cooking through Science* (New York: W. W. Norton, 2015). Some linked tightly to medical information, such as Alicia A. Romano and the Editors of America's Test Kitchen, *Cook for Your Gut Health: Quiet Your Gut, Boost Fiber, and Reduce Inflammation* (Boston, MA: America's Text Kitchen, 2021).

28. Mitchell L. Stevens, Cynthia Miller-Idriss, and Steteney Shami, *Seeing the World: How US Universities Make Knowledge in a Global Era* (Princeton, NJ: Princeton University Press, 2018): 6.

29. Morange, *A History of Biology*, 373–374.

30. John Kenneth Galbraith, *The Age of Uncertainty* (Boston, MA: Houghton Mifflin Harcourt, 1977).

31. Originally from *The Age of Uncertainty*, but should be read as part of a broader set of reprinted articles and chapters he wrote on a broad set of related issues, John Kenneth Galbraith, *The Essential Galbraith*, edited by Andrea D. Williams (Boston, MA: Houghton Mifflin, 2001): 224; Angus Burgin, "Age of Certainty: Galbraith, Friedman, and the Public Life of Economic Ideas," in Tiago Mata and Steven G. Medema (eds.), *History of Political Economy*, special volume on *The Economist as Public Intellectual* (Durham, NC: Duke University Press, 2013): 191–219.

32. Thaddus E. Weckowicz, "Ludwig von Bertalanffy (1901–1972): A Pioneer of General Systems Theory," *University of Alberta Center for Systems Research*, CSR

Working Paper No. 89–2 (2000), but originally published in 1989. This paper begins with the statement, "Ludwig von Bertalanffy, a distinguished biologist, occupies an important position in the intellectual history of the twentieth century. His contributions went beyond biology, and extended to psychology, psychiatry, sociology, cybernetics, history, and philosophy. Some of his admirers even believe that von Bertalanffy's general systems theory could provide a conceptual framework for all these disciplines," p. 2, available at http://www.richardjung.cz/bert1.pdf (accessed June 16, 2020).

33. At least, one might argue, until AI and the computers took over the world.

34. Ludwig von Bertalanffy, *General System Theory: Foundations, Developments, Applications* (New York: Braziller, 1968).

35. For two informative sources, see "Systems Theory," and "Ludwig von Bertalanffy," both in *Wikipedia*. Ludwig von Bertalanffy, *General Systems Theory: Foundations, Development, Applications* (New York: George Brazitter, 1968); Iniklas Luhmann, *Introduction to Systems Theory* (Oxford: Polity, 2013).

36. Lars Skyttner, *General Systems Theory: Problems, Perspectives, Practices* (Singapore: World Scientific, 2005): v.

37. Ibid., 41.

38. Ibid., 110–204.

39. Page, *The Model Thinker*, 118.

40. Quoted in Ibid., 117; but see her book too, Anne Marie Slaughter, *The Chessboard and the Web: Strategies of Connection in a Networked World* (New Haven, CT: Yale University Press, 2017).

41. Skyttner, *General Systems Theory*, 485.

42. Robert Lilienfeld, *The Rise of Systems Theory* (New York: John Wiley, 1978).

43. Already in the seventeenth century, the intellectual elites were complaining of information overloads and fragmentation into specialties.

44. Morange, *A History of Biology*, 282.

45. Harry G. Frankfurt, *On Bullshit* (Princeton, NJ: Princeton University Press, 2005): 62.

46. Ibid., 63.

47. For example, "Jimmy Kimmel Live," https://www.youtube.com/watch?v=umpalMtQE50, and see his "Lie Witness News" https://www.youtube.com/watch?v=bbiutHXmd9o (both accessed June 16, 2020).

48. One can read about this in "Pizzagate Conspiracy Theory," *Wikipedia* (accessed June 16, 2020). The story presented by this source is lengthy and buttressed with ninety-one references. The original incident occurred in 2016, but there remains sufficient interest that this entry was updated as recently as May 21, 2020; Whitney Phillips, "You're Fake News: The Problem with Accusations of Falsehood," in Melissa Zimdars and Kembrew McLeod (eds.), *Fake News: Understanding Media and Misinformation in the Digital Age* (Cambridge, MA: MIT Press, 2020): 55–69.

49. "'We Conclude' or 'I Believe?' Study Finds Rationality Declined Decades Ago" (January 12, 2022), https://phys.org/news/2022-01-rationality-declined-decades.html (accessed January 13, 2022), based on Martin Scheffer et al., "The Rise and Fall of Rationality in Language," *Proceedings of the National Academy of Science* (2021), 118, no. 51, pp. 1–8.

50. Colin Koopman, *How We Became Our Data: A Genealogy of the Informational Person* (Chicago, IL: University of Chicago Press, 2019).

51. Andrew Clark et al., *The Origins of Happiness: The Science of Well-Being over the Life Course* (Princeton, NJ: Princeton University Press, 2018): 33–152; Yew-Kwang Ng and Lok Sang Ho (eds.), *Happiness and Public Policy: Theory, Case Studies and Implications* (New York: Palgrave Macmillan, 2006): 193–208, 237–252.

52. The United Nations has sponsored such studies since the 1970s, but with respect to the United States, America's Climate Choices Panel on Limiting the Magnitude of Climate Changes, Board on Atmospheric Sciences and Climate, Division on Earth and Life Sciences, and National Research Council, *Limiting the Magnitude of Future Climate Changes* (Washington, D.C.: National Academic Press, 2010); United Nations, "Flagship UN Study Shows Accelerating Climate Change on Land, Sea and the Atmosphere," *UN News*, March 10, 2020, https://news.un.org/en/story/2020/03/1059061 (accessed June 19, 2020).

53. Diane Coyle, *GDP: A Brief but Affectionate History* (Princeton, NJ: Princeton University Press, 2014): 137–138.

54. Renn, *The Evolution of Knowledge*, 398.

55. Michael E. Porter, *Competitive Strategy: Techniques for Analyzing Industries and Competitors* (New York: Free Press, 1980); Clayton Christensen, *The Innovator's Dilemma: When New Technologies Cause Great Firms to Fail* (Boston, MA: Harvard Business School Press, 1997): 187–206; *Strategic Change* (New York: IBM Institute for Business Value, 2003).

56. James W. Cortada and Heather E. Fraser, "Mapping the Future in Science-intensive Industries: Lessons from the Pharmaceutical Industry," *IBM Systems Journal* 40, no. 1 (2005): 163–183.

57. Ibid.

58. Carl Zimmer, "How You Should Read Coronavirus Studies, or Any Scientific Paper," *New York Times*, June 1, 2020, https://nyti.ms/3doJ9S3 (accessed June 12, 2020).

59. Ibid.

60. Ibid.

61. In June two articles were retracted that had appeared in the prestigious *New England Journal of Medicine* and *The Lancet*, due to flaws and hasty reviews, Roni Caryn Rabin, "The Pandemic Claims New Victims: Prestigious Medical Journals," *New York Times*, June 16, 2020, https://www.nytimes.com/2020/06/14/health/virus-journals.html (accessed June 16, 2020).

62. Both quotes, Zimmer, "How You Should Read Coronavirus Studies, or Any Scientific Paper."

63. Colin Koopman, *How We Became Our Data: A Genealogy of the Informational Person* (Chicago, IL: University of Chicago Press, 2019): 2019): vii.

64. Ibid., 5.

65. "What Is a 'Healthy' Food? The F.D.A. Wants to Change the Definition," *New York Times*, September 30, 2022, https://www.nytimes.com/2022/09/29/well/fda-healthy-food.html.

For Further Reading

Information as a topic of discussion has a rapidly growing body of literature coming from many academic disciplines. The purpose of this bibliographic essay is to provide useful, but curated, selection of materials for further reading. It favors books that take a largely historical orientation and that are readily available and in English. These are organized largely by chapter topics for convenience. For specific citations to articles and online sources consult the endnotes.

DEFINITIONS AND ATTRIBUTES

For an introduction to what is information and about its various forms, see Luciano Floridi, *Information: A Very Short Introduction* (Oxford: Oxford University Press, 2010). To get quickly to the problem of having too much information see Evgeny Morozov, *To Save Everything, Click Here* (New York: Public Affairs, 2013), but also on Big Data and its issues, see Lisa Gitelman, ed., *"Raw Data" Is an Oxymoron* (Cambridge, MA: MIT Press, 2013), and a gorgeous book, Rick Smolan and Jennifer Erwitt, *The Human Face of Big Data* (Sausalito, CA: Against All Odds Productions, 2012). Other introductions to information, often with a similar emphasis on information almost as an object, are Jorge Reina Schement and Terry Curtis, *Tendencies and Tensions in the Information Age: The Production and Distribution of Information in the United States* (New Brunswick, NJ: Transaction Publishers, 1995); Toni Weller, *Information History in the Modern World: Histories of the Information Age* (New York: Palgrave, 2011) and her earlier book, *Information History—An Introduction: Exploring an Emerging Field* (New York: Neal-Schuman, 2008). Most influential on my thinking for many years, however, was the work of the late economist Fritz Machlup, through a half-dozen books he wrote on the subject, the most influential of which were *Knowledge: Its Creation, Distribution, and Economic Significance: Knowledge and Knowledge Production* (Princeton, NJ: Princeton University Press, 1980) and the sequel to an earlier book put together by his students after his death, Michael Rogers Rubin, Mary Taylor Huber, and Elizabeth Lloyd Taylor, *The Knowledge Industry in the United States, 1960–1980* (Princeton, NJ: Princeton University Press, 1986). For an introductory overview of how information is used today in business, see James W. Cortada, *Information and the Modern Corporation* (Cambridge, MA: MIT Press, 2011). On the economics of information, the most recent study is Joseph E. Stiglitz and Bruce C. Greenwald, *Creating a Learning Society: A New Approach to Growth, Development, and Social Progress* (New York: Columbia University Press, 2014). For a detailed discussion of the attributes of information, see the several chapters of James W. Cortada, *All the Facts: A History of Information in the United States since 1870* (New York: Oxford University Press, 2016).

Numeracy as an important form of information has recently been the subject of considerable attention. Useful examples of this literature include Ian Ayres, *Super Crunchers: Why Thinking-by-Numbers Is the New Way to Be Smart* (New York: Bantam Books, 2007) and Thomas H. Davenport and Jeanne G. Harris, *Competing on Analytics: The New Science of Winning* (Boston, MA: Harvard Business School Press, 2007). Two studies on the history of codifying information are particularly useful, David R. Headrick, *When Information Came of Age: Technologies of Knowledge in the Age of Reason and Revolution, 1700–1850* (New York: Oxford University Press, 2000); Markus Krajewski, *Paper Machines: About Cards and Catalogs, 1548–1929* (Cambridge, MA: MIT Press, 2011). For other useful discussions of these themes, there is a variety of materials, including Williamson Murray and Richard Hart Sinnreich, eds., *The Past as Prologue: The Importance of History to the Military Profession* (Cambridge, UK: Cambridge University Press, 2006); Mary Poovey, *A History of the Modern Fact: Problems of Knowledge in the Sciences of Wealth and Society* (Chicago: University of Chicago Press, 1998); Adrian Johns, *The Nature of the Book: Print and Knowledge in the Making* (Chicago: University of Chicago Press, 1998). For a scholarly review of the bibliography on the nature of its uses, see Donald Case, *Looking for Information: A Survey of Research on Information Seeking, Needs, and Behavior* (Bingley, UK: Emerald Group, 2012).

Charles Van Doren started the modern discussion of information versus knowledge with *A History of Knowledge* (New York: Citadel, 1991 edition). Do not overlook a useful article, M. K. Buckland, "Information as Thing," *Journal of the American Society for Information Science* 42, no. 5 (1991): 351–360. One recent publication that I had enormous difficulty understanding, because of its focus on technical issues, is James Gleick, *The Information* (New York: Pantheon, 2011). It is widely available and, therefore, should be recognized as an addition to our understanding of the nature of information, most specifically about information science. Also useful, and more focused on social and humanistic concerns, is Bonnie A. Nardi and Vicki L. O'Day, *Information Ecologies: Using Technology with Heart* (Cambridge, MA: MIT Press, 1999). An older book still useful is Alexandra Oleson and John Voss, *The Organization of Knowledge in Modern America, 1860–1920* (Baltimore, MD: Johns Hopkins University Press, 1979). No sequel was published. Finally, there is a magnificent study of early uses of information that can serve as a model for studies of the American scene, Jeremy Black, *The Power of Knowledge: How Information and Technology Made the Modern World* (New Haven, CT: Yale University Press, 2014), which covers many centuries and countries. A philosopher weighs in with useful case studies from the twentieth century, helpful in understanding how individuals are collections of information that shape their identity, Colin Koopman, *How We Became Our Data: A Genealogy of the Informational Person* (Chicago, IL: University Of Chicago Press, 2019).

For the best introduction to the theories of information societies, consult Frank Webster, *Theories of the Information Society*, 3rd ed. (London: Routledge, 2006). Linked to all of these kinds of discussions are economic ones, and for that begin with Brian Kahin and Dominique Foray, eds., *Advancing Knowledge and the Knowledge Economy* (Cambridge, MA: MIT Press, 2006). A team of scholars began exploring this supply side of information in a series of chapters in Alfred D. Chandler Jr. and James W. Cortada, eds., *A Nation Transformed by Information: How Information Has Shaped the United States from Colonial Times to the Present* (New York: Oxford University Press, 2000), which also includes an extensive bibliographic essay on these themes. On the role of networks, much has been published. I found useful Yochai Benkler, *The Wealth of Networks: How Social Production Transforms Markets and Freedom* (New Haven, CT: Yale University Press, 2006); Ramesh Subramanian and Eddan Katz, eds., *The Global Flow of Information: Legal, Social, and Cultural Perspectives* (New York: New York University Press, 2011). The giant in this topic is Manuel Castells, who has published extensively on the subject. For a useful summation of his ideas, see his *Communication Power* (Oxford: Oxford University Press, 2013). Finally, for a short tightly constructed discussion, see Michael Buckland, *Information and Society* (Cambridge, MA: MIT Press, 2017) and its useful bibliography.

Because professions have so much information embedded in their core, their role is crucial to understand. For that, begin with the leading expert on professions, Andrew Abbott, *The System of Professions: An Essay on the Division of Expert Labor* (Chicago: University of Chicago Press, 1988), followed by a reading of Eliot Freidson, *Professional Powers: A Study of the Institutionalization of Formal Knowledge* (Chicago: University of Chicago Press, 1986), Stephen R. Barley and Julian E. Orr, eds., *Between Craft and Science: Technical Work in U.S. Settings* (Ithaca, NY: Cornell University Press, 1997), and Keith M. Macdonald, *The Sociology of the Professions* (London: Sage, 1995).

Cities play important roles in shaping the nature of information and its use. For introductions relevant to our discussions, I suggest reading Keith M. Macdonald, *The Sociology of the Professions* (London: Sage, 1995), and at least one book by Richard Florida, such as *The Rise of the Creative Class and How It's Transforming Work, Leisure, Community and Everyday Life* (New York: Basic Books, 2002) or his *Who's Your City? How the Creative Economy Is Making Where to Live the Most Important Decision of Your Life* (New York: Basic Books, 2008). For the larger issue of the most educated living in urban centers and with some of the highest incomes and social standings, and implications, see, too, Donald Clark Hodges, *Class Politics in the Information Age* (Urbana: University of Illinois Press, 2000). Within that subject area, we again bump up against economics, and for that I would turn to George Gilder, *Knowledge and Power: The Information Theory of Capitalism and How It Is Revolutionizing Our World* (Washington, D.C.: Regnery, 2013), which is very approachable and insightful. An older book is a gem on this topic as well, Allan R. Pred, *Urban Growth and the Circulation of Information: The United States System of Cities, 1750–1840* (Cambridge, MA: Harvard University Press, 1973).

The role of standards is increasingly being seen as an important component of the broader issue of the nature and use of information. So it is time to integrate research done on the subject into our understanding about information. Three useful introductions, with extensive bibliographic citations to other research, are Lawrence Busch, *Standards: Recipes for Reality* (Cambridge, MA: MIT Press, 2011), and for specific business examples, see Andrew Russell, *Open Standards and the Digital Age: History, Ideology, and Networks* (Cambridge, UK: Cambridge University Press, 2014); JoAnne Yates and Craig N. Murphy, *Engineering Rules: Global Standard Setting since 1880* (Baltimore MD: Johns Hopkins University Press, 2019).

A fascinating, growing interest is emerging around the role of information as part of an individual's identity, such as the data collected on forms for pensions, to pay taxes, acquire drivers licenses, and so forth. For an excellent introduction to that line of research written by a philosopher who, as a warning, writes using the academic jargon of the day, nonetheless is very informative, see Colin Koopman, *How We Became Our Data: A Genealogy of the Informational Person* (Chicago, IL: University of Chicago Press, 2019).

Finally, Jeremy Black, *The Power of Knowledge: How Information and Technology Made the Modern World* (New Haven, CT: Yale University Press, 2014), covers many centuries and countries. It is worth examining, especially for the early centuries of Europeans in North America.

SECOND INDUSTRIAL REVOLUTION AND INFORMATION, 1860S–1930S

Historians and economists have been redefining this period of European and American history rather sharply over the past two decades, incorporating more analysis of economic, technological, and scientific events. To understand the role of information in this period, a number of studies are crucial to examine. Begin with Robert J. Gordon, *The Rise and Fall of American Growth: The U.S. Standard of Living since the Civil War* (Princeton, NJ: Princeton University Press, 2016), who also takes the story down to the present. For a shorter, but equally impressive examination of the period, there is Ian Morris, *Why the West Rules—For Now: The Patterns of History and What They Reveal about the Future* (New York: Farrar, Straus and Giroux, 2010) and also Edmund Phelps, *Mass Flourishing: How Grassroots Innovation Created Jobs, Challenge, and Change* (Princeton, NJ: Princeton University Press, 2013).

For a history of American information in this period, there is Cortada, *All the Facts*. For a smattering of a growing emphasis on the role of information across broad sweeps of history, see Emily S. Rosenberg (ed.), *A World Connecting, 1870–1945* (Cambridge, MA: Harvard University Press, 2012); and most useful about information, Jürgen Osterhammel, *The Transformation of the World: A Global History of the Nineteenth Century* (Princeton, NJ: Princeton University Press, 2014). On technology, information and control, key works continue to be James R. Beniger, *The Control Revolution: Technological and Economic Origins of the Information Society* (Cambridge, MA: Harvard University Press, 1986); JoAnne Yates, *Control through Communication: The Rise of System in American Management* (Baltimore, MD: Johns Hopkins University Press, 1989); James W. Cortada, *Before the Computer: IBM, NCR, Burroughs, and Remington Rand and the Industry They Created, 1865–1956* (Princeton, NJ: Princeton University Press, 1993).

Vaclav Smil, *Creating the Twentieth Century: Technological Innovations of 1867–1914 and Their Lasting Impact* (Oxford: Oxford University Press, 2005); David S. Landes, *The Unbound Prometheus: Technological Change and Industrial Development in Western Europe from 1750 to the Present* (Cambridge, UK: Cambridge University Press, 1969); Robert W. Fogel,

Railroads and American Economic Growth: Essays in Econometric History (Baltimore, MD: Johns Hopkins University Press, 1964); and David E. Nye, *Electrifying America: Social Meanings of a New Technology* (Cambridge, MA: MIT Press, 1990). For a defense of the role of government in creating information and hence economic value, see economist Mariana Mazzucato, *The Value of Everything: Making and Taking in the Global Economy* (New York: Public Affairs, 2018). To link the story of telegraphy, mapping the West, the army, and railroads, the essential study is by James Schwoch, *Wired into Nature: The Telegraph and the North American Frontier* (Urbana, IL: University of Illinois Press, 2018). On libraries, an early but useful study is Angus Campbell and Charles A. Metzner, *Public Use of the Library and of Other Sources of Information* (Ann Arbor: University of Michigan Institute for Social Research, 1952); and currently the most useful studies about weather, Kristine C. Harper, *Weather by the Numbers: The Genesis of Modern Meteorology* (Cambridge, MA: MIT Press, 2008); Robert Henson, *Weather on the Air: A History of Broadcast Meteorology* (Boston, MA: American Meteorology Society, 2010).

On the role of agricultural innovations in the United States, begin with Paul K. Conklin, *A Revolution Down on the Farm: The Transformation of American Agriculture since 1929* (Lexington: University Press of Kentucky, 2009); Alan L. Olmstead and Paul W. Rhode, *Creating Abundance: Biological Innovation and American Agricultural Development* (Cambridge, UK: Cambridge University Press, 2008); Peter D. McClelland, *Sowing Modernity: America's First Agricultural Revolution* (Ithaca, NY: Cornell University Press, 1997); Gladys L. Baker et al., *Century of Service: The First Hundred Years of the United States Department of Agriculture* (Washington, D.C.: Government Printing Office, 1963); and Wayne Rasmussen, *Taking the University to the People: Seventy-Five Years of Cooperative Extension* (Ames: Iowa University Press, 1989).

About the role of higher education, for comprehensive well-researched studies, see Roger L. Geiger, *The American College in the Nineteenth Century* (Nashville, TN: Vanderbilt University Press, 2000), also his *To Advance Knowledge: The Growth of American Research Universities, 1900–1940* (New York: Oxford University Press, 1986). For a reliable introduction to elementary education, consult William J. Reese, *America's Public Schools: From the Common School to "No Child Left Behind"* (Baltimore, MD: Johns Hopkins University Press, 2005) who takes his narrative to the end of the twentieth century. But most important of all is Claudia Goldin and Lawrence F. Katz, *The Race between Education and Technology* (Cambridge, MA: Harvard University Press, 2008). Also useful on parallel developments with education is an understanding of professional societies; one of the most useful histories of these continues to be Ralph Bate, *Scientific Societies in the United States* (Cambridge, MA: MIT Press, 1965).

LIBRARIANS AND INFORMATION

The literature on library history is extensive, but several surveys are useful for explaining events, organizations, and roles of librarians. For an international review, consult Pamela Spence Richards, Wayne A. Wiegand, and Marija Dalbello (eds.), *A History of Modern Librarianship: Constructing the Heritage of Western Cultures* (Santa Barbara, CA: Libraries Unlimited, 2015). On American public libraries, the standard work is Wayne A. Wiegand, *Part of Our Lives: A People's History of the American Public Library* (New York: Oxford University Press, 2015). The most useful biography of Dewey is by Wayne A. Wiegand, *Irrepressible Reformer: A Biography of Melvil Dewey* (Chicago, IL: American Library Association, 1996). But also for the broader history of the Dewy system, see M. P. Satija, *The Theory and Practice of the Dewey Decimal Classification System* (Oxford: Chandos Publishing, 2007). On the Library of Congress approach, there is Lois Mai Chan, *A Guide to the Library of Congress Classification* (Englewood, CO: Libraries Unlimited, 1999). There is also a biography on Cutter, Francis L. Miksa, *Charles Ammi Cutter: Library Systematizer* (Littleton, CO: Libraries Unlimited, 1977). More details on the early twentieth century can be found in W. Boyd Rayward, "The Origins of Information Science and the International Institute of Bibliography/International Federation for Information and Documentation (FID)," *Journal of the American Society for Information Science* 48, no. 4 (1997): 289–300.

On the most recent era, several books are essential. Begin with George E. Bennett, *Librarians in Search of Science and Identity: The Elusive Profession* (Metuchen, NJ: Scarecrow Press, 1988), then consult George Bobinski, *Libraries and Librarianship: Sixty Years of Challenge and Change, 1945–2005* (Lanham, MD: Scarecrow Press, 2007). These should be read in concert with Larry J. Ostler, Therrin C. Dahlin, and J. D. Willardson, *The Closing of American Library Schools: Problems and Opportunities* (Westport, CT: Greenwood Press, 1995); and for a sense of the rhetoric and discord within the profession, sample the writings of Jesse H. Shera, *Introduction to Library Science: Basic Elements of Library Service* (Littleton, CO: Libraries Unlimited, 1976). For a short overview of Information Science, see M. K. Buckland and Z. M. Liu, "History of Information Science," *Annual Review of Information Science and Technology* 30 (1995): 385–416. Finally, do not overlook useful historiographical articles, Stephen E. Atkins, "Subject Trends in Library and

Information Science Research, 1975–1984," *Library Trends* (Spring 1988): 633–658; W. Boyd Rayward, "The History and Historiography of Information Science: Some Reflections," *Information Processing & Management* 32, no. 1 (1996): 3–17; Gary P. Radford, "Trapped in Our Own Discursive Formations: Toward an Archaeology of Library and Information Science," *The Library Quarterly* 73, no. 1 (January 2003): 1–18; Kelly Blessinger and Michele Frasier, "Analysis of a Decade in Library Literature: 1994–2004," *College & Research Libraries* 58, no. 2 (March 2007): 155–169.

EARLY ENCOUNTERS BY COMPUTER SCIENTISTS AND BUILDERS

The history of computer science as a discipline and its identity apart from mathematics, engineering and physics, for example, is currently being studied in bits and pieces. Most of the research is still appearing in the form of articles, such as William Aspray, Andrew Goldstein, and Bernard Williams, "The Social and Intellectual Shaping of a New Mathematical Discipline: The Role of the National Science Foundation in the Rise of Theoretical Computer Science and Engineering," in Ronald Colinger (ed.), *Vita Mathematica: Historical Research and Integration With Teaching* (Washington, D.C.: Mathematical Association of America, 1996): 209–230; Peter A. Freeman, W. Richards Adrion, and William Aspray, *Computing and the National Science Foundation, 1950–2016: Building a Foundation for Modern Computing* (No City: Association for Computing Machinery, 2019): 4–26; Jesse T. Quatse, "Hardware Design in the Founding of Computer Science at CMU," *IEEE Annals of the History of Computing* 28, no. 3 (July–September 2006): 76–80; Jack Minker, "Forming a Computer Science Center at the University of Maryland," Ibid., 29, no. 1 (January–March 2007): 49–64; Gopal K. Gupta, "Computer Science Curriculum Developments in the 1960s," Ibid., 29, no. 2 (April–June 2007): 40–54.

For a useful introduction to many facets of the subject, consult Allen B. Tucker (ed.), *Computer Science Handbook*, 2nd ed. (Boca Raton, FL: CRC Press, 2004),). Jan van Leeuwen, *Handbook of Theoretical Computer Science* (Cambridge, MA: MIT Press, 1994), and the many editions of Anthony Ralston, Edwin D. Reilly, and David Hemmendinger (eds.), *Encyclopedia of Computer Science*, especially 4th ed. (Hoboken, NJ: John Wiley & Sons, 2003). For short course in its history, see Edwin D. Reilly, *Milestones in Computer Science and Information Technology* (Westport, CT.: Greenwood Press, 2003); Matti Tedre, *The Science of Computing: Shaping a Discipline* (Boca Raton, FL: CRC Press, 2014), Donald Knuth, *The Art of Computer Programming*, vol. 1, 3rd ed. (Boston, MA: Addison-Wesley, 1997); Peter

Brass, *Advanced Data Structures* (Cambridge, UK: Cambridge University Press, 2008), and one of the earliest studies, Niklaus Wirth, *Algorithms and Data Structures* (Englewood Cliffs, NJ: Prentice-Hall, 1985). For a bibliography, James W. Cortada, *A Bibliographic Guide to the History of Computing, Computers, and the Information Processing Industry* (Westport, CT: Greenwood Press, 1990).

A series of technical topics are relevant. The two key works on the role of standards are Martha Lampland and Susan Leigh Star, *Standards and Their Stories: How Quantifying, Classifying, and Formalizing Practices Shape Everyday Life* (Ithaca, NY: Cornell University Press, 2009); Andrew L. Russell, *Open Standards and the Digital Age: History, Ideology, and Networks* (Cambridge, UK: Cambridge University Press, 2014). On the design of computers, consult Thomas C. Bartree, Irwin L. Lebow, and Irving S. Reed, *Theory and Design of Digital Machines* (New York: McGraw-Hill, 1962); Bill Moggridge, *Designing Interactions* (Cambridge, MA: MIT Press, 2007); Robert Latham ad Saskia Sassen (eds.), *Digital Formations: IT and New Architectures in the Global Realm* (Princeton, NJ: Princeton University Press, 2005).

On the early history of computing in considerable detail, two fat tomes are useful by Charles J. Bashe, Lyle R. Johnson, John H. Palmer, and Emerson W. Pugh, *IBM's Early Computers* (Cambridge, MA: MIT Press, 1985; Emerson W. Pugh, Lyle R. Johnson, John H. Palmer, *IBM's 360 and Early 370 Systems* (Cambridge, MA: MIT Press, 2003). On benchmarking and measuring computer systems, see Bob Wescott, *The Every Computer Performance Book* (No City: CreateSpace, 2013); Jim Gray (ed.), *The Benchmark Handbook for Database and Transaction Systems*, 2nd ed. (Burlington, MA: Morgan Kaufmann, 1993); Raghunath Nambiar and Meikel Poess (eds.), *Performance Evaluation and Benchmarking* (Berlin: Springer-Verlag, 2009), and James W. Cortada, *Managing DP Hardware: Capacity Planning, Cost Justification, Availability, and Energy Management* (Englewood Cliffs, NJ: Prentice-Hall, 1983).

The literature on networked computing is vast, so to be tactical in learning about twentieth-century approaches, three well-written studies assist: Jiacun Wang, *Real-Time Embedded Systems* (Hoboken, NJ: John Wiley & Sons, 2017); Hagit Attiya and Jennifer Welch, *Distributed Computing: Fundamentals, Simulations, and Advanced Topics* (Hoboken, NH: John Wiley & Sons, 2004); Gerard Tel, *Introduction to Distributed Algorithms* (Cambridge, UK: Cambridge University Press, 1994). Other sources more focused on communications itself can be understood through Andrew S. Tanenbaum, *Computer Networks* (Englewood Cliffs, NJ: Prentice-Hall, 1989; Richard W. Watson, *Timesharing System Design Concept* (New York: McGraw-Hill, 1970); John Bellamy, *Digital Telephony*, 2nd ed. (New York: John Wiley & Sons,

1991); Eli M. Noam, *Interconnecting the Network of Networks* (Cambridge, MA: MIT Press, 2001), and on the specifics of information theory, John R. Pierce, *Signals: The Telephone and Beyond* (San Francisco, CA: W. H. Freeman & Co., 1981). There is a growing body of historical literature on the pre-Internet. Examples include Elaine B. Kerr and Starr Roxanne Hiltz, *Computer-Mediated Communication Systems: Status and Evaluation* (New York: Academic Press, 1982); Patrice Flichy, *Dynamics of Modern Communications: The Shaping and Impact of New Communication Technologies* (London: SAGE Publications, 1995); John Bray, *The Communications Miracle: The Telecommunications Pioneers from Morse to the Information Highway* (New York: Plenum, 1995); David E. Nye, "Shaping Communication Networks: Telegraph, Telephone, Computer," *Social Research* 64 (Fall 1997): 1067–1091; Philip L. Frana, "Telematics and the Early History of International Information Flows," *IEEE Annals of the History of Computing* 40, no. 2 (April–June 2018): 32–47. For the role of Bell Labs consult the appropriate endnotes for this chapter; the literature is extensive, but most of it focused on events within the labs and not on the specific nature of information.

For an introduction to databases as a technology see David M. Kroenke and David J. Auer, *Database Concepts*, 3rd ed. (Upper Saddle River, NJ: Prentice-Hall, 2007); for bibliographies of historically relevant materials, see James W. Cortada, *A Bibliographic Guide to the History of Computing, Computers, and the Information Processing Industry*, 446–448; and *Second Bibliographic Guide to the History of Computing, Computers, and the Information Processing Industry* (Westport, CT: Greenwood Press, 1996): 345–348. Useful case studies originating in science include Mary Ellen Bowden, Trudi Bellardo Hahn, and Robert V. Williams (eds.), *Proceedings of the 1998 Conference on the History and Heritage of Scientific Information Systems* (Medford, NJ: Information Today, Inc. for American Society for Information Science and the Chemical Heritage Foundation, 1999); Douglas S. Robertson, *Phase Change: The Computer Revolution in Science and Mathematics* (Oxford: Oxford University Press, 2003).

We lack a good biography of Ralph Hartley. Even a leading historian, Paul Ceruzzi, did not discuss his work in *A History of Modern Computing*, 2nd ed. (Cambridge, MA: MIT Press, 2003). Harry Nyquist also deserves serious bibliographic study. But others get more attention, for example, in Matti Tedre, *The Science of Computing: Shaping a Discipline* (Boca Raton, FL: Chapman and Hall, 2017); Jack W. Copeland, Carl J. Posy, and Oron Shagrir (eds.), *Computability: Turing, Gödel, Church, and Beyond* (Cambridge, MA: MIT Press, 2015). Turing has his biographers, and one could expect to see more in the future. Begin with Andrew Hodges, *Alan Turing: The Enigma* (New York: Simon & Schuster, 1983); Chris Bernhardt, *Turing's Vision: The*

Birth of Computer Science (Cambridge, MA: MIT Press, 2016). Then turn to Jack B. Copeland (ed.), *The Essential Turing* (New York: Oxford University Press, 2004); also his "Alan Turing's Forgotten Ideas in Computer Science," *Scientific American* 280, no. 4 (1999): 99–103; and with et al., *The Turing Guide* (New York: Oxford University Press, 2017), and for a biography by Copeland, see *Turing: Pioneer of the Information Age* (Oxford: Oxford University Press, 2012). On the Turing Test, Stuart M. Shieber, *The Turing Test: Verbal Behavior as the Hallmark of Intelligence* (Cambridge, MA: Bradford Books, 2004) and Rolf Herken (ed.), *The Universal Turing Machine: A Half-Century Survey* (New York: Springer-Verlag, 1995); Rod Downey (ed.), *Turing's Legacy: Developments from Turing's Ideas in Logic* (Cambridge, UK: Cambridge University Press, 2014). For John von Neumann, consult the relevant endnotes to chapter 3. The definitive anthology of Claude Shannon's work is N. J. A. Sloane and Aaron D. Wyner (eds.), *Claude Elwood Shannon: Collected Papers* (Piscataway, NJ: IEEE Press, 1993), but also useful and classic, Claude E. Shannon and Warren Weaver, *The Mathematical Theory of Communication* (Urbana: University of Illinois Press, 1949), reprinted for years by the press; 17th printing appeared in 1998. We do not yet have a biography of Gerard Salton, but we are better off regarding H. P. Luhn, Claire K. Schultz, *H.P. Luhn: Pioneer of Information Science: Selected Works* (New York: Spartan Books, 1968); Hallam Stevens, "Hans Peter Luhn and the Birth of the Hashing Algorithm" *IEEE Spectrum* 30 (January 2018): 42–47.

Regarding cards and tape storage, the literature is substantial and useful. For cards, consult Geoffrey Austrian, *Herman Hollerith: The Forgotten Giant of Information Processing* (New York: Columbia University Press, 1982); Harry P. Cemach, *The Elements of Punched Card Accounting* (London: Sir Isaac Pitman, 1951); Francis J. Murray, *Mathematical Machines*, vol. 1, *Digital Computers* (New York: Columbia University Press, 1961). For tape begin with James W. Cortada, *Historical Dictionary of Data Processing: Technology* (Westport, CT: Greenwood Press, 1987): 355–359. On databases, see for history C. J. Date, *An Introduction to Database Systems*, 6th ed. (Reading, MA: Addison-Wesley, 1995); Thomas Haigh, "'A Veritable Bucket of Facts': Origins of the Data Base Management System, 1960–1980," in W. Boyd Rayward and Mary Ellen Bowden (eds.), *The History and Heritage of Scientific and Technological Information Systems* (New Medford, NJ: Information Today, 2004): 73–88; and his, "How Data Got Its Base: Information Storage Software in the 1950s and 1960s," *IEEE Annals of the History of Computing* 31, no. 4 (October–December 2009): 6–25. An entire issue of this journal was devoted to the subject, 31, no. 4 (October–December, 2009). For related technologies underpinning databases, useful sources include John B. Bass and J. Kates, *Achieving Usability through Software Architecture*

(Pittsburgh, PA: Carnegie Mellon University, 2001); G. Lewis, S. Comella-Dorda, P. Place, D. Plakosh, and R. Seacord, *Enterprise Information System Data Architecture Guide* (Pittsburg, PA: Carnegie Mellon University, 2001). Sometimes the subject is linked to discussions about data warehousing, a development beginning in the 1960s, actualized in the 1980s, William Inmon, *Building the Data Warehouse* (New York: John Wiley & Sons, 1992) and subsequent editions. Finally, do not overlook Charles P. Bourne and Trudi Bellardo Hahn, *A History of Online Information Services, 1963–1976* (Cambridge, MA: MIT Press, 2003) or Peter A. Freeman, W. Richards Adrion, and William Aspray, *Computing and the National Science Foundation, 1950–2016: Building a Foundation for Modern Computing* (New York: ACM Books, 2019) and a massive collection of articles, Sergio Verdu and Steven W. McLaughlin (eds.), *Information Theory: 50 Years of Discovery* (New York: IEEE Press, 2000).

MATHEMATICIANS AND STATISTICIANS

On mathematics begin with some history: John Stillwell, *Mathematics and Its History*, 3rd ed. (London: Springer-Verlag. 2010). Understanding the Pythagorean theorem is a fruitful way of understanding the kind of new mathematical information that increasingly became available since the mid-nineteenth century, with Eli Maor, *The Pythagorean Theorem: A 4,000 Year History* (Princeton, NJ: Princeton University Press, 2007). For the nuts and bolts, useful texts include Ron Larson and Bruce H. Edwards, *Calculus: Early Transcendental Functions*, 6th ed. (Boston, MA: Cengage Learning, 2014); and Steven Strogatz, *Infinite Powers: How Calculus Reveals the Secrets of the Universe* (New York: Houghton Mifflin Harcourt, 2019). Because mathematics so stimulated the use of model thinking, it is essential to understand the concept, so for that consult Scott E. Page, *The Model Thinker: What You Need to Know to Make Data Work for You* (New York: Basic Books, 2018). On topography, there is David S. Richeson, *Euler's Gem: The Polyhedron Formula and the Birth of Topography* (Princeton, NJ: Princeton University Press, 2008).

To study statistics begin with Stephen M. Stigler, *The History of Statistics: The Measurement of Uncertainty before 1900* (Cambridge, MA: Harvard University Press; 1986); also his, *Statistics on the Table: The History of Statistical Concepts and Methods* (Cambridge, MA: Harvard University Press, 2002); for continuation of the story deep into the twentieth century, see Prakash Gorroochurn, *Classic Topics on the History of Modern Mathematical Statistics: From Laplace to More Recent Times* (Hoboken, NJ: John Wiley & Sons, 2016). The most detailed study is by Anders Hald in three volumes, *A History of Mathematical Statistics from 1750 to 1930* (Hoboken, NJ: John Wiley & Sons, 1998); and *History of Probability and Statistics and Their Application before 1750* (Hoboken, NJ: John Wiley & Sons, 1990); and *A History of Parametric Statistical Inference from Bernoulli to Fisher, 1713–1935* (Berlin: Springer-Verlag, 2007). Finally, two histories of statistics are essential by Theodore M. Porter, *Trust in Numbers: The Pursuit of Objectivity in Science and Public Life* (Princeton, NJ: Princeton University Press, 1995); and *The Rise of Statistical Thinking, 1820–1900* (Princeton, NJ: Princeton University Press, 2020).

For more narrowly focused but important studies about statistics, see Kevin Donnelly, *Adolphe Quetelet, Social Physics and the Average Men of Science, 1796–1874* (Pittsburgh, PA: University of Pittsburgh Press, 2015); Ian Hacking, *The Taming of Chance* (Cambridge, UK: Cambridge University Press, 1990); Donald MacKenzie, *Statistics in Britain, 1865–1930: The Social Construction of Scientific Knowledge* (Edinburgh: Edinburgh University Press, 1981); Alain Desrosières, *The Politics of Large Numbers: A History of Statistical Thinking* (Cambridge, MA: Harvard University Press, 1998, reprinted 2010), which fill in European developments. Emmanuel Didier, *America by the Numbers: Quantification, Democracy, and the Birth of National Statistics* (Cambridge, MA: MIT Press, 2020) demonstrates how policy and statistics evolved using the case of the American New Deal initiatives of the 1930s.

Textbooks have become more understandable and focused on specific audiences over the decades; see, for example, Russell T. Warne, *Statistics for the Social Sciences: A General Linear Model Approach* (Cambridge, UK: Cambridge University Press, 2018); for a standard text, see Mario F. Triola, *Elementary Statistics*, 13th ed. (London: Pearson, 2017); Brady T. West, Kathleen B. Welch, and Andrzj T. Galecki, *Linear Mixed Models: A Practical Guide Using Statistical Software*, 2nd ed. (Boca Raton, FL: CRC Press, 2015); Gareth James, Daniela Witten, Trevor Hastie, and Robert Tibshirani, *An Introduction to Statistical Learning* (New York: Springer-Verlag, 2017); Richard M. Heiberger and Burt Holland, *Statistical Analysis and Data Display* (New York: Springer-Verlag, 2015). But if you could read only one book on the subject, it is by David Spiegelhalter, *The Art of Statistics: How to Learn From Data* (New York: Basic Books, 2019). Its ties to information are crucial to understand, so for that begin with S. Kullback, *Information Theory and Statistics* (New York: Dover, 1968), a minor classic; then consult I. Vajda, *Theory of Statistical Inference and Information* (Dordrecht, Netherlands: Kluwer, 1989; R. E. Blahut, *Principles and Practices of Information Theory* (Reading, MA: Addison-Wesley, 1987).

Displaying information advanced enormously in the twentieth century thanks to the combination of mathematics and computing. Key works on the subject include by absolute favorites by Edward R. Tufte who self-published a series of books that are seminal, *Envisioning Information: Narratives of Space and Time* (Cheshire, CT: Graphics Press, 1990); *Visual Explanations: Images and Quantities, Evidence and Narrative* (Cheshire, CT: Graphics Press, 1997); *The Visual Display of Quantitative Information*, 2nd ed. (Cheshire, CT: Graphics Press, 2001); but see two other of his publications, the first a pamphlet with two case studies, *Visual and Statistical Thinking: Visual and Statistical Thinking: Displays of Evidence for Making Decisions* (Cheshire, CT: Graphics Press, 1997); and his criticism of PowerPoint presentations, *The Cognitive Style of PowerPoint: Pitching Out Corrupts Within* (Cheshire, CT: Graphics Press, 2006, 2011).

SCIENTISTS AND THE MEDICAL COMMUNITY

Science has its own culture, values, and ways of working that are not always understood by people not versed in the discipline, so a subject one should pause to consider before diving into the history of its evolution. For that purpose there is the convenient, short, and useful introduction by Jim Al-Khalili, *The Joy of Science* (Princeton, NJ: Princeton University Press, 2022). The most widely consulted general text on the history of science is James E. McClellan III and Harold Dorn, *Science and Technology in World History: An Introduction*, 3rd ed. (Baltimore, MD: Johns Hopkins University Press, 2015); and it includes a detailed bibliographic essay organized by chapter. Then for physics a useful place to begin with is Leonard Susskind and George Hrabovsky, *The Theoretical Minimum: What You Need to Know to Start Doing Physics* (New York: Basic Books, 2013). For a beautifully written short introduction to the subject one cannot do better than to read Jim Al-Khalili, *The World According to Physics* (Princeton, NJ: Princeton University Press, 2020). Since quantum Theory is largely a twentieth-century event, it must be understood, and a useful text for beginning is with Jagdish Mehra and Helmut Rechenberg, *The Formulation of Matrix Mechanics and Its Modifications, 1925–1926: The Historical Development of Quantum Theory* (Berlin: Springer-Verlag, 2001). But see also, Luciano Floridi, *Information: A Very Short Introduction* (New York: Oxford University Press, 2010).

A textbook on chemistry is always a useful place to explore modern concepts, so for that explore Rich Baur, James Birk, and Pamela Marks, *Introduction to Chemistry*, 5th ed. (New York: McGraw-Hill 2019); then for an historical perspective, see M. P. Crosland, *Historical Studies in the Language of Chemistry* (London: Heinemann, 1962); William H. Brock, *The Chemical Tree: A History of Chemistry* (New York: W. W. Norton, 1992); M. P. Crosland, *In the Shadow of Lavoisier: The Annales de Chimie and the*

Establishment of a New Science (London: British Society for the History of Science, 1994); Mary Ellen Bowden, Trudi Bellargo Hahn, and Robert V. Williams (eds.), *Science Information Systems: Proceedings of the 1998 Conference on the History and Heritage of Science Information Systems* (Medford, NJ: American Society for Information Science and Chemical Heritage Foundation, 1999); Theodore M. Porter, *Genetics in the Madhouse: The Unknown History of Human Heredity* (Princeton, NJ: Princeton University Press, 2018). Specifically about information, there is J. E. Ash and E. Hyde (eds.), *Chemical Information Systems* (Chichester, UK: John Wiley & Sons, 1974). About plastic, the standard source is now Stephen Fenichell, *Plastic: The Making of a Synthetic Century* (New York: HarperBusiness, 1996).

The literature on biology is now vast, but a few monographs are helpful in navigating through it, including even into an equally vast body of material about medicine: Jon Agar, *Science in the Twentieth Century and Beyond* (Cambridge, UK: Polity Press, 2012); Garland E. Allen, *Life Science in the Twentieth Century* (Cambridge, UK: Cambridge University Press, 1975); Peter J. Bowler, *Evolution: The History of an Idea* (Berkeley: University of California Press, 2003); Robert Bud, *The Uses of Life: A History of Biotechnology* (Cambridge, UK: Cambridge University Press, 1993); Kevin Davies, *Cracking the Genome: Inside the Race to Unlock Human DNA* (New York: Free Press, 2001); Stephen Jay Gould, *The Structure of Evolutionary Theory* (Cambridge, MA: Belknap Press of Harvard University Press, 2002); Lois M. Magner, *A History of the Life Sciences*, 3rd ed. (New York: Marcel Dekker, 2002); Jan Sapp, *Genesis: The Evolution of Biology* (New York: Oxford University Press, 2003). On computing's role, see R. M. Friedhoff and W. Benzon, *The Second Computer Revolution: Visualization* (New York: W. H. Freeman, 1989); L. Hunter (ed.), *Artificial Intelligence and Molecular Biology* (Menlo Park, CA: AAAI Press, 1993); and on early uses, R. S. Ledley, *Use of Computers in Biology and Medicine* (New York: McGraw-Hill, 1965). But do not overlook Jürgen Renn, *The Evolution of Knowledge: Rethinking Science for the Anthropocene* (Princeton, NJ: Princeton University Press, 2020). To understand how information crossed disciplines, you cannot do better than to read Harvey J. Graff, *Undisciplining Knowledge: Interdisciplinarity in the Twentieth Century* (Baltimore, MD: Johns Hopkins University Press, 2015). But if you want to begin with an overarching, clearly written masterful history, read Michael Morange, *A History of Biology* (Princeton, NJ: Princeton University Press, 2021).

Medicine, too, has a strong historical literature. For an overview, see the contributed essays in Roy Porter (ed.), *The Cambridge History of Medicine* (Cambridge, UK: Cambridge University Press, 2006), then Morris F. Collin and Marion J. Ball, *A History of Medical Informatics in the United States*

(Berlin: Springer-Verlag, 2015). Many of the sources cited about science include material on the role of medicine, including all three of Porter's books. For how the mind processes information, the role of bias, and errors in historical context, there is the highly readable authoritative account by Daniel Kahneman, Oliver Sibony, and Cass R. Sunstein, *Noise: A Flaw in Human Judgment* (New York: Little, Brown Spark, 2021).

BUSINESS AND GOVERNMENT

The way to start understanding the role of information in business and government is to become familiar with how large enterprises emerged in the late nineteenth century and expanded in the twentieth century. Historians do this by first turning to Alfred D. Chandler Jr., *The Visible Hand: The Managerial Revolution in American Business* (Cambridge, MA: Harvard University Press, 1977), then to good economic history, such as Robert J. Gordon, *The Rise and Fall of American Growth* (Princeton, NJ: Princeton University Press, 2016). Then to get specific about the role of information in such organizations, there is James W. Cortada, *The Digital Hand*, 3 vols. (New York: Oxford University Press, 2004–2008), which reviews developments from 1945 to the late 1990s across a dozen industries, including volume 3, which is devoted entirely to the public sector.

On models, you cannot do better for an introduction than Scott E. Page, *The Model Thinker: What You Need to Know to Make Data Work for You* (New York: Basic Books, 2018). Since models need data, also consult Cesar Hidalgo, *Why Information Grows: The Evolution of Order, from Atoms to Economies* (New York: Basic Books, 2015), and explanations in James W. Cortada (ed.), *Rise of the Knowledge Worker* (Boston, MA: Butterworth-Heinemann, 1998). A number of monographs provide specific case studies, particularly regarding the role of accounting. These include JoAnne Yates, *Control through Communication: The Rise of System in American Management* (Baltimore, MD: Johns Hopkins University Press, 1989); Peter Temin (ed.), *Inside the Business Enterprise: Historical Perspectives on the Use of Information* (Chicago, IL: University of Chicago Press, 1991); Lisa Bud-Frierman (ed.), *Information Acumen: The Understanding and Use of Knowledge in Modern Business* (London: Routledge, 1994); Margaret Levenstein, *Accounting Growth Information Systems and the Creation of the Large Corporation* (Stanford, CA: Stanford University Press, 1998); the now classic James E. Beniger, *The Control Revolution: Technological and Economic Origins of the Information Society* (Cambridge, MA: Harvard University Press, 1986). For business practices that evolved, begin with David A. Hounshell,

From the American System to Mass Production, 1800–1932 (Baltimore, MD: Johns Hopkins University Press, 1984); and for the late 1900s, see Robert E. Cole, *Managing Quality Fads: How American Business Learned to Play the Quality Game* (New York: Oxford University Press, 1999); and G. Hamel and A. Heene (eds.), *Competence-Based Competition* (Chichester, UK.: John Wiley & Sons, 1994): 11–33; J. Pfeffer and G.R. Salancik, *The External Control of Organizations: A Resource Dependence Perspective* (San Francisco, CA: Harper & Row, 1978).

Accounting and auditing has have been the subject of much research. For our purposes useful studies include Derek Matthews, *A History of Auditing: The Changing Audit Process in Britain from the Nineteenth Century to the Present Day* (London: Routledge, 2006); Lai Balkaran, *The Rise of Accounting, Auditing, and Finance: Key Issues and Events That Shaped These Professions for over 200 Years* (Hauppauge, NY: Nova Science, 2019). But also have a good accounting textbook nearby, preferably a recent edition. I consulted R. C. Moyer, F. H. deB. Harris, and J. R. McGuigan, *Managerial Economics*, 11th ed. (Mason, OH: Thomson Higher Education, 2007). For increased regulation and reporting of information, see Joel Seligman, *The Transformation of Wall Street: A History of the Securities and Exchange Commission and Modern Corporate Finance*, 3rd ed. (New York: Aspen Publishers, 2003); and Kees Camfferman and Stephen A. Zeff, *Financial Reporting and Global Capital Markets: A History of the International Accounting Standards Committee, 1973–2000* (Oxford: Oxford University Press, 2006). On the evolving relevance of business information reporting, see Baruch Lev and Feng Gu, *The End of Accounting and the Path Forward for Investors and Managers* (Hoboken, NJ: John Wiley & Sons, 2016).

On sales practices, there is the excellent study by Walter A. Friedman, *Birth of a Salesman: The Transformation of Selling in America* (Cambridge, MA: Harvard University Press, 2004); and on IBM's innovations, James W. Cortada, *IBM: The Rise and Fall and Reinvention of a Global Icon* (Cambridge, MA: MIT Press, 2019).

On Peter Drucker, begin with Jack Beatty, *The World According to Peter Drucker* (New York: Free Press, 1998); but then turn to Drucker himself and of his many books, the classic is his Peter F. Drucker, *Management: Tasks, Responsibilities, Practices* (New York: Harper & Row, 1973). For process management thinking, the sources most consulted by firms in the late 1900s included H. James Harrington, *Business Process Improvement* (New York: McGraw-Hill, 1991); Jack D. Orsburn et al., *Self-Directed Work Teams: The New American Challenge* (Burr Ridge, IL: Irwin Professional Publishing, 1990); W. Edwards Deming, *Out of the Crisis* (Cambridge, MA: MIT Center for Advanced Engineering Study, 1986); Armand V. Feigenbaum, *Total

Quality Control, 3rd ed. (New York: McGraw-Hill, 1991). But two other works are useful for twentieth-century events: Thomas K. McCraw, *American Business since 1920: How It Worked* (Wheeling, IL: Harlan Davidson, 2009); James Brian Quinn, *Intelligent Enterprise: A Knowledge and Service Based Paradigm for Industry* (New York: Free Press, 1992). For a large anthology of articles and chapters dealing with quality management and information in public and private sectors of the 1990s, see James W. Cortada and John A. Woods (eds.), *The Quality Yearbook* (New York: McGraw-Hill, 1994–2002), published annually for a total of nine volumes. These two authors also produced related volumes, *The Knowledge Management Yearbook, 1999–2000* (Boston, MA: Butterworth-Heinemann, 1999); and *The Knowledge Management Yearbook, 2000–2001* (Boston, MA: Butterworth-Heinemann, 2000). Combined the two sets of volumes include over 7,000 pages of material. On Deming, useful studies include Rafael Aguayo, *Dr. Deming: The American Who Taught the Japanese about Quality* (New York: Fireside, 1990); Cecelia S. Kilian and W. Edward Deming, *The World of W. Edwards Deming*, 2nd ed. (Boca Raton, FL: SPC Press, 1992); Mary Walton, *The Deming Management Method* (New York: Dodd, Mead, 1986), and Andrea Gabor, *The Man Who Discovered Quality: How W. Edwards Deming Brought the Quality Revolution to America* (New York: Penguin, 1992). However, there is no substitute for reading one of Deming's books, the classic being Deming, *Out of the Crisis*.

On inventory control and its issues, see J. Buchan, *Scientific Inventory Management* (Englewood Cliffs, NJ: Prentice-Hall, 1963); Thomas E. Vollmann, William L. Berry, and D. Clay Whybark, *Manufacturing Planning and Control Systems* (Homewood, IL: Irwin, 1988). For historical perspective the standard work is still David F. Noble, *Forces of Production: A Social History of Industrial Automation* (New York: Oxford University Press, 1986). On standards two studies stand out: JoAnne Yates and Craig N. Murphy, *Engineering Rules: Global Standard Setting since 1880* (Baltimore, MD: Johns Hopkins University Press, 2019); Andrew L. Russell, *Open Standards and the Digital Age: History, Ideology And Networks* (Cambridge, UK: Cambridge University Press, 2014).

ROLE OF ECONOMISTS

For the uninitiated into economics a good place to start is with David Leiser and Yhonatan Shemesh, *How We Misunderstand Economics and Why It Matters* (London: Routledge, 2018), followed up by consulting a couple of standard textbooks, such as Olivier Blanchard, *Macroeconomics Updated*, 5th ed. (Upper Saddle River, NJ: Prentice Hall, 2011); Ben Heijdra and Frederick van der Ploeg, *Foundations of Modern Macroeconomics* (New York: Oxford University Press,

2002). See also, Robin Bade and Michael Parkin, *Foundations of Microeconomics* (Boston, MA: Addison Wesley, 2001). I also found this book useful, Steven G. Medema and Warren J. Samuels, *Foundations of Research in Economics: How Do Economists Do Economics?* (Cheltenham, UK: Edward Elgar, 1996). If the reader is an economist and would like some background information and yet be able to jump in and debate an economist, I found a very well-written and organized introduction to many contemporary issues in Mariana Mazzucato, *The Value of Everything: Making and Taking in the Global Economy* (New York: Public Affairs, 2018). There are numerous histories of economic thoughts, I found these of use: William Milberg, *The Crisis of Vision in Modern Economic Thought* (Cambridge, UK: Cambridge University Press, 2005); Edward Nik-Khah, *The Knowledge We Have Lost in Information: The History of Information in Modern Economics* (New York: Oxford University Press, 2017). For critics of economic methods, see Philip Mirowski, *More Heat than Light: Economics as Social Physics, Physics as Nature's Economics* (Cambridge, UK: Cambridge University Press, 1989), but then Hugo A. Keuzenkamp, *Probability, Econometrics and Truth: The Methodology of Econometrics* (Cambridge, UK: Cambridge University Press, 2000); Peter Kennedy, *A Guide to Econometrics*, 5th ed. (Cambridge, MA: MIT Press, 2003); Campbell R. McConnell, Stanley L. Brue, and Sean M. Flynn, *Economics: Principles, Problems, and Policies*, 18th ed. (Boston, MA: McGraw-Hill Irwin, 2009); Steven Rappaport, *Models and Reality in Economics* (Cheltenham, UK: Edward Elgar, 1998).

For some useful biographies, see Peter Clarke, *The Twentieth Century's Most Influential Economist* (New York: Bloomsbury, 2009); Donald Markwell, *John Maynard Keynes and International Relations: Economic Paths to War and Peace* (Oxford: Oxford University Press, 2006). Other useful biographies include Michio Morishima, *Walras' Economics: A Pure Theory of Capital and Money* (Cambridge, UK: Cambridge University Press, 1977); Bert Mosselmans, *William Stanley Jevons and the Cutting Edge of Economics* (London: Routledge. 2007); Peter Groenewegan, *A Soaring Eagle: Alfred Marshall: 1842–1924* (Cheltenham, UK: Edward Elgar, 1995) is the near-definitive biography, but see his shorter biography, *Alfred Marshall: Economist, 1842–1924* (London: Palgrave, Macmillan 2007); Jha Narmadeshwar, *The Age of Marshall: Aspects of British Economic Thought, 1880–1915* (London: F. Cass, 1973);

Robert Loring Allen, *Irving Fisher: A Biography* (London: Wiley-Blackwell, 1993). Although not an economist Peter Drucker played an important role in moving some economic thinking into the business community, so I recommend Jack Beatty, *The World According to Peter Drucker* (New York: Free Press, 1998).

About GDP there is a delightful well-informed, short good read, Diane Coyle, *GDP: A Brief But Affectionate History* (Princeton, NJ: Princeton

University Press, 2014); for other new information ideas, see Richard H. Thaler and Cass R. Sunstein, *Nudge: Improving Decisions about Health, Wealth, and Happiness* (New Haven, CT: Yale University Press, 2008). On Machlup, his books are approachable by multiple disciplines and are foundational for modern notions of the information economy: Fritz Machlup, *The Production and Distribution of Knowledge in the United States* (1962), and *Knowledge: Its Creation, Distribution, and Economic Significance*, 3 vols. (Princeton, NJ: Princeton University Press, 1980–1984). How people in business applied his thinking, see Diane Cozel, *The Weightless World* (Cambridge, MA: MIT Press, 1997); Carl Shapiro and Hal R. Varian, *Information Rules: A Strategic Guide to the Network Economy* (Boston, MA: Harvard Business School Press, 1999). Non-economists gained large audiences, too, particularly in business circles, for example, James McGee and Lawrence Prusak, *Managing Information Strategically* (New York: Random House, 1993); Donald Tapscott, *The Digital Economy* (New York: McGraw-Hill, 1996). The literature on innovation is extensive, but for an entry point into the topic that includes a useful bibliography, consult James Bessen, *Learning by Doing: The Real Connection between Innovation, Wages, and Wealth* (New Haven, CT: Yale University Press, 2015).

On behavioral economics begin with Philip Corr and Anke Plagnol, *Behavioral Economics: The Basics* (London: Routledge, 2019), then consult Peter Diamond and Hannu Vartiainen (eds.), *Behavioral Economics and Its Applications* (Princeton, NJ: Princeton University Press, 2007); Robin M. Hogarth and Melvin W. Reder (eds.), *Rational Choice: The Contrast between Economics and Psychology* (Chicago, IL: University of Chicago Press, 1987); Andrew Shtulman, *Scienceblind: Why Our Intuitive Theories about the World Are so Often Wrong* (New York: Basic Books, 2017).

Artificial intelligence seems to spill over into all manner of disciplines. Specific to economics, however, there are useful explanations: Colin Camerer, *Behavioral Game Theory: Experiments in Strategic Interaction* (Princeton, NJ: Princeton University Press, 2003); Tshilidzi Marwala and Evan Hurwitz, *Artificial Intelligence and Economic Theory: Skynet in the Market* (Berlin: Springer-Verlag, 2017); and Scott J. Moss and John Rae (eds.), *Artificial Intelligence and Economic Analysis: Prospects and Problems* (Aldershot, UK: Edward Elgar Publishing, 1992).

ROLES OF POLITICAL SCIENTISTS AND HISTORIANS

To understand the issues explored by political scientists, begin with a standard introductory text, such as Michael G. Roskin, Robert L. Cord, James A.

Medeiros, and Walter S. Jones, *Political Science: An Introduction*, 13th ed. (Upper Saddle River, NJ: Prentice Hall, 2013). Then follow up with more detailed overviews, including Leonardo A. Morlino, Dirk Berg-Schlosser, and Bertrand Badie, *Political Science: A Global Perspective* (Thousand Oaks, CA: SAGE 2017); Robert E. Goodin (ed.), *The Oxford Handbook of Political Science* (New York: Oxford University Press, 2009). Oxford University Press has published a series like Goodin's on various aspects of political science; they are excellent and comprehensive.

Several monographs by leading experts set the tone for the type of research and information their discipline created and relied upon in the twentieth century. Examples include Robert A. Dahl, *Democracy and Its Critics* (New Haven, CT: Yale University Press, 1989), Arend Lijphart, *Democracy in Plural Societies: A Comparative Exploration* (New Haven, CT: Yale University Press, 1977); see also Gabriel A. Almond and Sidney Verba (eds.), *The Civic Culture Revisited* (Boston, MA: Little Brown, 1980); Juan J. Linz, *Totalitarian and Authoritarian Regimes* (London: Lynne Rienner, 2000); and the classic by Hannah Arendt, *The Origins of Totalitarianism* (New York: Schocken, 2004, originally published in 1948). A historian/political scientist, Barrington Moore Jr., added substantially to political science with a series of books, the most important of which are *Injustice: The Social Bases of Obedience and Revolt* (London: Routledge, 1978); *Social Origins of Dictatorship and Democracy: Lord and Peasant in the Making of the Modern World* (Boston, MA: Beacon Press, 1966); and *Political Power and Social Theory: Seven Studies* (New York: Harper Torchbooks, 1965); on his work, see Dennis Smith, *Barrington Moore, Jr.: A Critical Appraisal* (New York: Routledge, 2018, original edition Armonk, NY: M. E. Sharpe, 1983). On the discipline's work see Hans-Dieter Kingermann (ed.), *The State of Political Science in Western Europe* (Opladen, Germany: Barbara Budrich Publishers, 2007); S. F. Schramm and B. Caterino (eds.), *Making Political Science Matter: Debating Knowledge, Research, and Methods* (New York: New York University Press, 2006); David E. McNabb, *Research Methods for Political Science: Quantitative and Qualitative Methods* (Armonk, NY: M. E. Sharpe, 2004).

The literature on polling is now massive. However, a few texts introduce the information content and practices of polling. Two useful entry points are Paul Brace and Barbara Hinckley, *Follow the Leader: Opinion Polls and the Modern Presidents* (New York: Basic Books, 1992); Richard E. Neustadt, *Presidential Power and the Modern Presidents* (New York: Free Press, 1990); followed up with Claude E. Robinson, *Straw Votes: A Study of Political Predictions* (New York: Columbia University Press, 1932); George Horace Gallup (ed.), *The Gallup Poll: Public Opinion, 1935–1971*, 3 vols.

(New York: Random House, 1972); Kenneth F. Warren, *In Defense of Public Opinion Polling* (Boulder, CA: Westview Press, 1992); Howard Schuman, *Method and Meaning in Polls and Surveys* (Cambridge, MA: Harvard University Press, 2008); John T. Cacioppo and Richard E. Petty, *Attitudes and Persuasion: Classic and Contemporary Approaches* (London: Routledge, 1996, 2018); John G. Geer (ed.), *Public Opinion and Polling around the World: A Historical Encyclopedia*, 2 vols. (Santa Barbara, CA: ABC-CLIO, 2004), the first volume focuses on the United States, the second the rest of the world. For useful history, there is Jean M. Converse, *Survey Research in the United States: Roots and Emergence 1890–1960* (New York: Routledge, 2017).

Diplomatic behavior and information requires understanding international affairs, and so for that a good start is M. J. Grieve, *A Hundred Years of International Relations* (New York: Praeger, 1971), followed up immediately with any of the editions of Corneliu Bjola and Markus Komprobst, *Understanding International Diplomacy: Theory, Practice and Ethics*, 2nd ed. (London: Routledge, 2018); then with Joseph M. Siracusa, *Diplomacy: A Very Short Introduction* (New York: Oxford University Press, 2010). François De Callières, *The Practice of Diplomacy* (London: Constable & Co.,1919, originally published in 1716 as *De maniè de négocier avec les Souverains* [Amsterdam: La Compagnie]); Matthew S. Anderson, *The Rise of Modern Diplomacy, 1450–1919* London: Longman, 1993); Sir Harold George Nicolson, *The Evolution of Diplomatic Method* (New York: Praeger reprint, 1977, London: Constable, 1954); Abraham de Wicquefort, *The Ambassador and His Functions* (multiple editions in the 1700s in French); and a classic for over a century, Ernest Satow, *A Guide to Diplomatic Practice* (New York: Longmans, Green & Co., 1917); Paul Sharp and Geoffrey Wiseman, *The Diplomatic Corps as an Institution of International Society* (New York: Palgrave Macmillan, 2007). A classic short text, Harold Nicolson, *Diplomacy* (Oxford: Oxford University Press, 1936) was still in print late in the twentieth century; James Crawford, *Brownlie's Principles of Public International Law*, 9th ed. (Oxford: Oxford University Press, 2019), both used by diplomats today.

On the theory and practice of history time-honored sources include the blunt and clever great read by David Hackett Fischer, *Historians' Fallacies: Toward a Logic of Historical Thought* (New York: Harper Torchbooks, 1970); then the more serious proper studies by R. G. Collingwood, *The Idea of History* (New York: Galaxy Book, 1946) still in print; G. R. Elton, *The Practice of History* (New York: Thomas Y. Crowell, 1967); Jacques Barzun and Henry F. Graff, *The Modern Researcher* (New York: Harcourt, Brace & World, 1957). But do not overlook Richard Evans, *In Defense of History* (London: Granta Books, 2000); Michael J. Salevouris and Conal Furay, *The Methods and Skills of History: A Practical Guide*, 4th ed. (Oxford:

John Wiley & Sons, 2015): 13–26, 169–178; Simon Gunn and Lucy Faire (eds.), *Research Methods for History* (Edinburgh, UK: Edinburgh University Press, 2012); William H. McDowell, *Historical Research: A Guide for Writers of Dissertations, Theses, Articles and Books* (New York: Routledge, 2013); Martha Howell and Walter Prevenier, *From Reliable Sources: An Introduction to Historical Methods* (Ithaca, NY: Cornell University Press, 2001); James W. Cortada, *History Hunting: A Guide for Fellow Adventurers* (Armonk, NY: M. E. Sharpe, 2012); John Lewis Gaddis, *The Landscape of History: How Historians Map the Past* (New York: Oxford University Press, 2002); Peter Novick, *That Noble Dream: The "Objectivity" Question and the American Historical Profession* (Cambridge, UK: Cambridge University Press, 1988). Each discusses the changing nature of information and how it is created.

Von Ranke has been carefully studied by many scholars, such as by Andreas D. Boldt, *The Life and Work of the German Historian Leopold von Ranke (1795–1886): An Assessment of His Achievements* (Lewiston, NY: Edwin Mellen Press, 2015); and his, *Leopold von Ranke: A Biography* (London: Routledge, 2019); Iggers and J. M. Powell (eds.), *Leopold von Ranke and the Shaping of the Historical Discipline* (Syracuse, NY: Syracuse University Press, 1990); Leonard Krieger, *Ranke: The Meaning of History* (Chicago, IL: University of Chicago Press, 1977).

Oral history has a growing practitioner literature useful in understanding this new class of historical information. Always begin with Donald A. Ritchie, *Doing Oral History* (New York: Oxford University Press, 2002, 2015), Barbara Sommer, *The Oral History Manual*, 3rd ed. (Lanham, MD: Rowman & Littlefield, 2018); Thomas L. Charlton (ed.), *History of Oral History: Foundations and Methodology* (Lanham, MD: Rowman & Littlefield, 2007); Lynn Abrams, *Oral History Theory*, 2nd ed. (New York: Routledge, 2016); Patricia Leavy, *Oral History: Understanding Qualitative Research* (New York: Oxford University Press, 2011); or Ronald J. Grele et al., *Envelopes of Sound: The Art of Oral History* (Westport, CT: Praeger, 1991). There are also guides aimed at both professional and amateur historians worth consulting too, such as Robert Perks and Alistar Thomson (eds.), *The Oral History Reader* (London: Routledge, 1998); Linda Barnickel, *Oral History for the Family Historian: A Basic Guide* (No City: Oral History Association, 2010); and Laurie Mercier and Madeline Buckendorf, *Using Oral History in Community History Projects* (No City: Oral History Association, 2007).

On cliometrics there are Francesco Boldizzoni, *The Poverty of Clio: Resurrecting Economic History* (Princeton, NJ: Princeton University Press, 2011); John S. Lyons, Louis P. Cain, and Samuel H. Williamson (eds.), *Reflections on the Cliometrics Revolution: Conversations with Economic Historians* (London: Routledge, 2008).

Finally on contemporary issues and topics related to the history of information, see the still relevant Parson E. Tillinghast, *The Specious Past: Historians and Others* (Reading, MA: Addison-Wesley, 1972); William Aspray (ed.), *Chasing Moore's Law: Information Technology Policy in the United States* (Raleigh, NC: SciTech Publishing, 2004); and with Paul Ceruzzi (eds.), *The Internet and American Business* (Cambridge, MA: MIT Press, 2008); Aspray and Cortada, *From Urban Legends to Political Fact-Checking*; Aspray (ed.), *Historical Studies in Computing, Information, and Society* (Berlin: Springer-Verlag, 2020); Cortada, *All the Facts*.

EFFECTS OF INFORMATION AND COMPUTERS ON WORK

The diffusion of computing and digital information in workspaces has been studied by historians. Sources include James W. Cortada, *The Digital Flood: The Diffusion of Information Technology across the U.S. Europe, and Asia* (New York: Oxford University Press, 2012); Martin Campbell-Kelly, William Aspray, Nathan Ensmenger, and Jeffrey R. Yost, *Computer: A History of the Information Machine*, 3rd ed. (Boulder, CA: Westview, 2014); Paul E. Ceruzzi, *A History of Modern Computing*, 2nd ed. (Cambridge, MA: MIT Press, 2003); Martin Campbell-Kelly and Daniel D. Garcia-Swartz, *From Mainframes to Smartphones: A History of the International Computer Industry* (Cambridge, MA: Harvard University Press, 2015); James W. Cortada, *Before the Computer: IBM, NCR, Burroughs, and Remington Rand and the Industry They Created, 1865–1956* (Princeton, NJ: Princeton University Press, 1993), *The Computer in the United States: From Laboratory to Market, 1930–1960* (Armonk, NY: M. E. Sharpe, 1993); and *Information Technology as Business History: Issues in the History and Management of Computers* (Westport, CT: Greenwood Press, 1996); JoAnne Yates, *Structuring the Information Age: Life Insurance and Technology in the Twentieth Century* (Baltimore, MD: Johns Hopkins University Press, 2008). On the System 360, see Emerson W. Pugh, Lyle R. Johnson, and John H. Palmer, *IBM's 360 and Early 370 Systems* (Cambridge, MA: MIT Press, 1991); and Cortada, *IBM*. For by-products of the expanded computer industry, there is Jeffery R. Yost, *Making IT Work: A History of the Computer Services Industry* (Cambridge, MA: MIT Press, 2017); Charles P. Bourne and Trudi Bellardo Hahn, *A History of Online Information Services, 1963–1976* (Cambridge, MA: MIT Press, 2003).

For more contemporary views, which I documented, see James W. Cortada, *EDP Costs and Charges: Finance, Budgets, and Cost Control in Data Processing* (Englewood Cliffs, NJ: Prentice-Hall, 1980); *Managing*

DP Hardware: Capacity Planning, Cost Justification, Availability, and Energy Management (Englewood Cliffs, NJ: Prentice-Hall, 1983), *Strategic Data Processing: Considerations for Management* (Englewood Cliffs, NJ: Prentice-Hall, 1984). But see also, Leonard Rico, *The Advance against Paperwork: Computers, Systems, and Personnel* (Ann Arbor: Graduate School of Business Administration, University of Michigan, 1967); R. A. Hirschheim, *Office Automation: A Social and Organizational Perspective* (New York: John Wiley & Sons, 1985); J. F. Rockart and D. W. DeLong, *Executive Support Systems: The Emergence of Top Management Computer Use* (Homewood, IL: Dow Jones-Irwin, 1988); P. G. W. Keen and M. S. Morton, *Decision Support Systems: An Organizational Perspective* (Reading, MA: Addison-Wesley, 1978).

Implications of more digital technologies and information can be explored in publications influential on management when they appeared. See James M. Utterback, *Mastering the Dynamics of Innovation* (Boston, MA: Harvard Business School Press, 1994); Clayton M. Christensen, *The Innovator's Dilemma: When New Technologies Cause Great Firms to Fail* (Boston, MA: Harvard Business School Press, 1997); Carl Shapiro and Hal R. Varian, *Information Rules: A Strategic Guide to the Network Economy* (Boston, MA: Harvard Business School Press, 1999); Thomas S. Wurster, *Blown to Bits: How the New Economics of Information Transforms Strategy* (Boston, MA: Harvard Business School Press, 2000). More tactically about how computers were being used, James W. Cortada, *Best Practices in Information Technology: How Corporations Get the Most Value from Exploiting Their Digital Investments* (Upper Saddle River, NJ: Prentice Hall PTR, 1998); and *21st Century Business: Managing and Working in the New Digital Economy* (Upper Saddle River, NJ: Financial Times/Prentice Hall, 2001); Thomas H. Davenport, *Process Innovation: Reengineering Work through Information Technology* (Boston, MA: Harvard Business Review Press, 1992); Michael Hammer, *Beyond Reengineering: How the Process-Centered Organization Is Changing Our Work and Our Lives* (New York: Harper Business, 1996).

On supply chains and other collections of more recent types of information, useful introductions include Michael Hugos, *Essentials of Supply Chain Management*, 2nd ed. (Hoboken, NJ: John Wiley & Sons, 2006): 133–168; Jack R. Meredith and Scott M. Shafer, *Operations and Supply Chain Management for MBAs*, 7th ed. (Hoboken, NJ: John Wiley & Sons, 2019): 240–328; Victor Zarnowitz, *Business Cycles: Theory, History, Indicators, and Forecasting* (Chicago, IL: University of Chicago Press, 1996); Christopher M. Bishop, *Pattern Recognition and Machine Learning* (Berlin: Springer-Verlag, 2006) for a technical "how to" text; Cortada, *Information and the Modern Corporation*.

About the Internet I find many useful studies, but this in particular, Shane Greenstein, *How the Internet Became Commercial: Innovation, Privatization, and the Birth of a New Network* (Princeton, NJ: Princeton University Press, 2015). On the role of children and young adults a good place to start is with John Palfrey and Urs Gasser, *Born Digital: Understanding the First Generation of Digital Natives* (New York: Basic Books, 2008, 2016). Regarding the Cold war, see Paul N. Edwards, *The Closed World: Computers and the Politics of Discourse in Cold War America* (Cambridge, MA: MIT Press, 1996); Colin B. Burke, *America's Information Wars: The Untold Story of Information Systems in America's Conflicts and Politics from World War II to the Internet Age* (Lanham, MD: Rowman & Littlefield, 2018). Also essential are Brian McCullough, *How the Internet Happened: From Netscape to the iPhone* (New York: W. W. Norton, 2018); Katie Hafner and Matthew Lyon, *Where Wizards Stay Up Late: The Origins of the Internet* (New York: Simon & Schuster, 1996); Janet Abbate, *Inventing the Internet* (Cambridge, MA: MIT Press, 1999); Barry Wellman and Caroline Haythornthwaite (eds.), *The Internet in Everyday Life* (Oxford: Blackwell, 2002); Lee Rainie and Barry Wellman, *Networked: The New Social Operating System* (Cambridge, MA: MIT Press, 2012); William Aspray and Barbara M. Hayes (eds.), *Everyday Information: The Evolution of Information Seeking in America* (Cambridge, MA: MIT Press, 2011). One should not overlook Mark Muro, Sifan Liu, Jacob Whiton, and Siddharth Kulkarni, *Digitization and the American Workforce* (Washington, D.C.: Brookings Institution, November 2017) for a recent study. Finally, for descriptions of what kind of information required by hundreds of professions over the past 170 years, there is for the United States, U.S. Bureau of Labor Statistics, *Occupational Outlook Handbook*, published in many editions since the 1870s, and in recent decades online, https://www.bls.gov/ooh/.

LIVING IN THE INFORMATION AGE

A number of us have explored this issue. I have in James W. Cortada, *Living with Computers: The Digital World of Today and Tomorrow* (Cham, Switzerland: Springer, 2020); *How Societies Embrace Information Technology: Lessons for Management and the Rest of Us* (Hoboken, NJ: John Wiley & Sons, 2009); and in *All the Facts: A History of Information in the United States since 1870* (New York: Oxford University Press, 2016). But a useful book to not overlook is by Michael Buckland, *Information and Society* (Cambridge, MA: MIT Press, 2017). On the economics of a knowledge-centered society a recent addition to the literature is by Joseph E. Stiglitz and Bruce C. Greenwald, *Creating a Learning Society: A New Approach to Growth, Development, and*

Social Progress (New York: Columbia University Press, 2014). Where they also make suggestions for policy makers. However, if one could consult only a single source, let it be Frank Webster, *Theories of the Information Society*, 4th ed. (London: Routledge, 2014, first published 1996); and if only one history book, then by Toni Weller, *Information History—An Introduction: Exploring an Emergent Field* (Oxford: Chandos Publishing, 2008). For a more intellectual discourse, see Mario Perez-Montoro, *The Phenomenon of Information: A Conceptual Approach to Information Flow* (Lanham, MD: Scarecrow Press, 2007). For a detailed socio-technical analysis, one of the most widely respected students of the subject is Manuel Castells, and the crown jewel of his many publications is his trilogy, *The Rise of the Network Society, the Information Age: Economy, Society and Culture* (Oxford: Blackwell, 1996); *The Power of Identity, the Information Age: Economy, Society and Culture* (Oxford: Blackwell, 1997); and *The End of the Millennium, the Information Age: Economy, Society and Culture* (Oxford: Blackwell, 1997). Ronald E. Day's short book, *The Modern Invention of Information: Discourse, History, and Power* (Carbondale: Southern Illinois University Press, 2001) provides a useful window into modern thinking about information issues in modern society. It is quite thoughtful and not be overlooked.

There are many reminders that long before our time, earlier societies used information. For our project, I found the following relevant: Jürgen Habermas, *The Structural Transformation of the Public Sphere: An Inquiry a Category of Bourgeois Society* (Cambridge, MA: MIT Press, 1989); Daniel Headrick, *When Information Came of Age: Technologies of Knowledge in the Age of Reason and Revolution, 1700–1850* (New York: Oxford University Press, 2000); Anthony Giddens, *Social Theory and Modern Sociology* (Cambridge, UK: Polity Press, 1987); Edward Higgs, *The Information State in England: The Central Collection of Information on Citizens since 1500* (Basingstoke: Palgrave Macmillan, 2004), but do not overlook his other book, *Life, Death and Statistics: Civil Registration, Censuses and the Work of the General Register Office, 1836–1952* (Hatfield, UK: University of Hertfordshire Press, 2004); and Jon Agar, *The Government Machine: A Revolutionary History of the Computer* (Cambridge, MA: MIT Press, 2003).

Alvin Toffler's key works include *Future Shock* (New York: Random House, 1970) and *The Third Wave* (New York: William Morrow, 1980). I am not aware of a biography about him. On the French experience, we have Alain Minc's memoirs, *Voyage ou Centre du "Système"* (Paris: Bernard Grosset, 2019); and an accessible edition of the French study is available, Simon Nora and Alain Minc, *The Computerization of Society: A Report to the President of France* (Cambridge, MA: MIT Press, 1980). The standard work on the Minitel is now Julien Mailland and Kevin Driscoll, *Minitel: Welcome to the Internet* (Cambridge, MA: MIT Press, 2017).

THE EMERGENCE OF BIG DATA

Big Data is a relatively new form of information technology, so much of the literature on it focuses on explaining what it is or consists of technical publications on how to implement and use it. So much of the information about it has to be gleaned from technical journals and the trade press. The ones used in chapter 10 can be found in the endnotes. But a few books are beginning to appear. A useful entry point into the subject is David Weinberger, *Too Big to Know: Rethinking Knowledge Now that the Facts Aren't the Facts, Experts Are Everywhere, and the Smartest Person in the Room Is the Room* (New York: Basic Books, 2012), which is not a technical treatise. It might also be useful to consider how software is changing as Big Data rises, so for that consult D. M. Berry, *The Philosophy of Software: Code and Mediation in the Digital Age* (London: Palgrave Macmillan, 2011); and a surprisingly good read, Daniel E. Atkins et al., *Revolutionizing Science and Engineering through Cyberinfrastructure: Report of the National Science Foundation Blue-Ribbon Panel on Cyberinfrastructure* (Washington D.C.: National Science Foundation, January 2003). For insight on how scientists are reacting to Big Data, an excellent starting point is the short but very approachable report, David Bollier, *The Promise and Peril of Big Data* (Washington, D.C.: Aspen Institute, 2010). For a criticism of how firms and governments use Big Data, the key publication to explore is Shoshana Zuboff and James Maxmin, *The Age of Surveillance Capitalism: The Fight for a Human Future at the New Frontier of Power* (New York: PublicAffairs, 2019).

For more technical explanations, there are now numerous texts. I used O'Reilly Media, *Big Data Now* (Sebastopol, CA: O'Reilly Media, 2011). One cannot stray too far from how the mind works when dealing with such topics as Big Data, Nikolas Rose and Joelle M. Abi-Rached, *Neuro: The New Brain Sciences and the Management of the Mind* (Princeton, NJ: Princeton University Press, 2013). There are a series of publications that relate to Big Data that can help situate this new development into current technological and biological realities: Robert R. Korfhage, *Information Storage and Retrieval* (New York: John Wiley & Sons, 1997); Richard K. Belew, *Finding Out About: A Cognitive Perspective on Search Engine Technology and the W.W.W.* (Cambridge, UK: Cambridge University Press, 2000); Michael Lesk, *Understanding Digital Libraries*, 2nd ed. (San Francisco, CA: Morgan Kaufmann, 2005). For three texts on metadata, see Richard Gartner, *Metadata: Shaping Knowledge from Antiquity to the Semantic Web* (Berlin: Springer-Verlag, 2016); Marcia Zeng and Jian Qin, *Metadata* (New York: ALA Neal-Schuman, 2016); Steven J. Miller, *Metadata for Digital Collections* (New York: ALA Neal-Schuman, 2020).

FAKE FACTS, FAKE NEWS

Recent events supercharged interest in such topics as "fake facts," "alternative facts," and the more mundane issues of lies, rumors, misinformation, conspiracies, and gossip. Each existed for centuries and when studied by scholars, often in piecemeal fashion. The political scientists have done the most to understand the presentation and manipulation of truth and facts for political purposes, such as to win elections. In the past two decades experts on media and advertising have contributed to a more theoretically based understanding of the role of all manner of facts both truthful and not. Historians are just beginning to weigh in on the matter. William Aspray and I, both trained as historians, have recently weighed in with two studies, James W. Cortada and William Aspray, *Fake News Nation: The Long History of Lies and Misinterpretations in America* (Lanham, MD: Rowman & Littlefield, 2019); and William Aspray and James W. Cortada, *From Urban Legends to Political Fact-Checking: Online Scrutiny in America, 1990–2015* (Cham, Switzerland: Spring, 2019). A group of media experts have also provided varying perspective and brief case studies of related issues, focusing largely on recent examples, Melissa Zimdars and Kembrew McLeod (eds.), *Fake News: Understanding Media and Misinformation in the Digital Age* (Cambridge, MA: MIT Press, 2020). We did not discuss spying, espionage, or the work of governments to misinform each other, but it has a rich history. For a well-informed account of twentieth-century activities, see Thomas Rid, *Active Measures: The Secret History of Disinformation and Political Warfare* (New York: Farrar, Straus and Giroux, 2020).

For the language of the politician, a useful place to begin understanding political rhetoric is Murray Edelman, *Political Language: Words that Succeed and Politics that Fail* (New York: Academic Press, 1977). This political scientist wrote a raft of books on American political behavior, which are core to understanding the role of information in national elections; one of the most useful of which is *Politics as Symbolic Action: Mass Arousal and Quiescence* (Chicago, IL: Markham, 1971). But see also his *The Symbolic Uses of Politics* (Urbana: University of Illinois Press, 1985). Do not overlook Dan F. Hahn, *Political Communication: Rhetoric, Government, and Citizens* (State College, PA: Strata Publishing, 1998); and Bruce Bimber, *Information and American Democracy: Technology in the Evolution of Political Power* (Cambridge, UK: Cambridge University Press, 2003). All have rich bibliographies. Presidential assassinations are about conspiracies and have been studied extensively. On Lincoln's, the most useful is William Hanchett, *The Lincoln Murder Conspiracies* (Urbana: University of Illinois Press, 1983). On mythologizing him, see Gabor Borritt, *The Lincoln Enigma: The*

Changing Faces of an American Icon (New York: Oxford University Press, 2001); Philip B. Kunhardt III, Peter W. Kunhardt, and Peter W. Kunhardt Jr., *Looking for Lincoln: The Making of an American Icon* (New York: Alfred A. Knopf, 2008); and Merrill D. Peterson, *Lincoln in American Memory* (New York: Oxford University Press, 1994). On Kennedy's, there is Jim Marrs, *Crossfire: The Plot that Killed Kennedy* (New York: Basic Books, 2013). The best researched study, however, is by Philip Shenon, *A Cruel and Shocking Act: The Secret History of the Kennedy Assassination* (New York: Henry Holt, 2013).

The use of information by companies and industries has been explored. For a good introduction to a number of these, consult Ari Rabin-Havt and Media Matters for America, *Lies, Incorporated: The World of Post-Truth Politics* (New York: Anchor Books, 2016). The tobacco industry's behavior can be studied thoroughly with Richard Kluger, *Ashes to Ashes: America's Hundred-Year Cigarette War, the Public Health, and the Unabashed Triumph of Philip Morris* (New York: Knopf, 1996); Philip J. Hilts, *Smoke Screen: The Truth behind the Tobacco Industry Cover-Up* (Boston, MA: Addison-Wesley, 1996); David Kessler, *A Question of Intent: A Great American Battle with a Deadly Industry* (New York: Public Affairs, 2001); Allan Brandt, *The Cigarette Century: The Rise, Fall and Deadly Persistence of the Product that Defined America* (New York: Basic Books, 2007); and Naomi Oreskes and Erick M. Conway, *Merchants of Doubt: How a Handful of Scientists Obscured the Truth on Issues from Tobacco Smoke to Global Warming* (New York: Bloomsbury, 2010). This last book is the most authoritative study currently available based on a massive cache of industry documents.

On global warming, James Inhofe, *The Greatest Hoax: How the Global Warming Conspiracy Threatens Your Future* (Washington, D.C.: WND Books, 2012). For the alternative view, see National Research Council, *Limiting the Magnitude of Future Climate Change* (Washington, D.C.: The National Academic Press, 2010). Historical perspective combined with the use of a growing body of scientific evidence of the Earth's evolving climate over the millennia can be found in S. Fred Singer and Dennis T. Avery, *Unstoppable Global Warming: Every 1,500 Years* (Lantham, MD: Rowman & Littlefield, 2007). The most widely available discussion of the issues, demonstrating alternative uses of similar data, rhetoric, and opinions can be found in Al Gore, *An Inconvenient Truth: The Planetary Emergency of Global Warming and What We Can Do about It* (Emmaus, PA: Rodale, 2006) and a video he produced under the same title (New York: Melcher Media, 2006). For a more academic discussion along similar lines as Gore's, see National Research Council, *Climate Change: Evidence, Impacts, and Choices* (Washington, D.C.: National Research Council, 2011). Finally, on the manipulation of information, see David Michaels, *Doubt Is Their*

Product: How Industry's Assault on Science Threatens Your Health (New York: Oxford University Press, 2008).

On business uses of information, particularly public relations and advertising, begin with Stuart Ewen, *PR! A Social History of Spin* (New York: Basic Books, 1996) and Roland Marchand, *Creating the Corporate Soul: The Rise of Public Relations and Corporate Imagery in American Big Business* (Berkeley: University of California Press, 1998); but also consult Fred Koenig, *Rumors in the Marketplace: The Social Psychology of Commercial Hearsay* (New York: Praeger, 1985); and folklorist Gary Alan Fine, *Manufacturing Tales: Sex and Money in Contemporary Legends* (Knoxville: University of Tennessee Press, 1992). For a useful introduction to the history of advertising, see Daniel Pope, *The Making of Modern Advertising* (New York: Basic Books, 1983). Patent medicines has an extensive literature, but the authority is James Harvey Young, *The Toadstool Millionaires: A Social History of Patent Medicines in America before Federal Regulation* (Princeton, NJ: Princeton University Press, 1961); *The Medical Messiahs: A Social History of Health Quackery in Twentieth-Century America* (Princeton, NJ: Princeton University Press, 1967); and *American Health Quackery* (Princeton, NJ: Princeton University Press, 1992). For a study of nutrition and wellness information, see the early study by Victor Herbert, *Nutrition Cultism: Facts and Fictions* (Philadelphia, PA: George F. Stickley, 1980).

An excellent place to begin regarding the Internet and facts is by Laura Gurak, *Cyberliteracy: Navigating the Internet with Awareness* (New Haven, CT: Yale University Press, 2001), followed by Faithe Wempen, *Digital Literacy for Dummies* (Hoboken, NJ: John Wiley & Sons, 2015); Nicole A. Cooke, *Fake News and Alternative Facts: Information Literacy in a Post-Truth Era* (Chicago, IL: ALA Editions, 2018); and Daniel J. Levitin, *A Field Guide to Lies: Critical Thinking in the Information Age* (New York: Dutton, 2016). On metaliteracy, a key source is Thomas P. Mackey, *Metaliteracy: Reinventing Information Literacy to Empower Learners* (Chicago, IL: American Library Association, 2014).

Index

Note: Page numbers in *italics* refers to illustrations on the corresponding page.

Abel Prize, 253n14
abstracting services, 73
academic libraries, 59
academic research, 43–44
accounting, 49, 184, 189–96, *191–93*, 363n42
accurate information, 54
ACM. *See* Association for Computing Machinery
agencies, of information, 318n35
Age of Revolution, 55
The Age of Uncertainty (Galbraith), 295
agriculture: Department of Agriculture, 34, 38, 55, 186, 207, 256; digitalization in, 98; in education, 39–40; labor in, 32; in modernity, 246; in Morrill Act, 37
AI. *See* artificial intelligence
Aiken, Howard, 112
Akerlof, George, 237, 376n112, 377n119
ALA. *See* American Library Association
alcohol, *257*, 257–58
algebra, 138
algorithms, 338n37, 343n117
All the Facts (Cortada), 24–25, 68, 291
Alphabet Inc., 3

Amazon, 14, 95, 149, 171, 198, 215, 240
ambiguity, 10–11, 90–91
American Chemical Society, 164–65, 293
American Civil War, 6, 32
American Documentation, 79, 114
American Documentation Institute, 79
American Historical Association, 270–71, 292
American Library Association (ALA), 59, 62, 74. *See also* libraries
American Library Journal, 59
American National Standards Institute (ANSI), 117–18
American Political Science Association, 254
American Society for Information Science, 79–80
American Telephone and Telegraph (AT&T), 95–97, 99, 102, 108, 111–12, 113. *See also* Bell Labs
analog information, 339n50
anecdotal information, *286*
ANSI. *See* American National Standards Institute
Apple, 91, 97, 126–27, 238

427

applications, 7, 91, 92–93
applied mathematics, 134–35
applied research, 198
appropriations, 7
Arrow, Kenneth J., 224, 228–29
artificial intelligence (AI): computers and, 26, 124–25, 302–3; in culture, 14, 152, 296, 304; databases and, *284*, 284–85; history of, 19; humanity and, 105–6; information and, 280–81; in modernity, 297, 340n69; philosophy of, 105; research, 305; scholarship with, 93; science of, 242; society before, 29; tools, 123
Asia, 7
Aspray, William, 272–73, 362–63
Association for Computing Machinery (ACM), 90–91
assumptions, 241
Atiyah, Michael, 129, 137–39, *140*
AT&T. *See* American Telephone and Telegraph
auditing, 190–91

Babbage, Charles, 36, 130, 281–82
Bachman, Charles W., 89, 121–23, *122*
Bachman Information Systems, *122*, 122–23
Bacon, Francis, 64
Baeza-Yates, Ricardo, *115*
bandwagon effect, 260
banking, 199–200
Baran, Paul, 342n92
Barzun, Jacques, 264
basic research, 198
BEA. *See* Bureau of Economic Analysis
Becker, Carl, 274
behavior, 80, 379n145
behavioral economics, 217, 240–44, 270
Belgium, 69–71
Bell Labs: collaboration at, 341n79; culture at, 42–43, 96, 102;
discoveries at, 106, 133; engineering at, 104, 107, 111, 135; science at, 42–43, 110
benchmark polls, 259
Beniger, James R., 7
Benzoic acid, *166*, 166–67
Berners-Lee, Tim, *115*, 342n92
Bernier, Charles L., 167
Bernouvilli Urn Model, 201
Bertalanffy, Ludwig von, 296, 392n32
Berzelius, Jöns Jacob, 163
Bessen, James, 239
Bezos, Jeff, 211
bibliographies, 74–76, 125–26. *See also* libraries
Big Data, 5, 10, 175–76, 244, 285, 294, 311n29
binary digits, 312n32
bioinformatics, 175–79
biology: behavioral economics and, 240–44; bioinformatics, 175–79; concepts in, 392n32; history of, 154, 169–75; mathematics and, 225; physics and, 299–300; psychology and, 274–75, 380n151
BioScience Information Service (BIOSIS), 118–19
bits, of data, 312n32
Blaug, Mark, 218
BLS. *See* Bureau of Labor Statistics
Bohr, Niels, 86
bookless libraries, 314n56
books, 57–58, 73–77, 348n16
Boole, George, 99
Boolean algebra, 109–10
Boorstin, Daniel J., 9, 28, 186
Bowker, Geoffrey C., 177
Bradford, Samuel C., 65, 72–73, 76–77
Bradford's Law, 76–77, 79
Braudel, Fernand, 265
brushfire polls, 259
Buckland, Michael, 11, 84
Bureau of Economic Analysis (BEA), 230–34, 234–36, *235*, *236*

Bureau of Labor Statistics (BLS), 93–94, 230–31, 349n41, 361n6
Bureau of Statistics, 232
Burke, Colin B., 64, 72
Burke, Edmund, 218
Bush, George H. W., 263
Bush, Vannevar, 69, 73, 84, 340n64
business: culture, *298–99*; Deming on, 207–8; economics and, 189–96, *191–93*, 215–16, 219–20; government and, 183–84, 196–200, 208–12; information in, 365n73; information standards in, 203–7; innovation in, 187–89, 193; mathematical models for, 201–3, *203*; mathematics and, 240; STEM and, 202–3; technology and, 279–80, 372n41; TQM, 34, 184, 207–8; in U.S., 184–87
Butler, Pierce, 74

calculus, 134, *140*, 348n14
Car, E. H., 265
carbon, 317n14
Carnegie Corporation, 75
CAS. *See Chemical Abstracts Service*
cataloging, 326n28
Cato, Robert A., 266
Census Bureau, U.S., 186–87
central processing units (CPUs), 104–5
Cerf, Vinton G., 342n92
Ceruzzi, Paul, 272
Chan, Lois Mai, 64
Chandler, Alfred D., Jr., 31–32, 34, 211, 375n86
change, 133
Chaplin, Charlie, 14
Charles Babbage Institute, 121, 266, 269
Chemical Abstracts Service (CAS), 118–19, 163–69, *166*
Chemical Industry Notes (CIN), 120
chemical information, 161–69, *166*
chemistry, 44, 279, 293
Chicago Manual of Style, 265
children, 6, 59, 131, *139–40*, 252

China, 7
Churchill, Winston, 6, 103, 275
CIN. *See* Chemical Industry Notes
civil rights, 259
Clark, Andy, 29
Clark, John M., 227
classification, 326n28, 327n47.
 See also specific classifications
A Classification and Subject Index (Dewey), 64
Clinton, Hillary, 301
cliometrics, 267–70
codices, 272
coding, 335n8
cognitive scientists, 63
Cold War, 1–2, 35–36, 50, 77–78, 141
communication: AT&T for, 95–97, 111–12; communications theory, 110–11; with computers, 20; digitalization of, 99–101, *101*; in diplomacy, 261–62; discoveries in, 33; engineering and, 103; of information, 151–52; language and, 150; mathematical theory of, 79, 110; in modernity, 300–301; in nature, 3; technology for, 13–14, 46–51; telecommunications, 30–31; theory of, 11–12
community, 7
comparative politics, 252–53
computers: AI and, 26, 124–25, 302–3; coding, 335n8; in Cold War, 50, 77; commands, 338n36; communication with, 20; computational determinism, 179–80; computational mathematics, 135; computational methods, 228–29; Computer Age, 1–2; computer science, 60, 90–96, 116, 161, *203*, 279–80, 303–4, 392n24; data analysis with, 197; databases with, 116–23, *122*; data on, 99–101, *101*, 149–50; digitalization and, 89–90; documentation with, 177–78; economics and, 53; electrification and, 95–99; ENIAC computer, 106;

genetics and, 176–77; globalization of, 85–86; in higher education, 84; history of, 47–48, 51–52, 89–90, 123–27, 281–82, 292, 319n36; at IBM, 204, 211–12; industry of, 314n62; information on, 321n74; language of, 312n32, 337n28; library computing, 114–15; memory in, 273–74, 344n128; Nyquist for, 102–3; OCLC, 65–66, 119–20; personal, 16, 19–20, 92, 149, 297–98, *298–99*, 364n50; politics of, 325n14; programs for, 91–92, 105; research on, 85; Salton for, 112, 114–16, *115*; Shannon for, 109–12, *113*; smartphones and, 14, 19; statistics with, 338n37; for STEM, 94; theory of information and, 106–9; Turing for, 23, 69, 73, 103–6, 340n60
Computing-Tabulating-Recording Company (CTR), 42–43
Comrie, Leslie J., 51
Consumer Expenditure Survey, 231
Consumer Price Index, 231
control books, 205
Control Revolution, 7
corporations. *See* business
Cortada, James, 24–25, 68
Covid-19 pandemic, 54, 134, 174, 201, 267, 294–95, 303–6
Coyle, Dine, 234
CPUs. *See* central processing units
The Crack Up (Fitzgerald), 391n20
Crick, Francis, 163–64, 176
cross-disciplinary dependencies, 180–81
Crymble, Adam, 273–74
cryptology, 109–10
CTR. *See* Computing-Tabulating-Recording Company
culture: academic libraries in, 59; AI in, 14, 152, 296, 304; Apple in, 126–27; at AT&T, 102; at Bell Labs, 42–43, 96, 102; business,

298–99; digitalization in, 15–16; of Great Depression, 256; history of, 321n81; information and, 271–72; of libraries, 16, 325n10; in modernity, 294–302, *298–99*; Nobel Prize in, 41; personal computers in, 19–20; politics of, 23–24; popular, 12–13; progress in, 84; after Renaissance, 2; Second Industrial Revolution and, 12, 31–35, 53–56, 130; technology and, 272–73, 280–81; of U.S., 40–43, 68–69, 98; of Western Civilization, 45; after World War I, 27; after World War II, 13–14, 303
Cumberbatch, Benedict, 103
Current Employment Statistics, 231
Current Research Information System, 121
Cutter, Charles Ammi, 64–65, 66–67, 81

Dahl, Robert A., 253
Dalton, John, 163
Darwin, Charles, 169–70
data: from agriculture, 38; analysis, 142, 197; behavior of, 147; Big Data, 5, 175–76, 243–44, 285, 294, 311n29; bits of, 312n32; collection, 146; on computers, 99–101, *101*, 149–50; databases, 71–72, 92, 116–23, *122*, 124–26, 167–68, 197–98, *284*, 284–85; datum, 11; definitions of, 11; digitalization of, 81–82, 176–77; discoveries with, 160; economic, 246–47; in education, 5; entry clerks, 280; fake facts and, 12–13; for Google, 171; history of, 312n34, 313n41; at IBM, 204; IDC, 3; ideas and, 172; IDS, 122; information and, 11–12, *282*, 282–84, 288; knowledge and, 5–6, 8–9; language for, 345n137; management, 190; models, 290; numeric, 33–34; privacy with, 303; processing, 46–51, 54, 279–80; publishing,

271; research from, 294; in science, 50–51; signals, 339n56; specificity of, 33; statistics and, 49, 134–35; storage, 116–23, *122*; survey data presentation, *144*; technology for, 48–49; visualization of, 338n37; warehousing, 345n129
Davenport, Charles, 172
Davies, Donald, 342n92
DDC. *See* Dewey Decimal Classification
Deaton, Angus, 224
demand, *221*, 221–22, 369n11
Deming, W. Edwards, 34, 207–8, 211, 368n113
Deming Effect, 207–8, 211
demographic profiles, *143*, 148
Department of Agriculture, U.S., 34, 38, 55, 186, 207, 256
Department of Labor, U.S., 262
Department of State, U.S., 260–61, 263
Descartes, René, 157
descriptive statistics, 142–45, *143–44*
Desk Set (movie), 99
Dewey, Melvil, 23, 59, 63–66, 71, 81, 279
Dewey Decimal Classification (DDC), 59–60, 63–66, 328n68
Didier, Emmanuel, 146
The Diffusion of Knowledge, 75
digitalization: in agriculture, 98; in chemistry, 168–69; of communication, 99–101, *101*; computers and, 89–90; in culture, 15–16; of data, 81–82, 176–77; digital plumbing, 291, 293, 312n40; electrification and, 123–27; of information, 2–3, 15, 95–99, 338n40, 339n50, 364n50; of newspapers, 13–14, 98–99; of publishing, 305–6
diplomacy, 253, 260–63, 275–76, 384n37
Dirac, Paul A., 158, 353n23
discoveries: from academic research, 43–44; at Bell Labs, 106, 133; with data, 160; in economics, 379n145; genetics, 54, 163–64; at IBM, 48, 117; ideas and, 100–101, *101*; mass production of, 31–33; in medicine, 173–74, 363n33; in science, 27–29; by Shannon, *101*, 106–9, 158, 280, 297; in STEM, 177; in U.S., 125–26; after World War II, 46
documentation movement, 69–73, 79, 83–84, 114
Drucker, Peter F., 197–98, 237
DuPont Corporation, 44

East Germany, 1
Ebola, 150
Econometrica (journal), 224–30
economics: accounting, 49; BEA, 230–34, *235*, 236; behavioral, 217, 240–44, 270; Big Data in, 244; business and, 189–96, *191–93*, 215–16, 219–20; computers and, 53; discoveries in, 379n145; econometrics, 223–28; in education, 189–90, 223–24; in Europe, 317n12; GDP, 233–34, *235*, 236; globalization of, 54–55; Great Depression, 35–36, 52, 146, 256; in higher education, 97–98; history of, 215–17, 369n11, 374n66; of industry, 361n4; information from, 213–14, 222–28, 236–40, 245–48; of information technology, 93–94; language of, 246; macroeconomics, 215; management, 48; microeconomics, 215; neoclassical, 217–22, *221*; New Deal, 146; OECD, 231–32; philosophy of, 215–16; in politics, 219–20, 228–33; progress in, 227–28; research and, 214, 388n81; of scholarship, 362n28, 363n40; science of, 245; in Second Industrial Revolution, 218; of society, 28; in STEM, 213, 218, 238; of technology, 236; trend analysis, *144*; in U.S.,

230; in Western Civilization, 218; after World War II, 184–85
Edgerton, David, 15
Edgeworth, Francis Y., 248
education: academic libraries, 59; agriculture in, 39–40; applications of, 7; of children, 6, 59, 131; data in, 5; economics in, 189–90, 223–24; government and, 318n35, 319n43; higher, 39–45, 62–64, 75–76, 84–85, 97–98, 362n28, 363n40; history and, 38–39, 292–93, 316n1; humanity and, 155; innovation in, 210–11; iSchools, 330n98; libraries and, 36–37; organization in, 281; political science in, 254, *255*; professionalism and, *287–88*; publishing and, 4–5; religion and, 6–7; science in, 7; statistics in, 351n72; STEM, 94, 249–50; in U.S., 141–42, *144*; during World War II, 27. *See also* higher education
Einstein, Albert, 104, 107, *136*
elections, 256–60, *257*
electrification, 89, 95–99, 123–27, 341n82, 344n126. *See also* computers
Ellul, Jacques, 4
Elton, G. R., 264–65
Encyclopedia Britannica, 76
encyclopedias, 5
engineering, 50–54, 99, 103–4, 107, 109–11, 135
England, 28–29, 36, 149, 253, 385n47
ENIAC computer, 106
Enlightenment, 4–5
entertainment, 20
entropy, 111
environmentalism, 187, 303
Europe: documentation movement in, 69–73, 79, 83–84; East Germany and, 1; economics in, 317n12; historical societies in, 316n79; history of, 150, 278; knowledge in, 7, 62–63; language in, 12; politics in, 275; publishing in, 272; scholarship in, 83; U.S., and, 20, 40–41, 58, 69–70, 75, 86, 218–19, 291; after World War II, 385n47; World War I in, 2. *See also specific countries*
European Union, 262
evidence, 10–11, 264–67, 334n142, 372n37
evolution, 169–70
experimental information, *286*
Exponential Growth Model, 201

Facebook, 15, 60
facts. *See specific topics*
fake facts, 9–10, 12–13, 295–96
Fano, Robert M., *101*
FASB. *See* Financial Accounting Standards Board
Federal Bureau of Investigation (FBI), 120, 200
finances. *See* business
Financial Accounting Standards Board (FASB), 191
First Industrial Revolution, 29–31, 317n8
Fischer, David Hackett, 249
Fisher, Irving, 223–27, 373n45
Fisher, Ronald A., 148, 156
Fitzgerald, F. Scott, 391n20
Florida Agriculture and Mechanical University, 40
Floridi, Luciano, 179–80
Fogel, Robert William, 269
food, 363n33
Food and Drug Administration, U.S., 174–75, 179, 366n82
food research, 293
Ford Motor Company, 207
forecast models, *148*, 148–49, 339n43
forms, 206–7, 323n103
formulas, 162
France, 37, 261, 277–78, 385n47, 385n49

Frank, Anne, 267
Frankfurt, Harry G., 277, 300
Franklin, Benjamin, 36
Fraser, Heather, 305
Freud, Sigmund, 275
Friedman, Milton, 219
Frisch, Ragnar, 223–25

GAAP. *See* Generally Accepted Accounting Principle
Galbraith, John K., 219, 295
Galileo Galilei, 133, 157
Gallup, George H., 250, 256–57
Gallup Polls, 256–58, *257*
Galton, Francis, 146–47, 156, 172
Gardner, Howard, 342n94
GDP. *See* Gross Domestic Product
Geiger, Roger L., 44
General Electric, 365n74
Generally Accepted Accounting Principle (GAAP), 191
A General Mathematical Theory of Political Economy (Jevons), 219
General Motors, *298–99*
General Systems Theory, 24, 296–99
genetics, 29, 54, 163–64, 170–73, 176–77, 200, 299–300
geometry, 137–39
geopolitics, 1–2, 34–35, 303
George, Henry, 218
Gerard, R. W., 129
Germany, 69–70, 264, 267–68, 278
Gilded Age, 27–29, 316n6
globalization: of computers, 85–86; of economics, 54–55; England in, 29; history in, 270–71; of information, 51–52, 196–200; of language, 301–2; of libraries, 385n46; of literacy, 112
Goodman, Emily, 111
Google, 60–61, 71–72, 86, 116, 171
Gordon, Robert J., 28, 209
Gore, Al, 197–98
Gouraud, Charles, 147
government: auditing by, 190–91; of Belgium, 71; business and, 183–84, 196–200, 208–12; databases, 197–98; education and, 318n35, 319n43; genetics and, 200; humanity and, 288; information from, 35–40, 187–89, 361n6; information standards in, 203–7; mathematical models for, 201–3, *203*; research to, 54–55, 121; statistics, 184–87; U.S., 50, 183–86; war to, 200
Graduate Library School, 74
Graff, Henry F., 264
Grand Challenge movement, 24
Grand Unified Theory, 24
graphics, 93, 286, 372n37
graphite, 317n14
Great Depression, 35–36, 52, 146, 256
Green Revolution, 55
Grey, Edward, 29
Gross Domestic Product (GDP), 232–34, *235*, 236, 244, 247, 376n105

Hales, Thomas, *137*
Half-Life Model, 201
Hall, Marshall, *137*
Hanson, James C. M., 67–68
Harper, Richard, 16
Hartley, Ralph, *101*, 107–9
Hartley Oscillator, 107
hashing algorithms, 343n117
Hayek, Friedrich, 237
Hegel, George Wilhelm Friedrich, 3–4
hegemony, 30, 78
Heisenberg, Werner, 159, 354n26
Herzfeld, Charles M., 342n92
Hidalgo, César, 281
higher education, 39–45, 62–64, 75–76, 84–85, 97–98, 362n28, 363n40
Highway Research Information Services, 121
Hilbert, David, 104, 133, 138–39, 153–54
Hill, William Ely, *160*
history: of AI, 19; American Historical Association, 270–71,

292; of biology, 154, 169–75; of computers, 47–48, 51–52, 89–90, 123–27, 281–82, 292, 319n36; of computer science, 90–95; of culture, 321n81; of data, 312n34, 313n41; of economics, 215–17, 369n11, 374n66; education and, 38–39, 292–93, 316n1; of electrification, 95–99; of Europe, 150, 278; evidence from, 264–67; facts in, 25–26; of forms, 323n103; of Gallup Polls, 256–58, *257*; of GDP, 232–33; of genetics, 163–64, 170–73; in globalization, 270–71; historians, 5; historical societies, 316n79; of humanity, 274; of IBM, 198; of industry, 323n107, 375n86; information and, 267–73, 287–88, *287–88*; of Internet, 119–20, 125–26, 324n120; of labor, 27–28, 184, 208–11; of librarians, 60–61, 83–87; of mathematics, 135–36; modernity and, 1–2, 13–14, 249–51, 273–76, 384n37; of new information, 358n81, 389n96; oral, 267–70, 387n68; of organization, 63–69; of personal computers, 364n50; of physics, 157–61, *160*; of plastic, 321n76; of political science, 252–55, *255*, 382n12; of professionalism, 42; of programs, 105; of public policy, 228–33; of publishing, 2–3; quantitative, 267–70; of quantum physics, 158; of religion, 20; of research, 155–56, 252; of scholarship, 154–55, 386n63, 388n81; of science, 316n7; of Second Industrial Revolution, 2, 7; of society, 23; of specialization, 393n43; of statistics, 49, 130–31, 142–50, *143–44, 148*, 373n45; of STEM, 162; subjectivity of, 24–25; of technology, 15, 54; of Western Civilization, 133

Hitler, Adolf, 6
Holocaust, 267–68
Homology theory, 139
Huffman, David A., *101*
Human Genome Project, 171
humanity: AI and, 105–6; in databases, 124–25; education and, 155; government and, 288; in higher education, 85; history of, 274; information in, *18*, 294–302, *298–99*, 311n20; with Internet, 209; labor and, 172–73; language and, 151–52, 285; machines and, 93; philosophy and, 307; population increases, 55; registration of, 49–50; science and, 21, 45; in Second Industrial Revolution, 247–48, 281–82; society and, 5; in sociology, 7, 321n83; technology for, 316n7; typologies for, 4
Hume, David, 218
hypotheticals, 201–2

IBM: AT&T and, 97; computers at, 204, 211–12; data at, 96, *203*, 204; discoveries at, 48, 117; engineering at, 50–52; General Motors and, *298–99*; history of, 198; information processing at, 205; Internet and, 91; library computing at, 114–15; in modernity, 240–41; philosophy at, 183, 193–94, 366n92; research at, 28, 42–43, 87, 145; standardization at, 205–6, 208; strategy at, 188; technology at, 135, 340n69, 347n165
IDC. *See* International Data Corporation
ideas, 100–101, *101*
identity, 7, 206–7, 302
IDS. *See* Integrated Data Store
illusions, *160*
IMF. *See* International Monetary Fund
The Imitation Game (movie), 103
indexing terms, 343n113
Industrial Revolution. *See* Second Industrial Revolution

industry, 314n62, 323n107, 361n4, 375n86
inferential statistics, 142–45, *143–44*
inferior knowledge, 44
information: accounting, 184; accreditation of, 330n98; accurate, 54; agencies of, 318n35; AI and, 280–81; ambiguity of, 90–91; American Society for Information Science, 79–80; analog, 339n50; applications and, 92–93; attributes of, 13–16, *17–18*, 18–21; Bachman Information Systems, *122*, 122–23; behavior of, 80; biological, 175–79; about books, 57–58; in Bradford's Law, 76–77; in business, 365n73; chemical, 161–69, *166*; communication of, 151–52; on computers, 321n74; in computer science, 279–80, 392n24; culture and, 271–72; data and, 11–12, *282*, 282–84, 288; definitions of, 6–13; digitalization of, 2–3, 15, 95–99, 338n40, 339n50, 364n50; diplomacy and, 260–63; disaggregation of, 97; econometrics and, 223–28; economic, 223–28; from economics, 213–14, 222–28, 236–40, 244–48; ecosystems, 183–84; electrification of, 344n126; in genetics, 170, 299–300; in Gilded Age, 316n6; globalization of, 51–52, 196–200; from government, 35–40, 187–89, 361n6; in higher education, 40–45; Highway Research Information Services, 121; history and, 267–73, 287–88, *287–88*; in humanity, *18*, 294–302, *298–99*, 311n20; ISI, 119; knowledge and, 9, 271; large enterprises from, 31–35; management, 391n16; mathematical theory of, 79, 110; mathematics and, 112, *113*, 140–42; medical, 175–79; in modernity, 1–6, *17*, 19–20, 277–78, 281–82, 289–94, *290*, 302–7; to National Science Foundation, 337n28; in neoclassical economics, 217–22, *221*; new information ecosystem, 169–75, 358n81, 389n96; objectivity and, 82–83; observational, *286*; from opinion polling, 255–60, *257*; organization of, 62–69; in patents, 188–89; about people, 40; in political science, 67–68, 249–51, 273–76, 390n108; in PowerPoint presentations, *286*, 286–87; probability from, 285–86; processing, 205; in professionalism, 42, 153–54; publishing, 293; quality of, 329n84; quantification of, 91–92; research and, 254; retrieval, 92, 112, 114–16, *115*; scholarship on, 23–26, 315n75; science and, 61–62, 77–83, 154–57; from Second Industrial Revolution, 27–31, 279; Shannon for, 11–12, 124, 284, 307; shaping, 273; Smithsonian Science Information Exchange, 121; in society, 289; in sociology, 4; standards for, 203–7, 335n11; in STEM, 178; storage of, 118–19; studies, 378n123; systems, 78–79; in taxonomies, 21–23; technology and, 59–60, 93–94, *284*, 284–85; theory of, 106–9, 207; transformations, *290*; truth and, 264–67; typologies, 55–56; in U.S., 131–32, 317n12; weather, 339n43
Information Age, 1–2, 16, 181
Information & Culture, 26, 271–72, 315n75
innovation, 186–89, 193, 210–11
Institute for Scientific Information (ISI), 119
Integrated Data Store (IDS), 122
intellectualism, 72, 393n43
intelligence, 391n20
International Data Corporation (IDC), 3

International Monetary Fund (IMF), 216–17, 231–32
Internet: Amazon, 14, 95, 149, 171, 198, 215, 240; encyclopedias and, 5; history of, 119–20, 125–26, 324n120; humanity with, 209; IBM and, 91; OCLC, 65–66, 119–20; organization of, 71–72; publishing on, 272–73; scholarship on, 81; social media, 15, 60; web searching on, 81–82
intuition, 242
investing, 191
Iraq, 200
iSchools, 330n98
ISI. *See* Institute for Scientific Information
Isis (journal), 150–51

Japan, 7
Jardine, Lisa, 45
Jefferson, Thomas, 37
Jevons, William Stanley, 219, 224
Jewett, Charles C., 64
Jobs, Steve, 211
Johannsen, Wilhelm, 171
Johnson, Lyndon B., 266
Jones, Karen Spärck, 343n114
journalism, 13–14, 98–99, 305–7
Journal of the Association for Information Science, 79–80
Jung, Carl, 275

Kahneman, Daniel, 243
Kelvin (Lord), 157
Kennedy, John F., 266–67
Keynes, John Maynard, *136*, 216–17, 220–21, 245
Al-Khalili, Jim, 158
Khun, Thomas S., 289
Kim, Chai, 80
Kimmel, Jimmy, 300–301
Kissinger, Henry, 263
Klein, Lawrence, 224

knowledge: anonymous state of, *115*; concepts of, 287; data and, 5–6, 8–9; in Europe, 7, 62–63; Hilbert on, 153–54; inferior, 44; information and, 9, 271; intelligence and, 391n20; Knowledge Management, 283; in libraries, 22; mapping, 58, 62–69; organization of, 67–68, 83–87; in physics, 354n37; profound, 207–8; proliferation of, 51–52; of science, 8; in STEM, 180; in U.S., 68–69; wealth and, 317n9; wisdom and, 6–13, *282*, 282–84; workers, 45, 52
Koch, Robert, 173
Koopman, Colin, 13, 307
Krugman, Paul, 219, 245
Kuhn, Thomas, 2, 107
Kuwait, 200
Kuznets, Simon, 234

labor: in agriculture, 32; BLS, 93–94, 230–31, 349n41, 361n6; Department of Labor, 262; forces, 14; history of, 27–28, 184, 208–11; humanity and, 172–73; laws, 12; resources for, 86. *See also* business
La Fontaine, Henri, 69–70
Landon, Alf, 256
language: communication and, 150; of computers, 312n32, 337n28; for data, 345n137; of economics, 246; in Europe, 12; globalization of, 301–2; humanity and, 151–52, 285; of mathematics, 133–39, *136–37*, *139–40*, 348n14; in modernity, 129–30; in popular culture, 12–13; of probability, 285–86; programming, 92; of scholarship, 306; SQL, 118; of STEM, 177–78
large enterprises, 31–35
LCC. *See* Library of Congress Classification
libraries: academic, 59; ALA, 59, 62, 74; Big Data and, 10; bookless,

314n56; books in, 73–77; computer science and, 14; culture of, 16, 325n10; databases compared to, 92; DDC, 59–60, 63–66, 328n68; education and, 36–37; globalization of, 385n46; Graduate Library School, 74; in higher education, 75; information science in, 77–83; in iSchools, 330n98; knowledge in, 22; LCC, 59–60, 63, 65–69, 328n68, 328n70; librarians, 55–56, 59–62, 83–87; library computing, 114–15; library science, 304–5; NLM, 119, 178–79, 306; OCLC, 65–66, 119–20; organization in, 24, 57–58; political science in, 67–68; publishing and, 333n140; scholarship on, 26; statistics on, 325n6; UDC, 63, 69–74; in U.S., 58
Libraries of the Future (Licklider), 84, *115*
Library and Information Science (LIS), 78
Library & Information History, 26
Library of Congress Classification (LCC), 59–60, 63, 65–69, 328n68, 328n70
Licklider, Joseph C. R., 84, *115*, 125, 127
life sciences, 169–75
Lijphart, Arend, 253
Lilienfeld, Robert, 299
Lincoln, Abraham, 265, 267
Linz, Juan, 253
LIS. *See* Library and Information Science
A List of Books for College Libraries (Shaw), 75–76
literacy: globalization of, 112; mathematical, 131; in modernity, *17*, 18; rates, 18, *18*; religion and, 16; in U.S., 32–33
Literary Digest (magazine), 256, 258–60
Lloyd, Seth, 15
Locke, John, 218

Louisiana Purchase, 37
Lowell, A. Lawrence, 249, 254–55
Luenberger, David G., 22
Luhn, Hans Peter, 114–15, *115*

Machlup, Fritz, 198, 237–39, 313n44
macroeconomics, 215. *See also* economics
Malefakis, Edward E., 374n66
Malthus, Thomas, 201
management, 48
mandatory outlays, 195–96
mapping knowledge, 58, 62–69
marginal utility, 219–22, *221*
"The Market for 'Lemons'" (Akerlof), 376n112
Markov Decision Model, 201
Marshall, Alfred, 218, 220–22, *221*, 234, 372n37
Marx, Karl, 217–18
mass production, 31–33
"A Mathematical Theory of Communication" (Shannon), 110
mathematics: Abel Prize in, 253n14; biology and, 225; business and, 239–40; calculus, 134, *140*, 348n14; of economic information, 223–28; history of, 135–36; information and, 112, *113*, 140–42; language of, 133–39, *136–37*, *139–40*, 348n14; mathematical models, 201–3, *203*; mathematical theory of information, 79, 110; mathematicians, 129–31, 150–52, 247; numeracy, 131–33; physics and, 349n26; professionalism in, 349n41; Pythagorean theorem, 134, 202, 348n18; of ranking, 343n113; science and, 138, 150–51; statistics and, 145–46, 156, 222, 246, *290*. *See also* science
Maxwell, James C., *136*, 157
Mazzucato, Mariana, 219
McCloskey, Deirdre, 216–17
medicine: biology and, 169–75; chemical information and, 161–69, *166*;

Covid-19 pandemic, 54, 134, 174, 201, 267, 294–95, 303–6; discoveries in, 173–74, 363n33; medical information, 175–79; *Medical Subject Headings*, 179; MEDLINE, 178–79; NLM, 119, 178–79, 306; pharmaceuticals, 188; Porter on, 180–81; risk in, 171–72; science and, 43–44, 153–54, 179–81; statistics in, 174; in STEM, 186; viruses, 163
metadisciplines, 297
microeconomics, 215. *See also* economics
microfilming, 73–74
Minsky, Marvin, *101*
modernity: accounting in, 189–96, *191–93*; agriculture in, 246; AI in, 297, 340n69; CAS in, 163–69, *166*; communication in, 300–301; conflict in, 22–23; culture in, 294–302, *298–99*; after First Industrial Revolution, 317n8; GDP in, 247; historical evidence in, 264–67; history and, 1–2, 13–14, 249–51, 273–76, 384n37; IBM in, 241; information in, 1–6, *17*, 19–20, 277–78, 281–82, 289–94, *290*, 302–7; Knowledge Management in, 283; language in, 129–30; literacy in, *17*, 18; progress in, 23–24; publishing in, 9, 306–7; Shannon in, 23, 79–80, 195, 223, 271; society in, 53; statistics in, 156; technology in, 25
Modern Times (movie), 14
Monographic Principle, 72
Mooers, Calvin N., 78, *115*, 116
Moore, Henry L., 224
Moore's Law, 10, 54, 100
Morange, Michael, 154, 157, 357n75
Morrill Act (1862), 37
Morris, Ian, 270
Myth of the Paperless Office (Harper and Sellen), 16
"My Wife and My Mother-in-Law" (Hill), *160*

narrative facts, 290
National Aeronautics and Space Administration (NASA), 97, 119, 282, 305
National Cash Register Corporation (NCR), 47, 52, 188, 193
National Library of Medicine (NLM), 119, 178–79, 306
National Science Foundation, 337n28
National Union Catalog, 74
natural philosophy, 248
nature, 3
NCR. *See* National Cash Register Corporation
neoclassical economics, 217–22, *221*
networking, 92, 297–98, *298–99*
von Neumann, John, *101*, 104, 106, *136*, 161
New Deal, 146, 232
new information ecosystem, 169–75, 358n81, 389n96
newspapers, 13–14, 98–99
Newton, Isaac, 219–20
New York Times (NYT), 98–99
Nineteen Eighty-Four (Orwell), 127, 207
Nixon, Richard, 263
NLM. *See* National Library of Medicine
Nobel Prize, 41, 70, 219, 230, 243, 269, 377n119
Nonaka, Ikujiro, 1
North, Douglass Cecil, 269
Novick, Peter, 264
numeracy, 131–33
numeric data, 33–34
Nyquist, Harry, 100, *101*, 102–3
NYT. See New York Times

objectivity, 13, 82–83, 174–75, 228–29
observational information, *286*
OCLC. *See* Online Computer Library Center
OECD. *See* Organization for Economic Cooperation and Development
OED. See Oxford English Dictionary

Office of Management and Budget (OMB), 195
OMB. *See* Office of Management and Budget
On Bullshit (Frankfurt), 300
Online Computer Library Center (OCLC), 65–66, 119–20
operational research, 198, 214
opinion polling, 255–60, *257*
oral history, 267–70, 387n68
organization: with bibliographies, 74–76; in education, 281; Google for, 60–61; in higher education, 62, 63–64; history of, 63–69; of information, 62–69; of Internet, 71–72; of knowledge, 67–68, 83–87; in libraries, 24, 57–58; with microfilming, 73–74; in OCLC, 65–66, 119–20; research on, 81–82; with schemas, 21–22; of scholarship, 75–76; in science, 76–77; technology for, 86–87; after World War II, 77–83. *See also specific topics*
Organization for Economic Cooperation and Development (OECD), 231–32
Orwell, George, 127, 207
Otlet, Paul, 69–73, 74
Oxford English Dictionary (OED), 10, 12

Page, Scott E., 284–85, 297
Pareto's Law, 76
Paris Peace Conference, 47, 70
Pasteur, Louis, 173
patents, 188–89, 363n33
path dependency, 330n88
Patterson, George W., *101*
Patterson, John H., 193
Peano, Giuseppe, 133, *136*
Pearson, Karl, 146–47, 156, 172
peer-review scholarship, 306–7, 352n4
Peron-Frabenius Theorem, 201

Perry, James W., 168
personal computers, 16, 19–20, 92, 149, 297–98, *298–99*, 364n50
personality tests, 302
pharmaceuticals, 188
PhD degrees, 41, 94–95
philosophy: of Big Data, 311n29; of concepts, 3–4; of economics, 215–16; of fake facts, 295–96; of Gilded Age, 29; humanity and, 307; at IBM, 183, 193–94, 366n92; natural, 248; political science and, 373n45; of productivity, 277; religion and, 57–58; science and, 2; of Shannon, 1, 3; of social sciences, 249–51, 270, 274–75
physics: biology and, 299–300; computer science and, 96; Dirac Equation in, 353n23; knowledge in, 354n37; mathematics and, 349n26; quantum, 147–48, 158–61, 357n72
Pierce, Charles S., 147
Pigou, Arthur Cecil, 220–21
plastic, 321n76
Poincaré, Henri, 135, *136*, 138–39
political science: in diplomacy, 260–63, 275–76; in education, 254, *255*; history of, 252–55, *255*, 382n12; information in, 67–68, 249–51, 273–76, 390n108; in libraries, 67–68; opinion polling in, 255–60, *257*; philosophy and, 373n45
politics: of Big Data, 294; comparative, 252–53; of computers, 325n14; of culture, 23–24; economics in, 219–20, 228–33; of elections, 256–60, *257*; in England, 36; in Europe, 275; facts in, 12; GDP in, 233–34, *235*, 236; geopolitics, 1–2, 34–35, 303; of journalism, 305–7; political parties, 256–59, *257*; presidential elections, 256; public policy, 46–47; of publishing, 383n13; research in, 390n108; of Second Industrial Revolution,

35–40; surveys in, *257*, 257–58; treaties, 262; truth in, 301; in U.S., 255–56
polls, 256–59, *257*
popular culture, 12–13
population increases, 55, 140–42, *148*, 148–49
Porat, Marc Uri, 238
Porter, Theodore M., 132, 142, 145–51, 171–73, 180–81, 196, 248
PowerPoint presentations, *286*, 286–87
presidential elections, 256
Pricewaterhouse and Company, 206
privacy, 92, 303
probability, 285–86, 304
Producer Price Index, 231
productivity, 277
professionalism: education and, *287–88*; information in, 42, 153–54; in mathematics, 349n41; specialization in, 290–91; with STEM, 181, 205–6, 263; technology and, 85–86; in U.S., 60–61; in World War I, 47
profound knowledge, 207–8
programs (computer), 91–92, 105
progress, 23–24, 79, 84, 100, 227–28
prohibition, of alcohol, *257*, 257–58
projections, 304, 339n43
psychology, 240–43, 270, 274–75, 302, 342n94, 380n151. *See also* behavior
public policy, 46–47, 228–33
publishing: books, 73–77, 348n16; *Chicago Manual of Style*, 265; data, 271; digitalization of, 305–6; documentation movement in, 69–73; education and, 4–5; in Europe, 272; facts in, 266–67, 301; history of, 2–3; information, 293; on Internet, 272–73; libraries and, 333n140; in modernity, 9, 306–7; politics of, 382n13; before World War II, 75. *See also* libraries
Pythagorean theorem, 134, 202, 348n18

qualitative facts, 290
quantitative history, 267–70
quantities, 133–34, 151
quantum physics, 147–48, 158–61, 357n72
Quetelet, Adolphe, 146–47
Quinn, James Brian, 198

radio, 14, 33
Randolph-Macon College, 6
von Ranke, Leopold, 264–67, 278, 292
RBU. *See* Universal Bibliographic Repertory
reading, 8
registration, of humanity, 49–50
registry, in chemistry, 165–67, *166*
religion, 6–8, 11, 16, 20, 57–58
Renaissance, 2
research: academic, 43–44; AI, 305; by Aspray, 362n31; CAS, 168; during Cold War, 35–36; on computers, 85; from data, 294; diversity in, 198; economics and, 214, 388n81; food, 293; to government, 54–55, 121; in higher education, 362n28, 363n40; Highway Research Information Services, 121; history of, 155–56, 252; at IBM, 28, 42–43, 87, 145; information and, 254; innovation and, 186–88; operational, 214; on organization, 81–82; in politics, 390n108; projects, 79–80; scholarship and, 386n52; STEM, 85, 170, 243; after World War II, 210–11
resources, 86, 185
Ricardo, David, 218
Richie, Donald, 268
Rifkin, Jeremy, 52–53
Rijsbergen, C. J., *115*
risk, in medicine, 171–72
Robertson, Craig, 210
Roe v. Wade, 259
Roosevelt, Franklin D., 256
Roper, Elmo, 257

Salton, Gerard, 112, 114–16, *115*, 343n112, 343n117
sampling principle, 100, 102–3
Samuel, Raphael, 264–65
Samuelson, Paul, 224
Sardinas, August Albert, *101*
satellites, 97
schemas, 21–22, 63–69
Schmidt, Eric, 3
Schneider, Georg, 68–69
scholarship: with AI, 93; on diplomacy, 384n37; economics of, 362n28, 363n40; in Europe, 83; history of, 154–55, 386n63, 388n81; on information, 23–26, 315n75; information studies, 378n123; on Internet, 81; language of, 306; on libraries, 26; on *OED*, 12; organization of, 75–76; peer-review in, 306–7, 352n4; research and, 386n52; scholarly societies, 41–42; science and, 295; on statistics, 145; on STEM, 240, 274; surveys in, 279; in U.S., 385n50
Schrödinger, Erwin, 158, 357n72
Schumpeter, Joseph A., 213, 218, 223, 226, 236, 372n41, 374n59
science: of AI, 242; American Society for Information Science, 79–80; at Bell Labs, 42–43, 110; BIOSIS, 118–19; chemical information in, 161–69, *166*; cognitive scientists, 63; computer, 60, 90–96, 116, 161, *203*, 279–80, 303–4, 392n24; concepts in, 20–21; data in, 50–51; discoveries in, 27–29; of economics, 245–46; in education, 7; engineering and, 53–54; genetics, 29; history of, 316n7; humanity and, 21, 45; information and, 61–62, 77–83, 154–57; ISI, 119; knowledge of, 8; library, 304–5; LIS, 78; mathematics and, 138, 150–51; medicine and, 43–44, 153–54, 179–81; Moore's Law in, 100; at NASA, 97, 119, 282, 305; National Science Foundation, 337n28; organization in, 76–77; philosophy and, 2; political, 67–68; quantum physics, 147–48, 158–61, 357n72; scholarship and, 295; simulations in, 93; Smithsonian Science Information Exchange, 121; social sciences, 249–51, 270, 274–75; SSCI, 119–20; technology and, 317n14. *See also specific sciences*

SEC. *See* Securities and Exchange Commission

Second Industrial Revolution: copyrights in, 188–89; culture and, 12, 31–35, 53–56, 130; data processing in, 46–51; economics in, 218; fact production in, 40–45; First Industrial Revolution and, 29–31, 317n8; graphics in, 286; history of, 2, 7; humanity in, 247, 281–82; information from, 27–31, 279; politics of, 35–40; Third Industrial Revolution and, 30–31, 52–53

secularism, 7–8
Securities and Exchange Commission (SEC), 191
Selected Water Resources Abstracts, 120
Sellen, Abigail, 16
Sensenbrenner, Joe, 197–98
Shakespeare, William, 6
Shannon, Claude E.: for computers, 109–11, 112, *113*; discoveries by, *101*, 106–9, 158, 280, 297; Gardner on, 342n94; for information, 11–12, 124, 284, 307; mathematics to, 129; in modernity, 23, 79–80, 195, 223, 271; philosophy of, 1, 3; von Neumann and, 161; Wiener and, 127, 156–57
shaping information, 273
Shaw, Charles B., 75–76

Shera, Jesse H., 61–62, 65, 86
Shewhart, Walter A., 207
The Shock of the Old (Edgerton), 15–16
Sibley, John Langdon, 57–58
SIC system. *See* Standard Industrial Classification system
Skyttner, Lars, 298
Slaughter, Anne-Marie, 298
SMART. *See* System for the Manipulation and Retrieval of Text
smartphones, 14, 19, 91, 347n165
Smith, Adam, 215–18, 369n11
Smithsonian Institution, 269
Smithsonian Science Information Exchange, 121
Snow, C. P., 45, 340n61
social media, 15, 60
Social Science Citation Index (SSCI), 119–20
social sciences, 249–51, 270, 274–75. *See also specific social sciences*
society: before AI, 29; American Chemical Society, 164–65; digital plumbing in, 291, 293, 312n40; economics of, 28; hegemony in, 30; history of, 23; humanity and, 5; information in, 289; with literacy, 32–33; in modernity, 53; scholarly societies, 41–42; Statistical Society of London, 130; in U.S., 27, 329n84; women in, 60; after World War II, 294–95
sociology, 4, 7, 240–44, 321n83
Solomonoff, Ray, *101*
Solow, Robert, 224, 239
space, 133
Spain, 261–62, 277–78, 385n47, 385nn48–49
Spanish-American War, 262
specialization, 290–91, 393n43
Spence, A. Michael, 237
Spengler, Joseph J., 227–28
SQL. *See* Structured Query Language
SSCI. *See* Social Science Citation Index

Standard Industrial Classification (SIC) system, 231
standardization, 203–8
standards, for information, 203–7, 335n11
statistics: in accounting, 363n42; BLS, 93–94, 230–31, 349n41, 361n6; Bureau of Statistics, 232; with computers, 338n37; Current Employment Statistics, 231; data and, 49, 134–35; descriptive, 142–45, *143–44*; in education, 351n72; government, 184–87; history of, 49, 130–31, 142–50, *143–44, 148,* 373n45; inferential, 142–45, *143–44*; on libraries, 325n6; mathematics and, 145–46, 156, 222, 245, *290*; in medicine, 174; in modernity, 156; numeracy, 131–33; objectivity in, 174–75; of population increases, 140–42; Porter on, 132, 142, 146–48, 150–51; statistical methods, 155, 374n66; Statistical Society of London, 130; statisticians, 129–31, 150–52; variables in, 369n12; in work processes, 207. *See also* economics
Steiglitz, Ken, 8, 99–100, 105, 107, 111
STEM (science, technology, engineering, and mathematics): business and, 202–3; community, 212; computers for, 94; economics in, 213, 218, 238; education, 94, 249–50; history of, 162; knowledge in, 180; language of, 177–78; medicine in, 186; political science compared to, 254; professionalism with, 181, 205–6, 263; research, 85, 170, 243; scholarship on, 240, 274
Stigler, George, 237
Structured Query Language (SQL), 118
students, 38–39
subjectivity, 24–25
supply, *221*, 221–22, 369n11
survey data presentation, *144*

surveys, *257*, 257–58, 279
System for the Manipulation and Retrieval of Text (SMART), 114
systems theories, *290*

taxes, 200
taxonomies, 21–23
Taylor, Fredrick W., 47
Taylor, Robert, 125
Taylorism, 185–86
teachers, 38–39
technology: bookless libraries, 314n56; business and, 279–80, 372n41; for communication, 13–14, 46–51; computer science and, *17*, 19; culture and, 272–73, 280–81; for data, 48–49; data storage, 116–23, *122*; economics of, 236; for entertainment, 20; in higher education, 84; history of, 15, 54; for humanity, 316n7; at IBM, 135, 340n69, 347n165; information and, 59–60, 93–94, *284*, 284–85; microfilming, 73–74; in modernity, 25; for organization, 86–87; professionalism and, 85–86; progress in, 79; sampling principle for, 102–3; for satellites, 97; science and, 317n14; technological determinism, 330n88; in World War II, 103–4
telecommunications, 30–31
television, 1–2, 14
Tesla, Nikola, 27–28
Thaler, Richard, 379n145
theory of information, 106–9, 207
Third Industrial Revolution, 30–31, 52–53
The Third Industrial Revolution (Rifkin), 52–53
Tillinghast, Parson E., 273–74
Tinbergen, Jan, 224
Tirole, Jean, 224
Toffler, Alvin, 304
topology, 135, *137*, 138–39
totalitarianism, 253

Total Quality Management (TQM), 34, 184, 207–8
Trace, Ciaran B., 272
tracking polls, 259
transformations, of information, *290*
transportation, 185
treaties, 262
trend analysis, *144*
Truman, Harry S., 257
Trump, Donald J., 2, 267
truth, 264–67, 301, 329n84
Turing, Alan M.: for computers, 23, 69, 73, 103–6, 340n60; discoveries from, *101*; Licklider and, 127; progress from, 100; theories of, *136*
Twain, Mark, 27
typologies, 4, 44–45, 55–56

UDC. *See* Universal Decimal Classification
underdog effect, 260
United Nations, 262
United States (U.S.): American Chemical Society, 164–65; BLS, 93–94, 230–31, 349n41, 361n6; business in, 184–87; Census Bureau, 186–87; children in, 252; civil rights in, 259; Cold War in, 141; culture of, 40–43, 68–69, 98; Department of Agriculture, 34, 38, 55, 186, 207, 256; Department of Labor, 262; Department of State, 260–61, 263; discoveries in, 125–26; economics in, 230; education in, 141–42, *144*; England and, 36, 149; Europe and, 20, 40–41, 58, 69–70, 75, 86, 218–19, 291; Food and Drug Administration, 174–75, 179, 366n82; GDP, 234; in geopolitics, 34–35; Germany and, 278; Gilded Age in, 27–29; government, 50, 183–86; Great Depression in, 35–36, 52, 146, 256; information in, 131–32, 317n12; knowledge in, 68–69; libraries in, 58; Library

of Congress in, 59–60, 63, 65–69, 74; literacy in, 32–33; Morrill Act, 37; NASA, 97, 119, 282, 305; New Deal in, 146, 232; OMB, 195; in Paris Peace Conference, 47; PhD degrees in, 94–95; politics in, 255–56; population increases in, 55; professionalism in, 60–61; scholarship in, 385n50; SEC, 191; society in, 27, 329n84; Spain and, 385n48; after World War I, 29–30
Universal Bibliographic Repertory (RBU), 70
Universal Decimal Classification (UDC), 63, 69–74
U.S. *See* United States

valves, 99
Verdú, Sergio, 112
Vietnam, 385n49
viruses, 163

Wall Street, 280
Walras, Léon, 219, 224
war, 200
Watson, James, 163–64, 176, 358n81
Watson, Thomas J., Sr., 193
wealth, 317n9
weather, 339n43
Weaver, Warren, 79–80
WebDewey, 65–66
Weber, Max, 301
web searching, 81–82
Western Civilization, 4–5, 7, 45, 76, 133, 218, 253

Wheatley, Margaret J., 21
Wheeler, Tom, 3
Whittemore, Bruce J., 80
Wiegand, Wayne A., 66–67
Wiener, Norbert, 3, *101*, 110, 127, *137*, 156–57
Wikipedia, 4, 71–72
Williams, James, 80
Williamson, Charles C., 62
wisdom, 6–13, *282*, 282–84
women, 60
Woolf, Harry, 150–51
World War I, 2, 6, 27, 29–30, 33, 47
World War II: cryptology in, 109–10; culture after, 13–14, 303; discoveries after, 46; economics after, 184–85; education during, 27; Europe after, 385n47; Frank in, 267; Holocaust in, 267–68; numeric data after, 33–34; organization after, 77–83; publishing before, 75; research after, 210–11; scholarly societies after, 41–42; society after, 294–95; technology in, 103–4; telecommunications after, 30–31; U.S. government in, 50
writing, 8

YouTube, 99

Zatocoding, 116
Zinn, Howard, 32
Zins, Chaim, 80–81

About the Author

James W. Cortada is a senior research fellow at the Charles Babbage Institute, University of Minnesota. He is the author of many books on the history and use of information, computing, and business practices. He is also the author of *Building Blocks of Society: History, Information Ecosystems, and Infrastructures* (Rowman & Littlefield, 2020), and co-author with William Aspray, *Authenticity: Understanding Misinformation Through the Study of Heritage Tourism* (Rowman & Littlefield, 2022).

www.ingramcontent.com/pod-product-compliance
Lightning Source LLC
Chambersburg PA
CBHW070006010526
44117CB00011B/1442